Standard	Key Elements of the Standard	Chapter and Topic
		8: Creating a Learning Environment, p. 265 8: Different Children—Different Places, p. 277 8: Time, p. 296 9: Understanding Play, p. 306 9: Why Do Children Play?, p. 309 9: The Role of Play in Development, 316 9: Facilitating Play, p. 320 9: The Special Role of Outdoor Play, p. 327 9: Issues in Play, p. 327 10: What Is Curriculum?, p. 340 10: The Physical Development Curriculum, p. 347 10: The Communication Curriculum, p. 354 10: The Creative Arts Curriculum, p. 361 10: The Inquiry Curriculum, p. 371 11: Planning Considerations, p. 385 11: Writing Plans, p. 398 12: Preparing Yourself for Inclusion, p. 435 12: Implementing Inclusion, p. 440 12: Characteristics and Strategies for Working with Young Children with Disabilities, p. 447 12: Other Special Needs, p. 455 13: Understanding Families, p. 464 13: Involving Families, p. 482 13: Helping in Times of Stress, p. 486 13: Strengthening Families, p. 487 14: Know About Children and Best Practice, p. 494 14: Reflect and Set Goals, p. 495 *All chapters:* Reflection Boxes
5. Using Content Knowledge to Build Meaningful Curriculum	5a. Understanding content knowledge and resources in academic disciplines 5b. Knowing and using the central concepts, inquiry tools, and structures of content areas or academic disciplines 5c. Using their own knowledge, appropriate early learning standards, and other resources to design, implement, and evaluate meaningful, challenging curricula for each child	5: Sharing Information with Families, p. 180 10: What Is Curriculum?, p. 340 10: The Physical Development Curriculum, p. 347 10: The Communication Curriculum, p. 354 10: The Creative Arts Curriculum, p. 361 10: The Inquiry Curriculum, p. 371 11: Planning Considerations, p. 385 11: Influences on Curriculum Choices, p. 386 11: Organizing Curriculum, p. 391 11: Writing Plans, p. 398
6: Becoming a Professional	6a. Identifying and involving oneself with the early childhood field 6b. Knowing about and upholding ethical standards and other professional guidelines 6c. Engaging in continuous, collaborative learning to inform practice 6d. Integrating knowledgeable, reflective, and critical perspectives on early education 6e. Engaging in informed advocacy for children and the profession	1: Who Is the Early Childhood Educator?, p. 4 1: Working as Part of a Team, p. 8 1: The Teacher as a Person, p. 8 1: The Teacher as a Professional, p. 16 1: Guidelines for Ethical Reflection, p. 23 1: Finding Your Path, p. 24 2: Overview of Programs for Young Children, p. 36 2: Programs for Children from Birth to Age 5, p. 37 2: Programs for Children Ages 5 Through 8, p. 43 2: The Standards Movement, p. 45 2: Issues and Trends in Early Childhood Education, p. 47 5: What Is Assessment?, p. 144 5: Issues in Standardized Assessment, p. 177 5: Confidentiality, p. 180 5: Reflect on your ethical responsibilities, pp. 180, 181 6: Spanking Is Never a Choice, p. 221 7: Protect Children from Abuse and Neglect, p. 238 7: Reflect on your ethical responsibilities, pp. 239, 244 9: Reflect on your ethical responsibilities, pp. 332, 334 10: Reflect on your ethical responsibilities, p. 357 12: Inclusion and the Law, p. 434 12: Preparing Yourself for Inclusion, p. 435 12: Collaboration, p. 447 12: Reflect on your ethical responsibilities, pp. 454, 459 13: Reflect on your ideas about child-rearing practices, p. 470 13: Reflect on the ways your family was involved in your education, p. 485 13: Supporting Families, p. 486 13: Reflect on family involvement you have seen, p. 486 13: Understanding Legal and Ethical Responsibilities, p. 488 13: Reflect on your strengths and challenges in supporting families, p. 488 14: Make a Commitment to Children, p. 494 14: Understand and Use a Code of Ethics, p. 495 14: Make a Commitment to Yourself, p. 496 14: Connect with Colleagues, p. 497 14: Make a Commitment to Your Profession, p. 498 14: Stand Firm in What Is Right for Children, p. 502 Appendix A, p. 507

Who Am I in the Lives of Children?

NINTH EDITION

Who Am I in the Lives of Children?

An Introduction to Early Childhood Education

Stephanie Feeney
University of Hawai'i at Mānoa, Emerita

Eva Moravcik
Honolulu Community College

Sherry Nolte
Honolulu Community College

PEARSON

Boston   Columbus   Indianapolis   New York   San Francisco   Upper Saddle River
Amsterdam   Cape Town   Dubai   London   Madrid   Milan   Munich   Paris   Montreal   Toronto
Delhi   Mexico City   São Paulo   Sydney   Hong Kong   Seoul   Singapore   Taipei   Tokyo

Vice President and Editorial Director: Jeffery
  W. Johnston
Senior Acquisitions Editor: Julie Peters
Development Editor: Bryce Bell
Editorial Assistant: Andrea Hall
Vice President, Director of Marketing:
  Margaret Waples
Senior Marketing Manager: Christopher D. Barry
Senior Managing Editor: Pamela D. Bennett
Senior Project Manager: Linda Hillis Bayma
Senior Operations Supervisor: Matthew Ottenweller

Senior Art Director: Diane C. Lorenzo
Text and Cover Designer: Candace Rowley
Cover Image: Jeff Reese
Media Project Manager: Rebecca Norsic
Full-Service Project Management: Thistle Hill
  Publishing Services, LLC
Composition: S4Carlisle Publishing Services
Printer/Binder: R.R. Donnelley & Sons Company
Cover Printer: Lehigh Phoenix/Hagerstown
Text Font: ITC Garamond Std Book

Credits and acknowledgments for materials borrowed from other sources and reproduced, with permission, in this textbook appear on the appropriate page within the text, or below.

The Standards and Key Elements in the Learning Outcomes section of each chapter are from NAEYC. "NAEYC Standards for Early Childhood Professional Preparation Programs." Position Statement. Washington, DC: Author. Reprinted with permission from the National Association for the Education of Young Children (NAEYC). Copyright © 2009 NAEYC. Full text of all NAEYC position statements is available at www.naeyc.org/positionstatements

Every effort has been made to provide accurate and current Internet information in this book. However, the Internet and information posted on it are constantly changing, so it is inevitable that some of the Internet addresses listed in this textbook will change.

Photo Credits: Details from Pieter Bruegel, *Kinderspiele,* Kunsthistorisches Museum, Vienna, pp. 60, 66; *J. A. Comenius in his study,* by Vaclav Nedbal, 1911, oil on canvas, The National Pedagogical Museum and Library of J. A. Comenius, Praha 1, Czech Republic, p. 67; Orbis sensualium pictus, Nürnberg 1660, publisher: Michael Endter – *Children's Plays,* The National Pedagogical Museum and Library of J. A. Comenius, Praha 1, Czech Republic, p. 68; Copyright © North Wind / North Wind Picture Archives — All rights reserved, p. 70; courtesy of the Library of Congress, pp. 73, 81; provided by the authors, p. 76; © Bettmann / CORBIS, p. 85; courtesy of the Centenary of the Montessori Movement, p. 86; Anthony Magnacca / Merrill, p. 87. All other photos by Jeff Reese.

Library of Congress Cataloging-in-Publication Data
Feeney, Stephanie.
  Who am I in the lives of children? : an introduction to early childhood education / Stephanie
Feeney, Eva Moravcik, Sherry Nolte. — 9th ed.
    p. cm.
  Prev. ed. cataloged under title
  Includes bibliographical references and index.
  ISBN-13: 978-0-13-265704-4 (casebound)
  ISBN-10: 0-13-265704-X (casebound)
1. Education, Preschool—United States. 2. Preschool teaching—United States.
3. Child development—United States. 4. Early childhood education—United States.
I. Moravcik, Eva. II. Nolte, Sherry. III. Who am I in the lives of children? IV. Title.
LB1140.23.F44 2013
372.210973—dc23

                                                                    2011047415

10 9 8 7 6 5 4 3 2

ISBN-13: 978-0-13-265704-4
ISBN-10:   0-13-265704-X

Dear Reader:

Welcome to the ninth edition of *Who Am I in the Lives of Children?,* an introduction to the field of early childhood education. Our purpose in writing this book is to support you in becoming a professional who can enhance the development of young children in early childhood education programs.

It is not our intention for everyone to come to the same conclusions or to work with children in the same way. We feel strongly that in order for you to become a skilled early childhood educator, you must develop your own style and a professional philosophy that reflects your values and guides your actions. Your journey toward becoming an early childhood educator will be an exciting one. We encourage you to take time to think carefully about what you know, believe, and value regarding young children and their families and your role as a teacher. There is much to learn about this field, and our knowledge about it grows and evolves continuously. It is impossible to include everything you might need to know in this book. Rather, we offer you a lens through which to view information, ideas, and the many choices you will make in your work with young children and with their families. We are confident that as you thoughtfully reflect on what you are learning,

carefully consider your attitudes and beliefs about children and education, and practice and hone your skills, you will find both satisfaction and joy in participating with others in the important work of the early childhood educator.

About the Authors

When we read a book, we like to know about the authors—who they are and why they wrote the book. We want to share some of that information with you. Among us we have filled the roles of preschool teacher, social worker, kindergarten teacher, center director, education coordinator, parent and child center program director, consultant, parent educator, CDA trainer, Head Start regional training officer, college professor, and author. We have worked in parent cooperatives, child care centers, preschools, infant-toddler programs, Head Start programs, military child care programs, public schools, government agencies, and college settings. We have been board members of our local and national early childhood organizations and child advocates.

Stephanie, now retired, was professor of early childhood education at the University of Hawaii for many years. Since her retirement she has been coeditor of the third edition of *Continuing Issues in Early Childhood Education* and has written *Professionalism in Early Childhood Education: Doing Our Best for Young Children* (both published by Pearson). She continues to be involved in writing and teaching about ethics and professionalism.

Eva is a professor at Honolulu Community College, where she teaches courses and coordinates a small child development lab school. Her daily work with children, family, staff, and college students continues to provide her with grounding in the reality of life in a program for young children.

Sherry, who joined us as contributor to the seventh edition and coauthor in the eighth edition, brings extensive experience working in programs for military families, low-income children, and infants and toddlers. She also is a professor at Honolulu Community College, where she teaches and supervises practicum students.

Eva and Sherry, with a little help from Stephanie, have just finished writing *Meaningful Curriculum for Young Children,* a companion book to this text. Their in-depth reading, research, and writing on curriculum informs this edition.

Stephanie Feeney, Eva Moravcik, and Sherry Nolte

As of this edition, Doris Christensen has retired from writing; however, we continue to appreciate her contributions that have so long been a part of *Who Am I in the Lives of Children?* Dr. Linda Brown assisted us in the revision of Chapter 12, "Including Diverse Learners." We are once again joined by our longtime friend and colleague, Mary Goya, professor of early childhood education at Hawai'i Community College in Hilo, who updated the *Instructor's Resource Manual, Test Bank*, and *Online PowerPoint Slides* for this edition.

This book grows out of our experiences as children, as adults, as learners, and as teachers. Our early schooling included experiences in child-oriented nursery schools much like those we describe in this book, as well as in large public schools, private schools, and a small multinational school. Although our childhood experiences were different, our values are similar, and we have many of the same ideas about education. We have all long held a strong commitment to ensuring that all children experience programs that are nurturing and challenging, that support all aspects of their development, and that welcome their families as partners.

We began writing because we wanted an introductory text consistent with our belief that the personal and professional development of early childhood teachers are inextricably linked, and that emphasized the importance of reflection on values and educational choices—an approach that was not common at the time, although today we are pleased that others have adopted this perspective. This ninth edition, like the previous eight, reflects a process of reading, reflection, and integration of new information and experiences.

About the Book: A Child-Centered Approach

Since the first edition in 1979 and through eight subsequent revisions, *Who Am I in the Lives of Children?* has been used by us and by others in a variety of programs and in a number of different places. It has been used across the United States and in countries as diverse as Canada, Australia, Japan, Singapore, and China. Each edition has reflected developments in our field, the feedback of our students and colleagues, and our own growth as educators and child and family advocates.

Because we want to speak to our readers in as comprehensible a way as possible, we write in an informal, direct, and personal voice. In this edition, as in all of the previous ones, we continue to emphasize the development of personal awareness and the ongoing process of reflection on values and choices.

The cornerstone of this book and our work with children is what we refer to as a *child-centered* approach to early childhood education. This approach has its roots in a long tradition of humanistic and progressive education and in the unique history and philosophy of early childhood education. Our ideas have been profoundly shaped by educators, psychologists, and philosophers who have advocated child-centered educational practice, including (in chronological order) Friedrich Froebel, John Dewey, Maria Montessori, Lucy Sprague Mitchell, A. S. Neill, Lev Vygotsky, Jean Piaget, Erik Erikson, Abraham Maslow, Barbara Biber, Sylvia Ashton-Warner, James L. Hymes, Loris Malaguzzi, John Holt, and Howard Gardner.

Programs that evolve from the child-centered tradition are dedicated to the development of the whole child—physical, social, emotional, and intellectual. Such programs are characterized by a deep respect for the individual and the recognition that individual differences need to be honored in educational settings. They reflect the understanding that children learn best from direct experience and spontaneous play. Educators in child-centered programs begin with children as they are and focus on getting to know each individual's strengths, interests, challenges, and circumstances. They then support each child in growing and learning in ways that are in harmony with who they are rather than according to a predetermined plan. These educators see each child as a member of a family, a community, and a society, and their choices reflect these understandings.

We subscribe to a constructivist approach to providing learning experiences for young children and to the importance of intentional teaching. We continue in this edition to affirm our values and commitment to a respectful, culturally sensitive, child-centered, and family-friendly approach to working with young children. We strive to make the values and guiding principles of early education visible and affirm our commitment to them. Over the years it has become clear to us that this approach is broader than just a way of viewing early childhood education—it is an approach to working with people of all ages, to learning at all stages, and to life.

What's New in This Edition

- In Chapters 4 through 13, which concern the day-to-day work of the early childhood educator, we have included more classroom-based anecdotes and integrated new examples of how constructivism and intentionality can be translated into classroom practice.
- Because of the importance of partnerships with families, we have included a new feature, "Connecting with Families," which can be found in Chapters 4 through 13.
- Chapter 1's coverage of professional ethics has been updated and includes a new section, "Finding Your Path."
- Chapter 2's discussion of programs and standards and issues in the field has been updated and a new section on trends in early childhood education has been added.
- Chapter 4 includes an updated and expanded discussion of brain research and its relevance to early childhood education, including the importance of the executive functions of the brain.
- Updated and expanded Chapter 5 includes new content on rubrics, children's work

samples, digital portfolios, portfolios for children in the primary grades, documentation panels, and authentic assessment in kindergarten and the primary grades.
- Chapter 6 has an expanded discussion of family systems theory, a new emphasis on social and emotional competence as a goal for guidance, and a discussion of practices that support this learning, including a discussion of the Teaching Pyramid (CSEFEL).
- Chapter 7 includes an expanded discussion of obesity prevention and fitness activities in early childhood programs.
- New in Chapter 9 is a discussion of levels of make-believe play based on work by Vygotsky and Elkonin. The idea of flow in play, Eberle's processes of play, play's role in brain development, and discussion of rough-and-tumble play have also been added.
- Strengthened chapters on curriculum and curriculum planning include examples of integrated curriculum in a constructivist early childhood program. (Videos showing this approach in action can be viewed on the MyEducationLab website at myeducationlab .com, which requires a unique access code for each student.) Other additions to Chapter 11, "Curriculum Planning," include an expanded discussion of DAP, content standards, basing plans on observation, writing weekly plans, and a comparison of integrated approaches to planning.

Our Vision for You

Many approaches can be taken in teaching others to work with young children. In this book we want to help you discover who you are as an educator and what you value for children instead of focusing exclusively on content and skills. Like creating a clay figure in which each part is drawn out of a central core, we strive to help your work be an integral part of who you are. Without this foundation, it is difficult to know how to respond to a group of real children. A figurine constructed by sticking head, arms, and legs onto a ball of clay often falls apart when exposed to the heat of the fire. Similarly, a teacher whose education consists of bits and pieces may fall apart when faced with the reality of the classroom.

You will play an important part in the lives of the children and families with whom you will work.

We hope that this ninth edition of *Who Am I in the Lives of Children?* will help you become a competent, nurturing, and reflective early childhood educator and an active and committed advocate for young children.

Acknowledgments

We have been writing and revising *Who Am I in the Lives of Children?* since 1977, and during that period of time we have been influenced and supported by many colleagues, friends, and students. Our list of individuals to acknowledge continues to grow, as does our gratitude.

We offer thanks to educational leaders who have contributed to our thinking and practice since we launched this book: Barbara Bowman, Sue Bredekamp, Harriet Cuffaro, Lilian Katz, Elizabeth Jones, Gwen Morgan, and Karen VanderVen. We remember with fondness Docia Zavitkovsky, Jim Greenman, Elizabeth Gilkeson, and Elizabeth Brady, and we honor the memory of Jean Fargo for helping us to realize that values must lie at the heart of the work of the early childhood educator. And we continue to be inspired by the respectful attitude toward children and the eloquent words of the late Fred (Mister) Rogers.

We wish to thank the following friends and colleagues for their assistance with this and previous editions: Georgia Acevedo, Steve Bobilin, Linda Buck, Spring Busche-Ong, Svatava Cigankova, Robyn Chun, Jane Dickson-Iijima, Richard Feldman, Marjorie Fields, Nancy Freeman, Amy Garma, Jonathan Gillentine, Kenneth Kipnis, Miles Nakanishi, Robert Peters, Julie Powers, Larry Prochner, Jackie Rabang, Alan Reese, Beth Rous, Kate Tarrant, and Lisa Yogi.

Our students in the early childhood/elementary education program at the University of Hawai'i at Mānoa and the early childhood program at Honolulu Community College have given us insight, asked thought-provoking questions, and provided us with the viewpoint of the future educator.

Like you, we learn by doing. Our attitudes, values, knowledge, and skills have developed as we have worked with the children, families, and staff at programs in Hawai'i: the Leeward Community College Children's Center, the Keiki Hauoli Children's Center at Honolulu Community College, University of Hawai'i at Mānoa Children's Center, the Early School, and St. Timothy's Children's Center.

We would also like to thank the reviewers of this edition for their insights and comments: Victoria Candelora, Brevard Community College; Jody Lawrence, Davidson County Community College; Barbie Norvell-Johnson, Coastal Carolina University; Sharon Pyeatt, Oklahoma City University; Patricia Roiger, SUNY Cortland; and Emily Stottlemyre, McLennan Community College.

The images that bring this book to life are the work of Jeffrey Reese, a talented photographer who took photographs for this and the previous four editions. The pictures were taken in Oregon at South Coast Head Start in Coos Bay and at Helen Gordon Child Development Center in Portland; in Olympia, Washington, with the family of Kona and Ed Matautia; and in Hawai'i at the Leeward Community College Children's Center, the Keiki Hauoli Children's Center at Honolulu Community College and Kaneohe Marine Base Child Development Center. Video for MyEducationLab was taken by Steve Bobilin in Hawai'i at Leeward Community College and at Honolulu Community College. The artwork that adds such vibrancy to this edition is the work of the children of Leeward Community College Children's Center. We appreciate the cooperation of the children, staff, and families of these schools. We are grateful to the National Pedagogical Museum and Library of J. A. Comenius, Prague, Czech Republic, for graciously allowing us to use images from their collection in Chapter 3.

Special thanks to our editor, Julie Peters, for all of her guidance during this revision.

No book is written without affecting the lives of the families of the authors. We especially want to thank our husbands and children, Don Mickey, Jeffrey Reese, and David and Miles Nolte, who have encouraged us and supported our efforts with patience and good humor.

Stephanie Feeney

Eva Moravcik

Sherry Nolte

Waldport, Oregon, and Honolulu, Hawai'i

FEATURES of this book

Reflection Boxes

There are two types of reflection boxes in the chapters of this book. These boxes pose questions for you to think, write, and talk about.

◀ "Reflect on . . ." Boxes

These questions are intended to help you engage with what you are learning. Thinking and reflecting is a cornerstone of the learning process. Discussing and writing about these topics is a good way to focus your learning and clarify your thinking.

Reflect on your experience

Reflect on your experiences in preschools and kindergartens. How did the programs that you attended as a child, or that you have observed or taught in, seem to reflect what is described in the history of these programs? What were the programs like? What were your reactions to them?

"Ethical Reflection" Boxes ▶

Early childhood educators often encounter ethical issues in their work. An overview of professional ethics and discussion of ethical dilemmas that teachers of young children might experience can be found in Chapter 1, "The Teacher." These boxes describe ethical dilemmas and ask you to think about the conflicting responsibilities in each situation and to reflect on what the "good early childhood educator" might do to resolve it using guidance from the NAEYC Code of Ethical Conduct.

Reflect on your ethical responsibilities

You have a 6-year-old in your class who is frequently absent from school. When you ask her about her many absences, she tells you that she had to stay home to take care of her baby sister because her mom was sick or had to work. Using the guidelines on page 23, reflect on your ethical responsibilities in this situation.

Golden Rules ▼

"Golden Rules" boxes contain important principles and practices for teaching, summarized and presented in a clear and useful format.

GOLDEN RULES FOR CREATING INDOOR LEARNING ENVIRONMENTS

1. Arrange the environment so it can be easily supervised, cleaned, and maintained.
2. Make sure there is water to drink, toilets/diapering facilities, sinks, and quiet places for resting.
3. Choose child-sized furniture and include comfortable seating for adults.
4. Organize the classroom in areas.
5. Select safe, good-quality, sturdy equipment and materials and discard or repair broken, incomplete ones.
6. Store materials children can use at their eye-level on low, open, uncrowded shelves and store teacher materials out of reach.
7. Rotate play materials.
8. Regularly reevaluate and change the environment.
9. Add items of beauty to the environment.
10. Include materials that reflect the children, their families, and geographic location.

Connecting with Families ▼

A new feature of this edition: ideas contained in boxes that we call "Connecting with Families." These give you practical ideas for ways to include families in your program.

CONNECTING WITH FAMILIES

About Guidance Practices

Families use a variety of ways to teach their children about their expectations and the ways that they want them to behave. Some of these may be similar to what you know about and understand; others may be quite different. Here are some ways you can get to know more about their goals, values, and discipline practices:

- Include a question in your enrollment packet asking families to tell you about ways they handle inappropriate behavior at home.
- Make time for a get-to-know-you meeting during the child's first days and ask them about their discipline methods; take time to share ways that you handle inappropriate behaviors in your classroom.
- Ask them what social skills they most wish their child to master and invite them to share ideas for how you can support them in teaching them.
- Plan family meetings around discussion of common challenges such as bedtime, meals, saying no, and so on. Ask for their input regarding what the topic should be.
- Invite professionals with expertise in child guidance or knowledge of the cultures of families in your program to lead a family meeting or to offer a parenting class.

End-of-Chapter Features

- **Learning Outcomes:** We had a purpose and specific learning outcomes in mind as we wrote each chapter of this book. These learning outcomes relate to the NAEYC Standards for Early Childhood Professional Preparation Programs that are included at the end of each chapter.
- **To Learn More:** This section suggests projects to help you learn more about the chapter's content.
- **For Your Portfolio:** This section suggests items that you might wish to put in your professional portfolio. Today, professionals in many fields create portfolios in which they document for employers and themselves their qualifications, skills, experiences, and unique qualities. Portfolios are "living documents" that will change as you grow, learn, and have new experiences. Guidelines for starting a portfolio can be found in Chapter 1.
- **Investigate Related Websites:** This section lists websites that might be of interest if you want to follow up on what you have learned.

At the back of the book you will find a *Bibliography,* which lists the books and articles that we referred to or consulted as we wrote each chapter. We hope you will have the opportunity to read some of these references as you develop into a committed early childhood educator.

MYEDUCATIONLAB™

The Power of Classroom Practice

In *Preparing Teachers for a Changing World*, Linda Darling-Hammond and her colleagues point out that grounding teacher education in real classrooms—among real teachers and students and among actual examples of students' and teachers' work—is an important, and perhaps even an essential, part of training teachers for the complexities of teaching in today's classrooms. **MyEducationLab™** is an online learning solution that provides contextualized interactive exercises, simulations, and other resources designed to help develop the knowledge and skills teachers need. All of the activities and exercises in MyEducationLab are built around essential learning outcomes for teachers and are mapped to professional teaching standards. Utilizing classroom video, authentic student and teacher artifacts, case studies, and other resources and assessments, the scaffolded learning experiences in MyEducationLab offer pre-service teachers and those who teach them a unique and valuable education tool.

For each topic covered in the course you will find most or all of the following features and resources:

Connection to National Standards

Now it is easier than ever to see how coursework is connected to national standards. Each topic on MyEducationLab lists intended learning outcomes connected to the appropriate national standards. And all of the activities and exercises in MyEducationLab are mapped to the appropriate national standards and learning outcomes as well.

Assignments and Activities

Designed to enhance student understanding of concepts covered in class and save instructors preparation and grading time, these assignable exercises show concepts in action (through video, cases, and/or student and teacher artifacts). They help students deepen content knowledge and synthesize and apply concepts and strategies they read about in the book. (Correct answers for these assignments are available only to the instructor only under the Instructor Resource tab.)

Building Teaching Skills and Dispositions

These learning units help students practice and strengthen skills that are essential to quality teaching. After presenting the steps involved in a core teaching process, students are given an opportunity to practice applying this skill via videos, student and teacher artifacts, and/or case studies of authentic classrooms. Providing multiple opportunities to practice a single teaching concept, each activity encourages a deeper understanding and application of concepts, as well as the use of critical thinking skills.

IRIS Center Resources

The IRIS Center at Vanderbilt University (iris.peabody .vanderbilt.edu), funded by the U.S. Department of Education's Office of Special Education Programs (OSEP), develops training enhancement materials for pre-service and in-service teachers. The Center works with experts from across the country to create challenge-based interactive modules, case study units, and podcasts that provide research-validated information about working with students in inclusive settings. In your MyEducationLab course we have integrated this content where appropriate.

Teacher Talk

This feature emphasizes the power of teaching through videos of master teachers, each speaker telling his or her own compelling story of why he or she teaches. These videos help teacher candidates see the bigger picture and consider why what they are learning is important to their career as a teacher. Each of these featured teachers has been awarded the Council of Chief State School Officers' Teacher of the Year award, the oldest and most prestigious award for teachers.

Study Plan Specific to Your Text

A MyEducationLab Study Plan is a multiple-choice assessment tied to chapter objectives, supported by study material. A well-designed Study Plan offers multiple opportunities to fully master required course content as identified by the objectives in each chapter:

- **Chapter Objectives** identify the learning outcomes for the chapter and give students targets to shoot for as they read and study.
- **Multiple Choice Assessments** assess mastery of the content. These assessments are mapped to chapter objectives, and students can take the multiple-choice quiz as many times as they want. Not only do these quizzes provide overall scores for each objective, but they also explain why responses to particular items are correct or incorrect.
- **Study Material: Review, Practice, and Enrichment** gives students a deeper understanding of

what they do and do not know related to chapter content. This material includes text excerpts, activities that include hints and feedback, and interactive multimedia exercises built around videos or scenarios.

New! CourseSmart eTextbook Available

CourseSmart is an exciting new choice for students looking to save money. As an alternative to purchasing the printed textbook, students can purchase an electronic version of the same content. With a CourseSmart eTextbook, students can search the text, make notes online, print out reading assignments that incorporate lecture notes, and bookmark important passages for later review. For more information, or to purchase access to the CourseSmart eTextbook, visit coursesmart.com.

SUPPLEMENTS to this text

The supplements package for the ninth edition is revised and upgraded. All online ancillaries are available for download by adopting professors via pearsonhighered.com in the Instructor's Resource Center. Contact your Pearson sales representative for additional information.

Instructor's Resource Manual This manual contains chapter overviews and activity ideas for both in and out of class, as well as instructions for assignable MyEducationLab material.

Online Test Bank The Test Bank includes a variety of test items, including multiple choice, true/false, and short essay, and is available in various LMS formats.

Pearson MyTest This powerful assessment generation program helps instructors easily create and print quizzes and exams. Questions and tests are authored online, allowing ultimate flexibility and the ability to efficiently create and print assessments anytime, anywhere! Instructors can access Pearson MyTest and their test bank files by going to pearsonmytest.com to log in, register, or request access. Features of Pearson MyTest include:

Premium assessment content

- Draw from a rich library of assessments that complement your Pearson textbook and your course's learning objectives.

- Edit questions or tests to fit your specific teaching needs.

Instructor-friendly resources

- Easily create and store your own questions, including images, diagrams, and charts using simple drag-and-drop and Word-like controls.

- Use additional information provided by Pearson, such as the question's difficulty level or learning objective, to help you quickly build your test.

Time-saving enhancements

- Add headers or footers and easily scramble questions and answer choices—all from one simple toolbar.

- Quickly create multiple versions of your test or answer key, and when ready, simply save to MS-Word or PDF format and print!

- Export your exams for import to Blackboard 6.0, CE (WebCT), or Vista (WebCT)!

Online PowerPoint Slides PowerPoint slides highlight key concepts and strategies in each chapter and enhance lectures and discussions.

brief CONTENTS

CONTENTS

4 Child Development 101

9 Understanding and Supporting Play   305

12 Including Diverse Learners   431

13 Partnerships with Families   463

14 Becoming an Early Childhood Professional   493

SPECIAL features

Who Am I in the Lives of Children?

We teach who we are.

JOHN GARDNER

1

The Teacher

Welcome to the field of early childhood education! You are embarking on the important career of educating and caring for young children. The kind of person you are and the kind of professional you will become will have a lasting impact on children, families, and society. The purpose of this book is to help you become an educator who can nourish the growth of children; support families; work amicably with colleagues; advocate for children and families; and in the future, make contributions to your field. In this chapter we provide a brief introduction to the field of early childhood education (which will be expanded in Chapter 2) and introduce you to the role of the early childhood educator and to some of the responsibilities that accompany that role. We then look at the teacher of young children from two different and interconnected perspectives—who they are as people (what they bring to work with children) and who they are as professionals (the kinds of educators that they will become). In the section on the teacher as a person we encourage you to look at your personal attributes, attitudes, skills, values, and morality. These things will play an important role in who you will be in children's lives. In the last part of the chapter we look at some careers in early childhood education and the educational experiences you will need to pursue the path you choose. In the process of learning more about yourself and about the field of early childhood education and care, you will acquire the knowledge, skills, and behaviors that will help you to grow into a dedicated early childhood educator who can provide high-quality nurturing, education, and care.

MyEducationLab

Visit the
MyEducationLab for
*Who Am I in the Lives
of Children?* to enhance
your understanding
of chapter concepts
with a personalized
Study Plan. You'll also
have the opportunity
to hone your teaching
skills through video-
based Assignments and
Activities, as well as
Building Teaching Skills
and Disposition lessons.

What we call things is important because words create an image of who we are and what we do. So we begin this first chapter with some basic definitions regarding who we serve and what we call the field and the people who work in it. *Early childhood* is generally defined as the period in the life span that includes birth through age 8. The field is generally referred to as "early childhood education," "early childhood education and care," or "early care and education" to emphasize the dual focus on learning and care that distinguishes early childhood programs and educators from other educators and schools.

In this edition we will use the term *early childhood education* (ECE) to refer to education and care provided in all settings for children between birth and age 8. We prefer this term because education is a core function of our work and because it brings us into direct alignment with other arenas of education (elementary, secondary, post-secondary) while suggesting that we are unique in our focus on young children. Additionally, the role of education is the one most valued in our society. When programs are viewed as educative they are seen as worthy of respect, and the children who are cared for and educated are viewed as learners. This term reflects the view that those who implement early childhood education support development and help children learn in the context of caring relationships.

Early childhood educators provide education and care for young children in a number of different kinds of settings. Most provide care with an educational focus with the goal of promoting positive development and learning. These programs are found in diverse facilities, including child development centers designed for the care and education of young children, schools, and homes. Programs for children under the age of 5 may be called *preschools, child care centers, child development centers,* or *prekindergartens*. Programs where young children and their parents come together to learn are called *family–child interaction programs*. Programs for children 5 through 8 years of age are generally referred to as *kindergartens, primary programs* (kindergarten through grade 3), *elementary schools* (kindergarten to grade 6), and *after-school programs*.

People who work with young children are called a variety of things including teacher, caregiver, provider, practitioner, and early childhood educator. We call this chapter "The Teacher" because we believe this best reflects you, a student reading this text, and your career aspirations, whether you are considering working with infants or 8-year-olds. We use *teacher* as an umbrella term because it emphasizes the things that unite us as a group of people who work with young children. Sue Bredekamp (2011) makes a case for the use of the term *teacher* because "*teacher* is the broadest term, it captures most of the job responsibilities, commands society's respect, and is, after all, what children usually call the adults who care for them and educate them no matter what the setting" (Bredekamp, 2011, p. 21). It also is a term that the general public—people like your family and friends—will understand and are likely to have positive associations with. We hope to convey the importance and seriousness of your chosen vocation to you; and we hope that, in turn, you will convey the value of this work to others. In this book we will use the terms *teacher, early childhood educator,* and *practitioner* interchangably to refer to everyone who is employed to educate and care for children between the ages of birth and 8 including infant and toddler caregivers, family child care providers, home visitors, preschool, kindergarten, and primary grade teachers.

Because programs for children under the age of 5 are most often found in preschools and child care centers while kindergarten through grade 3 programs are usually housed in elementary schools, it can be challenging to see the field of early childhood education as a whole. It might be helpful as you construct your understanding of the field to keep in mind that all programs for young children have the overriding purpose of supporting children's growth and development. No matter what they are called or where they are housed, programs for young children provide both care and education. People who work with young children, regardless of their job title or the age of the children, strive to support all aspects of development, promote learning, and provide nurturing care.

The Work We Do

Working with young children is varied and challenging; it demands knowledge, skill, sensitivity, creativity, and hard work. If these challenges excite you, you have probably chosen the right field. Early childhood education is especially rewarding for those who enjoy the spontaneous teaching and learning opportunities that abound in daily life with young children. It may not be as enjoyable for people who think that teaching is a matter of dispensing subject matter or for those who like work that is tidy and predictable. Sometimes college students who begin their careers with visions of shaping young minds become discouraged when they discover how much of their time is spent mixing paint, changing pants, arbitrating disputes, mopping floors, and wiping noses. But while working with young children can be demanding and tiring, it can also be invigorating and gratifying. For in addition to more mundane tasks you will get to have conversations with children, tell and read stories, sing, observe nature, explore neighborhoods, plant gardens, and provide inspiration for creative expression. You will have the opportunity every day to plan and implement interesting and meaningful learning experiences. We have found that this wide range of tasks makes work with young children endlessly interesting and challenging.

While your most important task as an early childhood educator is working with children, you will also interact with families, colleagues, and community agencies. If you embarked on a career in early childhood education because you enjoy being with young children, you might be surprised at the extent to which early childhood educators work with adults as well. You will interact with families and work with other staff members daily. You might also communicate with people in agencies concerned with children and families (like child welfare workers and early intervention specialists) and engage with other professionals as you further your own professional development.

Early childhood programs resemble one another in the breadth of their responsibilities to children. We hope that you, as one of tomorrow's early childhood educators, will make a commitment to providing high-quality programs for young children (the chapters of this book will explain what that entails). Eventually, you may also want to develop knowledge of broader societal issues and become involved in policy decisions and publicly advocating for the rights and needs of young children.

Working with Children

The first and most important of your many tasks is working with children. Each day that you work with young children you will communicate with them, play with them, care for their physical needs, teach them, and provide them with a sense of psychological comfort and security. The younger the children with whom you work, the more you will need to provide nurturing and physical care.

Reflect and write about your current ideas about early childhood teachers*

What do you see in your mind when you think of a teacher of young children? What is the teacher like? What is the teacher doing?

*This is the first of many reflections that you will find in this book. Reflecting on the questions asked and writing down your ideas will help you become a good teacher of young children. Your instructor might assign reflections as a formal part of your class. If not, you might want to get a notebook and briefly write down your ideas. They will form a valuable way to document your own growth as an early childhood educator and start you on the road to becoming a reflective teacher.

Your work with young children will begin before the first child arrives and will continue each day after the last child has gone home. It starts when you create an environment that is safe, healthy, and stimulating. The learning environment is the primary teaching tool in programs for children age 5 and younger. You will also design the daily schedule, plan learning experiences, and collect and use resources. This stage setting is an essential part of working with young children. After children have arrived you will observe and support them as they play, mediate relationships between children, model the way you want people to treat one another, and help them develop skills and learn about the world. In a single day you might function as a teacher, friend, secretary, parent, reference librarian, interior designer, colleague, nurse, janitor, counselor, entertainer, and diplomat.

Developmentally Appropriate Practice

In early childhood care and education we regard all areas of development—social, emotional, intellectual, and physical—as important and interconnected. Because young children are vulnerable and dependent on adults for responsive care, you will be expected to nurture and support all aspects of development. We call this attention to overall development concern for "the whole child," an idea you will encounter over and over in this book. Responsive care and education that is mindful of the development of the whole child is known today as *developmentally appropriate practice* (often referred to as DAP) (Copple & Bredekamp, 2009). We will discuss how to provide developmentally appropriate practice in the pages of this book.

Most early childhood educators believe that the best kind of program for children has a whole-child emphasis. Current attention to standards has made preschool teachers more aware of the importance of subject matter learning than they were in the past when programs were more likely to be based on play in a planned environment. This approach to education has disappeared in many kindergarten through third-grade programs due to demands for accountability and academic achievement. We, the authors of this book, believe that children thrive in programs that address all areas of development and regard them all as important. We look forward to the day when this approach to education returns to all programs for young children.

Intentional Teaching

There is growing emphasis on the need for early childhood educators to have a repertoire of intentional teaching strategies for every child they encounter (Epstein, 2007; NAEYC, 2009). According to Ann Epstein (2007), intentional teachers have a purpose behind every decision they make and skill in articulating the reasons for their actions. The intentional teacher decides on goals for children's development, thinks through possible actions, and then decides on strategies that will achieve these goals. This teacher also has a solid base of knowledge of development, research and pedagogy, and relevant standards and knows how to draw on these to meet goals while also adapting to individual differences in children. An important part of your preparation to be a teacher will be learning to select appropriate teaching strategies and to practice explaining why you chose them in a way that is easily understood by children's family members, colleagues, and others interested in the development of young children.

Addressing Standards

Early childhood teachers have always planned curriculum, assessed children, and followed program guidelines. Because of the current public attention to early childhood education and demands for accountability, these are now a bigger part of your teaching responsibility. Many early childhood programs have begun to pay more attention to early learning standards, academic content (especially literacy), and the instructional role of the teacher. As part of the current emphasis on standards you will probably be expected to:

- Know what standards are used in your program and in your state
- Design curriculum that addresses early learning standards
- Assess what children have learned in terms of standards
- Identify how you are meeting standards

Even though these tasks are very similar to what teachers have done in the past, they mean that today you can expect your work to be more visible, more public, and more likely to be evaluated. You might also be asked to provide evidence of program quality as described by a variety of quality rating systems or be expected to develop classroom portfolios for preschool programs that seek national accreditation.

Differences Between Preschool and Primary Programs

If you are in a teacher education program that assigns students to practice teaching in both preschools and elementary schools, you are likely to notice differences in philosophy and practices between programs for younger and older children. Programs for preschool children are generally informed by research on child development. They arrange the learning environment into activity centers filled with toys and materials to explore and create with, regard play as an important medium for learning, emphasize child-choice and hands-on activities, view the role of the teacher as facilitator, and base assessment of children on observation. In elementary programs, as you probably remember from your childhood, teachers focus more on the acquisition of skills in subjects like reading and math and knowledge of science and social studies. A typical elementary classroom may be furnished with desks or worktables. Teaching is likely to involve more reading and verbal instruction. Children do more assigned paper-and-pencil work and are frequently assessed with graded paperwork and tests. Of course these generalizations are not true of every program. There are exceptions in every community.

Working with Families

Young children cannot be separated from the context of their families, so relating to and working with parents and other family members is an important part of the role of the early childhood educator. Because early childhood programs often provide the child's first experience in the larger world away from home, you will play an important role in the transition between home and school—helping families and children learn to be apart from one another for a period of time each day. In fact, you may be the second professional (the first is usually the pediatrician) who has a relationship with the family and the child. A partnership between home and the early childhood program is absolutely essential in programs for infants, toddlers, and preschoolers. It should also be an important component of programs for older children.

Just as your work with children brings with it diverse roles and demands, your work with families involves a range of skills both similar to and different from those you need in your work with children. In your work with families, you may find yourself being a consultant, a social worker, an advocate, a teacher, a reporter, a librarian, a mediator, a translator, a social director, and a postal carrier, making your work with families another way that your job will be varied, engaging, and challenging.

Working as Part of a Team

An important feature of the role of most early childhood educators is working collaboratively with other adults. Working as part of a team involves collaborating with coworkers, supervising volunteers, interacting with program administrators, and working with a host of others from custodians to counselors. Some early childhood educators report that participating in a team gives them support, stimulation, and a sense of belonging. Team support can reduce stress, contribute to a pleasant work environment, minimize conflict, and increase motivation (Rodd, 1994). The ability to work productively on a team is an important professional skill you will need to learn.

In effective teams, people work together on behalf of a shared goal. They support and respect one another despite differences. They acknowledge and make best use of one another's strengths and contributions. They understand their roles and fulfill their responsibilities. Perhaps most important, they communicate productively and resolve the conflicts that inevitably occur when people work in close proximity every day.

Being a part of a team is more than just turning up for work each day. It involves an understanding of team roles and responsibilities and taking an active role in the work situation. It means being a good colleague by treating others with respect, doing a fair share of the work, and appreciating your colleagues' contributions.

The Teacher as a Person

Because who you are as a person is the foundation for the professional you will become, we begin by considering what the early childhood educator is like as a person and ask you to take a careful look at yourself. Then we examine what it means to be an early childhood professional. As you enter the field, you bring with you the sum of your experiences—your personal qualities, gender, race, culture, family circumstances, values, beliefs, and life experiences. These aspects will blend over time with your professional training and experiences working with children and families to forge your identity as an early childhood educator.

What Qualities Make a Good Teacher of Young Children?

Are you intellectual? Thoughtful? Practical? Are you active and outgoing? Are you quiet and reserved? Are you creative and dramatic? You can become a good teacher with any of these traits. Many kinds of individuals can work successfully with young children. There is no one "right" personality type, no single set of experiences or training that will impart the required traits, no one way of being a good teacher of young children. No single mold produces a good early childhood educator.

Though many people from many different backgrounds *can* be good early childhood educators, not everyone finds success and satisfaction in this field.

What *does* make a good early childhood teacher? What combination of attitudes, knowledge, skills, and personal qualities—including *dispositions* (tendencies to respond to experiences in certain ways)—contribute to the ability to work effectively with young children? Successful early childhood educators have been described as having the following characteristics: positive outlook, curiosity, openness to new ideas, enthusiasm, commitment, high energy, physical strength, a sense of humor, flexibility, self-awareness, the capacity for empathy, emotional stability, warmth, sensitivity, passion, perseverance, willingness to take risks, patience, integrity (honesty and moral uprightness), creativity, love of learning, and trust in children (Cartwright, 1999; Colker, 2008; Feeney & Chun, 1985; Katz, 1993). Teachers of young children need to love what they do, communicate effectively with children and adults, be good role models, provide unconditional caring for children, and at the same time be able to view them objectively.

Many early childhood scholars have explored the characteristics that early childhood teachers need. We have included this statement written by Barbara Biber in 1948 in every edition of this text because it so eloquently addresses what we think early childhood educators should be like:

> A teacher needs to be a person so secure within herself that she can function with principles rather than prescriptions, that she can exert authority without requiring submission, that she can work experimentally but not at random and that she can admit mistakes without feeling humiliated. (p. 282)

There is no end to the list of desirable teacher qualities. We agree with the authors cited in this chapter and many others who have written movingly about the qualities of good early childhood teachers. We are firmly convinced that a deep appreciation for children and childhood lies at the core of the good early childhood teacher. Respect—a way of relating to others that is based on the belief that every human being has value and deserves to be appreciated—is fundamental. In early childhood education, it is not necessary (or possible) to love every child, but it is imperative that early childhood educators respect the worth and value of every child and family member. It is also important that teachers of young children are able to be altruistic—to focus consistently on the best interests of others—and have the capacity for caring because nurturing others is at the core of the work of the early childhood educator.

We know that appreciation and respect for children paired with a caring nature and an inquiring mind and spirit lead to a sense of joy, hope, and commitment that can turn teaching young children from a job into a calling.

Personal Characteristics

As we have said, people with a wide range of personal characteristics can be effective as teachers of young children. What is important is for you to be willing to look at yourself as objectively as possible, understand your personal characteristics and how they might impact your work with children and families, and be willing to work to overcome anything that may be hinder your ability to work effectively with children and maintain good relationships.

Over the years we have asked beginning students in our college classes to think about the characteristics of the teachers they had as children whom they liked best and liked least. We have found that many of their memories are about the distinctive personal qualities of their former teachers. The teachers that they liked best were kind, fair, compassionate, warm, and listened to them. The teachers they liked least were uncaring, inconsistent, uninteresting, inattentive, and sometimes humiliated them. The memories from childhood that our students report are often vivid, and some still elicit strong emotions. Exploring this question has reinforced our belief that who a teacher is as a person has a strong and lasting impact and is the first thing that should be considered as you embark on your career as a teacher.

Temperament

We have found the research of pediatricians Alexander Thomas and Stella Chess on the temperament of infants, adapted to adults by therapists Jayne Burks and Melvin Rubenstein (Burks & Rubenstein, 1979), a good place for our college students to begin to look at their personal characteristics. Thomas and Chess refer to *temperament* as an individual's behavioral style and characteristic ways of responding. They found that newborns show definite differences in traits that tend to persist over time. Though modified through life experiences, the nine dimensions of temperament are helpful in explaining personality differences in adults as well as children.

Figure 1.1 gives a brief description of the nine traits as they apply to adults, and a continuum accompanying each trait. We have used the continua in our teaching as a tool for personal reflection. Traits of temperament are neither good nor bad; they are simply part of you. However, some characteristics like positive mood, a high activity level, and ease in adapting to new situations will be helpful in working with young children.

FIGURE 1.1 Thomas and Chess's Nine Dimensions of Temperament

1. ACTIVITY LEVEL—Level of physical and mental activity.
   very active _____ very inactive/quiet

2. REGULARITY (Rhythmicity)—Preference for predictable routines or spontaneity.
   highly regular/predictable _____ highly irregular/unpredictable

3. DISTRACTIBILITY—Degree to which extraneous stimuli affect behavior, readiness to leave one activity for another.
   easily distracted _____ very focused despite distractions

4. APPROACH-WITHDRAWAL—Ways of responding to new situations.
   enjoys new experiences _____ avoids new experiences

5. ADAPTABILITY—Ease of adjustment to new ideas or situations (after initial response).
   adapts very easily to change _____ has difficulty adapting

6. PHYSICAL SENSITIVITY (Threshold of Responsiveness)—Sensitivity to changes in the environment including noise, taste, smell, and temperature.
   very aware of changes _____ not too attuned to changes

7. INTENSITY OF REACTION—Energy level typical of response, both positive and negative.
   very high intensity _____ very low intensity

8. PERSISTENCE/ATTENTION SPAN—The amount of time devoted to an activity, even when it is difficult, and the ability to continue working when distracted.
   not easily distracted _____ very easily distracted

9. QUALITY OF MOOD—General optimism or pessimism; tendency to enjoy things uncritically or to be more selective about situations enjoyed.
   generally happy or optimistic _____ generally sad or pessimistic

Source: Information from J. Burks & M. Rubenstein, *Temperament Styles in Adult Interaction*, 1979.

Consider two teachers:

Ruby and Michelle teach together in a classroom of 3- and 4-year-olds. Ruby arrives at school an hour before the children and families arrive; she likes to be alone in the classroom to gather her thoughts and get materials ready. Michelle rushes in at the last minute with a bag of intriguing items she has gathered related to their curriculum on plants. A half-hour after the school has opened Ruby is quietly reading to a few of the younger children, including Joshua, who has been having a hard time separating from his mom. Michelle is leading the rest of the children on a hunt through the yard for flowers.

Ruby and Michelle display some quite different temperamental characteristics, particularly rhythmicity and intensity of reaction. Realizing that a child, parent, or colleague has a temperament that is different from your own (as in the case of Ruby and Michelle) can keep you from finding their behavior negative or difficult. To heighten your awareness of your own temperament, you may wish to plot yourself on the continua in Figure 1.1 and think about the implications of what you find.

Multiple Intelligences

Howard Gardner's conception of multiple intelligences is another resource you can use to understand children and to understand yourself. Gardner describes intelligence as culturally defined, based on what is needed and valued within a society. When you realize your unique talents and strengths (your intelligences), you are better able to maximize them. Figure 1.2 presents the eight categories identified by Gardner.

Understanding that people can be intelligent in different ways can also help you in your work with colleagues. If Ruby and Michelle, from the earlier

FIGURE 1.2 Gardner's Multiple Intelligences

- **Musical intelligence:** The ability to produce and respond to music. This might be you, if you are especially sensitive to the aural environment of the classroom and play instruments and sing easily as you work with children.

- **Bodily-kinesthetic intelligence:** The ability to use the body to solve problems. This might be you, if you demonstrate good coordination and play actively with children.

- **Logical-mathematical intelligence:** The ability to understand the basic properties of numbers and principles of cause and effect. This might be you, if you love to invent challenges for yourself and children.

- **Linguistic intelligence:** The ability to use language to express ideas and learn new words or other languages. This might be you, if you are very articulate and enjoy word play, books, storytelling, and poetry.

- **Spatial intelligence:** The ability to form a mental image of spatial layouts. This might be you, if you are sensitive to the physical arrangement of a room, are able to easily see how to rearrange the classroom, or especially enjoy working with children in blocks.

- **Interpersonal intelligence:** The ability to understand other people and work with them. This might be you, if you are attentive to relationships and demonstrate sociability and leadership.

- **Intrapersonal intelligence:** The ability to understand things about oneself. This might be you, if you have strong interests and goals, know yourself well, are focused inward, and demonstrate confidence.

- **Naturalist intelligence:** The ability to recognize plants and animals in the environment. This might be you, if you know all about the flora and fauna in your community and have an especially well developed science curriculum and science area in your classroom.

Source: Information from H. Gardner, *Frames of Mind*, 1983.

Reflect on your personal characteristics

Consider your personal characteristics using the temperament continua and your intelligences using Gardner's model. What are you like? What are your preferences for activity and setting? What are you good at? What is challenging for you? What might be the implications of what you learned about your personality for relating to children, families, and colleagues?

example, are wise, they will build on one another's strengths and learn from one another. Ruby with her inclination to reflect and plan in advance and her strong interpersonal intelligence is likely to become the expert on addressing children's social-emotional needs, and Michelle with her strong naturalist intelligence will become the expert in motivating children and creating science curriculum. If they are not wise, they might come to resent each other for their differences.

Learning more about yourself can help you be more sensitive to, and accepting of, differences among people, more aware of the impact of your personality on others, and better able to consider the kinds of work settings in which you might function most effectively.

If you are interested in learning more about your personal qualities, abilities, and characteristic ways of responding, there are instruments, such as the Myers-Briggs Type Indicator (MBTI), which examine the way that people characteristically look at the world and make decisions. Other assessment instruments are available in most college counseling centers. You can also take the MBTI on the Internet, formally for a fee or informally in modified versions (see the website information at the end of this chapter).

Personal Values and Morality

Values are principles or standards that a person believes to be important, desirable, or worthwhile and that are prized for themselves (for example truth, integrity, beauty, love, honesty, wisdom, loyalty, justice, respect). You develop your values during a complex process that draws on your family background, culture, religion, community, and life experiences. In countless ways values underlie major and minor life decisions. The things you do each day, the foods you eat, the place you live, the magazines and books you read, the TV programs and videos you watch, and the work and play you choose are all influenced by your values. Your professional values will grow out of these personal values. If you spend some time reflecting, you will be able to identify your personal values and see the kind of impact they have on your life.

You are very likely to have chosen early childhood education because you care deeply about children. You might be motivated by religious values, a commitment to world peace, a concern for social justice, or a passion for learning. You might have a desire to help children enjoy fulfilling lives, to be successful students, or to become productive members of society. Awareness of your personal values will help you to be clear about what you are trying to accomplish in your daily work with children.

It is sometimes surprising to discover that other people do not share values that you believed were universal—one of the reasons the first year in a new community or a new relationship (for example, with a new spouse) and the first year of working in an early childhood program can be difficult. Awareness can help you to realize that values are very much a part of who you are and that the values you hold dear might not be held by everyone you encounter in your life and work.

Morality involves a person's views of what is good, right, or proper; their beliefs about their obligations; and ideas about how they should behave (Kidder, 1995; Kipnis, 1987). Morality involves making decisions about what is right and wrong. From an early age people learn that moral issues are serious because they concern our duties and obligations to one another. We quickly learn, for example, how we *ought* to treat others and that adults expect even children to behave in these ways.

The roots of personal morality can be found in the early childhood years. You can probably identify the standards of behavior that were established by the adults you looked up to in your home, place of worship, and neighborhood. *Telling the truth, helping others, being fair, respecting elders, putting family first,* and *respecting differences* are all examples of some of the earliest lessons that many people learn from their families and community and religious leaders.

As you begin your preparation for becoming an early childhood educator, it is worthwhile to consider what values have brought you to this decision and how your values are likely to influence the ways you will work with and for young children.

Attitudes Toward Diversity

Closely related to people's values are their attitudes toward groups of people whose culture, religion, language, class, ethnicity, sexual orientation, appearance, or abilities are different from their own. Attitudes toward these and other kinds of differences grow from our values, the messages we get as children from the adults in our lives, and from our own experiences (or lack of them) with different kinds of people.

We all develop preferences and expectations about people. The inclination to favor or reject certain individuals or groups of people (*biases*) may be based simply on the human tendency to feel comfortable with those who are similar to us. Unlike other values and preferences, biases can lead to stereotypes and prejudices that may have a negative impact and even lead to unfair or unjust treatment of individuals or groups of people. A *stereotype* is an oversimplified generalization about a particular group of people. It is an unjustified fixed mental picture that is not based on direct experience. *Prejudice* is "an opinion, or feeling formed without adequate prior knowledge, thought or reason. Prejudice is prejudgment for or against any person, group or sex" (Derman-Sparks, 1989, p. 3). If you can recall the experience of having been rejected or negatively judged because of your family, ethnicity, age, culture, gender, religion, language, appearance, ability, status, or any other personal characteristic, you will be aware of the powerful effect of prejudice. We usually think of prejudice as negative feelings about a group, but it can also be harmful to be prejudiced in favor of a group. When this occurs members of the favored group may get an unrealistic sense of entitlement and those who are not favored may perceive themselves as unworthy.

Most of us fail to recognize our own biases, but we all have some. If we are aware of our biases we might deny them or feel embarrassed by them. This does not make them go away. They influence our relationships with children, families, and colleagues.

Working to identify your biases will help you to recognize when you might be having negative effects on children or their families. When you become aware of a bias, simple awareness may be enough to help you to be more accepting of diversity or to correct a tendency to react negatively to a child or family. Indeed, many fine teachers actively work to dispel these feelings by identifying the things they like about the child or family member who triggers a negative reaction. When you focus on positives, you are more easily able to develop a

Reflect on your values and the moral messages you received as a child

Make a list of your values. How do you think you developed these values? Which values were directly taught in your home, place of worship, or community? Were there any that were taught in indirect ways? What everyday behaviors do you think of as moral or immoral? How do these reflect your childhood and upbringing? Can you think of ways that your values have changed over time?

Reflect on your attitudes toward diversity

In what ways and in what circumstances have you experienced bias or prejudice in your own life? How did it influence your view of yourself and other people?

Are there people you tend to dislike or with whom you feel uncomfortable? What are the characteristics of these people? Do you tend to prefer children of one race, culture, economic background, sex, or style of behavior?

When you consider working with diverse children, what opportunities interest you? What challenges worry you?

special affection for a child or adult whom you were once inclined to dislike. Your newfound appreciation of a child or family can also influence your feelings about other members of a group.

D.G. was a 3-year-old in the Dancing Bears room. With his pale blue eyes and nearly white crew cut he stood out dramatically from the other children. His teacher, Marie, found D.G. physically unappealing. In addition to looking different, his behavior was different. He spoke little and refused to participate in group activities or to cooperate when asked to clean up. Marie worked hard to find things she liked about D.G. She noted that he built elaborate block structures and painted colorful pictures. One day she noticed that he helped younger, smaller children. Marie made a point of telling D.G. that she had noticed those things. Over time she found herself liking him more. By the last day of the school year, the hugs they exchanged were a sincere expression of appreciation and affection.

It is also a good idea to ask yourself if there are any particular children or groups of children with whom you prefer not to work. If you find that you have strong prejudices toward groups of children or families that you can't overcome, you may need to consider seriously whether it is a good idea for you to enter the field of early childhood education.

We live in an increasingly diverse world. As an early childhood educator you are very likely to have close contact with people who have different racial, economic, cultural, and linguistic backgrounds, sexual orientation, abilities, and lifestyles. This diversity offers both challenges and opportunities. Although you may have moments of discomfort and self-doubt, you also have the possibility of gaining new appreciation and insights as you learn to value a wide range of human differences.

The Impact of Life Experiences and the Ability to Reflect on Them

You bring your whole history to your work with children and their families. Who you are as a person includes the characteristics you were born with, your personality, culture, life experiences, attitudes, and values. These things will have an impact on the early childhood professional you will become. You might not be fully aware of these aspects of yourself if you do not reflect on them. However, you must come to understand yourself if you are to understand others. Self-knowledge and the ability to reflect on the impact of your personality and behavior on others are essential attributes of caring and competent early childhood educators.

Cheryl grew up as an only child. Both of her parents were teachers and she always pretended to be teacher to her dolls and toy animals. Cheryl loved school but she was shy and did not make friends easily. She volunteered at a neighborhood preschool when she was in high school and discovered that she didn't feel shy with children. She decided to become a preschool teacher. She completed her degree in early childhood education and became a teacher in the preschool where she did a practicum placement. No one who meets her today can believe that she was ever shy and lacked friends.

Sue is a first-grade teacher who grew up in the inner city. Her parents did not speak English. She has vivid memories of her first unhappy days in kindergarten. But Sue soon loved school. When she was 8, Sue's father died. Later her brother died of a drug overdose. There was never enough money, and there were many sad days in Sue's life. But she did well in school and earned a scholarship to go to the state college. Sue was the first person in her family to earn a degree. Sue loves her job and often talks about the ways in which she feels she is making a difference to children from families like hers.

Sarah is a preschool teacher who came from an abusive family. She left home before she was 16, but Sarah managed to go to school and earned an A.S. degree. She is now a teacher of 3-year-olds. She is fiercely protective of the children in her class and says most parents don't deserve to have children. She is negative about authority figures like her director and the preschool board. She is frequently absent and often comments on the poor quality of her program. Sarah complains that she is paid too little to put in extra hours to fix up the classroom or meet with parents.

As you enter the early childhood field, remember that you were once a child and that the ways you feel about yourself and others were profoundly influenced by your early experiences. Working with children and their families may generate long-forgotten feelings and attitudes. It is a good idea to reflect on your early experiences and how they might impact your relationships before they crop up in unexpected and destructive ways. If you had your basic needs met in childhood, you are most likely to see the world as a good and nurturing place and it may be easy for you to support the growth and development of children. If—like Cheryl, Sue, and Sarah—you encountered problems in growing up, you may need to spend some time working through these issues, either on your own or with a friend or counselor. All of us have both happy and unhappy memories of our early lives. Many fine early childhood educators, like Sue, dedicate themselves to giving children the positive early experiences that they missed. Some, like Sarah, are not able to overcome their early experiences and current challenges without insight and help.

Educators who have the capacity for caring, compassion, and nurturing know and accept themselves. Self-knowledge depends to a great extent on the ability to observe yourself in the same honest and nonjudgmental way that you observe children and to realistically appraise your areas of strength and those in which change is needed. Self-knowledge means recognizing that everyone experiences negative feelings and strong and unpleasant emotions such as anger and fear. These feelings need to be identified, accepted, and expressed in productive ways (for example, in discussion with caring friends and relatives, with a counselor, or by writing or creating art about them) or they may become destructive.

The capacity for self-knowledge and acceptance is the cornerstone for the quality of compassion that is so important in a person who works with young children and their families. The importance of compassion is expressed in this quote from developmental psychologist Arthur Jersild, which we have included in every edition of this book because it expresses the idea so eloquently:

> To be compassionate, one must be able to accept the impact of any emotion, love or hate, joy, fear, or grief—tolerate it and harbor it long enough and with sufficient absorption to accept its meaning and to enter into a fellowship of feeling with the one who is moved by the emotion. This is the heroic feature of compassion in its fullest development: to be able to face the ravage of rage, the shattering impact of terror, the tenderest prompting of love, and then to embrace these in a larger context, which involves an acceptance of these feelings and an appreciation of what they mean to the one who experiences them. (Jersild, 1955, pp. 125–126)

Reflect on who you are and who you want to be in the lives of children

What events and experiences in your childhood most influence who you are today? What, if any, unhappy or difficult experiences have you had to work to overcome? What might be the connections between your childhood experiences and your desire to teach young children? Who do you want to be in the lives of children?

Part of the process of professional development (and the central theme in this book) is to ask yourself: "Who am I in the lives of children? Who do I want to be?" No one is completely self-aware, mature, wise, compassionate, and insightful all the time. Everyone has tendencies to be hostile and defensive. It is important to learn to look at yourself as objectively as you can and to accept feedback from others as valuable information that can help you to grow instead of something to defend against or to use to berate yourself.

The Teacher as a Professional

You are learning to be an early childhood educator, which means that you are planning to enter a *profession* and to become a *professional*. We hear these terms used every day, but their meanings are not always clear. A profession is an occupation that provides an essential service to society. A professional is an individual who has received training and who uses personal skills and abilities to serve society through realizing the commitments of the profession.

There is some debate today about whether ECE is a "true profession"— meaning whether it meets most of the criteria that are used to determine if an occupation is a profession. Some of these criteria are a specialized body of knowledge and expertise, prolonged training, rigorous requirements for entry into training and admission to practice, agreed-on standards of practice, commitment to unselfish dedication to society and meeting the needs of others (altruism), recognition as the only group in the society who can perform its function, autonomy (self-regulation and internal control over the quality of the services provided), and a code of ethics.

Those who work with young children generally meet the criterion of altruism admirably. As a field we have a knowledge base and training based on it. We have a code of ethics that spells out early childhood educators' moral obligations and identifies the distinctive values of the field (these are listed in Figure 1.4) and provides guidelines for ethical conduct. We do not fully meet criteria for professional status with regard to training and entry into the field. Training is often quite brief, requirements for entering the field vary in different places and different settings, and they are usually not rigorous. Early childhood programs are rarely autonomous or self-regulated because most private programs for children 5 and younger are licensed by social welfare (not early childhood) agen-

cies, and public school policies are not made by educators but by community members who serve on boards of education. And the codes of ethics used by early childhood educators are not enforced as are those of established professions.

While our field may not meet all of the criteria used to define professions, there is no doubt that we make important contributions to society by nurturing and educating young children during a critically important period in the life cycle. Awareness of the value of our contributions is growing. Because early childhood educators have a powerful impact on all aspects of children's development it is imperative that their behavior reflects the professional ideals of dedication to service, priority to the interests of children and families, upholding standards of competence, and provision of high-quality services.

Specialized Knowledge and Skills

The possession of specialized knowledge and skills is the central defining feature of every profession. Over the last few years quite a lot of work has been done on defining the knowledge base of early childhood education. There is growing agreement and an extensive body of literature that describes what is needed to support young children's development and enhance their learning.

Knowledge and skills are described in teacher preparation standards that were developed to ensure that teachers were adequately prepared to work effectively with children. These include CDA competencies administered by the Council for Professional Recognition, Early Childhood Professional Preparation Standards developed by the National Association for the Education of Young Children (NAEYC),[1] Standards for Accomplished Early Childhood Teachers created by the National Board for Professional Teaching Standards (NBPTS), and Standards for Special Education Teachers of Early Childhood Students developed by the Council for Exceptional Children (CEC). In addition to the standards produced by national groups, most states have created professional development systems to increase the expertise of educators who work with children from birth through age 5 (Bellm, n.d.).

In 2010 NAEYC *Standards for Initial and Advanced Early Childhood Professional Preparation Programs* (2011), the NAEYC addresses what graduates of early childhood training programs in two-year, four-year, and advanced programs need to know and be able to do. Figure 1.3 presents a summary of the NAEYC standards. It should come as no surprise to you that the content they represent comprises much of the substance of this book. We will indicate at the end of each chapter which of the NAEYC standards it addresses.

The centerpiece of the knowledge base of the skilled early childhood educator is child development. The commitment to basing work on knowledge of child development goes back to the child study movement of the 1920s and is a characteristic that distinguishes us from most other educators. This and other essential knowledge is reflected in the chapters of this book. It includes history and characteristics of ECE; observation, assessment, and documentation; guiding a group of young children; health; safety and nutrition; designing learning environments; supporting play; designing and implementing curriculum; inclusion of children with disabilities; and working with families.

Professional Commitment and Behavior

Being a professional goes beyond an accumulation of knowledge and skills. It involves commitment, knowledge, ethical behavior, and the willingness to continue to learn and grow.

Professional behavior involves *being a good employee*. It means being punctual, dressing appropriately, taking your work seriously, being aware of your responsibilities, following through on commitments, applying the knowledge you have acquired to your work with children, and representing your program and the field positively in the community. It also involves *behaving collegially,* keeping

---

[1]National Association for the Education of Young Children (NAEYC) is an association dedicated to improving the well-being of young children, with focus on the quality of educational and developmental services for children from birth through age 8. Founded in 1926, NAEYC is the world's largest organization working on behalf of young children.

FIGURE 1.3   Summary of NAEYC's Standards for Early Childhood Professional Preparation Programs

Standard 1.   Promoting Child Development and Learning
Key elements of Standard 1
1a: Knowing and understanding young children's characteristics and needs
1b: Knowing and understanding the multiple influences on early development and learning
1c: Using developmental knowledge to create healthy, respectful, supportive, and challenging learning environments

Standard 2.   Building Family and Community Relationships
Key elements of Standard 2
2a: Knowing about and understanding diverse family and community characteristics
2b: Supporting and engaging families and communities through respectful, reciprocal relationships
2c: Involving families and communities in their children's development and learning

Standard 3.   Observing, Documenting, and Assessing to Support Young Children and Families
Key elements of Standard 3
3a: Understanding the goals, benefits, and uses of assessment
3b: Knowing about and using observation, documentation, and other appropriate assessment tools and approaches
3c: Understanding and practicing responsible assessment to promote positive outcomes for each child
3d: Knowing about assessment partnerships with families and with professional colleagues

Standard 4.   Using Developmentally Effective Approaches to Connect with Children and Families
Key elements of Standard 4
4a: Understanding positive relationships and supportive interactions as the foundation of their work with children
4b: Knowing and understanding effective strategies and tools for early education
4c: Using a broad repertoire of developmentally appropriate teaching/learning approaches
4d: Reflecting on their own practice to promote positive outcomes for each child

Standard 5.   Using Content Knowledge to Build Meaningful Curriculum
Key elements of Standard 5
5a: Understanding content knowledge and resources in academic disciplines
5b: Knowing and using the central concepts, inquiry tools, and structures of content areas or academic disciplines
5c: Using their own knowledge, appropriate early learning standards, and other resources to design, implement, and evaluate meaningful, challenging curricula for each child

Standard 6.   Becoming a Professional
Key elements of Standard 6
6a: Identifying and involving oneself with the early childhood field
6b: Knowing about and upholding ethical standards and other professional guidelines
6c: Engaging in continuous, collaborative learning to inform practice
6d: Integrating knowledgeable, reflective, and critical perspectives on early education
6e: Engaging in informed advocacy for children and the profession

Source: NAEYC. 2009. *NAEYC Standards for Early Childhood Professional Preparation Programs.* Washington, DC: Author. www.naeyc.org/files/naeyc/file/positions/ProfPrepStandards09.pdf. Reprinted with permission from the National Association for the Education of Young Children (NAEYC). Full text of all NAEYC position statements is available at www.naeyc.org/positionstatements.

personal feelings and grievances out of the classroom, and knowing about the *legal* and *ethical* responsibilities that are described in the sections that follow.

Legal Responsibilities

Early childhood teachers have legal responsibilities. We need to know laws and policies relevant to our work with children, and like every citizen we must follow the laws of our country and community. Early childhood educators are mandated reporters of child abuse or neglect. This means that you have a legal and ethical responsibility to report suspected abuse or neglect, such as a child who comes to school with visible injuries that you suspect are the result of being physically abused by a family member or other adult.

One of your first important tasks as a new teacher is to find out the child abuse reporting procedures for your particular workplace. Although you may fervently wish never to have to use this information, it is critical that you know what to do in order to fulfill your legal and moral responsibilities to children's welfare.

Professional Values and Ethics

Personal values and morality cannot always guide professional behavior because not everyone has the same values and life experiences, nor has everyone learned the same moral lessons. Even those who have the same values and moral convictions may not apply them in the same way in their work with children. Early childhood educators need more than personal attitudes, values, and morality to guide their work. These need to be supplemented with professional values that give clear guidance on how to behave when faced with moral issues and that let early childhood educators speak with one voice about their professional commitments.

Professional Values

The values of a profession are not a matter of preference but are agreed-upon statements that members believe to be essential. Professional values spell out the beliefs and commitments of a profession. The National Association for the Education of Young Children has developed a *Code of Ethical Conduct and Statement of Commitment* (Revised April 2005, Reaffirmed and Updated May 2011) to guide its members in responsible professional practice. The NAEYC Code identifies core values, presented in Figure 1.4, that express early childhood educators' central beliefs, commitment to society, and common purpose.

These core values make it possible to reach agreement on issues of professional ethics by relying on *professional* values that apply to all early childhood educators, not personal values or beliefs.

Most people who choose early childhood education as a career find themselves in agreement with the spirit of these values. As you merge your personal values with the professional values of the field, you will join other early childhood practitioners in their commitment to supporting the positive growth and development of children and their families.

When values conflict. When you encounter conflicts in your work, they often will involve professional values. One kind of values conflict occurs within yourself. For example, you may face a conflict regarding the needs and demands of your professional and personal life (such as when an important staff meeting is scheduled on your spouse's or child's birthday). In your work with children, you may value freedom of expression (for example, allowing children to engage in dramatic play about things that engage them) versus the value of peace

Reflect on your professional values

Brainstorm a list of values that you think all early childhood educators should hold. Compare your list to the NAEYC core values in Figure 1.4. Think about why these lists are similar to or different from each other.

FIGURE 1.4   Core Values in Early Childhood Education

Standards of ethical behavior in early childhood care and education are based on commitment to the following core values that are deeply rooted in the history of the field of early childhood care and education. We have made a commitment to:

- Appreciate childhood as a unique and valuable stage of the human life cycle
- Base our work on knowledge of how children develop and learn
- Appreciate and support the bond between the child and family
- Recognize that children are best understood and supported in the context of family, culture*, community, and society
- Respect the dignity, worth, and uniqueness of each individual (child, family member, and colleague)
- Respect diversity in children, families, and colleagues
- Recognize that children and adults achieve their full potential in the context of relationships that are based on trust and respect

*The term culture includes ethnicity, racial identity, economic level, family structure, language, and religious and political beliefs, which profoundly influence each child's development and relationship to the world.

Source: Reprinted from the NAEYC Code of Ethical Conduct and Statement of Commitment, revised April 2005, reaffirmed and updated May 2011. Copyright © 2011 by the National Association for the Education of Young Children. The full text of all current NAEYC position statements is available at www.naeyc.org/positionstatements.

(forbidding war play because it brings violence into the classroom). Or you may face the predicament of having to choose between work that pays well and work you love. In these situations it will be helpful to analyze the conflict and decide which value is most important to you.

It is also important to be sure your actions are consistent with your values. Sometimes teachers are not aware of the ways in which their behavior might contradict their values. A teacher we know thought that she valued independence and child-initiated learning. But when she looked at her classroom, she realized children were not allowed to choose their own materials from the open shelves.

At some point you will find yourself facing value conflicts with others. It helps to recognize that differences in values are a natural and healthy part of life in a diverse society. You can learn to address values conflicts thoughtfully, though it is not always easy to arrive at a solution. You may find yourself in a situation in which an administrator's actions (such as minimizing the risk of allegations of sexual abuse by forbidding staff to hug children) are in direct conflict with an important value (giving young children the affectionate physical contact you know that they need). You may find yourself in conflict with colleagues whose values lead them to different ideas about how to work with children (demanding quiet at mealtime while you think meals are a perfect time to develop language and conversational skills).

You might also find yourself caught in a conflict between your beliefs and pressures from families who want you to teach and treat children in ways that violate these beliefs. At some time you are likely have to deal with family members who want you to do things that you feel are not in the child's best interests. For example, they may be anxious about their children's success in school and want them to master academic content that you have learned is developmentally inappropriate.

When people from different backgrounds and with different values work together to care for children, conflicting viewpoints inevitably arise. When you encounter a conflict, it is helpful to decide whether it is about values. Values conflicts can be best handled by suspending judgment (the inner voice that says, "No! They're wrong! I'm right!") and listening carefully to the other person's viewpoint. Our friend and colleague, the late Jean Fargo, used to suggest to her college students that they learn to "be curious, not furious." Often values conflicts involve cultural differences, such as whether to hold a crying child or give the child space and time to comfort him- or herself. Cultural differences need to be acknowledged and discussed. When you work together you can seek a solution that is respectful to both parties. Keep in mind that when competing views are based on strongly held value differences, especially those relating to culture, solutions might not be easily found and you may simply have to agree to disagree.

Occasionally, differences about teaching practices are so serious that you will find you do not want to continue to work in a program. For instance, one of our students chose to leave a good-paying job when her school adopted a curriculum that did not allow her to teach in ways that were consistent with her commitment to hands-on learning and child-choice. Coming to this conclusion can be painful, but it may be your only alternative if the value difference is too extreme. You might find that, like the student we just described, you are happier teaching in a setting that more closely reflects your values and commitments to children.

Professional Ethics

Ethics is the study of right and wrong, duties and obligations. Professional ethics address the moral commitments of a group, extending and enhancing the personal values and morality of educators through shared, critical reflection about right and wrong actions in the workplace. Standards of ethical conduct are not statements of taste or preference; they provide a shared common ground for professionals who strive to do the right thing.

The ethical commitments of a profession are contained in its code of ethics. An ethical code is different from program policies, regulations, or laws. It describes the aspirations of the field and the obligations of individual practitioners. It tells them how they should approach their work, and some things that they should and should not do. A code of ethics helps professionals do what is right—not what is easiest, what will bring the most personal benefit, or what will make them most popular. When followed by the members of a profession, a code of ethics assures the public that practice is based on sound and agreed-upon standards and is in the best interest of those being served and of society.

Codes of ethics. There are several codes of ethics available for educators today. Those of the American Montessori Society and of the National Education Association can be used by teachers who work with students of all ages (preschool through grade 12). Codes developed by NAEYC and the Division for Early Childhood (DEC) of the Council for Exceptional Children are specific to work with young children. If you live or work in a country other than the United States, you may also have a code of ethics that reflects local values and culture. (See the list of websites at the end of this chapter for information on some of these codes.)

The NAEYC Code of Ethical Conduct and Statement of Commitment is included in most American early childhood textbooks and in the curricula of early childhood teacher education programs. The NAEYC Code has been adopted by the National Association for Family Child Care (NAFCC) and endorsed by the Association for Childhood Education International (ACEI). Anyone who works with young children should learn which code applies to their program, read it carefully to understand its ethical commitments, and refer to it when ethical guidance is needed.

The most compelling reason for early childhood educators to have a code of ethics is that young children are vulnerable and lack the power to defend themselves. The adults who care for them are larger and stronger and control the valuable resources that children want and need. Katz (1993) pointed out that the

Reflect on a values conflict

Can you remember a time when you and another person had a disagreement based on values? What values did each of you hold? What did you do? Were your values or the relationship changed by the conflict?

more powerless the client is with regard to the practitioner, the more important the practitioner's ethics become. Young children cannot defend themselves from teachers who are uncaring or abusive. For that reason it is extremely important that those who work in early childhood programs act fairly and responsibly on children's behalf.

Another reason that it is important for early childhood educators to have a code of ethics is that they serve a variety of client groups—children, families, employing agencies, and the community. Most early childhood educators would agree that their primary responsibility and loyalty is to the children. But it can be hard to keep sight of this priority when parents, agencies, or administrators demand that their concerns be attended to first.

The NAEYC Code is widely used in early childhood programs. It was first adopted in 1989 and it has been updated every 5 years since then with the most recent version approved in 2011. The NAEYC Code has been expanded to include a supplement for teacher educators (2004) and a supplement for administrators (2006). The code and supplements are designed to help you answer the question, "What should the good early childhood educator do when faced with a situation that involves ethics?"

The code is organized into four sections describing professional responsibilities to children, families, colleagues, and community and society. The items in the code are designed to help practitioners make responsible ethical decisions. It includes *ideals* that describe exemplary practice and *principles* that describe practices that are required, prohibited, and permitted. (The complete NAEYC Code can be found in Appendix A.)

Ethical responsibilities. Ethical responsibilities are clear-cut. They are those things that must or must not be done. The first, and most important, of the responsibilities that are spelled out in the NAEYC Code and most other codes is that early childhood educators should do no harm to children. The first item in the NAEYC Code (P-1.1) reads, "Above all, we shall not harm children. We shall not participate in practices that are emotionally damaging, physically harmful, disrespectful, degrading, dangerous, exploitative, or intimidating to children. *This principle has precedence over all others in this Code*" (NAEYC, 2011). This item in the code means that the first priority of every early childhood educator must be the well-being of children, and that every action and decision should first be considered in the light of potential harmful consequences.

A second very important ethical responsibility is the obligation to keep information about children and families that you acquire at work strictly confidential (confidentiality is a hallmark of every profession). Nothing erodes trust faster than divulging private information given by family member. An early childhood educator should never share confidential information, for example knowledge about an impending divorce shared by a parent, with a person who does not have a legitimate need to have it.

Other responsibilities include being familiar with the knowledge base of early childhood education and basing what you do upon it; being familiar with laws and regulations that have an impact on children and programs; respecting families' culture, language, customs, and beliefs and their child-rearing values and their right to make decisions for their children; attempting to resolve concerns with coworkers and employers collegially; and assisting programs in providing a high quality of service.

Facing a decision with an ethical component sometimes makes you realize that the "right" thing to do may be difficult. For example you may feel that your colleagues will not like you if you protest when they do things that you do not think are good for children (for example: having children watch cartoons on rainy days, not allowing the children use the bathroom except at scheduled times, demanding that children not talk at meal times).

Ethical dilemmas. When you encounter an issue or problem at work, one of the first things you will want to do is determine whether it involves ethics. Ask yourself whether the problem or issue has to do with right and wrong, rights and responsibilities, and human welfare. Not all conflicts that arise at work involve ethics. If the teacher next door fails to change the artwork on the bulletin board on a regular basis, she may not meet your standards or provide the best experiences for children, but she is not being unethical. A conflict with a team member over whether to read children a story after lunch or after breakfast involves deliberation but probably does not involve ethics. If the conflict or concern is an ethical issue, however, you need to determine whether the code clearly spells out what you must or must not do, whether it involves a responsibility, or if it is an ethical dilemma.

An ethical dilemma is a workplace predicament that involves competing professional values and has more than one defensible resolution. Deciding on the right course of action can be difficult because a dilemma puts the interests of one person or group in conflict with those of another. For instance, it might mean placing the needs of a child above those of the parent. Whatever choice you make in an ethical dilemma involves some benefits and some costs. Ethical dilemmas cannot be resolved easily by applying rules and relying on facts. In fact, rules and regulations may even give contradictory directions. There may not

GUIDELINES FOR ETHICAL REFLECTION

A feature in this book, "Reflect on Your Ethical Responsibilities," is designed to give you experience in thinking through what an early childhood educator should do when faced with a professional ethical dilemma. When the dilemma occurs in the workplace, decisions about what to do need to be based on the collective ethical wisdom of the profession, not on your personal view of the right thing to do. The question changes from "What should *I* do in this situation?" to "What should *the good early childhood educator* do in this situation?" Although it may not tell you exactly what to do, the NAEYC Code of Ethical Conduct can help you grapple with the ethical issues that you encounter and remind you that the primary commitment of an early childhood educator is to the well-being of children. When faced with an ethical

dilemma the best course of action is sometimes obvious, but at other times you will need to think hard to come up with the best alternative. The NAEYC Code will help you clarify responsibilities and prioritize values.

Ethical reflections are found throughout the chapters in this book. Use the following steps to think about each of the situations presented:

- Who are the people involved in the situation? What are the conflicting responsibilities of each one?
- What core values apply to the situation?
- How is this issue addressed in the NAEYC Code? (Be sure to look at the ideals and principles in all four sections of the code.)
- Based on your review of the code and your reflection about the situation, what do you think would be the most ethical resolution to the situation?

be ready resolutions for many of the dilemmas you face in your early childhood workplace in this or any other book. Rather, these dilemmas require careful deliberation using guidance from a code of ethics in combination with your best professional judgment. Guidance for addressing ethical dilemmas can be found in the NAEYC Code of Ethical Conduct. The box, Guidelines for Ethical Reflection (on page 23–24) provides direction for thinking about the ethical dilemmas presented in this book.

Finding Your Path

Every early childhood educator has a story.

Fred always enjoyed being with children. He took a child development class in high school and loved the time he spent with kids in a preschool. Like his older brother, Fred went into auto mechanics and became a certified mechanic. His family approved and he made good money. But Fred was dissatisfied; working as a mechanic was not fulfilling. After 3 years he decided to go back to school to train to be an early childhood educator. He realized that he wouldn't make as much money, but he knew this was what he wanted to do.

As a young mother Ann enrolled her son in the campus child care center while working on her B.A. in French. She often stayed at the center and helped out. One day the staff asked her if she wanted to work part-time at the center. The next semester Ann changed her major to education. Today she is a kindergarten teacher.

Ruth always knew she wanted to be a teacher. She enrolled in pre-ed classes as soon as she entered college. She worked in a child care program as a part-time aide while she was going to college. Ruth became a preschool teacher after she graduated and soon went on to graduate school. Today she is the education director for a small preschool.

In college Laurel had a double major in psychology and anthropology. She decided that she wanted to communicate her love of learning by becoming a teacher. Through a practicum placement in a preschool she learned about the strong impact that early childhood programs could have on children's development. She decided to become a preschool teacher because she wanted to make a difference. After teaching preschool for several years she realized that while she enjoyed teaching she was fascinated by the philosophy and theory of early education. She decided that she could also serve young children by working with future teachers. She went back to school for a master's degree and now teaches early childhood education in a community college.

In this chapter so far we have discussed the role of the early childhood educator, desirable personal qualities, the importance of reflection, and some professional expectations that accompany work with young children. In this last section we explore career options, look at training requirements for various roles, and the stages of development that early childhood educators may pass through in the course of their careers.

Roles

There are many settings in which you can work with young children, and many different roles you can take. And there are two broad categories of roles in early childhood education: *Working with children and families* involves daily interactions and direct responsibility for children's care and education. These positions include family child care provider, classroom teacher for infant-toddler programs (also called caregiver), preschools, kindergarten, or in primary grades (1–3). Early childhood teachers also work with children in bilingual and special education classrooms.

Early childhood expert Sue Bredekamp (2011) identifies the many other roles that support children's development and education as *working* for *children*. In these roles you may work in proximity to the children as you do when you are a child care center director, curriculum specialist or school principal, or school counselor. Other roles include serving children at a further distance, as you do as an education specialist in an agency, teacher educator, resource and referral specialist, curriculum developer, or parent educator.

There are other roles in which a person can support young children but need significantly different training and are not considered an early childhood educator. These include therapists, child care licensing workers, librarians, social workers, or counselors.

The great majority of early childhood students are preparing to work directly with young children and will find this work satisfying for their entire career. Others take on other responsibilities after working with children for a time. They may want to try a new challenge, or may realize that they are more suited for other roles. The experiences that they have in working *with* young children will provide a solid foundation for working effectively in positions that involve working *for* children.

Educational Requirements

You will gain knowledge and skill through specialized training in early childhood education. This training is essential to becoming an educator who can provide positive experiences for young children. Teaching experience alone or a degree in another field (even a related field like elementary education) does not provide those who work with very young children with the necessary knowledge and skill.

Research has demonstrated that higher levels of teacher education result in better classroom quality and greater gains in children's cognitive and social development (Barnett, 2004; Early et al., 2007; Kontos & Wilcox-Herzog, 2001). This research has led to recent efforts to require more training, especially in Head Start and state-funded prekindergarten programs.

Those who are concerned with the education and welfare of young children and trained in early childhood education can do many different kinds of jobs. Each person has to find the career that best reflects his or her interests, talents, and style. Different roles require different kinds and levels of training and provide different working conditions and compensation. Educational requirements vary depending on the position; the age of the children; how the program is administered; the agency that regulates the program; and the community, state, and country in which you live. Requirements for working in programs for younger children are quite different, and usually less rigorous, than those for school-age children. In some places regulations require specialized training for teachers who work with children younger than 3. It is helpful for you to understand this distinction as you plan for your career. Teachers of young children are usually trained either in programs for children from birth to age 5 (usually offered in two-year colleges), or for prekindergarten through third grade (usually in four-year university schools of education). Some programs in four-year institutions focus on the entire birth to age 8 age group.

Preschool and child care programs for children from birth to age 5 generally require the Child Development Associate (CDA) credential or an associate's

Reflect on your path

Where are you coming from as an early childhood educator? Have you always known you wanted to be a teacher? Did you receive training in another field and then discover early education by happy accident? Did you come to early childhood education with your own children? How do you think the path that brought you to early childhood education might influence your perspective as a teacher?

(two-year) degree in early childhood education. The CDA is a nationally awarded early childhood credential that requires 120 clock-hours of approved training (from a community college, agency, or distance learning organization), a standard exam, and demonstrated competency in working with young children.

Associate degrees in early childhood education require coursework in education and child development; practical experience working with infants, toddlers, and preschoolers; and general education courses. A bachelor's degree in education or child and family studies may also qualify students to teach in programs for children younger than 5.

Within the early childhood community the two-year degree is not regarded as a terminal degree but rather as the first step in a professional development continuum that, in early childhood education, is referred to as a "career lattice." Since the 1980s there have been efforts underway to create a seamless system for early childhood professional development that can begin with community-based training, progress to a two-year degree program, then articulate to a four-year degree program, and, finally, lead to a graduate degree (NAEYC, 2009).

Teaching prekindergarten through grade 3 in public schools generally requires a four-year teacher preparation program that leads to a bachelor's degree in education. These programs follow an approved course of study that leads to a teaching certificate (sometimes called a license). Some states offer a teaching license or endorsement in early childhood education. These programs require coursework in early childhood education and child development, as well as student teaching in an early childhood setting.

Colleges that offer early childhood programs may apply for NAEYC Early Childhood Associate Degree Accreditation (ECADA) or NCATE/NAEYC recognition of baccalaureate and graduate degrees as part of the National Council for Accreditation of Teacher Education (NCATE) accreditation for programs leading to initial or advanced teacher licensure (NAEYC, 2009). Both kinds of accreditation are based on the professional development standards that were mentioned in this chapter.

Awareness of the importance of early childhood education in children's development has led to an increased interest in the qualifications of those who work with young children. Two recent developments illustrate this attention. Head Start, a federally funded program for low-income children, recently increased requirements for teachers. As of 2008 all newly hired and half of all current Head Start teachers must have a bachelor's degree in early childhood education or a related field. Revised standards for NAEYC-accredited teacher programs also propose that all teachers of preschool children should have at least a bachelor's degree. However, state licensing standards usually do not include this requirement.

Table 1.1, Roles and Training Required to Work with Children in Early Childhood Programs (see page 27) lays out recommended training for a variety of roles in early childhood settings.

Not everyone enters the early childhood education field with specialized training. People come to it in a variety of ways. It is estimated that only 25% of early childhood educators began their careers in the "traditional"

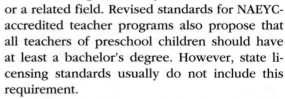

TABLE 1.1   Roles and Training Required to Work with Children in Early Childhood Programs

Setting	Role	Required Training
Homes	Family Child Care Provider	Most states—no formal training required CDA credential in family child care and accreditation by the National Association for Family Child Care Small business administration Infant/child CPR and first aid
	Nanny	Most states—no formal training required Nanny training programs in colleges and private agencies—can vary from 6 weeks to a year in length
	Home Visitor	Most states—no formal training required CDA credential or higher degree required for some home visitor programs for low-income and at-risk children
Centers (early childhood programs for children under the age of 5, and after-school programs for elementary school children)	Teacher Aide/Assistant	Orientation and on-the-job training or CDA credential
	School-Age Program Leader	High school diploma or equivalent1 Orientation and on-the-job training
	Assistant Teacher/Assistant Caregiver	Some training in working with young children May require a CDA (infant and toddler, preschool, or bilingual) or a degree Usually less training or experience than the supervising teacher
	Teacher/Caregiver	Specialized training in working with young children Most states—college degree required (sometimes in education, early childhood education, or child development) Some states—CDA accepted
	Master, Lead, or Head Teacher in a program for children birth to age 5	Same as teachers Employer may require specialized training Positions involving staff supervision or curriculum development may require bachelor's or master's degree
	Special Education Preschool Teacher	A bachelor's degree in education with specialized training in special education
Elementary Schools	Educational Assistant	Requirements vary from state to state—in some states 2 years of college required
	Teacher (pre-K, kindergarten, grades 1–3 in a public school)	Bachelor's degree and elementary teacher certification Specialized training may include training in early childhood education Licensure varies by state—may cover infancy through third grade, preschool through third grade, kindergarten through sixth grade, or early childhood or kindergarten endorsement in addition to an elementary certificate
	Resource Teacher or Specialist	Degree and teaching credential, plus training to prepare in subject area

STARTING YOUR PROFESSIONAL PORTFOLIO

Today in education, and in many other fields, one way to demonstrate your professionalism is through the creation of a professional portfolio. A professional portfolio documents your skills, knowledge, and training. In some colleges you will be asked to create a portfolio for the purpose of assessing whether you have accomplished the required performance outcomes for a class or program.

Regardless of whether or not you are required to create a professional portfolio, we recommend that you keep one as a convenient way to keep track of your accomplishments to share with future employers, as well as a tool for recording your growth as an early childhood educator. At the end of each chapter we suggest additions to your professional portfolio that relate to the content of the chapter and that demonstrate your learning. Here are some ideas to help you begin:

Start Your Portfolio Select an open, flexible format that is easy to organize and modify (such as a three-ring binder) to hold your portfolio.

Introduce Yourself Use the reflections in this chapter to help you get started—writing ideas you'd like to include (1) in a brief *autobiography* that outlines the significant events in your life that led you to choose early childhood education as your career, (2) in a *personal mission statement* that explains your vision for yourself as an early childhood educator and your hopes and dreams as a professional, and (3) in a statement of *educational philosophy* describing what you value in the education and care of young children. Remember, these will change as you progress from beginning student to beginning professional. Periodically go back to these to see how your ideas have evolved, and make revisions that reflect new insights.

Collect Letters of Recommendation Letters of recommendation from people who know your work and your character are independent evidence of your ability. When an employer, supervisor, or college professor gives you a favorable evaluation or compliments you on your work, it is a good moment to ask them to formalize their appreciation by writing you a letter for your portfolio.

Create a Resume A resume is a short outline of your qualifications and experience. It is useful to include an updated resume in your portfolio if you plan to use the portfolio as a part of a job application. It gives a prospective employer a quick way to see if you are suitable for a position. Guidance for resume preparation for early childhood educators, examples of resumes and suggestions for links to helpful websites are available from New York State's Early Childhood Career Development Resource Guide, which can be accessed at earlychildhood.org/cdrg/prep_employ.cfm.

Document Your Qualifications Make a section in your portfolio for degrees, certificates, personnel registry cards, and diplomas. Remember that training in other fields (for example, music, water safety) can be useful supplements to your formal training in working with young children.

Begin an Ongoing Training Record Over the course of your career you will have many opportunities for ongoing training. Your portfolio is an excellent place to keep track of this training and keep any certificates of attendance that you receive. For each training entry be sure to note the date of the training, the name of the trainer and sponsoring organization, and the number of hours of training. Remember to make a note of any ways in which you improve your practice as a result of the training.

Document Your Knowledge and Competence Use the statements of core knowledge and skills for your state,

manner by majoring in early childhood education before they began work in the field. Some (about 25%) were introduced to the field as parents, observing the benefits of a good program for their young child and then going to school to get training in early care and education. Others (about 50%) have come by what can be called a serendipitous route, discovering the field as a happy accident, often after receiving a degree in another field and later obtaining the necessary education to become an early childhood professional (Bredekamp, 1992).

We, the authors of this book, reflect two of these typical paths. Stephanie did what we like to refer to as "worked her way up" to early childhood education. She studied secondary social studies, and only after receiving her degrees and working as a social worker in the Head Start program did she find her way to early childhood education. Eva and Sherry completed early childhood training the CDA competency standards, or the NAEYC program standards as a framework for the knowledge and competency sections of your portfolio. In each section provide examples of what you have learned and work you have done in this area. Document your work through photographs (for example, a photograph of children's work or a classroom environment that you designed), written descriptions (for example, a description of a situation in which you successfully guided a child who was having difficulties), or a sample of your written work (for example, a lesson plan, a paper that demonstrates your knowledge, or a newsletter for families). Your portfolio should include only items that have a direct bearing on your professional abilities and growth. Each item for the knowledge and competence section of your portfolio should have a brief explanatory statement that ties your work to the standard that is being illustrated, so that a reader can understand why it has been included.

Sample Portfolio Table of Contents

Introduction to a Teacher

Autobiography

Philosophy and mission

Professional letters of recommendation

Qualifications

Resume of education and experience

Personnel registry card

College degrees and certificates

First aid and CPR certification

NAEYC or other professional association membership card

Ongoing Training Record

Certificates of attendance at workshops and conferences (be sure to include date)

Knowledge and Competence (this could be put in two columns labeled "Competency Area" and "Examples")

Growth and development (for example, photograph of a toy you made for a child of a particular age)

Professionalism (a sample of a reflection you wrote after attending a workshop)

Diversity (a plan for a child with disabilities or who speaks a language other than English)

Observation and assessment (an observation you made and a plan based on it)

Health, safety, and nutrition (a plan for teaching children about health)

Learning environments (a sample floor plan for a classroom)

Relationships and guidance (a reflection on a situation in which you guided a child)

Planning learning experiences (a sample integrated study plan you created)

Working with families (a newsletter or family conference outline you wrote)

Program management (a sample of some ways that you maintain records)

Notes: Your portfolio should not include brochures or handouts that you have gathered—only those you have produced yourself. Avoid including the names of children and family members in portfolio materials.

---

before they entered the field. Eva always knew she wanted to become a preschool or kindergarten teacher and entered college with that as her career goal. As an undergraduate majoring in sociology, Sherry took a child development class as an elective and switched her major to child development when she became interested in working with young children.

Our observations over the years are consistent with Laura Colker's assertion that early childhood educators often enter the field because they have always felt that it was their "calling," because they believe it is important to make a difference in children's lives, and because they have a commitment to making a difference in the world (2008).

In order to document your growing professionalism, we recommend that you keep a portfolio and update it regularly, as described in the box "Starting Your Professional Portfolio." on pages 28–29.

Stages of Professional Development

Just like the children with whom you will work, you will pass through developmental stages and you will continue to grow and learn. Like the children, you need appropriate stimulation and nurturing to reach your full potential at each stage. Knowing that there are stages can help you to understand that you will have different professional needs at different times in your career. As a beginning teacher, you will be focused on your direct work with children and the network of relationships that go with it. With experience, day-to-day tasks get easier and you will have different needs and seek new challenges.

Lilian Katz (1995) describes four stages of development of teachers of young children that focus on changes in the need for professional support and education, as follows:

Stage 1: Survival. The first year of working with young children is a time when you need to apply the knowledge that you gained in college. It is often hard and stressful because everything is new and also because you may have unrealistically high expectations of yourself. As a beginning practitioner you are likely to want advice and lots of practical suggestions. You need to feel appreciated and connected to other professionals.

Stage 2: Consolidation. When you have become adept at basic "survival" in the classroom, you begin to bring together what you know to create a more personal approach to working with children. During this time you may find on-site assistance, consultants, and the advice of colleagues helpful.

Stage 3: Renewal. When you have been working with children for 3 to 5 years, you may begin to feel somewhat bored or dissatisfied. At this stage you may enjoy doing professional reading, going to conferences or workshops, doing action research, and joining professional associations. Visits to other schools may renew your enthusiasm and give you new ideas as well as a greater sense of belonging and professionalism.

Stage 4: Maturity. After 5 or more years of working with children, you may find yourself less interested in practical details (which you have mastered) and more interested in consideration of the values, theories, issues, and philosophy that underlie your work. At this stage attending seminars, working on advanced degrees, and more theoretical professional reading may renew your sense of excitement and provide new areas of interest and involvement.

Katz's stages apply best to individuals who are working in programs that serve children on a daily basis. Those who move from work *with* children to work *for* children go through similar stages and seek similar challenges as they gain professional experience and maturity.

Reflect on your ideal job

Imagine a perfect job for you in early childhood education. What age group would you like to work with? What kind of program appeals to you most? What would the job be like? Why does it appeal to you? What training would you need for this job?

Final Thoughts

You are at the beginning of your career as an early childhood educator and have much to learn and many rewarding experiences ahead of you. You already know that you will need to work in your college classes. There will be books to read, papers to write, projects to create, programs to visit, children to teach, and exams to study for. But you may not be thinking about the work you will continue to do once your college work is over. Good teachers are lifelong learners, by necessity and by disposition. If you aspire to be a good teacher, and we assume you do, you will continue to learn about children and teaching for your whole career.

A job becomes a "calling" when it involves an important purpose, deep values, and a strong sense of what and how one wants to contribute to the world. When you get paid to do work that has meaning in your life, work you love, you have a calling. We hope that you will find that work in early childhood education is a way you can experience personal fulfillment as you serve young children and their families.

The children are waiting.

Learning Outcomes

When you read this chapter, and then thoughtfully complete selected assignments from the "To Learn More" section and prepare items from "Starting Your Professional Portfolio" (see the box on pages 28–29), you will be demonstrating progress in meeting **NAEYC Standard 6: Becoming a Professional** (NAEYC, 2009).

Key elements:

6a: Identifying and involving oneself with the early childhood field

6b: Knowing about and upholding ethical standards and other professional guidelines

6c: Engaging in continuous, collaborative learning to inform practice

6d: Integrating knowledgeable, reflective, and critical perspectives on early education

To Learn More

Remember a Teacher: Write about a teacher you remember from your own childhood. Describe the following:

- Her or his personal qualities
- What you think your teacher valued and why
- His or her effect on children
- His or her effect in your life
- How you would like to be similar to or different from this teacher and why

Write a Newspaper Article About a Professional Early Childhood Educator: Interview an early childhood educator who has been working in the field for at least 5 years. Ask about the following:

- **Basic information**—job title, responsibilities, employer, training for the position
- **Career path**—education, experiences, and philosophy that led the individual to early childhood education

- **Professional joys and issues**
- **Contributions**—professional accomplishments, participation in the professional community
- **Vision**—what the person sees as the state of early childhood education and what the future holds for the field

Compare Two Programs: Observe two early childhood programs for at least a half a day for each one. Write a paper in which you compare the programs briefly and list what seem to be the primary values of each program. Explore the specific things you saw that led to your conclusions.

Write a Book Review: Read one of the books about teachers and teaching listed below. Write a short review of the book as if you were writing for a newsletter or journal for teachers. Don't tell the whole story; give the highlights, share the personal meaning for you, and motivate your audience to read it for themselves.

Ashton-Warner, Sylvia. 1963/1986. *Teacher.*

Ayers, William. 1989. *The Good Preschool Teacher: Six Teachers Reflect on Their Lives.*

Glover, Mary Kenner. 1993. *Two Years: A Teacher's Memoir.*

Hillman, Carol B. 2011. *Teaching Four-Year-Olds: A Personal Journey.* Updated and revised edition.

Kane, Pearl Rock. 1991. *My First Year as a Teacher.*

Kidder, Tracy. 1989. *Among Schoolchildren.*

Kohl, Herbert. 1968. *Thirty-six Children.*

Nieto, Sonia. 2003. *What Keeps Teachers Going?*

Paley, Vivian. 1979. *White Teacher.*

———. 1981. *Wally's Stories—Conversations in the Kindergarten.*

———. 1988. *Mollie Is Three—Growing Up in School.*

———. 1990. *Boy Who Would Be a Helicopter.*

———. 1991. *Bad Guys Don't Have Birthdays: Fantasy Play at Four.*

———. 1992. *You Can't Say You Can't Play.*

———. 1995. *Kwanzaa and Me.*

———. 1997. *The Girl with the Brown Crayon.*

———. 1999. *The Kindness of Children.*

Pappas, Sophia. 2009. *Good Morning Children: My First Years in Early Childhood Education.*

Pratt, Caroline. 1948/1970. *I Learn from Children.*

Van Cleave, Mary. 1994. *The Least of These: Stories of Schoolchildren.*

Write an Autobiography: Briefly describe yourself using the characteristics of effective teachers described in this chapter, Thomas and Chess's Nine Dimensions of Temperament, and Gardner's Multiple Intelligences. You may also wish to use your reflections from this chapter. Review the experiences and relationships in your life at home and in the world that led you to choose early childhood education as a career.

Write About Values: Discuss how your values impact the way you work, or hope to work, with children. Discuss values you are acquiring as a professional. Where have they come from? What are your thoughts about the core values of the early childhood field as written in the NAEYC Code of Ethical Conduct? What do you see as you look ahead to becoming an early childhood educator (or as you continue your career)?

Investigate Related Websites:

Associations that provide information and seek to improve professional practice:

National Association for the Education of Young Children (NAEYC): naeyc.org

Association for Childhood Education International (ACEI): acei.org

Southern Early Childhood Association (SECA): southernearlychildhood.org

The Myers & Briggs Foundation: myersbriggs.org/my-mbti-personality-type/mbti-basics

New York State Early Childhood Career Development Resource Guide: earlychildhood.org/cdrg/prep_employ.cfm

Codes of ethics:

American Montessori Society Code of Ethics: amshq.org/About%20AMS/Who%20We%20Are/Code%20of%20Ethics.aspx

Division for Early Childhood (DEC) of the Council for Exceptional Children Code of Ethics: dec-sped.org/uploads/docs/about_dec/position_concept_papers/Code%20of%20Ethics_updated_Aug2009.pdf

National Association for the Education of Young Children: naeyc.org/positionstatements/ethical_conduct

Early Childhood Australia: earlychildhoodaustralia.org.au/code_of_ethics/code_of_ethics.html

Canadian Child Care Federation: cccf-fcsge.ca/practice/practice_en.html#CodeofEthics

New Zealand Teachers Council: teacherscouncil.govt.nz/required/ethics/

Association of Early Childhood Educators (Singapore): aeces.org

 **For Your Portfolio**

Include one of the assignments from the "To Learn More" section as a demonstration of your understanding of the field of early childhood education.

MyEducationLab

Go to Topic 12: Professionalism/Ethics in the MyEducationLab (myeducationlab.com) for *Who Am I in the Lives of Children?* where you can:

- Find learning outcomes for Professionalism/Ethics along with the national standards that connect to these outcomes.
- Complete Assignments and Activities that can help you more deeply understand the chapter content.
- Apply and practice your understanding of the core teaching skills identified in the chapter with the Building Teaching Skills and Dispositions learning units.

- Access video clips of CCSSO National Teachers of the Year award winners responding to the question, "Why Do I Teach?" in the Teacher Talk section.
- Listen to experts from the field in Professional Perspectives.
- Check your comprehension on the content covered in the chapter with the Study Plan. Here you will be able to take a chapter quiz, receive feedback on your answers, and then access Review, Practice, and Enrichment activities to enhance your understanding of chapter content.

It takes a village to raise a child.

AFRICAN PROVERB

2

The Field of Early Childhood Education

Early childhood education touches the lives of many people in our society. Those who are most intimately affected are the children and families who participate and the educators who work in programs for young children. It also impacts employers, educational systems, and everyone else who deals with the children and families who are served by early education programs. Families need programs that provide their young children with worthwhile experiences and help them to develop their potential and succeed in later schooling. Family members benefit from having supportive teachers who communicate with them about their children and who offer them guidance in supporting children's school participation and development into productive citizens.

In this chapter we lay out the broad outlines of the field of early childhood education as it exists in the United States today, with an emphasis on those programs that might be of interest to beginning teachers seeking to find their place in the field. In it we describe some ways that programs for young children can be classified and look at programs for the care and education of children ages 5 and younger, programs for the care and education of children ages 5 to 8, and programs for children with disabilities in each of these age groups. We discuss approaches used to regulate programs, ways of recognizing competence in teachers, current views about the importance of quality in programs, and the impact on U.S. education of the movement to develop standards for student achievement. The chapter concludes with a look at some recurring issues in early childhood education and a few current trends.

As you learn to be early childhood educator, you will find out about and work in different kinds of programs for young children. We recommend that you visit and work in as many of these programs as you can to get direct experience of the variety of approaches available in early childhood education today. Your growing understanding of the many aspects of the field and the important contributions it makes to our society will play a role in your growth as an educator who can support the positive development in young children.

MyEducationLab

Visit the MyEducationLab for *Who Am I in the Lives of Children?* to enhance your understanding of chapter concepts with a personalized Study Plan. You'll also have the opportunity to hone your teaching skills through video-based Assignments and Activities, as well as Building Teaching Skills and Disposition lessons.

Overview of Programs for Young Children

Programs for young children today can be classified in terms of the age and other characteristics of the children they serve, by their purposes, by the places in which they are housed, and by their sponsorship and funding.

Children

Early childhood is a period in the life cycle that includes birth through age 8. This stage can be divided into four different age groups:

- Infants and toddlers—birth to 36 months
- Preschoolers—3- and 4-year-olds
- Kindergartners—5- and 6-year-olds
- Primary grade children—first through third graders—6-, 7-, and 8-year-olds

The children served in early childhood programs include those who are typically developing and those who have special needs.

Purposes

The two primary purposes for early childhood programs are (1) to support children's learning and development and (2) to provide care for children in families where adults are working or in training. Care for children's physical and psychological needs and early education are inextricably linked—preschool, child care, early intervention, prekindergartens, kindergartens, and primary classrooms are their major modes of delivery. Some early childhood programs have secondary goals such as support or education of parents and the provision of health, nutrition, and social services to children and families. Another program goal—indigenous language revitalization—has emerged in community-based programs led by groups of people who want to preserve their language and culture and pass it on to future generations.

Facilities

Early childhood education and care programs can be found in settings that are dedicated to the care of children (centers and schools) and in family homes. Center-based programs for children between birth and 5 years of age may be located in sites that were specifically designed to care for groups of young children; in spaces found in religious facilities like churches, mosques, and synagogues; in community and recreational facilities such as the YWCA and YMCA; in public housing complexes and in workplaces. Home-based care may be located in a family's own home or the home of a caregiver. Most programs for children aged 5 and older (and an increasing number of 3- and 4-year-olds in prekindergarten programs) are housed in public and private school facilities.

Sponsorship and Funding

Sponsorship and funding of early childhood programs may be public (federal, state, or county) or private. Over the years, and continuing today, the greatest percentage of programs for children under age 5 are private and supported by tuition paid by the families of the children who attend. Private programs may be *not-for-profit*, intended as a service to children and their families. Many of these programs are housed in religious facilities and may be partly subsidized by churches, mosques, and synagogues. Programs may also be *for-profit*, designed as a service-oriented business. Some of these centers are owned and operated by nationwide chains that attempt to make child care affordable and profitable by using standardized building plans, bulk purchase of equipment and supplies, and a standardized curriculum. These for-profit chains have become an increasingly common type of privately sponsored child care.

Because they have found that the provision of child care contributes to a reliable and productive workforce, employers in some large corporations, hospitals, and government agencies sponsor child care programs for their employees. The U.S. Department of Defense—the largest employer sponsor of child care— offers programs for children of personnel who serve in the military. Colleges and universities may sponsor and subsidize early childhood programs for the children of faculty, staff, and students as well as for teacher education and research. Some high schools sponsor early childhood programs to serve students' children and/ or as laboratories for students to learn about child development.

Children between ages 5 and 8 attend kindergarten through third-grade programs that provide educational experiences. These programs are offered in state-funded public schools and in private schools that are supported by tuition paid by families. Programs for children with disabilities are generally housed in public schools and receive a combination of state and federal funding.

Programs for Children from Birth to Age 5

There are a number of kinds of education and care programs available for children 5 years of age and younger. These programs are delivered in homes, child care centers, and schools. The majority of them offer care for the children of working families combined with planned educational experiences. Some programs are funded by state and federal governments in order to address the educational needs of children from low-income families and children with disabilities. Another kind of program provides education about parenting and child development for family members. These programs may also provide educational experiences for children.

Child Care

Child care is a fact of life for a significant portion of children and families in our country. A 2011 report by the National Association of Child Care Resource and Referral Agencies stated that the number of children potentially needing child care was approximately 14.8 million children under age 6, about 62% of a population of 23.8 million (NACCRRA, 2011).

Of children in care, approximately 60% are in center-based care, 35% in relative care, and 22% in nonrelative family child care. Many children attend more than one family child care setting or are in multiple child care arrangements with center-based programs supplemented by care provided by relatives (NACCRRA, 2008; U.S. Census Bureau, 2005).

Care and education for young children whose family members work may be provided in full- or part-day center-based programs, family child care homes, and/or informal arrangements (care provided by relatives or friends, sometimes referred to as *kith and kin* care). Because there is no one system for delivering and funding these programs, their availability and quality varies greatly from community to community and from state to state.

Center-Based Child Care

Facilities that are dedicated to the care and education of young children are referred to as child care centers, child development centers, and preschools. They may also be referred to as *day care*—a term left over from the 1900s, when it was used to distinguish care offered during the day from overnight boarding care. We prefer the term *child care,* which is a more accurate description of what programs actually do.

Programs for children under 5 have the challenging task of providing a safe, nurturing environment and educational experiences to support children's development, often for long hours each day. Today the majority of centers care for children for a full day while members of their families are at work or in training to enter the workforce.

Until the 1980s most early childhood education programs served children between 2½ and 5 years of age. As more and more women entered the workforce, the demand for out-of-home care for infants and toddlers became widespread. In order to meet children's needs and ensure their safety, experts believe—and most states require—that programs for infants should have a ratio of 1 caregiver to every 3 to 4 children. For this reason the cost of infant care in centers is much higher than care for older preschoolers. In 2007 the national average fee for children aged 0 to 2 was $8,150 per year, compared to $6,420 for 3- to 5-year-olds. This means that, even though infant-toddler care may be available in most areas, its high cost makes it inaccessible for many families (Ackerman & Barnett, 2009).

At one time some families hesitated to place their children in infant-toddler care based on research that suggested that out-of-home care negatively impacted infants' and toddlers' attachment to their parents (Belsky, 2001). Subsequent research found that child care did not necessarily present a risk to the mother-child attachment relationship. This research did show that poor quality care combined with insensitive parenting seems to have negative effects on attachment (NICHD, 1997).

In some communities, other kinds of programs are available to meet the needs of working families. Some programs are available late hours for family members who work in hotels and factories; others, often housed in hospitals, care for children with mild, noncontagious illnesses.

Home-Based Child Care

Home-based care is the least visible, yet most common, form of privately sponsored child care in the United States. Throughout history, children have been cared for in their own homes and in the homes of relatives, friends, and paid caregivers. Home-based care can be provided in family child care homes (usually three to eight children), in group child care homes (generally 12 to 15 children), in the homes of close relatives or family friends (kith and kin care), or in the child's own home by either a trained caregiver (like a nanny) or an untrained caregiver.

Recent surveys report that children spend more hours per week (26.7) in nonrelative care than in relative care (24.3 hours per week) or center-based care (24.8 hours) and that relatives regularly provide child care to almost half of the more than 19 million preschoolers (Iruka & Carver, 2006; U.S. Census Bureau, 2005).

Home-based care is usually available from early morning to early evening and may also be offered on evenings and weekends. It is typically less expensive than center-based care and nearly always more flexible in schedule and provision of care for children who have mild illnesses. These programs are often chosen by families of infants and toddlers who prefer that their children be cared for in the small, intimate environment of a home. It is also employed as an alternative to a center-based care for preschool-age children whose families prefer this alternative.

Until recently the expense of in-home care was borne by the families of the children served. Since the advent of welfare reform in the early 1990s, government subsidies have been available for child care for women who are leaving welfare rolls to enter the labor force. The majority of these women choose kith and kin care, which is generally more obtainable in low-income neighborhoods than licensed care, especially for infants and toddlers. The Department of Defense also offers the option of in-home care to military children in recognition of the fact that many families prefer to have their children cared for in home settings. In 2008 there were more than 9,000 trained in-home care providers delivering child care services to children of military parents (Department of Defense, 2008).

Head Start and Early Head Start

Head Start is a federally funded program that was originally designed to ameliorate the effects of poverty on young children and to help prepare them to be successful in school. Head Start provides a comprehensive child development program that includes education and support services for children from low-income families who meet income eligibility requirements.

"Head Start programs promote school readiness by enhancing the social and cognitive development of children through the provision of educational, health, nutritional, social and other services to enrolled children and families. They engage parents in their children's learning and help them in making progress toward their educational, literacy and employment goals. Significant emphasis is placed on the involvement of parents in the administration of local Head Start programs" (ACF/OHS, 2004).

Since its inception in 1965, Head Start has served more than 27 million children throughout the country (ACF/OHS, 2010). In 2009, it served more than a million children: 92% in centers, 5% in home-based programs, and 1% in family child care homes (CLASP, 2010a).

In recognition of research demonstrating the importance of development from birth to age 3, *Early Head Start* was established in 1995 to serve low-income pregnant women and families with infants and toddlers. The purposes of the Early Head Start program are to enhance children's development, enable parents to be better caregivers and teachers to their children, and help parents work toward economic independence. The program includes educational experiences; home visits, especially for families with infants; parent education, including parent-child activities; comprehensive health services; nutrition; and ongoing support for parents through case management and peer support groups. In 2009 the Early Head Start program served just under 84,000 children—fewer than 3% of those who were eligible (CLASP, 2010b).

Research on the Impact of Early Childhood Programs on Children from Low-Income Families

Since it began, there has been public debate over whether or not Head Start "works." This debate continues today (Klein, 2011). Whether or not Head Start is a success is based in large part on what measures of success are used. Longitudinal research on children from low-income families who participated in high-quality early childhood programs (predominantly Head Start) has demonstrated that these programs have a significant and lasting impact on children's cognitive development, social behavior, and health—and benefit their families as well. Moreover, it has been demonstrated that the cost is more than compensated by savings in later remedial education programs and correctional institutions. Studies report that for every dollar spent, $7 is saved (Lazar & Darlington, 1983; McKey, 1985; Schweinhardt & Weikart, 1997). The Abecedarian Study, conducted by researchers at the Frank Porter Graham Child Development Center, showed long-lasting benefits for children from low-income families who participated in an experimental program from infancy through age 5. Researchers found significant differences in abilities and achievements between children who attended the program and members of a control group. At age 21, those who had been enrolled in the program were more likely to score higher on IQ and reading and math tests, to be enrolled in or graduated from in a four-year college, to have delayed parenthood, and to be gainfully employed (Frank Porter Graham Center, 1999).

Positive results like these were linked to the high quality of the program—which included high ratios of adults to children, ongoing professional development, good salaries for staff, and individualized curriculum for children based on learning games. A national longitudinal study of the development of Head Start children was conducted in 1997, using a battery of instruments called FACES (Family and Child Experiences Survey). The study reported that children who attended Head Start showed significant gains in vocabulary, writing skills, and social skills over the Head Start year. The program also had a positive impact on child health and readiness for school and on families. Head Start parents reported reading to their young children 3 to 5 times a week. Follow-up studies in 2000 and 2003 documented significant gains in vocabulary, early math, and early writing skills (Administration for Children and Families, 2001, 2003, 2006).

Reflect and write about programs for children from birth to age 5

Think about a program for children under 5 that you know. What are its purposes? Who runs it? Who pays for it? Do you think it is a high-quality program? How can you tell? Would you enjoy working in it? Why?

Early Childhood Family Education

Another type of program for young children is based on the assumption that parents are children's first and most important teachers. Programs that involve families, especially in combination with a high-quality program for children, have been demonstrated by research to be beneficial both to children and to family members (Barnett, 1995). Programs may encourage family members to work with children in their classrooms or provide information to help them to support their children academically or deal with parenting issues. Some programs for infants and toddlers are offered by trained visitors who work with parents and children in their homes.

Family literacy programs, another mode of parent education, are designed to break the cycle of poverty and illiteracy and improve the opportunities of low-income families. This approach integrates a program for children with literacy instruction and parenting education for family members. A review of research by Padak and Rasinski (2003) reported positive outcomes of these programs for both children and families.

Family education programs may be designed for parents whose children are functioning normally but who want additional knowledge about parenting. They may also focus on specific parenting issues, such as substance-abuse prevention, appropriate discipline, and antisocial behavior. Some of these programs are aimed at specific populations of parents, such as those with children at critical periods of development, single parents, or parents with low incomes, while others target specific populations of children, such as children with disabilities.

Programs for Children 0 Through 5 with Disabilities

The federal Education for All Handicapped Children Act, passed in 1975, marked the beginning of an alliance among families of children with disabilities and professionals and other advocates in the field of special education. In 1990, it was replaced by the Individuals with Disabilities Education Act (IDEA), which has guided the provision of early childhood special education services since that time. The purpose of IDEA is to ensure that all children with disabilities have access to a free, appropriate public education (FAPE). Services are also mandated under the Americans with Disabilities Act (ADA), which requires access to public accommodations for all individuals regardless of disability. Public accommodations for early childhood programs include child care centers and family child care homes (Haring, McCormick, & Haring, 1994).

Today programs and services for young children with disabilities are available in all states, supported by a combination of federal and state funding. Children from birth to age 3 may attend early intervention programs, which are offered by a variety of community agencies for children who have disabilities or who are at risk for developing disabilities. Preschool programs for 3- to 5-year-olds are most often housed in public schools, although some can be found in community preschools and Head Start centers.

Public Prekindergarten Programs

A significant new development in programs for children under 5 is the rapid growth of state-funded prekindergarten (pre-K) for 3- and 4-year-olds. These programs are designed to help children get ready to meet the academic expectations they will encounter in kindergarten. They may be housed in public schools, in child care centers, and in some communities in both schools and centers. Availability and eligibility vary greatly between states. In some states programs are intended for low-income children who are at risk for school failure; others seek to serve all age eligible children. The movement to make these programs available for all 4-year-olds before they enter kindergarten is referred to as *universal pre-K*.

The proliferation of pre-K programs can be attributed to the body of research demonstrating the positive effects of early education programs on children's subsequent academic performance. Based on this research, educators and policy makers have concluded that children who attend pre-K programs will be better prepared to meet school expectations and ultimately better able to perform well on the tests that are increasingly important in American schools. Increased parental demand based on information about the benefits of early childhood programs is also a factor in the growing number of pre-K programs.

A report on public school enrollment (NACCRRA, 2008) states that the fastest public school growth between 1985 and 2005 occurred in the elementary grades (prekindergarten through grade 8), and that the most dramatic part of this increase was in pre-K programs. The percentage of children enrolled in public pre-K programs continues to increase, from 17% of 4-year-olds in 2005 to 27% in 2010 (Barnett et al., 2010).

In the 2009–2010 school year 40 states (up from 38 the previous several years) had state-funded pre-K programs; enrollment in these programs increased in 23 of these states; 27% of all 4-year-olds attended pre-K programs; six states served more than half of their 4-year-olds; and 4% of 3-year-olds attended pre-K programs—though about half the states have no program for 3-year-olds (Barnett et al., 2010)

The amount and reliability of pre-K funding varies from state to state; programs thrive when state budgets are healthy, but states tend to reduce or eliminate programs when times get hard. Moreover, "Children and families in the states with no provision for state pre-K are increasingly disadvantaged relative to those in the rest of the nation" (Barnett et al., 2007, p. 10).

Program Regulation and Quality Enhancement

Because young children are dependent and vulnerable, families and society want to be assured that the programs that serve them are committed to their welfare and will protect them from harm. The method used to ensure a minimal level of quality in programs for children under age 5 is licensing of programs. "Governments can regulate programs that are operated in the private market. Regulatory policy enables governments to protect the public and to set a floor of quality for programs in the private sector" (Morgan, 2003, p. 65). Some programs may also seek to demonstrate that they meet additional standards that are used to define high quality.

Regulations governing state-funded programs are determined by the state in which the program is delivered. If the program is housed in a community pre-school it will be subject to state licensing rules. If, like most special education and prekindergarten programs, it is located in a public school setting, it will fall under the regulations that govern educational programs for older children.

Licensing

Licensing of programs for children under 5 is based on standards developed in each state. In some states, all programs are required to be licensed; in others, certain categories of programs are exempt from licensing. Because early childhood programs have, until recently, been viewed as a social service for families, licensing is generally managed by human services departments rather than departments of education. Licensing originally focused on programs for preschool-age children, but it now includes programs for infants and toddlers and before- and after-school care. Most states also have provisions for licensing or registering family child care homes, though these requirements are difficult to enforce because it is hard to know who is offering care if providers do not assent to be regulated.

In most states licensing provides a "safety net" to ensure that the physical environment is safe and healthy and that there are enough adults available to supervise children. In some states standards are higher and support for children's development is included in program requirements. Standards for licensing and for enforcement of standards vary greatly by state, and licensure in itself is no guarantee of quality. Unlike many other Western nations, the United States has no nationally mandated child care standards, even for federally funded child care programs.

The National Association for the Education of Young Children (NAEYC, 1997) position statement on licensing and public regulation of early childhood programs emphasizes children's right to care in settings that protect them from harm and promote their healthy development. It states (1) that all facilities including centers and family child care homes should be licensed, (2) that licensing standards should be clear and reasonable and reflect current research, (3) that licensing standards should be vigorously and equitably enforced, and (4) that licensing agencies should have sufficient staff and resources to do their job.

Quality Standards

Some programs strive to reach a higher level of program quality than is required for state licensing. *Accreditation* is a voluntary process that enables programs to measure themselves against a national set of standards and assists families in identifying high-quality placements for their children. The accreditation process requires extensive self-study and validation by professionals outside of the program being reviewed.

In 1985, NAEYC established an accreditation system for recognizing programs that meet criteria for high quality. These standards were revised in 2006 in order to make the process more reliable and accountable. The changes included requirements for annual reporting, program and classroom portfolios, more rigorous performance criteria, and higher teacher qualifications. As of June 2011 there were approximately 7,000 programs accredited by NAEYC in all states, including child care centers, military programs, Head Start programs, and public school programs (NAEYC Academy).

Interest in accreditation as a way to improve program quality has led to the development of a number of national accreditation systems in addition to that of NAEYC. Systems have been developed by the National Association for Family Child Care (NAFCC), National Early Childhood Program Accreditation (NECPA), the American Montessori Society (AMS), the Association of Christian Schools International (ACSI), and the National Lutheran Schools Association (NLSA).

Some programs that receive government funds may be required to have standards that are different from or exceed state licensing standards. Child care facilities run by branches of the armed services for the children of military personnel are subject to regulations that are higher than those for most states. At present, 93% of military-sponsored child care programs meet NAEYC accreditation standards. Family child care providers are certified according to a set of military standards and are encouraged to obtain NAEYC accreditation (Hruska, 2009). Head Start programs are required to meet state licensing requirements *and* follow national Head Start performance standards. These standards address the broad categories of early childhood development and health services, family and community partnerships, and program design and management (Administration for Children, Youth, & Families, 2008).

Another approach being used by states to improve the quality of early childhood programs is the development of quality rating and improvement systems (QRIS) that recognize levels of quality above those required for licensing. They are discussed later in this chapter.

Programs for Children Ages 5 Through 8

Although there is great diversity in programs for children under the age of 5, the majority of 5- to 8-year-olds, including those with disabilities, attend kindergarten through third grade in state-funded elementary schools (public schools). Some families (about 12% in 2008) (NCES, 2011) opt out of the public school system and send their children to religious or secular private schools. And a small minority of children in this age group are homeschooled. Before- and after-school programs are available in many school districts to provide child care for families who need care for children outside of school hours.

Kindergarten Through Primary Grade (K–3) Programs

Historically kindergartens have served as a transition for 5-year-olds between home or an early childhood program and the more academically demanding first-grade classroom. According to the National Center for Education Statistics, enrollment of 5- to 6-year-olds has been about 96% for a few decades (NCES, 2011).

Kindergarten began as a half-day program, but since the 1970s the percentage of full-day kindergartens has increased greatly. In 2009, approximately 61% of all kindergarten programs nationwide were considered full-day (NCES, 2011). It is difficult to know exactly what "full-day" means, however, because there is a wide variation among states in how this term is defined. In most states kindergarten is available for families who wish to send their children, but school attendance is not mandatory until first grade.

Although there have been kindergartens in the United States since the middle of the 19th century, there is still no consensus about what their purpose should be or the kinds of educational experiences they should provide. Policy specialist Kristie Kauerz (2005) wrote, "kindergarten is not firmly established either as an integral part of the K–12 system or as an integral part of states' emerging systems of early care and education. Kindergarten in the United States straddles both worlds" (p. 1). According to Kauerz, this is not surprising given the history of the kindergarten, which was introduced as a nurturing, play-based program intended to help children make the transition into formal schooling and now tends to be viewed as the beginning of the academic school program. Until recently reading wasn't taught until first grade, because children before the age of 6 were not considered "ready" to read. That has changed and today almost all kindergartens teach reading.

First grade has long been considered the beginning of the serious work of school. In the United States school attendance is compulsory from 6 or 7 years of age. The first through third grades are an integral part of the public school system, though children in these grades are still included in the age definition of early childhood. The curriculum in the primary grades has always tended to be more academic than that of the preschool or the kindergarten.

Charter Schools

Growing concern with the ability of public schools to meet the needs of all children has led to attention to the provision of charter schools. Charter schools are independently operated, publicly funded programs that have greater flexibility than regular schools in meeting regulations. A charter is a performance contract that describes the mission of the school, the educational programs it will follow, and methods that will be used for assessing students' and program effectiveness. If a program can demonstrate successful performance the charter may be renewed. Charter schools have received grants from the U.S. Department of

Education since 1995 and continue to be a focus of educational reform efforts. The underlying concept is that in exchange for being granted a higher degree of autonomy than other public schools a program must demonstrate the effectiveness of its practices (U.S. Charter Schools, n.d.).

Many legislators and policy makers regard public school systems as being too slow to embrace change. They see charter schools as a way to speed up the process and believe that they will improve public education. Advocates for charter schools maintain that they provide more choices for families, increase opportunities for learning, encourage innovative teaching, and improve education. Critics maintain that charter schools attract the best students and leave the regular public schools to deal with those who have the greatest needs, and that they take needed resources away from already overburdened public schools.

Programs for Children Ages 5 Through 8 with Disabilities

The majority of 5- to 8-year-old children with disabilities are educated in public school classrooms. An increasing number of these children are included in regular classrooms for at least part of the day. Many school districts implement *full inclusion*—which means that all children with disabilities are placed in general education classrooms for the entire school day. Most educators today believe that this practice is beneficial for both children who have disabilities and their peers who are not disabled. When children with disabilities are included in regular classrooms, it is imperative that school districts provide adequate support services for the teachers involved. If this is not done, inclusion adds another responsibility to the load of already overburdened classroom teachers.

Homeschooling

Prior to the advent of universal public education in the United States, educating children at home was the only option for families who lived in isolated locations or could not afford to send their children to private school. Some families in the United States today choose to homeschool their children for these or other reasons. NCES (2011) reports that 2.9% of all students were homeschooled and that 3.1% of kindergartners were homeschooled.

The most common reasons that families give for homeschooling their children are (1) to teach a particular set of values and beliefs, (2) to increase academic achievement, (3) to individualize curriculum, (4) to enhance family relationships, and (5) to provide a safe environment. Some research suggests that homeschooled children do somewhat better on standardized tests than those who are educated in schools, and there is no reported evidence of negative consequences of homeschooling (Ray, 2006).

Many states have established standards and requirements that families must meet in order to homeschool their children. These requirements vary greatly. Some states and school districts require a particular curriculum or adherence to an approved plan of instruction.

The Standards Movement

All education in the United States has been profoundly influenced by the movement for school reform that began three decades ago with the publication of the report *Nation at Risk* (National Commission on Excellence in Education, 1983).

Reflect and write about programs for 5- to 8-year-olds

Think about a kindergarten or primary grade program that you know. What is the program like? Do you think that it provides a good experience for the children? Would you enjoy working in it? Why?

This report examined the state of American education and declared that a "rising tide of mediocrity" threatened the nation. The authors reported that test scores were falling, that academic expectations were too low, and that students educated in the United States were not competing favorably with those in other countries. Recommendations included the development of higher and measurable standards for academic performance and higher standards for teacher preparation.

In the years since *Nation at Risk* was released, accountability for school performance has become a national priority. The federal government has become increasingly involved in educational policy, which until the 1980s had been the realm of state and local governments. In 1989 the National Educational Goals Panel (NEGP), a bipartisan group of political leaders, took up the cause of educational reform and initiated the creation of eight national education goals. In 1994 the NEGP was charged with monitoring and facilitating progress in reaching the eight goals (National Education Goals Panel, 1997). This initiative resulted in the development of current state systems for linking standards, assessment, and accountability.

The National Education Goals Panel promoted the development of content standards intended to help states and school districts ensure that worthwhile subject matter was being taught. *Content standards* address goals and objectives for each subject area for each grade. Standards were originally developed by professional associations including the National Council for the Social Studies, National Council for Teachers of Mathematics, International Reading Association, and others. States then developed their own standards, drawing on the national standards but tailoring them to their own educational priorities. *Performance (or achievement) standards* and assessments, usually in the form of tests, were later developed by states to determine the extent to which children had mastered the prescribed content. Standards are now a feature of every public school system in the United States.

Common Core Standards

The Common Core Standards Initiative, a state-led effort coordinated by the National Governors Association Center for Best Practices (NGA Center) and the Council of Chief State School Officers (CCSSO), promotes the development of consistent standards for students in kindergarten through 12th grade. Groups including teachers and administrators worked together on the development of these standards, which are intended to provide consistency of expectations throughout the country (Common Core Standards Initiative, n.d.).

The Alliance for Childhood, an early childhood advocacy organization, supports the concept of core standards but has expressed strong reservations about the content relating to young children in the standards as they are currently written. It is concerned that the standards will lead to unrealistic expectations for kindergarten and primary-age children, will lead to unwarranted pressure for academic achievement, and will move early education further away from the hands-on active learning that early childhood educators believe is most appropriate for young children (Alliance for Childhood, 2011).

Early Learning Standards

When elementary school administrators and others became aware of the impact of preschool experiences on children's ability to meet kindergarten expectations, they began to call for early childhood educators to develop their own standards. *Early learning standards* (also called content standards and early learning guidelines) describe learning experiences that should be provided in programs to give children a well-rounded educational experience and to help prepare them for later school expectations. These standards are intended to help early childhood educators design worthwhile curriculum for preschool programs. They include examples of what most children are able to do at a particular age when exposed to appropriate learning experiences.

NAEYC (2003) developed a position statement identifying principles or criteria for developing, adopting, and using early learning standards. It states that "standards can help practitioners and policy makers create a clear focus on what is truly important in early education" (Hyson, 2003, p. 66).

There has been tremendous growth in the development and implementation of early learning standards over the last decade. In 1999 only 10 states had standards for children's learning prior to entering kindergarten. By 2005 some 39 states had developed standards (Kagan, Scott-Little, & Stebbins Frelow, 2003), and by 2007 49 states plus the District of Columbia had them (Scott-Little, Lesko, Martella, & Milburn, 2007). The majority of these standards were developed for use by state-funded early childhood programs. States vary in the focus of their standards (some address only language and literacy; others address all domains of development) and in the extent to which their use is mandated. In all states, the early learning standards are linked to K–12 standards.

A number of states have also developed infant-toddler standards, called *early learning guidelines*. The Zero to Three organization, a nonprofit group dedicated to promoting the healthy development of infants and toddlers, has developed recommendations intended to promote beneficial standards that will not be used to push academic expectations down to the youngest children. Some of their recommendations are that standards should (1) address a range of developmental domains, (2) be inclusive of the culture and languages of the children's homes, and (3) incorporate items addressing the critical nature of relationships for infant and toddler development. Zero to Three also stresses that early learning guidelines for infants and toddlers should be aligned with pre-K and K–12 standards in a way that illustrates how foundations of learning are established in the first years of life (Zero to Three, 2008).

Standards are helpful when they emphasize worthwhile content for curriculum. Unfortunately, they can also lead to inappropriate expectations and narrowly focused teaching. It is increasingly important that early childhood educators and policy makers work together to ensure the effective development and use of standards so that they lead to positive outcomes for children and the field (Kagan et al., 2003).

Issues and Trends in Early Childhood Education

In this chapter so far we have introduced you to the field of early childhood education, the roles and responsibilities of people who work with young children, and educational standards that inform curriculum and teaching in early childhood programs. In this last section we will share some information that will help you to understand and navigate in the real world of working in an early childhood program. We will introduce you to some vital issues and current trends that you are likely to encounter as you move into your career in early childhood education.

Reflect and write about your experience with standards

Have you ever had an experience with content standards as a student or in a program for young children that you have visited or worked in? What do you remember about the standards? What do you remember about the effect they had on students and teachers?

Issues

Early childhood educators do not always agree with one another. And like any field that has an impact on the public, not everyone agrees with early childhood educators. *Issues* are those matters where there is debate or disagreement, discussion or concern. Most of the issues we address here have been the subject of lively discussion since we entered the field of early childhood education and it is likely that they will continue to be deliberated about for some time to come. We include brief descriptions of recurring issues here to give you a bit of a heads-up so that they don't take you by surprise.

Goals of Early Childhood Education

Reflect and write about the goals of early childhood programs

Think about the early childhood programs that you remember from your childhood and that you have observed and/or worked in. What do think were the goals of those programs? What do you think was the justification for these goals?

One issue that you are very likely to encounter has to do with the fundamental question of what the goals of early childhood education should be. There is general agreement about broad purposes of programs for young children—they are intended to provide care and education. Care involves meeting children's need for a safe environment and for activity, nutrition, and rest and is a necessary component of all programs. The controversy tends to be about the goals for education offered in early childhood programs.

Education is an expression of social values and can be the means to accomplish many kinds of societal goals. What should be the goal of early childhood education? Heated debates regarding the appropriate curriculum and methods used in early childhood programs are often the result of differences about goals.

Educators who have been trained in early childhood education tend to embrace the view that the most appropriate goal for programs is the "development of the whole child" with a focus on social, emotional, and physical as well as intellectual development. These educators are concerned with the actualization of children's potential; they believe that healthy, happy children grow into healthy, happy, and productive adults; and they agree with philosopher John Dewey's contention that school is not preparation for life but that it *is* the life of the child. Historically, this was the goal of the nursery school, which has evolved into today's child development centers for children under 5 years of age. Many early childhood educators today continue to hold this view (including the authors of this book).

A second goal for early childhood education is academic learning—providing children with skills that will prepare them for success in later schooling. Preschool programs that serve families who are concerned about having their children gain admission to private schools and colleges tend to promote this goal. Academic achievement is today the goal of most public K–6 programs and many private schools in the United States. This view is held by many educators whose training and focus is on elementary education.

The third goal for early childhood programs is the amelioration of the effects of poverty and deprivation on children. Like those with an academic focus, these programs are dedicated to preparing children for success in later schooling. They also emphasize helping children to develop the behaviors and skills that will need when they enter school in kindergarten. Some of these programs, like Head Start, also offer comprehensive

services that include child health and nutrition and parent education. This is most often the view of educators and policy makers who are concerned with providing equal opportunities for children who are at risk for school failure.

The fourth goal for early childhood programs involves inculcating culture or values. Schools based on a particular religious belief and programs designed to teach children about or preserve a language or culture fall into this category. This is most often the view of members of a particular community—for example, a religious or cultural group.

Being aware of these different goals may help you to understand the conflicting claims and different opinions that you are likely to encounter when you enter the early childhood workforce. Debate about appropriate goals for ECE has been going on for as long as we have been in the field and is likely to continue into the future.

The Nature of the Curriculum

The nature of curriculum for young children has been the subject of debate since the first preschools and kindergartens were founded in our country. Controversy regarding appropriate curriculum and methods for early childhood programs are often the result of differing goals.

Early childhood educators in programs for children 5 years old and younger have most often been trained in child-centered philosophy that emphasizes learning through play and helping children learn to live and work with others. They have learned to base their work on the child development theories of Erik Erikson, Jean Piaget, Lev Vygotsky, and others that emphasize the importance of social, physical, and mental activity. Traditionally early childhood teachers based their curriculum on observations of children's interests and developmental capabilities and on knowledge of early childhood pedagogy. Programs today are working to combine the child-centered, play-based curriculum that characterized ECE in the past with the newer goal of helping children to acquire a common set of knowledge and skills described in standards. Lynn Kagan and Kristie Kauerz (2007) describe this as a shift toward "specifying what children should know and be able to do" rather than "evoking" the curriculum from the children themselves (p. 21).

The child-centered approach to early childhood curriculum stands in contrast to the prevalent view in elementary education and special education that curriculum should be based on clear objectives and focus on the acquisition of knowledge and skills. Many teachers of older children and school administrators believe that the purpose of the curriculum in the kindergarten and early grades is to prepare children for the expectations they will encounter in later grades.

Responsibility for Early Childhood Education

Another issue that you are likely to encounter when you enter the field of early education (especially if you work in a preschool program that is funded by tuition) has to do with whose responsibility it is to help families provide care and education for their children. It has always been assumed in the United States that families were responsible for taking care of their children before they entered public school. Government involvement was limited to extreme circumstances: care for orphans, child care at times of national crisis, protection for abused children, and food and housing for the children of the poorest in society.

Our society today has made a commitment to government's responsibility for the education of all children once they reach school age. Public education for children 5 years of age and older is generally agreed to be the responsibility of

Reflect and write about curriculum

What do you remember about the curriculum in the early childhood programs from your childhood? Do you think it reflected a child-centered focus or an academic focus? What were your feelings about it?

Reflect on the responsibility for early childhood education

Who do you think should be responsible for early care and education? Is it a family responsibility or a societal responsibility? Why? Would your family, friends, and members of your community agree with your view? What do you think policy makers should do to meet the needs of young children in our society?

the states. A well-defined legal structure outlines the authority and responsibility of the federal, state, and local governments for the education of school-age children. Because the care and education of children under the age of 5 was seen as a family issue and not a societal issue, these children have received less attention and programs for them have received much less funding than programs for older children.

Before the 1960s, government assumed a small role in programs for children under kindergarten age. In response to specific problems, the federal government formulated public policies and created and funded initiatives designed to address the welfare of poor children who were at risk for school failure and those with disabilities. The federally funded Head Start program for low-income children and other demonstration programs for this population of children were created in the 1960s and 1970s.

Today, there is more widespread recognition than ever before of the importance of early experiences and the value of early education programs for young children. Over the last decade this awareness has led to more local and state support for early childhood education. During this period many states have begun to implement state-funded programs for 4-year-olds. Some even include 3-year-olds in these programs. In spite of these efforts, participation in the majority of programs for infants, toddlers, and preschool-age children is funded by tuition paid for by families.

Societal views about responsibililty for early childhood education are going through a period of tremendous change, as awareness of the importance of development in the early years and the important role early childhood programs can play in supporting it has moved to the forefront of national consciousness. You can expect that now, at the beginning of your career, there will be more discussion and change as our society confronts this issue.

Quality, Compensation, Affordability

The next three issues are interconnected and relate to programs for children 5 years of age and younger. In our fast-paced society where many parents are working two or more jobs, it is frequently difficult for families to find the kind of care they want for their children or to find care that they can afford. Three critical issues related to programs for children aged 5 and younger have sometimes been referred to as the *trilemma of child care*. Trilemma refers to the interrelationship of three different needs: (1) the need for *quality* programs to support children's development, (2) the need for adequate *compensation* for staff, and (3) and the need for *affordable and accessible* child care programs for families. These issues are sometimes referred to by the letters QCA—Quality, Compensation, and Affordability.

Quality. A number of large-scale studies have documented the positive, long-term effects of high-quality early childhood programs on children and families. Research has shown that carefully designed programs produce gains in children's social, emotional, and cognitive development and have a long-lasting impact on children's ability to succeed in school and to function later in life. Cognitive benefits are that children who attend high-quality programs score higher on assessments of school readiness and language development, show gains in IQ, and are less likely to be placed in special education or be retained in a grade. Social outcomes include fewer behavioral problems and less contact with the criminal justice system. Other benefits include increases in parents' economic self-sufficiency, reduced rates of criminal activity, and improvements in children's health (Barnett, 1995; Cryer, 2003; Gomby, Larner, Stevenson, Lewit, & Behrman, 1995; Karoly et al., 1998; NICHD, 1999).

The needs of working families, the push for school readiness, and the widespread recognition of the developmental benefits of high-quality programs have combined to raise interest in the issue of quality in early childhood education. Programs that meet standards for quality are thoughtfully organized; responsive to the needs of children and families; staffed by well-trained and caring educators; and provide safe, healthy, developmentally appropriate experiences for children.

Unfortunately, research also reveals that many programs that are available today are not delivering high-quality care. In their influential study, researchers from the National Institute of Child Health and Human Development (NICHD, 1999) found that most of the classrooms observed did not meet quality standards. They also reported that children in classes that did not meet any quality standards achieved lower-than-average language comprehension scores in tests, while children in centers that met all guidelines had above-average scores. It is well known today that quality in early childhood programs can make a great difference in children's lives and initiatives are under way (described later in this chapter) to improve quality in early childhood programs.

Compensation. Teacher salaries in privately run center-based programs for children under age 5 are almost always lower than those for comparable positions in publicly funded programs because they come from tuition paid by families. Low teacher salaries, inadequate benefits, and lack of opportunity for advancement make it difficult to recruit and retain competent teachers in many private early childhood programs. Other consequences of inadequate compensation are lower program quality and high staff turnover. The latter is especially unfortunate, because children's lives are disrupted each time a teacher leaves. Frequent staff turnover undermines the stability of relationships that is so critical for young children's development and ability to thrive in child care settings.

The National Child Care Staffing Study conducted in the late 1980s (Whitebook, Howes, & Phillips, 1990) made the case that program quality is affected by the education of teaching staff and the adequacy of their wages. It reported that funding for child care had decreased in the previous decade, and that during the same period staff turnover had nearly tripled. A follow-up study (Whitebook, Howes, & Phillips, 1998) found that wages for child care staff had remained mostly stagnant over the ensuing decade. These authors reported that teaching staff continued to earn low wages (even in high-quality programs), and though some improvements in health benefits were seen, high turnover continued. A 2008 report indicated that salaries remain low. The average pay of those who provide child care in homes was reported to be $9.05 per hour ($18,820 annually) and the average pay of teachers in center-based programs was $12.45 per hour ($25,900 annually) (NACCRRA, 2008). Low pay in early childhood programs is primarily a woman's issue because 99% of caregivers in family child care homes are women, as are 97% of preschool teachers (NACCRRA, 2008). It is also a large part of the reason that few men choose to teach in early childhood programs, even though many might find it rewarding.

Affordability. The third issue relating to the provision of care of children age 5 and younger has to do with families' ability to pay for it. Families need care for their children while they are at work, and they want programs that will support children's healthy development and learning. "Yet finding and affording quality child care is a challenge for all families, particularly low-income working parents for whom the cost of quality child care is a real and daily barrier" (Schulman, 2000, p. 1).

A report from NACCRRA (2007) makes the case that child care continues to be expensive, and paying for it is a heavy burden for families. It says: "The high price of child care strains household budgets and forces parents to make sacrifices—often in the quality of care their children receive" (p. 1). For many families, child care expenses are more than they spend on food. Care for two children can exceed the median cost of rent and in some cases mortgage payments. Moreover, in many states the price of child care for an infant in a center is more than a year's tuition in a public university. In every state the average annual price for care for two children is greater than 50% of the median household income for single parents.

The high cost of care results in poor children not being able to attend early childhood programs at all, or receiving the least expensive, poorest quality (often unlicensed and unmonitored) care. "Too many children are cared for in unstimulating or even unsafe settings. . . . It is particularly alarming given that children from low-income families are at greatest risk for school failure and are most in need of the strong start that high-quality care can provide" (Schulman, 2000, p. 1). When early childhood education and care costs are high, even middle-income parents are likely to turn to nonregulated sources that offer no assurance of quality.

School Readiness

Readiness is a frequently discussed issue that involves the interface between the preschool and kindergarten programs. The term refers to whether children who are about to enter kindergarten will be ready to meet school expectations. Today 5-year-olds in kindergarten programs are generally expected to learn to read and do paper-and-pencil tasks, things that in the past were not expected until first grade.

Elementary school administrators who became concerned when they noticed that some children were having a hard time meeting raised academic expectations in kindergarten began to devise policies to ensure that children would not begin kindergarten until they were "ready." Some school districts raised the age of kindergarten entry because it was believed that older children would do better at meeting the higher expectations. In other places, assessment tests were used to exclude children who were judged to be "unready" for kindergarten. And more and more children were retained in kindergarten because they weren't ready for the increasingly rigorous expectations of first grade.

As a result of these practices, educators began to discuss the question "How should readiness be defined?" (Lewit & Baker, 1995). How readiness is defined in large measure determines where the responsibility for improving readiness lies—with the child, the school, or the supports that each receives. The definition of readiness that is decided upon has practical consequences. It affects decisions about assessment, about the kinds of investments that communities and states should make, and about how to judge educational progress.

A general consensus regarding the broad components of readiness has emerged at the national level. The National Educational Goals Panel (1997) recommended three components: (1) readiness in the child, (2) schools' readiness for children, and (3) family and community supports that contribute to children's readiness. NAEYC's position statement on school readiness (National

Reflect and write about readiness

Reflect on your first days of kindergarten and first grade. Were you ready for school? How did you know? What made it easy or hard for you when you started school? What did the school or teacher do to help, or to hinder, your first school experiences? What other experiences have you had with school readiness?

Association for the Education of Young Children, 1993, p. 2) states: "Schools must be able to respond to a diverse range of abilities within any group of children, and the curriculum in the early grades must provide meaningful contexts for children's learning rather than focusing primarily on isolated skills acquisition." In other words, schools should meet the needs of all of the children who are age-eligible to attend without consideration of their ability to perform academic tasks.

For a number of years states have been engaged in efforts to define the components of readiness and to decide how progress in each one will be evaluated. Readiness initiatives in the states have included providing high-quality preschool for more children (especially those at risk for school failure), using more developmentally appropriate curriculum in the kindergarten, educating families about things they can do to help their child to be successful in school, training teachers and principals in child development (including realistic academic expectations for young children), and developing procedures for helping children make a smooth transition from home or preschool to the kindergarten program.

Trends

A trend is the general direction in which something is developing or changing. As we look at the field of early childhood education in the early years of the 21st century we can see a number of interconnected trends that are likely to continue into the future and have a significant impact on the field. Among these are growing diversity among families in our society, the development of coordinated early childhood systems including child care Quality Rating and Improvement Systems (QRIS), alignment of pre-K programs with early elementary grades, continuing pressure to raise teacher qualifications, and accountability for results in publicly funded programs.

Family Stress and Diversity

A trend in our field that will impact you as a teacher is that nearly every problem confronting families of young children has become more pressing in recent years. Virtually all families of young children work and need child care. Many live in poverty and are without health insurance. Increasing numbers are homeless and experience violence in their communities. There is also greater strife and more uncertainty in our society. You will feel the impact of these trends because the children and families in your class will live with them.

There is greater diversity culturally, linguistically, and in lifestyles today than there was in the past. Early childhood educators are called on to work with children who have a range of abilities, who come from different cultures, from a range of socioeconomic backgrounds, and from families who speak many languages. As a teacher, you will need to understand and embrace this diversity and be prepared to focus on the best interests of young children in our rapidly changing, fast-paced, and increasingly interconnected world.

Systems Development

Support for early childhood education grew dramatically in the first decade of the new century as the public gained new understanding of the importance of early brain development, and learned about research demonstrating the positive impact of high-quality programs and the economic return on the investment in early learning. In order to respond to this new interest and new demands, the early childhood field needs to commit itself to overcoming the fragmentation of the current early childhood "nonsystem," a patchwork of uncoordinated programs and services that are confusing to families and inefficient as delivery systems.

Early educators are now challenged to learn to think more comprehensively about the needs of the children and families that we serve. States are struggling to create and sustain systems to support the coordination of programs for young children. The federal government established an effort to support state system building through the 2007 Head Start reauthorization. The Improving Head Start Act required that governors designate state advisory councils on early childhood education and care but this remained an "unfunded mandate" (no money was provided for the councils in the act) until 2010 when start-up grants through the American Recovery and Reinvestment Act (ARRA) became available. Forty-five states and five territories received funding. Governors were required to formally designate a council and appoint its leadership.

Philanthropic organizations have played a large role in helping to move state efforts forward with initiatives such as BUILD, created by the Early Childhood Funders Collaborative in 2002 to help states to develop comprehensive early childhood systems. The Early Childhood Systems Working Group, composed of leaders in the field and supported by BUILD, has developed a model of comprehensive early childhood system building based on a set of agreed-upon values and principles that addresses early learning and development, health, and family leadership and support (BUILD Initiative, n.d.).

Two system-building efforts within the Early Learning and Development system are child care Quality Rating and Improvement Systems, and P–3 or Pre-K–3 Systems that work to coordinate and align prekindergarten through grade 3 in public education systems.

Quality Rating and Improvement Systems

Quality rating and improvement systems (QRIS) are intended to support children's development through raising the quality of care and education in early childhood programs. QRIS create, align, and strengthen the components of early care and education with the goal of improving children's experiences. These components include quality standards, a process for monitoring standards, a process for supporting quality improvement, a system that identifies pathways to professional development for those who work with young children, data management and reporting systems, provision of financial incentives and other supports to meet higher standards, and dissemination of information about program quality to parents and the public. Participation is usually voluntary and many kinds of early childhood programs can participate including center-based child care, family child care, school-age, prekindergarten, and Head Start (QRIS National Learning Network, n.d.).

As of 2011, all states either were operating a QRIS or had one in development. The Office of Child Care (Federal Department of Health and Human Services, Administration for Children and Families) now requires states to report on their progress in developing or implementing QRIS in their annual Childcare and Development Block Grant Plans. These plans are mandatory in order for states to access federal funding for child care (Administration for Children and Families, n.d.). Trends relating to the development of new early childhood systems are likely to persist in spite of the current uncertain economic climate, though they may progress more slowly than if the country were facing a better economic situation.

Coordination and Alignment of Pre-K Through Grade 3 Programs

For most of the history of early childhood education there has been a divide between programs for children between birth and age 5 and children 5 to 8 years of age in kindergarten through grade 3 programs. Recently, philanthropy has played an important role in efforts to systematically link these two systems. The Foundation for Child Development is a leader in the pre-K–3rd, or P 3, initiative to build bridges between programs that serve children across the early childhood age span by creating continuity between ECE programs and public elementary schools (Foundation for Child Development, 2008; Thorman & Kauerz, 2011). These efforts are intended to ensure that what children learn in preschool provides a good foundation for later learning and to offer children an easier transition between preschool and kindergarten.

Efforts to integrate and align QRIS and P 3 movements are also supported by philanthropy (Thorman & Kauerz, 2011), and, in an unprecedented move, in 2010 the U.S. Department of Health and Human Services, which oversees child care and Head Start, and the U.S. Department of Education, announced the creation of a Joint Interagency Policy Board on Early Learning. The purpose of the board is to bring greater coherence to policies and "to improve the quality of early learning programs and outcomes for young children; increase the coordination of research, technical assistance and data systems; and advance the effectiveness of the early learning workforce among the major federally funded early learning programs across the two departments" (U.S. Department of Health and Human Services, 2010). Later these two agencies jointly sponsored the Race to the Top Early Learning Challenge grants designed to "reward states that create comprehensive plans to transform early learning systems with better coordination, clearer learning standards, and meaningful workforce development" (U.S. Department of Health and Human Services, 2010). At this writing the winners of the grant competition have not been announced, but 35 states and the District of Columbia had indicated their intention to apply.

Raising Teacher Education Requirements

Educational requirements for teachers in programs for children 5 years old and younger are rarely as high as those for educators who work in public school systems. This has been the case because, until recently, early childhood education was seen as a service for working families rather than as an educational program for children. Recent research demonstrating that higher levels of teacher education result in better classroom quality and greater gains in children's cognitive and social development (Barnett, 2004; Burchinal, Cryer, Clifford, & Howes, 2002; Early et al., 2007) has resulted in efforts to require higher educational qualifications, especially in Head Start, state-funded prekindergarten programs, and some quality rating and improvement systems.

Efforts to improve teacher qualifications in private early education programs are included in NAEYC program accreditation standards. By 2015 50% of teachers in NAEYC-accredited programs will be required to hold a bachelor's degree and the remainder must have a minimum of an associate's degree (NAEYC, 2009).

Higher teacher qualifications will lead to improvement in the quality of programs and make it more likely that children benefit from their early educational experiences. Unfortunately, this trend could also have negative consequences if attention is not also paid to compensating early educators commensurate with their education and experience. It is likely to be very difficult to attract qualified early educators to low-paying jobs. In addition, the trend could result in the exclusion of some who are already in the workforce but who may not have the means to acquire higher qualifications. This trend also challenges a long-held value of inclusiveness in the workforce that has characterized the field of early childhood education.

Accountability

Policy makers who invest public dollars in education want to be assured programs that receive funding can demonstrate their effectiveness. This focus on accountability has been a strong part of the educational landscape since the advent of the standards movement in the 1980s. The federal No Child Left Behind (NCLB) Act of 2001, which expanded previous policies related to school accountability, led to a focus on assessment that was unprecedented in American public education. This legislation required states to measure every public school student's progress in reading and math, yearly, in grades 3 through 12 and report their progress on an annual report card. While most educators and policy makers agreed that it was important to ensure that all children were making adequate progress in school, many were concerned that NCLB would lead to the temptation for teachers to "teach to the test" and would focus teaching on isolated facts that are easy to assess rather than thinking skills that are harder to measure. They were also troubled by lack of attention to and, hence, devaluing of the arts, social studies, physical education, and social development (Graves, 2002; Kohn, 2000).

In an effort to inform the development of policy around accountability in publicly funded early childhood programs, The National Early Childhood Accountability Task Force, made up of national leaders in child development, early education, and assessment, has recommended a unified system of early childhood education including a single, coherent system of standards, assessments, data, and professional development across all programs; alignment of high-quality and comprehensive standards; curriculum and assessments as a continuum from pre-K through grade 3; and the requirement that all assessments of children and programs be valid, reliable, and well suited for their intended purposes. It is hoped that the wisdom of these experts will be heeded as states compete for the Early Learning Challenge grants.

Economic Issues

As we write this ninth edition, awareness of the value of early childhood education and the desire to support it is greater than it has ever been. Even with the slow recovery of the U.S. economy and state and federal budget deficits, there continues to be hope that the initiatives begun in the last decade will continue, albeit at a slower pace.

Employment, fiscal restraint, and the deficit are the primary concern of every legislator. At the time of this writing there have already been significant cuts to state child care subsidy programs. Pre-K programs which until recently had been enthusiastically promoted in states are having their budgets cut or are facing elimination, and there are distant rumbles of opposition to continued funding for Head Start and other programs for children, especially poor children. Advocates such as the Children's Defense Fund and NAEYC are working hard to minimize the impacts on early childhood programs and services. We are hopeful that as policy makers wrestle with economic issues, they will be mindful of the value of investing in the future by supporting programs for young children.

Final Thoughts

Over the last century, our understanding of the needs of young children has changed dramatically. At the beginning of the 20th century, most people believed that they were not ready to learn anything important until the age of 6, when they entered school. Few people were aware of the impact of the early years on children's development. The work of early childhood educators was generally not understood or appreciated. Today we have entered a new era of awareness of the impact of early experiences on human development. New studies of child development, especially brain development, have demonstrated that the early years are critically important in human development. Compelling research has shown the impact of programs on children who are at risk for failure in school. Policy makers have discovered early childhood and are beginning to realize that investment in programs for young children can have significant social benefits.

As you can tell from reading this chapter, early childhood education is a diverse field with much to contribute to our society. And while it is receiving greater recognition than it has in the past, is also subject to the economic forces that are impacting our society. As we write this edition we see some new developments that bode well for young children. States are funding and implementing more prekindergarten programs; work is being done to develop infrastructure for the early childhood field; more collaboration and coordination is occurring among organizations that work with children and families; and efforts are under way to align programs across the 0–8 age span. We are also facing a period of limited resources and partisan battles about which programs will be funded, which cut, and which eliminated.

Early childhood educators, more than any other group, have an obligation to consider children's needs and to support them in growing into fully functioning human beings. Knowledgeable and caring early childhood educators have much to contribute and *can* make a difference. The early childhood field is entering a new era. You who are entering it now will see many new developments. There will be new opportunities, challenges, and important contributions for you to make.

 ## Learning Outcomes

When you read this chapter, and then thoughtfully complete selected assignments from the "To Learn More" section and prepare items from the "For Your Portfolio" section, you will be demonstrating progress in meeting **NAEYC Standard 6: Becoming a Professional** (NAEYC, 2009).

Key element:

6a: Identifying and involving oneself with the early childhood field

To Learn More

Visit a Program: Observe and write a description of a program for young children in your community. Find out about its history, philosophy, sponsorship, tuition, staff-child ratios, teacher qualifications, and salaries. How is it regulated? Is it accredited? If so find out by whom and what the process was. How does it involve families? What are the major challenges it faces? Reflect and write about what you learned.

Survey Program Regulations: Survey your neighborhood and report on the kinds of programs that are available for children from birth to 8 years of age (preschools, child care, programs for low-income children, public and private school programs). Find out who is responsible for regulation of each kind of program. How do regulatory standards differ? Find out whether any programs in your community are accredited by NAEYC. Reflect and write about what you learned.

Research a Program: Research and report on one of the following topics:

- The history of Head Start in your community (number of centers, number of children served, teacher qualifications, current status, and issues)
- Parent education programs in your community
- Requirements for homeschooling in your community
- How early childhood education and care is administered in another country or in several other countries

Research Training Opportunities: Research and report on training programs available for teachers of young children in your community and on typical salaries for teachers in different kinds of programs. What thoughts and issues are raised by your findings?

Research Policies: Research and write about what is being done in your state with regard to one or more of the following initiatives: state-funded programs for 3- and 4-year-olds, quality rating and improvement systems, infrastructure for coordination of early childhood programs and services, school readiness initiatives, early learning standards.

Investigate Related Websites:

Alliance for Childhood: allianceforchildhood.org

Association for Childhood Education International (ACEI): acei.org

Association for Supervision and Curriculum Development (ASCD): ascd.org

ASCD Whole Child Initiative: wholechildeducation .org/about

Children's Defense Fund: childrensdefense.org

Children Now: childrennow.org

Foundation for Child Development: fcd-us.org

The Future of Children: futureofchildren.org

Head Start/Early Head Start: acf.hhs.gov/programs/ohs

National Association for the Education of Young Children (NAEYC): naeyc.org

National Child Care Information and Technical Assistance Center: http://nccic.acf.hhs.gov

National Institute for Early Education Research (NIEER): nieer.org

Pre-K Now: preknow.org

Zero to Three Policy Center: zerotothree.org

For Your Portfolio

Include one of the assignments from the "To Learn More" section as a demonstration of your understanding of the field of early childhood education and care.

Write an introduction explaining why you chose this assignment and how it contributes to your professional development.

MyEducationLab

Go to Topic 1: History in the MyEducationLab (myeducationlab.com) for *Who Am I in the Lives of Children?* where you can:

- Find learning outcomes for History along with the national standards that connect to these outcomes.
- Complete Assignments and Activities that can help you more deeply understand the chapter content.
- Apply your understanding of the important concepts identified in the chapter with the Building Teaching Skills and Dispositions learning units.

- Check your comprehension on the content covered in the chapter with the Study Plan. Here you will be able to take a chapter quiz, receive feedback on your answers, and then access Review, Practice, and Enrichment activities to enhance your understanding of chapter content.

What is past is prologue.

WILLIAM SHAKESPEARE

3

History and Educational Models

Knowledge of the history of early childhood education gives you a sense of your roots in the past and an idea of how current approaches to working with children and families have grown out of previous thought and practice. Knowing about the history of the field can help you realize that much of what is called "innovation" in current practice has been thought about, written about, and tried before. Similarly, it may help you face the challenges you will encounter when you learn that current philosophical debates are not new—they mirror issues that have been going on for a long time. Knowledge of history can give you a sense of connection to the past and to the field that you are entering. It can also give you a vantage point for looking at many of the things you will encounter as you begin to explore programs and work with young children.

Early childhood education is a fairly new field, although it has old roots and emerges from a long historical tradition. In this chapter, we discuss the evolution of some of the important ideas and trends that have contributed to the field today. In it we will describe:

- what educators and philosophers from different historical eras thought about how young children learn and how their ideas influenced early childhood education and continue to influence the field today.
- three educational movements that profoundly influenced the nature of the early childhood education: the kindergarten, the nursery school, and progressive education.
- three approaches to early childhood education that had their origins in Europe and are still practiced, and that continue to influence current programs around the world.
- the history and influence of two important components of early childhood education in the United States (child care and Head Start).

MyEducationLab

Visit the MyEducationLab for *Who Am I in the Lives of Children?* to enhance your understanding of chapter concepts with a personalized Study Plan. You'll also have the opportunity to hone your teaching skills through video-based Assignments and Activities as well as Building Teaching Skills and Disposition lessons.

Many of our current ideas about early education were shaped by Western—largely European—views about children and worthwhile educational approaches. We will focus on how these have evolved and continue to influence the field of early childhood education in the west, particularly in the United States today. However, every country has its own unique history of early education and care. Other places and other cultures within our country have their own distinct educational history and values. You might want to talk with elders in your family or read about ways of teaching young children that were characteristic of your family's culture or country of origin, and compare and contrast them to the ideas presented here. Think about how they are consistent or inconsistent with the views of the educational thinkers discussed in this chapter.

It is always helpful to remember that what actually occurred in history is communicated in the voice and viewpoint of the person who wrote about it. In the case of early childhood education, women did most of the caring for children and men did most of the writing about it. As you read, it may broaden your perspective to think about who is *not* represented and whose voices are *not* heard—and to think about how they might have told their story.

The Humanistic Tradition

Early education as a specialized field in Western countries is generally thought of as having begun in Europe in the early 19th century. However, many of the values and practices found in today's programs grow from beliefs about children and child rearing that have been passed down from generation to generation and from the ideas of religious leaders, philosophers, scholars, social reformers, and educators of the past.

Many of today's programs have their roots in what is sometimes called the *humanistic* approach to education—a system of thought that reflects concern for the values, potential, well-being, and interests of human beings. Those who contributed to this tradition were concerned with issues like respect for human dignity, the role of education in contributing to all aspects of children's development, the connection between mind and body, the value of observing children, the importance of play in development, support for individual freedom, and the important role of families in children's development. Some educational innovators believed in universal education rather than educational opportunity only for males and for the rich. Some saw childhood as a valuable time in its own right, not just as a preparation for adulthood. All of these ideas emerged in antiquity in Greece and Rome and were reborn and elaborated during a number of different periods in history, especially the 19th and 20th centuries. They continue to resonate today.

Humanistic ideas were slow to be accepted, particularly during the lifetimes of their originators. These innovators were often regarded as radical and treated with suspicion and hostility. At only a few times in history has the dominant practice in teaching young children reflected humanistic ideals. Today, as we will describe in this chapter, we can still see the influence of the humanistic tradition in the United States and in many other parts of the world.

In order to put our historical discussion into perspective, it helps to realize that today's concept of childhood is the product of centuries of social and economic change. In the past many different and conflicting ideas prevailed about the place of children in society and their appropriate education. A prevailing view for much of Western history was that children were almost the same as small adults and that childhood was something a person had to get through on the way to the much more desirable state of being an adult.

In Europe and North America during the historical eras described in this chapter, the treatment of children was predominantly harsh, and most education was based on rote learning. Physical punishment prevailed as the means by which adults controlled children's behavior. At different times and in different places, philosophers and educational innovators recognized shortcomings in the dominant approaches and suggested humane alternatives. Though they influenced some educators and philosophers, none fundamentally changed the day-to-day education and treatment of most young children. However, the idea of educating young children in more humane and meaningful ways has been reinvented or rediscovered over and over again. The work of each of the educational philosophers we describe here has been influential. Taken altogether they have created the humane, child-centered approach that many young children enjoy today.

Reflect on why history is important

Think about ways that the history of your family, community, culture, or country has influenced your life. Reflect on why it might be important to know about your own history and history in general.

The Origins of Early Childhood Education

During different eras some notable historical figures shaped the field of early childhood education. These philosophers, religious leaders, scholars, physicians, and educators were influential, though a number of them were concerned with education in general rather than the education of young children in particular.

Ancient Greece and Rome (400 B.C.–A.D. 200)

Our Western tradition of education can be traced back to ancient Greece. In ancient Mediterranean societies, children younger than 7 tended to be cared for by their mothers and other members of their extended family. Many were enjoyed, loved, and left to play or asked to do simple tasks near home. At about age 7 specific training for an occupation would begin. Such training differed widely between genders and among social classes.

The ideal of a well-rounded education was first clearly expressed in ancient Greece. The Greek word *paideia* (from which we get our words *pedagogy* and *encyclopedia*) was used to express this cultural ideal. The Greeks believed that free human beings should strive for excellence in body, mind, and spirit.

Plato

The philosopher **Plato** (428–348 B.C.) founded a school in Athens in a grove of trees, called the Academy. This first academic believed that the early childhood years provided a splendid opportunity to shape a child's future social, cultural, and intellectual life. In *The Republic* (Plato's book on the ideal state), he said that state nurseries should be established to foster a spirit of community. Plato recognized different stages of childhood (Lascarides & Hinitz, 2000) and proposed that curriculum should include games, music, stories, and drama that would illustrate the values needed by all good citizens. Children's progress would be monitored to identify gifted children and provide them with an enriched program. Plato believed that children came into the world with all essential knowledge dormant within them. Education helped children to "remember" this knowledge and apply it to their daily lives.

Plato broke with the tradition of his own time by insisting on the education of girls and by criticizing the use of corporal punishment as a means of discipline.

63

Plato's realization of the importance of early childhood in shaping future social and political views would come to influence many later thinkers including Jean Jacques Rousseau, Robert Owen, and John Dewey. Plato's view that knowledge of geometry and geometrical shapes was essential to understanding the order of the cosmos would later play a role in the spheres (balls) and the cylinder, rectangle, and square blocks created by Friedrich Froebel for the first kindergartens.

Play was considered a worthwhile activity in Greece. Structured physical play in the form of games and gymnastics began in childhood and continued to be important as recreation for adult men. The free play of young children was viewed as necessary and a way of learning. Plato suggested gathering together all of the village children between the ages of 3 and 6 for group play under adult supervision.

Aristotle

Plato's pupil **Aristotle** (384–322 B.C.) also examined the nature and purpose of education. Like his teacher, Aristotle recognized the importance of beginning education with young children, believed in the potential excellence of human beings, emphasized the development of mind and body, and valued children's play. But whereas Plato was primarily interested in leading students and society to the contemplation of "the Good," "the True," and "the Beautiful," Aristotle was interested in the world visible to the senses and the logical organization of thought. He held that human beings could be defined as "rational animals." Aristotle valued the education of young children because he believed that good habits must be established early in life. Aristotle's most famous student was Alexander the Great, who spread Greek educational ideas throughout a vast empire that extended to India.

After the collapse of Alexander's empire, the Romans came to dominate the entire Mediterranean and West European world. The Romans adapted much from the Greeks. By the 2nd century A.D. the Roman state subsidized an educational system for boys in cities throughout their empire.

Quintilian

In Rome, Quintilian (A.D. 35–95) was the foremost educator of his time. His ideas about education were similar to those of the Greek educational philosophers. From observation he realized that children younger than 7 benefited little from the customary educational practices. Accordingly, he encouraged parents to allow young children to play. He suggested that it was important to pick good nurses and tutors, so that young children could learn correct speech and behavior by imitation rather than intimidation. Figure 3.1 highlights the ideas and impact of Plato, Aristotle, and Quintilian.

FIGURE 3.1   **The Ideas and Impact of Plato, Aristotle, and Quintilian**

The Ideas of Plato, Aristotle, Quintilian

- Education should begin with the young child.
- Human beings are essentially good.
- Both boys and girls should be educated.
- Development of both mind and body are important.
- Play is a valuable tool for learning.

The Impact of Plato, Aristotle, Quintilian on ECE

- Later educational philosophers incorporated these ideas in their work.

While these Greek and Roman philosophers played a role in advocating some new and humane forms of early childhood education, their views did not reflect the whole picture of Greek and Roman society. Both societies practiced slavery and tolerated infanticide.

The Middle Ages (500–1450)

The Middle Ages, generally defined as the period between the Roman Empire and the Renaissance, is also referred to as the *medieval era*. This period was characterized by a feudal economic system—the granting of land in exchange for military service and the powerful influence of the church.

In the 4th century, the Roman Emperor Constantine became a Christian and began a series of reforms that put Christian leaders and their values in positions of moral and legal authority. Christians recalled how Jesus had once scolded his disciples for keeping the little children from coming to him. Although most Christians believed that children were born in sin, the ritual of baptism was believed to restore their original goodness. Christian emperors soon made all forms of infanticide illegal. Land and money were given by the Roman state to the church so that it could provide social services for the poor.

The Western Roman Empire collapsed in the late 5th century. The church under the leadership of the pope (the bishop of Rome) managed to convert the barbarian tribes that conquered the West. For the thousand years of the medieval era, the Catholic Church struggled to carry on the traditions of literacy and learning in an age of darkness.

Monks and nuns in monasteries labored to copy books that had survived the destruction of the ancient world and to pass on their knowledge to the young children who were chosen to live a religious life. These children, known as *oblates,* were the future of the monastery—and their education was considered to be an important part of the community's activities. Boys and girls were educated separately but received the same education in grammar and the liberal arts. Monastic teachers (most of them former oblates) came to appreciate the psychology of young children to the extent that they sometimes abandoned corporal punishment in favor of gentler methods that would foster the love of learning and the desire for God. Singing, laughter, and play were part of the daily life of the monastery school. Exposure to the brightly colored illuminated manuscripts produced by the monastic script writers developed the child's sense of beauty. Many of these young people chose to remain in the monastery and become monks and nuns.

In the later Middle Ages, new religious orders such as the Franciscan friars no longer lived in monasteries but went into communities to work among the poor. They often provided care and primary education to abandoned or orphaned children. St. Francis in the early 13th century emphasized devotion to the child Christ that helped to inspire more concern for the children of the poor.

Among the noble families of the medieval era, boys were often sent away from home at an early age, to learn as *pages* (child servants) in the households of other nobles. Girls remained at home longer and were taught to sing, play musical instruments, and weave tapestries. Some were taught to read and write by educated nuns in convent schools. Both boys and girls were expected to learn courtly manners by the example of adults.

Most people during that period were peasants who worked land that belonged to the rich and powerful. Peasants and poor townsfolk needed the help of their young children. Boys and girls as young as 3 were expected to feed and

Children with hobby horse detail from Children's Games painting by Pieter Bruegel, 1560

tend animals and to work in kitchen gardens. Children in the towns were taught the basics of their parents' trade early and were formally apprenticed to a craft at age 7. However, toys and art depicting children at play are the tangible evidence that even in the middle ages childhood and childhood pastimes were distinct from those of adults.

The Renaissance and the Reformation (1300–1600)

During the Renaissance and Reformation in Europe (which began in Italy in the 1300s and moved westward until the early 1600s), cities continued to grow and became powerful centers for trade and for the arts. Attention turned from the church to the individual and the arts, stimulating a revival of the literature of the ancient Greeks and Romans (Gutek, 1972). Renaissance men and women placed a high value on education. The invention of the printing press about 1485 helped make many books available, so that knowledge was no longer the monopoly of the church. The ancient languages—Latin, Greek, and Hebrew—were held to be the key to all the lost knowledge of antiquity. In order to help young children make a good beginning in their study of Latin (the universal language of educated Europeans), men such as *Sir Thomas More* of England (1478–1535) and his friend *Desiderius Erasmus* (1466–1536) encouraged parents and teachers to avoid using severe physical punishments as a way to motivate children. Both men believed that children would want to learn if an effort was made to make the subject matter enjoyable. Thomas More, for example, made archery targets shaped like the letters of the alphabet for his children to shoot at. His daughter Margaret later was able to converse in both Latin and Greek. Erasmus was so impressed that he became an early advocate for the higher education of women.

Martin Luther

In 16th-century Europe, religious reform was tied to new ideas about education. *Martin Luther* (1483–1546), a former monk whose biblical scholarship caused him to break with the Catholic Church, began a movement of religious reform known as the Protestant Reformation. Luther was a strong advocate of universal education. He believed that boys and girls should be taught to read so that they could read the Bible for themselves. Luther believed that schools should develop the intellectual, religious, physical, emotional, and social qualities of children. An extensive school system was developed in Germany in response to Luther's views, but his goal of universal education did not become a reality until 19th-century America. Figure 3.2 highlights the ideas and impact of Martin Luther.

FIGURE 3.2 **The Ideas and Impact of Martin Luther**

The Ideas of Martin Luther

- Education should be for all children.
- Individual literacy is important.
- All aspects of development are important.

The Impact of Martin Luther on ECE

- Later educational philosophers, particularly Comenius, incorporated these ideas in their work.

During the 16th and 17th centuries, efforts by the Catholic Church to respond to the Protestants led to a renewal of Catholic culture known to historians as the Counter-Reformation. This movement had an immense impact on the history of education in the early modern era, for it led to the creation of new religious societies dedicated to good works including the education of orphans, children of the poor, and non-Christian peoples in the New World. Both Protestant and Catholic schools in this period tended to emphasize the sinful nature of the child. Christian missionary schools were culturally insensitive to indigenous peoples they came to serve and sought to eliminate their cultural practices and beliefs. The great exception to the severity of 17th-century education was the gentle and learned **Comenius**.

John Amos Comenius—The Father of Early Childhood Education

John Amos Comenius (the Latinized version of Jan Amos Komensky) (1592–1670) was born and raised in what is now the Czech Republic and was a bishop in the Protestant Moravian church *(Unitas Fratrum; Czech or Bohemian Brethren)*. As a result of the Thirty Years' War (1618–1648), Comenius and many other Protestants were forced to become lifelong refugees. In the hope that he could help teachers provide effective and humane education, Comenius began to write about education, which he believed could be an important vehicle for improving society. He developed teaching methods that anticipated elements of modern early childhood education and produced some of the earliest materials for teaching children.

John Amos Comenius
(Komensky)

Comenius's work was well received in Europe and his books were widely translated. Like Luther, he believed in universal education. He saw all people as being equal before God and believed, therefore, that all individuals—rich or poor, common or noble, male or female—were entitled to the same education. Comenius believed that up to the age of 6 children should not leave the family and should be taught in their native languages, not in Latin. In his work *School of Infancy (Schola infantiae)* Comenius suggested that in addition to teaching young children to be pious and virtuous they should develop simple practical knowledge consistent with today's good early childhood curriculum, such as the names of body parts, words for the geography of their home (hill, river, valley), simple arithmetic (many, few, knowing that three is more than two), and simple short songs. He believed that schools should prepare children for life and for further education that he envisaged as taking place in a series of ascending grades, where at each level the child would be exposed to an ever-widening circle of knowledge. He hoped that by providing universal education he could bring about a world of peace and goodwill among those of differing faiths.

Long before the development of modern theories of child development, Comenius wrote about how young children learned. He closely observed them and recognized that the period from birth to age 6 was of the highest importance for human development. The "roots of all arts and sciences," he wrote, "though we seldom do anything about it, begin at this age" (Deasey, 1978, p. 35). He believed that language was the foundation for later learning and designed programs for language and concept acquisition that were intended to begin in infancy and

Ludi pueriles.

Kinderspiele.

Orbis Pictus—
children's games

carry on through later childhood (Gutek, 1994). Schooling for the youngest began in the maternal school, the "school of the mother's knee." The mother was to attend to her child's physical needs and encourage play. She might show the child a book designed by Comenius that had woodcuts illustrating words and concepts. His book, *Orbis Pictus,* is considered to be the first picture book.

Comenius observed that learning seems to occur spontaneously when children are allowed to play. He encouraged classroom use of puzzles, building materials, and other concrete objects as learning tools. Contemporary evolution of these practices can be seen in the ideas that children learn best when knowledge is personally relevant and that concrete experiences must precede abstract tasks. These ideas are important today in what we refer to as *developmentally appropriate* educational practice. The ideas and impact of Comenius are outlined in Figure 3.3.

After the Reformation, basic schooling under civil or church auspices in reading, writing, and arithmetic was provided for the young before they began their training for specific vocations. Churches also founded charity schools for 5- through 11-year-old children to teach reading, writing, and arithmetic in local languages.

The Age of Enlightenment (1700s)

During the 18th century, the scientific revolution led to a new emphasis on humankind's potential to understand the universe and transform society. Men and women of the Enlightenment tended to emphasize human reason and to doubt traditional sources of authority. This period was characterized by a movement away from the influence of religion to a more humanistic (person-centered) view of life. The Enlightenment led to efforts to make education more practical and scientific and generated the new and influential idea that the education of young children was a naturally unfolding process that needed adult support.

John Locke—The Child Is a Blank Slate

John Locke (1632–1704)—academic, doctor, philosopher, and political theorist—was an influential thinker of the Enlightenment. He developed the theory, based

FIGURE 3.3 **The Ideas and Impact of Comenius**

The Ideas of Comenius

- The period from birth to age 6 is of the highest importance for human development.
- Language is the foundation for later learning.
- Education begins with nurture at the "school of the mother's knee."
- Learning should be meaningful/personally relevant.

The Impact of Comenius on ECE

- Use of picture books
- Use of toys (puzzles, blocks) in education
- Later educational philosophers, particularly Pestalozzi, incorporated these ideas.

FIGURE 3.4   The Ideas and Impact of Locke

The Ideas of Locke

- The child enters the world as a blank slate or "tabula rasa."
- Knowledge is received through the senses.
- Nurture more important than nature.
- Prolonged swaddling is not good for children.
- Respectful loving relationships rather than corporal punishment.

The Impact of Locke on ECE

- Playful teaching
- Focusing on the child in education

on his medical knowledge, experience, and emerging philosophy of human understanding, that the child comes into the world with a mind like a blank slate (*tabula rasa*) and that knowledge is received through the senses and is converted to understanding by the application of reason. This view was in direct contradiction to the opinion generally held during his time that people entered the world with some aspects of their character already formed. Locke's belief in the importance of "nurture" over "nature" in determining the direction of human development led him to emphasize the influence of early training and education and to advocate for changes in parental care and education of children. He believed that infants should not be restricted by the common practice of swaddling them in tight strips of cloth, that young children should not be restrained from physical exploration, and that gentle forms of discipline rather than corporal punishment should be used. Locke believed that respectful, loving relationships are the best way for parents and teachers to inspire the child to imitate their examples and that learning should never become a task imposed on the child. Locke's ideas, highlighted in Figure 3.4, anticipated the modern notion of the role of education in the shaping of human potential (Cleverley & Phillips, 1986; Weber, 1984).

Jean Jacques Rousseau—Belief in the Child as Inherently Good

Jean Jacques Rousseau (1712–1778)—French philosopher, writer, and social theorist—had a powerful impact on educational thought. He eloquently challenged the prevalent view of his time that children came into the world with original sin and needed to establish habits of obedience, even if doing this required harsh treatment. He opposed the Enlightenment views that reason was more important than emotion and that civilization was more valuable than nature. He disagreed with Locke's belief that one should always reason with children. Rousseau did not believe that people were born evil, but rather that their inherent goodness was spoiled by civilization. In his famous novel *Emile,* Rousseau presented his view that goodness will flower when people are raised out of contact with corrupt society. Rousseau formulated a stage theory of development and believed that education should begin at birth and continue into adulthood. He believed in basing educational practice on knowledge of the nature of the child, whose ways of learning are different from those of adults. Educational practice, according to Rousseau, should be based on the understanding that children learn best from direct experience and exploration of the environment—ideas that are still held in early education today. He envisioned children learning through their own natural, undirected play, free of adult interference and guidance. He encouraged parents and educators to express their confidence in the natural growth process

FIGURE 3.5 The Ideas and Impact of Rousseau

The Ideas of Rousseau

- The child is inherently good.
- Education should begin at birth and continue into adulthood.
- Children learn best from direct experience and exploration of the environment.
- Children learning through their own natural, undirected play.
- There are developmental stages.

The Impact of Rousseau on ECE

- Focus on direct experience
- Belief in free play

by allowing for the interests and spontaneous activities of children. Given his progressive views, it is surprising that Rousseau sent his own illegitimate children to be raised in an orphanage. In spite of his human limitations and somewhat unwarranted optimism about the impact of unlimited freedom on children, Rousseau's ideas—viewed as radical in his time and by many in ours—had tremendous impact on the educators who followed and were a precursor to later research on developmental stages. Figure 3.5 outlines Rousseau's ideas and impact.

The Industrial Revolution (1800s)

During the 19th century, national school systems were evolving in Europe and the beginning of public education was under way in the United States. New theories of education had widespread impact. Two notable influences were Johann Pestalozzi and Robert Owen.

Johann Pestalozzi—Early Childhood Education Begins

Early childhood education as a distinct discipline began with Johann Pestalozzi (1746–1827), a Swiss educator who had been influenced by the views of Rousseau and the Romantic movement he helped to inspire. Pestalozzi experimented with Rousseau's ideas in the education of his own son. However, when his son still could not read at the age of 11, Pestalozzi concluded that Rousseau's ideas about teaching were not effective and went on to develop his own teaching methods. His ideas laid the foundation for the reform of 19th-century education and had a strong impact on development of progressive education in the United States and Europe. Like Luther and Comenius before him, Pestalozzi believed that all children had the right to education and the capacity to profit from it. He devoted his life to education, particularly for the orphaned and poor, and established several schools in which his ideas could be implemented. He believed that education could help to awaken the potential of each child and could thereby lead to social reform. He wrote that the first year of life was the most important in a child's development. He

Johann Pestalozzi

FIGURE 3.6 **The Ideas and Impact of Pestalozzi**

The Ideas of Pestalozzi

- All children have the right to education and the capacity to profit from it.
- Education can help to awaken the potential of each child.
- The first year of life is the most important in a child's development.
- Instruction should be adapted to each child's interests, abilities, and stage of development.

The Impact of Pestalozzi on ECE

- Focus on sensory exploration
- Allowing self-paced learning

proposed that instruction should be adapted to each child's interests, abilities, and stage of development. He rejected the practice of memorization and advocated sensory exploration and observation as the basis of learning. The learning experiences he designed were sequenced from concrete to abstract. He believed that children learned through self-discovery and could pace their own learning. Pestalozzi was also concerned with teaching human relationships. He wrote, "My one aim was to . . . awaken a feeling of brotherhood . . . [and] make them affectionate, just and considerate" (Braun & Edwards, 1972, p. 52). Figure 3.6 highlights the ideas and impact of Pestalozzi.

Robert Owen

Welsh industrialist and social reformer Robert Owen (1771–1858), a disciple of Pestalozzi, became concerned with the condition of families who worked in the cotton mills during the Industrial Revolution. Owen worked for reforms in labor practices and the establishment of schools to improve the lives of factory children who, from the age of 6, were required to labor for long hours in the mills. He provided humane living conditions and abolished child labor in his own textile factory in Wales.

Owen believed that the education of young children, combined with an environment that allowed people to live by the principle of mutual consideration, could transform the nature of people and society. His *infant school,* the first in England for children 3 to 10 years of age, offered a nurturing and emotionally secure setting. Owen did not believe in pressuring children to learn or in punishing them. Rather, he thought that the natural consequences of their actions would teach children right from wrong. Sensory learning, stories, singing, dance, nature study, and physical exercise were included in the school program.

Owen's ideas were considered extreme in his time, and his schools did not survive in England. Later in his life Owen moved to the United States, where he thought he would find more support for his ideas about society and schooling. He was one of the founders of New Harmony, a utopian community in Indiana. Although the schools he created did not survive, many of the ideas that originated in them can still be found in today's early childhood programs. These include periods of time during which children choose their activities, emphasis on a caring and nonpunitive teacher, and the use of spontaneous play as a vehicle for learning.

Pestalozzi and Owen, who were directly involved in the education of young children, both have had a strong influence on later educational practice. They were idealists, deeply humanitarian, and concerned with social reform as it affected the poor. Owen's concern for the education of his factory workers' children led to the creation in Britain of the Infant School Society (ISS) in 1825.

FIGURE 3.7   The Ideas and Impact of Owen

The Ideas of Owen

- An "infant" school for children under 5 should be established.
- Education of young children (in combination with other factors) can transform the nature of people and society.
- Natural consequences will teach children right from wrong.
- Do not pressure children to learn.

The Impact of Owen on ECE

- Sensory learning, stories, singing, dance, nature study, and physical exercise
- Periods of time during which children choose their activities
- Play valued as a vehicle for learning
- Caring and nonpunitive teachers
- Influence on later educational systems particularly in the American kindergarten, the Lanham Act schools, and the British Infant School

This society later became a model for efforts to educate the children of working mothers in the United States. See Figure 3.7 for an outline of Owen's ideas and impact.

Educational Movements That Shaped the Field of Early Childhood Education

Some programs and ideas that originated at the beginning of the 20th century have had a profound and long-lasting impact on the field of early childhood education in the United States and in other places in the world. These include the kindergarten, created in Germany by Friedrich Froebel; the nursery school, founded in England by Margaret and Rachel McMillan; and progressive education, which began in the United States and was based on the progressive political movement and the philosophy of John Dewey. Although these programs originated in different places and in response to different societal and educational needs, all three share the caring and respectful attitudes toward children that characterized many of the educational reformers we described on the previous pages.

Froebel and the Kindergarten

Friedrich Wilhelm Froebel (1782–1852) established the first kindergarten program in Germany in 1837. Froebel's mother died before he was a year old and he suffered a lonely childhood as the only child of a Protestant minister. Before becoming interested in education he studied mathematics, philosophy, and sciences and was trained as an architect. After working in a number of different settings, he discovered that he had a talent for teaching. He attended a training institute run by Pestalozzi and embraced many of his ideas. After further study in science and linguistics, Froebel devoted his life to education. Froebel's views on the importance of play, toys, and games in the intellectual, social, and spiritual development of young children were in part inspired by his study of Comenius (Deasey, 1978). He founded several innovative schools and directed an orphanage. Over the years he developed a philosophy of education and a program for 4- to 6-year-olds that he envisioned as a transition between home and school and between infancy and childhood. Because it was intended to be a place where children were nurtured and protected from outside influences, as plants might be in a garden, he called his school *kinder* ("child") *garten* ("garden"). This term is still used for all programs for young children in many parts of the world and for programs for 5-year-olds in the United States.

Like Comenius, Rousseau, and Pestalozzi, Froebel believed that children were social beings, that activity was the basis for knowing, and that play was an essential part of learning. Froebel, a deeply religious man, believed that the education of young children should differ in content and teaching methods from that of older children, and wanted children to have the opportunity to develop those positive impulses that came from within. He also thought that the mother's relationship to the infant and young child was very important in the child's development.

Friedrich Wilhelm Froebel

The Froebelian Kindergarten

Froebel described three forms of knowledge that he saw as the basis for all learning: Knowledge of *forms of life,* such as gardening, care of animals, and domestic tasks; knowledge of *forms of mathematics,* such as geometric forms and their relationships with each other; and knowledge of *forms of beauty,* such as design with color and shape, harmonies, and movement.

Children's play was guided by the teacher, who carefully presented special materials and activities designed by Froebel to enhance sensory and spiritual development. The materials, called *gifts,* included yarn balls, blocks, wooden tablets, geometric shapes, and natural objects (see Figure 3.8). Among the gifts were the first wooden blocks used as tools for children's learning. These objects were intended to encourage discovery and manipulation and to lead children to an appreciation for people's unity with God. Froebel embraced the view that each child was inherently good and born with innate knowledge that could be awakened by exposure to the fundamental principles of Creation. The outward symbols of Creation were the basic shapes of geometry. Froebel's blocks and other gifts were designed to expose children to these shapes and allow for the exploration of their symbolic truths.

Handwork activities, called *occupations,* included molding, cutting, folding, bead stringing, and embroidery. They were intended to foster discovery, inventiveness, and skill. Songs and finger-plays (many written by Froebel), stories, and games were selected to encourage learning the spiritual values underlying the program. Froebel held that education must begin with the concrete and move to greater abstraction and that perceptual development precedes thinking skills.

The early kindergartens emphasized the importance of cleanliness and courtesy, the development of manual skills, physical activity, and preparation for later schooling. Kindergarten children were not made to sit still, memorize, and recite as older children were. The teacher's role was not that of taskmaster, but of affectionate leader.

The Kindergarten Movement

Having conceived of the kindergarten as a nurturing place for the cultivation of children's natural goodness and an extension of the home, Froebel proposed the idea of training young women to be kindergarten teachers. Educators from

FIGURE 3.8 Froebel's Gifts

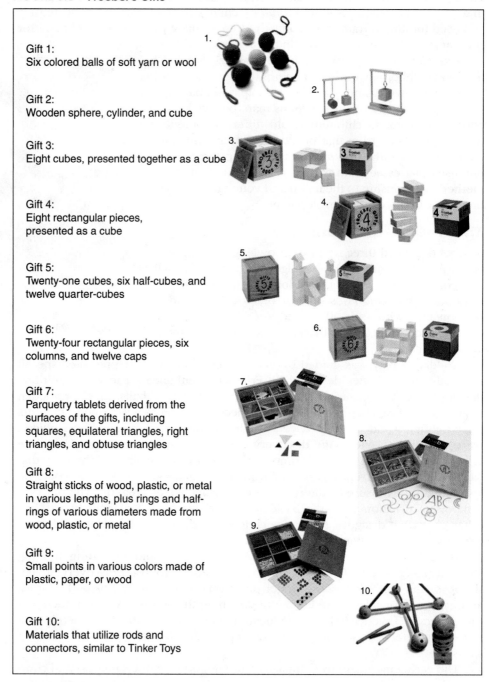

Gift 1:
Six colored balls of soft yarn or wool

Gift 2:
Wooden sphere, cylinder, and cube

Gift 3:
Eight cubes, presented together as a cube

Gift 4:
Eight rectangular pieces,
presented as a cube

Gift 5:
Twenty-one cubes, six half-cubes, and
twelve quarter-cubes

Gift 6:
Twenty-four rectangular pieces, six
columns, and twelve caps

Gift 7:
Parquetry tablets derived from the
surfaces of the gifts, including
squares, equilateral triangles, right
triangles, and obtuse triangles

Gift 8:
Straight sticks of wood, plastic, or metal
in various lengths, plus rings and half-
rings of various diameters made from
wood, plastic, or metal

Gift 9:
Small points in various colors made of
plastic, paper, or wood

Gift 10:
Materials that utilize rods and
connectors, similar to Tinker Toys

Source: Used by permission of Scott Bultman, Froebel USA, froebelusa.org

Europe and the United States studied his methods and returned to their homes to begin kindergartens. Graduates of Froebel's teacher training institute brought the ideals and practices of the kindergarten to the United States and many other countries.

Two sisters, **Bertha Meyer Ronge** and **Margarethe Meyer Shurz,** brought the kindergarten to the English-speaking world. In 1851, Bertha started the first kindergarten in England. Margarethe founded the first American kindergarten in Watertown, Wisconsin, in 1856 (Lascarides & Hinitz, 2000). The early American kindergartens were private, often established in homes and taught in German by teachers who had studied with Froebel (Beatty, 1995, pp. 53–54).

Elizabeth Peabody founded the first English-speaking kindergarten in Boston in 1860. Later, after studying with Froebel's disciples in Germany, she founded the first kindergarten teacher education program in the United States and was influential in winning public support for kindergartens in this country. The first publicly supported kindergarten was opened in St. Louis in 1873 and was followed by rapid expansion of kindergartens between that year and 1900. Peabody was also a reformer who worked to provide education for the children of slaves in the South and Native American children (Lascarides & Hinitz, 2000).

Two aspects of the society of the late 1800s appear to have contributed to the rapid growth of the kindergarten. The first was the idea that children are inherently good, which was gaining wider acceptance at that time. If children are viewed in a positive way it follows that they require a nurturing and benevolent environment in their early years. The second was a concern for the social problems created by the large influx of poor immigrants, which gave rise to the field of philanthropic social work. Mission kindergartens for children of the poor were established by social workers with the expectation that if children were taught the appropriate values and behaviors, they and their families would be more successful in assimilating into American society.

Many of the first professional associations concerned with promoting early childhood education in the United States grew out of the kindergarten movement. One of these was the American Froebel Union, established by Elizabeth Peabody in 1878. Another was the International Kindergarten Union (IKU), begun in 1892. The IKU merged with the National Council of Primary Education in 1930 to become the Association for Childhood Education International (ACEI), still an active organization today. The National Kindergarten Association (NKA), another early professional association, was founded in 1909 and was active in working for universal acceptance of the kindergarten until it was disbanded in 1976 (Williams, 1993).

Patty Smith Hill (1868–1946), one of the founders of the Institute of Child Welfare Research at Columbia University Teachers College, worked to bring innovation to the Froebelian kindergarten when it came under fire for being rigid and teacher dominated. She combined ideas from a number of approaches and was able to move kindergartens in a direction more consistent with the progressive ideas of her time. One of Hill's significant contributions was the development of a professional organization for nursery educators, the National Association for Nursery Education (NANE), in 1926. This organization has evolved into the large and influential National Association for the Education of Young Children (NAEYC). Her other notable and long-lasting contribution was cowriting with her sister the song "Good Morning to All," the tune of which became popular as "Happy Birthday to You."

Kindergartens in the United States were influential in other countries. The first kindergarten in Canada, inspired by those in the United States, began in Toronto in 1883 by James Laughlin Hughes. The first kindergarten in Australia was founded by Margaret Windeyer in 1895 following a visit to a kindergarten in San Francisco. And New Zealand's first free kindergarten was established in the 1880s following visits by educators to the kindergartens of the United States (Prochner, 2009).

American kindergarten, 1920s

Issues Related to the Kindergarten Movement. Froebel's ideas dominated the kindergarten movement in the United States until they were challenged by the progressive education movement at the beginning of the 20th century (which we will discuss a little later in the chapter). The program that Froebel created represented a radical departure from the schools of his day. Although the kindergarten allowed children to learn through play, it was far more structured than the individualized, free-play approach later advocated by progressive educators, and it little resembled what we consider to be developmentally appropriate practice today. It could, however, be considered as the beginning of contemporary early childhood practice in much of the world, and it was profoundly influential (Weber, 1969; Williams, 1993).

A period of ferment caused by conflicting philosophies began in the kindergarten movement in the 1890s and lasted for more than 20 years. Progressive educators challenged supporters of Froebel's approach and expressed the concern that kindergarten practices were rigid and didn't reflect their ideas about how children develop and learn. By 1920, the progressive approach had achieved dominance. The reformed kindergarten curriculum reflected many of Froebel's original ideas but added a new emphasis on free play, social interaction, art, music, nature study, and excursions. New unstructured materials, including large blocks and dollhouses, encouraged children's imaginative play. Books and songs reflected children's interests, rather than conveying a religious message, and activities were inspired by events in the children's daily lives.

The Impact of Kindergarten

The impact of Froebel's kindergarten and the kindergarten movement are profound. Although publicly supported kindergartens had existed in the United States since 1873, they were not widespread. As kindergartens gradually moved into public schools, they met with grudging acceptance. Today school for 5-year-olds is accepted and universally available in the United States and most other countries, though it is not mandatory in all. In many countries the word

FIGURE 3.9 The Goals, Principles, and Impact of the Froebelian Kindergarten

Founded by Friedrich Froebel in Germany in 1837

Goals of the Froebelian kindergarten:

- To awaken the child's senses to the perfection of the God-given structure underlying all of nature
- To provide a common ground for all people and advance each individual and society into a realm of fundamental unity*

Pedagogical principles of the Froebelian kindergarten that are still prevalent today:

- Activity is the basis for knowing.
- Play is an essential part of the educational process.
- The role of the teacher is to support the development of positive impulses in children.
- Teaching of young children should differ in content and process from teaching older children.
- The teacher is an affectionate leader.

Froebelian kindergarten practices that are still used today:

- Teaching materials and activities (Froebel called them *gifts* and *occupations*) including clay work, paper cutting, block building, finger-plays, songs, and drawing
- A preparation program for teachers

*Brosterman, 1997, 12–13.

kindergarten is synonymous with early childhood education (Education Commission of the States, 2011).

The child-centered approach of the kindergarten has had an impact on the education of young children in both primary grades and in preschool programs. The rigid atmosphere of the traditional primary schools, with their emphasis on drill and practice of academic skills, was sharply contrasted to the approach of kindergartens. However, the gap gradually narrowed. Many kindergarten activities found their way into the primary grades, even as primary activities filtered down into the kindergarten. Today kindergarten and first-grade classrooms resemble one another.

Froebel's kindergarten has also had an impact on preschools. The preschool curriculum that includes play, handwork, songs, and rhymes clearly is the descendent of Froebel's gifts and occupations. Figure 3.9 summarizes the goals, principles, and impact of the Froebelian kindergarten.

Margaret and Rachel McMillan and the Nursery School

Margaret McMillan (1860–1931) and her sister **Rachel** (1859–1917) were social reformers in England who spent their lives trying to address the problems of poverty brought about by the Industrial Revolution in England. The sisters were born in the United States to parents who were originally from Scotland. After the death of her husband, their mother returned to Scotland when the sisters were still young children. As adults the sisters moved to England to find employment. During the 1890s they began to visit the homes of the poor, which led them to lives of social activism with a focus on improving the welfare of the "slum child." They campaigned for school meals and opened Britain's first school health clinic.

In 1911, the sisters started the **Open-Air Nursery School and Training Centre** in London, attended by 30 children between the ages of 18 months and 7 years. This open-air, play-oriented nursery school was their response to health problems they witnessed in children who lived in poor communities and was intended to be a model for other schools and a site for educating teachers. They called their new program a *nursery school* to show that they were concerned with care, nurture, *and* learning The McMillan sisters recognized that many poor children in England needed both care and education in their first few years to give them a good foundation for later life. (Interestingly enough, in the 1980s Americans revived this notion with the addition of the word *care* to early childhood education.) The nursery school had its foundation in the work of Darwin, Plato, Rousseau, Froebel, and Owen. It was designed to identify and prevent health problems and to enhance children's physical and mental development before they entered formal schooling. The McMillan sisters were concerned with basing education on the child's "sense of wonder" and believed that teachers must know what attracts and engages children (Williams, 1993). They also wanted to assist parents in interacting positively with their children.

Rachel was primarily in charge of the school until her death in 1917. Margaret was devastated by the loss of her sister, but she continued to run their nursery school. She also served on the London County Council and wrote a series of influential books that included *The Nursery School* (1919) and *Nursery Schools: A Practical Handbook* (1920). In 1930, Margaret established the Rachel McMillan College to train nurses and teachers.

In providing for children's physical needs, the McMillans strongly emphasized the value of active outdoor work and play. They also stressed health and nutrition, perceptual-motor skills, aesthetics, and the development of imagination. The teacher's role was both to nurture and to informally teach children. A planned learning environment that children could explore was an important mode of learning (McMillan, 1919). The nursery school included materials for sensory development, creative expression, gardening, nature study, and sand play.

Early Nursery Schools in the United States

At the same time that kindergartens were gaining hold in the United States, the nursery school movement began as an effort to meet the needs of even younger children. Nursery schools in the United States were inspired by the English nursery school. They were also influenced by Sigmund Freud's ideas about psychosocial development and by the philosophy of progressive education.

One of the first nursery schools in the United States was the City and Country School, established in New York City in 1913 by **Caroline Pratt**. In 1916, the Bureau of Educational Experiments opened its laboratory nursery school under the direction of **Harriet Johnson**. In the 1920s, a number of other laboratory nursery schools were established in the United States, including one organized by Patty Smith Hill at Columbia University Teachers College in New York City, and the Ruggles Street Nursery School and Training Center directed by **Abigail Eliot** in Roxbury, Massachusetts.

Abigail Eliot studied with Margaret McMillan and observed her nursery school for children in the slums of London. Early in 1922 she returned to Boston to continue her education. In 1930 she was among the first women to receive a doctorate from Harvard University. The Ruggles Street Nursery School founded by Abigail Eliot combined elements from Froebel, Montessori (discussed later in this chapter), the McMillan sisters, and others. Eliot emphasized the use of scissors and paste, plasticene, hammer and nails, and several kinds of blocks (Paciorek & Munro, 1999, p. 62).

Unlike most laboratory nursery schools, which served middle-class children, the Ruggles Street Nursery School followed the McMillans' example of providing a full-day program for children in a low-income neighborhood. Whereas the McMillans concentrated on the physical health of the children, Eliot thought that more should be done to create an intellectually stimulating, child-centered environment. She also actively sought to involve parents in the school. Some of the mothers later went on to become teachers (Beatty, 1995, pp. 143–144).

Parent cooperative nursery schools began in 1916 with the creation of the University of Chicago cooperative nursery school. These were like other nursery schools in that they provided supervised learning and socialization experiences for young children. They differed in that they were cooperatively run by a teacher and parents who were required to assist in the daily program. The benefits of these programs were low tuition, more free time for mothers, opportunities to gain new insights and skills in working with young children, a sense of community, and the continual development of new leaders. The schools became popular and spread rapidly throughout the United States (Byers, 1972).

Also founded during this period were prominent child-study institutions with laboratory schools: Yale University's Clinic of Child Development, the Iowa Child Welfare Research Station, and the Merrill-Palmer Institute in Detroit. **Edna Noble White**, who visited the McMillans' nursery school in England in 1921, established Merrill-Palmer Institute. She was interested in extending the mission of her school beyond the children by providing "motherhood training." Merrill-Palmer later became "world famous as a center for parental and pre-parental education" (Beatty, 1995, p. 153).

During the 1920s and 1930s, nursery schools were established in many college home economics departments to train future homemakers and to serve as centers for child development research. These programs were multidisciplinary in orientation because the early pioneers came from a number of fields, including nursing, social work, medicine, psychology, and education. The earliest nursery schools emphasized children's social, emotional, and physical development—hence the whole-child orientation described in this book. The intellect received less attention because of the common belief that significant cognitive development did not occur until children entered school at the age of 6. Children played freely indoors and outdoors in a learning environment that was designed especially for them.

The Impact of the Nursery School

Early childhood education still reflects the legacy of the early nursery schools. In those programs, and in today's programs, children are seen as growing and learning through interactions with people and with a planned learning environment. The role of the school is to keep the paths of exploration open so children can develop in their own unique ways. The daily schedule is characterized by blocks of time in which children are free to choose activities and engage in them for long periods. The classroom is divided into activity areas—typically those for block construction, dramatic play, art, water play, sand play, science, math, and language and literacy. The role of the teacher is to create an environment that facilitates learning and to support cognitive, language, and literacy development by giving children many things to explore, think about, talk about, and read about. Teachers support children's social and emotional development by providing a safe and nurturing environment, valuing each child's contributions, encouraging children to work and play together cooperatively, and to verbalize their feelings.

The traditional nursery school has continued to evolve since the 1960s in response to the needs of less advantaged children and in recognition of the importance of early experiences for cognitive development. What remains constant is the insistence that children can benefit from play in a carefully designed environment under the guidance of a caring and sensitive teacher.

FIGURE 3.10   The Goals, Principles, and Impact of the Nursery School

---

Founded by Margaret and Rachel McMillan in England in 1911

Goals of the nursery school:

- To provide nurture (loving care) to children
- To support the health, nourishment, and physical welfare of children
- To assist parents in improving their ways of caring for and interacting with their children
- To provide a model for teachers of how to work with young children*

Pedagogical principles of the nursery school that are prevalent today:

- It is important to stimulate the child's sense of wonder and imagination.
- Play in a planned learning environment is an important vehicle for education.
- Outdoor work and play are important.
- Aesthetics are an important part of the curriculum.
- The teacher's role is to nurture and teach informally.
- Children need trained and qualified teachers.

Nursery school practices that are still used today:

- Programs like Head Start for low-income children
- Sensory activities
- Outdoor activities including sandbox and gardening
- A focus on children's health, including personal hygiene and nutrition
- Creative expression activities

---

*Lascarides & Hinitz, 2000, 121.

Parent Cooperative Nursery Schools can still be found throughout the United States (as well as in Canada, Australia, New Zealand and Great Britain) although there are many fewer since the 1970s when women's participation in the labor force began to increase rapidly. A number of leaders in early childhood education found their way into the field as parents in co-op nursery schools.

Today the terms *nursery school, preschool,* and *child development center* are used in the United States to describe programs that evolved from the McMillan nursery school. Programs such as Head Start and state-funded preschools for low-income children embody the purpose of the original nursery schools and the McMillan sisters' vision and commitment to poor children. The Head Start program, described in Chapter 2 and at the end of this chapter, is the best contemporary example of this legacy. The comprehensive design of the Head Start program, which includes health and nutrition, reflects the concern of early nursery education with children's health and well-being. See Figure 3.10 for an overview of the goals, principles, and impact of the nursery school.

John Dewey and Progressive Education

Progressive education was part of the progressive movement, begun in the late 19th century to seek social and political reforms for problems that resulted from industrialization in the United States. Progressive theorists sought to use science and reason to improve mankind. Progressive education evolved from a combination of the ideas of Rousseau, Pestalozzi, and Froebel and from 19th-century social reform movements (Williams, 1993). The founders of the movement desired a "progressive" society in which people could develop their full potential. Their goal was to improve society through fundamental changes in the schools. They attempted to transform dreary educational environments that offered a skills-based curriculum learned by drill and recitation.

John Dewey (1859–1952), though not the founder of the movement, became its most influential spokesperson. Dewey taught high school before studying for a doctorate in philosophy. He then taught at the University of Chicago, where he was instrumental in setting up a laboratory school for experimentation with innovative educational concepts. Later he moved to Columbia University in New York and continued to write about education and philosophy for the rest of his career.

Dewey wanted schools to be places where children would grow physically, intellectually, and socially and be challenged to think independently. He called for classrooms to be places in which children investigated the world around them and engaged with subject matter that expanded their natural curiosity. He believed that schools should reflect the life of the society and that education should be viewed as the life of the child in the present, not just as preparation for the future. He also believed that, in addition to their instructional role, schools should play a role in helping immigrants learn to adapt to a new culture.

Progressive educators advocated techniques of instruction that were based on children's interest, involved hands-on activities, recognized individual differences, and were to the greatest extent possible initiated by the child, not the adult.

John Dewey

What Is Progressive Education?

In Dewey's view, the school community offered children an opportunity to practice democratic ideals in a group situation and to learn through activities that were interesting and meaningful. Although early childhood programs at the University of Chicago laboratory school that he founded included some Froebelian kindergarten materials, they were used in different ways. Dewey's approach emphasized greater freedom and spontaneity in play and involvement in the social life of the classroom instead of highly structured activities. An important instructional approach, still used today, was to have children in the elementary school work on collaborative projects related to their own interests.

Progressive educators were concerned with "teaching the whole child"— addressing physical, social, and emotional as well as intellectual development. In programs based on progressive education children learned through doing— through experiencing and experimenting with real materials and self-directed activities. In *My Pedagogic Creed,* published in 1897, Dewey wrote that "the child's own instinct and powers furnish the material and give the starting points for all education." This mirrors today's views of developmentally appropriate practice in which children's interests and needs are an essential component of curriculum planning. But Dewey cautioned that enjoyment and fun were not legitimate educational purposes—educational activities always needed to support children's development and learning.

In progressive education programs, the role of the teacher was to provide a carefully designed learning environment and curriculum that prepared children to be members of a democratic society. The curriculum included "real experiences" such carpentry, weaving, cooking, and the study of local geography. Teachers were expected to observe children and, based on their observations, ask questions and provide experiences designed to integrate different subject areas and help children expand their understanding of the world around them.

The role of the teacher was to serve as a guide and observer, not instructor and disciplinarian.

The Impact of Progressive Education

The ideas of progressive education combined with research in child development triggered a great deal of educational experimentation. A number of schools based on progressive ideas were established at the end of the 19th and beginning of the 20th centuries. These included the Laboratory School at the University of Chicago, which began in 1896 as a small experimental school; the Francis Parker School in Chicago in 1883; the Horace Mann School in New York City in 1887; the Bureau of Educational Experiments (later called Bank Street School) in 1916; and the Lincoln School at Teachers College, Columbia University, in 1917.

The ideas of progressive education gained acceptance in American school systems during the first half of the 20th century and were also influential in European schools. From its beginnings, however, progressive education had its critics. One of the major criticisms was that it did not emphasize systematic study of the academic disciplines. Eventually progressive education came under fire from those who felt that students were not gaining sufficient mastery of basic school subjects. The movement had become associated with permissiveness, rather than with its guiding principles that curriculum must challenge children intellectually and help them to develop self-direction and responsibility. The progressive influence on American education waned after World War II as more academic, skill-based teaching practices gained prevalence. Progressive education in public schools came to a halt after the launch of the Soviet satellite *Sputnik* in 1957, which focused American education on producing scientists who could compete with the Soviet Union.

Progressive education had a profound impact on American education, particularly on the kindergartens and nursery schools, many of which remain more closely allied ideologically with progressive philosophy than with more traditional academic approaches. A number of highly respected private schools continue to reflect the philosophy of progressive education, including the Bank Street School for Children and the City and Country School in New York City; Shady Hill School in Cambridge, Massachusetts; and Hanahau'oli School in Honolulu. These programs are based on the progressive beliefs that curriculum should be integrated instead of based on distinct subject areas, that children should be active learners who have many opportunities to pursue their own interests, that schools should help children to gain understanding of their world, and that classrooms are places where children can live and learn democracy.

There was a resurgence of interest in progressive approaches to education when American educators visited England in the mid-1960s and 1970s to learn about state-supported schools for 5- to 8-year-olds (called *British infant schools*), which combined the ideas of progressive education with Swiss psychologist Jean Piaget's views of child development. In British infant schools young children learned from active involvement in tasks or projects.

Current interest in the developmental-interaction approach (DIA) as developed and implemented at Bank Street College in New York City, in the Reggio Emilia preschools in Italy (both of which we will discuss later in this chapter), and in the Project Approach (similar to the Reggio approach, with focus on children's extended exploration of a topic) has its roots in progressive ideas and indicates that progressive education continues to have a strong impact on early childhood education today. See Figure 3.11 for an outline of progressive education goals, principles, and impact.

FIGURE 3.11 The Goals, Principles, and Impact of Progressive Education

Promoted by John Dewey, Lucy Sprague Mitchell, Harriet Johnson, Caroline Pratt in the United States in the 1890s

Goals:

- To improve society through schooling
- To help people to develop their foil potential
- To prepare citizens to live in a democratic society

Progressive pedagogical principles that are still prevalent today:

- Education is the life of the child in the present, not just preparation for the future.
- Cooperation and problem solving are important aspects of the curriculum.
- Children learn through doing.
- All aspects of development are important.
- The role of the teacher is to be a guide.

Progressive teaching practices that are still used today:

- Curriculum based on children's interests and needs
- Projects and active exploration as the core of the curriculum
- The community as a source of curriculum
- Unit blocks used to represent what is learned

Contemporary Examples

Do the three programs just described still exist? Though all have changed over time in some ways, each still exists. Though kindergarten is the most widespread and its influence is great, there are few Froebelian kindergartens in existence today. However, two programs, well known today, evolved from the educational movements that we just described: (1) the High/Scope model, which is based on the Piaget's theory of development and embraces many of the goals of the McMillans' nursery school, and (2) the developmental-interaction approach, a present-day example of progressive education.

High/Scope

High/Scope was one of the first programs designed in the 1960s to ameliorate the effects of poverty on children's development. This approach, created by David Weikart and his colleagues in Ypsilanti, Michigan, draws its theoretical foundation from the work of Jean Piaget. In the late 1960s the U.S. government authorized two studies to assess the impact of different educational approaches on the development and learning of low-income children. The first study, "Planned Variation," focused on Head Start programs. The second, "Follow Through," looked at the effects of continuity in programming from preschool through third grade. Weikart and his colleagues built on their previous experience working with low-income, at-risk children and developed an educational model as part of this research.

The High/Scope curriculum, which continues to be implemented today, was based on key experiences related to the acquisition of concepts like classification, seriation, number, spatial relationships, and time. These key experiences provide the basis for planning and adapting the learning environment, making decisions about teacher-led group activities, and assessment of children's progress.

In a High/Scope classroom children are actively engaged in learning centers for building, dramatic play, art, mathematics, reading and writing, music and movement, sensorial exploration, science, and motor development. The environment is consciously planned to enable children to actively manipulate and experiment with objects and then to represent what they have learned.

The role of the teacher is to carefully design the learning environment and support children in learning from it. Attention is given to providing materials and activities that expose children to the key experiences. For example, teachers might foster seriation by providing three or four different sizes of the same materials and bringing relative sizes to children's attention during the play period. A pretend area might include several different sized spatulas. Where relationships are observable between materials, such as different sized pots and pans, they are displayed in gradually ascending order from smallest to biggest, so the relationships are evident to children.

During a typical day children engage in a three-step process called "plan-do-review." They talk about their plans before the work period and then meet to recall or represent them afterward. A typical morning begins with children gathering. Teachers work with all children to generate plans for the play period. As children carry out their plans during the work period, teachers observe, encourage, and extend children's ideas. After the play period ends, children once again gather to review their activities in a teacher-facilitated review time. The developers of this approach believe that this process makes children more conscious of their actions and fosters the connection between language and action. Representation of work is considered important and children's work is posted on classroom walls.

A notable aspect of the High/Scope program is the research it has conducted. Since the early 1970s and continuing to the present day, longitudinal studies of High/Scope program benefits have demonstrated the impact of high-quality early childhood programs on poor children that continues into their adult lives. In the 30-year follow-up study of the original group, researchers reported that in comparison to a control group, adults who had attended the program had higher monthly earnings, a higher percentage of home ownership, a higher level of schooling completed, a lower percentage receiving social services, and fewer arrests by age 27 (Schweinhart, Barnes, & Weikart, 1993). Contemporary evidence from research on the long-term impact of programs for poor children bears out the power of the original vision of the nursery school.

The Developmental-Interaction Approach

Many preschools and elementary schools today embody the philosophy of progressive education. Bank Street School for Children in New York City is a noteworthy example. The educational program developed at Bank Street had its roots in progressive education and also drew heavily from child development theory including the work of Anna Freud, Erik Erikson, Barbara Biber, and Jean Piaget. The Bank Street School for Children and the Bank Street College of Education both continue to operate in New York City (though now moved to 112th Street) and the approach they pioneered is still taught in early childhood teacher education programs and implemented in many classrooms for young children by teachers who studied at Bank Street.

In New York in 1916, Harriet Johnson, Caroline Pratt, and Lucy Sprague Mitchell organized the Bureau of Educational Experiments, which was the forerunner of the Bank Street College of Education, as an agency for research on child development. Mitchell, a friend of Dewey and a strong advocate of progressive education, directed the Bank Street School for Children and was influential in its evolution into a teacher training institution. Mitchell was deeply committed to young children's learning about their world through direct experience. Her book *Young Geographers* introduced the study of geography to young children through direct experiences in their communities. This community study still characterizes the curriculum of Bank Street School for Children and the educational model based on its practices. Caroline Pratt's and Harriet Johnson's observations of preschool children at play led to the development of the wooden unit blocks that continue to be standard equipment in early childhood programs today. Johnson's *The Art of Block Building* described her observations of nursery school children's stages of block building skill (Beatty, 1995, pp. 140–142).

The founders of this approach emphasized the development of the "whole child," the interaction of different aspects of development, and the interaction of the child with other people and with the environment. In the 1970s the name of this method was changed from the Bank Street approach to the developmental-interaction approach (DIA) to call attention to its emphasis on interactions rather than its geography (Goffin & Wilson, 2001, p. 67). The developmental-interaction approach was another of the models implemented and studied as part of the Planned Variation and Follow Through research conducted in the 1960s.

The DIA approach is based on the progressive principle that the classroom must allow children the social experience of living within a democratic community. Its creators believed that children need to be actively involved in thinking and reasoning with real experiences that begin with direct experience in the community and extend outward to situations that are further removed.

Lucy Sprague Mitchell

A DIA classroom is viewed as a representation of society, with social studies and learning trips forming the core of the curriculum. Children explore topics they can experience directly in their communities such as the bakery, grocery store, harbor, and public works. Other subject areas are generally integrated into the exploration of social studies topics. If, for example, the children in a DIA classroom were studying the nearby harbor, they would first take a learning trip to the harbor and then follow up in the classroom with various ways of representing what they observed and learned. Follow-up activities might involve reading books about harbors, writing, drawing, role-playing, and block building.

A DIA classroom is set up in centers where children can make choices about their own learning. While there are class meetings and group activities facilitated by a teacher, there is also much independent, productive play. Play is an essential part of the curriculum—especially block building and dramatic play. These forms of play allow children to symbolically represent their growing knowledge of the world. They also provide teachers with insight into how children interpret their experience.

Educators who advocate this approach stress the importance of a child functioning as a member of the group. Teachers are expected to provide children with the experience of living within a democratic community, and to be sensitive interpreters and facilitators who respond to the needs and interests of each child. In addition to knowing what and how to teach, teachers are expected to be able to reflect on why each decision is made (Cuffaro, 1995).

The whole-child and real-world curriculum advocated by Bank Street College has had a strong impact on early childhood education in the United States for many years and remains a strong influence today. A number of the curriculum examples we use in this book reflect the developmental-interaction

Reflect on your experience

Reflect on your experiences in preschools and kindergartens. How did the programs that you attended as a child, or that you have observed or taught in, seem to reflect what is described in the history of these programs? What were the programs like? What were your reactions to them?

approach. It is also possible to observe it in action in the Bank Street School for Children, in the classrooms of teachers who were trained at Bank Street College, and in other schools that base their practice on the philosophy of progressive education.

Three Influential European Approaches

Three educational approaches that emerged in Europe in the 20th century are based on many of the same ideas and values that characterized the kindergarten, the nursery school, and progressive education. Each of these programs was developed by an inspired and creative thinker and added significant new elements to what had gone before. The programs are the Montessori method developed in Italy by Maria Montessori, the Waldorf education method conceived in Germany by Rudolf Steiner, and the Reggio Emilia approach founded in Italy by Loris Malaguzzi. Many schools today directly implement or base their programs on these approaches and each of them has had a profound influence on educational thought and practice. Each of these programs has its own educational philosophy including ideas about nature of the child, curriculum content, teaching methods, design of the learning environment, and role of the teacher. As you study early childhood education and observe programs, you might hear someone say, "We base our program on Reggio," or "I work in a Montessori program," or "My child attends a Waldorf school." We hope that you will be able to visit and/or work with children in one or more of these programs to see them in action.

The Montessori Method

Maria Montessori (1870–1952) overcame the opposition of her family and her society to become, in 1896, one of the first women in Italy to receive a medical degree. Early in her medical career she devised effective approaches for teaching children with serious cognitive delays, previously regarded as incapable of learning. In 1907 she founded the *Casa dei Bambini* (Children's House) in Rome, where she explored the applicability of her educational methods to typically developing children. The program she designed was based on her observations of young children and how they learned. She reached the conclusion that intelligence was not fixed and could be either stimulated or stifled by the child's experiences. Further, she believed that children learn best through their own direct sensory experience of the world. The foundation for her interest in education was her study of the writings of French physicians Seguin and Itard about their humane methods for educating children who have mental retardation. Although Montessori's training was in medicine, the contributions she made to education have been her lasting legacy.

Montessori was interested in the first years of life and believed that children went through sensitive periods during which they had interest and capacity for the development of particular knowledge and/or skills. She believed that children had an inherent desire to explore and understand the world in which they lived. She saw these young explorers as self-motivated and able

Maria Montessori

to seek out the kinds of experiences and knowledge most appropriate for their stage of development. Concerned with preserving the dignity of the child, she valued the development of independence and productivity.

Montessori Programs

Montessori's educational approach was distinguished by the provision of a child-sized learning environment, carefully designed and sequenced learning materials, learning experiences that actively involved the child, and a teacher role that involved observing and guiding rather than direct instruction. Because the role of the teacher is to observe and direct children's learning rather than to instruct, a Montessori teacher is called a *directress* or *director*.

In a Montessori classroom, children are grouped in mixed ages and abilities: 0–3, 3–6, and 6–12. Children learn from firsthand experience—by observing and by doing. Practical life experiences such as buttoning, zipping, cutting, and gardening enable children to care for themselves and the environment while building skills that will be useful throughout their lives. All learning in a Montessori classroom is cumulative. Each activity paves the way to future, more complex experiences. Activities are organized primarily for individual work, rather than group interaction. Children move freely about the classroom and choose their own activities.

The classroom learning environment based on Montessori's principles is attractive and equipped with child-sized, movable furniture. Montessori stressed the importance of an orderly environment that helps children to focus on their learning and develop the ability to concentrate. Classrooms are equipped with didactic materials designed by Montessori to help children develop their senses and learn concepts. These carefully crafted materials continue to be the basis of the curriculum in a Montessori school. They are treated with care and respect and are displayed on open shelves so children can use them independently. The materials are graded in difficulty, sequenced from known to unknown and from concrete to abstract. Each concept to be taught is isolated from other concepts that might be confusing or distracting. For example, if the child is learning the concept of shape, the materials will be of uniform size and color so that the attribute of shape can be readily perceived. Materials are also designed to have immediate, self-correcting feedback, so children know if they have successfully completed a task.

Purposeful activity is characteristic in a Montessori classroom. Children's work is taken seriously and is not considered play. Children can work on any material they have learned to use at any time. Teachers do not make assignments or dictate what activities children should engage in, nor do they set a limit as to how far a child can pursue an interest. Adults and children are expected to respect concentration and not interrupt someone who is busy at a task. Children are free to move around the room. A child can work at an activity for an unlimited time but is expected to approach tasks in sequence.

The Impact of Montessori Programs

Montessori's schools were successful in Italy and the Netherlands (where she had her headquarters for many years), and they eventually spread throughout the world. During World War II Montessori lived in India, where she worked in classrooms and trained teachers in her approach. Although private Montessori schools have operated in the United States since 1915, it remains a separate movement that has not been integrated with other educational approaches.

Historically, Montessori education was quite controversial in the United States, possibly because it differed from some of the basic tenets of the nursery school and progressive education. Most Montessori programs do not allow for a great deal of social interaction, and classrooms have little or no provision for the development of creativity in the arts or in the way that the didactic materials are used. Montessori schools share with nursery and progressive schools the view that children are inquisitive, self-motivated learners, capable of selecting activities appropriate for their current needs and developmental stage. Montessori was an important educational innovator, and a number of her ideas—such as the provision of a child-size environment and the use of sensory materials—have found their way into most contemporary early childhood programs.

Montessori carefully prescribed the teaching techniques and materials for her schools. Teachers in these programs are expected to have specialized Montessori training. During this training, teachers learn about the Montessori view of the child and how to use the specialized Montessori materials.

Two major professional associations are involved in the training of Montessori teachers and accreditation of schools and teachers. One is the original organization, Association Montessori Internationale (AMI), which has headquarters in the Netherlands, and the other is the American Montessori Society (AMS), founded in 1956 to adapt Montessori methods to an American style of working with children. Today Montessori programs can be found in both private and public settings in the United States and in many other places throughout the world. It is estimated that there are approximately 20,000 Montessori schools worldwide, including 4,500 in the United States (North American Montessori Teachers Association, n.d.).

Waldorf Education

Rudolf Steiner (1861–1925) was a German philosopher, scientist, and educator whose method is known today as Waldorf education. As a young man Steiner studied mathematics, physics, and chemistry. He then earned a doctorate in philosophy. He was interested in the intersection of science and spirituality. Steiner was a prolific thinker, lecturer, and writer and made contributions to philosophy and education. He was the founder of a school of philosophy called *anthroposophy,* which explores the role of spirituality in contemporary society. He was deeply interested in the individual's search for self and the development of human potential.

After World War I, the owner of the Waldorf Astoria Cigarette factory in Germany invited Steiner to create a school to serve the workers' children. The first Waldorf school was opened in 1919 with the goal of educating people to build a free, just, and collaborative society.

Steiner believed that childhood is a phase of life important in its own right. His theory of human development is based on 7-year cycles that combine physical, mental, and spiritual development. Steiner's philosophy emphasized balanced development, imagination, and creativity. The schools he developed were designed to promote healthy, unhurried learning experiences for children based on their stage of development.

Waldorf Programs

Steiner's school stressed the development of the child's body, mind, and spirit. The focus was on educating the "whole" child because Steiner realized that engaging with a variety of academic, artistic, and handicraft subject areas would, over time, engender a balance of the human faculties of thinking, feeling, and will.

Steiner believed that in the first 7 years of life the most important development had to do with the child's body and will (inclination to activity), and that educational activities should, therefore, be practical, imitative, and hands-on in nature. The Steiner kindergarten program takes place in an ungraded setting for children 3 to 6 years of age. The curriculum consists of storytelling, puppetry, artistic activities (painting, drawing, modeling), imaginative play, and practical work (finger knitting, bread baking, gardening).

Steiner thought it was important for the young child to experience a feeling of warmth and security. Therefore, classroom environments for young children are like an extension of a home. Classrooms tend to feature soft colors, natural materials, and simple learning materials like homemade dolls that encourage imaginative use. Early childhood classrooms are beautifully appointed and aesthetically pleasing; they do not include plastic toys, academic materials, or modern technology like computers and video players.

In the Waldorf educational system, young children are allowed to remain childlike. Steiner believed that there is a time for every aspect of development and that children under the age of 7 should not receive formal academic instruction. Children in Waldorf schools often do not learn to read and write until well after their peers in other school settings. Waldorf educators maintain that they catch up in learning these subjects by second or third grade (Williams & Johnson, 2005).

Teachers in Waldorf schools stay with a group of young children for 3 years. This allows teachers to create a community of learners and promote continuity of experience. It provides opportunities for older children to be role models for younger children and to take on a nurturing role. The role of the teacher is to design the learning environment, to establish predictable routines, and to support and nurture the individual growth of each child. The focus is on self-discovery and sensory experience rather than direct instruction, with the goal of helping children develop a sense of responsibility and the ability to regulate their own behavior. The teacher in a Waldorf school is viewed as an important role model for children.

The Impact of Waldorf Education

Today, Waldorf education occurs in independent, self-governing schools (preschool through 12th grade) based on the ideas of Rudolf Steiner. Currently there are approximately 1,000 Waldorf schools in more than 60 countries (including more than 200 in the United States, 44 of which are publicly funded) (Association of Waldorf Schools International, 2011). There are 60 teacher training institutions worldwide. Waldorf education attracts teachers, and families choose it for its views of child development and profound respect for childhood. It is one of the fastest growing educational movements in the United States today (Williams & Johnson, 2005).

Waldorf education has been criticized for having a spiritually based pedagogy (though it is not considered to be a religious school), for the lack of emphasis on skills in the early grades, for lack of formalized assessment procedures, and for lack of attention to the role of technology in modern life. Some critics regard anthroposophy as a dangerous pseudoscience. Others believe that the Eurocentric origin of some of the curriculum—the gnome- and giant-laden fairy tales, for example—are out of date and inappropriate in today's multicultural society.

There have been some discussions about whether Waldorf education could be adopted in contemporary public schools. Questions are raised about whether it could work if parts of it were taken out of context and whether its spiritual underpinnings bring it into conflict with requirements for separation of church and state.

The Reggio Emilia Approach

Since the 1980s educators from around the world have visited the publicly funded infant-toddler centers and preschools in the small northern Italian city of Reggio Emilia. American educators were excited and inspired by what they saw in Reggio and have brought home ideas that revitalize progressive educational concepts about working with young children.

After World War II, as part of its reconstruction, the city of Reggio Emilia developed an educational system for young children. A school was built in 1948 by parents who hired an innovative educator named Loris Malaguzzi (1920–1994) as its director. By 1963, under Malaguzzi's leadership, the original school had become a municipal-government-funded system of early childhood programs. By the 1980s educators from all over the world were visiting Reggio Emilia to observe their preprimary schools.

The Reggio Emilia schools are characterized by a set of values and philosophical assumptions that are informed, in part, by constructivist theories and the progressive education movement, and by a deep commitment to honor the rights of children, parents, and teachers. Key concepts of this philosophy are (1) that the child is a strong and competent individual who has a right to receive the best education and care that a society can offer; (2) that education is based on relationships, especially the interrelationships among children, teachers, and parents; and (3) that education is based on the interaction of young children working and playing together in small groups.

Reggio Emilia Programs

In Reggio Emilia the school is seen as an amiable community in which teachers' dialogue with children, with each other, with the community, and with families is an essential part of the educational process. The curriculum is not established in advance but emerges from children's intellectual curiosity, social interactions, and interests. Projects and curriculum goals are based on teachers' observations of children. The teachers view themselves as children's partners in learning; together, they "co-construct" understanding and enjoy discovering with the children.

The Reggio approach promotes the intellectual development of children through a systematic focus on symbolic representation. The focus of the curriculum is in-depth project work emerging from the interests of the children. The children are encouraged to represent their environment through many "natural languages," or modes of expression, often referred to as "The Hundred Languages of Children" (Edwards, Gandini, & Forman, 1998). These modes of expression may include drawing, painting, working in clay, sculpting, constructing, conversing, and dramatic play. Educators in Reggio Emilia believe that these languages must be cherished, nurtured, celebrated, and documented. They actively encourage children to explore the possibilities of working with a wide variety of materials.

Educators in Reggio schools often refer to the learning environment as the "third teacher," because children construct knowledge through their interactions with it. The goal is to provide an environment that promotes partnerships, social interaction, and constructive learning. Important elements of school design are the art studio, called the *atelier,* and a large central gathering area, called the *piazza,* where children can gather and can play independently. The schools of Reggio Emilia have skylights and floor-to-ceiling windows so that the classrooms are flooded with natural light. Schools are designed with the idea of "transparency" so children can see from one area of the school to another. Mirrors and plants combine to create a bright and cheerful environment. High-quality art supplies, including paints and clay as well as recycled materials and natural objects, are beautifully arranged, often by color, on open shelves within the children's reach. Children's work is prominently displayed. The physical environment created at the Reggio Emilia schools honors the child's right to have a beautiful, functional space in which to work and play.

Teachers are responsible for day-to-day administration of the schools with support from a team of educational coordinators, or *pedagogistas,* who work to create continual exchanges of information among teachers, families, and children. These coordinators also interact with policy makers and serve as advocates and lobbyists for children, parents, and teachers. Each school also has an art teacher, or *atelierista,* who helps teachers to support children in expressing their knowledge through symbolic representation. The atelierista works with small groups of children as they investigate and explore topics through a variety of media.

Teachers in Reggio programs are collaborators with the community, children, and other teachers in the construction of curriculum. They regard themselves as researchers who conduct systematic study in the classroom by collecting and preparing documentation of the children's work for the purpose of better understanding children, curriculum planning, teacher development, and connecting with families and communities. Photographs of the children working, and transcriptions of the children's questions and comments, are mounted and displayed with their actual work so that children and parents can examine them. Teachers also assemble portfolios of the children's work, listen to tape-recorded sessions with the children, and review videotape of the children working and playing.

The Impact of Reggio Emilia

The early childhood programs of Reggio Emilia reflect a distinctly collaborative approach to working with children, families, and the community. This approach is entirely consistent with the social and political systems of the city of Reggio Emilia and its province, Emilia Romagna, which are among the most progressive and prosperous in Italy.

Unlike the previous models (Montessori and Waldorf) just discussed, there are no "Reggio" schools outside of Reggio Emilia, Italy. Instead there are many schools and teachers that can be said to be "Reggio-inspired." As already stated, many delegations of educators from the United States and other countries have visited Reggio since the 1980s to study their educational system. Leaders of the Reggio schools caution against efforts to replicate their system or to follow its provisions without question (in fact questioning, or *provocation,* is an essential component of the Reggio approach). They have avoided publishing curriculum or teacher manuals and insist that education in Reggio, as in every other community, must be constantly evolving and changing based on the unique characteristics of that community. American interest in these programs raises questions about whether educational practices from one country can retain their vitality when

Reflect on historical influences

Think about the Waldorf, Montessori, and Reggio programs described here. What are your reactions to each of them? How are the programs you have visited or worked in similar to them? Have you had any experience of a Waldorf, Montessori, or Reggio Emilia program? Was it a program that you would like to work in or send your own child to?

transplanted to another country that has a different educational history, traditions, and goals. In spite of these cautions, American enthusiasm for Reggio continues.

Early childhood education in Reggio Emilia can be seen as a reaffirmation of the progressive roots of American early childhood education and it offers a reminder about how important it is for educators to thoughtfully examine and discuss their practices. The commitment of the municipal government of Reggio Emilia to the welfare of young children makes Reggio more than just another educational innovation. It is also a model of a society that cares for and nurtures the potential of young children.

Reflection on the Three Approaches

Each of these approaches to early childhood education was created in western Europe as a response to specific historical circumstances, but each is unique and has qualities that made it universally appealing and led to continued interest in it.

Some of their common elements were explored in an article by Carolyn Edwards:

> All three approaches represent an explicit idealism and turn away from war and violence toward peace and reconstruction. They are built on coherent visions of how to improve human society by helping children realize their full potential as intelligent, creative, whole persons. In each approach, children are viewed as active authors of their development, strongly influenced by natural, dynamic, self-righting forces within themselves, opening the way toward growth and learning. Teachers depend for their work with children on carefully prepared, aesthetically pleasing environments that serve as a pedagogical tool and provide strong messages about the curriculum and about respect for children. Partnering with parents is highly valued in all three approaches and children are evaluated by means other than traditional tests and grades. (2002, p. 1)

We are not surprised that these approaches are gaining attention in the United States at this time. Each of them epitomizes the respect for and valuing of children, and childhood itself, that have characterized early childhood education for centuries. Each is, in many ways, consistent with our current conceptions of developmentally appropriate practice.

Table 3.1 compares the educational approaches described in this section.

Two Significant Components of the History of American Early Childhood Education

Even before you began learning about early childhood education you had probably heard of child care (which you may have thought of as day care) and Head Start. And you probably had some idea of what these two kinds of programs are like. No overview of the history of American early childhood education is complete without reflecting on the impact of child care and Head Start.

Child Care

The history of the early education field is not just about creative thinkers who developed educational programs. There is another history—one that chronicles the efforts to provide for working families who needed care for their children,

TABLE 3.1   Comparison of the Educational Approaches

Approach	The Montessori Method	Waldorf Education	Reggio Emilia
Originator	Maria Montessori (physician)	Rudolf Steiner (philosopher and architect)	Loris Malaguzzi (educator and psychologist)
Where and When	Italy, 1907	Germany, 1919	Italy, 1948
First School	Casa dei Bambini—Children's House	School for employees of the Waldorf Astoria cigarette factory	Started by parents in Reggio Emilia in northern italy
Goals	To preserve the dignity of the child To develop the child's independence and productivity The psychological health of the child	To build a free, equal, and collaborative society To develop free human beings who have purpose and direction in their lives To achieve balanced development of young children (mind, body, and spirit)	To work collaboratively in a community To develop the child's potential To develop children's symbolic languages To ensure the young child is visible to community and society
Significant Ideas	Education begins at birth—and the first 6 years are critical. There are sensitive periods for development of skills. Intelligence is stimulated by experience. Children learn best through sensory exploration. Children are intrinsically motivated and seek out appropriate learning experiences. Learning is sequential.	Childhood is important in its own right. From birth to 7 years, children respond through movement and are sensitive to the environment. Warmth and security are important. Emphasis is on development of inner strength. Imitation and example are important strategies for learning. Teachers should protect early childhood.	Child is "strong, rich, and competent"; respect for the child is important. Systematic focus is on symbolic representation. The learning environment is a teacher. The teacher is learner, researcher, and co-collaborator.
Distinctive Features	Orderly, child-sized learning environment Self-correcting, sequenced materials designed to teach a concept or skill Children work independently, choosing activities based on level of complexity Space delineated by mats or trays Mixed age grouping Teacher (directress) is observer and guide	Warm, homelike, aesthetic environment Natural materials for children to use in sensory and creative pursuits Storytelling, puppetry, artistic activities, imaginative play, and domestic activities Ritual and rhythms of life and seasons are important Mixed age grouping (3 years with same teacher in preschool/kindergarten) Teacher as a warm, steady focal point for the program	Aesthetic learning environment (light and transparency) Wide variety of open-ended materials used as tools and resources In-depth project work based on children's interests Emphasis on using the arts for representing ideas Looping (3 years with same teacher) Documentation of children's work shown throughout the school Trained artist (*atelierista*) as guide in addition to teacher

and for children who were poor, had disabilities, were non-English-speaking, or otherwise at risk for failure in our society.

The Origins of Child Care in the United States

In colonial America, as in Europe, prior to the Industrial Revolution (which brought about the mass production of goods and moved the workplace from the home to the factory) most women were able to keep their children at home while they produced domestic goods and helped with farm work or the family's craft or trade. In some cases, children were sent to a "dame school," where an older woman would gather children from 2 to 6 years of age to teach them some reading, writing, and arithmetic (the "three R's").

The need for child care for poor families and widows greatly increased with the rise of industrial production and merchant capitalism in the late 18th century. While Americans came to idealize motherhood in the period after the Revolutionary War, changes in economic life made it increasingly difficult for mothers to make a living at home. Many poor women were forced to choose between leaving their children at home alone or seeking charity from the community. As the number of poor increased, many communities no longer gave them money and food, but forced them to enter workhouses to earn their keep. Children were not allowed in the work-houses, so mothers were forced to give up their children to be raised as indentured servants (a form of time-limited slavery) for other families. Women who tried to keep their children found that the only work available was so poorly paid that they could not afford to hire anyone to care for them. Some poor women pooled their resources to pay for care or had older children mind the younger ones. Others left their children to beg in the streets or even locked them indoors during the workday.

Quaker women in Philadelphia tried to help poor working women with child care by founding the Society for the Relief and Employment of the Poor. In 1798 this society built a house that provided religious education for children while their mothers worked at spinning in another portion of the house.

The Boston Infant School founded in 1828 is an early example of the positive influence of new ideas concerning child care and education in the United States. Philanthropists in Boston who hoped to provide good care for the children of working mothers took Robert Owen's British infant schools as a model. In the

1830s other infant schools were established in several U.S. cities. Two cities established separate infant schools for the children of African Americans. Support for the infant schools was not sustained past 1850, however. By that time most middle-class Americans thought that young children should stay at home with their mothers. They failed to grasp the reasons that made working outside the home essential for so many women.

Although the infant schools did not survive, the day nurseries of the mid-19th century served the most needy of the great waves of immigrants arriving in the United States.

The first of these was New York's Nursery for the Children of Poor Women, founded in 1854. Its mission was to provide care for the children of women temporarily forced to provide for their families (Michel, 1999). These privately run programs enabled immigrant parents employed in urban factories to keep their families together. Personnel in the day nurseries were largely untrained, worked long hours with high child-adult ratios, and provided minimal care for children. In the eyes of society, the great virtue of the day nursery was that they gave the children a reprieve from even more harmful environments. These programs were primarily concerned with the health of children and not with educational goals.

In 1878, **Pauline Agassiz Shaw**, a wealthy Boston woman influenced by the success of the American kindergarten movement, established a day nursery with educational programs for children of different ages (Michel, 1999). Some day nurseries followed Shaw's trend in providing comprehensive services with long hours of operation, infant care, family education and training programs, and even counseling.

Unfortunately, most day nurseries did not include services for infants in addition to 3- to 6-year-olds. An attempt to meet this need was made by **Frances Willard** as part of her work with the Women's Christian Temperance Union in the 1880s. Willard's day nurseries were provided free of charge to poor mothers. The day nurseries were not open to all racial and ethnic groups, however, and never to the children of unwed mothers. Such discrimination left many working mothers with no option but to send their children to orphanages or to unsatisfactory arrangements in the homes of strangers (Michel, 1999).

The National Association of Colored Women (NACW) became active in the 1890s in establishing day nurseries for urban African American children. Many African American women had a history of domestic servitude, first as slaves before the Civil War and then as domestic servants. In most cases they had been required to care for white children while leaving their own babies in the care of only slightly older children (Michel, 1999).

The 19th century witnessed a number of experiments in child care, which enabled many women to avoid the worst extremes of poverty by working outside the home. The general attitude in American society was that child care was a stopgap measure that a decent mother would use only in the direst circumstances. While mass public schooling was winning acceptance as a necessary condition for the rights of citizenship, the provision of care for young children remained mired in its association with social welfare (Michel, 1999).

Child Care in Times of National Emergency

Child care in the United States has never been seen as a basic service that government should help provide, except as a temporary response to families in need of aid or during times of national political or economic crisis. During the Depression in the 1930s, federal child care centers, called Emergency Nursery Schools, were established to provide relief work for teachers, custodians, cooks, nurses, and others who needed employment. These programs were terminated as the Depression ended.

Again, during World War II, the U.S. government became involved in the business of sponsoring child care. This time, the purpose was to meet the needs of the large numbers of women employed in defense plants. Under the Lanham Act (1942–1946), federally funded child care centers served children in 41 states.

Employer-sponsored child care, which was common in Europe, also emerged as part of the response to the demand for female workers during the war. Most notable were the two child care centers run from 1943 to 1945 by Kaiser shipyards in Portland, Oregon. The Kaiser centers were outstanding for their comprehensive, high-quality services made available to employees with children aged 18 months to 6 years.

The Kaiser company made a commitment to providing the best services possible to children and families. They hired **Lois Meek Stolz**, an early childhood expert who had been director of the Child Development Institute at Columbia University and professor of psychology at Stanford University, as director. **James L. Hymes Jr.**, graduate of the Child Development Institute and highly respected early childhood educator, was manager of the programs. Teachers trained in early childhood education were hired, and the centers were especially designed by an architect to serve young children. The centers functioned 24 hours a day, all year long (except Christmas). They included an infirmary, provided hot meals for mothers to take home when they picked up their children, and offered other services that helped families combine work in the defense industry with caring for their children. During the short time they were in operation, the Kaiser centers served almost 4,000 children (Hymes, 1996). The centers were closed down after the war when women workers were no longer needed, but their legacy remains and reminds us that we as a nation can provide high-quality, comprehensive programs for children and families if we choose to do so.

Government- and industry-sponsored child care were temporary measures, intended only to support the war effort. They were largely phased out as peace brought a return to the image of the "traditional family" with mothers in the home, tending to their children. Of course, many mothers did not return home, but continued their employment. As child care facilities either closed or were reduced to prewar levels, these employed mothers had limited options for child care. A patchwork of private arrangements was the common solution. The California Children's Centers were among the few survivors of the Lanham Act provisions and were eventually merged into California's child care system.

Child Care After World War II

The postwar view that a woman's appropriate role was homemaker, combined with the belief that children of employed mothers suffered from a lack of maternal care, gave strength to the contention that child care was at best unnecessary and at worst harmful to children. Between 1950 and 1965, it received little attention or support. Meanwhile, family life in America started to undergo major changes. The extended family system began to disintegrate as family mobility increased and the divorce rate soared. More and more women entered the workforce either out of financial necessity or because of a desire to find meaningful work outside the home. Single parents, if employed, could no longer assume complete responsibility for their young children, but had to share this responsibility with other caregivers, usually nonrelatives.

The Evolution of Child Care

Today's child care programs grow out of the historical streams we have just discussed: the nursery school, which focused on the health and development of the child, and the day nursery, which served families by providing care for children while family members were at work. Today we join the terms *education* and *care* to define the early childhood field. This terminology indicates ongoing efforts to bring these two strands together into a coherent system that will meet the needs of young children and their families.

Head Start

A significant landmark in the history of early childhood education in the United States was the creation of the Head Start program. Head Start is a comprehensive child development program that provides education and support services for eligible children from low-income families. In order to address all aspects of development, Head Start includes an educational program, support for social-emotional development, physical and mental health services, and a nutrition component. It also emphasizes strengthening the family and involving the community.

The History of Head Start

In January of 1964, President Lyndon B. Johnson declared a "War on Poverty." Born of the civil-rights movement, the *War on Poverty* reflected the idea that government should help disadvantaged groups to compensate for inequality in social or economic conditions. It included a basic belief in education as a solution to poverty. In January of 1965, a committee of specialists in all fields involving children was brought together to design a program to assist children to overcome setbacks or obstacles caused by poverty. The name of this program was Head Start. In the summer of 1965 Head Start ran as an eight-week part-day summer program in low-income communities for 560,000 4- and 5-year-olds. Head Start was soon expanded to a full-year program when it became obvious that one summer was not enough time to achieve its goals.

The Head Start program represented a new view of child development as a valuable end in itself and an unprecedented mobilization of resources on behalf of children. It provided preschool children of low-income families with a comprehensive program to meet their emotional, social, health, nutritional, and psychological needs. And it represented a new philosophy that low-income people should help plan and run their own programs.

Head Start grew and changed with time. Soon after it started, Head Start programs for Native American and migrant farm workers were added. In the 1990s it was expanded from part-day to full-day in response to provisions of national welfare reform that required parents who were receiving welfare assistance to pursue job training and employment opportunities. In 1994 in recognition of research demonstrating the importance of development from birth to age 3, *Early Head Start* was established to serve low-income pregnant women and families with infants and toddlers.

The Impact of Head Start

Since the 1960s the millions of children who have attended Head Start have benefited from its high-quality, comprehensive program. Head Start has demonstrated the effectiveness of providing a wide range of services and has provided a model for other programs. Many of the practices today associated with high-quality programs including nutritious meals and family involvement are outgrowths of the Head Start Program. And much as the word *kindergarten* became the generic term for early childhood programs in much of the world, so too *Head Start* has become synonymous with preschool programs for low-income children in many places.

Head Start can be viewed as a 20th-century expression of many of the themes that have characterized the history of the field of early childhood education in the past: attention to children's health, involvement of families in the education of their children, curriculum that addresses all areas of development, and, especially, early childhood education as a way to improve society by ameliorating the effects of poverty on young children.

You are entering a field with a long history and a tradition of concern for the needs of children and their families. The pioneers in the field were often ahead of their time in their recognition that education had to address the "whole child," not just the child's intellect, and in their treatment of children in ways that were respectful and based on knowledge of child development. Some of the distinctions you will find between early childhood education and other levels of education result from the fact that significant contributions to the field came from diverse disciplines like medicine, health, and philosophy. Many of the innovators described here recognized the important role of play in learning. They also advocated for universal education, recognizing that the education of young children was a valuable strategy for overcoming the effects of an impoverished background. They were concerned with improving society and saw that the creation of a caring and humane world must begin with the children. These values of respect for children and their development and the vision of a better, more humane world have been at the center of early childhood education and care since its beginning and are still embraced by many in the field today. The programs for young children that we described in this chapter are part of this legacy.

Over the years slow progress has resulted in more humane and egalitarian treatment of young children. We have become more aware of children's needs and the importance of meeting them in their early years; we have learned more about how children grow and learn and how to provide educational experiences based on this knowledge; and we have learned more about the kind of support that families need in order to do the important work of giving their children a good beginning in life.

Learning Outcomes

When you read this chapter, and then thoughtfully complete selected assignments from the "To Learn More" section and prepare items from the "For Your Portfolio" section, you will be demonstrating progress in meeting **NAEYC Standard 6: Becoming a Professional** (NAEYC, 2009).

Key elements:

6a: Identifying and involving oneself with the early childhood field

6c: Engaging in continuous, collaborative learning to inform practice

To Learn More

Explore an Educational Approach: **Read more about one of the educational approaches described in this chapter. If possible visit a program that follows the approach. Reflect and write about what you see as the major features of the program and its benefits to children. Include your thoughts and reactions to what you experienced and learned and the implications for you as an early childhood educator.**

Research a Historical Figure: **Research one of the historical figures mentioned in this chapter. Write a paper explaining who the person was and how he or she influenced the field of early childhood education. Include your thoughts and reactions to what you learned and the implications for you as an early childhood educator.**

Research Early Childhood Education in a Non-European Society: **Research and write about the history**

of early childhood education in a Non-European cultural or ethnic group (African Americans, Native Americans, Asians, Hispanics, Native Hawaiians, or some other group). Include your thoughts and reactions to what you learned and the implications for you as an early childhood educator.

Research Early Care and Education in Another Country: Do some research on the history and characteristics of early childhood education in a country that is of interest to you. Include your thoughts and reactions to what you learned and the implications for you as an early childhood educator.

Read a Biography: Read a biography of one of the historical figures mentioned in this chapter. Write a review of the book that includes your thoughts about what you learned and implications for you as an early childhood educator.

Read a Book: Read a book about one of the three educational approaches discussed in this chapter. Write a review of the book that includes your thoughts and reactions to what you read and the implications for you as an early childhood educator.

Observe a Classroom: Visit one of the following:

- a nursery school or a kindergarten based on the principles of progressive education.
- a program that is based on one of the educational approaches described in this chapter (Waldorf, Montessori, Reggio Emilia, High/Scope, Developmental Interaction Approach).

Observe and describe classroom practices and analyze how what you observed reflects the history of early childhood education described in the chapter. Include your thoughts and reactions to what you learned and the implications for you as an early childhood educator.

Investigate Related Websites:

The Pedagogical Museum and Comenius Library: pmjak.cz:80/new/index.php

Froebel Foundation USA: froebelfoundation.org

Froebel Web: froebelweb.org

Rachel MacMillan Nursery School: rachelmcmillannursery.co.uk

John Dewey Society: doe.concordia.ca/jds

The Association for Experiential Education: aee.org

High/Scope Educational Research Foundation: highscope.org

Bank Street College of Education: bankstreet.edu/theory-practice

Why Waldorf Works (website of the Association of Waldorf Schools of North America): whywaldorfworks.org

American Montessori Society: amshq.org

Association Montessori Internationale: montessori-ami.org

North American Reggio Emilia Alliance (NAREA): reggioalliance.org

National Head Start Association: nhsa.org

 **For Your Portfolio**

Include one of the assignments in "To Learn More" that demonstrates your understanding of the history of early childhood education and care.

MyEducationLab

Go to Topics 1: History and 5: Program Models in the MyEducationLab (myeducationlab.com) for *Who Am I in the Lives of Children?* where you can:

- Find learning outcomes for History and Program Models along with the national standards that connect to these outcomes.
- Complete Assignments and Activities that can help you more deeply understand the chapter content.

- Apply your understanding of the important concepts identified in the chapter with the Building Teaching Skills and Dispositions learning units.
- Check your comprehension on the content covered in the chapter with the Study Plan. Here you will be able to take a chapter quiz, receive feedback on your answers, and then access Review, Practice, and Enrichment activities to enhance your understanding of chapter content.

In all the world there is no other child exactly like you.
In the millions of years that have passed, there has
never been a child like you.

PABLO CASALS

4

Child Development

Fascination with young children is a defining characteristic of early childhood educators. They are intrigued as they watch a toddler's intent expression as he plucks and examines grass, listen to preschoolers trying to decide who gets to be the dad in the dramatic play area, or observe the concentration of a 7-year-old as she carefully creates a clay sculpture. The joy you find in watching children as they grow and learn will make teaching not only your job but your calling; it is a part of the way you build your skills and hone your craft as a teacher.

You are becoming a specialist in understanding how young children grow and learn. You are learning about them today, and you will continue to learn about them throughout your career. Knowledge of child development in combination with your experiences in early childhood programs will give you a basis for understanding children and providing good experiences for them. As you work with children and their families, you will draw on this knowledge base as a foundation for professional decision making.

Because knowing about children's growth and development is an essential part of being a competent early childhood teacher, in most programs of study you will take one or more courses focused on the study of child development. This chapter is a review if you have completed such a course and a reference if you have not yet done so.

The Study of Child Development

People have studied children for centuries. A growing body of research on children's development conducted over the last 75 years has given educators insight into how children grow and learn and a greater understanding of the patterns

Reflect on your interest in child development

How did your interest in young children begin? What did you first notice about them? What interested you then? What intrigues you now about young children?

and sequences of children's development. It has taught us to see how all young children grow in ways that are similar to one another and how each individual is unique. It has encouraged us to identify the factors and circumstances that support children's growth as well as those that may impede it. Child development research has shown us the uniqueness of individual children and has encouraged us to examine the circumstances that influence each child's development.

Studying child development theory can be exciting! As you learn more you will see how children you know display characteristics and milestones related to what you have learned. You will find you are increasingly interested in observing children. Understanding theory will help you to understand and organize your observations of young children and help you to plan activities and experiences that will support their development.

A part of the study of child development is learning about the characteristics of children at different ages. This knowledge is one of the foundations of *developmentally appropriate practice* (DAP). As a teacher of young children, you will strive to make your practice (what you do) a good fit for the children you teach. When you know about milestones typical for particular stages of development, are attentive to children's individual characteristics, and know about their family and culture, you can thoughtfully develop learning experiences are meaningful, relevant, and respectful of children (Copple & Bredekamp, 2009).

Principles of Child Development

There are six underlying principles, or main beliefs, that serve as a framework for the contemporary study of child development.

The Child Develops as a Whole

In early childhood education we often refer to the development of the *whole child*. By this we mean that we consider all domains (or areas) of development as we look at how the child grows and learns.

> *Three-year-old Sterling is playing in the sand. As he digs and dumps, he demonstrates his **physical** ability. He cups his hand, stretches out his arm, scoops, and makes vrooming noises replicating the action of a backhoe. This shows his understanding of how things work and his **cognitive** skill. He engages **socially** as he calls to his friend and beckons him into the play. As Sterling plays, he reveals his **emotional** state—his eyes gleam with satisfaction and he uses his **language** skills to tell you, "I'm a backhoe man."*

Children use their bodies to move and their senses to explore the world (physical development). They acquire and order information and learn to reason and problem-solve (cognitive development). They learn to talk with others about what they are thinking, experiencing, perceiving, and doing (language development). They learn to relate to others and make moral decisions (social development). And they learn to trust, to recognize and express their feelings, and to accept themselves (emotional development). Early childhood educators recognize the importance of each of these areas of children's development and know that they are interconnected and influence one another. They believe that these areas cannot be addressed separately and that no single area is more important than another.

Development Follows Predictable Patterns

Children acquire skills and achieve milestones in a predictable sequence.

> *For the first time today Sidney, 32 months, picks up the scissors. He holds them awkwardly, struggles to open and close the blades and ineffectively cuts small*

snips in the paper, giving up after a few tries. Kim, his teacher, goes to the cupboard and gets out cotton balls and tongs. She invites Sidney to try to pick up the cotton with the tongs and he experiences much greater success than he did with the scissors. Over the next weeks Kim provides other tong activities and brings in a variety of sturdy paint sample cards that Sidney enthusiastically cuts. Sidney is not yet a master cutter, but each day he gains skill and confidence in using scissors.

Development is sequential and cumulative. For example, before children can learn to skip, they must have mastered the large-muscle coordination required to hop and run. New experiences that do not build from previous experiences can be meaningless or overwhelming to a child, while experiences that are not challenging or interesting may lead to boredom and restlessness. J. McVicker Hunt (1961) described the concept of an *optimal match* between a child's present level of understanding or skill and the acquisition of new knowledge or skill. New experiences need to provide just the right amount of novelty or challenge in order to engage the child.

You support and encourage children's development by planning experiences that provide challenge and by avoiding experiences that children find extremely frustrating (because they are too difficult) or boring (because they are too easy). Such planning requires that you make use of knowledge of the sequence of children's typical development.

Rates of Development Vary

A child's age in years and months (chronological age) and the child's stage of development are only approximately related. The direction and sequence of development are similar for every child, but each individual develops at his or her own rate.

Ella was born 2 weeks after Shane. Both children started at the community college child development center when they were 6 months old. Shane's teeth emerged 3 months before Ella's and he accomplished each milestone of physical development well ahead of Ella. Ella was a vocally responsive baby and by her first birthday had a vocabulary of about 25 words and syllables that she used skillfully in her interactions with people. Shane was cheerfully wordless until well into the middle of his second year. Now at 2½, both are healthy, verbal, active toddlers.

Each infant enters the world with a unique biological endowment, and because the interplay of physical and environmental forces is different for every person, no two children (even identical twins in the same family) are exactly alike.

What a child can do and understand today is the basis of future development. As you study development, you will gain knowledge of milestones (developmental achievements) that mark children's development. This understanding will help you to plan a program that takes into account the wide variety of abilities you are likely to encounter, even among children who are close to the same age. In order to have appropriate expectations, you need to observe and become acquainted with the competencies of each child in your group and add that information to what you know about child development in general.

Development Is Influenced by Maturation and Experience

Development results from changes in the child based on the interplay of maturation and experience.

Gabriella, 22 months old, is taking apart a knobbed puzzle of farm animals. She has been dumping the pieces out of puzzles for several weeks now, then

saying "Help!" to her caregiver, who patiently works with her to pick up the pieces and fit them back in the spaces. Day after day she repeats this activity. Today without assistance she manipulates each animal piece back in its space. "I did it!" she cheerfully announces.

Maturation is the unfolding of genetically determined potential that occurs as the child grows older. *Experience* is made up of a person's interactions with the environment, with people, and with things. During the early childhood years, children's bodies increase in size and mass, and the child gradually develops increasingly more complex responses and skills. Although it is not clear whether such development can be enhanced through special training, it can be delayed by factors such as poor nutrition, serious illness, and the lack of opportunities to explore the world.

Maturation and experience influence cognitive development. For example, infants lack the concept of *object permanence*—the awareness that even when an object is not in sight it still exists. As the child matures, this concept develops, but no amount of training seems to significantly accelerate its acquisition. However, a lack of experience with objects that can be seen, handled, and then removed may delay the development of this concept. Gabriella, in the preceding example, learned to do the puzzle both because she had many experiences with it and because she was physically and cognitively ready.

Early childhood educators understand that they must provide a safe, healthy, stimulating program and then trust the children to take what they need to grow and learn. Your increasing skills in observing children, coupled with your understanding of child development theory, will provide you with the knowledge base you will need to provide appropriate environments and experiences for the children you will teach.

Development Proceeds from Top Down and from Center Outward

Physical development proceeds from the top downward (the *cephalocaudal pattern*), seen most clearly in the development of the fetus. In the early stages of fetal development, the head is half of total body length, whereas at birth the head is one-quarter the body length. This same top-down pattern is seen in motor development. Infants develop control of their heads before sitting and walking.

Growth and motor control also proceed from center of the body and move outward toward the extremities (the *proximodistal pattern*). The large muscles closest to the center of the body grow and develop coordinated functions before the small muscles of the hands and fingers.

When Monica was 3 she loved to paint. Each time she went to the easel she covered her hands with paint and used them to swirl the colors around the paper. Now that Monica is 5 she draws detailed pictures of people, animals, houses, and objects using fine-tipped marking pens.

The proximodistal pattern is reflected in Monica's developing skills in painting and drawing. Younger children paint or draw using their whole arm in large circular motions. As they get older they are better able to control the brush or pen and use their wrists and fingers to make more precise movements.

As children mature and engage in motor activities, they become more capable of coordinating their movements. It is important to be aware of physical capabilities so that you provide children with the challenges that they need to grow but do not frustrate them by expecting them to perform tasks for which they are not ready.

Culture Affects Development

Leanne, a teacher in a program with a large Samoan population, brings out a long rope to mark off a playground area. Four-year-olds Mele, Sione, and Talisa pick it up and skillfully begin to jump rope. Leanne looks on in amazement and comments to Sione's father, who has just dropped him off, that she has never seen preschool children jump rope. Sione's father smiles proudly and tells her that he always knew that young children could jump rope but was amazed when Sione began to talk so much after being in school a few months. He tells her that he did not expect children to talk that much until about age 8.

CONNECTING WITH FAMILIES

Understanding Individual Development

Families want their children to do well! They want to know that their children are meeting developmental milestones in a timely fashion and accomplishing tasks at the same time as (or ahead of) other children of the same age. Family members may compare their child's progress to the achievements of others—siblings, cousins, or other children in the classroom or community. You can help families to have appropriate expectations for their children's development. Here are some strategies:

- Share information with families about children's successes and achievements. *"Connor was so excited this afternoon when he stacked 12 blocks into a tower."*

- Explain what is important about children's actions. *"Connor is showing rapidly increasing fine motor skills and eye hand coordination. These will be important later as he does more writing."*

- Document children's work for families through pictures and written observations. These help families to see children's progress. *Take a photograph of a Serena as she successfully climbs to the top of the climber and share it with her father at pick-up time.*

- Focus on the individual nature of development; remind families that when children are very focused on development in one area (such as climbing and or socializing) they may show less interest in another area (such as language or fine motor practice). *"Lisa Marie is so focused on learning to stand! She'll begin babbling again once she masters learning to walk."*

- Remind families that every child develops at an individual pace and that most differences do not mean that a child is delayed or won't be successful. *"Bryson may not be reading yet, but he's showing such an interest in stories. Children develop skill in reading over time and with many opportunities to learn about words."*

- Let families know that all children have important individual skills and strengths and help them celebrate their child's unique talents. *"Alex is so thoughtful of other children. He always seems to know when someone is upset and shows them kindness and concern."*

Reflect on optimal match in your own education

Think of a time when a teacher gave you an experience that was challenging and interesting for you. What made the experience an "optimal match" for you at that time? How was it different from other kinds of learning experiences?

Children's development is influenced by the culture in which they live and grow. Values and beliefs of each culture determine many of the experiences and opportunities that are provided for children. Developmental expectations also have a cultural component.

Applying Principles to Practice

Your understanding of developmental characteristics and principles will guide many of the choices that you make as a teacher. Perhaps most importantly, this knowledge provides a lens through which you view every experience you provide for children. You will choose materials and activities with knowledge of stages of development in order to provide challenges and experiences that enhance the growth and development of each child. Over time you will gain the ability to articulate your reasons for making each choice.

Foundations of Development

We know that the foundation for healthy development is laid down prenatally, before birth. Research has reinforced our understanding of the strong relationship between the health and well-being of the mother and other family members during pregnancy and the later development of the infant, child, and adult (Berk, 2008). We also know that when infants and young children have their basic needs met, when they are nurtured by the adults in their environment, and when they have adequate opportunity to explore the world, they are most likely to grow and develop optimally. Contemporary research confirms that brain development is enhanced when infants experience nurturing relationships and opportunities to interact with people and objects (Lurie-Hurvitz, 2009, cited in Woolfolk & Perry, 2012).

The history of thought about human development has been characterized by shifts in belief about the relative impact of biological (internal/inborn) factors versus environmental (external/experiential) forces on personality and behavior. Biological forces on development (sometimes referred to as *nature*) are genetic or inborn traits that influence growth and maturation. For example, a person's adult height is determined by his or her genetic inheritance. Environmental forces (referred to as *nurture*) have to do with the kinds of interactions and experiences that enhance or restrict the development of biological potential. For example, every child is born with the capacity to learn any language but will only learn those that he or she hears spoken.

Historically people engaged in heated debate (often called the *nature-nurture controversy*) over whether the biological endowment or the environment is the primary force in shaping human behavior. Today we know that both biology and environment have powerful influences on the development of each individual. The way that children interact with their environment and organize their understanding from these interactions is determined by their biological attributes, their current stage of development, and their past experiences and interactions.

The Biological Basis of Development

Jonah and Megan are twins born into a large and loving biracial family. Their grandparents, aunts, uncles, cousins, and friends all visit to see the babies, to see who they look like. Megan has her daddy's chin and her mommy's nose.

Jonah has his mommy's eyes and daddy's nose. But somehow both babies look uncannily like baby photos of their dad. During the first week home their mom reports that Megan is a calmer, "sunnier" baby, and Jonah is a fussier and more sensitive baby. Megan nurses easily, Jonah is harder to console.

Infants are born into the world with a complex combination of traits that derive from genetic inheritance. Each baby has some characteristics and needs that are universal and others that are unique.

Inherited Characteristics

No one questions that biological factors play an important role in development. The hereditary basis of development includes physical characteristics such as eye, hair, and skin color. Other characteristics—height, weight, predisposition to some diseases, and temperament—are significantly determined by individuals' inheritance, but can be influenced by environmental factors as well. Studies of identical twins reared separately who select similar careers and lifestyles raise intriguing questions about the impact of heredity (Santrock, 2009).

Although we do not know the extent to which genetics influence behavior and development, we do know that each young child comes with a unique genetic inheritance, and no two are alike. In developmentally appropriate early childhood programs, children are not expected to be the same. Differences are respected and valued. The teachers offer a variety of learning activities to address children's interests and learning preferences and adjustments are made constantly to meet individual needs. These programs welcome children with diverse characteristics and abilities. Adjustment to schedules, routines, and activities can allow typically developing children, those with disabilities, and those with special gifts and talents to grow and flourish in the same program.

Basic Needs

In their first weeks, Jonah's and Megan's lives consist of a host of needs expressed and met. They nurse, they sleep, they are held and rocked, and they are changed and bathed. Their mother nurses the babies, and her life is an almost constant pattern of feeding and caring for their needs. Their dad delights in caring for the babies. He holds, rocks, and sings to them, and he changes and bathes them.

An undeniable factor in development is physiological need. Every human being has basic needs for air, water, food, and shelter. If these needs go unmet, the individual will not survive.

An additional prerequisite for an infant's healthy development is warm physical contact with a caregiver (which we discuss in greater in greater detail on pages 110–111). Research motivated by the high mortality rates of unhandled research animals first established the significance of comforting tactile experiences in the early development of all species of mammals. A classic study conducted by Harry Harlow in the 1950s found that baby monkeys had a marked preference for contact with a terrycloth surrogate mother who provided contact comfort but no food over a wire mother who had the advantage of providing milk but little else to recommend her in the eyes of the baby monkeys (Santrock, 2009).

The first and most important task of any early childhood program is to ensure that children's basic needs are met. Though the emphasis varies depending on the age of the children, all early childhood educators understand and devote a considerable amount of attention and time to making sure that needs are addressed. Young children of any age thrive in programs that that provide safe environments, nutritious and regular meals, appropriate physical activity and rest, and warm physical contact.

Reflect on your own basic needs

Think about a time when you were unhappy and under stress and another time when you were especially happy and productive. How well were your basic needs being met during these times? What made it possible for you to be happy and productive? What do these conclusions suggest for your work with young children?

Temperament

By the time Megan and Jonah are 10 weeks old they are clearly different individuals. Megan sleeps, eats, and eliminates on a predictable schedule. She is soothed by being rocked in a baby swing outside in a tree. She stares contentedly at the patterns of a mobile and rests quietly inside when she can hear the sound of people's voices. Jonah's sleeping, eating, and elimination are much less regular than Megan's. He is calmed by a mechanical swing that does not vary in span or pace. He nurses and rests better if he is away from the sounds of people.

An aspect of development that has its basis in biology is called *temperament*. Temperament is "an observable, biologically based pattern of behavior and emotions, a characteristic way of experiencing and interacting with the world" (Kaiser & Rasminsky, 2012). Several researchers have constructed models of temperament. The most widely used, and the one we find most useful, was described by physicians Alexander Thomas and Stella Chess (1970, 1977, 1996) based on the New York Longitudinal Study. Thomas and Chess reported that babies are not all alike at birth (something that parents have always known) and that distinct and observable differences in temperament are evident among newborn infants in their first days and weeks of life. According to Thomas and Chess, babies can be seen to differ in nine personality characteristics, listed in Figure 4.1.

The individual differences tend to cluster together in three basic types of temperament in children, labeled by Thomas and Chess as follows:

- The *Easy Child* (about 40%) quickly establishes regular routines in infancy, is generally cheerful, and adapts easily.
- The *Difficult Child* (about 10%) has irregular daily routines, is slow to accept new experiences, and tends to react negatively and intensely.
- The *Slow-to-Warm Child* (about 15%) has a low activity level, has mild or low-key reactions to stimuli, is negative in mood, and adjusts slowly.

Another 35% of children did not match any of these clusters but seemed to have unique blends of temperamental traits. Megan, in the preceding examples, appears to fit the profile of an "easy" child, while Jonah has more of the characteristics of the "difficult" child.

FIGURE 4.1 Thomas and Chess's Temperament Dimensions

- **Activity level:** The proportion of inactive periods to active ones
- **Rhythmicity:** The regularity of cycles of hunger, excretion, sleep, and wakefulness
- **Distractibility:** The degree to which new stimulation alters behavior
- **Approach/withdrawal:** The response to a new object or person
- **Adaptability:** The ease with which a child adapts to the environment
- **Attention span and persistence:** The amount of time devoted to an activity and the effect of distraction
- **Intensity of reaction:** The energy of response regardless of its quality or direction
- **Threshold of responsiveness:** The intensity of stimulation required to evoke a response
- **Quality of mood:** The amount of friendly, pleasant, joyful behavior as contrasted with unpleasant, unfriendly behavior

Source: Information from L. E. Berk, *Child Development* (8th ed.), 2009.

Studies support the idea that temperament is genetic. For instance, one study found that Asian babies tend to be less active, irritable, and vocal, but more easily soothed and better able to quiet themselves than Caucasian infants of the same age (Kagan et al., 1994; Lewis, Ramsay, & Kawakami, 1993). Infant boys tend to be more active and less fearful than infant girls (Berk, 2008). This supports the idea that some temperamental traits are present from birth.

The *longitudinal* (long-term) nature of the Thomas-Chess research shows that the characteristics are moderately stable throughout childhood and later in life. However, contemporary research (Rothbart, Ahadi, & Evans, 2000) indicates that early behaviors tend to change somewhat over time and become established by age 2. This suggests the effect of the environment on children's temperamental dispositions. With repeated experiences, certain temperamental traits and patterns tend to become more stable.

We have found the concept of temperament valuable in helping us to understand the wide range of personalities in the young children we have taught. We have also found the idea of "goodness of fit" (Thomas & Chess, 1977) very useful when considering the impact of temperament. *Goodness of fit* refers to the interaction between children's characteristics and the expectations of the adults who live and work with them. Children experience "goodness of fit" when teachers are aware of and sensitive to their temperament, accept characteristic temperamental behaviors, and help them to adapt to their environment. Early childhood teachers who are respectful of temperamental difference will prepare routines and environments that support the needs of children with a range of characteristics. For example, teachers who recognize that some children have a very high activity level will arrange their schedules to ensure that these children have frequent opportunities for vigorous play, rather than expecting them to sit quietly for long periods of time.

Max was a "difficult" infant and young child. His high energy level and his intense personality were often challenging for family members and teachers. Max's parents were careful to ensure that he had many opportunities to use physical energy in acceptable ways. They worked closely with his preschool and elementary teachers to encourage them to simultaneously hold high expectations and provide avenues for success that fit well with Max's personality and learning style. Max, at 17 years of age, is a relaxed young man, enthusiastic about his upcoming choices for college and happy in his relationships with friends and family. His energy, drive, and enthusiasm are seen as assets.

In this example, Max's family and teachers saw his individual traits as strengths and made sure to provide him with acceptable ways to express them. Understanding temperament will allow you to provide programs that value and nurture children as individuals. You can respond flexibly to individual children and find ways to modify the environment and your own behavior to provide a good match for each child's temperament.

The Impact of Environment

Jonah and Megan's parents are able to give their babies attention, time, and a safe and healthy home. By the time the babies are 3 months old, Megan sleeps happily alone in the crib while Jonah sleeps better in the family bed. Both babies love to be sung to and read to. Their sensitive and attentive parents have modified their lives in response to their children's needs. In addition, mom's Asian culture encourages the perspective that the child is the center of the home.

Reflect on a child you know

Think about a child you know well. Can you characterize him or her as easy, difficult, or slow to warm? How well do this child's characteristics fit with the expectations of his or her parents or caregivers? How do you respond to the child's temperament? What could you do to support this child if you were his or her teacher or caregiver?

Each baby is born into a particular family, culture, and set of circumstances. Children are shaped by and will shape their environment in a reciprocal dance that begins the first day of life.

The Critical Nature of Nurturing Relationships

A prerequisite for healthy development is a warm, intimate, continuous relationship between a child and his or her primary caregivers. Care given in the context

of a loving relationship is essential to normal physical, cognitive, social, and emotional development and helps a child learn that the world is a safe and trustworthy place. A classic study of babies raised in an orphanage in Romania points to the vital importance of warm, nurturing relationships. While these children were fed, bathed, and changed regularly, they received limited interaction from adults and had few playthings or activities. Researchers found that development was significantly delayed in all areas (Dennis, 1973).

John Bowlby (1969) identified attachment to a primary caregiver (usually the mother) as foundational to healthy social and emotional development. He defined *attachment* as a close emotional bond between two people, and identified stages of infant attachment. Bowlby noted that infants are born with behaviors that engage adults and promote attached relationships. Crying, gazing, and smiling are all infant behaviors that tend to engage adults and help them form intense bonds with infants. Mary Ainsworth (1979) found that the degree of attachment between mothers and their children ranged from securely attached to not attached at all and that well attached infants were more likely than those with insecure attachments to explore independently and exhibit positive interaction patterns. More recent research indicates that secure attachment is strongly related to children's development in all domains and that mothers are not necessarily the only attachment figure. Fathers and other important adults provide important nurturance and securely attached infants may have strong multiple attachments rather than a single bond with only the mother.

A central conclusion from the landmark report *From Neurons to Neighborhoods* (Shonkoff & Phillips, 2000) is that human relationships are the "building blocks of healthy development." The authors highlight the significance of responsive adult-child interactions, noting that caring adults are critical for healthy development and that children's achievements occur in the context of close relationships with others.

While establishing positive relationships with children is pivotal for teaching young children of all ages, the significance of attachment is of particular concern to those who work with infants and toddlers. The work of Magda Gerber and the RIE (Resources for Infant Educators) Institute as well as Ronald Lally at the Center for Child and Family Studies, WestED/Far West Lab affirms the critical nature of attachment for infants and toddlers both at home and in out-of-home care settings. Responsive interactions experienced by well-attached children have been shown to foster the development of strong neural pathways in children's brains, as well as provide a foundation for all areas of development. Programs for very young children foster attachment when they use a *primary caregiving system*—a staffing plan where a very small group of infants and/or toddlers are assigned to one adult who handles the majority of their care. Primary caregivers are able to learn the particular needs and styles of each child. Children and caregivers form strong bonds and learn one another's ways of communicating. Primary care groups allow caregivers and children to develop warm relationships, the hallmark of quality care for young children. Some people worry that children in child care settings become overly attached to caregivers and that these relationships interfere with family-child bonds. However, studies indicate that out-of-home care in quality programs for infants does not undermine children's attachment to their parents and that a secure attachment to a teacher may enhance infant-parent bonds (McDevitt & Ormrod, 2010). In an ongoing longitudinal study of early child care and its effects on children's development researchers from the National Institute of Child Health and Human Development (NICHD, 2006), found that higher quality child care programs are positively related to better mother-child relationships.

The Importance of Early Experiences

Until the mid-1900s, the prevalent view of development was that people matured in predictable ways according to a biologically predetermined plan. In the classic work *Intelligence and Experience* (1961), J. McVicker Hunt countered that view and cited many studies demonstrating the powerful effects of early experience on children's development. In the last 60 years, research has validated these conclusions and demonstrated resoundingly that experiences in the first 5 or 6 years of life have a critical impact on all areas of children's subsequent development (Shonkoff & Phillips, 2000).

In particular, numerous studies have shown that in order for infants and young children to develop normally they need an environment that provides them with an appropriate amount of novelty and stimulation and includes opportunities for sensory exploration. Interactions with people and objects in the course of play—the important work of infancy and childhood—have positive effects on later development (Berk, 2008).

Critical and Sensitive Periods. Animals generally exhibit *critical periods,* times during which the normal development of an organ or structural system must take place. If development does not occur during a critical period, permanent damage may occur or growth may be retarded. For example, research with kittens and monkeys shows that if their eyes are covered or they are kept in darkness during the early months of life, normal vision will not develop later even when their eyes are uncovered or they are put into lighted environments. Human beings also have critical periods. For example, during prenatal development if the growing embryo or fetus is exposed to *teratogens*—environmental agents that cause prenatal damage—or maternal diseases during particular times of growth, serious physical and/or mental impairments are likely. Although critical periods in human beings are quite significant, there are relatively few of them. More prevalent, however, are *sensitive periods*, times during which the child is especially responsive to particular types of environmental influences and experiences. Sensitive periods that occur during the early years include a sensitive period for attachment (birth through age 3), brain development (birth through age 3) and language development (birth through age 5) (Berk, 2009; McDevitt & Ormrod, 2010; Shore, 1997).

Recent studies of human neurological development indicate that sensitive periods are "windows of opportunity," times when an individual can most easily learn a particular skill or mental function. For example, it is easiest for an individual to learn language during the first few years of life. It is possible to become fluent in languages learned later but will require more effort to master a language acquired after age 5 or 6. These "windows" are longer than originally thought.

McCall and Plemons (2001) suggest that even with long windows of opportunity, developmentally appropriate experiences should be available from the time the window opens, even if it may be years before the window closes.

Resiliency. Inner strength and the ability to handle difficult circumstances with competence is called *resiliency*. Children who are resilient are able to "bounce back" from adversity and handle challenging life situations with competence.

> *Maureen is the first child in a family of six siblings. Both her parents used alcohol and drugs from the time that she was very young and she assumed the role of caregiver for her younger siblings. She experienced regular episodes of parental anger and neglect. However, she was very close to her maternal grandparents, who visited her often and created special family events for her and for her siblings. As an adult, Maureen is a successful executive of a large corporation. She is well liked by employees, friends, and associates. She is a loving wife and enjoys a warm relationship with her two teenage children.*

Studies suggest that inadequate nurture and stimulation in the early years does not necessarily cause irreversible deficiencies later in life (Kagan, 1984). A longitudinal study of children from the Hawai'ian island of Kaua'i identified characteristics of children who are resilient in the face of adversity (Werner, Bierman, & French, 1971; Werner & Smith, 1992). Resilient children have a combination of inherited characteristics, such as a positive disposition, and significant environmental factors, the most important of which is a long-term, trusting relationship with a caring adult. In the preceding example, Maureen's relationship with her grandparents coupled with her inborn easy temperament contributed to her success both as a child and as an adult, despite many challenges. Although repeated experiences of extreme and early deprivation can cause serious damage to the developing child, studies suggest that human beings can be remarkably resilient, and that early deprivation does not necessarily result in lifelong problems.

The contemporary view is that the development of resilience is a dynamic process and that most children can learn to cope with some stress. Resilient children have a sense that they can control much of what happens to them and are willing to persist even when they encounter challenges. They are able to identify their strengths and use them to create positive outcomes. They usually display a sense of humor and playfulness (Breslin, 2005; Kersey & Malley, 2005). Resilient children are able to understand cause and effect and see the world as a positive place where events have reason and meaning. As a teacher you support resilience in young children when you form meaningful personal relationships with each child and help them to identify their strengths. You can then use your knowledge of children to create experiences that encourage the children in your care to believe they are competent people and that the world is an interesting place (Gonzalez-Mena & Eyer, 2009).

Brain Research and Its Implications for Early Childhood Programs

During the last two decades there has been a growing body of research on the development of the brain. Once it was assumed that the structure of the brain was genetically determined and fixed at birth. Today we know that only the brain's main circuits are determined at birth. The brain of a newborn is only 25% of its adult weight. At birth the baby's brain has all the neurons (brain cells) that it will ever have. It will not grow more cells; instead each neuron expands in size and develops more connections—called *synapses*—to other brain cells. Synaptic connections are what enable us to think and learn. The brain continues to grow and change significantly during the early years (and beyond) in response to experience.

Brain research has yielded a great deal of information about how young children grow and learn. Much of the information gathered from studies of the brain can be useful to you as you work with and plan for young children. Some of the points we have found most helpful follow.

- **The complex interaction between people's inborn biological traits (nature) and their experiences (nurture) profoundly affects all of human development, including brain development.** This interplay begins before birth and continues throughout life. It is most significant during childhood. According to Jack Shonkoff (2000), "it is the ongoing communion between our heredity and our experiences that shapes us" (in Galinsky, 2010). This complex interaction is especially important to brain development because as children interact with the people and objects in the environment, their brains create new synapses, thus becoming more dense and consequently better able to think and learn. The child reaches a maximal brain density at about 3 years of age. This density is maintained during the first decade of life, after which a "pruning" of excess synapses occurs. The brain keeps the connections that have a purpose—those that are being used—while eliminating those that are not in use. Pruning increases the efficiency with which the brain can do what it needs to do. In this way the brain actually "creates" itself based on the individual's experiences. Because the brain removes synapses that are not in use, an "over-pruning" of these connections can occur when a child is deprived of positive interactions with others and hands-on experiences in the early years (Hawley, 2000).

- **Early experiences have a decisive and long-lasting impact on the architecture of the brain, and directly affect the way the brain is wired, the ability to learn, and the capacity to regulate emotions** (Shore, 1997). The ways in which significant adults relate to children have a direct impact on the formation of neural pathways. In other words, a secure attachment to a nurturing, consistent caregiver who provides stimulating experiences has a protective function. It supports brain development and helps a child learn impulse control and ways to handle stress.

- **The whole-child approach to child development is supported by current brain research.** Brain imaging studies show that many areas of the brain are engaged when people complete specific tasks. For example, when children focus on cognitive tasks, the areas of the brain related to emotion are also activated (Galinsky, 2010). It is important that early childhood teachers are aware of this interplay between cognitive and emotional learning and understand how children's feelings are related to their cognitive skills and abilities.

- **Brain research helps us to understand the importance of the executive functions of the brain. Executive functions are a set of mental processes that help people connect past experience with present action.** Executive functions, located in the prefrontal cortex of the brain, are the neurological processes that allow people to successfully engage in a range of important activities such as planning, organizing, strategizing, paying attention to and remembering details, and managing time and space. They emerge during the preschool years and don't fully mature until early adulthood. Executive functions allow people to manage their attention, emotions, and behavior. They are not just intellectual skills but include interplay between social, emotional, and intellectual abilities. Executive functions allow people to manage their feelings and their behavior in order to

FIGURE 4.2   The Importance of Executive Functions of the Brain

Executive functions in the brain are what allow people to:

- Pay attention & focus on tasks
- Keep track of time and finish work on time
- Keep track of more than one thing at once
- Remember rules
- Inhibit a first response in order to meet a larger goal
- See another's point of view or perspective
- See connections between past events and new experiences; put ideas together in new ways
- Evaluate ideas and reflect on past work

Sources: Information from E. Galinsky, *Mind in the Making*, 2010; National Center for Learning Disabilities (NCLD), 2010.

meet goals. In *Mind in the Making: The Seven Essential Life Skills Every Child Needs,* Ellen Galinsky offers an extensive and readable review of the contemporary research about children's learning and brain development. Her work stresses the fact that studies consistently find that executive function is strongly related to children's abilities to be successful in an array of arenas including academics and relationships with others (2010). Figure 4.2, The Importance of Executive Functions of the Brain, lists some of the tasks and behaviors that executive function supports.

- **A growing body of research indicates that teachers and parents can offer children experiences that increase executive function, specifically skill in understanding perspectives of others, paying attention, critical thinking, and self-control.** Children who develop these skills during the preschool years and early in kindergarten have been shown to have stronger interpersonal skills as well as greater gains in literacy and math than children without these abilities (Galinsky, 2010).

- **At certain times during childhood, negative experiences or the absence of appropriate stimulation are more likely to have serious and sustained effects on development than at other times.** The developing brain is vulnerable. Trauma and neglect can lead to impairment of the brain's capacity. Excess cortisol, a hormone that increases when stress levels rise, can destroy brain cells and lessen brain density. Maternal depression, trauma, abuse, and/or prenatal exposure to substances such as cocaine, nicotine, and alcohol can all have harmful and long-lasting effects on brain development (Shore, 1997). Studies indicate that when children are in high-stress situations for a prolonged period they are less able to pay attention, to remember, and to have self-control (Galinsky, 2010).

- **Evidence amassed over the last two decades indicates that early intervention can promote healthy brain development, increase cognitive abilities, and lead to more positive academic outcomes.** Intensive, timely, and well-designed intervention can create significant and long-lasting improvement for children who are at risk of impairment.

For example, the University of North Carolina's "Abecedarian Project," a longitudinal study, soundly demonstrated the positive effects of early intervention on children whose mothers had low income and low education levels. Children who received an intensive 5-year program of full-day, full-year child care and whose families participated in parent involvement activities beginning in the first few months after the child's birth had dramatically higher IQs than those in a control group who received only free formula and diapers. The children receiving

FIGURE 4.3   Implications of Brain Research for Early Childhood Practice

1. Provide safe, healthy, stimulating environments and good nutrition to children.
2. Develop warm and caring relationships with children and support strong attachment between children and their families.
3. Ensure that each small group of infants or young toddlers has a consistent primary caregiver.
4. Engage in frequent and warm verbal interaction with young children and read to them often.
5. Adopt a whole-child approach; focus on children's experiences and learning of physical, social, emotional, communication, and cognitive skills.
6. Design activities, environments, and routines to allow children of diverse abilities, backgrounds, interests, and temperaments to experience consistent acceptance and success.
7. Encourage exploration and play.
8. Involve families in the program in meaningful ways.
9. Limit television exposure (even "educational" TV) and encourage families to do the same.
10. Identify children who may have developmental delays or special needs; assist families in locating resources for support and early intervention.

the intervention demonstrated significantly better school achievement through elementary and high school. Clearly, this intensive early intervention had a long-lasting impact on these children's lives (Ramey, Campbell, & Blair, 1998). Several other longitudinal studies, including the recent Chicago Longitudinal Study of the Chicago Child-Parent Centers have demonstrated similar positive outcomes for children who are enrolled in high-quality early care and education programs (Reynolds & Ou, 2011).

Increased interest in the implications of brain development research has encouraged additional study and review by neuroscientists, psychologists, and linguists. Some researchers suggest that the information about brain development has been overapplied to policy decisions that affect funding for children's programs (Bruer & Greenough, 2001). While there is debate as to the particulars of how the brain builds and destroys synapses as a result of experience, "a large body of research over five decades shows that education enrichment for children and family in the early years of life promotes healthy development in many domains from school entry to adulthood" (Reynolds & Ou, 2011) (see Figure 4.3, Implications of Brain Research for Early Childhood Practice).

Theories of Development

Child development researchers and scholars have developed *theories*—a group of related ideas or principles that describe and explain how children grow and learn. Theories show us the relationship between facts (what has been empirically observed) and a thoughtful interpretation of what these facts might mean. Theories help us to understand the past and predict the future. Theories of child development offer frameworks for understanding children's growth and learning.

As you study theories of development, it is helpful to remember that theorists' research and conclusions were influenced by their own circumstances, including when and where they lived, their culture, and their values. As a student, you will study child development theories. You should reflect on them seriously, think about how they do and do not support your existing beliefs about children and families, and consider whether they are consistent with what you have observed.

As you learn and reflect, you may find your philosophy of education and teaching, as well as your practice, changing in response to the insights you have gained.

Arnold Gesell and Maturational Theory

Arnold Gesell (1896–1961) and his associates, Frances L. Ilg and Louise B. Ames, pioneered the scientific study of child development in the 1930s. By gathering information on dozens of children at each age level, they identified growth and behavioral characteristics (developmental norms) of children from birth through adolescence. The resulting guidelines for what can be expected of children at various ages and stages of development serve as the basis for many developmental charts (like the ones included in this chapter) and screening instruments that are in use today (Gesell, 1940; Gesell & Ilg, 1974).

Gesell claimed that genetic inheritance and maturation determined a major portion of an individual's development. This view, sometimes known as *maturational theory,* postulates that genetic differences determine the rate at which children attain the growth and maturation necessary for learning skills and concepts. Progress cannot be made until the prerequisite growth and maturation have occurred, and attempts to hasten development are futile. Those who embrace this theory also maintain that environmental factors can influence development positively or negatively. They suggest that children need protection from disease, injury, and environmental hazards with day-to-day care supplemented by periodic medical examinations to ensure that health is good and growth patterns are normal.

Gesell's work led to the concept of *readiness,* a period of development in which a specific skill or response is most likely to occur. The notion of readiness

is one that influences our thinking in many areas of children's growth and learning. Decisions about when children should be expected to learn to use the toilet, read, or drive an automobile are influenced by our understanding of and beliefs about readiness.

Critics of maturational theory have challenged Gesell's methods of data collection and have suggested that the small size and limited diversity of the population studied restricts the applicability of the conclusions. Other reviews have cautioned that the maturationist approach can be taken to mean that environmental stimulation is not important.

Implications of Maturational Theory for Practice

Understanding that development follows a predictable sequence allows you to plan activities that encourage children to practice the skills they are building and to move on to the appropriate next steps when they are ready. Children grow and thrive in environments that invite the practice of emerging skills but avoid rushing or pushing children to reach new milestones before they have fully mastered prerequisite ones. One of the wonders of development is that when children engage in appropriate activity at any one stage, they are naturally building the skills needed to successfully enter the next. For example, the infant lying on her stomach, kicking vigorously, is strengthening the lower back muscles needed to begin to sit up.

Information about developmental norms can help you to determine whether children are developing according to schedule and offer guidelines for determining when you might be concerned with a child's overall progress or with a particular aspect of development. Developmental norms can guide your decisions about when children can realistically be expected to acquire abilities and to learn skills.

As a teacher of young children, it will be imperative that you apply developmental norms with sensitivity to the groups of children with whom you work. You will get to know the circumstances of the families of the children in your care. You will learn about the values that they hold for their children's achievements and you will understand how these influence the opportunities and experiences that they provide for their children's growth and development. Your thoughtful reflection on individuals will allow you to use information about developmental norms appropriately and effectively.

Jean Piaget and Constructivist Theory

The process by which the helpless newborn becomes a talkative, reasoning child is amazing, immensely complex, and not readily apparent. We cannot watch an idea grow or see thoughts develop. Understanding how children think and learn has been and continues to be a significant focus of study for child development theorists.

Tomas (age 2½) and Janae (age 4) sit down at the table. Their teacher gives them each a ball of play dough. Janae breaks up her dough into three small balls. Tomas looks over at Janae's dough and begins to wail, "I want plenty like Janae!"

Perhaps the best known cognitive theorist is Jean Piaget (1896–1980). Piaget was originally trained as a psychologist who specialized in understanding the nature of knowledge (epistemology). Piaget's interest in children began when he worked at the Binet Laboratory, studying intelligence testing. As part of this work, Piaget noticed and became intrigued with the consistency of children's incorrect answers to certain questions. This led him to focus his research on understanding how children think. From careful study of his own three children he came to the significant conclusion that children actually think in ways that are substantially different from adults (Piaget, 1966). Earlier theorists had focused on opposing beliefs that knowledge is either *intrinsic* (coming from inside the child—nature) or *extrinsic* (coming from the external environment—nurture). Piaget thought that neither of these positions explained how children actually think and learn, but instead that the interaction of the child's physical and genetic abilities (brain growth, reflexes, motor skills) and the child's experiences (people and objects in the environment) created knowledge and understanding. Piaget's theory is based on his conclusion that children create or *construct* their own understanding of the world. They do this through their interactions with people and objects. As they grow and develop, they continue to revise and expand their understanding. Because of this core tenet, Piaget's theory is referred to as *constructivist theory*.

Piaget believed that children can create understanding only when they are actively engaged in interacting with people and objects. Constructivist theory supports a hands-on, interactive approach to teaching as opposed to instruction that focuses on telling or showing. Piaget believed that understanding must be discovered and constructed by the activity of the child rather than through

Reflect on symbolic play

Think about a time when you have observed children engaged in pretend play. How were they learning to use symbols? How did this play help them to explore their understanding of how the world works?

passive observation. His position supports the importance of play as the most relevant way for children to learn. Through play, children encounter a variety of opportunities to interact with their environment and create logical understanding of how the world works. As they engage in pretend play, children are beginning to use symbols—the block represents a telephone; the play dough a pizza. These playful experiences allow the child to build the knowledge base needed for later academic success.

Kinds of Knowledge

Piaget postulated that children acquire three kinds of knowledge as they grow: physical, social, and logico-mathematical.

Physical knowledge, the knowledge of external reality, is gained from acting on the physical world. For example, by holding and playing with a ball, children experience and learn about its properties—texture, shape, weight, squishiness, and tendency to roll away and bounce.

Social knowledge is learned from others. It includes language, rules, symbols, values, ideas about right and wrong, rituals, and myths. It is learned by observation, through being told, and for older children and adults by reading. For example, children learn that balls are used to play games, that certain kinds of balls are used for certain games, and particular types of balls have particular names.

Logico-mathematical knowledge is the understanding of logical relationships constructed as children observe, compare, and reason. When children categorize and order, and observe the relationships between things, they are developing logico-mathematical knowledge. For example, children will observe the relationship between a tennis ball and a playground ball (similar shapes, roll, and bounce, but different size, color, texture, and weight). Through the experience of many balls, a child develops the idea of *ball* as a single category based on shared characteristics. Logico-mathematical knowledge requires direct experience but is based on the internal process of reflecting on what is experienced.

Processes for Construction of Knowledge and Understanding

Piaget theorized that as children interact with the environment, they develop organized ways of making sense of experiences. Piaget referred to these organizing structures as *schemata* (sometimes called *schema* or *schemes*). Early schemata become the basis for more complex future mental frameworks. Infants use mostly behavioral or physical schemes such as sucking, looking, grasping, and shaking. Older children move from physical or action-based schemes to the development of mental schemes that allow representational thought and the ability to solve problems. Piaget identified two processes—*assimilation* and *accommodation*—that children use to organize their experience into structures for thinking and problem solving. These processes are summarized in Table 4.1.

Piagetian Stages of Cognitive Development

Piaget proposed that children progress through a series of developmental stages that build from the interaction among three elements: existing mental structures, maturation, and experience. Stages occur in the same predictable sequence for everyone, although the exact age at which a child enters the next stage varies with the individual and the culture. The characteristics of the stages are summarized in Table 4.2.

Most children in early childhood education and care programs will be in the *sensorimotor* and the *preoperational* stages of cognitive development. During the sensorimotor period, children create understanding when they touch, taste, see, hear, and feel the many objects and people in their environment. They use their

TABLE 4.1   Piaget's Model of Cognitive Change

Child's Experience	Cognitive Process/ Adapation	Child's State of Cognition
Child has many experiences with dogs.	Child creates a mental schema, a "dog scheme" that includes the information that dogs walk on 4 legs.	Equilibrium: *Definition: A balanced and comfortable state.*
Child sees a sheep for the first time and calls it "dog."	Assimilates: *Definition: Includes new information into existing schemes or behavior pattern, but does not change the existing mental structures or patterns.* Child includes the goat into her existing "dog scheme."	Equilibrium: Child has successfully adapted to the new information by including it into an existing mental structure.
Child notices that sheep have different characteristics from dogs. She has experiences with other 4-legged creatures.		Disequilibrium: *Definition: A state of imbalance where new information does not fit into existing mental structures.*
She calls sheep "maa."	Accommodates: *Definition: Creates a new scheme, or rearranges one or more existing ones, so that new information will fit accurately into the mental structures.* Child makes a new mental structure for these 4-legged animals that do not bark or wag their tails.	Equilibrium: By creating a new scheme, the child has successfully adapted her mental structures to new information.

emerging motor skills to manipulate objects and learn about their properties. At first their responses are mostly a result of reflex actions. Very quickly, however, they begin to pay attention to how their actions are associated with interesting events. The baby lying beneath a mobile notices movement and sound as she kicks the dangling objects above her. As understanding of cause and effect expands and motor control develops, babies actively seek to re-create interesting or pleasurable outcomes. Experience teaches them that even though people or objects are out of sight, they still exist (*object permanence*). As they enter the preoperational stage, children are beginning to use symbols (words) to represent experiences. According to Piaget they are still bound to their perceptions and are *egocentric*—able to see things only from their own viewpoint. The primary way they learn is through direct experiences that involve sensory exploration and manipulation. During this period children are likely to focus on only one characteristic of an object or experience at a time, so they are easily deceived by appearances. Tomas, in the example at the beginning of this section, did not

TABLE 4.2 Piaget's Stages of Cognitive Development

Stage	Developmental Hallmark	Characteristics of the Child
Sensorimotor stage (birth to 2)	*Object permanence*—understanding that objects exist even after they are out of sight	• Changes from a reflexive organism to one capable of thought and language • Has primarily motor behavior • Depends on physical manipulation to gain information about the world • Is not able to form mental images for events that cannot be heard, felt, seen, smelled, or tasted • Learns to differentiate self from others • Learns to seek stimulation • Begins to develop the concept of causality
Preoperational stage (between ages 2 and 7) **Preconceptual phase (between 2 and 4)** **Intuitive phase (between 4 and 7)**	*Conservation*—realization that the amount or quantity of a substance stays the same even when its shape or location changes	• Is *egocentric*—unable to take the viewpoint of others • Evolves from one who relies on actions for understanding to one who is able to think conceptually • Learns labels for experience • Develops the ability to substitute a symbol (word, gesture, or object) for an object or an event that is not present • Thinks based on the way things appear rather than on logical reasoning • Tends to classify by a single salient feature • Begins to develop moral feelings and moral reasoning
Concrete operations period (between ages 7 and 11)	*Transitive inference*—the ability to mentally arrange objects into a series	• Develops the ability to apply logical thought to concrete problems • Is developing more stable and reasonable formal thought processes • Still has to think things out in advance and try them out through direct manipulation
Formal operations period (between ages 11 and 15)	*Hypothetico-deductive reasoning*—the ability to systematically analyze and deduce outcomes based on a general theory	• Is able to apply logic to all classes of problems • Can weigh a situation mentally to deduce the relationships without having to try it out

have the ability to "conserve" so he was fooled by the appearance of the dough. One of our favorite stories that illustrates this concept concerns a child on his first plane ride who turned to his mother after the plane had completed its ascent and asked, "When do we start getting smaller?"

Jeremy, age 7, has gathered rocks and pebbles since he was a preschooler. During a family vacation to the mountains, he collected a number of different rocks, which he carefully wrapped and brought home with him. He added these to his other rocks and he now delights in sorting and arranging his growing collection. He has organized the rocks in increasingly complex ways: by color and hue, from smallest to largest, and by where he found them. With the help of his dad, Jeremy is using an elementary geology book and is beginning to categorize his rocks using some geological terms.

As children approach their seventh birthday, their thinking becomes more logical, flexible, and organized than it was during the preschool years. They are now able to mentally organize concepts and images. This allows them to solve more complex problems mentally without the need to physically manipulate objects. However, their understanding is still tied to concrete concepts, those they have experienced. Children in this cognitive stage, which Piaget referred to as *concrete operations,* are developing a more accurate understanding of space and they can order objects in a more complex manner than younger children.

Piaget was also concerned with how language influenced the development of thinking. He observed that preschool children's speech was more often egocentric (talking aloud to oneself) rather than socialized speech (dialogue with others). He suggested that egocentric speech is an accompaniment to activity that reflects thinking. That is, children become capable of acquiring and using language *only* as they develop concepts. Language is acquired in social contexts *after* concepts are in place. From this perspective, experience is essential and cognitive development creates language.

Piaget's Contributions to Understanding Social and Moral Development

Constructivist theory is also helpful in explaining how children construct understanding of the social world (Edwards, 1986). *Social cognition—* thoughts and understanding about social behaviors and relationships—develops during the early childhood years as children move from an egocentric perspective toward comprehension of the thoughts and feelings of others. They become capable of seeing the relationship between their own behavior and the responses of other people. They become capable of envisioning relationships as persisting over time.

Constructivist theory also contributes to our understanding of children's moral development, their development of a set of standards about what is right and wrong. Piaget (1965) proposed that children construct concepts about fairness and justice through their interactions with peers. He associated moral development with children's growing ability to interpret rules, and he described stages and a sequence of moral development.

> *Jerrick is the lunch helper. He is carefully carrying a pitcher of milk to the table. Another child runs up behind Jerrick and bumps him; the pitcher of milk spills. Taylor, another child in the group, observes the disaster and exclaims, "I'm gonna tell! Teacher, Jerrick spilled the milk."*

According to Piaget, children younger than 6 base their judgments about what constitutes naughty behavior on the amount of damage done and not on intention, because their focus is on concrete and observable outcomes. By middle childhood, children are able to take intentions into account when forming conclusions. According to Piaget, both the child's stage of cognitive development and previous social experiences contribute to moral development. His research demonstrated that children move from the view that rules are unchangeable and derived from higher authority to the more mature perspective that rules are made by people and can be changed. A number of other scholars have studied how children think about authority and fairness and how the development of morality can be supported by the adults in their lives (Damon, 1988; Edwards, 1986; Eisenberg, 1992; Lickona, Geis, & Kohlberg, 1976). See a discussion of Kohlberg's theory later in this chapter.

Implications of Constructivist Theory for Practice

Piaget's work has helped parents and professionals become aware that children's thinking is fundamentally different from that of adults and that it relies on experience. As children have direct, repeated sensory experiences they construct their understanding about the world. Constructivist theory has helped educators understand that children's cognitive development proceeds through stages, just as their physical development does. It is as foolish to attempt to rush a child into thinking like an adult as it would be to attempt to teach a crawling infant to high-jump. This understanding has helped educators refine the construct of *readiness*. Although cognitive development cannot be rushed, research suggests that it can be impaired. Children need intellectual stimulation to learn to think and reason (Healy, 1990).

Piaget's insistence that young children are always trying to construct a more coherent understanding of their world through their experience has led many educators to the belief that educational practices should allow ample opportunity for children to explore, experiment, and manipulate materials. Piaget was adamant that we cannot directly instruct children in the concepts that characterize the next developmental stage. These concepts are acquired as a result of a complex interaction between experience, maturation, and adult mediation.

As a teacher who has learned about constructivist theory, you will understand that you cannot pour knowledge into children. You will find that it is not effective to try to "cover" a concept in your teaching. Instead, you will select materials and experiences that encourage each child to build his or her own understanding of important ideas. Piaget stressed that children are naturally curious; when you offer children opportunities to solve problems and search for their own meanings, you support them in constructing knowledge.

Piaget's study of the development and structure of knowing and thinking created a new methodology for the study of cognitive development. His careful observations of the strategies that children use in their thinking and his description of the processes and stages of development have made an important contribution to our understanding of how young children learn and have generated much fruitful thought and research about cognitive development.

The interest and debate that Piaget's work has generated attests to its significance. His studies have been replicated in many settings and his work has been extensively critiqued. Later research has determined that some or all of the cognitive milestones he identified occur earlier than Piaget determined. Another criticism focuses on his idea of distinct stages of cognitive development, suggesting that stages are not distinct and that skills develop gradually with experience and familiarity with particular materials and content. Nonetheless, his work has significantly shaped contemporary understanding of human intelligence and learning (see Figure 4.4, Implications of Constructivist Theory for Practice).

Laurence Kohlberg and Moral Development Theory

Laurence Kohlberg's (1927–1987) work on moral reasoning elaborates and extends Piaget's theory of children's moral development (Kohlberg, 1984).

FIGURE 4.4   Implications of Constructivist Theory for Practice

1. Provide materials for sensory play and exploration.

2. Offer open-ended materials that can be organized and combined in many ways.

3. Develop a daily schedule with large blocks of time for children to play.

4. Ask questions and encourage children to solve their own problems.

5. Provide meaningful experiences and opportunities for study based on children's real-world experiences.

Kohlberg focused on how people make moral decisions across the life span. He describes three stages of moral development that relate to developing views of moral conventions—the rules about what is right and wrong. In this view, people move from stage to stage as a result of their own reasoning, which grows with experience. As they mature they are able to see contradictions in their own beliefs. Like Piaget's stages, Kohlberg's model is a hierarchy—that is, each person must pass through each stage in order, and each is dependent on the preceding one (see Figure 4.5, Kohlberg's Stages of Moral Development). Kohlberg's model assumes that people move from making decisions about behavior based on external controls (punishments or negative consequences) to choosing behavior based on internal standards and principles.

Carole Gilligan and others have been critical of Kohlberg's work because the subjects were primarily male and because research was based on hypothetical, not real-life, situations. Gilligan did follow up research that led her to conclude that males are more oriented toward fairness and justice in their moral decision-making, and females are more concerned with caring and responsibility (Gilligan, 1982). Further research offered compelling evidence that both males and females include a caring and a justice orientation in their moral decision-making (Smetana, Killen, & Turiel, 1991; Walker, 1995). Others have noted that Kohlberg's theory emphasized the Western value of individual rights, ignoring other cultures' focus on group values (Berk, 2009).

FIGURE 4.5   Kohlberg's Stages of Moral Development

Level One: *Preconventional morality* (characteristic of children from 2 to 7)—moral decisions are based on self-interest—on emotion and what the child likes. At this stage children have no personal commitment to rules that they perceive as external. They will do something because they want to, or not do it because they want to avoid being punished. By age 4 children begin to understand reciprocity—if I am nice to you, you might respond by being nice to me.

Level Two: *Conventional morality* (characteristic of children between 7 and 12)—people choose to conform to and uphold the rules and conventions of society because they exist. They are concerned with group approval and consensus. Action is guided by concern with the general good and a desire to maintain the social order by doing one's duty.

Level Three: *Postconventional morality* (adolescent and older, though not everyone reaches this stage)—people accept rules and laws that are agreed on in society and based on underlying moral principles. When the highest level is reached, individuals may make decisions based on conscience, which places universal morality above law or custom.

Source: Information from L. Kohlberg (ed.), *The Philosophy of Moral Development: Moral Stages and the Idea of Justice*, 1981.

Lev Vygotsky and Sociocultural Theory

Lev Semenovich Vygotsky (1896–1934) was a Russian psychologist whose work focused on the manner in which children develop thought and language. His *sociocultural theory* looks at the ways that children's development is influenced by their culture. A foundational tenet in this theory is that social and cognitive development are interactive and that language influences learning (Vygotsky, 1962).

> *Skye, age 3, is building with blocks. She builds a low building with a roof. Her teacher, Val, sits down next to her and also constructs a building with a roof. Then Val says, "I think I need more space in my house." Val puts a unit block at each corner and places a roofboard on top to create a second story. Skye looks on with great interest and tries to add a second story to her house using three units and a half-unit block for the corners. Her top floor collapses. Val says to her, "Help me find four that are just the same size for the next floor."*

Like Piaget, Vygotsky believed that children are active participants in their own learning and that they construct their knowledge and understanding. However, unlike Piaget, who believed that children's development is bound by their maturational stage, Vygotsky suggested that children's learning is shaped by their social experiences and by interactions with and expectations from peers, older children, and adults.

According to Vygotsky, *social context*—the circumstances of the family, the values of the school, the geographic location of the community—all influence both what children think about and the ways that their thinking is structured and focused (Bodrova & Leong, 2007). As examples, children who live in rural settings may learn to think about time based on crop cycles whereas those in urban settings may understand time based more on seasonal activity. Children raised in families where spoken language is valued as the primary way to communicate will understand and organize experiences and information differently from a child raised in a family where nonverbal communication is more customary.

In Vygotsky's view the development of language allows children to organize and integrate experiences and to develop concepts, making language central for thinking. Communication with others is vital because children develop language in relationships with more competent speakers (adults and older children). Whereas Piaget believed that cognitive development creates language, Vygotsky postulated that language is the means for developing thoughts and creating understanding. Like Piaget, Vygotsky observed the egocentric speech of childhood; however, he interpreted it as the *means* by which children develop concepts and plan actions. Most adults are aware of talking to themselves internally and may occasionally find themselves "thinking out loud," particularly when faced with a new or challenging task. For children, *private speech* is audible and gives them a tool for regulating their actions and their behaviors (Bodrova & Leong, 2007). As children get older, this audible speech diminishes and becomes internalized.

Vygotsky believed that every function in development occurs first at the social level and then at the individual level. Children develop through what he referred to as the *zone of proximal development,* the range of behaviors between what a child can accomplish independently and what the child can do with help. In *Thought and Language* Vygotsky wrote, "What the child can do in cooperation today he can do alone tomorrow" (1962). In this view adults support learning by providing a small amount of assistance, a *scaffold,* to allow children to successfully complete a task, as in the earlier example of Skye. As the child becomes more competent, less assistance is offered until the child can do it alone. For example, when children are first learning to ride a two-wheeled bicycle, they may use training wheels that are close to the ground. As skill and confidence increases, an adult may raise the wheels. After additional practice the wheels are removed and an adult holds the bike and runs as the child rides. Finally the child is able to balance and pedal independently.

Implications of Sociocultural Theory for Practice

Vygotsky's theory helps us understand that adults play a vitally important role in young children's learning and development because they are actually helping them to construct meaning. Through relevant conversation, adults help each child find a personal meaning in the activities offered. This theory, which is very influential today, makes us aware of the importance of the child's social context for learning. The family and culture of the child must be a welcome part of the program.

Vygotsky's concept of a zone of proximal development (ZPD) is immensely useful to early childhood educators. The practitioner who understands this concept knows how to support a child in a task, as illustrated in the example in the beginning of the section. Teachers apply this theory when they "take into account [children's] physical, emotional, social and cognitive development . . . and identify goals for children that are both challenging and achievable" (Copple & Bredekamp, 2006). This is a cornerstone of developmentally appropriate practice.

Vygotsky's belief that children's abilities should be analyzed both quantitatively and qualitatively supports careful observation of children as a valid assessment of their skills and abilities (Mooney). Teachers will identify children' skills, then guide their learning using a variety of techniques. They will also encourage cooperative learning by arranging activities where small groups of children with varying skills work and talk together to complete tasks (Berk, 2009). Time, materials, and support for fantasy and pretend play are also included in classrooms that embrace this theory.

Urie Bronfenbrenner and Ecological Theory

Urie Bronfenbrenner (1917–2005) was a psychologist and one of the founders of the Head Start program. His *ecological theory* describes systems of social and cultural contexts that influence development. Bronfenbrenner suggests that children's development can be understood only in the context of social, political, legal, and economic systems and that these are can be thought of as nested layers around the child. Each of these systems influences the other as well as the growing child (see Figure 4.6).

According to Bronfenbrenner's model, the *microsystem,* at the center of the figure, is where the child has the most interactions. This includes the family, school, and peers. These relationships influence the child and the child influences others in the

FIGURE 4.6   **Bronfenbrenner's Ecological Theory**

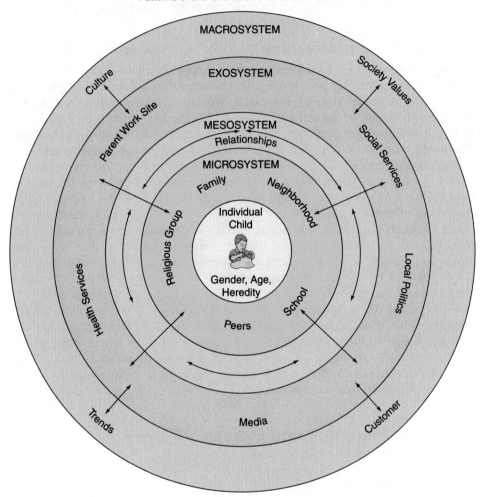

CHRONOSYSTEM
Patterns of Life Events and Circumstances

microsystem. The next layer, the *mesosystem,* involves the relationships between the microsystem and the broader environment, such as the family's relationships to the school or to children's peers. For example, a family's positive relationship with the child's school is likely to encourage academic success for children. Moving outward, the *exosystem* includes social settings that affect but do not directly include the child—for example, a parent's work place or agencies that provide services to the family. Conditions experienced by a parent at work such as a change from a day to an evening shift or a new and more demanding boss are likely to cause changes in the parent-child relationship at home. The next layer, the *macrosystem,* is the culture in which the child lives—the behavior patterns, beliefs and values, laws and customs that are transmitted from one culture to another. For example, the type of discipline that families use is influenced by the values and beliefs that are part of their culture. Finally, the *chronosystem* refers to timing of events and circumstances and how it affects individual development. For example, a young child will be influenced differently than an older one by the death of a parent or a divorce.

Implications of Ecological Systems Theory for Practice

Ecological systems theory reminds us that children can be understood only within the context of their relationships to family, peers, the community, their culture, the society, and the time in which they live. Understanding that changes in family circumstance affect the child and that a child's behavior and development also affects the family is helpful to teachers who want to support positive growth and learning. Ecological systems theory supports the practice of basing curriculum on significant aspects of the child's family, neighborhood, and culture.

Howard Gardner and Multiple Intelligences Theory

Howard Gardner's research in cognitive development and neuroscience led to the creation of a theory called *multiple intelligences theory*. This theory suggests that, instead of a single general intelligence, each person's intellectual capacity is actually made up of different faculties that can work individually or in concert with one another.

> *Phyllis drives into a town she visited once briefly several years ago. The gas is low and she remembers that a gas station is located on the corner a few blocks away. She navigates to it without a wrong turn. The week after she returns home, Ann, a creative and talented colleague who has lived in Phyllis's neighborhood all her life, agrees to pick her up on the way to a meeting. Ann is 20 minutes late. When she arrives she apologizes, "I stopped at the store, and I didn't know how to get to your house from there."*

FIGURE 4.7 **Gardner's Multiple Intelligences**

- **Musical intelligence:** The ability to produce and respond to music. It is seen in children who are especially sensitive to sound and who frequently play with instruments and music.

- **Bodily-kinesthetic intelligence:** The ability to use the body to solve problems (e.g., in playing a game or dancing). Children who have high bodily-kinesthetic intelligence demonstrate good coordination at a young age, demonstrate expressiveness with their bodies, and have a hard time sitting still.

- **Logical-mathematical intelligence:** The ability to understand the basic properties of numbers and principles of cause and effect. Children who love puzzles and show an early interest in numbers are demonstrating this intelligence.

- **Linguistic intelligence:** The ability to use language to express ideas and learn new words or other languages. Children who have strength in linguistic intelligence may play with and be capable with language from an early age, love reading and rhymes, be imaginative, and able to tell stories.

- **Spatial intelligence:** The ability to be able to form a mental image of spatial layouts. A young child with good spatial intelligence may be able to read maps and draw at a young age, construct imaginatively with blocks, and be sensitive to the physical arrangement of a room.

- **Interpersonal intelligence:** The ability to understand other people and work with them. A child who notices the relationships between others and demonstrates sociability and leadership is demonstrating interpersonal intelligence.

- **Intrapersonal intelligence:** The ability to understand things about oneself. A child with intrapersonal intelligence has strong interests and goals, knows him- or herself well, is focused inward, and demonstrates confidence.

- **Naturalist intelligence:** The most recently identified intelligence is the ability to recognize plants and animals in the environment. Children with this intelligence may want to collect animals and plants, long to be outdoors, and show a highly developed ability to discriminate between different animals and plants. They also have a highly developed ability to identify specific cars, planes, dinosaurs, and so forth.

Source: Information from H. Gardner, *Multiple Intelligences: Theory and Practice*, 1993.

**Reflect on
your areas of
intelligence**

Consider the eight
areas of intelligence
that Gardner describes.
Which are your areas of
strength? What areas
are most challenging
for you? What were
your best learning
experiences in school?
What were your worst?
How might knowledge
of multiple intelligences
theory influence how you
will teach?

Gardner has identified eight "intelligences" (Gardner, 1983, 1991, 1993) and believes that more will be identified in the future (see Figure 4.7). Ann and Phyllis in the preceding example vary in spatial intelligence.

Intelligence is culturally defined based on what is needed and valued within a society. Imagine for a moment how different cultures may view diverse types of intelligence. For example, people from ancient Polynesian cultures used the stars to navigate from place to place. They put a high value on spatial intelligence. Individuals from cultures that were dependent on hunting for food valued those who had the bodily-kinesthetic intelligence necessary to be successful hunters. People who possessed these needed abilities were valued and children were taught these skills. Euro-American societies have typically valued linguistic and logical-mathematical intelligences. American teachers have, to a great extent, taught for those who have language and math abilities.

Implications of Multiple Intelligences Theory for Practice

Multiple intelligences theory supports the viewpoint that individuals have unique talents that should be acknowledged and maximized. It also reinforces the view that we should plan a variety of ways for children to learn the same skills and concepts. It encourages schools and teachers to expand their definition of success to go beyond traditional academic outcomes. When we have identified children's strengths, then we can provide a number of effective ways to nurture their potential.

This theory has particularly important ramifications for the way learning is designed for children in elementary school and beyond. Educators who embrace the multiple intelligences constructs will ensure that children have learning opportunities that develop intelligence in all areas. Consideration of diverse intelligences could result in more attention to and funding for curriculum and programs that focus on the arts and physical education.

Erik Erikson and Psychosocial Theory

Primary among the contributors to our understanding of children's emotional development is psychoanalyst Erik Erikson (1902–1994), whose 1963 work *Childhood and Society* continues to influence educators today. Erikson's *psychosocial theory* describes eight stages of social and emotional development that cover the human life span. The first four are described in Figure 4.8. Erikson believed that basic attitudes are formed as individuals pass through these stages, and that serious problems at any stage will lead to difficulty in mastering the next stage. Each stage is characterized by a major task or challenge. In infancy, the major task is the development of basic trust; for the toddler, it is the development of autonomy; for the preschooler, the development of initiative; and for the school-age child, the development of industriousness (Erikson, 1963).

For each stage, Erikson described a continuum with the potential for healthy development at one end and the potential for development of negative and self-defeating attitudes at the other. He saw development as a product of the tension between the two extremes, with more positive than negative experiences necessary for healthy progress. He believed that strengths developed at one stage allowed individuals to move successfully to the next and that it is possible for individuals to return to earlier stages and revisit and resolve those conflicts.

Implications of Psychosocial Theory for Practice

Insights from psychosocial theory have important implications for early childhood educators. Because crucial aspects of development occur in the first 8 years, when

**Reflect on the role
of trust**

Can you recall
experiences from your
childhood that helped
you learn to trust or to
mistrust others? How do
you feel when you are
with people you trust?
What can you do when
you are with individuals
you trust that you cannot
do when you are with
those you do not trust?
What would your life be
like if you did not trust
people?

FIGURE 4.8   Erikson's Stages of Childhood Psychosocial Development

Trust vs. Mistrust (Infant): During the first stage of development infants learn, or fail to learn, that people can be depended on and that they can depend on themselves to elicit nurturing responses from others. Nurturing, responsive relationships in the first year of life are essential to the development of basic trust. Through the love, nurture, and acceptance received, the infant learns that the world is a good and safe place. Infants who do not receive such care may lose hope and the ability to trust themselves or others.

Autonomy vs. Shame and Doubt (Toddler): During the second stage of life, which begins at 12 to 15 months, children develop a basic sense of autonomy that can be defined as self-governance and independent action. Rapidly growing toddlers are learning to coordinate many new patterns of action and to assert themselves as human beings. Conflict during this period centers on toilet training and self-help skills. If parents and caregivers are accepting and easygoing and if they recognize the child's developing need to assert independence, the child will move successfully through this stage. If adults are harsh and punitive and if the child is punished for assertive behavior, then shame and doubt may become stronger forces in the child's life.

Initiative vs. Guilt (Preschooler): This period is one of interest, active exploration, and readiness for learning. Children need to express their natural curiosity and creativity during this stage through opportunities to act on the environment. If explorations are regarded as naughtiness and if parents or teachers are overly concerned with preventing children from getting dirty or destroying things, a sense of initiative may not be developed and guilt may be the more prevalent attitude.

Industry vs. Inferiority (School Age): During this period, children are ready for the challenge of new and exciting ideas and of constructing things. They need opportunities for physical, intellectual, and social accomplishment. They need many and varied interactions with materials. Success and a feeling of "I can do it!" result in a sense of competence. When children's attempts to master new skills and situations result in repeated failure, they may develop a sense of inferiority.

Source: Information from E. Erikson, *Childhood and Society* (rev. ed.), 1963.

a child is greatly dependent on adults, the relationships between children and significant adults in their lives are extremely important. Understanding that the young child is in the process of becoming a distinct individual can help you understand and support children's conflicting needs for connectedness and independence.

Many practices found in high-quality early childhood programs support children in moving successfully through Erikson's developmental tasks. Low ratios of children to adults and the designation of a primary caregiver in programs for infants and toddlers are important because contact with a limited number of warm, caring adults is a necessary condition for the development of the sense of **trust**. Infant caregivers who respond promptly and respectfully allow infants to develop a sense of safety needed to move to the next stage. Offering many opportunities for toddlers and young pre-school-age children to make choices about play activities, materials, playmates, and self-help routines encourages the development a sense of autonomy. Skilled toddler teachers accept the toddler's need to say no while maintaining clear and consistent limits. They encourage toddlers to demonstrate increasing **independence** and remain available to them for physical and emotional support. During the preschool and early elementary years, teachers must provide adequate time and resources to encourage children to explore, to plan, and to carry out play episodes so that the sense of **initiative** can develop. Initiative blossoms when children experience a curriculum that allows them to practice their emerging skills and provides them with tools and materials for success. And during the school-age years, providing opportunities for children to participate in many kinds of creative projects helps develop the sense of **industry**. Elementary teachers who deemphasize mistakes, focus on successes, and encourage children to try new things are fostering positive development in this stage of development.

As you develop skill in helping children to move through these developmental tasks, be aware that in many cultures, families place a high value on interdependence and support of the group. These families may not support developing autonomy and initiative in their young children and may prefer that you employ practices that focus on encouraging children to be supportive members of a group. Open and sensitive communication with families will help you to determine their preferences and to select practices that are congruent with families' culture and values.

Abraham Maslow and Self-Actualization Theory

Psychologist Abraham Maslow (1908–1970) developed a theory regarding the development of human motivation and potential. His *self-actualization theory* was based on the view that there is a hierarchy of basic needs (Maslow, 1968, 1970) (see Figure 4.9, Maslow's Hierarchy of Human Needs). At the base of the hierarchy are the physiological needs for air, water, food, and shelter. If these needs go unmet or are only partially met, individuals may not survive or may focus all of their energy in meeting these needs. When basic physical needs are satisfied, security becomes a more pressing issue. According to Maslow, the highest human need is for self-actualization. When people are free from threats in their environment, when they are surrounded by others who are caring and predictable, they feel secure and can achieve self actualization—the ability to focus on giving and receiving love, the pursuit of an understanding of the world, and self-knowledge. Maslow's model suggests that individuals who are self-actualized are able to

FIGURE 4.9   Maslow's Hierarchy of Human Needs

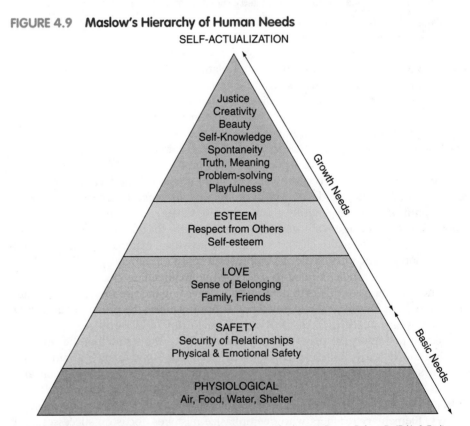

Source: Diagram based on *The Hierarchy of Needs* from Maslow, Abraham H. Frager, Robert D. (Ed.), & Fadiman, James (Ed.), *Motivation and Personality (3rd ed.),* 1987. Reprinted by permission of Pearson Education, Inc., Upper Saddle River, NJ.

perceive reality clearly, are open to new experiences, and can make choices that support the growth of their own potential. They have the ability to be spontaneous and creative and to form and maintain positive relationships with others.

Maslow's theory has been promoted as universally applicable. However, it rests on a Western philosophy of individualism. Cultures that take a more collective perspective would argue that the needs of the family or group should take precedence over those for individual potential and personal growth.

Implications of Self-Actualization Theory for Practice

Have you have ever tried to study for a test or learn a new task at a time when you were tired, not feeling well, or worried about an important relationship? If so, you are already aware of the applicability of Maslow's theory. Awareness of this theory will remind you to be attentive to children's need for regular and nutritious meals and snacks. It will lead you to pay careful attention to creating and maintaining an environment that is safe and healthy. In addition, it will help you understand that children who do not feel loved and accepted may have difficulties learning. When children are isolated you will take steps to help them experience social acceptance. You will foster children's feelings of self-esteem and approval from others by providing a variety of ways for them to achieve success. As you model curiosity, appreciation for aesthetics, and enthusiasm for learning, you support children's movements toward becoming self-actualized individuals.

Development of the Whole Child

Children at different ages have different characteristics. Studies of development, such as the ones done by Gesell and many others, have identified typical behaviors and characteristics of children at each age.

Periods of Development

We have found it most helpful in our work to think of four distinct periods of early childhood:

- *Infants* range in age from birth through approximately 12 months.
- *Toddlers* are 12 months through 36 months (1 to 3 years).
- *Preschoolers/kindergartners* range from 3 years to 6 years.
- *School-age children* are those whose ages are between 6 and 8.

Each of these stages of development has distinct milestones (important developmental events that herald the transition to a new stage). But it is important to remember that timetables for development are highly individual. Children will achieve developmental milestones based on their own internal genetic clocks as well as the opportunities they have for experience and practice. Children with disabilities may achieve some milestones simultaneously with their peers while acquiring others later.

Domains of Development

In order to clarify and define children's development it is useful to identify aspects or "domains" of development—physical, social/emotional, and cognitive (including language). These divisions are not universal—social and emotional development are often considered distinct; development of language is often

Reflect on developmental norms

What do you know from your family or from your memories about your own development? For example, when did you first walk? Talk? Ride a bike? Read? Was your development considered "typical" or "normal"? Did your development cause concern for your family? What might you imagine that families feel when they suspect their child's development is not proceeding "on schedule"?

separated from cognitive development; creative development is sometimes identified as a separate domain. Regardless of how they are categorized by educators and theorists, in a real child they are parts of a whole that interact with and influence one another.

> *Five-year-old Janine has experienced frequent middle ear infections, a physical condition that has limited her ability to hear since early infancy. Because of this, her speech and language development are not as advanced as those of many other 5-year-olds. She has fewer words than most and it is sometimes difficult to understand what she says. This has limited her play with other children, and her social skills are not as advanced as many of her peers. Her delayed language also means that sometimes she doesn't understand spoken information as quickly as other children do.*

In this example, the physical condition of the ear infections has influenced a number of domains of Janine's development.

The charts of developmental milestones on the following pages are meant to give you a "snapshot" of development during each period of early childhood. When you use them, keep in mind the principles of development discussed at the beginning of this chapter and recall that every child is different and that development is influenced by the unique circumstances of his or her life.

Understanding Infants' Development

During the first year of life, infants experience extremely rapid growth in all developmental domains. They move from being totally dependent at birth to being able to move independently, communicate, and engage in relationships with others. During their first 12 months of life, infants start to understand fundamental principles of cause and effect and ways to organize and make sense of the world around them. They transform from babies who are usually eager to please adults to young toddlers who are taking their first steps toward independence.

Infants' Physical Development

In the first year of life, children grow faster than they will at any other time of their lives. Their height increases by approximately 50%, their weight triples, and their brain size doubles (Berk, 2008). Several teeth emerge from their gums. They develop the ability to sit, crawl, stand, and perhaps take first steps.

Infants' Cognitive and Language Development

Infants explore the world using all of their senses and begin to organize these experiences into categories that have meaning. As they explore objects and people, they begin to identify characteristics and develop concepts—mental images that help them make sense of their experiences. Initially they gaze at caregivers, attending to facial expressions and speech. They play with sounds themselves and begin to engage in sound dialogue with trusted adults. By the end of the first year they understand many spoken words and may begin to name some familiar people and objects.

Infants' Social and Emotional Development

During the first year of life, infants develop attachments to important people in their lives. When their needs are met promptly, when they are nurtured, played with, and responded to, they develop a sense of trust, essential for healthy emotional and social development. From birth, babies carefully observe the actions of

TABLE 4.3 Milestones of Development for Infants

Age	Domain		
	Physical and Motor	**Cognitive and Language**	**Social and Emotional**
Birth–5 months	• Rapidly gains height and weight ***Large Motor*** • Lifts head • Sits with support • Rolls over ***Small Motor*** • Gazes at, then reaches for objects • Examines hands and fingers • Grasps objects • Transfers objects from hand to hand	• Gazes at faces and objects • Tries to repeat behaviors that cause interesting results (e.g., kicks at a mobile when it moves) • Indicates recognition of familiar people, places, and things • Cries, coos, and responds to human language • Babbles strings of consonants and vowels • Begins to imitate sounds	• Smiles; uses smile to respond and get responses • Copies adult expressions • Responds more actively to familiar people • Responds more to people than to objects • Begins to laugh • Cries when distressed • Begins to show emotions such as surprise, fear, and anger
6–12 months	***Large Motor*** • Sits unassisted • Crawls • Stands with assistance • Stands alone; cruises • Takes some steps ***Small Motor*** • Uses pincer grasp • Coordinates two hands	• Shows awareness of cause and effect by repeating actions to create an outcome • Imitates simple actions such as waving bye-bye • Demonstrates object permanence; searches for objects and people; protests when they disappear; removes a toy that has rolled behind something by removing the object • Understands familiar words; looks at objects when they are named • Responds appropriately to simple requests (e.g., "kiss mommy") • Speaks first words	• Engages in interactive games such as peek-a-boo • Demonstrates awareness of, then anxiety with, unfamiliar people • Shows awareness of caregivers' different moods • Demonstrates attachment to caregivers • Uses caregivers as "home base" to provide security • Shows anxiety when separated from familiar caregivers • Responds to other children; may touch them, verbalize, take or offer toys • Responds to others' distress

people around them. They begin to be aware of themselves as separate from others; they experience differences in their own emotions and they become sensitive to the feelings of others around them. Table 4.3 shows milestones of infant development.

Understanding Toddlers' Development

During the toddler years children explore and learn about the world with great eagerness and curiosity. During this brief period they acquire many skills, organize a great deal of information, and have a lot of energy! This constant on-the-go behavior and their need to demonstrate independence has resulted in the unfortunate label of "terrible twos." As you observe toddlers and come to appreciate how fast they are growing and learning, you may decide, as many toddler teachers have, that this name should be replaced with "terrific twos."

Toddlers' Physical Development

Although they are not growing as rapidly as they did as infants, toddlers experience significant height and weight gain and master many large motor skills. They progress from clumsy tottering to speedy running. It is easier for toddlers to start than to stop or turn, so they often bump into objects and people as they move. As toddlers gain control of the small muscles of their hands and fingers, they learn to feed themselves with skill. They become masterful at undressing, although they still struggle with putting on clothes and shoes. As their growth slows, so does their appetite, and during this stage they may become fussy about what they eat. By the end of the third year, most children have mastered using the toilet during the daytime, although accidents are still common. Because they are practicing so many new motor skills and learning about the world with their senses, they are "into everything." This means that caregivers must be particularly attentive to ensuring that environments are safe for active exploration.

Toddlers' Cognitive and Language Development

Like infants, toddlers are sensory learners. They learn about the world using all five senses. Their memory for objects and events increases dramatically. Younger toddlers enjoy imitating the actions of others and will hold a play phone to their ear and babble or pretend to drink coffee as they have seen adults do. As their memory and cognitive skills increase, they add their own ideas and plans to make-believe play events. For example, a toddler might use blocks as pretend food and invite an adult to taste the dinner. Their language skills expand rapidly as they engage with adults and with other children. Toddlers often use *overgeneralized speech*—the use of a single word for a variety of similar objects. For example, a toddler we know referred to the family cat as *mao* and overextended the word to label the neighbor's dog, a furry toy, and the lady across the street who had three cats.

Toddlers' Social and Emotional Development

The toddler years are a time of growing independence. As their physical and cognitive skills develop and mature, toddlers move from away from being acquiescent infants and begin exerting autonomy. Shouts of "No!" and "Me do it!" are familiar to adults who spend time with toddlers. Opportunities to make choices and time to complete tasks successfully are crucial for developing toddlers. They often feel frustrated because their emerging but still immature skills lead to situations where they cannot yet accomplish what they wish to do. Toddlers usually experience higher expectations and more limits from adults than they did as infants; this often results in feelings of frustration. Consequently, tantrums are common during these years as toddlers struggle to learn to control their bodies and emotions. Table 4.4 outlines milestones of toddler development.

TABLE 4.4 **Milestones of Development for Toddlers**

Age	Domain		
	Physical and Motor	**Cognitive and Language**	**Social and Emotional**
12–24 months	• Grows rapidly but slower than the first year ***Large Motor*** • Walks with increasing steadiness • Has a wide "tottering" stance • Climbs onto furniture • Squats to pick up objects • Begins to run with stiff gait • Walks up stairs with assistance, one step at a time • Uses riding toys by pushing feet on ground ***Small Motor*** • Picks up and drops small objects into containers • Scribbles • Turns pages in a book, 2–3 at a time • Feeds self with fingers or spoon • Stacks 2–3 small blocks	• Imitates simple adult behaviors when adult models • Uses sensory trial and error to solve problems • Points to objects in a storybook • Follows a one-step direction • Imitates behavior that has been seen in the past • Has 4–5 words at 15 months; 15–20 by 18 months; 200 by 24 months • Combines two words; simple sentences by 24 months • Uses words broadly (e.g., calls all beverages milk) • Fills in words in familiar stories	• Shows strong attachment to familiar caregivers and works to maintain physical closeness with them • Continues to use primary attachment figures as "home base" and is willing to venture further from them • Prefers to play alone (solitary play) • Begins to play beside others (parallel play) • Refers to self by name • Understands ownership of personal possessions, "mine" • May try to comfort someone in distress; hugs, pats, or brings a favorite toy to them
24–36 months	***Large Motor*** • Walks on tiptoe • Leans forward while running • Kicks large balls • Climbs • Throws a ball with two hands • Jumps in place • Begins to pedal a tricycle ***Small Motor*** • Hand preference is emerging but not stable • Stacks 6 or more blocks • Strings large beads • Uses a spoon and fork • Uses thumb and forefinger to draw with crayons or markers • Snips with scissors	• Identifies several objects in a single picture • Distinguishes one object from many • Begins to understand aspects of space and time (e.g., the park is near, Grandma's is far; we will go to the park tomorrow) • Overextends concepts such as calling all animals dogs • Begins to match objects by similar characteristics • Substitutes one object for another in make-believe play (e.g., uses a block for a telephone) • Uses telegraphic speech ("Daddy bye-bye") • Sings parts of familiar songs • Understands prepositions ("over, on, behind") and pronouns ("mine, his, yours") • Uses 3–5 word sentences • Uses question words ("who, what, why") • Begins to use past tense and plurals • Recognizes and repeats simple rhymes • Recognizes and names a few colors	• Enjoys playing alongside others; carefully observes other children • Engages in behaviors to elicit responses from others (e.g., runs from adults to engage them in chase games) • Insists on doing things independently • Identifies self as a boy or girl • Engages in simple role playing games (e.g., pretends to drive to the store) • Begins to show preference for certain children as friends

Understanding Preschoolers'/Kindergartners' Development

The increasing physical and cognitive skills of children aged 3 to 5 allow them to be more self-sufficient than toddlers. Their interest in peer relationships has expanded and they are starting to understand how the social world works. Preschoolers and kindergartners are unfailingly curious about both the physical and social world and may exhaust adults with their many questions. Their rapidly developing sense of humor makes interactions with them lively and fun.

Preschoolers'/Kindergartners' Physical Development

During the preschool/kindergarten years, children gain approximately 4 to 6 pounds and grow 2 to 3 inches each year. Their legs lengthen and their physical appearance becomes leaner and more adult-like. Preschoolers' brains continue to grow and will reach 90% of adult size by age 5. Most enjoy using their rapidly developing large-motor skills. Throwing, jumping, hopping, running, and skipping are favorite activities for most children of this age. Preschoolers are building dexterity in their hands and fingers so that by age 5 most use scissors and drawing materials with skill. At age 4 they typically start to write letters and numbers and include details in their drawing and painting. The many examples of children's art that you see in this book were created by 3-, 4-, and 5-year-olds. By age 5 most children have developed consistent hand preference called "hand dominance."

Preschoolers'/Kindergartners' Cognitive and Language Development

Preschoolers and kindergartners learn about the world directly through their experiences; they are often referred to as *concrete learners,* meaning that they need many real interactions with people and objects to develop knowledge. They understand only what they can see, hear, and experience (known as *perceptually bound thinking*); logic and abstract thought develop only after many hands-on experiences. The 3-year-old who insists that her friend has more spaghetti because she has spread her mound around her plate is demonstrating this perceptually bound thinking. Children organize their experiences by sorting and classifying objects, people, and events. As they near age 5, children can begin to sort and order using two or more characteristics.

Both their spoken (expressive) and understood (receptive) vocabularies are expanding rapidly and they use words both to give and to ask for information. They use many rules of grammar but may occasionally overextend these. The child who tells you she "sitted" or "runned" is demonstrating understanding of how past tense is applied. Because language is closely tied to culture, it is important to remember that children from families who place high value on nonverbal learning and communication may not demonstrate the same type or quantity of expressive language as children whose families use extensive spoken language. English language learners, children who are learning to speak English at the same time they learn another language, may appear less verbal than their monolingual peers as they are first learning English, but given opportunities to use both languages will show similar language development to children who are only learning to speak English (Tabors, 2008; Youngquist & Martinez-Griego, 2009).

Preschoolers'/Kindergartners' Social and Emotional Development

Children's sense of initiative grows during this period. They take great pleasure in creating and carrying out plans, particularly during fantasy play. Sensitive teachers make sure that children have ample time and assistance for planning things; they provide interesting and functional materials to support children's projects and make-believe play. Preschoolers are interested in friendships with other children, although their concrete thinking often creates challenges in these first friendships. For a young preschooler, a friend is the child who is playing with them now, offers a desired toy, or sits by them at lunch. Older preschoolers and kindergartners develop decided preferences for certain peers—and conflict over friendship is common during this period. Three- through 5-year-olds develop increasing awareness of the needs and feelings of other people and are able to engage in more empathetic behaviors and play more cooperatively. They are learning to regulate their behavior but still need adult support to help them to verbalize feelings and delay gratification. Table 4.5 summarizes the developmental milestones for this age group.

Understanding Young School-Age Children's Development

Children aged 6 to 8 are increasingly social and are rapidly developing logic and reasoning skills. This is the time in childhood when peers become much more important and children define themselves increasingly by how other children relate to them. Most young school-age children enjoy physical activity, and participation in organized sports and competitions becomes important to many. Their early experiences in formal school settings will frame their beliefs about who they are as learners. Wise teachers will search for ways to ensure that all children experience success in their early academic endeavors. This requires that you attend to their different learning styles and diverse strengths and interests.

Understanding School-Age Children's Physical Development

Healthy 6- to 8-year-olds grow 2 to 3 inches and gain approximately 5 pounds each year. Their legs are lengthening, giving them a somewhat "leggy" appearance. Their muscles are strengthening. Because their growing ligaments are not yet firmly attached to their bones, they are extremely flexible. They typically exhibit a strong need for physical activity and may find it difficult to sit for extended periods of time. In addition to increased large-muscle strength and skill, they are gaining increasing control of the muscles in hands and fingers. Their writing skill is growing, and their drawings and paintings include greater detail. This increased dexterity allows them to enjoy a wide range of crafts and construction projects.

Understanding School-Age Children's Cognitive and Language Development

School-age children are typically enthusiastic and eager to learn new things. Their increasing attention span and memory allows them to focus on more complex concepts than younger children. They are beginning to use logic and reasoning to solve problems and can understand more abstract ideas. However, they still need learning experiences that are related to what is familiar to them. They enjoy

TABLE 4.5 Milestones of Development for Preschoolers and Kindergartners (3–5 years)

Age	Domain		
	Physical and Motor	**Cognitive and Language**	**Social and Emotional**
3–4 years	• Growth slows; body elongates *Large Motor* • Walks swinging arms • Balances on one foot • Pedals and steers a tricycle • Gallops • Climbs quickly and smoothly with alternating steps • Throws a ball overhand with accuracy • Bounces and catches a ball *Fine Motor* • Dresses with occasional assistance • Uses scissors to cut • Copies vertical lines and circles • Draws simple picture of a person	• Organizes and groups objects by a single characteristic (e.g., color, size, shape) • Judges quantity by appearance • Develops one-to-one correspondence • Rote counts to 10 • Understands that numbers refer to a specific amount • Attention span lengthens; notices increasing detail • Carries out a three-step direction • Distinguishes between day and night • Enjoys and attends to books and stories • Uses self-talk • Has rapidly expanding vocabulary • Uses "s" for plurals, "ed" for past tense, sometimes overgeneralizes (e.g. "I putted on my shoes") • Uses 4–5 word sentences • Understands relational words ("on, in, under")	• Begins to share and take turns • Engages in some small group and cooperative play • Wants to please adults • Understands that others have thoughts, ideas, and memories • May assume that what they know and feel is the same as what others know and feel • Shows gender-stereotyped beliefs and actions • Often expresses strong feelings physically (e.g., hits when angry)
4–5 years	• Legs lengthen; body proportions become more adult-like *Large Motor* • Displays increased speed and agility in large-motor activity • Walks up and down stairs unassisted, alternating feet • Skips using alternating feet • Shows mature climbing and running patterns • Catches and throws balls using only hands and fingers • Dribbles and bounces balls	• Visualizes space from the perspective of others • Is increasingly able to create a plan and predict outcomes of actions • Begins to categorize objects based on function • Begins to sort objects by more than one attribute (e.g., color size, shape, weight) • Begins to develop understanding of difference between reality and fantasy • Understands time concepts of yesterday, today, and tomorrow; begins to use clocks and calendars • Rote counts to 20; can count groups of objects up to 10	• Begins to prefer same-age peers to adults • May have special or best friends • Is able to express strong feelings using words • Shows rapid mood shifts • Becomes aware of the effect of their actions on others • Is increasingly cooperative in play and actions • Obeys rules in order to avoid negative consequences
	Fine Motor • Cuts with scissors following a straight line • Copies a triangle and cross • Begins to show mature pencil grip • Demonstrates hand preference	• Knows that letters and numbers are different • Recalls some letter and number sequences • Recognizes several printed words • Tells familiar stories • Defines some words • Asks questions and wants answers that give useful information • Has growing vocabulary of approximately 10,000 words	

researching ideas and planning complex projects. They may collect such things as shells, rocks, beads, or sports-star cards, using their increasingly sophisticated classification and seriation skills as they sort and organize these collections. Their vocabulary is increasing at a faster rate than that of younger children and many average 20 new words a day (Berk, 2008). They learn that words often have several meanings and take great delight in puns, riddles, and jokes. They are increasingly able to communicate in writing, often using invented spelling as they begin to understand rules of phonics.

Understanding School-Age Children's Social and Emotional Development

The years from 6 to 8 are a time of significant growth in social skills and competence. Children who have well-developed social abilities tend to do better in school than those who are less socially adept (Lin, Lawrence, & Gorrell, 2003). Peers are of vital importance, and children begin to define themselves by the ways they believe that others see them. It is important that children feel included and have ways to make contributions to the group. This is of particular importance for children of differing abilities and those with special needs.

Young school-age children understand the concept of fairness: Everyone in the group should have the same resources and privileges. They begin to expand this concept to include the idea that those who work harder or show particular achievement

TABLE 4.6   Milestones of Development for School-Age Children (6–8 years)

Domain		
Physical and Motor	**Cognitive and Language**	**Social and Emotional**
• Exhibits steady height and weight gains • Has high energy; strong need for physical activity ***Large Motor*** • Demonstrates increasing strength, flexibility, and agility in large-motor control • Shows increased balance; rides a two-wheeled bike, walks a balance beam, skates • Enjoys active games and activities requiring physical skill • Engages in rough and tumble play • Coordinates many movements and engages with increasing skill in sports ***Fine Motor*** • Prints clearly; few reversals • Includes more detail in drawings • Begins to include some depth cues in drawings • Eye-hand coordination matures; cursive writing begins	• Uses symbols as tools for thinking and for literacy • Develops conservation of quantity (e.g., realizes that quantity remains the same even if form changes) • Demonstrates logical thinking • Enjoys collections and organizes, sorts, and categorizes items in increasingly complex ways • Reads with increasing skill • Learns beginning number concepts • Begins to read for information • Has rapidly expanding vocabulary • Begins to grasp multiple meanings for words; puns, riddles, jokes, and metaphors are enjoyed • Changes speech and language patterns to be appropriate for individual listeners • Enjoys telling and writing stories	• Becomes increasingly influenced by peer relationships; peer pressure and a need for belonging are common • Has a growing interest in fairness, equality, and justice • Begins to evaluate self by what others think • Also views self in terms of own abilities • Recognizes that people can experience more than one emotion at a time • Shows increasing awareness of the subtleties of behavior; understands that actions do not always indicate thoughts and feelings • Has beginning understanding of social concepts such as laws and justice • Continues to need adult approval but may resist accepting it

merit additional rewards. As they near the end of this period of childhood, they begin to understand social justice in a broader way and their social problem-solving skills expand. They may learn to value offering opportunities to those who are less advantaged or who have experienced losses or disabilities. Teachers of children in this age group can help them to understand and value *altruism*—unselfish concern for the welfare of others. School-age children can successfully plan and participate in community service projects and other activities that provide assistance to people in need—and they benefit when encouraged to do so. Table 4.6 summarizes school-age children's development.

Final Thoughts

Reflect on how you will apply child development knowledge

Think about a concept from one of the theories discussed in this chapter that helped you to understand something important about children. How will you use that knowledge in your work? How do you think that your knowledge of child development might influence what you do in the classroom?

Understanding the ways that children grow and learn contributes to your skills as an early childhood educator. As you move ahead in your professional development, there are two important things to keep in mind. First, the information about children that you acquire as a college student is just the beginning. You will continue to learn about children throughout your career. Child development knowledge, like the children themselves, is always growing and changing. New research is being conducted—old theories are being refined and new ones created. Be aware of, and keep an open mind about, new information. Sometimes you will discover information that is immensely helpful. At other times a popular new theory will simply be a discredited old idea in a new guise. We find that an inquiring but somewhat cautious approach serves teachers and children best.

Second, keep in mind that you are in the process of personal and professional development. As you study and as you work directly with young children, your understanding will grow. Your daily experiences and observations of children will combine with what you read to give you an ever deeper and richer understanding. Working with young children involves a constant and dynamic interplay of information that combines the work of others with insight you develop based on your own observations. Keep watching and listening to children and know that your understanding will continue to grow and that you can supplement the conclusions of the experts with the knowledge you are gaining from experience.

Learning Outcomes

When you read this chapter, and then thoughtfully complete selected assignments from the "To Learn More" section and prepare items from the "For Your Portfolio" section, you will be demonstrating progress in meeting **NAEYC Standard 1: Promoting Child Development and Learning** (NAEYC, 2009).

Key elements:

1a: Knowing and understanding young children's characteristics and needs

1b: Knowing and understanding the multiple influences on development and learning

1c: Using developmental knowledge to create healthy, respectful, supportive, and challenging learning environments

To Learn More

Observe a Young Child: Observe a child for 45 minutes to an hour. Write notes on what you see, and interpret and report on the child's behavior in terms of one or more of the theories of development presented in this chapter.

Observe a Second Child Who Is in a Different Period of Development: Observe for 45 minutes to an hour and write notes on what you see. Compare and contrast behaviors of this child with those of the child in the first observation and report on differences that you noted in each developmental domain.

Investigate Related Websites:

Information about autism: First Signs: firstsigns.org

Information for helping children and families overcome adversities: ResilienceNet: resilnet.uiuc.edu

Society for Research in Child Development: srcd.org

National Child Care Information and Technical Assistance Center: nccic.acf.hhs.gov

National Center for Infants, Toddlers, and Families: Zero to Three: zerotothree.org

For Your Portfolio

Create an Activity Plan for Different Ages: Plan and implement an activity for a preschooler. Indicate how you would modify it for a toddler or a school-age child and implement it again with a child of that age group. Document how the two children respond to the activity through photographs, work samples, or anecdotal records.

Make a Poster for Parents: Illustrate the milestones of development for one age group of children (infants, toddlers, preschoolers, kindergarten, or primary children) in one area of development (social/emotional, physical, or cognitive/language). Post it in a classroom. Photograph it and write a paragraph about it.

MyEducationLab

Go to Topics 2: Child Development/Theories and 8: DAP/Teaching Strategies in the MyEducationLab (myeducationlab.com) for *Who Am I in the Lives of Children?* where you can:

- Find learning outcomes for Child Development/Theories and DAP/Teaching Strategies along with the national standards that connect to these outcomes.
- Complete Assignments and Activities that can help you more deeply understand the chapter content.
- Apply and practice your understanding of the core teaching skills identified in the chapter with the

Building Teaching Skills and Dispositions learning units.
- Listen to experts from the field in Professional Perspectives.
- Check your comprehension on the content covered in the chapter with the Study Plan. Here you will be able to take a chapter quiz, receive feedback on your answers, and then access Review, Practice, and Enrichment activities to enhance your understanding of chapter content.

Bring with you a heart that watches and receives.

WILLIAM WORDSWORTH

5

Observing, Documenting, and Assessing Children

Because you care about young children, you are studying them. You are learning about their growth, development, and learning. In this chapter we will look at the nature of assessment as it is practiced in early childhood programs today, how observation and documentation fit into the assessment picture, and your role in the assessment process.

Assessment is a part of life. We assess children formally and informally from the moment of their birth. In the first minutes of life, we observe and evaluate: *Does he have all his fingers and toes?* Each moment of your life involves taking in information, making comparisons, evaluating situations, and making decision based on them. For example, your assessment of the weather and your planned activities helps you to select the clothes you wear.

Observation is the foundational assessment skill, the one that all teachers practice. Carefully and sensitively observing helps you to understand, assess, and plan for children. Historically, early childhood educators have believed that observation conducted during the course of daily life in the classroom is the best way to gain the information needed to understand children and thus design responsive and appropriate programs. We honor this history and reflect the high value we place on the skill of observation by placing *observing* first in the title of this chapter.

Documentation is the process of making a record. In early childhood education, a *document* is tangible evidence of work, learning, and activity collected by teachers. Documentation is related to one of the important purposes of assessment—to make visible to families, policy makers, and members of the community the development and ability of children, and the power of the work we do. Written observations, photos, video and audio recordings, and children's work are all examples of

MyEducationLab
Visit the MyEducationLab for *Who Am I in the Lives of Children?* to enhance your understanding of chapter concepts with a personalized Study Plan. You'll also have the opportunity to hone your teaching skills through video-based Assignments and Activities as well as Building Teaching Skills and Disposition lessons.

documentation. Teachers may also document the work of the group and the life of the classroom community, including families.

When people think about assessment, they most often think of *standardized assessment*, measuring and quantifying children's development and learning using standardized instruments like tests. Standardized assessment usually takes the form of tests that focus on well-defined target behaviors or achievement in a specific area of knowledge or skill.

What Is Assessment?

In education assessment is a multipart process that is used for the purpose of appraising young children's development and learning. It has three interconnected components (Jones, 2004; McAfee & Leong, 2010; McAfee, Leong, & Bodrova, 2004; Wortham, 2011). The first component is **collecting and recording** information about children's learning and development. It can come from observation, interviews, examples of children's work, tests, checklists, photographs, and recordings. The second component involves **interpreting and evaluating** the information gathered. The third part of the process has to do with **using** the information that you have acquired from your assessment. This may involve making choices about instructional practice, providing information to families, deciding whether a child needs a referral for special services, and making a placement decision. It can also be used for program evaluation.

There are two broad approaches to assessment. The first is called *authentic assessment* (also called **classroom assessment**, **alternative assessment**, and **performance-based assessment**). This type of assessment occurs in the ongoing life and daily activities of the early childhood classroom. The second approach, known as *standardized assessment* (also called **formal assessment**), employs instruments (a test or other tool) that in some way measure children's development and learning.

Because assessment is part of early childhood program practice and state and national policy, it is essential for you to understand it. In fact, it is a part of your ethical responsibility to do so, and to do so appropriately. As stated in the NAEYC Code of Ethical Conduct (see Appendix A):

> **P-1.5**—We shall use appropriate assessment systems, which include multiple sources of information, to provide information on children's learning and development.

Why Do We Assess Children? The Purposes of Assessment

The better you understand an individual child, the more able you will be to provide a program that meets that child's needs and that serves all the children in your program. This is the ultimate goal of assessment of all kinds—*to better understand and thus better serve children*. Keeping this goal at the forefront of your mind will help you to understand and use assessment appropriately.

When you watch a child on her first day of school and go to comfort her as she begins to look fearful, you are using assessment **to understand** an individual. When you observe a group of children and write notes on how they play and interact in a classroom, and then use this information to modify the learning environment, you are using assessment **to guide your decision making**. When you evaluate a child's abilities using a checklist and then use the data **to make a plan** that builds upon these strengths, you are using assessment to inform curriculum planning. Assessment carried out while you are teaching, to inform and improve instruction, is called *formative assessment*. Assessment that is designed to evaluate a child's acquisition of knowledge or skills after teaching is completed is called *summative assessment*.

When you conduct a screening test and use the results to refer a child for further testing, you are using assessment **to identify** a child who may need special services. In each of these cases assessment helps you to support development and learning and ensures that you are meeting the needs of children.

Assessment has other purposes as well. Assessment information is used **to report** to a child's family how a child is progressing in school and whether or not a child has achieved learning goals. Giving a family information about the learning, growth, and development of their child enables them to better support their child at home.

Administrators and policy makers often use assessment for **program evaluation**. It can guide them in determining goals for improvement and deciding how to allocate resources. These goals and resources may help programs to better serve children. One measure of program quality is the quality of child assessment conducted by teachers. At this time in the history of education, standardized assessment (in the form of test scores) is being used to determine how effective teachers and school are in achieving mandated goals.

Authentic Assessment

Authentic means *genuine*. *Authentic assessment* is evaluation of a child's development or performance in the context of everyday life. In a natural or authentic approach, the teacher observes and documents real-life examples in which skills and knowledge are demonstrated in tasks that are meaningful to the child. Authentic assessment is not a onetime event. Instead, it is an ongoing process. It uses the input of teacher, parent, and child. Thus actual performance—rather than responses to artificial tasks as is required on tests—is the measure by which children's knowledge and skill are assessed.

Authentic assessment includes multiple kinds of information, collected throughout the day while children are engaged in a range of activities including self-selected play, teacher-directed activities, routines, and transitions. In authentic assessment, a variety of methods are used to record or document what children do—but the most important is teachers' observations of children engaged in meaningful activities. Photographs, videotapes and audio recordings, interviews with children and family members, and examples of children's work (called *work samples*) also can provide authentic evidence of a child's understanding and ability.

Reflect on authentic assessment

Consider one of your skills or accomplishments. How could you demonstrate this achievement or ability to someone else? Is this demonstration more authentic (real) than taking a test? What is the best way to show what you know and can do?

Observation

You see, but you do not observe.

Arthur Conan Doyle

As a student of early childhood education, learning to observe is a part of your education. You use the skill of observation to understand children's development, to make theory come alive. You observe teachers, learning environments, and activities to learn about teaching strategies and how these work (or don't work) in the real world.

As a teacher, you will observe to assess children and to assess your own teaching. So, observation is one of an early childhood teacher's most important tasks. However, the practice of observation is more than a task. It is a disposition, a habit of mind that you are cultivating in yourself. Once acquired, it will help to make you a better teacher and will bring you joy and satisfaction in your work.

How did you discover that you wanted to work with young children? You probably came to this field because you found children intriguing. You may have seen things about them that your friends didn't notice. If so, you are already an amateur observer of children. *Observation* (systematically watching and noting what children do) is your most effective technique for understanding children. It is the foundation of all the ways that you will learn about them. One reason it is such an important technique is that many things that children cannot express through spoken words can be inferred by watching them in their natural settings.

> *Paul is a fragile-looking, curly-haired, just turned 3-year-old. He drags a laundry basket into the shade of a tree. He sits down in the basket and stretches his legs. "I fit! I'm 3!" he says, holding up three fingers. Paul rocks his body and the basket back and forth: "I'm rocking the cradle. I'm rocking the cradle." He rocks and rocks till the basket tips, and with a look of surprise he spills onto the ground. Paul stands up and smiles. He turns the basket over and hits it on the top several times, listening to the hollow drumming sounds that his thumping makes. Then he lifts up the basket and crawls underneath. He crouches under the basket, peers out through the holes, and announces, "I'm going to hatch the cradle." He stands up wearing the basket like a turtle's shell. "I hatched!"*

The ability to observe—to "read" and understand children—is one of the most important and satisfying skills that you can develop. It will help you to know and understand individuals, plan more effectively, and evaluate your teaching. More important, observation is the window that enables you to see into the world of the child. By observing Paul and his laundry basket with open heart and mind, you learn many things. You learn that he is a child who, like many 3-year-olds, enjoys solitary play. You note that he uses and enjoys language that is slightly more sophisticated than many 3-year-olds'. You learn that he knows some things about cradles, drums, and eggs, and that he has a concept of "three," "fit," and "hatch." You discover that he is able to use materials in innovative ways. You note that he has the control of the large muscles in his arms, legs, and torso that you would expect in 3-year-olds. And you see that he can handle simple problems independently. Based on this, you might evaluate your own teaching (the rock-a-bye-baby activity seems to have taught a concept!) and plan new experiences for him (perhaps use more rhymes and language games with Paul because he seems to be attuned to words). You gain an empathy toward him that helps you to be his advocate and his friend. You develop insight into how Paul (and many 3-year-olds) feels about and understands the world—insight that you can share with other adults who did not have the opportunity to observe Paul.

Observation can provide you with information that will help you to respond effectively to the needs of a frightened or angry child, to intervene, to mediate recurring problems between two children, to know what a child is experiencing as a member of a family, and much more (see Figure 5.1). Observation lets you know what children are learning and experiencing today and helps you to plan for tomorrow. It also helps you to identify a child who needs more stimulation,

Through observation you develop:

- Increased sensitivity to children in general—awareness of the range of development and a heightened awareness of the unique qualities of childhood and the world of children **to give you greater understanding of and empathy for children**

- In-depth understanding of individual children—how they think, feel, and view the world, and their interests, skills, characteristic responses, and areas of strength and weakness—to use in **planning curriculum that meets the child's needs** and in **communicating the child's progress** to others

- Understanding of social relationships—among children and between children and adults—**to enable you to better facilitate relationships** in the classroom

- Awareness of the way the environment is used by children, families, and staff **so that you can improve it**

- Increased ability to share meaningful aspects of children's development and the ability to make visible the power of children's learning **to help you to be a better advocate for children**

or who might be troubled, have special needs, or be abused or neglected and in need of help. Observation will help you to communicate about children with other adults who share a concern about their well-being.

Observation is the basis for decision-making in much of your work with young children and their families. It is used in some form in almost every chapter in this book. You will observe many different children and use what you see to help you understand the child development theories you have learned. You will observe children's characteristics, abilities, and interests, and in response you will plan for their development. You will observe them as you teach and will modify your teaching and your plans in response to what you see. You will observe their interactions with others and modify your behavior to help them to build good relationships. You will observe them with their families and use this information to help them build strong bonds with the most important people in their lives. And when you observe that their needs are significantly different from those of other children, you will use your observations to help you communicate with others to determine whether or not they require special services.

The Observation Process

To observe is to take notice, to watch attentively, to focus on one particular part of a complex whole. It means perceiving both the total picture and the significant detail. Learning to observe involves more than casual looking, and it is not nearly as easy as one might think. To make useful observations of children, their significant relationships, and their environments requires training and practice. You must be clear about why you are

Remember a time when you observed something with fresh eyes (for example, a new home, a new city, or a new baby). What did you notice? How was this different from everyday looking? Look around at the place where you are right now and focus on the different colors and sounds in the environment. What do you notice? How is observation different when you focus? What might happen if you observed a child in this way?

observing and be willing to gather information and impressions with a receptive eye and mind.

The consistent practice of observation will help you develop *child-sense*—a feeling for how individual children and groups of children are feeling and functioning. This deep understanding is based on a great deal of experience in observing individuals and groups of children over time. Observing can generate a sense of connection and greater understanding, and hence empathy, caring, and concern.

To observe more objectively and separate out feelings and reactions from what is actually seen, it is useful to divide the observation process into three parts:

1. **Observing:** Purposefully gathering information
2. **Recording:** Documenting what you have observed in a variety of ways
3. **Interpreting:** Reflecting on what your observations might mean

Observing. The first and most essential step in the observation process is to experience as completely as possible. This process involves consciously focusing on watching and listening while quieting the inner voice that adds a running commentary of explanations and evaluations. This is sometimes called *childwatching* or *kidwatching* and it is different from everyday seeing and the purposeful classroom scanning that teachers do to anticipate problems. It is most like the "fresh eyes" and heightened senses one brings to a new experience, such as you do when you travel or go to a new place

An effective observer of young children has the ability to wait to see and hear what is really happening instead of hurriedly drawing conclusions. To really watch and listen requires that you suspend expectations and be receptive—to separate what you *actually* see and hear from what you want, expect, or fear that you will see and hear.

You must suspend judgments and try to reduce the distortions that result from biases, defenses, and preconceptions. Objectivity is difficult in part because you are a participant in the life of the children, families, and settings that you observe, and you both influence the people and things in it and are influenced by them. It is also difficult because you have spent a lifetime making judgments about the world. If you are aware of your impact on the situation and its impact on you, you can work toward becoming a more objective observer while realizing that it is impossible to be completely objective.

It is also helpful to be aware of your characteristics as an observer. When you realize what you tend to focus on, you can also get an idea of what you characteristically ignore. We have our college students observe a bowl of goldfish and describe what they see. Some notice the minute detail of fish anatomy like a biologist, some see the fish in relation to their environment, and some are aware of the interactions among the fish. They learn about what they tend to observe and they are surprised at how different the observations of the same fish can be. By doing these kinds of observation exercises, you increase the range of things that you attend to and become a more keen observer.

The more you know about children, the more specific and accurate your observations become. You will start to look beyond what is obvious. Experienced observers know that children communicate a great deal through their bodies—facial expression; body tension; the language of hands, fingers, and eyebrows; the tilt of a head or shoulder; the slight protuberance of a tongue—as much as through their spoken words and obvious actions. You will learn to notice a child's body, build, posture, tone of voice, appearance, ways of moving and manipulating objects, mood, interactions with others, and many other attributes.

As you observe, you may become aware of your own biases. Are you drawn to children who are neat and tidy? Are you bored by children who are quiet and compliant? Do you have preferences for children of one race or one gender? As you practice observation you are likely to discover that there are things you like about every child you observe. This is one of the important benefits of observing. It helps you to appreciate diverse children and thus makes you a better teacher.

Skillful early childhood educators observe all the time and adjust what they do in response to what they see.

Karen observes 4-year-old Arisa during her third morning in school. Arisa does not talk to anyone but her eyes follow Shan, another 4-year-old, playing in the dramatic play area. With a sigh, Arisa lies down in the library corner and stares blankly into space. "Hey, come try the kitty-cat puzzle," Karen invites Arisa, remembering that yesterday she observed both Arisa and Shan playing with this puzzle at different times. Shan approaches the table and soon Shan and Arisa are playing together.

Observing will give you helpful information about a child or a situation. Like Karen in the example above, you will sometimes use what you have observed immediately to respond to a child. At other times you will consciously and purposefully observe with a specific focus (a child, behavior, kind of learning, interaction, practice, or situation) and gather observations over time for a specific purpose (to learn what a child can and cannot do, to plan curriculum, to assess the environment).

Recording. Because few of us have good enough memories to accurately remember all that we observe, we also need to have skill in recording. We record so that we can remember, share, and make sense of what we have observed. Recording what you have observed, compiling and organizing what you have recorded, and then using it to inform teaching turns observation into a powerful tool to use on behalf of children.

A number of techniques can be used to make a record of an observation. In the sections that follow we will describe three ways to record what you have observed: writing a narrative record, using a simple structured record, and using technology to make an electronic record. *Narrative observation records* are open-ended written documents. They provide rich detail and a vivid picture of children and require skill in writing. *Structured observation records* are closed-ended documents that require little or no writing. They tally if, how frequently, or how long specified behaviors occur. They can help you to understand patterns of behavior but are usually quite narrowly focused and give relatively little detail. *Electronic observation records* are visual or audio documentation. They provide accurate and vivid representations but require equipment, technical skill, and time to put together.

Interpreting. The third step in the observation process is to make interpretations (sometimes called conclusions, inferences, or comments) based on what you have seen and heard. Although behavior is observable, the reasons for behavior are not visible and may only be inferred. You need to observe closely and then seek the relationship between the child's behavior that you have observed and its unobservable cause. You can never truly know why a child behaves as he or she does, but you will make decisions based on your understanding of children's development and behavior every day. It is important that you develop skill in making interpretations based on what you actually observe.

Understanding a child's behavior is difficult because many factors—stage of development, health, culture, and individual experience—combine in complex

ways to determine how a child acts in a given situation. One of the first things that you will consider in interpreting what you observe is what you know about children's development in general. This understanding, which will increase as you have more experience and education, helps you to distinguish between and interpret behavior that is typical of a toddler but unusual in a 4-year-old (e.g., biting another child) or vice versa (e.g., creating an ABA pattern in a string of beads). Your knowledge of child development will be helpful as you write interpretations of your observations.

The same behavior can mean different things in different children. Edwin's downcast eyes might mean that he has been taught to show respect to adults by avoiding eye contact when spoken to, while the same behavior from Joanie might mean that she is avoiding acknowledging what you are saying. Individual observers may interpret the same behavior or incident in dissimilar ways, depending on their knowledge and their own cultural backgrounds. If your cultural background is the same as Edwin's you are likely to understand his behavior, but if your background is more similar to Joanie's you might mistakenly assume he is trying to avoid hearing or acknowledging what you are saying.

It is best to be tentative in your interpretations. We have seen situations in which several individuals observed the same incident and made significantly different interpretations. For example, several of our college students noticed a little girl lying down in the shade of a play structure at a program they were visiting. One thought she was withdrawn and antisocial; another was convinced she was lonely, unhappy, and in need of comforting; a third felt that she was tired and taking a few moments to relax; another thought that she was looking at bugs. Like the men in the fable of the blind men and the elephant, they needed more information about the child and the events that preceded their observation in order to make accurate, useful interpretations.

Narrative Observation Records

Written observations tell a story. They are called *narrative observations*. Like a story, a narrative observation begins with a setting—where and when the observation occurs. It has characters—a child or children and the adults and materials with whom they interact. And it has action—the child's activities and interactions.

Early childhood professionals use the skill of writing narrative observations to communicate with parents and other professionals. The ability to write clear, concise, meaningful description, like the ability to teach, comes with lots of practice and lots of feedback. Good narrative observations use clear language and convey the uniqueness of children and their activity.

When you first start writing narrative observations it may feel awkward, and you may have difficulty deciding how much of what you observed to record. It also can be hard to clearly separate what you observed (objective description) from what you think about it (subjective interpretation). The three examples in Figure 5.2 demonstrate the range—one is too subjective and filled with personal opinions and interpretation, another is lacking in detail, and a third is objective and vivid.

A good description is specific. Broad general statements are not effective in capturing important qualities of the child or interaction. For example, the

Subjective
Sasha is a cute little girl with beautiful curly hair. She is happy because she is in the sandbox. Sasha is making birthday cakes. She sings "Happy Birthday." She wishes it was her birthday. Carson gets mad, he walks up to Sasha and says, "Hey it's not your birthday! It's my birthday!" He scares Sasha and kicks over her birthday cake. Sasha gets mad back and throws some sand at Carson. Carson and Sasha don't know how to be nice to one another.

Lacking in Detail
Sasha is playing in the sandbox. Carson walks up and yells at her. Sasha throws sand at him. Carson and Sasha cry.

Objective
Sasha sits in the sandbox playing with a bucket and shovel. She slowly fills the bucket with sand. After each scoop she peers into the bucket and pats the sand. When the bucket is filled to the brim she pats the top several times. She looks at the ground and picks up three small sticks that she pokes into the top of the bucket of sand. She sings, "Happy Birthday to Sasha." S. looks around the sandbox and smiles a wide smile. Carson, a classmate who turned 4 today, stomps up and says, "Hey it's not your birthday! It's my birthday!" He kicks over the bucket. S.'s eyes widen and fill with tears. She picks up a handful of sand and throws it at C. C. yells, "Teacher!" He and S. both burst into tears.

statement that *"Sasha is playing with sand"* does not tell the reader much. We have a better picture of the child and situation when the observer tells us, *"She fills the bucket with sand. After each scoop she peers into the bucket and pats the sand."* Details such as when Sasha played in the sandbox, how long she played, who she played with, and how she played increase the reader's ability to understand the child and the situation.

Remember that you are not only recording what you see but also what you observe using your other senses. It is especially important to note the words children use. If these are not included, you have only described a part of the picture and only told half the story. The addition of expressive detail can communicate a great deal more. It takes practice to balance vivid imagery and objectivity. The language should capture the subtleties and complexities of children's behavior. Carefully chosen words convey the essence of the person and situation and are an important part of writing vivid descriptions; they enhance our ability to visualize the subject of the observation.

> *Sasha's eyes widen and fill with tears. Then she picks up a handful of sand and throws it at Carson.*

Notice how much more easily you can picture the scene, compared to this description:

> *Sasha throws some sand at Carson.*

In choosing modifiers, avoid words that have a strong emotional impact or bias built into them (*Sasha is a cute little girl*). Describe what the child *does* (*Sasha sits in the sandbox playing with a bucket and shovel*), instead of giving your views of what he or she *is, feels, wishes,* or *intends* (*She is happy because she is in the sandbox*), none of which you can see. Opinions of children such as *pretty, cute, bright, attractive, good, messy, slow, mean,* or *naughty* are to be avoided in written observations because they are value judgments. Describing a child in these terms tells more about the values of the observer than the nature of the child. Because the descriptions you write may be shared with others, you have the responsibility to convey useful information that is free from personal bias or unsubstantiated evaluations.

When you are learning to observe in a college class you may also be asked to write physical descriptions of children. This exercise is done to build your sensitivity to the unique qualities of individuals and to increase your ability to write vividly and objectively. In writing physical descriptions you will note basic physical attributes and write about them to help the reader to visualize the child: age, sex, size, build, facial features, coloring, and distinguishing markings. A plain physical description gives little sense of the distinctiveness of a child: "She is an Asian girl, 4 years of age, shorter than her peers." You will convey a better picture of the child as a unique individual if you elaborate the basic physical description with some of the child's unique qualities: body stance, way of moving, facial expression, gestures, tone of voice. The following additions convey a much more vivid sense of the child:

> *K. is an Asian girl, 4 years of age, shorter than her peers. She has black eyebrows, lashes, and hair, almond-shaped eyes, a fair smooth complexion, thin lips, and a small upturned nose. She is slim and has a delicate build. She strolls from activity to activity with quick, light steps. Her arms hang slightly away from her body and swing with the rhythm of her stroll.*

It is usually neither necessary nor desirable to describe specific details of children's clothing. They will be wearing something else the next time you observe!

Running records and *anecdotal records* are the narrative observation methods traditionally used by early childhood educators. When you hear other early childhood educators talk about making observations, they are usually referring to these methods.

Running Records. When you see a teacher or student teacher with a clipboard writing down everything a child says and does, that teacher is writing a form of observation called a *running record,* sometimes called a *specimen record.* When you first learn to observe young children, you will usually learn to write a running record.

Running records are written while you are watching. They are open-ended and detailed narrative accounts of behavior and events. When you sit down to write a running record, you will observe a particular child engaged in a particular activity at a particular time. You observe and write down everything that the child says and does for the time you are observing. We often compare a running record to a video recording. You record what happens while it is happening, with as much fidelity as possible. Because it is written while it is happening, a running record is always written in the present tense. The skill you are developing is the ability to write vivid description quickly while avoiding interpretation and judgment. Learning to do this type of written observation well requires considerable practice.

When you are writing a running record, you can do little else. For this reason, running records are rarely used by practitioners who are "on the floor" and responsible for a group of children. As a student, you will have opportunities to practice and master the skill of writing running records in order to develop sensitivity to and knowledge about children. As a practicing professional, you may use this skill only when you need to do an in-depth study of a particular child and when you have assistance. For ordinary purposes, you will select more efficient and less time-consuming methods.

The format used in Figure 5.3 shows a standard way to write running records. During the actual observation, use the middle column to record what you see. As soon after observing as possible, write comments and note any feelings or other impressions in the right-hand column. With this format you are able to review your description, add other comments, and decide whether you have enough information. If not, you can observe the child in other settings to see whether the behaviors are repeated and characteristic or simply the outcome of a particular situation.

Anecdotal Records. If observations are important but practitioners rarely write running records, you may be asking yourself what they do instead. The form of written observation most frequently used by practitioners is the *anecdotal record*. If a running record is the written equivalent of a video recording, an anecdotal record is the written equivalent of a photograph. Like a running record, an anecdotal record is an open-ended, detailed narrative describing incidents, behaviors, and interactions. An anecdotal record, however, is brief and describes a single incident, the way a photograph captures a single moment (the word *anecdote* means "a brief story"). An anecdotal record is written after the fact. In other words, you write an anecdotal record *after* you notice something worthy of documenting. For this reason anecdotal records are written in the past tense.

Anecdotal records are helpful for early childhood practitioners who need to document events and changes in children. It is valuable to learn how to write them, and important to develop strategies to make them a part of your daily work with children.

What belongs in an anecdotal record? Like any other observation, an anecdotal record has a focus, is dated, includes the name of the child and the observer, and includes some context (place/time). And like any other observation, it should be as objective as possible and free of bias and judgment. Because anecdotal records are brief and are usually read by those who know the child already, it is unnecessary to give much background information. Tell what happened briefly

FIGURE 5.3 Example of a Running Record

Child: _John A._   Date: _10/10_   Observer: _Lisa L._

Time/Setting	Observation	Comment
10:30 art area New play dough set out on table. Each chair has a plastic place mat, ball of dough, apron hanging over back of chair. Teacher has told children new play dough available.	J. runs to table and sits down without putting on an apron. Starts to pinch the ball of dough apart. Teacher says, "Hey J., I think you forgot something." J. smiles, "Oh yeah." Stands up and takes yellow plastic apron and pulls it over head—wearing it backwards (long part behind). Teacher makes no comment. J. sits back down and picks up the dough.	Complies with reasonable requests
	J. rolls a teaspoon-sized "pinch" of dough into a ball. Eyes are fixed on the dough and his hands as he rolls. He rolls the dough with his right hand against the mat. He rolls and rolls the ball until it is a nearly perfect sphere. With a little smile, he picks it up and places it on the edge of his mat and glances up at other children.	Shows good fine motor coordination and persistence
10:35	J. continues pinching and rolling little balls of dough, placing them along the edge of the mat. His eyes stay fixed on the dough. J. glances up after completing each ball but does not interact with other children who are chattering to one another.	Doesn't seem too interested in the other children
10:45	When entire big ball of dough has been turned into little balls, J. stands up and walks to the collage shelf. He picks up container of straws and toothpicks and carries back to table.	Seems to have a plan
	J. pokes a toothpick into first ball of dough. Then he pokes another ball of dough onto the other end of the toothpick. He sticks a second toothpick into the second ball of dough and continues to link the balls with toothpicks.	Attempting to symbolize?
	He gets to the fourth ball of dough and it falls apart. J. says to the teacher, "Help me."	Uses adults as resources
	Teacher says, "What are you trying to do?"	

but completely. We also suggest that you note why you wrote this observation, as you see in the examples that follow:

Behavior or interactions that seem typical for a child:
9/5—During outside play Bryce (4 yrs.) walked quickly up a plank. Then he jumped across a tire to another plank. He walked across that plank and down the final plank. "Ta-da!" he said holding his arms out. "That's how you do it!"
Comment: Demonstrates a good sense of balance. Enjoys large-motor challenges.

Behavior or interactions that seem atypical for a child:
9/4—At circle time a teacher sang "Old MacDonald" with finger puppets. The teacher held up one of the puppets and sang, "On this farm he had a cow." Emily (3½ yrs.) protested, "It's not a cow! It's a donkey." She lay on the carpet and cried while the group sang the song.

Comment: Unusual behavior—angry/unhappy and upset. Emily is usually very enthusiastic at circle time.

The achievement of a developmental milestone:
8/23—At 10:00 this morning Tevin (10 mos.) was on his hands and knees next to a low table. He sat back on his heels and reached up so that he was grasping the edge of the table. He pulled himself to a standing position. His eyes grew wide, he grinned and then his knees buckled and he sat down fast. He repeated this five more times during the next half-hour.

Comment: First time Tevin has pulled himself up at the center.

Incidents and interactions that convey the child's strengths, interests, and needs:
9/20—After lunch at his desk, Ethan (5½ yrs.) drew a detailed picture of a car. The drawing included a tailpipe with exhaust, a spoiler, door handles, head-lights, and tires with elaborate hubcaps. Ethan wrote RASG CR on his drawing.

Comment: Shows understanding of and interest in cars. Is able to make de-tailed representations in drawings. Uses inventive spelling.

Incidents and interactions that convey the nature of social relationships and emotional reactions:
11/14—During outside play this afternoon Bryan (4 yrs.) was riding on the rick-shaw trike. He zoomed past Kengo (4 yrs.) who was shoveling sand into a bucket. He stopped and said to Kengo, "The garbage truck is collecting the garbage. You want to be a garbage man?" Kengo answered by picking up his bucket, sitting on the rickshaw seat, and yelling, "Let's go!" The two boys drove to one end of the yard where they filled the bucket with leaves, which they packed to the other end of the yard. They continued to play garbage man until Bryan's mom came, about 20 minutes.

Comment: Cooperative friendships.

Behavior or interactions relating to an area of special concern:
3/3—While working on an addition exercise Stanley (6 yrs.) put his head down on his desk. I asked, "What's up, Stanley?" He said, "I'm just so dumb."

Comment: This is the second or third time that Stanley has said this in the last 2 weeks—each time it was associated with seat work.

Anecdotal records can also be made with special emphasis on children about whom you have questions or concerns and those children who sometimes seem "invisible"—so inconspicuous that they tend to be forgotten.

Making Anecdotal Record Writing a Part of Every Day. To help you to understand children and how they develop, it is valuable to have anecdotal records written over time. To have these it is necessary to observe and write anecdotal records on a regular basis—if possible, every day. With all the other things that you will have to do as a teacher, you may wonder how to find time to write anecdotal records. Some teachers write them while they are supervising children, during naptime, or during break time. In some programs teachers are given dedicated time to write anecdotal records. But there will never be enough time unless you have made a commitment to writing observations. Once you have made this commitment you will write consistently until the practice of writing ob-servations has turned into a habit, a part of your daily routine like washing your hands and brushing your teeth. To do this it is necessary to create a convenient and systematic way to write and keep them organized (see "Golden Rules for Writing Anecdotal Records"). We have used and seen a number of ways to make anecdotal record writing a part of everyday practice:

- **Clipboards posted throughout the classroom.** Clipboards with pencils attached are posted conveniently throughout the classroom with an anecdotal record sheet for each child on each clipboard. You then can reach for the clipboard and make a few notes right after you have observed something of significance. In this method an anecdotal record form like the one shown in Figure 5.4 is helpful. The forms are filed weekly or when they are filled up in a folder/notebook. When you do this, it is essential to use a cover sheet to ensure confidentiality.

FIGURE 5.4   Example of an Anecdotal Record Form

Observations of N.L.	
Domain I: Physical Development **Secondary Domain:** Personal/Social **Date:** 01/30 At the woodworking table NL used both hands to hold a hammer. She hammered repeatedly until the nail was securely in the wood. **Comment:** Demonstrates physical strength and coordination. Shows persistence in completing tasks.	**Domain II: Personal/Social Development** **Secondary Domain:** Cognitive **Date:** 01/31 NL and V. were playing with a big cardboard box. They took turns getting in the box. When V. was in the box and it was closed up tight NL told V. that she was going to tell the other children that no one was inside. "Don't say a word," she cautioned V. Then she said to other children, "There's no one inside, there's only air." **Comment:** Plans for play. Engages in cooperative play. Able to take viewpoint of others.
Domain III: Communication (Language/Literacy) **Secondary Domain:** Cognitive **Date:** 01/30 The children and teacher were observing a monarch caterpillar. The teacher asked why the caterpillar appeared to have two sets of antennae. NL said, "Maybe it is two caterpillars." Then the teacher said she didn't know but that she was going to find out. NL suggested, "Check on the computer." **Comment:** Literacy: Demonstrates awareness of different sources of information. Science: Hypothesizes	**Domain IV: Cognitive Development** **Secondary Domain:** Personal/Social **Date:** 02/01 NL said, "I want a booster. But, you know, my mom won't let me. She said I have to stay in my car seat. But V. is only four and she has a booster." **Comment:** Seems to understand that rules should have a logical foundation. Makes logical arguments. Advocates for herself. Has concepts of fairness.
Domain V: Creative Development **Secondary Domain:** Personal/Social **Date:** 02/05 NL mixed colors on her palette. With the colors she mixed she painted a scene that included a rainbow, sun, grass, and rain. When she was through she took her painting to each teacher and showed her work. Then she placed the painting on the drying rack. **Comment:** Purposefully expresses ideas through art. Uses work to communicate with others. Takes responsibility for her own work.	

- **Notebooks.** Each child has a notebook in which you write anecdotal records. Notebooks are kept in the classroom. Sometimes they are used as the basis of a portfolio and at other times they are kept where families can read them every day.
- **Classroom laptop.** A laptop computer (used only by the teachers) with a file for each child is kept in the classroom on which you input anecdotal records after an observation has been made, at a time that is convenient and appropriate. A safe and convenient location in the classroom where you can keep the computer ready to use is required.
- **Self-stick labels, index cards, or notebooks.** Teachers wear aprons with pockets, or fanny packs, and keep a pen and a stack of large self-stick labels, index cards, or a small notebook in the pocket. Anecdotal records are made with the child's name and the date. At the end of the day or week notes are filed. They can be organized chronologically and/or by developmental domain. Some teachers later add selected self-stick labels directly to the child's portfolio. (See the section on portfolios later in this chapter, on pages 166–171.)
- **Digital voice recorders.** Small, inexpensive digital voice recorders are kept in a pocket (as described previously) to record observations. These allow you to describe what you see happening and capture children's words verbatim. Because recordings must be transcribed and organized, they may be more time-consuming that on-the-spot written observation.
- **Handheld computers,** smart phones, or PDAs are kept in pockets, aprons, or fanny packs and are used to write observations while you are on the floor with children. A format for observation can be built in. These save you from having to transcribe observations later. However, the process of inputting information may distract you from interacting with children.

The anecdotal records you create in the course of your day may be just a few words or fragments of information with details that you fill in later (when written these are sometimes referred to as jottings). It is important to go back on the same day to any that are incomplete, or you will lose the details that make records useful. Anecdotal records, like all observations, are a part of your collection of information about each child. They need to be carefully monitored and filed with all other confidential records.

Interpreting Narrative Observation Records. Descriptions of what you observed, accompanied by interpretations, make it possible for others to read what you have observed and decide whether they agree with your conclusions. Descriptions created by different observers can be helpful because each of us tends to notice different things. Two people viewing or reading about the same child or incident will often have different perceptions. It is also helpful to discuss your interpretations with someone else. Becoming aware of different perspectives can help you realize how difficult it is to interpret accurately. We encourage you to make liberal use of the words *might* and *seems to* in your interpretations to underscore the tentative nature of conclusions about children's needs, feelings, and motivation.

Interpretations should be based on several observations. State your conclusions concisely, and cite the descriptive data on which they are based. A teacher who has made many observations of N.L. (the child in our sample anecdotal records in Figure 5.4) might summarize with something like this:

> *As can be seen in observations dated 1/30, 1/31, 2/1, and 2/5, N.L. seems to have a strong sense of self. She plays with other children but also can be independent and comfortable on her own. She often expresses ideas and her own point of view to adults. When something seems unfair she advocates for her rights.*

GOLDEN RULES FOR WRITING ANECDOTAL RECORDS

1. Write after you observe a typical behavior or interaction.
2. Write after you observe a new behavior or interaction.
3. Write after you observe an unusual behavior or interaction.
4. Describe what happened. Include only what you saw, heard, or otherwise experienced through your senses. Avoid generalizations (*always, usually, never*).
5. Omit the words *I* and *me* unless the child spoke those words (remember that the observation is about the child, not you).
6. Refrain from saying why you think the child behaved or interacted in this way.
7. Exclude your opinions of the child, the behavior, or interaction (remember, it's not about you).
8. Leave out your feelings about what happened.
9. Write a separate comment that explains why you thought this behavior or interaction was important to record and what you think it might mean in terms of this child's development and program goals for children.
10. Keep anecdotal records confidential.

Using Narrative Records. The point of writing narrative records (both running and anecdotal) is to improve the quality of the educational experience you provide for children. They help you to understand and be more responsive to individuals and are the most useful kind of observation to guide you in planning curriculum and assessing whether the curriculum is currently meeting children's needs. To use narrative records for curriculum planning, bring together the narrative observation records of a child and read through them to help you determine the child's strengths, interests, and needs. Plan activities that build on the strengths and interests and that provide opportunities to address the needs. Observations of all the children in the class can be used to inform the selection of a topic of study in an integrated curriculum.

Narrative records form the basis of the child portfolio described later in this chapter. In a portfolio you assemble observations, organize them, and summarize them to present a coherent picture of the child in school. The interpretation of the observation of N.L. on page 157 is an example of how you might present observations in a portfolio.

Structured Observation Records

Narrative observation records help you to create a picture of a child over time. As you observe in many areas, the picture grows. Sometimes, however, you may need or want to learn more about a child more quickly in order to make a referral or work on a particular problem. When this is the case, some form of structured data gathering may be useful or necessary. *Structured observations* can reveal trends and patterns in behavior. Designed well, they increase your objectivity and can correct for misperceptions or biases.

Time samples, event samples, checklists, rating scales, rubrics, and interviews are some of the most commonly used structured methods of gathering information. They differ in the degree to which they are systematized, their most appropriate use, and their advantages and disadvantages. The particular technique that you choose will depend on what you want to know and how you think you might best find it out. If you understand what information each provides and think carefully about the purpose of the observation, you will be able to select the method that generates the information you need.

Time Samples. A time sample (also known as a *frequency count*) is a method for tracking behaviors that occur at regular intervals and in rapid succession (see Figure 5.5). It is not a record of everything that happens, but rather a system for collecting information on a predefined behavior or set of behaviors displayed by an individual or group. For example, you might use this technique to find out how often a particular behavior (trike riding, focused work, hitting, fantasy play, thumb sucking) is actually occurring.

A time sample uses a grid on which you tally the occurrence of particular behavior(s) during a short time period. A simple checklist or code will be devised to help you quickly record what type of behavior is occurring. For example, ✓ could stand for *a positive interaction* and x could stand for *a negative interaction*. A time sample must be conducted often enough to get a good idea of the frequency of the behavior—a minimum of three sample days are needed as the basis for any interpretation. You may want to then sample weeks or months later to determine whether change has occurred.

Time sampling is an efficient method of gathering information. It can be used for observing more than one child at a time. The information from a time sample can be used as a basis for drawing conclusions about the frequency and relative importance of particular behaviors. However, the behavior(s) being studied must occur frequently. Because information about the cause of behavior is not gathered, you cannot draw conclusions about the reasons a behavior occurs.

We once designed a time sample to test our belief that 4-year-old Michael was initiating an excessive number of conflicts with others. Several staff members felt that they spent a great deal of time each day intervening in the conflicts that he provoked. Another teacher had difficulty understanding our frustration because she perceived Michael as a very positive and cooperative person. The time sample was simple. We agreed to track how frequently Michael initiated interaction with

FIGURE 5.5   Example of a Time Sample

Children: _Michael, Teddy, Philip_

Target: ✓ = engages in positive interaction   x = engages negative interactions
          0 = noninteraction   * = initiates interaction

Date: _3/3_

15 min. time sample	Michael	Teddy	Philip
0–3 min.	✓ * ✓	0 ✓	✓
3–6 min.	✓ x ✓	✓ * x	✓ ✓
6–9 min.	x * ✓ ✓ *	x ✓ *	0 ✓ *
9–12 min.	✓ * x	0	x* ✓
12–15 min.	✓ ✓ * x	x * ✓	x ✓ ✓ *

two friends and whether it was positive (play or conversation with another child) or negative (physical or verbal argument). The three 15-minute time samples uncovered that Michael had many more positive than negative interactions, as did his friends. We discovered, however, that Michael initiated interactions three times more frequently than his two playmates. This time sample helped explain our different perceptions and helped us to understand why we felt taxed by our frequent interventions. Our increased understanding helped us to become more trusting and to allow Michael more opportunity to handle interpersonal problems on his own.

Event Samples. An event sample is used to help you understand more about a behavior (see Figure 5.6). You watch for a particular behavior or interaction and then record what preceded the event, what happened during the event, and what happened after the event (called the *consequence*). The sample is made while it is occurring or immediately after. The purpose is to collect information about the relationship between the behavior and the context of the behavior so that you can understand the cause and possibly devise a way to alter the course of events.

Like a running record, an event sample relies on your skill in making detailed observations. For example, if you think a child has been engaging in a lot of

FIGURE 5.6 Example of an Event Sample

Child's Name ___Mari___   Age _4.5_   Date(s) _Sept.–Oct._

Date/Time	Preceding Event	Behavior	Consequence
9.24/7:48	M. was pouring juice at pitcher the snack table. She tipped over the paper cup and spilled a small amount.	M. set down the pitcher and struck out at a stack of paper cups, knocking them from the table.	Jim quickly grabbed M. in his arms and said, "It's OK, it was just a little spill."
9.26/8:07	M. entered the block area and began placing trucks from the shelf on the structure Pua and Jenny were building. Pua said, "You can't play."	M. ran from the block area past the art area on her way out the back door. On her way past the watercolor table she made a wide sweep with her arm and knocked over a cup of water.	Ginger, who witnessed the block corner scene, followed her out. She took M. in her arms and told her, "I bet it made you mad when Pua told you that you could not build with them."
10.6/7:5Q1	M. placed her blanket in her cubby on top of a plastic container. The blanket fell out as she turned to walk away.	M. shoved the blanket back into the cubby and pulled the entire contents of the cubby onto the floor and ran out the door to the gate.	Jim, who was greeting the children, followed M. out and said, "Please let me help you get your blanket in straight."
10.8/8:15	M. was playing with the tinker toys. Jenny joined her and accidentally bumped her construction and several pieces fell off.	M. screamed at Jenny and said she was stupid. With a single sweep of her arm M. knocked the pieces to the floor and threw herself on the rug.	Ginger gently rubbed M.'s back until she calmed.

aggressive behavior, you might want to note what precedes every aggressive act, exactly how the aggression occurs, and what teachers and other children as well as the child do after the aggressive behavior. You may discover that the behavior is happening only before lunch or nap or at the end of the day. It might be triggered by interaction with one child or group, or you may discover that there are unintended consequences that are encouraging the continuation of the aggression. Event sampling is not time-consuming, and it can provide useful information for figuring out the causes of behavior. It can be the basis for generating plans to help children and staff change their behavior.

Checklists, Rating Scales, and Rubrics. Checklists are lists of traits, behaviors, concepts, and skills on which an observer puts dates or check marks next to each item to indicate if or when it is observed (see Figure 5.7). They are a useful, relatively simple way to record the skills and knowledge children demonstrate in the classroom. A checklist can also provide an informal profile of each child in a class if it is constructed to cover the different areas of development in the usual sequence. You can create your own checklists to help in documenting the progress of individual children. A customized checklist is a good strategy for reviewing the milestones of development. A well-designed checklist ensures that you have a systematic guide to observing and recording information about the aspects of development that you wish to emphasize in your program. It also can be designed to help you to assess how effective your program is in meeting curriculum and content standards.

Rating scales are nearly identical to checklists in purpose and uses (see Figure 5.8). The only significant difference is that a rating scale provides a mechanism for indicating the degree to which a behavior or characteristic is present.

You are probably familiar with rubrics as they are used in your college classes. In early childhood settings rubrics are similar to rating scales (see Table 5.1). Typically a rubric provides a way to indicate the characteristics of a skill and the extent to which it has been demonstrated. A rubric differs from a rating scale in that very specific criteria for different levels are included within the rubric. Rubrics are often used as grading tools in the primary grades. They can also be created to evaluate preschooler's abilities. Like all assessment their appropriate use is to improve the quality of instruction for children.

Interviews. Informal conversations with children often provide you with insight into their ideas and learning. These can be documented in anecdotal records.

FIGURE 5.7 **Example of a Checklist**

Child's Name _____   Age _____

Observer _____

Instructions: Enter the date on which you first observe the listed behavior.

___ / ___ / ___ Scribbles

___ / ___ / ___ Paints with whole arm movement

___ / ___ / ___ Holds crayon with thumb and fingers

___ / ___ / ___ Paints with wrist action

___ / ___ / ___ Cuts with scissors

___ / ___ / ___ Holds cup with one hand

FIGURE 5.8   Example of a Rating Scale

Child's Name _____   Age _____

Observer _____   Date _____

Indicate the degree of success the child has with the following by marking the place on the scale that best represents the current level of functioning.

Scribbles:

easily   somewhat easily   with difficulty   not able to do

Paints with whole arm movement:

easily   somewhat easily   with difficulty   not able to do

Holds crayon with thumb and fingers:

easily   somewhat easily   with difficulty   not able to do

Paints with wrist action:

easily   somewhat easily   with difficulty   not able to do

Cuts with scissors:

easily   somewhat easily   with difficulty   not able to do

Holds cup with one hand:

easily   somewhat easily   with difficulty   not able to do

When you ask a child to tell you about a block building or a painting or to show you a specific skill, you are conducting an informal interview.

Formally interviewing children, on the other hand, is a planned technique for gathering information. Their answers can give you insight into language, social-emotional development, understanding of concepts, and perception of the world. An interview may be repeated after an interval of time to help you to understand and document a child's growth.

In a formal interview you select a focus (math concepts, feelings about friends, language development) then plan a series of questions and ask them of all the children. This allows you to compare children's responses and better understand how different children understand a concept. If you decide to conduct an interview, it is important to carefully consider what it is you are trying to discover and how to best communicate it to the children. For example, if you were trying to assess the value of a trip to the zoo during a study of birds, you might interview children as a group by asking a broad open-ended question ("What do you remember about the birds we saw at the zoo?") to find out whether they had acquired the concept *There are many different birds with many colors, shapes, and sizes.* Children's responses could then be recorded on a group chart kept in the form of a facsimile (e.g., a rewritten chart on letter-size paper) or a photograph. Or you might interview children individually to elicit a more targeted response aimed at a specific skill—for example, the ability to observe and describe, by asking a child, "Tell me what you noticed about the hornbill." Thus, like all authentic assessment, interviews serve a dual purpose: assessment and advancing children's learning. The box "Golden Rules for Interviewing a Child for Assessment" gives you ideas for ways to make interviews with children successful.

TABLE 5.1 Pre-K Math Rubric

	Advanced	Proficient	Basic	Not Yet
Matching	Matches groups of identical item (e.g., a group of plates to a group of cups)	Matches related items (e.g., fork to knife)	Matches identical items	Does not match items
Sorting and Classifying	Independently sorts and classifies by more than one attribute (e.g., says . . . these are round and red)	Consistently groups items that have shared attributes (e.g., puts all the round ones together)	Inconsistently groups similar objects together (e.g., puts round ones together then adds red ones that are not round)	Does not group similar items
Rote Counting	Rote count more than 10	Rote count to 10 consistently	Rote count to 5 consistently	Does not rote count
Quantity (More/Less)	Consistently compares sets verbally (more/less, bigger/smaller)	Inconsistently uses words to compare sets	Points to bigger/ smaller sets on request	Does not compare sets
Patterns	Notices and re-creates more complex patterns (abcabc)	Notices and re-creates simple patterns, with objects (abab)	Inconsistently notices and re-creates simple patterns with objects	Does not recognize or re-create simple patterns with objects

Electronic Observation Records

People have been taking photographs of children in school for as long as cameras have existed. Today, technology is available (still and video cameras, audio recorders, scanners, and computers) that can help you record children's activities and work. Creating a photographic, video, or audio record of a child engaged in school serves much the same purpose as other forms of observation and requires the same level of understanding of its purpose. Just as written observations require skill and judgment, so, too, do electronic observations. Skill in managing technology is a new basic required of teachers of young children. The acquisition of the up-to-date equipment that it entails, and the teacher time required to effectively make use of the technology, are new expenses that must be included in program budgets.

Photographs. As the saying goes, a picture is worth a thousand words. But is it? Photographs are valuable documentation when they show something happening or provide a

GOLDEN RULES FOR INTERVIEWING A CHILD FOR ASSESSMENT

1. Don't interrupt a child who is actively involved with friends or play activities; instead, invite the child to join you during an interlude after play.
2. Choose a quiet corner for the interview where you can sit at the child's level.
3. Plan questions in advance and relate them to your objectives for children— remember you want to know what children understand and can do, not whether they liked an activity or the way you teach.
4. Use open-ended questions that have many possible answers to avoid the child feeling there is a "right" answer. Start with phrases like "Tell me about..." and "What do you think...?"
5. Use language that is easy for the child to understand.
6. If the child doesn't answer a question, try rephrasing the question and asking it again.
7. Use the child's answers and interests to guide the interview.
8. Record children's behavior as well as their words.

record of a child's work. They can quickly and accurately show something that is difficult to describe clearly—for example, a photograph of a child's elaborate block structure.

Photographs are valuable only when they are genuine representations of what children can do, not when posed to be cute to adults. They are also not particularly useful as observation when they record an event that is not meaningful in terms of children's development—for example, the entire class dressed up for Halloween or 2-year-olds eating gooey cupcakes and getting icing on their faces. Exercise the same criteria for using photographs that you use for writing anecdotal observations. Photograph children engaged in something typical, something new (a milestone), or something that is of concern.

The term ***annotated photograph*** (McAfee, Leong, & Bodrova, 2004) is used to describe a photograph that is accompanied by an anecdotal record, as shown in Figure 5.9. The annotation should include the child's name and the date of the photograph, the setting or context of the photograph (e.g., in the dramatic play area), an anecdote explaining what happened (e.g., what you observed when the photograph was taken), and what the photo tells about this child. Without annotation a photograph may not be enough to help another person understand its significance. It is valuable to take several pictures of a child engaged in an activity to show the process as the child engages in play or work to create a product.

Video and Audio Records. Like photographs, video and audio records are valuable documentation when they show something happening or provide a record of a child's ability. They are particularly useful in documenting nuances of movement and for recording subtleties of language and interactions. They allow a number of observers to view or hear the same child engaged in the same activity.

02/13 N. pedaled the rickshaw trike with two friends on the back demonstrating large-motor strength

FIGURE 5.9 **Example of an Annotated Photograph**

Because they capture everything, they are not dependent on writing skill and not as subject to the bias of the observer. You may notice detail in a recording that you would not have observed while writing an observation. Creating audio recordings for the purpose of documentation is different from using a digital voice recorder as a spoken alternative to writing an observation.

Video and audio recordings have some disadvantages, however. Equipment can be distracting to children, especially if a large camera or a tripod is being used. Editing video requires some technical skill, and it can be time-consuming to cull the few significant minutes or seconds from larger recordings. Recording made in a typically noisy classroom environment can be difficult to understand.

In order to use video or audio records effectively, decide in advance what activity or interaction you want to record. Give children time to get used to the camera or tape recorder before you try to capture the significant event. Record a few children away from the rest of the group if possible. Ask another teacher, a volunteer, or a parent to help you videotape if you are recording while you are teaching. Finally, be sure to select only short relevant sections to share with others. Editing in this way can make the resulting video or audio records useful as documentation.

Selecting an Observation Recording Technique

Each of the techniques described in the preceding sections is particularly useful for one or more purposes. You are likely to use all of them at different times. Remembering what you are trying to accomplish can help you to select an observation recording technique. Figure 5.10 is designed to help you choose.

Work Samples

Work samples (children's drawings, paintings, cutting, writing, journals, dictated stories, maps, computer work, word banks, and so forth) serve as a powerful form of authentic assessment. They provide tangible evidence of a child's learning.

FIGURE 5.10 Selecting an Observation Method

In order to . . .	Use . . .
Create a vivid record of a child's activity	Running record; videotape
Record a behavior or interaction or the achievement of a milestone	Anecdotal record; annotated photograph
Ascertain how often a type of behavior occurs	Time sample
Understand why or when a particular behavior occurs	Event sample
Gather information about children's play preferences, individual progress, how materials and equipment are being used	Checklist
Evaluate the extent to which a child has reached particular milestones	Rating scale
Compare how different children understand a specific concept	Interviews
Quickly and accurately document something that is difficult to describe	Annotated photographs; videotape
Document movement, language, or interactions (or related abilities, such as musical skill) in order to share them with others	Running record; videotape or audio recording

FIGURE 5.11 Annotated Work Sample

A pot of mums was placed in the center of the art table. J. took a Sharpie marker and drew a flower, then embellished the center with a face. She requested yellow liquid watercolor paints and carefully painted in each petal. "It's a happy flower!" she said to the teacher.

Collect samples of each child's work on a regular basis. Remember to collect a variety of items. Be sure to label, date, and annotate all work samples before storing them. Like annotated photographs, annotated work samples should include the child's name and the date, the setting or context in which it was created, a written description explaining what happened (e.g., when it was created), and your interpretation of what it tells about this child. Large or three-dimensional work samples (like easel paintings and woodworking projects) can be captured in a photograph. Some teachers prefer to scan children's work so that they have an electronic copy.

Portfolios

One of the most common ways to meaningfully organize the rich data that authentic assessment provides is in a *portfolio,* a term derived from the portfolios that artists create to present their work to others. Just as an artist's portfolio gives a fuller understanding of the artist's abilities, so a child's portfolio gives a fuller understanding of who the child is and what the child knows and can do. Educators using the words *authentic assessment* are usually thinking of portfolios and may use the term *portfolio assessment* as a synonym for authentic assessment.

The term *portfolio* is also used to refer to the documentation that teachers and others gather to represent their own training and ability—usually called a *professional portfolio.* More recently, the terms *program portfolio* and *classroom portfolio* have been used to describe an organized assemblage of plans, documents, and records that provide evidence of implementation in a program for children of accreditation criteria. In this chapter, however, we are talking about *child* portfolios. In preschool programs these are sometimes called *developmental portfolios,* to reflect their purpose (to illustrate a child's development), their organization (according to developmental domains), and to distinguish them from portfolios for older elementary students organized by academic subject areas and designed to show achievement of academic objectives.

Portfolios are, flexible, systematically organized compilations of evidence of a child's learning, ability, growth, and development (observations, work samples, photographs, etc.) collected over time. They are a logical extension of the observational approaches that traditionally have been used to learn about children in early childhood programs. A portfolio becomes *portfolio assessment* when it contains evidence to evaluate whether and to what degree a child has acquired skills, knowledge, and dispositions. In elementary school settings, portfolios represent an alternative to tests, report cards, and letter grades, although they may be used in addition to these more traditional methods. Portfolios focus on what children can actually do. They provide a far more complete and authentic picture of a child than a checklist or a test.

Portfolios help you to look at children's work over time to gauge how they are developing—socially, emotionally, physically, and cognitively. They give you a deeper understanding of a child and can help to guide your planning. Portfolios also assist you as you share your understanding with families and other professionals, and they represent the child's strengths and potential and can be shared with the staff of the next program to which the child moves.

Creating Portfolios

Portfolios can include the narrative, structured, and electronic observation records, work samples, and interviews we have previously described. What you collect for each child's portfolio will depend on program goals and your purpose in creating portfolios.

To make meaningful and useful decisions about what to collect for a child's portfolio, you must identify goals and objectives for children and decide what materials and information will indicate that these have been accomplished. For example, if a program goal is the enhancement of literacy, you might collect work samples in which a child has incorporated print or print-like marks, keep records of books read to or by the child, and write anecdotal records when the child uses pens or pencils to communicate.

You are likely to collect more items than you will actually include in a portfolio. Each item included should be meaningful and informative—that is, it should tell something about the child's development, abilities, and learning. Because the purpose of a portfolio is to document the individual child's development, samples will not be the same for every child. School-age children can participate in selecting and explaining the work samples they include in their portfolios.

It is important that a portfolio create a complete and authentic representation of the child's understanding and skill in the categories you have determined to be important. Having an outline of items that are essential to include will help. It is frustrating to discover that you are missing critical observations, photographs, or work samples when you are ready to put together the portfolio. Figure 5.12 is a basic list of items that we collect for a preschool child's portfolio. Your list will reflect the age of children you teach as well as your program's goals and values.

A folder full of random and disorganized "stuff" is not a portfolio, nor is a "scrapbook" decorated with stickers and winsome photos of the child grinning into the camera. To turn a collection into a portfolio, you organize and interpret the evidence that you have collected. In many programs a structure for portfolios is established. In settings for children under 5, domains of development are often used as the organizing framework. In primary schools, subject areas are often used. When your program has such a structure in place, you may be asked to do the following:

- Collect certain items at the same time from all children, such as a drawing from the first week of school and another from the last week of school—sometimes called *core items*.

FIGURE 5.12   Sample Portfolio Contents for a Preschool Child

Background Information	
Child's date of birth	Date started school/class
Language(s) spoken in the home	Ethnic/racial/cultural identification

Evidence of Physical Development and Health: *Observations, photographs, work samples that show . . .*	
Size/weight compared to others of his/her age	Typical, food intake/preferences
Toileting routines/accidents	Length of typical nap
Large-motor activity	Fine-motor activity
Sensory activity	Preferred hand and grip

Evidence of Personal/Social Development: *Observations, photographs, work samples, or recordings that show . . .*		
Self-regulation and self-help	Self-initiated activities	Friendships (also child-reports)
Making choices	Showing awareness of feelings	Interactions w/ others
Separation from family	Cooperative behavior	Solving a social problem
Pretend play		Formal group activity

Evidence of Language and Cognitive Development: *Observations, photographs, work samples, or recordings that show . . .*		
Reading or writing	Dictated notes or stories	Writing samples (one per month
Listening to or telling stories	Talking or storytelling	Conversations with others

Evidence of Cognitive Development: *Observations, photographs, work samples, or recordings that show . . .*		
Noticing a natural phenomenon	Discovery or exploration	Sorting, counting, or classifying
Examples of maps or illustrations		Identifying a problem

Evidence of Creative Ability and Aesthetic Awareness: *Observations, photographs work samples, or recordings that show . . .*		
Engaged in music	Painting (one per month)	Musical expression in song
Engaged in movement	Creative art or construction	Drawing (one per month)

CONNECTING WITH FAMILIES

Families have an important role in assessment. They are not merely "the audience" to whom you present a portfolio. They have valuable contributions to make. Invite families to participate in tangible ways. Have incoming families tell the child's story, describe what the child was like last year, share who the child is in the family today. You might want to design a questionnaire for incoming families to complete to include in a portfolio.

- Collect evidence of a child's ability in specific activities—such as a drawing, an observation of a social interaction, a written or taped language sample, a photograph of a block building, or a writing sample.
- Have children select examples of a favorite or "best" work to include in their portfolios.

Creating portfolios for a class of children is a lot of work! It is easier when you develop a system for compiling items to be included. A large accordion folder that includes several file folders to organize different kinds of materials serves well as portfolio storage. Some teachers use file boxes, and others organize materials into notebooks that have folders and pocket sheets in which to store work samples. All of these systems work well for managing works in progress such as anecdotal records, checklists, and rating scales. Large items that must be stored elsewhere can be indexed in the system with a note about where they are stored. Some teachers construct cardboard or wooden files that are sized to fit the easel paintings so that everything can be stored together.

The next steps in creating a portfolio are to reflect on what you have collected, analyze what it means, and finally write a description of the child's abilities and characteristics based on the evidence that you have collected. This description can be called an *individual profile,* a *developmental description,* or a *summary statement.*

The individual profile provides a picture of what makes this child unique. It should include a general description of the child's ability, interests, progress, and patterns of engaging in each of the areas included in the portfolio. It should incorporate the teacher's appraisal of where the child is in terms of program goals and note any areas of concern that need to be monitored. School-age children can begin to take a role in this process. They can consider their own strengths, interests, and weaknesses, select work samples, and add their point of view to the summary (see "Golden Rules for Creating Child Portfolios").

Digital Portfolios

In some programs portfolios are created electronically without physical materials. Instead, photos, observations, rating scales, and such are entered or scanned into a computer. These are then assembled into a digital document that can be shared electronically. These *digital* portfolios (sometimes called *electronic portfolios,* or *e-portfolios*) have the advantage of requiring little physical space and they require no storage boxes, binders, sheet protectors, toner, or photo paper. The

---

FIGURE 5.13 Sample Portfolio Contents for a Primary School-Age Child

For each subject area (typically reading, writing, math) include:

1. Statement describing the standards, program goals, curriculum objectives and expectations in this subject area for this grade level
2. Representative work samples/formal assessments from the beginning, middle, and end of the year
3. Key assignments and related rubrics
4. Notable work samples chosen by child or teacher
5. Observations, jottings, captioned photographs, and video related to the subject area
6. Child reflections/summaries (from first grade); e.g., "One thing I'm good at is _____. One thing I want to work on is _____."
7. Summary statement by the teacher

disadvantage of a digital portfolio is that it requires technical expertise on the part of the teacher as well as the family who ultimately is given the portfolio. Lack of computer access may place it out of reach for some families. As with all forms of digital storage, the computer program that created the portfolio will eventually be outdated, rendering the portfolio difficult, if not impossible, to access.

Portfolio Blogs. Another strategy for creating digital portfolios is to create a blog for each child. Instead of a "finished product" portfolio that is presented to the family periodically, a blog is ongoing. The teacher inputs observations and photographs each week. Both teacher and family have access to the blog and are able to input their observations and insights.

Using Portfolios

How do you use the portrait of a child that the portfolio provides? One of the most valuable things you can do is to use it to share your understanding of the child with families and other professionals. The portfolio itself vividly depicts the child and his or her work. It provides a focal point for a conference with the family or other professionals. The summary description that you write for the portfolio can be used as part of a narrative report given to families at a conference.

The portfolio can also be used to guide planning for the child and for the group. The individual profile that you created includes the child's abilities, strengths, interests, and challenges. These will help you plan for this specific child. Taken together, the portfolios created for the group give you a picture of what curriculum content might benefit the class as a whole.

GOLDEN RULES FOR CREATING CHILD PORTFOLIOS

1. Decide on domains or subject areas to be used as a structure.
2. Involve families in the portfolio process from the start by explaining what you plan to do and having them participate when possible.
3. Set aside a special place for collecting portfolio evidence. It should have a section for each child and be large enough to hold larger examples of children's work.
4. Establish a time line for collecting evidence and writing summaries, including how and when the portfolio will be shared and passed on.
5. Identify evidence of a child's ability—such as drawing, an observation of a social interaction, an observation or taped language sample, a photograph of a block building, or a writing sample.
6. Create a checklist or other system to ensure that you collect observations of each child and samples of their work in every domain or subject area on a regular basis.
7. Collect *core items* at the same time from all children, such as a drawing or writing sample from the first week of school and another from the last week of school.
8. Annotate each item you collect with the date and a brief explanation of its significance.
9. Have older children select examples of a favorite or "best" work to include in their portfolios.
10. Find a colleague to be your portfolio partner so that you can share, edit, and review one another's written work.

Portfolios are not static documents. They are typically updated at specific times. You might, for example, begin the portfolio at the start of the year, write an initial profile at midyear, continue to add items to the portfolio throughout the year, and review and update it the end of the year. Finally, the portfolio becomes a part of the documentation that moves with the child to the next class or into the archives of his or her family.

Authentic Assessment Systems

It is relatively easy to complete a checklist on each child in a preschool group or give a standardized test to a group of first graders. It can be daunting to authentically assess a class of young children. Some programs devise structured ways for teachers to organize their observations and collection of evidence to create portfolios. A number of commercial systems have been designed to aid early childhood educators in this task. These systems are valuable because they systematize and guide observations and collections of photographs and work samples with specific criteria and procedures. They stand at the border between authentic assessment that we have just described and standardized assessment in which a consistent, uniform (i.e., standard) method is used so that results can be compared.

The portfolio systems described next involve structured methods for collecting evidence. All require teacher training, and all ask you to collect data about children in natural and nonintrusive ways. They also provide computer-generated reports and/or lesson plans through software or online programs. The examples that follow are a sampling of a few of the better known systems.

The High/Scope Child Observation Record (COR). The High/Scope Child Observation Record (COR) (High/Scope, 2003) is an example of a system designed to help teachers and caregivers determine the developmental status of young children ages 6 weeks to 6 years. It is an observational assessment that includes six categories. For infants and toddlers, these include broad domains of child development: (1) sense of self, (2) social relations, (3) creative representation, (4) movement, (5) communication and language, and (6) exploration and early logic. For preschool-age children, the categories are slightly different: (1) initiative, (2) social relations, (3) creative representation, (4) music and movement, (5) language and literacy, and (6) logic and mathematics. Activities that typically occur in a program day are used

for assessment. The teacher or caregiver takes a series of brief notes over several months and at the end of that time rates the child's behavior using a 30-item questionnaire. Scores must be interpreted by a test administrator, who is specially trained to evaluate the COR. There are online alternatives for recording observations and generating reports and plans.

The Work Sampling System. The Work Sampling System (Dichtelmiller et al., 2001) is a more comprehensive performance-based assessment system designed to be used from preschool through the primary years (ages 3 to 11). It consists of three components: (1) developmental guidelines and checklists, (2) portfolios, and (3) summary reports. The developmental guidelines and checklists are designed to assist teachers in observing and documenting individual children's growth and progress. They are structured around developmentally appropriate activities and are based on national, state, and local curriculum standards. Each checklist covers seven domains: (1) personal and social development, (2) language and literacy, (3) mathematical thinking, (4) scientific thinking, (5) social studies, (6) the arts, and (7) physical development. The checklists and guidelines create a profile of children's individualized progress. Checklists, observations, and digitized work samples are entered online, and a digital portfolio is created that replaces report cards as a means of communicating children's progress to families. They include performance and progress ratings in each domain, along with teachers' comments about the child's development.

The Ounce Scale (Meisels, Dombro, Marsden, Weston, & Jewkes, 2003) is the infant-toddler version of work sampling to be used with children from birth to 3½ years. It includes three components: an observation record in which teachers record their observations; a family album in which families collect observations, photos, and mementos of their child's growth and development; and a rating scale used to evaluate children's growth and development at the end of eight age levels. The online version generates ideas for families to try at home.

The Ounce Scale includes six areas of development: (1) personal connections (trust), (2) feelings about self, (3) relationships with other children, (4) understanding and communicating (language development), (5) exploration and problem solving, and (6) movement and coordination. Family involvement in the assessment is an integral part of the Ounce Scale. It is designed to be used in group programs, home visiting programs, and family support programs.

Teaching Strategies Gold. Teaching Strategies Gold is designed to accompany *The Creative Curriculum for Preschool*, Fifth Edition (Dodge, Colker, & Heroman, 2010), and *The Creative Curriculum for Infants, Toddlers & Twos* (Dodge, Rudick, & Berke, 2006). It is a preschool and infant-toddler observational assessment system based on skills related to development (e.g., *understands and follows directions*). It uses a rating scale that includes examples of ways in which children might demonstrate the skills. These range from "forerunner" behaviors (*associates words with actions—says "throw" when sees a ball thrown*) to "mastery" behaviors that would typically occur when children have mastered the specific skill (*follows directions with more than two steps—e.g., follows directions to put clay in container, wipe table, and wash hands when the activity is finished*).

Teachers using Teaching Strategies Gold must use a Web-based system for recording and interpreting observations that are then used for the development of portfolios and curriculum plans. Because it is tied to a curriculum manual, it makes a clear connection between assessment and planning.

Public Documentation

A way to authentically assess your curriculum is to create public *documentation*. One form of public documentation (called *documentation panels*) is associated with the preschool programs of Reggio Emilia, Italy. *Documentation panels* are posters in which photographs, children's work, observations, and teacher-authored text are put together to illustrate an aspect of the program. Often, though not always, documentation panels are used to present how curriculum studies/projects led to children's growth and learning. They can also be used to show how the questions of a group of children led to investigation, to illustrate how children learn by using a particular piece of equipment, or to show how children learn from their interactions with others. Documentation panels can be hung in hallways, classrooms, and entryways.

A well-crafted documentation panel is more than a pretty wall decoration. It powerfully illustrates the depth of children's learning, as well as your curriculum and teaching. It shows your respect for children and makes visible to family members and visitors that "real" education is going on in early childhood programs. Other forms of documentation that can be used of public education include power point presentations, videos, books, and gallery displays.

Authentic Assessment in Kindergarten and the Primary Grades

While portfolios and the authentic assessment strategies that we have described here are not new they are not universally used in programs for primary school-aged children, particularly in public schools. If you come to teach in a public school setting, authentic assessment may feel like a time-consuming luxury that you have difficulty justifying. Your school may require you to write report cards. With the greater emphasis on accountability and testing requirements, you may have to administer standardized tests and may feel obliged to focus on the content and process of taking tests. What should you do?

Remembering that the purpose of assessment is to improve instruction. You can observe, document, and interpret what you observe in addition to administering standardized tests and completing report cards. And, if you think of authentic assessment more broadly you can use it as a way to support developmentally appropriate practices in your classroom.

In their thoughtful article *Joyful Learning and Assessment in Kindergarten*, Hughes and Gullo (2010) suggest some ways to think about authentic assessment to ensure both accountability and joyful, appropriate learning:

1. View assessment as a **continuous process**—in other words, use ongoing authentic assessment of children's activities as a vehicle for assessing their growth and informing your teaching.
2. Understand assessment as a **comprehensive process**—in other words, realize that true assessment needs to include children learning in different ways—not just on a test.
3. Consider assessment as an **integrative process**—that is, authentic assessment shows the effectiveness of instruction. When children use what they have learned in lessons and self-selected activity and you document their responses, then you are powerfully assessing the children and your teaching.

While this understanding does not give you more time, it provides you with a powerful justification for both developmentally appropriate practices and authentic assessment. As Hughes and Gullo note, "Appropriate assessment can lead to joyful learning *and* joyful teaching" (2010, 59).

Standardized Assessment

Childhood is a journey, not a race.

Anonymous

In standardized assessment all children are given the same tasks in the same way. And they are evaluated or scored using the same criteria. This is because standardized tests are intended to objectively compare children's development and learning to a norm. McAfee, Leong, and Bodrova point out, "We do assessment that is standardized when we do our best to be consistent and uniform, or *standard* in our methods so results can be compared. . . . Standardization saves time, as well as increases the reliability and fairness of our assessments" (2004, 57).

Early childhood educators have historically been committed to using observation and authentic assessment as their primary means for learning about and reporting children's development and learning. In this section we will tell you about some of the kinds of standardized assessment instruments that are currently used in early childhood settings, discuss the appropriate function of each type, and explore some of issues associated with their use.

Kinds of Standardized Assessment Instruments

A *test* is a systematic procedure for sampling a child's behavior and knowledge that usually summarizes the child's performance with a score. Standardized tests have clearly defined purposes and have some distinguishing characteristics that set them apart from other approaches to learning about children. Each item on a standardized test has been carefully studied to establish the dependability of the test. Two kinds of data are used to establish dependability: (1) *validity* or accuracy, the degree to which a test measures what it claims to measure, and (2) *reliability* or consistency, how often identical results can be obtained with the same test. Standardized tests are either *norm-referenced* or *criterion-referenced*. Norm-referenced tests compare an individual child's performance on the test with that of an external norm, which was established by administering the test to a large sample of children (for example, the SAT test). Criterion-referenced tests relate the child's performance to a standard of achievement (for example, whether or not a child can skip) but do not compare the child to a reference group.

A standardized test should have a well defined purpose, a manual with information on standard procedures, data that confirm reliability and validity, and clear directions. Those who select the test need to have carefully considered the appropriateness of the purpose of the test for the children who will be tested. The language used in the test (both the particular language and the vocabulary level) should be comprehensible to the children being tested.

An assessment *instrument* or *tool* (the terms are interchangeable) is a systematic means of collecting and recording information about young children. Checklists, rating scales, and performance assessments, as well as tests, are instruments. Keep in mind that while all tests are assessment instruments/tools, not all assessment instruments are tests.

Some commonly used standardized assessment tools are screening instruments, developmental assessments, diagnostic tests, academic readiness tests, and individual and group intelligence and achievement tests. Standardized assessment instruments reflect the values of the people who created them—what they believe to be worthwhile for a child of a particular age to know, to do, or to have experienced. If you are ever called on to select or use one of these assessment tools, you will want to determine whether it is a good fit for your purposes and the child or children you wish to learn about.

Screening Instruments

Screening instruments are designed to identify children who may need specialized services. They compare a child's development to that of other children of the same age. Screening is a relatively fast and efficient way to assess the developmental status of children. Every child is screened, in some way, beginning at birth. The newborn is observed for obvious defects. Simple screening such as observation and testing of heart rate, muscle tone, and respiration occur in the first few minutes after birth. As children grow and develop, they encounter other forms of screening in the course of regular medical care.

Another important kind of screening occurs in school settings to identify children who might have developmental delays or medical conditions requiring correction, such as a vision or hearing impairment. Appropriate screening can bring about improvements in children's lives. Generations of children entering the Head Start program have been screened. Many with hearing losses, vision impairments, and other medical problems have been identified and given appropriate treatment. Children who are identified by the screening process as being at risk for learning problems can be evaluated and receive special services to help them do better in school.

Educational screening instruments are relatively short, have few items, address a number of developmental areas, and can be administered and interpreted by trained professionals or trained volunteers. Screening identifies children who need to be looked at more carefully. A child should *never* be labeled on the basis of screening, because screening *cannot* predict future success or failure, prescribe specific treatment or curriculum, or diagnose special conditions. It should not be used to determine individual development plans or as the basis for curriculum planning.

Good screening instruments are valid and reliable and focus on performance in a wide range of developmental areas (speech, understanding of language, large and small motor skills). They should also involve information from families who know the child best and have important information to contribute. Screening instruments are most likely to appropriately identify children if they use the language or dialect of the child's family. Children who are not tested in their first language will not be able to communicate their true abilities. Similarly, instruments should reflect the experiences and cultural background of the children.

Screening services vary from community to community and from state to state. Many communities provide screening when children enter kindergarten or first grade. Some have Childfind programs to make parents and other adults aware of the importance of early identification. As an early childhood educator, you may participate in choosing or administering a screening instrument and be involved in follow-up. If formal screening is not available in your school or community, informal screening through sensitive observation can also identify children who need further assessment.

No screening instrument is foolproof. Some children with developmental delays will remain undetected, while others who have no serious delays will be identified as needing further evaluation. For this reason it is important that screening instruments be chosen carefully and that great care is taken in reporting results to families.

Some screening instruments are specific to age and stage of development, while others address a range of ages. Examples of this type of screening instrument are the Bayley Scales of Infant Development and the Peabody Developmental Motor Scales. Multidomain developmental screening tests include all areas of development and are among the most commonly used. The Early Screening Inventory, the DIAL (Developmental Indicators for Assessment of Learning), and the Early Learning Accomplishment Profile are examples of these instruments.

Developmental Assessments

Developmental assessments include checklists and rating scales that have been created for appraising children's skills and abilities. They are designed to help you learn about children's actual functioning in the classroom by identifying patterns of strengths and weaknesses in a number of developmental domains. They are criterion referenced—that is, they reflect a child's degree of mastery over a skill or sequence of skills, rather than comparing them to a norm. Developmental assessments are not meant to label children; rather, they give you information so that you can design appropriate experiences for individual children and groups.

A developmental assessment is usually administered, interpreted, and used by program staff. It may take weeks or even months to completely administer a developmental assessment in a number of areas. In some programs it may be a process that continues throughout the school year. It may be administered early in the year to identify skills the child already has and then used as the basis for designing experiences and activities to help the child to move to the next step. The child may be assessed again later in the year.

Developmental assessments often include guidelines for lessons and materials that are designed to develop specific skills. Although these may provide good ideas, teachers should never teach assessment items in isolation or use them as the basis for curriculum. Examples of commonly used assessments include Batelle Developmental Inventory and the Learning Accomplishment Profile, Third Edition.

Developmental assessment may also serve a screening purpose, especially if no other screening has been done. Results can indicate that a child may have a problem. If a delay is observed, the child should be carefully watched and should receive additional support in the area of concern. The child may need a diagnostic evaluation if the delay persists.

Like screening instruments, developmental assessments measure only what can be observed and what their authors believe to be important. They may not assess what you or your colleagues value. If you decide to use a developmental assessment instrument, be aware of the limitations of the instrument and continue to use your own observations to create a more comprehensive picture of a child.

A developmental assessment instrument that is appropriate for a given program will have goals for children that are similar to or compatible with the goals of the program. Good instruments provide guidelines for use and can be easily administered and interpreted by staff—criteria for success are clearly spelled out. They can be used with the language or dialect of the program's population and can be adapted to reflect the culture and typical experiences of its children. Good assessments involve manipulative and verbal rather than written responses, and short testing periods followed by rest intervals.

Diagnostic Tests

Diagnostic tests are in-depth evaluations used to assess what children actually can do in specific areas of development. They are used to identify children with special needs, and serve as the basis for making decisions about instructional strategies and specialized placements. These tests vary from those designed to help understand a child's functioning in a single developmental domain to others that are more general. For example, a speech-language specialist might administer a diagnostic test to determine a child's receptive language capabilities, and a psychologist might administer a developmental inventory that assesses a half-dozen or more domains.

Diagnostic tests are often conducted as part of the comprehensive evaluation process carried out by an interdisciplinary team. The team may include a physician; psychologist; speech, hearing, and physical therapists; family members; and the classroom teacher. The team will evaluate whether a serious problem exists, what it seems to be (diagnosis), and the kind of strategies, placement, and services that would be most appropriate for the child (treatment).

Readiness and Achievement Tests

Readiness and achievement tests examine children (individually or in groups) to make judgments regarding their performance in comparison to some standard. They are standardized tests that are administered and scored using a prescribed procedure that is not a part of the regular program activity.

Readiness tests focus on a child's existing levels of skills, performance, and knowledge. Their proper purpose is to facilitate program planning. Achievement tests measure what a child has learned—the extent to which he or she has acquired information or mastered identified skills that have been taught. Achievement tests are designed to determine the effectiveness of instruction. Most of the tests that are administered as part of No Child Left Behind requirements are achievement tests.

Issues in Standardized Assessment

In recent years there has been a dramatic increase in the use of standardized testing of young children. Standardized assessment has become the focus of intense interest and concern in the field of early childhood education. Part of the reason lies in a national concern with educational accountability that has filtered into early childhood education. The No Child Left Behind Act of 2001 created a federal mandate requiring testing of children in federally funded programs. Although originally written to require testing of children beginning in third grade, it now affects hundreds of thousands of 4-year-olds in Head Start programs (Meisels & Atkins-Burnett, 2005). Some pressure comes from families and policy makers who want to be reassured that children are learning and will be able to compete with peers in other communities and countries. Increased understanding of the significance of early experience in children's intellectual development has also led to the desire to find out more about what children are learning and to develop standards by which achievement must be assessed.

Those who advocate the use of tests maintain that having comparative data and a national frame of reference is helpful in assessing the effectiveness of instruction and in making decisions about school admissions and placements. They also claim that data on standardized tests are helpful in justifying programs and proving accountability to funding agencies.

When the primary purpose of assessment is to identify developmental problems or to gather information about children's progress in a systematic way, then standardized tests may be called for. Unfortunately, standardized testing is also being used to determine which children fit existing programs and to exclude those who do not "make the grade," rather than to make educational programs responsive to all children's needs and developmental stage.

Critics of standardized testing (Cryan, 1986; Graves, 2002; Kamii, 1990; Kohn, 2000; Wortham, 2011) raise a number of issues and concerns. Some of the most frequently cited are the following:

- Test results may not be valid and reliable because it is difficult to administer tests to young children. The tests may be beyond children's developmental capabilities, or the children's behavior may be unduly influenced by mood or by the test situation.
- Tests measure a narrow range of objectives—mostly cognitive and language abilities—and miss important objectives of early childhood education such as creativity, problem-solving, and social and emotional development.
- Many tests are culturally biased. Children who do not speak English as a first language and those from minority groups frequently not do as well on the tests.
- Tests are often inappropriately administered and interpreted because most early childhood professionals are not trained in the appropriate use and interpretation of standardized tests.
- Teachers who want children to do well on tests may introduce skills too early or alter their curriculum and "teach to the test," resulting in teaching methods and content that are inappropriate for young children.
- Tests are often used for purposes for which they were not intended. Test results are inappropriately used to keep children out of school, retain them in the same grade, place them in remedial classes, or make unwarranted placements in special education classrooms rather than for improving classroom practice.

High-Stakes Testing

Early childhood educators strenuously object to **high-stakes testing,** using the scores on tests to make decisions that have long-term consequences such as rejecting, retaining, or tracking children. Perhaps equally destructive is when schools become narrowly focused on test results curriculum and children's school experiences are limited. In order to prepare children to take tests successfully, some programs eliminate recess, play, story reading, art, music, and physical education. Children's love of learning and true education itself become the victims of high-stakes testing. Concern with high-stakes testing is so great that it has been added to the NAEYC Code of Ethical Conduct for early childhood educators:

> **P-1.6**—We shall strive to ensure that decisions such as those related to enrollment, retention, or assignment to special education services, will be based on multiple sources of information and will never be based on a single assessment, such as a test score or a single observation.

The National Association for the Education of Young Children (NAEYC) and the National Association of Early Childhood Specialists in State Departments of Education (NAECS/SDE) have developed a position statement to address these issues and to help ensure that assessments of all kinds are used appropriately. Their position states:

> The National Association for the Education of Young Children and the National Association of Early Childhood Specialists in State Departments of Education take the position that policy makers, the early childhood profession, and other stakeholders in young children's lives have a shared responsibility to make ethical, appropriate, valid, and reliable assessment a central part of all early childhood programs. To assess young children's strengths, progress, and needs, use assessment methods that are developmentally appropriate, culturally and linguistically responsive, tied to children's daily activities, supported by professional development, inclusive of families, and connected to specific, beneficial purposes: (1) making sound decisions about teaching and learning, (2) identifying significant concerns that may require focused intervention for individual children, and (3) helping programs improve their educational and developmental interventions. (NAEYC & NAECS/SDE, 2003)

The position statement goes on to give the following guidelines for decisions related to testing in early childhood settings (NAEYC & NAECS/SDE, 2003):

Ethical principles guide assessment practices—do not deny children opportunities or services, or make decisions on the basis of a single assessment.

Assessment instruments are used for their intended purposes—make sure instruments have been shown to be valid for those purposes for which they are used.

Assessments are appropriate for ages and other characteristics of children being assessed—make sure instruments were designed and validated with children whose ages, cultures, home languages, socioeconomic status, abilities and disabilities, and other characteristics are similar.

Assessment instruments are in compliance with professional criteria for quality—make sure instruments adhere to measurement standards set forth by the American Educational Research Association, the American Psychological Association, and the National Center for Measurement in Education.

What is assessed is developmentally and educationally significant—make sure instruments have comprehensive, developmentally, and educationally important goals aligned with early learning standards, program goals, and curriculum, rather than a narrow set of skills.

Assessment evidence is used to understand and improve learning—make sure instruments lead to improved knowledge about children and translate into improved curriculum and teaching practices.

Assessment evidence is gathered from realistic settings and situations that reflect children's actual performance—make sure instruments use real-world classroom or family contexts that are consistent with children's culture, language, and experiences.

Assessments use multiple sources of evidence gathered over time—make sure to use repeated, systematic observation, documentation, and broad, varied, and complementary assessment methods.

Screening is always linked to follow-up—make sure referral or other intervention follows screening, and never diagnose or label based on a brief screening or onetime assessment.

Use of individually administered, norm-referenced tests is limited—make sure instruments are appropriate and potentially beneficial, such as identifying potential disabilities.

Staff and families are knowledgeable about assessment—make sure staff are given resources that support their knowledge and skills, that they see assessment as a tool to improve outcomes for children, and that families are partners in assessment.

As a teacher of young children you need to be aware of different ways of gathering and using information, know the strengths and limitations of a range of assessment options, and remain sensitive and flexible in the ways you learn about children. No single technique or instrument will disclose everything that you need to know about a child. Understanding the uses, and abuses, of assessment can help you to become a better teacher and, when necessary, an advocate for children.

The first thing to think about in using any kind of assessment instrument is what effect it will have on children and their families. Ask yourself if the information you are collecting will lead to positive experiences for children and better

Reflect on your ethical responsibilities

The governing body of your school has decided that all the children in your age/grade level will be tested using a lengthy paper-and-pencil test. You believe the test is inappropriate and might even be harmful to your children's well-being. Some of the other teachers agree with you but do not want to complain. Using the "Guidelines for Ethical Reflection" on page 23, reflect on your ethical responsibilities in this situation and think about an ethical response that you might make.

teaching and learning. And be sure to keep in mind the ideals and principles in the NAEYC Code of Ethical Conduct that relate to assessment.

Sharing Information with Families

The first purpose of assessment is to improve children's educational experience by providing instruction that is most appropriate for them. The second purpose is to use assessment to share with families.

Families want to understand their child's experiences in the early childhood program. They need to know how their child is growing and learning. Most programs have some system for sharing information with them. A conference with family members is the most effective way of sharing information and planning how to mutually support the child's development. Conferences enable families and staff to share and participate in a joint problem-solving process. They often culminate with a summary of the discussion and decisions of the conference and are followed up with a written report.

In some programs written progress reports are the primary way families receive information about their child's progress. Written reporting methods that are frequently used include report cards and narrative summaries. Report cards are most commonly found in programs for primary-age children and are often criticized because they distill large quantities of information about a child into a single letter grade. In most early childhood programs, some combination of conferences and written summaries are used to regularly report on a child's progress. And increasingly the portfolio, including its written summary statement, shared at a conference among parent, teacher, and child, is coming to be an accepted way of sharing information in programs for preschool and primary children.

Confidentiality

When and how you share information that you have gained from observations and standardized assessments with others, the degree to which you protect the information you collect, and the uses to which you put it are all important issues. When you do share such information, it is important to consider your ethical and legal[1] obligations to children, families, and society.

Written observations, assessments, and tests are confidential, and should be stored in such a way as to protect the privacy of children and families. Families have an undisputed right to access this information. And it is generally considered appropriate to share observations and assessment results with other teachers and administrators who work with the child. Who else has a "need to know"? Therapists, teachers in the next school, physicians, and others concerned with the child's welfare may have a genuine reason for being given information. Generally, before sharing information you will get the written permission of the family. The NAEYC Code of Ethical Conduct provides you with guidance.

Everyone enjoys telling a funny or endearing story about a child with whom they have worked. However, it is never acceptable to gossip or discuss a child in a way that may be injurious to the child or in a way that identifies the child to others. Even

---

[1] The Family Educational Rights and Privacy Act (FERPA) is a federal law that protects the privacy of student education records. The law applies to all schools that receive funds under an applicable program of the U.S. Department of Education. Generally, schools must have written permission from the parent or eligible student in order to release any information from a student's education record.

in your college observation papers, it is important to change the child's name or to use his or her initials to avoid breaching confidentiality. Specifically, here is what the NAEYC Code of Ethics states about confidentiality:

> **P-1.4**—We shall use two-way communications to involve all those with relevant knowledge (including families and staff) in decisions concerning a child, as appropriate, ensuring confidentiality of sensitive information.

and

> **P-2.13**—We shall maintain confidentiality and shall respect the family's right to privacy, refraining from disclosure of confidential information and intrusion into family life. However, when we have reason to believe that a child's welfare is at risk, it is permissible to share confidential information with agencies, as well as with individuals who have legal responsibility for intervening in the child's interest. (See Appendix A for the complete NAEYC Code of Ethical Conduct.)

Reflect on your ethical responsibilities

A mother of a child in your class asks you to share how a relative's child (also in your class) is doing in school. She shares that she is concerned about this child's development. You've been worried about the child, too. Using the Guidelines for Ethical Reflection on page 23, reflect on your ethical responsibilities in this situation and think about an ethical response that you might make.

Final Thoughts

You are becoming an early childhood educator, someone who understands and supports the development of children. You will learn about children in many ways through reading, study, practice, and discussions with others. However, the authentic assessment of children, particularly through observation, will teach you the most. The rewards of observing children are great. Like anything worth doing, developing observation skill takes time and work. We urge you to observe children consciously and frequently. And we encourage you to practice writing observations. As you hone these skills, you will discover that you feel more joy and compassion in your work, teach with enhanced skill, and communicate with greater clarity.

Your ability to understand and use the range of observation and assessment strategies discussed in this chapter will help you to better understand children and make sound educational decisions. Knowledge of both authentic assessment techniques makes you a more competent professional and provides the basis for becoming an advocate for children.

 ## Learning Outcomes

When you read this chapter, and then thoughtfully complete selected assignments from the "To Learn More" section and prepare items from the "For Your Portfolio" section, you will be demonstrating progress in meeting

NAEYC Standard 3: Observing, Documenting, and Assessing to Support Young Children and Families (NAEYC, 2009).

Key elements:

3a: Understanding the goals, benefits, and uses of assessment
3b: Knowing about and using observation, documentation, and other appropriate assessment tools and approaches

3c: Understanding and practicing responsible assessment to promote positive outcomes for each child
3d: Knowing about assessment partnerships with families and with professional colleagues

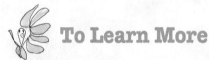 To Learn More

Observe a Child: Select a young child you do not know in an early childhood program. Observe the child for a period of at least half an hour on three different occasions (engaged in outdoor play, an indoor work period, and one other time). Make notes on what you observe each time. Keep a running record of everything the child says and does while you are observing. When you are finished, rewrite your notes in the form of three narratives that include the following:

- A description of the physical attributes of the child and what makes him or her unique
- Where and when you observed, including the setting and the other people present during each observation
- A detailed account of all the things the child did and said during each observation

Summarize What You Observed: Write about what this child can do and what seems to be important for him or her right now. What did you observe that led you to these conclusions?

Reflect on the Child: Write about your interpretations. What do you think the child is thinking and feeling? What did you observe that led you to this conclusion?

Reflect on Your Own Learning and Reaction: Write a reflection on what you learned through these observations and what you think it means. Note any feelings or reactions you had to the child or the observation process. Why do you think you had these reactions? What did you discover about observation?

Use a Structured Observation Method: Use two or more of the structured observation methods described in the chapter to study a child you know. For example, you may wish to use a time sample of the kinds of play the child engages in. Observe the child at least three times on different days. Write about what happened and comment on the following:

- What you learned about the child
- What you didn't learn that you might want or need to know
- What might be done to support this child

- What the experience suggests about the possible advantages and/or disadvantages of using structured observation methods

Use a Standardized Assessment Instrument: Review the manual/instructions and try using a standardized assessment instrument with a child you don't know. If the instrument has a large number of items, use just one developmental area. Interview the child's teacher or parents and find out what they think the child can or cannot do. Write about what happened and comment on the following:

- What you learned about the child
- What you didn't learn that you might want or need to know
- How consistent or inconsistent the results were with the teacher's or parents' experiences of the child
- What the experience suggests about the possible advantages and/or disadvantages of using standardized assessment instruments

Create a Portrait of a Child (Case Study): Select a child to observe over at least an 8-week period as the subject of your portrait. Make observations of all aspects of the child's development on a regular basis. Write a narrative in which you summarize the observations. Describe what the child does without making judgments, assumptions, or interpretations of his or her interests or motivation. Refer to Chapter 4 for information about areas of development. Your portrait should include the following:

- **Physical description:** Include the child's age, gender, and a brief description of the child's physical appearance and characteristic facial and body expressions. Convey what the child is like, and how he or she is unique.
- **Physical development:** Observations of how the child responds to sensory experiences, skill in the use of hands and fingers, how the child uses his or her body in physical activities. Comment on how

the child compares to peers in areas of physical development.

- **Social/emotional development:** Observe the child's relationship to children and adults, the extent to which the child is independent/dependent on others, how the child demonstrates self-control or lack of it, evidence of sharing, cooperation, and other prosocial behavior. Comment on the mood/emotional tone that the child characteristically projects.
- **Cognitive development:** Observe the child's ways of interacting with the world and his or her approach to problem-solving. Select other observations that indicate the child's stage of cognitive development and knowledge and understanding of the world.
- **Supplemental data:** Supplement your narrative observations with developmental checklists, work samples, and any other additional information (e.g., time samples) that you have collected.
- **Summary and conclusions:** Summarize what you have learned and share your thoughts about how the child is progressing developmentally and what the staff might do to continue to support the child's development. What did you learn about yourself and about children from this observation experience?

Create a Child's Portfolio: Create a practice portfolio for a child that includes observations in every developmental area, photographs, and work samples. Write a developmental summary based on these data. Share the portfolio with the child's family.

Interview a Teacher About Assessment: Talk to a teacher about the way he or she assesses children. Ask specifically about how authentic assessment and standardized assessments are used. Ask the teacher to tell you about the ways in which assessment supports instruction. If possible, have the teacher show you examples of the assessment(s) she or he has created.

Investigate Related Websites:

Early Childhood Education Assessment (ECEA) Consortium: ccsso.org/Resources/Programs/Early_Childhood_Education_Assessment_(ECEA).html

"Preschool Assessment: A Guide to Developing a Balanced Approach" available from the National Institute for Early Education Research: nieer.org/resources/policybriefs/7.pdf

National Center for Fair and Open Testing: fairtest.org

 **For Your Portfolio**

A Narrative Observation Record: Include a copy of a narrative observation record of a child (with the name changed or eliminated to preserve confidentiality). Describe how you used the information from this observation to meet this child's needs (e.g., by changing your way of interacting, adding an activity, modifying the environment).

Structured Observations: Include a copy of structured observations that you completed on a child (with the name changed or eliminated to preserve confidentiality) or group of children. Explain how you might use the

information from these observations to better meet children's needs (e.g., by changing your way of interacting, adding an activity, modifying the environment).

A Child's Portfolio: Take a photograph of a portfolio you have created for a child. Include a copy of the developmental summary (with the name changed or eliminated to preserve confidentiality). Write a short paragraph explaining how you used the portfolio to share information in a conference with the family or other professionals, or used it to guide planning for this specific child.

MyEducationLab

Go to Topic 4: Observation/Assessment in the MyEducationLab (myeducationlab.com) for *Who Am I in the Lives of Children?* where you can:

- Find learning outcomes for Observation/Assessment along with the national standards that connect to these outcomes.
- Complete Assignments and Activities that can help you more deeply understand the chapter content.
- Apply and practice your understanding of the core teaching skills identified in the chapter with the

Building Teaching Skills and Dispositions learning units.

- Listen to experts from the field in Professional Perspectives.
- Check your comprehension on the content covered in the chapter with the Study Plan. Here you will be able to take a chapter quiz, receive feedback on your answers, and then access Review, Practice, and Enrichment activities to enhance your understanding of chapter content.

Nothing I have ever learned of value was taught to me by an ogre. Nothing do I regret more in my life than that my teachers were not my friends. Nothing ever heightened my being or deepened my learning more than being loved.

J. T. DILLON

6

Relationships and Guidance

Warm, positive relationships between children and the important adults in their lives are the foundation for children's overall emotional well-being. Building effective relationships with young children and with their families is one of your most essential and rewarding tasks as an early childhood educator. The relationships you create will influence children's learning and their relationships with others, will contribute to their decisions about whether school is a safe and trustworthy place, and will determine how they view themselves as learners and as members of a community. The model you provide and the social climate you create will influence many of the choices children will make about their own actions and relationships.

In this chapter, we will explore the pivotal role of teacher-child relationships in guiding young children's behavior. We will offer suggestions for building and maintaining relationships with the children in your classroom and will describe practices and strategies that help children learn to shape their own relationships with others. We will discuss ways to help children learn to cooperate and to negotiate the inevitable conflicts that arise when people live, work, and play together. We will identify some strategies for successfully managing groups of young children. Finally, we will look at ways to guide children whose behavior is difficult to manage and identify strategies and practices that can help children in early childhood settings learn to relate positively to others.

What Is Guidance?

Early childhood educators often use the term *child guidance* rather than behavior management or discipline. *Guidance* means assisting or leading another person to reach a destination. A *guide* accompanies others in order to show points of interest and to explain meaning. Child guidance is about supporting young children as they learn the difficult skills required to direct and manage their own behavior.

Child guidance encourages children to learn about the needs and feelings of others as well as their own needs and feelings. When you guide young children, you lead them toward understanding themselves and developing self-control. You help them to understand the effects of their behavior on others, and you teach them the skills they need for engaging in satisfying relationships with others—both with peers and adults.

In quality early childhood programs, teachers choose *guidance practices* (what they say and do to guide children's actions) based on: (1) knowledge of child development, including understanding of brain development and its relationships to behavior, (2) appreciation for each individual child, (3) understanding of what families value and believe is important for their children, and (4) knowledge about appropriate guidance practices.

Early childhood teachers have specialized knowledge about how children's development affects behavior, and they gear their expectations to reflect this understanding. They value and enjoy childhood behaviors and believe children have a right to be childlike. They provide supportive guidance based on the understanding that children learn through experiences appropriate to individual age, temperament, learning style, interest, culture, and family choice.

Early childhood educators also understand that children must construct their understanding of the world, including the nature of social relationships. They learn through play and exploration. Children learn social skills through being part of a group and by interacting with people. They learn to treat others with respect and to take responsibility when they are treated respectfully and welcomed into the classroom community. As you learn to provide these opportunities to children in your classroom, you guide them to become cooperative, productive people.

Relationships Are the Foundation for Guidance

As an early childhood teacher, you will come to understand that the relationships that you build with each child are your most effective guidance tools. When you engage in warm, genuine, and caring relationships with children, they begin to learn the social skills necessary to become a member of the classroom community and you learn to appreciate their individual strengths and challenges. When you have a positive relationship with a child, when you like and trust one another, you are able to effectively model ways to interact with others and to help them learn to manage strong emotions appropriately.

The relationship between child and teacher is a significant factor in children's perception of their early learning experiences. Although most young children enter early childhood programs with lively and inquisitive minds, only some come to feel successful as students, to love learning, and to regard education as a rewarding experience. Children are most likely to retain their eagerness and curiosity when they experience teachers who genuinely appreciate and respect them and who base their actions and decisions on knowledge about how children grow and learn.

Good relationships between children and early childhood educators, like all good relationships, are characterized by honesty, empathy, respect, trust, and warmth. They are authentic, not forced or artificial. In good relationships children feel safe from fear of physical and/or psychological harm. No one can be productive when they feel threatened, anxious, or uncertain. Good early childhood programs promote caring relationships between young children and their teachers; harmful tactics such as humiliation or corporal punishment are never used. Shaming or physically punishing children damages both the teacher-child relationship and children's feelings of emotional well-being.

The most effective early childhood educators we know genuinely like children and have clear, developmentally appropriate expectations of them. They are playful, enjoy and often share young children's viewpoints, and gain children's cooperation without demanding unquestioning obedience. They see children as partners, not adversaries, and view the process of helping children grow, through pleasant as well difficult as times, as central to their job. They are careful to promote positive relationships with and between children, families, and staff.

Guidance Is Based on Trust

Trust is foundational to all social and emotional growth. Children develop a sense of trust through positive relationships with the important people in their lives. Work by Howes and Ritchie (2002) draws on premises of attachment theory (Bowlby, 1982) and applies them to teacher-child relationships. These researchers stress that for children of all ages and life circumstances, a trusting relationship with the teacher is necessary in order for children to learn. Further, their research indicates that the quality of the attachment relationship between teachers and children significantly influences children's long- and short-term development. When children trust their teachers, they are able to use them as resources to support their learning (Howes & Ritchie, 2002). In classrooms where teachers create strong teacher-child relationships and support positive peer interactions, children are more likely to behave in socially acceptable ways. In these settings, "classroom management" is about positive relationships rather than finding ways to manage conflict and difficult behaviors (Howes & Ritchie, 2002).

Guidance Honors Differences

Each child and teacher brings to the classroom a unique set of life experiences. Your own family, your past experiences, and your individual characteristics will influence how you relate to young children and the choices you make about how to guide their behavior. Your awareness of the primacy of the family in the child's life will play a key role in your ability to guide children appropriately.

Diverse Beliefs About Guidance

Families hold widely different beliefs and values about how children should behave. They most often choose guidance strategies based on what they have been taught by their parents and grandparents. Discipline and guidance practices reflect the values families have about what is important for children to learn and their beliefs about how individuals should behave toward other people.

The methods that families use to discipline their children reflect a variety of family and cultural circumstances. In some families and cultures, respect for authority is a foundational value. Families with this value expect children to do what they are told promptly, politely, and without questions. Children from these families may learn that obedience is expected and disobedience is often punished. Other families value individual decision-making and teach their children to question authority. Children from these families may learn early that making choices and asking questions are behaviors that are expected and rewarded. Some children may be taught that conformity is important and that most decisions should be made based on what is best for the group, which might be the family, the classroom, or the society. These children may be uncomfortable asking questions. Families who value the interdependence of group members may discourage independence and engage in practices that discourage children's autonomous actions. For example, they might hand feed or carry an older toddler or continue to dress a preschooler who is able to manage dressing him- or herself. Children from these families may develop self-help skills later than children from families who place a high value on independence.

You have values and beliefs about child rearing, too. Your family and your culture have taught you about expectations for children's behavior and about adults' roles in guiding them. You will bring these beliefs and values with you into your classroom and they will affect your expectations and practices. These will also be influenced by what you are learning as a student of early childhood education. There will be times when your personal beliefs, what you have been taught (and are learning) about child guidance, and the beliefs and values of children's families will be in conflict. In these instances it is important to remember that competent early childhood educators learn to honor the beliefs of the families of all children in their care. This does not mean that you will engage in practices that you believe to be inappropriate or unethical. Rather, you will listen thoughtfully when families tell you their beliefs and you will respectfully share your own. When teachers are insensitive to the differences in values between home and school, children may receive messages that indicate to them that their families' ways are "wrong" or "bad." Every child deserves to feel that what is learned at home is valued in school.

You are likely to have children in your classroom whose families have taught them behaviors that are different from the ones that are familiar to you.

Two-and-a-half-year-old Ajut has been enrolled in a full-day program for 4 months. Despite his teacher's warm overtures, he has not spoken directly to her. She has heard him speak to other children during play time. When his teacher looks at him, he looks away quickly and he resists her invitations to talk or play with her.

Because they are unfamiliar, these differences in behavior styles and ways of relating to others may make you feel uncomfortable, or upset. As a teacher you may encounter differences such as those described in Table 6.1.

Use these examples, along with others you will experience, to begin to think about and expand your acceptance of differences. Engaging in dialogues with

Reflect on your family's expectations

What did your family expect of you when you were a child? How did your family want children to behave in public places and in gatherings with other adults? What did they expect from you at school? How did they let you know when they were pleased with what you did? How did they communicate disapproval?

TABLE 6.1 Children's School Responses to Family Guidance Practices

What Families May Do at Home	How Children May Respond at School
Give directions; discourage or forbid questions Require unquestioning obedience	Confused when you ask them to make choices Unwilling to express personal wants Test limits often
Expect children to ask questions Encourage children to make independent decisions	Question adult decisions and reasons Take initiative; may seem to "get into everything"
Use discipline that is harsh and may include spanking or other kinds of physical punishment	Appear to ignore or disregard verbal requests
Have very few limits for or expectations of young children	Distressed or confused when told "no" by adults
May see young children as "babies" and enjoy interacting with them in this manner	Stressed and upset when separating from family members Limited self-help skills Resist or be upset when teachers expect them to feed, dress, and/or toilet independently
Expect independence	Difficulty sharing space, materials, or play activities Act without permission (e.g., leave the classroom, take food from the refrigerator)
Express feelings openly and often	Yell, scream, throw a tantrum
Encourage self-restraint and control of expression	Appear shy, reticent, and quiet Reluctant to speak in a group Unwilling to share ideas or opinions
Encourage strong sense of family pride, honor, and respect	Extermely fearful when they feel they may have misbehaved or disappointed an adult; have a high need for adult approval
Discourage children from calling attention to themselves; require children to demonstrate a humble or modest attitude	Reluctant to speak in group settings; uncomfortable when called on by the adult
Use language that may appear to "put children down" or avoid emphasizing their strengths and skills as a way to avoid bragging (e.g., "my lazy daughter")	Uncomfortable when praised or acknowledged

families about their child-rearing beliefs and practices will help you continue to build relationships that will provide the basis for appropriate guidance.

Differences in Children

You will base your expectations for children's behavior and your choices of guidance practices on the age and developmental stage as well as on individual need and circumstances of each child. Just as you would not expect a 1-year-old to ride a bicycle, you should not expect a 5-year-old to be able to sit at a desk engaged in an activity for an extended period of time.

Learning to tell the difference between an unacceptable behavior and one that may be annoying but is age appropriate is an important skill that all early childhood practitioners need to develop. The following behaviors are typical, although they may be trying to adults:

Infants:	Sob when parent is out of sight
	Refuse to communicate with unfamiliar adults
Toddlers:	Joyfully empty containers
	Respond to most requests with a forceful "NO!"
	Treat all objects as "mine"
Preschoolers:	Resist adult schedules; dawdle through routines
	Do not always tell the truth
	Tell others, "You're not my friend" or "You can't play"
School-age:	Become very competitive; love to be the winner
	Boss other children
	Say, "You can't make me" or "I hate you"

Guidance Is Not Punishment

Punishment can be defined as a rough or injurious penalty. It is designed to stop unwanted behavior by inflicting retribution that is painful or unpleasant. While punishment may achieve immediate results, it will not teach children alternatives or enhance their understanding of what should be done. "Good" behavior resulting from punishment is motivated by fear. Physically painful or corporal punishment is never acceptable in an early childhood program. Physical punishment demonstrates that it is all right to hurt someone if you are big enough. Additionally, although children who have been physically punished may behave appropriately when an adult is watching them, at later times they tend to show increased aggressive behavior (Honig, 1985). According to the American Academy of Pediatrics, "spanking increases aggression and anger instead of teaching responsibility. While it is true that many adults who were spanked as children

CONNECTING WITH FAMILIES

About Guidance Practices

Families use a variety of ways to teach their children about their expectations and the ways that they want them to behave. Some of these may be similar to what you know about and understand; others may be quite different. Here are some ways you can get to know more about their goals, values, and discipline practices:

- Include a question in your enrollment packet asking families to tell you about ways they handle inappropriate behavior at home.
- Make time for a get-to-know-you meeting during the child's first days and ask them about their discipline methods; take time to share ways that you handle inappropriate behaviors in your classroom.
- Ask them what social skills they most wish their child to master and invite them to share ideas for how you can support them in teaching these.
- Plan family meetings around discussion of common challenges such as bedtime, meals, saying no, and so on. Ask for their input regarding what the topic should be.
- Invite professionals with expertise in child guidance or knowledge of the cultures of families in your program to lead a family meeting or to offer a parenting class.

may be well-adjusted and caring people today, research has shown that, when compared with children who are not spanked, children who are spanked are more likely to become adults who are depressed, use alcohol, have more anger, hit their own children, hit their spouses, and engage in crime and violence. These adult outcomes make sense because spanking teaches a child that causing others pain is OK if you're frustrated or want to maintain control—even with those you love" (American Academy of Pediatrics, 2009).

It is more consistent with the early childhood core values of respect, trust, and appreciation for childhood to choose strategies to guide behavior rather than techniques that are punitive.

Guidance is a process designed to help children develop self-control—to understand and use constructive behaviors instead of negative ones. When you frame your thinking about guidance around this goal, you will select practices that nurture, support, and teach—and avoid those that harm or punish vulnerable young children.

Goals for Guidance

Skilled early childhood educators reflect carefully on their goals for children. They think about long- and short-term goals and they consciously choose practices that are congruent with these goals.

Most teachers and families will agree that the following are appropriate long-term goals for child guidance:

- To foster social and emotional intelligence
- To build inner control, self-discipline, and the ability to self-regulate
- To develop resiliency, self-confidence, and a positive sense of self
- To support the development of critical thinking skills
- To teach positive social skills and the ability to be an effective member of a community

It is important to keep in mind the fit between what you actually do in daily practice and your long-term goals for children. Without this awareness you can accumulate a grab bag of techniques that "work" (that is, control immediate behavior problems) but fail to have long-term positive effects.

Short-term goals for child guidance are more immediate. They often include objectives for controlling behavior and ensuring children's safety during day-to-day interactions. Short-term goals may include teaching children to behave in ways that:

- Ensure their safety and the safety of others
- Respect and show care for the feelings and rights of others and of themselves
- Use toys, tools, and materials carefully

How were conflicts and misbehavior dealt with in the schools you attended? What strategies were used? Were they effective? What were your feelings about them? Recall an incident in which you were punished in school. What happened? How did you feel? What were the effects on you? What do you wish had happened? How did the teacher's ways of handling problems affect how you felt about your teachers and school?

**Reflect on your
long-term goals
for children**

What do you feel are
the most important
long-term social and
emotional goals for
educators to have for
the young children
that they teach? Why
did you choose these?
How might they affect
the types of guidance
practices that you use?

Teachers need to think about both long-term and short-term goals when creating relationships and selecting guidance practices. Consider these examples:

Dallas begins climbing on the upper railing of the slide. His teacher is worried that he may fall and hurt himself badly.

Marissa grabs a large block and is holding it in a threatening manner over the head of Kaleo.

Mei is merrily tossing the magnets into the aquarium.

In each instance, the teacher's immediate goal must be to ensure the safety and well-being of the children and of the classroom materials. When there is an immediate risk, teachers do not wait to allow the child to think about their actions and do independent problem-solving. They take action. Dallas's teacher will insist that he get down from the railing immediately. Marissa's teacher will prevent her from using the block to hit Kaleo. Mei's teacher will stop her from dropping the magnets into the aquarium. It is the *manner* the teachers use, the words they choose, the way they use their voices and bodies and their subsequent actions that will determine what children learn from the experience. When the immediate danger is past, skilled teachers then use these experiences for teaching important social and emotional skills.

Fostering the Development of Social and Emotional Intelligence

A primary goal of guidance is to help children develop social and emotional intelligence. Social intelligence is that ability to understand what is happening with other people and to respond to that understanding in a personally and socially effective manner (Livergood, n.d.). This includes the ability to understand the social cues of others, to resolve conflicts, and to engage in prosocial and cooperative behavior. Emotional intelligence is the understanding of feelings, both one's own and those of others. The ability to manage personal feelings and emotions is often referred to as social and emotional competence (CASEL, 2011).

Effective guidance practices promote the growth of social and emotional competence by supporting children's growing abilities to:

- Identify their feelings and the feelings of others
- Demonstrate care and concern for others
- Develop warm and caring relationships
- Handle challenging situations calmly and constructively

Young children are just learning to handle their own feelings and to read and respond to the feelings of others. Consequently, you will want to develop ways to help children learn to calm themselves when angry, make friends with other children, resolve conflicts successfully, and make good choices (CASEL, 2011).

Sometimes teachers lament the amount of time they need to spend helping children learn to deal with upsets, to resolve social problems, and to cooperate. They may view this as time away from curriculum or planned activities. Teachers who value social and emotional learning, and who recognize the importance of these skills, believe that they are an integral part of the curriculum of equal if not greater importance than literacy, math, or other curriculum areas. Recent findings from a large study in Chicago indicate that when children receive specific instruction in social and emotional learning, they not only demonstrate significantly improved skills in these areas of development but also show meaningful gains in academic achievement (Durlak, Weissberg, Dymnicki, Taylor, & Schellinger, 2011).

Building Inner Control

An important hallmark of development during early childhood is growth in the ability to self-regulate. Children aren't born knowing how to control their impulses or how to make acceptable choices of behaviors. These are skills that must be learned. In the past decade, there have been a number of studies designed to help us understand how children learn to regulate their actions. Researchers have determined that self-regulation emerges as a result of both maturation and appropriate experiences that allow children to learn to take deliberate actions, plan ahead, and consciously control their responses (Bronson, 2000). Bronson suggests that there are particular practices teachers can use that support the development of self-regulation at each stage of development (see Table 6.2).

Emotional and social competence and the ability to self-regulate have been shown to be essential elements of children's readiness for elementary school and foundational for developing cognitive skills (Hyson, 2002; Mitchel & Glossop, 2005, cited in Willis & Schiller, 2011). Children learn to control their emotions and their behavior when teachers and other important adults create environments that are warm and trustworthy and where responsible actions are expected, modeled, discussed, and valued.

Promoting the Development of Resiliency and a Positive Sense of Self

Another guidance goal is to help children develop inner strength, confidence, and a positive sense of self. Children who develop these traits are equipped to make healthy life choices and to resist peer pressure to engage in dangerous behaviors. Children who have a clear understanding of their developing strengths and abilities are more likely to be able to overcome obstacles and challenges—in other words, to be resilient (Breslin, 2005).

As children grow and have experiences with others, they develop a set of beliefs about who they are based on their perceptions of how others see them. This *self-concept* includes perceptions of one's physical self, social and cognitive qualities, and competence. Self-concept is greatly influenced by the "mirror" held up by significant people—family members, other important adults, and peers. It begins to develop in the first days of life and continues to grow and change. Families are children's first and most influential sources of information about who they are. It is from families that children begin to establish their identities as individuals of a gender, race, and culture. As they get older, messages from peers become important to children's emerging concepts of themselves. When most of the messages that children receive from others indicate that they are competent and valued, they begin to build a sense of *self-esteem*—a positive sense of themselves. Genuine self-esteem is not about thinking highly of oneself, no matter what the circumstance; rather, true self-esteem is based on a realistic internal self-appraisal, an accurate understanding and acceptance of strengths and weaknesses, and an overall positive sense of self-worth.

Reflect on self-control

Think about a time when you felt very angry. How did you cope with that feeling? Did you use self-control? What were the consequences? What experiences helped you learn to control your feelings?

TABLE 6.2 Supporting Self-Regulation

	Milestones in the Development of Self-Control	Practices to Support Children's Development of Self-Regulation
Infants Birth through 12 months	Not able to self-regulate Beginning control of motor abilities Begin to learn that self is separate from others Begin to anticipate events Begin to connect their motor actions with specific outcomes	Provide predictable schedules and routines based on individual needs Offer opportunities to interact with people and objects in their environment in ways that allow them to create interesting and pleasurable results
Toddlers 12–24 months	Begin to be able to start, stop, and/or maintain an action Begin to communicate and to understand the requests of others	Model actions that toddlers can repeat to successfully complete tasks independently Provide opportunities to make choices of play materials and experiences
24–30 months	Can remember what someone has done or said in the past Developing behaviors indicating autonomy Can carry out simple requests Can label own actions and those of others	Give simple cause-and-effect reasons for desired behavior: "If you pour the milk on the table, you won't have any to drink" Use suggestions rather than commands Use language to describe actions and routines and to emphasize the relationships between actions and outcomes
Preschoolers	Can wait a bit for something they want Can sometimes control their emotions Can make choices between several options Understand cause and effect of physical and social events Are learning to understand that others have feelings different from their own Can follow increasingly complex directions Understand and follow clear rules Becoming consciously aware of their ability to control their actions and thoughts	Give simple responsibilities, such as opportunities to feed the classroom fish or set the table Provide choices of activities and playmates Provide materials and supplies that allow them to carry out a variety of plans and tasks successfully Model and describe appropriate ways to solve problems and deal with feelings Provide reasons for rules and limits Help children make connections between their behavior and the outcome it produces Encourage families to limit exposure to media violence Discuss strategies and assist them with making conscious choices Deemphasize or limit competition
School-Age Children	Can use more complex strategies for solving problems Can consciously choose strategies to allow them to delay gratification Are beginning to compare themselves to others and use internal standards to judge behavior and achievements	Allow individual choices among appropriate learning activities Provide assistance that supports children's independent effort Expect, model, and teach respectful, responsible behavior Model and teach increasingly complex problem-solving strategies

Source: Bronson, M.B. 2000. "Recognizing and Supporting the Development of Self-Regulation in Young Children." Research in Review. *Young Children* 55(2): 32–37. Adapted and reprinted with permission from the National Association for the Education of Young Children (NAEYC). www.naeyc.org.

This self-respect is not the momentary pleasant feeling that some children have when an adult praises them or gives them a treat or a reward. An authentic and positive sense of self is built as children have many experiences that tell them they are valued for who they are. This sense of self supports their ability to accurately identify their own strengths and to accept their challenges and limitations.

Educational researchers have determined that such realistic and optimistic self-appraisal can help children develop *resiliency*—the ability to effectively deal with difficulty and to bounce back from challenging situations. Resilient children demonstrate confidence in their own ability to overcome challenges and frustrations (Kersey & Malley, 2005). Studies of resilient children point to the fact that a caring, involved adult is a consistent feature in the lives of children who deal effectively with adverse life circumstances. When adults let children know they are loved and accepted, acknowledge their skills and accomplishments, support emerging independence, explain the reasons for rules, and model empathy, they are promoting the development of resilience (Pizzolongo & Hunter, 2011). As an early childhood teacher, you will help children become resilient when you consistently express your faith in them and your belief that they can and will be successful. When you help them to accurately assess their own progress and to set goals for future growth, you are supporting the development of healthy sense of self.

Supporting the Development of Critical Thinking Skills
Appropriate child guidance teaches children to think carefully and logically about how to behave. If children are always told what must be done and how to do it, they will have no reason to learn how to determine appropriate behaviors for themselves. Offering children choices, helping them to predict outcomes, and encouraging them to evaluate results invites children to ultimately assume responsibility for their own actions.

Developing the Ability to Be an Effective Community Member
A primary goal of guidance is to help children learn how to be contributing members of a community. Children are not born with the ability to work cooperatively with others. Children learn *prosocial behavior*—cooperation, responsibility, empathy, and altruism—when teachers and other adults value and model these actions.

We will explore some practices for supporting these behaviors in subsequent sections of this chapter.

The Teaching Pyramid

The Center on Social and Emotional Foundations for Early Learning (CSEFEL) has developed a framework to help teachers use classroom practices that promote children's social and emotional competence. This model, The Teaching Pyramid, is shown in Figure 6.1. It is based on the principle that when teachers put the majority of their time and energy into the foundational tiers—relationships and classroom environment, less will need to be expended on the ascending levels. The foundation of the pyramid is the relationships that teachers build with young children. Warm and positive relationships are key to supporting children's growing ability to relate to others in a positive and cooperative manner and to preventing negative behavior.

195

FIGURE 6.1 **The Teaching Pyramid Model for Supporting Social Competence and Preventing Challenging Behavior in Young Children**

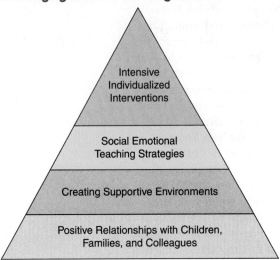

Source: L. Fox, G. Dunlap, M. L. Hemmeter, G. E. Joseph, & P. S. Strain. 2003. "The Teaching Pyramid. A Model for Supporting Social Competence and Preventing Challenging Behavior in Young Children," *Young Children 58*(4): 48–52. Adapted and reprinted with permission from the National Association for the Education of Young Children (NAEYC). www.naeyc.org.

The second tier of the pyramid is providing supportive classroom environments. The ways teachers structure the physical space, the daily schedule, classroom routines, and the methods used to present curriculum all have a strong influence on children's sense of self-confidence and their growing ability to manage their emotions and behavior competently. The Teaching Pyramid framework reminds teachers that the combination of positive relationships and a classroom environment designed to meet the needs of individuals and groups of young children encourages their engagement and can prevent or limit challenging behavior.

The third tier of the pyramid, social and emotional teaching strategies, illustrates the fact that many young children need specific instruction in ways to manage their emotions and to interact cooperatively with others. Teachers should develop activities and select literature that helps children identify and talk about emotions. Positive communication strategies and skills for cooperative play and problem solving should be a prominent part of the planned curriculum.

The last and smallest tier of the pyramid, intensive individualized intervention, is the use of carefully planned intervention strategies for children whose behavior is challenging. Research demonstrates that when the three lower levels of the pyramid are in place, only about 4 percent of the children in a classroom or program will require more intensive support (Sugai et al., 2000).

The pyramid provides you with a tool for evaluating your practices to ensure that you are putting your focus on strategies that will promote positive behavior and social and emotional learning for the children in your classroom.

Subsequent sections of this chapter include discussion of practices that align with each level of the Teaching Pyramid Model.

Positive Communication Builds Healthy Relationships

Good communication is the foundation for healthy relationships and a key practice in effective early childhood classrooms. Communicating with children requires some special techniques and an investment of time and attention. Another significant element of an effective classroom is the development of a positive social environment. By this we mean creating settings where children and adults understand and share information with one another in supportive and meaningful ways.

Communication Strategies

One way that teachers create positive social environments is through persistent use of positive and effective communication strategies. Young children communicate through physical interaction as well as through words, so you must learn to pay attention to facial expressions, sounds, body posture and tension, and touches. Children communicate most easily with adults who are physically on their level; therefore, early childhood teachers spend a great deal of time stooping, squatting, and sitting on low chairs or on the floor.

Respectful communication conveys to children that you value their feelings and thoughts and you trust their capacity to learn. Adults sometimes speak to children in ways that are condescending and insincere or brusque, bossy, and rude. You may have felt insulted when someone spoke to you "as if you were a child." When you talk to children "like people" you will find that you enhance communication and relationships, although it may feel awkward when you first try. When you strive to relate authentically to children—in a real and genuine manner—and show them that you are committed to listening to them and understanding their communication, they learn important skills for communicating with others.

We have found the following strategies to be useful.

Time and Attention

Relationships are built on the small, shared individual experiences you have with children each day. Reading a story, having a conversation, feeding a guinea pig, watching the goldfish swim, digging in the sand, taking a walk around the yard to look for bugs, or singing a song together—these are the kinds of experiences that build relationships. Shared experiences—the workings of the plumbing, the quality of the easel paint, the traits of a favorite character from a story, the foods for a favorite meal, and thousands of others—make up the content of worthwhile conversations you can have with children. In many schools, adults make contact with children only to give directions, handle problems, pronounce facts, or teach skills and concepts. These things will be part of your day, but they are not the stuff of which genuine relationships are built.

Children need plenty of time and opportunities to talk. Teachers often talk a great deal and leave little time for children's responses, perhaps because they feel it is a part of their role, because they are uncomfortable with silence, or because they are not interested in what children have to say. Continual teacher talk gives little chance or encouragement for children to express themselves. Be certain to find times each day to engage in genuine conversations with the children in your classroom.

Respectful and Authentic Speech

Speak with children in a sincere way. Use a conversational tone and clear and straightforward speech. "Cute," condescending, or artificially sweet ways of talking send the message to children that they are not worthy of respect. Educators who have a genuine interest in children speak to them without such artificiality and never cut a conversation short because the subject matter isn't "nice."

Avoid using the same words and phrases over and over. Some examples that we hear often when we visit children's programs are: "Use walking feet," "Use helping hands," and the ever-present "Use your words." While we applaud that these requests are stated positively, we believe that many teachers become so accustomed to using these stock phrases that they forget to use authentic and real language to communicate. When children hear the same phrase repeatedly, it begins to fade into the background and fails to communicate effectively. Instead, think of a number of different meaningful ways to phrase requests, such as: "Tell him what you mean," "Let her know what you need," "You can talk instead of hitting," and "Thank you for remembering to walk."

Effective Listening

An essential skill for good communication is the ability to listen. Listening means paying attention to the message another person is conveying. Although it seems commonplace, listening requires concentration and effort. When we visit schools, we frequently hear teachers describe an upsetting relationship with a child by telling us, "she never listens."

> *Mandy was sitting at the art table. "Look, teacher," she said, "look at my magic seeds!"*
>
> *Her teacher, Alyce, was nearby gathering materials. "That's nice, honey," she said to Mandy.*
>
> *"Teacher, my sister and I found these magic seeds and we're gonna use them to grow a whole big dinner," Mandy explained. Still looking into the cupboard, Alyce murmured an "um-hum." Mandy picked up a cup beside her and dumped its contents onto her paper, which was damp from using watercolors. Out came some sandy dirt along with a few small seeds. Mandy rubbed the dirt around on her wet paper, trying to find all of the seeds.*
>
> *Looking up, Alyce exclaimed, "Oh, Mandy, you've gotten your paper and the table all dirty. Please throw that dirt away and then you can paint nicely on the paper."*
>
> *"But teacher," Mandy said, looking very worried, "these are my magic seeds!"*
>
> *"There's sand and dirt all over the art table," Alyce responded. "Please listen to what I'm telling you. You need to get that mess cleaned up so other children will be able to paint."*

Who didn't listen? True listening is a most powerful tool for building relationships with children and creating a peaceful, productive classroom.

Listening involves being obviously attentive to a child's meaning and feelings. You can demonstrate attentiveness and listen better if you look at children, crouch or sit at their level, and give verbal and nonverbal feedback that communicates that you really hear them. Timing, the quality and register of your voice, facial expression, gestures, and body posture often convey more to a child than the words you use. Responding with a nod, smile, or word of encouragement gives the child time to express ideas and feelings and gives you time to try to piece together words and body language. Statements like "I see," "Tell me more," "Yes," "Is there anything else you want to tell me?" and "Thank you for telling me" are encouraging responses. These general listening behaviors can be used in concert with the strategies discussed below to help you create an environment where all children and adults are learning to be skilled communicators.

Nonverbal Messages. Listening well requires that you pay careful attention not only to words, but also to gestures, body stance, movement, and tone of voice. One message can be sent by a person's words while body and expression convey something else. Nonverbal messages are frequently your best source of information about children's thoughts and feelings. This is particularly true if you work with infants and young toddlers. Even highly verbal preschoolers were nontalkers only a year or two ago. Despite their increasingly sophisticated language, primary school children also speak with their bodies. English language learners will appreciate your attempts to listen with your eyes as well as your ears.

The more you know about a child (age, social and language habits, culture, family background, and experiences), the better you will be at really understanding the child. The combination of general knowledge plus attention to the immediate situation will enable you to comprehend the meaning behind words and behavior.

At the beginning of the school year, 3-year-old Noa's morning was punctuated by bouts of crying, "I want my mommy!" As children left circle time to play, Noa's crying started again, and the cry for Mommy took on a new and more desperate tone accompanied by a dance-like motion. His observant teacher approached him, spoke with him quietly, and then led Noa to the bathroom.

This teacher's observations, her awareness of Noa's routine, and her knowledge of 3-year-olds helped her to understand what the problem really was.

The term *active listening* was first developed by Thomas Gordon and described in his seminal work that teaches communication skills to teachers (2003). Gordon taught that it is useful to think of words and body language as a code for feelings as well as thoughts. Active listening involves responding to the feelings as well as the content of a message. By asking a question or making a statement, you give the child the opportunity to clarify the meaning and express the feelings involved.

Consider these examples:

Two-year-old Erin, during the first month of school, was absentmindedly stacking blocks. Her teacher walked by, and Erin said, "When my Mommy come?" Erin's face and body slumped and her voice sounded worried and sad. The teacher responded, "It sounds like you wish you could see her right now." Erin nodded and a tear spilled out. She whispered, "I miss Mommy."

Four-year-old Chloe, during her fifth month of school, was intently building an elaborate block structure. The teacher walked by, and Chloe said, "When is my Daddy coming?" Chloe's body was tense, her eyes focused on her structure, and her voice was high pitched and anxious. The teacher responded, "Sounds like you are worried." Chloe said, "Yeah, I want to finish my building and Daddy always wants me to hurry up."

While the questions spoken were quite similar, the feelings that each child was experiencing were different. Active listening allowed the teachers to clarify and understand each child's meaning.

Six-year-old Ciara returned to the classroom after recess and put her head down on her desk, ignoring her teacher's request to find her writing journal. She turned her face away when her teacher approached. "Looks like you're upset," her teacher remarked. "Rest for a minute while I help the other children start their writing, then if you'd like, we can talk about it."

Active Listening. Active listening teaches children the very important lesson that all feelings are OK. It provides children with words to express feelings and models talking about feelings, which is an important element of social and emotional intelligence. Children whose feelings are validated in this way come to feel good about who they are. Fred Rogers reminded us of the importance of honoring all children's feelings when he said, "Children can't be expected to leave the unhappy and angry parts of themselves at the door before coming in. We all need to feel that we can bring the whole of ourselves to the people who care about us" (Rogers, 2003).

Reflective and Responsive (R & R) Statements

In addition to listening carefully, good early childhood educators are skilled at responding to children's messages in ways that support their sense of self and their learning about people and relationships. An effective way to do this is to use *reflective and responsive statements* (Kostelnik, Whiren, Soderman, Stein, & Gregory, 2003). These deceptively simple responses are very powerful communication tools: "You are climbing so carefully up the slide." "You used all of the red paint to make your dragon painting." "You finished that math job very quickly today." "You are waiting patiently for your turn on the tricycle." Simply put, "R & R statements" are words that tell children that you see and are paying attention to what they are doing (see Figure 6.2). When you use these statements frequently, children are aware that you value their actions and interests. Regular use of R & R statements also helps children make sense of what they are experiencing.

Encouragement Instead of Praise

During a recent 1-hour visit to a classroom, one of us heard more than 30 instances where adults praised children. We heard phrases such as: "I like the way that Desiree is sitting so nicely at circle." "You're our best cleaner, Bernie." "You're a great artist, Lorenzo." "Madison, that's a beautiful drawing." "Great building, Danisha." And repeatedly: "Good job. Good job. Good job!"

What's wrong with praise? For many years educators were taught to use praise generously with children in their classrooms. Praise was viewed as a tool to make children feel good about themselves and to motivate learning and good behavior. But there is research that indicates that the consistent use of praise actually has the reverse effect, and that when children are praised repeatedly they may become anxious about their ability to perform and may be less likely to repeat positive actions (Hitz & Driscoll, 1988; Kohn, 2001). Moreover, praise is often not genuine. Teachers use it not as a way to express genuine pleasure

FIGURE 6.2   R & R (Responsive and Reflective) Statements

> ### Say What You See
>
> R & R statements are ...
>
> - Nonjudgmental statements that describe what a child is doing or experiencing:
>   "You're way up at the top of the climber."
>   "You have been using lots of red paint."
>   "You've been working on your story for a long time."
>
> - Statements that show interest in the child and the child's activity:
>   "You've used a lot of Logos to make that building."
>   "You seem to especially enjoy the fossil book."
>   "You and Alex spent all of play time in the block corner this morning."
>
> - Statements that help children understand what they are doing or feeling:
>   "You're trying to figure out a way to balance a big block on top of a tiny one."
>   "You're wondering how you can get a turn with the trike."
>   "You wish your Mom could have stayed longer."
>
> - Statements that judge or evaluate are not R & R statements. Examples:
>   "You're a great climber."
>   "Your picture is pretty."
>   "You are smart with puzzles."
>   "What a good boy you are."
>
> When you "say what you see"—that is, use R & R statements—children feel that their actions, speech, and ideas are valuable.

about a child's actions, but rather as a means to manipulate future behavior or the behavior of other children (Meece & Soderman, 2010).

If your goal is to help children build inner control, then praise is not an effective practice. Praise can teach children to act to receive approval from adults, not because they feel an action is correct or worthy. In some cases, children become so dependent on external evaluation from adults that they can't determine what they like or value. We have known children who ask for adult approval constantly: "Do you like my picture?" "Am I climbing good?" "Am I a good helper, too?" These children appear to be "praise junkies," dependent on praise as the only way to feel good about themselves.

In the example at the beginning of this section, the teacher who commented on Desiree's "nice sitting" appeared more interested in using words to encourage other children to come to circle than giving Desiree meaningful feedback about her behavior. In other instances, this type of praise is intended to encourage children to repeat a positive action in the future, not as a sincere acknowledgment of effort or skill. Used this way, praise becomes an external reward.

Several studies have indicated that although praise may encourage children to continue an activity while an adult is watching, children are less likely to continue the activity when the adult leaves or to repeat the activity in the future (Kohn, 2001). Rather than increasing children's commitment to positive behavior, praise encourages children to find ways to get future verbal "goodies" from important adults.

Less obvious, but equally important, is the fact that praise can diminish children's sense of pride and self-worth. Those who are praised excessively may lose the ability to evaluate their own progress or to feel intrinsic joy and delight in an activity.

Praise is like the large pink icing rose in the center of a cake. It is appealing, and at first bite its sweetness tastes wonderful. A couple more bites still might taste good, but it quickly becomes overly sweet. It has only one simple flavor; we soon tire of it and if we eat very much at any one time, we might even feel slightly ill. It may provide some quick energy but it provides no nourishment and doesn't support growth or health.

Encouragement, on the other hand, is like a warm soup. It has many complex flavors and eating it gives us nutrients we need to feel strong and to have sustained energy. While it may not have the initial appeal of the sweet icing, its long-term effects strengthen us and encourage our growth. Teachers use encouragement when they comment on children's efforts (*you spent such a long time working on that drawing*), rather evaluating the product (*that picture is just beautiful*). Encouragement helps children to identify their own strengths and interests (*it seems like you enjoy building very tall towers*), rather than relying on adults' assessments (*you are one of the best builders*).

For a comparison of encouragement versus praise, see Table 6.3.

I-Messages

When you have a problem with a child's behavior you can use an *I-message*, a technique described by Gordon (2003) as a way to communicate your concerns without blaming children. An I-message invites a child to participate in solving the problem rather than telling them what to do. When you give an I-message, you maintain your rights, get your point across, and avoid hurting children or your relationship with them. An effective I-message has three elements:

1. It states the specific condition or behavior that is problematic.
2. It states your feelings.
3. It explains how the behavior affects the adult.

I-messages communicate that, although you don't like a particular behavior or situation, you trust that the child is capable of dealing with it. Often the behavior will stop once the child knows that it causes a problem. The order and wording of an I-message is not as critical as communicating the three pieces—behavior, feelings, and effect—and the implied invitation to the child to find a mutually acceptable solution. For example:

"It's hard for everyone to hear when there's so much noise."

"It makes me feel frustrated if I have to shout so others can hear the story."

"I'm disappointed. There's too much noise for everyone to hear the story."

These statements do not send a negative evaluation and they leave the solution in the hands of the child. A more common response might be to use a directive: "Stop talking! You're bothering everyone. You will have to leave if you can't be quiet." Such a "you-message" denies the child the opportunity to solve the problem. It focuses on the child in a blaming, shaming, or evaluating manner, ignores the effect of the behavior on others, and imposes a solution on the child, rather than allowing him or her to solve the problem.

When you use an I-message, be careful to avoid overstating your feelings or attempting to make the child feel guilty with your statement. Use feeling words that accurately and professionally state your feelings, but avoid strong statements

TABLE 6.3 Differences Between Encouragement and Praise

Encouragement is . . .	Praise is . . .
Specific: "Thank you. You helped pick up all the blocks and put them away where they belonged."	**General:** "That's beautiful."
Descriptive and nonjudgmental: "You did the pilot puzzle. It's a tricky one."	**Making a judgment:** "You're a great puzzle solver."
About feelings and motivation: "It's really satisfying when you finish a painting that you have worked on so hard, isn't it?"	**About external products or rewards:** "I'll put the best paintings on the bulletin board to show the parents."
Thoughtful and individual: "That was the first time you slid down the twisting slide by yourself."	**The same for all and holds little meaning for the individual:** "Good job."
Encouragement focuses on . . .	**Praise focuses on . . .**
The process, experience, and effort: "You really worked hard on scrubbing that table."	**The person or outcome:** "That's the best job of cleanup I ever saw."
Growth of the individual: "You wrote the names of everyone in our class. I remember when you could only write your name."	**Comparison of children:** "You're the best printer in our class."
Self-evaluation: "It looks like you feel proud of that picture." "How did you feel about finishing your science project?"	**Judgment from others:** "I love your picture!" "Good work!"

telling children that they "hurt your feelings" or "made you sad" as these tend to be more manipulative than expressive of a true emotion.

Children will learn to use I-messages as a way to communicate with one another, when they hear this model used frequently. The use of I-messages is helpful in teaching children to resolve problems and conflicts with one another. Teachers who use R & R statements and active listening create a foundation for the use of I-messages because they have modeled describing situations and labeling feelings.

Communicating with Infants and Toddlers

When you relate to infants and toddlers, you communicate with your whole being—voice, body, and heart. A relationship with an infant involves being attentive and responsive by returning coos, smiles, and babbles. The best educators of infants relate to even the youngest child with the respect.

> *"Time for lunch," Darcy says to 8-month-old Reiko, who is sitting on the carpet exploring a box of rattles. Reiko looks briefly at Darcy then returns her attention to the rattles. Darcy walks over to her, stoops, and watches her quietly for a few minutes. "You're really busy listening to those sounds," she tells her. She watches for another minute then says, "It's lunchtime now. I'm going to pick you up and take you to wash hands then eat lunch. We have carrots today—your favorite!" Darcy watches as Reiko looks up and reaches an arm toward her. "You're ready—up we go," says Darcy, lifting Reiko to her shoulder.*

Darcy was careful to acknowledge that the play Reiko was engaged in was interesting. She made sure to let her know what was coming and gave her time to respond before lifting her. In play as well as during care routines, skilled infant-toddler teachers give time and attention to communicating with each child. They learn each child's communication style and respond appropriately. It is impossible to "spoil" a baby by responding to his or her needs (something some adults fear). When you learn the meaning of a cry, a gurgle, a gesture, or a grunt, you know what is needed and can act appropriately. This responsive caregiving tells the baby that you care about her, that her needs and wishes are valued. Responsive caregiving does not mean jumping at every cry. Instead, by knowing the infant and his or her typical needs and behavior, you can acknowledge feelings and create routines and activities that meet the baby's needs.

Speak to infants and toddlers as you would speak to other people you know and care about. Although the conversation may be one-sided, the relationship is mutual. Just as you do with older children, build a relationship based on the things you do together. Learn to read nonverbal messages and to acknowledge and interpret their meanings. As their babbles and sounds increase, your language will provide a scaffold for the sounds to become talk. Not only does this verbal interaction build relationships, but it is also the way that human beings learn language.

The I-messages that we discussed earlier are useful with infants and toddlers as well as preschool and school-age children. For example, a toddler with minimal language who pulls your hair can be told "Ouch!"—with an exaggerated sad expression—"It hurts when you pull my hair," followed by a gentle guiding of the hand in a patting motion and a smile: "I like it when you touch me gently." When a toddler behaves in an unacceptable way or an infant's action must be stopped, teachers who understand development will gently and clearly explain what must be done and why: "I can't let you pull my hair. That hurts me. Here,

Reflect on your relationship with a teacher

Recall a teacher with whom you had a positive relationship. Recall another teacher relationship that you felt was negative. What contributed to your positive or negative feelings about each teacher? How did each teacher communicate with you? How did these relationships affect how you felt about teachers and school?

Reflect on your feelings about conflict

How do you tend to deal with conflict in your life? Do the ways you deal with disputes and upsets usually work well for you? What do you want children to learn about conflict resolution?

you can pull the raggedy doll's hair." Do the children understand? Infants and toddlers, like the rest of us, understand kindness and respect; understanding the words will come later.

Cultural Differences in Communication

Cultural differences exist in the manner in which individuals communicate with one another. Nonverbal behaviors such as eye contact, smiling, and touch can mean different things. In Euro-American cultures direct eye contact with an adult is usually interpreted as a cue that a child is listening attentively, while in some other cultures it can be interpreted as a sign of disrespect. Likewise, you may assume that a smile indicates happiness, pleasure, and joy. However, the smile of a child from some backgrounds may be used to mask shame or anger. It is important that you learn about the communication styles of families whose children are in your care and learn to understand and respond appropriately to both their verbal and nonverbal communications.

Guiding Children's Social Interactions

As a teacher of young children, an important part of your job is to ensure that children have productive group experiences. In addition to what we have already discussed about strategies for effective relationships with individuals, you will need to create a positive social environment in the classroom, help children learn to get along with each other, and address the problems that inevitably arise in any group of young children.

Dealing with Conflict

> *"But I need to have them now; they are mine!"* Nadia sobbed, pointing to the shiny red shoes that Vivian was dancing in.
> *"I have them; you can't use them."* Vivian said, dancing away.
> *"But I really, really need them! I need them right now,"* Nadia cried, running after Vivian. *"I can't do my dance without those shoes. You **have** to give them to me!"*

Problems and conflicts are an inevitable aspect of group life, both in and outside of early childhood programs. The way that teachers deal with conflict provides an important model for young children. When teachers view conflict as a learning opportunity, children can learn that it is a part of life and they can learn skills for problem resolution.

How you feel about conflict is a reflection of your experiences, values, and culture. Reflecting on how you feel about and deal with conflict in your own life may be helpful in considering what you will model for children.

Help Children Identify and Express Their Feelings

Conflict is often accompanied by anger, a powerful emotion that can be hard to understand and express. Anger is a second-level reaction—a response to hurt, threat, frustration, or anxiety. Young children may not have words to express the feelings that lie behind their conflicts or may have been taught not to express feelings. Before you can help children learn to resolve conflicts peacefully, you must help them to identify and acknowledge their feelings. The accompanying box, "Ways to Help Children Understand and Express Feelings," suggests some ways to help children learn and talk about their feelings as a prelude to conflict resolution.

When disputes between young children occur, it is wise to watch first and refrain from intervening too soon. Children who are not hurting one another can often work out their own solutions. Although it is tempting to step in to solve problems for them, this intervention does not help them learn to be problem-solvers. Recall that two of the long-term goals for child guidance are promoting inner control and developing skills for living in a community. If children learn that the teacher is always going to solve problems for them, they will neither learn these skills nor be motivated to do so. Teachers who support these guidance goals allow children the time, space, and authority to resolve problems independently. We find it helpful to remember this phrase: *"You can't teach children to think by telling them what to do"* (source unknown).

Be sensitive to the fact that, in some cultures, it is considered rude to show feelings openly. If children are uncomfortable with labeling or discussing feelings, never insist that they do so. Discussions with families regarding their preferences about expressing feelings and handling conflict can help you select strategies that meet the needs of all children in the group.

When conflict threatens to cause serious harm, you must act. Intervene swiftly and place your body between children who are hurting one another or threatening to do so. Talk with the children to help them begin to identify a solution. It is more effective to ask *what* can be done, so that children can return to their activities, than to ask *why* they came into conflict, *who* had the toy first or *who* hit first. This helps the children find a solution to their problem instead of focusing on who is right and who is wrong. *"How can you get a turn with the trike?"* and *"What's another way to ask if you can play?"* are more supportive of problem solving than *"Who had it first?"* and *"Why did you hit him?"*

Even very young children can be given time and opportunity to deal with conflict. We recently observed a teacher who simply put her arm between two toddlers who were hurting one another. She kept her arm there, saying little except, "You both want the white purse, but there's just one here," and "I can't let you hurt one another." Very quickly one child found another purse and peaceful play resumed.

WAYS TO HELP CHILDREN UNDERSTAND AND EXPRESS FEELINGS

- Accept and name children's feelings for them: "You feel disappointed that Calder has the ball you wanted."
- Model expressing your own feelings: "When puzzles are tossed on the floor, I worry that the pieces will get lost."
- Invite children to talk to you and to one another about how they feel: "Your face looks sad. Would you like to tell me how you are feeling?"
- Point out similarities and differences in feelings: "You both like to write stories. Briana likes to write by herself. Aaron prefers to work with a writing team."
- Provide opportunities for children to identify and express feelings through conversations, art, music

movement, dramatic play, and writing: "Would you like to make a painting that shows how you felt after you watched the sad movie about the dog?"

- Rehearse expressing feelings through activities like role-playing: "Let's pretend that it is time to clean up and you aren't finished with your construction project. How would you feel? Show me some of the things that you could do."

With practice, children can learn to tell each other how they feel and what they want instead of striking out or running to an adult when a confrontation occurs. Even very young children benefit when teachers give names to the emotions they are feeling. As they get older this helps children build a vocabulary for expressing and understanding feelings.

When children are "stuck" and cannot reach a solution on their own, a well-timed word can sometimes help them resolve the conflict. Following are some examples of things to say when you are talking with children who are in conflict situations:

"Stop. I won't let you hurt Harrison. You can tell him that it makes you mad when he takes your truck. Ask him to give it back to you."

"I can see you're angry about what happened. What do you want to tell her?"

"Hitting hurts. Let's think of some other ways to handle this problem."

"You have different ideas about how to construct the model. What can you do to decide how to get back to building?"

"That hurt Alethea's feelings and she's really sad now. Please stay with me—maybe we can help her feel better."

"There isn't room for five children in the tire swing. Would you like to choose who goes first? Shall I help?"

"What can you do to solve this problem so you can go back to playing restaurant?"

Teach Peaceful Conflict Resolution

We want children to learn to be cooperative and to solve problems constructively even when we are not present. By guiding them repeatedly through the process of peaceful conflict resolution, teaching negotiating skills, and offering encouragement, we can enable them to reach this goal. Refer to the accompanying box, "The Conflict Resolution Process," to help you learn the steps in this process.

We find that young children are interested in this process, and with patient facilitation from trusted adults they will learn to use it with skill. When we have involved children in handling problems with us, we have found that they also start to do it quite effectively in their own problems with peers. In addition to being consistent with our goals of developing inner control and the cooperation skills that children need to live effectively in a community, teaching children this process relieves the teacher of the onerous role of being the "classroom police."

Build a Classroom Culture That Promotes Respect and Fairness

What children learn about dealing with others is taught most meaningfully by what they see modeled. The words, behaviors, and daily choices you make are the most powerful teachers. Listen attentively to the words you use with children: Are you polite? Respectful? Are you careful that everyone is included in classroom routines and activities? Are children who are less appealing, less skilled, or more challenging welcomed into discussions and activities with the same warmth as easy, well-mannered youngsters? Are those with disabilities given meaningful ways to participate?

Children learn to treat others with respect and fairness when teachers

THE CONFLICT RESOLUTION PROCESS

Jayson and Paul are happily playing a game of X-Men in the pretend area. Olivia and Stacey come in and sit at the table, starting to pretend that they are getting ready for a party. "Hey," Jayson shouts, "You can't be there. That's the X-Men house."

"Yeah, get away," Paul says. "We are playing here and no girls can come here."

"Uh-un," Stacey says. "We can play here if we want to. You've been here a long time and Olivia and I want to get our dresses on and play party."

1. **Cool down.** Everyone involved may need a moment to take several deep breaths and relax, particularly if the conflict has included children hurting one another: "I can hear that you are all upset. Let's figure out what we can do. Take three big breaths to get calm, then we'll talk about how we can solve this problem."

2. **Identify the problem.** Figure out what the problem is and what needs to be solved without making judgments: "Olivia and Stacey want to play in the home area. Jayson and Paul say 'No' because they're playing X-Men."

3. **Describe the underlying feelings, worries, concerns, and values.** These must be acknowledged before solutions can be generated: "Olivia and Stacey are worried they might not get a turn if they don't play now. Jayson and Paul like playing here, too. They're afraid they won't get to play X-Men if you join them."

4. **Brainstorm solutions.** Ask the children what they can think of to solve this problem: "Olivia has thought of two plans. Jayson and Paul can play X-Men outside, or she and Stacey can be X-Men, too. Paul has thought of two plans, also. He thinks that Olivia and Stacey can play in the block area now and play in the pretend area tomorrow, or they can play in the pretend area in 10 minutes."

5. **Choose one and try it.** "What do you want to try? What do you think might work for all of you?" Encourage the children to follow one of the suggested solutions. "Okay, Olivia and Stacey will try playing X-Men in the home area for 10 minutes with Jayson and Paul. Then they will play another game."

6. **Follow up.** If necessary, encourage and support children as they try the solution. At a later time invite children to reflect on what could be done to prevent problems in the future and on how their solutions worked: "What do you think we could do so that this problem doesn't happen again?" or "How did it work out when all of you played X-Men?"

strive both to model and to teach these beliefs and values. Many teachers use daily class meetings as a means of creating a positive social environment. When meetings are structured so that everyone is encouraged to talk and share feelings honestly but with kindness, children learn the skills they need as communicators, negotiators, and problem-solvers. Class meetings help teachers create an environment where children feel emotionally safe and as a result are able to concentrate and learn (Gartrell, 2004; Vance & Weaver, 2002). This method of social problem solving is congruent with those used in Hawaiian and other native cultures. In Hawai'i some classrooms include a *ho'oponopono*, a time and place for individuals to gather to talk through differences when they arise. Such practices strengthen the sense of community and trust that children experience.

Carefully chosen children's literature can also contribute to a classroom culture that promotes fairness, justice, and equality. Children can be encouraged to discuss and dramatize their understanding of these social concepts.

Guiding Groups: Strategies for Positive Classroom Management

Guiding a group of young children, sometimes called *classroom management*, is an art that requires knowledge, skill, sensitivity, and self-confidence. Like any art, it is one that you will acquire through learning and experience, and it becomes easier with practice. As your skill increases and you become comfortable using some of the strategies discussed in this chapter, you will find that you will need to devote less of your time to "managing" and will be able to spend more of your time on relationships and learning experiences. Your enjoyment of young children will serve you well! Following is a discussion of attitudes and practices that can assist you in keeping groups running in a smooth and amicable manner.

Make the Environment and Schedule a Partner in Guidance

The physical environment of a program sends strong messages to children about how they are expected to act and whether they are welcome and accepted. A carefully arranged environment and an appropriate daily schedule (see Chapter 8) can help you set up physical spaces that invite children to work and play together in harmonious ways. When you notice that children are having difficulties, it is useful to look at the environment and schedule to determine whether either one is the source of the problems.

For example, in a preschool class we know, the block center was in the middle of the room. To get to any other area, children had to walk through the block center, often bumping into structures. Children whose buildings were knocked down responded angrily, often using blocks as defensive weapons. Children who walked through the block area regularly picked up blocks as props for other centers and deposited them far away. Creating a more sheltered block area reduced these problems. In a toddler program we recently observed, staff provided few duplicate materials and toddlers were often in conflict over toys. Replacing highly prized single toys with two to four similar toys minimized conflicts. In a primary program, children's behavior improved noticeably after the schedule was changed from two consecutive and lengthy seated activity periods to a routine where quiet seat work was interspersed with time outside and in learning centers.

Use Authority Wisely

By virtue of your role as an educator, society confers on you a certain authority, the right to exercise power, make decisions, take actions, give commands, and expect obedience. The most obvious source of this authority is adulthood. You are larger, stronger, and older, so most children acknowledge your right to give direction. Although authority is given by society as part of your role, it is strengthened by your education, knowledge, skills, and commitment.

You have probably experienced teachers, bosses, family members, or others in authority who treated you fairly and kindly. It is also likely that you have encountered those who were harsh, punitive, or unfair. You may have experienced people in authority who were unclear and inconsistent, unable to provide direction about what you were supposed to do. Unfair and unclear approaches to authority leave adults and children feeling confused and upset. Early childhood educators should strive to use authority humanely, fairly, and with clarity. We call this use of authority *authoritative* to distinguish it from unfair or unkind *authoritarian* uses of power.

In his first weeks as a practicum student in a kindergarten class, Miguel actively engaged in play with the children. On the playground, he took the role of the chasing monster, resulting in many giggles and calls of "Catch me, catch me, Mr. Miguel." His tickles and jokes and high-fives were enthusiastically welcomed by the children and he became their favorite play partner. In

Reflect on teacher authority

Think about a teacher you liked and a teacher you didn't like. How did each exercise authority? Did he or she win your respect and gain your cooperation? If so, how? If not, why not? What were the implications of this experience?

sharing his experiences in his college seminar, Miguel expressed frustration. While the children were delighted to play with him, they ignored his directions and seemed to completely disregard his requests for them to engage in academic tasks.

Becoming comfortable with authority is one of the first issues that any prospective educator faces. Our college students often struggle with authority as they learn to work with children. The way they approach authority involves their values and expectations. Some try to deny their authority. Like Miguel, they behave as if they were one of the kids and become confused and frustrated when children do not respect them or cooperate with them. Others expect children to grant them authority simply because they are the teacher. They make demands without first building a respectful relationship and are surprised when children are rebellious and resistant.

Authority that is authentic and lasting is based on mutual respect; it is used wisely and with compassion. There is no single right way to exercise authority and no one way that is appropriate for each age and individual. Some early childhood practitioners invite children's cooperation with a shared joke and a smile, and children seem delighted to join them. Others calmly state appropriate expectations in a friendly, no-nonsense voice and gain willing compliance. Still others almost silently step in to redirect children with a word or gesture that prevents a blow, encourages a friendship, or assists in a routine. Each of these approaches is grounded in respect and knowledge of children.

Dana, a practicum student, is reading a story to a small group of children. Across the room, Wayne, age 4, takes a crayon and draws on top of the art shelf. Dana leaves the group and reminds him, "We don't draw on the furniture."

Later that morning Wayne says to another child, "C'mon!" as he grabs play dough from the table and runs with it to the library area, giggling and looking back at Dana who is calling, "We don't do that."

Your first experiences in trying to manage a group of children are likely to be somewhat challenging. Children will test you to find out what they can expect from you so they can feel secure. They may intentionally "misbehave" to see how you will respond. Experienced teachers are usually clearer about their expectations of children and communicate those expectations with kind authority from the beginning in words, body language, and behavior. They clearly state what is expected rather than telling children what not to do or offering vague messages like Dana used in the vignette above when she told the children, *"we don't do that."* Less experienced individuals often hesitate and send mixed messages. Children respond with more testing. When you are clear about your expectations and communicate them with authority, your work becomes easier. Authority comes with time, practice, and patience.

Create Guidelines for Behavior

It is important for all people—adults and children—to understand what is expected of them in particular situations. Understanding expectations creates a sense of safety. It allows people to make informed choices about how to act and to feel a sense of control over themselves. Young children feel safe when they know that there are *limits*—boundaries that allow for personal choice within the confines of safety. Limits protect rights and property, make the program predictable, and help children learn to respect and get along with others. When fairly and consistently applied, they help children feel safe and comfortable. Janet Gonzalez-Mena (2011) equates limits with the guardrails on a high bridge. While you may never actually need them to keep you from driving off into the water, without them it would be a frightening experience to cross the bridge. Young children need to know about and understand classroom limits. When you explain them clearly and enforce them firmly but with kindness, most children will gradually feel safe within them and their need to test them will dissipate.

We find that children are best served when teachers develop a set of guidelines—positively stated expectations that help them choose appropriate behaviors in a variety of situations. While many teachers call these *rules,* we prefer the term *guidelines.* These need to be simple enough so they can be easily understood, few enough to remember, and general enough to apply to a wide variety of situations. For example:

- Take care of others.
- Take care of yourself.
- Take care of our things—toys, books, tools, and the environment.

Or, "Treat yourself gently, treat one another gently, treat our environment with care," or "Be safe, be kind, be thoughtful." Using any of these, adults and children together can decide what constitutes safe, kind, thoughtful care for people and the environment they share. Guidelines should always be stated in the positive; they should provide direction about what *to* do rather than what *not* to do. More limited rules such as *"don't run"* or *"don't hurt"* can be confusing to young children who may only focus on and recall the last word they hear.

Older preschool and primary children can participate in creating and modifying agreements about desirable behavior. A good way to start this process is to ask the children, "What do we all need to agree to do so that everyone feels safe, and can learn in school?" Agreements created by the group are not permanent; instead, the group considers them and changes them in response to different situations. As they do so, they are likely to develop greater commitment to following agreements as along with an understanding of the principles of group living. This can be done quite successfully in class meetings.

You will need to communicate the guidelines with clarity and simplicity. Children are more likely to respect and follow the guidelines when they understand the reasons for them and when the behavior required is within their ability.

Here are some examples of guidelines, how they might be applied, and reasons that children can understand:

Guideline: Treat each other kindly.
Application: "Use words to tell her you want a turn."
Reason: "No one can work and play if they are afraid of getting hurt."

Guideline: Use toys, books, and games carefully.
Application: "Put the puzzles on the shelf when you finish using them."
Reason: "Toys, books, and games can get lost or damaged. Then we would not have them to play with anymore."

Guideline: Be safe.
Application: "Slide down when there is no one on the sliding board."
Reason: "Everyone needs to be safe at school."

Guidelines help children to develop skills for regulating their own behavior. They provide a framework for children to use when making decisions about what is right. These are pivotal skills for living and working successfully in a community.

Redirect Instead of Distract

When children are behaving in ways that are unsafe or damaging to the environment, you can redirect their energy and attention to an activity similar to the one that is unacceptable.

Eighteen-month-old Kea stands at the sink, pouring water from a cup onto the floor. Her teacher says, "You are really enjoying pouring that water. Someone might slip when water is on the floor—let's get out the water table and do some pouring there."

In this example, Kea's teacher respects her interest in pouring. She offers her a similar activity that will allow her to continue her interest in a way that is safe. Children who are running in a block area can be directed to a movement activity; shouting can be refocused by playing a game with voice sounds including whispers and songs. This technique is more respectful than distracting a child by offering an activity that has no relationship to what the child is interested in. Distraction tells children that their interests are not worthy or valued; redirection respects children's focus and energy while helping them to engage in an activity that is acceptable and appropriate.

Anticipate Problems

Thinking about what children are like and anticipating their needs and probable behaviors will go a long way toward ensuring smooth classroom experiences. You can make sure children have worthwhile and interesting things to do, sufficient time to engage in activities, and experiences that require no more adult supervision than you have available. A particularly useful skill is to develop what we call "teacher eyes"—an awareness of what is taking place throughout the classroom. This means attending to a number of things simultaneously. You must learn to be aware of what is happening with the entire group while paying attention to small groups and individuals.

For example, in a typical preschool or kindergarten class you might need to attend to all of the following situations at once:

Yusuke and Monte are building a large block structure and wearing the construction hats they use for playing police, which sometimes leads to rough and tumble play.

Teale and Harrison are painting at the easel, giggling with one another as they look at one another's work. Harrison holds up a wet paintbrush and drips purple paint on the floor.

Sarah, Tyrone, Dominic, and Emilia are listening to a story read by Dominic's mom in the library corner.

Kellen, Max, and Nermeen are in the dramatic play area, dressed up in finery, feeding the dolls when Kellen announces, "No boys!"

Jon and Tiffany are staring intently at Squeakers, the mouse, while Tiffany pokes a piece of Tinkertoy at Squeakers.

Anna, Mishka, and Colin are at the writing center enthusiastically calling you to come write their words.

As the teacher in this classroom, you would need to make on-the-spot decisions in response to what children need, what will help individuals, and what is needed for the class as a whole. You would have to continue to attend to the rest of the group after you have made your decision, and you would need to have an interesting alternative ready for each group of children as they were ready for a change

The box "Suggestions for Classroom Management" lists some techniques that we have found helpful in managing a group of young children.

Orchestrate Transitions

Transitions are times when children are asked to move between types of activities and sometimes from one location to another. Throughout a school day, children move from meals to center time, from centers to group activities, from group time to outside, and so on. Teachers are often busy and distracted. Aggressive and destructive behaviors often escalate at these times. However, with advance planning, transitions need not be times of peril.

Reading time is over for the kindergarten class. Mrs. Lester has asked the children to put away their books and line up quietly in the area in front of the door so they can go outside. She gathers her materials from the circle area, then goes to the table where the children did an art activity earlier in the day. She begins

---

SUGGESTIONS FOR CLASSROOM MANAGEMENT

- Position yourself so you can see what is happening throughout the room.
- Get children's attention by moving close to them, crouching down, and speaking directly to them. Avoid shouting across the room or yard.
- Use children's names positively and frequently in conversation so they don't fear something negative when you address them by name.
- Indicate what to do rather than what not to do when correcting behavior and include a reason for your direction. Children often feel rebellious and challenged when told what not to do. For example:

Instead of saying:	Substitute:
"Don't run with the scissors."	"Please walk when you carry scissors so no one will get hurt."
"Don't sit down until you wash."	"Wash your hands before you sit down to eat so you can stay healthy."
"Don't tear the book."	"Turn the pages carefully so they won't tear.
"Don't poke the guinea pig."	"Use very gentle pats and quiet voices so you don't scare the guinea pig. We want him to feel safe at school."

- Offer children two acceptable choices as a way to help them respond positively to adult requests. Choices help children to feel powerful and in control. For example:

"Please walk when you carry scissors so no one will get hurt. I'd be happy to carry the scissors while you go outside to run."

"Wear a smock so you won't get paint on your clothes. You may use pens or crayons if you don't want to cover up your new shirt today."

"Touch the poster gently—you can use newspaper if you'd like to tear."

- Avoid giving children choices that you are unwilling or unable to allow. "Would you like to give me the knife?" is not appropriate when you mean "I must have the knife right now—it is dangerous."
- Use choices to help children comply with adult requests and retain a sense of independence: "Would you like to walk inside using great big giant steps or tiny quiet baby steps?" Notice that the choice is not whether or not to come inside, but how to move your body to get there.

wiping the table, telling the children to get ready to go outside in just a few minutes. As she is cleaning, the children are becoming increasingly restless. Jackson grabs Lexi's ponytail and tugs on it as she steps on his toes trying to cut into the line. Sasha is shouting at Jerome, who is insisting that it is his turn, not hers, to be the line leader. Liane and Juan Carlos are singing loudly and beginning to do a vigorous dance. Liane's elbow accidentally pokes Jacob's eye and he shouts at her to "Cut that out now, you dummy!" Genee, who has been struggling with her sweater, starts to cry when a sleeve rips. As the commotion level rises, Mrs. Lester raises her voice and says loudly, "I said to wait quietly in the line by the door! If you can't line up quietly, you will miss recess."

It is all too easy for situations like this one to occur when transition times are not planned with thought and care. The following strategies can help you to orchestrate peaceful classroom transitions:

- **Let children know before a transition will occur.** Young children do not understand time well and have difficulty predicting when one event will end and another begin. It helps them to take control of their own actions if they know when a change is coming. For younger children, a reminder just a few minutes before a transition is helpful. It is best if the reminder is made in terms of something concrete that the child can understand: "You have time to ride the tricycle around the path two more times before we go inside." Telling very young children that a transition will occur in 5 minutes is less helpful. It alerts them that the change is coming; but since 5 minutes is a very abstract concept, it is not especially useful in helping them to plan their remaining time in an activity.

Older preschoolers and primary-age children are developing a sense of time. They appreciate a longer advance reminder and can understand when you tell them that they have 10 minutes before a change is coming. This allows them to have time to organize how they will complete an activity.

- **Use music, movement, and/or fantasy.** It's much easier to help children move from a classroom to a playground when they fly like birds or swim like dolphins than when they must walk quietly in a straight line. Singing or pretending to be construction vehicles as you pick up blocks makes the activity more fun and encourages participation.

- **Keep the transition as short as possible.** Children are not good at waiting. Once you begin the movement from one activity to the next, do it as quickly and with as much focus as possible. In the example at the beginning of this section, Mrs. Lester's class would have handled the transition much more easily had she been present to assist them and then taken them outside as soon as all were assembled. When children are asked to wait, upsets are likely to occur.

- **Plan games or transition activities.** These help children focus and will encourage them to move individually rather than in a large, disorganized mass. The accompanying box, "Some Ideas for Transition Games," offers more suggestions.

SOME IDEAS FOR TRANSITION GAMES

These ideas are especially useful when dismissing children from circle time or a group activity and helping them move to another location.

- **Clues and Riddles:** Give a clue about the child's family, vacation, pet, or home: "A child whose mom is named Donna and whose dad is named Skip can go." Ask a riddle about something related to the curriculum theme: "What grows in the ground, gives shade to sit in, makes a good place to climb, and is a place for birds to build their nests? The first correct guesser can go."

- **Create a Verse:** Sing "Old MacDonald" (or a similar endless song). Ask children to think of a verse, and they can go when their verse has been sung.

- **Props:** To help children move into learning centers or activity time, bring items from the various centers for each child. As you bring out the item ask a child to describe it, name its place, and take it there to play.

- **Friends:** Select a child to pick a friend with whom to leave the group.

- **Games:** For example, the Lost-and-Found game: Choose a child. Say, "Police Officer Maya, there's a lost child who's wearing blue shorts and a Batman T-shirt. Can you help me find him?" When Maya finds the child, she leaves and the found child becomes the police officer.

- **Name Songs:** Sing a name song like "Get on Board Everybody" or "Hello" and have children leave when their name is sung.

- **Plan for children who struggle with transition.** Almost every class has children who have difficulty with transition. You'll learn quickly who these children are. You can help them by assigning them a role during the transitions and when possible remaining near them until they are reengaged in the next activity.

We recently visited a classroom and heard a teacher saying, "Duncan, we'll be going outside soon and I would really appreciate it if you could help me take the hoops outside today. They're kind of large so it would be great if you could carry them with me." We had seen Duncan struggle during transitions on previous days, but with this guidance, he moved from indoors to outdoors with success.

Manage Large Group Times

Additional skills are needed when you lead a large group (often at a daily event called "circle time," "morning circle," "morning meeting," or "group time"). Group times work best when they have a wide appeal, allow children to be active, and are relatively short (10 to 15 minutes for younger preschoolers). As children grow older, their ability to participate for longer periods of time increases (up to a half-hour for primary children). Structured group activities are not appropriate for infants and toddlers although a group may gather spontaneously if you do something interesting, such as playing a guitar, reading a story, or bringing in a puppy to visit. Teachers of toddlers and 2-year-olds will have much more effective group experiences if they are prepared for spur-of-the-moment gatherings rather than spending time herding resistant toddlers to a group area and insisting that they sit down.

Group times work when children are comfortable (which means not too hungry, tired, or crowded) and when group size and teacher-child ratios are appropriate to age and abilities. Consider children's development and interests in selecting group activities that match their ability to participate. For example, a typical group of 3-year-olds will be more interested in moving and making noises like animals than in animal habitats and eating patterns. A group of 7-year-olds might be exactly the opposite.

Appropriate group activities for preschool and primary children have the following characteristics:

- They encourage active participation.
- They include physical activity.
- They include something to look at or explore with other senses.
- They contain an element of novelty.

Singing songs, doing finger-plays, reading stories, presenting flannelboard stories or puppets, engaging in creative movement activities, writing group stories, playing games, and discussing something that is of interest are all potentially good activities for group time.

When leading a large group, you are the center of the learning experience and the children respond to your direction. Your sensitivity to their mood and energy and your ability to respond to it will determine whether the children stay involved and are cooperative. A large group will fail if it requires too much waiting or if children lack interest. When you reach the limits of children's interest, you need to say "That's all for today." Do so cheerfully and without blaming children or showing disappointment. Learning to read and respond to a group takes time, experience, and self-confidence.

Young children who are not ready for group experiences will tell you by wiggling, getting up, lying down, or walking away. These behaviors give you valuable feedback—something (the activity or the timing) is not appropriate to their needs. Sometimes one or two children have difficulty while the rest enjoy group time. If so, you can provide an alternative activity for these children. Both you and the children will have a better time if expectations are appropriate and clear and if alternatives are available for children who aren't ready for group experiences. Another successful strategy for some children is to allow them to hold something in their hands during group time, such as a small toy car or stuffed animal. While this may seem distracting, it actually may help them to focus and participate.

"Golden Rules for Group Times" offers some suggestions for making group times successful.

Dealing with Difficult Behaviors

Building positive relationships, communicating respectfully, and using the practices discussed in this chapter will go a long way toward helping children behave in cooperative and productive ways. However, even when you do all of these things, you will sometimes encounter children whose behaviors will difficult to handle. In this section we will look at behaviors that teachers often find annoying, irritating, or disruptive.

GOLDEN RULES FOR GROUP TIMES

1. **Make a plan.** Plan the activities you will do in advance; have a backup activity to do if something you planned doesn't work.

2. **Have an "attention grabber."** Start groups times with something you know will capture children's interest: a new action song, a large shell, a picture of an anteater. Gaining children's interest at the beginning helps to ensure a successful group time.

3. **Be organized.** Have all your materials gathered and ready so that when you bring the children together they do not have to wait while you locate needed items.

4. **Demonstrate enthusiasm.** If you present a group activity as something that is fun and desirable and you expect everyone to cooperate, the children are likely to believe you're right and act accordingly.

5. **Mix it up.** Focus children's attention by keeping the activities moving without long pauses. Include lots of movement, and do different things.

6. **Be flexible.** Make changes in response to what children do. Skip a planned activity, add movement, or insert a song or finger-play as you notice children's responses.

7. **Be positive.** Focus on things children do right—don't focus on the negative.

8. **Be dramatic.** Use your voice for effect (change volume and pitch to catch interest). Use your face to communicate—eyes, eyebrows, and mouth can express feelings and ideas without words. Some practitioners even dress to interest children. A teacher we know has a collection of T-shirts and earrings that she wears to go with the day's activity.

9. **Use the unexpected.** See the classroom from a child's point of view; anticipate what's going to interest children and incorporate it into what you are doing. If a fire truck drives by or a visitor walks in, make this a part of the group activity.

10. **Quit while you're ahead.** Group times often fall apart when they go on too long. When children's interest flags, save your activity for another day.

We will describe some of these behaviors and explore strategies for helping children learn more positive ways to behave. *Challenging behaviors*—persistent behaviors that harm the child, other children, or adults—will be discussed at the end of this section.

Find Your "Button Pushers"

Teachers vary in their perceptions of what constitutes difficult behavior. One teacher may be upset when children spit. Another may deal with spitting easily but be unnerved when children swear. The difference in your acceptance of children's behavior comes from your own beliefs about how children should behave. It's helpful to identify those behaviors that you find particularly upsetting before you have to deal with them.. We call this "finding your button pushers." *Button pushers* are actions that cause you to become angry or upset very quickly. Many children seem skilled in identifying those buttons and pushing them. It gives children a sense of power when their actions create an immediate and strong response in adults. If you know which behaviors cause you to have a strong reaction, you can plan how you will react to them. A calm response lacks drama, is thoughtful, and is much less interesting for children than an unplanned outburst. Because of this they may be less motivated to repeat the behavior. This does not mean that you should be insincere about your feelings. A thoughtfully worded but honest message is the key: "Spitting makes me angry and it spreads germs. Tell me you are feeling upset by using words."

The Child Is Different from the Behavior

There are several points to keep in mind when dealing with child behaviors you find challenging. First, always remember that it is the behavior, not the child, that is the problem. When children's behavior is upsetting, it is easy to confuse *what* the child does with *who* the child is. It's tempting sometimes to think of Keiko as an annoying child, Jillette as the naughty one, Jake as cooperative, and Aaron as a good boy. Some teachers begin to think of the child as characterized by the behavior. Rory is a biter. Yun Mi is a talker. Children are better served if we avoid these labels. Keiko's behavior has been upsetting. Rory has been biting lately. Even positive labels like "good girl" put adults in the role of judges and may not have positive results. It helps children make appropriate choices about how to behave when you view them as good, worthy, and lovable people who sometimes make mistakes and need help choosing appropriate behavior.

Another thing to remember is that all behavior has a reason. Even though you may not be conscious of it, there is a reason for everything a child does. Your job is to be a detective and find out how an annoying behavior is serving a particular child. Once you understand the purpose, it is easier to help the child find a less disturbing way to get his or her needs met.

Mistaken Behavior

Dan Gartrell (1995, 2001, 2004) suggests that it is helpful for teachers to think about unacceptable behavior as *mistaken behavior* instead of labeling it with the more familiar term *misbehavior*. He explains that misbehavior implies the children's behavior is intentional and that the children must, therefore, be punished for their "bad" actions. Teachers who think of misbehavior in this way may then label children as naughty and punish them in an attempt to get them to end the misbehavior.

Mistaken behavior, on the other hand, suggests that children are learning to behave acceptably and are therefore subject to making mistakes. This perspective is more congruent with the principles of child guidance that we have discussed in this chapter. A teacher who adopts this viewpoint assumes the role of a guide who helps children, rather than taking on the role of a judge who scolds and criticizes.

> *Mikayla and Cherise are in the dramatic play area. Mikayla puts on a lacy tutu and turns to sit on a small sofa next to Cherise. Cherise sees the skirt and shrieks, "That is mine!" She begins tugging on the tutu as Mikayla holds it tightly around her. Mikayla stands and starts to try to move away and as she does, Cherise reaches over and slaps her face.*

The girls' teacher can choose to view Cherise's behavior as "mistaken." She knows that it is hard to learn ways to get what you want. While she does not condone or accept behavior that hurts others, she does not judge Mikayla as "bad" because she hasn't yet learned more cooperative ways. As she moves to assist the girls, she asks herself, "What can Cherise and Mikayla learn from this experience?"

> *Walking quickly to the dramatic play area, the teacher stoops and places an arm around each girl. She asks Mikayla, who is crying, to show her where it*

Reflect on your "button pushers"

Think about a particular behavior that causes you to become upset and angry. What are you likely to do when a child acts in this way? Would this response help the child to choose a more appropriate, less annoying behavior? Does it show anger? Is it punitive? Plan a more reasoned response you might make when a child "pushes your buttons."

hurts. She asks both children to tell her what has happened. She empathizes with each, telling Mikayla, "You felt upset when Cherise tried to take the tutu and it hurt when she hit you." She is also empathetic to Cherise, "You were using the tutu earlier and you did not want Mikayla to take it." She says, "Cherise, I can see that you really want to use that tutu. You were trying to let Mikayla know that you did not want her to have a turn. Mikayla is crying now because her face is hurting where you hit it."

She includes both girls by asking, "What do you think you can do now?" After the negotiations are concluded, the teacher ensures that both Cherise and Mikayla are reengaged in an activity before moving to other responsibilities.

Understanding behavior as "mistaken" encourages the problem-solving approach that we discussed earlier in this chapter. It has the following characteristics of effective guidance:

- It avoids judging, labeling, or victimizing either child.
- It does not require a forced apology but invites the child who offended to make amends if she or he so chooses.
- It takes a learning-focused approach; the situation is viewed as an opportunity for each child to learn behaviors that work well in relationships.

Strategies for Dealing with Difficult Behaviors

There are several guidance methods that can be effective in dealing with difficult or mistaken behaviors. Also see the accompanying box, "Golden Rules for Responding to Difficult Behavior."

Natural and Logical Consequences

Children learn to behave appropriately when they have opportunities to make connections between their behavior and the outcomes that it produces. The

GOLDEN RULES FOR RESPONDING TO DIFFICULT BEHAVIOR

1. **Observe the child closely and think carefully about what the behavior means.** There is always a reason for it.
2. **Emphasize that school is a safe place.** Let children know that you will not allow anyone to hurt them or permit them to hurt others.
3. **Offer two acceptable choices when you want children to change their behavior.** "You can paint at the easel or at the table."
4. **Give real choices.** If it is time to clean up, an appropriate choice might be, "Would you rather put the blocks away or help clean up the pretend area?" Don't ask, "Do you want to put your toys away now?"
5. **Allow children to save face.** For example, if a child has loudly proclaimed that he won't hold your hand as you cross the street, allow him to hold the hand of another adult or the child next to him.
6. **Focus on solutions rather than causes.** Ask, "What can we do since you both to use this toy?" instead of "Why did you take her block?"

use of natural and logical consequences can help children make this association. Sometimes known as the *democratic approach* to guidance, this practice is based on the work of Alfred Adler, as interpreted and applied to classrooms by Rudolf Dreikurs (1969). Dreikurs noted that children become discouraged and disrupt the group when they do not know how to be cooperative members of the class. The democratic approach can help children understand the unproductive strategies that they have adopted and allow them to redirect their behavior more positively.

Natural Consequences. Some consequences are the natural result of a child's actions and require no intervention on the part of an adult. For example, if a child pours his yellow paint down the drain, the natural consequence is that the paint is gone. Natural consequences allow a child to learn from experience. This approach is appropriate when the consequence does not endanger a child and when it does not unfairly penalize another person or the group. Natural consequences seem simple, but they require restraint. It can be hard to see a child naturally disappointed, uncomfortable, or unhappy. It also can be difficult to refrain from voicing a smug "I told you so" when a child experiences natural consequences that you foretold. We find that active listening, discussed earlier in this chapter, is a good response in these kinds of situations. For example, to a toddler who has dumped her juice onto the table: "You wish you had more juice, but it's all gone." Or to a 5-year-old who has thrown the balls over the fence: "You would really like it if we had more balls to play with." Your task is not to fix the situation or sympathize with the child; allow the child to experience the circumstances and feelings related to his or her own actions.

Logical Consequences.   Some negative behavior does not lead to any natural or acceptably safe consequences. In this situation you may choose to create related consequences. With older preschoolers and primary-age children you can do this effectively as a group process. For example, in an after-school group the children got tired of not being able to find pieces of board games because the games were often not put away. They decided that the consequence for leaving a game out would be no games for the rest of the week. By confronting the direct consequences of their behavior, children learned the laws of being a member of a group.

Younger children can benefit from situations where teachers use clearly related consequences such as, "Because you are breaking crayons, you will need to leave the art area and find another place to play." In following through on a consequence, you need to be calm and simply say, "You may not be in the block area now because you are throwing the blocks. You can come back when you are ready to play safely." Logical consequences must be reasonable, fair, and directly related to behavior: "You threw the books off the shelf. When you are calm you can put them back on the shelf." Such consequences are consistent with the values of justice and responsibility. Be sure to apply them calmly and to avoid using them in a punitive manner or one that isolates children. A logical consequence becomes a punishment when you angrily shout, "No books for you; you tore the pages!."

The Problem with Time Out

For many years, teachers were taught that time out was a logical consequence that could be used to help children learn appropriate behaviors. The premise was that children could learn that if they could not behave in socially approved ways, they would be separated from the group. Programs using this technique sometimes send children to a "time out" chair where they are instructed to sit for a period of time and "think about" their behavior. Some child development experts have suggested that time out, as it is frequently used in early childhood classrooms, is not a child-centered guidance technique but rather one that punishes children who have not yet learned how to behave acceptably in group situations. Katz (1984) has argued that time out confuses young children because they cannot understand the relationship between their "bad" behaviors and the forced removal to the chair.

Although many teachers who use time out intend it to be a strategy that helps children learn appropriate social behaviors, there are some undesirable outcomes of time out:

- Because it is imposed by others ("go sit in the chair"), time out does not encourage children to develop internal control or self-regulation skill.
- While sitting in time out, the child may feel confused, isolated, and/or lonely, making it punitive rather than instructive.
- Children in time out are not learning about alternative strategies for handling upset or dealing with social situations.
- Other children may view the child in time out as "bad" or a troublemaker.
- Time out diminishes a child's feeling of confidence and self-worth. (Schreiber, 1999)

When classrooms have a "time out" chair where misbehaving children are sent, some children are seen as bad and others may fear that they will be shamed if they make mistakes (Gartrell, 2004). On a recent classroom visit, one of us spoke with a child who pointed to another and said, "That's Vince; he's bad. He has to go to time out every day." We did not think that Vince felt accepted or encouraged by this characterization. Additionally, his recurring mistaken behaviors during the observation confirmed for us that the practice of time out was simply not effective in helping this child to learn productive ways of interacting with others.

A Place to Calm Down

Providing a safe, comfortable space for a child to regain composure can be helpful. Different from time out, offering a place for calm reflection and "cooling off" can be an effective way to help children gain self-control. It is particularly useful when teachers help children learn to take themselves there at times when they are upset or need a quiet place. The differences between this practice and time out are that offering a place to calm down is not punitive and that it is self-regulated—the child determines when to go and when return to the group. Dragging a kicking and screaming child to the "calm place" is not effective. Sometimes you may need to forcibly (and as gently as possible) remove a child from an emotional or physically aggressive situation. When this happens, remain with the child, offering encouragement and support as he or she works to regain enough self-control to return to the group. You can offer the child some criteria to determine readiness: "When your body is relaxed and you can keep your hands from hitting other people then you will be ready to come back." Be sure to offer a returning child some assistance in reentering the group. Contrast these practices with those of traditional time out where children hear, "Sit in the time out chair and think about what you did until I tell you to get up."

Behaviorist Approaches

Over the years reinforcement techniques originally developed by B. F. Skinner have been applied to the classroom. This approach is known as *behaviorism*. Behaviorists believe children misbehave because they have been taught to do so by improper rewards, or *reinforcement*. To change or *extinguish* old behaviors, new ones must be taught and rewarded.

All early childhood educators use behaviorist principles some of the time. When you smile at a shy child who attempts a new activity, you are providing reinforcement. When you ignore a child whose demanding behavior is disruptive, you are choosing not to reinforce it. The phrase "catch them being good" is a simple way of suggesting that you encourage, reward, or provide social reinforcement to children for desired behavior.

Systematic reinforcement—offering a reward or other positive support every time a behavior occurs—can be effective, but it is also highly manipulative and counter to values of respect and freedom of choice. We do not believe that systematic reinforcement is appropriate for typically developing young children who are engaged in normal interactions. These children will respond to approaches more consistent with the core values and goals of early childhood education. Behaviorist techniques can be helpful when chosen with care to deal with extreme or challenging behavior and are sometimes used to help children with cognitive disabilities learn appropriate ways to behave.

Spanking Is Never a Choice

Neither spanking nor any other type of physical punishment is ever appropriate in early childhood programs. Not only are such practices illegal in many states, but they also have harmful effects on children and are in direct opposition to the long-term goals of teaching children to be self-directed individuals who can resolve conflicts peacefully. When children are spanked they learn that it is acceptable to hurt people who are younger, smaller, or more vulnerable. They learn that hands are more powerful than words. Because children imitate the important adults in their lives, children who have been spanked are more likely to deal with problems in an aggressive manner than those who have consistently experienced other forms of discipline (Straus, Sugarman, & Giles-Sims, 1997).

The NAEYC Code of Ethical Conduct (2005/2011) strongly supports this position in the first item in the code addressing principles relating to children. P-1.1—Above all, we shall not harm children. We shall not participate in practices that are emotionally damaging, physically harmful, disrespectful, degrading, dangerous, exploitative, or intimidating to children. This principle has precedence over all others in this Code.

Challenging Behaviors

Some children exhibit challenging behaviors—persistent behaviors that prevent them from being able to function in a group or that threaten their own safety or the safety of others. Generally, the term *challenging behavior* refers to behaviors that persist over time and are disruptive, damaging to others or to the environment, and resistant to teacher intervention.

Kaiser and Rasminsky (2012) identify challenging behaviors as those that:

- Interfere with children's cognitive, social, or emotional development
- Are harmful to the child, to other children, or to adults
- Put a child at high risk for later social problems or school failure

These behaviors are challenging for the children themselves, who are unable to be successful in a group and who probably feel helpless to control their behavior. They are also challenging for the adults who deal with them daily and who may feel helpless and overwhelmed by such behaviors.

It is important to remember that many young children engage in challenging behaviors at some time in their lives, and that in most instances consistent use of the positive guidance techniques discussed in this chapter will help them to learn more acceptable behavior. In some cases, however, challenging behavior indicates on going difficulties that may require intervention strategies.

Causes of challenging behaviors are complex and still being debated by researchers. Children with developmental delays and attention deficit disorders have a higher biological risk for developing challenging behaviors than other children. Certain temperamental traits tend to be associated with challenging behavior. Children whose mothers used drugs and alcohol during pregnancy may also be at risk. Environmental factors that increase children's risk of developing challenging behavior include poverty; exposure to violence; frequent exposure to harsh, inconsistent, discipline; family interactions that model antisocial dispute resolution; viewing violent television; and low-quality child care (Kaiser & Rasminsky, 2012).

Children who are aggressive to others need to know that you will not allow them to hurt themselves or other people. Children who are destructive need know that you will not allow them to destroy materials or harm the environment. These things need to be emphasized each time aggressive or destructive incidents occur or appear imminent.

"It's my job to keep everyone safe at school. I won't let you hurt Freddie and I won't let anyone hurt you."

"I won't let you tear children's artwork. Everyone's work is cared for at school."

"Even though you are very mad, it is never okay to hurt someone. I will help you calm down."

"I'll help you find a way to safely put the trikes in the shed; they get dented when you slam them against the wall."

"Come with me to find a place where you can calm down and get control of your body. I can't let you hurt other children.

As children learn that their feelings will be respected, that their needs will be met, and that they will be protected from retaliation and isolation, they may turn less to aggressive and destructive behaviors.

The techniques you have been studying will help you guide children with challenging behavior—but they will take time and a "stick-to-it" disposition. Change does not happen overnight, and you may find that you need support as you help these children to become functional members of the group.

Dealing with challenging behavior is increasingly identified as a source of concern for early educators (Hemmeter, 2007). In a 2005 study, researchers at Yale University Study Center found that approximately 7 of every 1,000 prekindergarten students were being expelled from early education programs due to

Dealing with Challenging Behaviors

- Identify what you genuinely like about the child, and tell team members, the family, and the child.
- Identify for the child what he or she is doing right.
- Let the child know you are committed to helping him or her make it in the classroom and that you believe it will happen.
- Have sincere, positive physical contact with the child every day.
- Recognize your own aggravation and find ways to release it away from the child.
- Find a coworker to talk to during the days when the child's behavior is upsetting you.

unacceptable behaviors. This translates to more than 5,000 expulsions per year (Gilliam, 2005).

In response to this need, the Center on the Social and Emotional Foundations for Early Learning (CSEFEL) at Vanderbilt University developed the Pyramid Model for Supporting Social Emotional Competence, which was discussed earlier in this chapter. The top level of the pyramid, *Intensive Individualized Interventions*, provides strategies for supporting children with persistent challenging behavior. The authors of this model advocate including the parent, teacher, administrator, and an individual with behavior support expertise to work collaboratively to develop a plan for the child that includes "strategies for preventing challenging behavior, teaching the child new skills he or she can use in place of the problem behavior, . . . and responding in a way that increases appropriate behavior and decreases inappropriate behaviors" (Hemmeter, 2007). Additional information about positive behavior support plans can be found at the CSEFEL website, vanderbilt.edu/csefel.

When children need intensive support, it is important to work with your program administrators and the child's family in order to get outside help. State offices of child development, special education services in public schools, and state departments of health are possible sources of assistance. For children under age 3, support may be available from early intervention services, often administered by either departments of health or education. You can work as a team to plan for appropriate intervention. Remember that it is never helpful or productive to blame the child or the parents for the challenging behavior. All children deserve opportunities to learn the skills they need to function in our society.

Final Thoughts

As you make decisions about the approaches you will use to build relationships and to guide children, we urge you to give thoughtful consideration to your values, the ways you use authority, and your long-term goals for children. We encourage you to support children's inner strength and to be aware of cultural and individual differences. We remind you that building the complex skills needed to control strong feelings and to cooperate with others takes time and practice. We hope that you will find joy in your relationships with the young children you teach and that you will use encouraging practices to promote their social and emotional growth. Working with young children is a voyage of discovery. The ways you relate to and guide children will determine whether or not it is a peaceful voyage taken with friends.

Learning Outcomes

When you read this chapter, and then thoughtfully complete selected assignments from the "To Learn More" section and prepare items from the "For Your Portfolio" section, you will be demonstrating progress in meeting **NAEYC Standard 4: Using Developmentally Effective Approaches to Connect with Children and Families** (NAEYC, 2009).

Key elements:

4a: Understanding positive relationships and supportive interactions as the foundation of their work with children

4b: Knowing and understanding effective strategies and tools for early education

4c: Using a broad repertoire of developmentally appropriate teaching/learning approaches

4d: Reflecting on their own practice to promote positive outcomes for each child

To Learn More

Observe an Early Childhood Educator: Visit an early childhood educator whom you have reason to believe is skilled at child guidance. Observe him or her working with children for at least 2 hours. Notice this teacher's ways of communicating and relating in the following situations: (1) with one child at play, (2) with a child during a routine, (3) mediating or preventing a dispute, and (4) leading a group activity. Be aware of what the teacher and children say and do; how she or he listens, responds, and communicates about problems. Write about what you saw and comment on the goals and values that this practitioner might hold. Describe how he or she appeared to influence children's self-concepts, relationships, and feelings about school and learning.

Interview an Early Childhood Educator: Talk to an educator who has been working with young children for several years. Ask about the guidance strategies used most often, where they were learned, and why they were chosen. Ask which guidance problems are encountered frequently, and how difficult behaviors are addressed. Find out what this teacher thinks is the most important thing to know about guiding young children. Write about what you learned and comment on how this educator might influence children's self-concepts, relationships, and feelings about school and learning.

Create a Child Guidance File: Gather articles about children's behavior and ways to build positive relationships with young children. What can you infer about the author's views about how children learn and philosophy

of guidance? Organize those that you think would be helpful in the future into a file for easy reference. Include articles that you could share with families.

Read a Book: Read a book about one of the aspects of child guidance described in this chapter. Reflect on the book and write about what you have learned and its implications for your own child guidance practices. Some suggested books are these:

The Irreducible Needs of Children: What Every Child Must Have to Grow, Learn, and Flourish (Brazelton & Greenspan, Perseus).

Me, You, Us: Social-Emotional Learning in Preschool (Epstein, NAEYC & High Scope Press).

The Power of Guidance: Teaching Social-Emotional Skills in Early Childhood Classrooms (Gartrell, Delmar, & NAEYC).

A Matter of Trust: Connecting Teachers and Learners in the Early Childhood Classroom (Howes & Ritchie, Teachers College Press).

The Emotional Development of Young Children: Building an Emotion-Centered Curriculum (Hyson, Teachers College Press).

Challenging Behavior in Young Children: Understanding, Preventing, and Responding Effectively (Kaiser & Rasminsky, Pearson).

Create a List of Resources: Find out what agencies in your state or city provide support and assistance for families and teachers of children with challenging behavior.

Record contact information about these programs and include it in your Community Resource file.

Investigate Related Websites:

Technical Assistance Center on Social Emotional Intervention for Young Children (TACSEI): challengingbehavior.org

Center on the Social and Emotional Foundations for Early Learning: vanderbilt.edu/csefel

Collaborative for Academic, Social, and Emotional Learning: casel.org

National Network for Child Care: nncc.org

Never, Ever Hit a Child: neverhitachild.org

Positive Discipline: positivediscipline.com

U.S. Department of Education, Partnership for Family Involvement in Education: ed.gov/pubs/whoweare/index.html

 # For Your Portfolio

Problem Solving: In your work or practicum setting, find several opportunities to facilitate problem solving between two children involved in a conflict over play materials. As soon as possible after each event, spend a few minutes making an anecdotal record of it—how the children behaved, what you said and did, how the children responded, how the problem was resolved (or not), and how you felt about the role you played. After recording this information over several weeks, read over your notes to evaluate your progress. Observe and write down the effect it has had on your skill as a facilitator and on the behavior of the children. Keep these notes in your portfolio.

Guidance Philosophy: Write one or two paragraphs that describe your beliefs about relating to and guiding young children. Include discussion of your long-term goals for children, how you respond to what diverse families value for their children, and the communication and guidance practices you use or plan to use.

MyEducationLab

Go to Topic 9: Guiding Children in the MyEducationLab (myeducationlab.com) for *Who Am I in the Lives of Children?* where you can:

- Find learning outcomes for Guiding Children along with the national standards that connect to these outcomes.
- Complete Assignments and Activities that can help you more deeply understand the chapter content.
- Apply and practice your understanding of the core teaching skills identified in the chapter with the Building Teaching Skills and Dispositions learning units.
- Check your comprehension on the content covered in the chapter with the Study Plan. Here you will be able to take a chapter quiz, receive feedback on your answers, and then access Review, Practice, and Enrichment activities to enhance your understanding of chapter content.

If our American way of life fails the child, it fails us all.

PEARL S. BUCK

The greatest wealth is health.

VIRGIL

7

Health, Safety, and Well-Being

Among the many goals we have for the young children in our programs, none are more important than the achievement of a sense of well-being—a state of wellness of the body, mind, and soul. Ensuring that children are safe from physical harm, have limited exposure to disease, and have experiences that support physical and emotional wellness are your most important responsibilities as an early childhood teacher.

This chapter focuses on the ways that teachers in early childhood programs can keep children healthy and protect them from physical and psychological harm. Early childhood teachers are responsible for:

- Protecting young children from hazards
- Providing attentive supervision
- Maintaining a healthy, safe, and appropriately challenging environment
- Developing and practicing wellness routines
- Teaching children about ways to keep themselves safe
- Helping children learn to care for their bodies, particularly by choosing healthy foods and staying active
- Identifying signs of illness and of abuse
- Helping children develop strategies to cope with disasters and with violence

Children and families have a right to have access to programs that:

- Have safe facilities
- Have policies and procedures in place to ensure health and wellness
- Provide nutritious meals and snacks
- Offer resources to teachers to safeguard their own health and safety

As a good early childhood educator, you need to be aware of these responsibilities. You will want to be certain that you are doing all that you reasonably can to protect children and to advocate for their health, safety, and well-being.

More than 11 million children in the United States under age 5 are in some type of child care arrangement (NACCRRA, 2010), and most children over the age of 5 are enrolled in an elementary school program. Many are also enrolled in after-school care programs. Whether in full-day child care, part-day preschool, kindergarten, elementary school, or after-school care, all young children need to be safe and secure, and in settings that promote their health and well-being.

Physical Safety and Health

Keeping children safe and healthy is, in large measure, a matter of common sense. Protect children from hazards. Supervise them well. Make sure they have nutritious food, water, and clean facilities needed for health. Teach them how to follow routines that will keep them safe and well. Although at first glance these things appear simple, they are actually somewhat complex and implementing them can be challenging in settings that serve groups of young children.

If you teach in a program for children 5 years of age and under, you will have particular responsibilities to implement health and safety practices. Special vigilance and care must be taken with infants and toddlers, who are especially vulnerable. As children enter kindergarten and move into the primary grades, they are better able to attend to their own health and safety needs. Kindergarten and primary teachers still need to practice routines for safety and wellness but have fewer tasks in this area than teachers and caregivers of younger children.

We recommend that you use a resource such as *Caring for Our Children: National Health and Safety Performance Standards: Guidelines for Out-of-Home Child Care* (AAP, APHA, & NRC, 2011). This recently updated manual provides comprehensive health and safety guidelines for early childhood programs. It is available both online and in hard copy. A number of websites listed at the end of the chapter offer additional information regarding health and safety.

Creating Safe Places for Children

When a family entrusts the care of their child to an early childhood program, they expect the physical environment to be safe. They believe that the program will have sound policies in place to ensure that their child will not be hurt. They trust that you, the teacher, are knowledgeable and skilled in selecting safe equipment, materials, and activities; that you follow policies and procedures designed to protect children from harm; and that you have training in first aid. They assume that you will take precautions to prevent accidents and supervise children in order to ensure their safety.

What Is Safe?

Young children build physical skill and strength as they master challenges. Learning to walk, climbing on playground structures, riding a bicycle, and using scissors, knives, and woodworking tools—all involve a certain amount of risk. *Risk* is defined as exposure to the chance of injury or loss. While we want to protect children from injury, we know that children learn from challenging activities that require developmentally appropriate risk-taking. The educator's role is to ensure that the activities are well matched to the children's skill and ability level as well as to make certain that the environment is free of hazards. A *hazard*—as differentiated from a risk—is a danger that a child cannot anticipate or see and, therefore, cannot evaluate. A sharp table edge, a hot metal slide, a broken stair, a balloon fragment—all of these are examples of hazards. Children do not have the experience to know that these things may be harmful. Consequently, hazards must be immediately repaired or removed from environments where children work and play.

When you make decisions about safety and which risks to allow, you will use your knowledge about children along with individual circumstances as guides for making appropriate choices for each situation.

Developmental Differences and Safety

Characteristic behaviors of each stage of development are often the ones that put children at risk. Infants and toddlers explore the world by putting things in their mouths—so choking is a common hazard. An eager preschooler may grab a glass jar to use as a bug house and get cut when she drops it onto the pavement. In the midst of a competitive game, a school-age child may accidentally injure a playmate with sports equipment or a playful shove.

Safety precautions change with children's developmental stages. For example, covering electric outlets is essential with mobile infants, toddlers, and preschoolers but is unnecessary with typically developing kindergarten and primary-age children. Young children may be injured because of undeveloped physical skill, strength, and coordination. Their natural inclination to learn through exploration encourages risk-taking behavior. Toddlers' rapidly developing large-motor skills encourage climbing, sometimes resulting in falls. Three- and four-year-olds are curious and active, and so bruises and scrapes are common during vigorous exploratory play. Kindergarten and primary-age children usually have well developed motor skills and have great confidence in their own abilities, so injuries may occur during their investigations of materials, equipment and their growing physical skills. Children with disabilities may explore and play in ways that are more typical of younger children and may need more supervision and protection than their normally developing peers.

Part of your job will be to evaluate the safety of the environment, keeping the characteristics of the group of children in mind. Jim Greenman reminds us that, "There are often serious consequences if a program eliminates opportunities for children to use their bodies and materials in ways that involve some risk. . . . In a sterile, padded world with insufficient stimulation or challenge, humans either turn themselves off or turn to and on each other for stimulation" (2007). In settings where there is little opportunity for physical challenge or appropriate risk-taking, children will invent these experiences for themselves. When you notice children climbing on railings, jumping from shelves or balancing atop slide rims, they are telling you that they need additional large-motor challenges. Ensuring safety is important, but it is also important to provide opportunities for children to test their own abilities and begin to learn to assess danger accurately. If we remove most challenges from children's environments, we deprive them of opportunities to build confidence and learn ways to keep themselves safe.

Safe Outdoor Environments

The outdoor environment provides children with rich and varied learning opportunities. In fact, in the most recent edition of the *National Health & Safety Performance Standards,* the section on *Preventing Childhood Obesity in Early Care and Education* states that all children, including infants and toddlers, should play outdoors every day except when weather and air quality conditions create a significant health risk (AAP, APHA, & NRC, 2011). Outdoor environments must be free of hazards and be outfitted with equipment that is safe and is age- and stage-appropriate. Although you may have little control over the characteristics of your program's outdoor environment, it is important that safety be a guide for your decisions about how you will use the space and for the outdoor experiences you will plan for children.

Playgrounds should satisfy several safety criteria. They should be:

Secure: Play yards for infants, toddlers, and preschool children must have sturdy fences with gates and childproof latches to ensure that children do not leave without supervision. Remind families that only adults are allowed open gates. When possible, locate latches out of children's reach. Playgrounds for school-age children may use less structured boundaries such as plants and hedges to define outdoor play spaces.

Hazard-Free: Check for and remove dangerous items such as broken glass or cigarette butts. Be sure that chemicals, fertilizers, tools, and other dangerous equipment or substances are locked out of children's reach. Many common plants are toxic if handled or swallowed by young children. Ask your local poison control center or cooperative extension service for information about poisonous plants and arrange for removal of any that you find.

Safely Equipped: Playground equipment such as swings, slides, and climbers provides opportunities for children to develop physical skills. It is important that equipment is appropriate for the skills of the children using it and that it meets current guidelines for safety. The U.S. Consumer Product Safety Commission's *Public Playground Safety Handbook* (CPSC, 2010), available online (http://www.cpsc.gov/cpscpub/pubs/325.pdf) provides comprehensive standards for outdoor play structures.

Each year, more than 200,000 children go to U.S. hospital emergency rooms with injuries associated with playground equipment (CPSC, 2010). Many of these injuries occur when a child falls from the equipment onto the ground. The risk of injury from falls is reduced when play structures are surrounded by railings and have the proper type, depth, and area coverage of impact-absorbing materials beneath them.

The Consumer Product Safety Commission provides information about appropriate types of impact-reducing materials and requirements for their installation and maintenance. Grass, concrete, asphalt, soil, turf, and carpeting are unacceptable as impact material. Sand, wood chips, and commercially installed soft surfaces are among the types of materials recommended for cushioning falls. If your playground has sand or wood chips, part of your job may be to turn and rake them regularly. If your playground does not have appropriate impact material, you can advocate for improving this important safety feature.

Practices That Promote Outdoor Safety

Regular routines can go a long way toward ensuring that children's outdoor experiences are safe. You can work with administrators and other teachers to establish and follow such routines.

Complete Regular Safety Checks.   Outdoor play areas should be checked daily for dangerous substances and these should be removed. Use a checklist such as the one included in Appendix B to regularly check outdoor equipment to ensure safety.

Check Weather Conditions.   Unless there is a wind chill below 15 degrees F, a heat index above 90 degrees F, or local health authorities report air quality risk, plan to take children outside for some part of every day (AAP, APHA, & NRC, 2011).

For safe play in warm weather:

- Play outside before 10:00 or after 2:00.
- Offer water frequently.
- Check equipment to be certain that it will not burn children's skin, and prevent access to equipment that is too hot.
- With parental permission, apply a sunscreen with a sun protection factor (SPF) guarding against UVB and UVA rays about 30 minutes prior to outdoor play. For infants younger than 6 months, sunscreen is not safe. Instead, keep infants in shaded areas and dress them in light clothing that covers their bodies completely, including a wide-brimmed hat.
- Ask families to provide hats and encourage children to wear them.

On cold days, ensure that children have dry, warm clothing. Layers work well for active play, as children can remove clothing if they become too warm. Be sure scarves are tucked into jackets and hoods do not have strings, as these can get caught on playground equipment and cause strangulation. When there is snow, encourage children to enjoy digging, exploring, and playing with it, but do not allow them to eat it.

Supervise Attentively.   Even the safest playgrounds can't protect children from injury. Constant, attentive supervision by adults is necessary. We have visited schools where teachers spent much of the outdoor time talking with one another instead of supervising the children. This puts children at risk and limits teachers' opportunities for enhancing learning. Early childhood staff should develop a plan for outdoor supervision that will ensure that adults are close to play structures and alert to children's activity at all times.

Help Children Learn to Be Safe.   When young children play outside they run, jump, and climb. They test themselves. Most of the time their activity is safe and appropriate, but not always. It is important for teachers to work together to determine acceptable behaviors that ensure safe outdoor play in their setting. Develop guidelines (some teachers call them rules) that are stated positively—so that they tell children what *to* do—and worded so that each has a reason that a young child can understand. Use the "Guidelines for Using Outdoor Equipment Safely" in the accompanying box to talk to children about outdoor safety. Teach children that that there are two basic guidelines that everyone needs to follow—*keep yourself safe* and *keep other people safe*. It is also important to teach children to keep all plants and plant materials such as seeds or flowers out of their mouths and to bring broken or damaged toys to an adult right away.

Safe Indoor Environments

Indoor environments need to be safe as well as attractive and functional. Like the outdoor environment, some aspects of the classroom environment will be beyond your control—but you should be aware of risks inherent in it, do all that is possible to create an inside space that is safe for children's activities, and work with administrators to eliminate hazards.

Prevent falls by ensuring that carpets and other floor coverings are secure. Avoid throw rugs. Windows and glass doors should be made of safety glass. If they are not, be sure to limit children's access to them. Glass doors should have vision strips at both children's and adults' eye-levels to protect against collisions. Prevent children from opening doors by installing safety covers over doorknobs that are within their reach.

In classrooms for children under 5, all electrical outlets should be covered with safety plugs when not in use. Fans should be located well out of the reach of children. Ensure that children do not have access to radiators. If space heaters are used, place them in areas that are inaccessible to children and away from curtains or other flammable materials. Water temperature in classroom taps should be kept below 120 degrees to eliminate the possibility of burns. Draperies and carpets should be flame resistant.

You can prevent accidents by removing or locking away hazardous materials, such as cleaning supplies, medications, and plastic bags. Knives, adult scissors, and other tools should never be left where children can get to them without supervision, even for a moment. Hazardous items should be stored in a sturdy, lockable cabinet, mounted out of children's reach.

Material Safety. As a classroom teacher, you will have more control over which toys and materials you offer to children than you do over the conditions of the building and its furnishings. You increase children's safety when you are aware of manufacturer recommendations regarding the intended age group for

GOLDEN RULES FOR ENSURING SAFE TOYS AND MATERIALS

1. Choose toys and art materials that are labeled nontoxic. Crayons and paints should say "ASTM D-4236-94" on the package, which means that they've been evaluated by the American Society for Testing and Materials.
2. Choose water-based paint, glue, and markers.
3. For papier-mâché and similar projects, use only newspapers and magazines with black ink.
4. Avoid battery-operated or electrical toys that can cause shock.
5. Do not use toys with strings or cords longer than 10 inches.
6. Check all toys regularly to ensure that they are in good repair with no cracks, rips, sharp edges, or loose parts.
7. Avoid materials with small removable or loose parts that could be swallowed; for children under 3, choose toys that are larger than 1.5 inches and balls that are larger than 1.75 inches in diameter. Remove button- or google-eyes from stuffed toys.
8. Avoid toy chests, which may trap children or pinch limbs.

a toy and when you are attentive to publications from government agencies and consumer groups that are concerned with toy safety. Because new information about safety is always coming out, it is important to keep up-to-date. The U.S. Consumer Product Safety Commission lists recalled toys on its website, cpsc.gov. A recently launched website, http://saferproducts.gov/Search/Result, allows users to easily search for recalls by product name and/or type.

Because young children, particularly infants and toddlers, explore objects with their mouths, you must be especially aware of potential choking risks. Small toys, broken pieces of toys, buttons, coins, and other small objects are choking hazards. Balloons are a particular danger for young children who are likely to put them into their mouths in an attempt to inflate them. Balloons should never be brought into an early childhood program, not even for birthdays or celebrations. Latex or vinyl gloves should also be kept out of children's reach. Foods that can pose choking risks will be discussed later in this chapter. Classrooms should be checked daily to ensure that all items accessible to children are safe for them to use.

The suggestions in the "Golden Rules for Ensuring Safe Toys and Materials" box will help you select safe items.

Safe Equipment and Furnishings. Furniture and equipment in early childhood programs should be comfortable, durable, and appropriately sized. Chairs should allow children's feet to touch the floor, and tables should be at a comfortable height for eating and working. Young toddlers need chairs that prevent them from falling out; cube chairs are well suited for this younger age group. School-age children are most comfortable at tables with movable chairs. Shelving should be sturdy, stable, and low enough for you to see over. Corners and edges should be rounded. If you have an indoor climber, be careful to position it in an open area away from furniture, and place large foam mats under and around it to cushion falls.

Programs that serve infants should select cribs that meet the new CPSC safety standards that were approved in 2011. In addition to more stringent requirements for safe crib construction of newly manufactured cribs, the regulations require that as of December 2012 all cribs used in child care centers must meet these new requirements. For a summary of these standards, go to cpsc.gov/onsafety/2011/03/the-new-crib-standard-questions-and-answers.

Caring for Our Children: National Health and Safety Performance Standards (2011) prohibits the use of infant walkers and "jumpers" (seats attached to a door frame or ceiling that encourage the infants to jump or bounce). There have been several reports of springs or clamps breaking on various models of jumpers. Infant walkers are dangerous because their upright position can cause children to tip over. Children in walkers can move around very fast, making them likely to bump into furniture, objects or people and cause pain or injury. Many injuries, some fatal, have been associated with infant walkers. There have been several reports of springs or clamps breaking on various models of jumpers (AAP et al., 2011).

Establish Systems to Ensure That Equipment and Facilities Are Safe. Naturally you will always act immediately to remove hazardous equipment from your classroom. In addition, a system for completing safety inspections on a regular basis will help you and others on your teaching team to ensure that hazards are noticed and removed or repaired promptly. Toys and materials should be checked at least weekly for splinters, broken parts, and sharp edges. Furnishings and equipment should be checked at least once each month. See Appendix B for recommended intervals for inspections and for sample checklists.

Supervise for Safety. An important way to keep children safe is to arrange your classroom so that you can see children at all times and so that pathways and exits are clear and uncluttered. It also necessary to remain aware of individual differences between children—Enrico may need a guiding hand and watchful eye when he snips with scissors, while Monica is be able to use them safely—and supervise appropriately. Attentive supervision will also limit injuries that occur as a result of children's conflicts. If you are paying close attention, you may be able to intervene before a child throws a block or bites another child.

Vehicle and Trip Safety

Learning trips extend children's educational opportunities beyond the program site and should be a regular part of the curriculum. Whether you travel by school bus to visit the seashore, take the city bus to a nearby shopping mall, or go on a neighborhood walk to find leaves and insects, you need to take precautions for children's safety.

Safe learning trips require a low adult-child ratio and small group size. The age and characteristics of the children determine the ratio and group size required to ensure their safety. A walk that includes crossing a busy street with a group of six 8-year-olds and one teacher may be safe and reasonable. That same walk with six toddlers and one teacher would be unsafe.

Plan trips carefully. If possible, visit the site before the trip so that you will be aware of possible hazards as well as points of interest. Locate bathrooms and sources of water. Carefully prepare children before the trip to be certain that they know the safety rules. We find that pretending to go on a trip before the actual event helps children follow rules and know what to expect. Notify families in advance of each excursion and, if school policy permits, invite them to join you. Extra adult hands can be a welcome addition on excursions!

Always take a well-stocked first aid kit and emergency contact information for each child and adult. Develop an agreed-on plan for how to manage emergencies and take a working cell phone. Diapers and clothing changes for younger children may be needed. Be sure that children will have access to drinking water and plan for a meal or snack if the trip is during a time when they usually eat. Plan drop-off and pick-up spots to minimize exposure to traffic.

All vehicles used to transport children should run well, be fitted with appropriate safety restraint systems (based on children's height and weight) and have all safety features operational. Child safety seats should be appropriate for the children's size and meet the Federal Motor Vehicle Safety Standards. The use of child safety seats reduces risk of death by 71% for children younger than 1 year of age and by 54% for children ages 1 to 4 (AAP, APHA, & NRC, 2011).

Walking trips are a wonderful way of enriching the curriculum and help children learn how to be safe as pedestrians. Ensure children's safety on walking trips by assessing all points along the route carefully before walking it with children. Determine potentially risky areas and develop a plan to ensure safe walking. Use buggies or strollers to take infants and young toddlers on trips around the neighborhood. Check these carefully before each trip to ensure that they are in good repair and that each child has a working seat belt.

Practices That Promote Safety

Safety requires constant attention to children's characteristics, and the ways they interact with the program environment. The practices you adopt and the routines that you implement will help keep the children in your program safe.

Safe Group Sizes and Teacher-Child Ratios. It is difficult to keep children safe if the group is large and there are not enough adults to provide adequate supervision. Young children are more comfortable in small groups, and teachers and caregivers can best meet their individual needs when the group is a manageable size. Although as a teacher, you may have little control over the number of children in your group, it is important for you to know the standards for appropriate group sizes so you can advocate for them. The Early Childhood Program Standards and Accreditation Criteria developed by the National Association for the Education of Young Children (2007) offer guidelines for appropriate group size and teacher-child rations for each age group (see Table 7.1).

Monitor Access. It is important to protect children by monitoring people who enter the program. This enables you to prevent children from leaving with non-authorized adults, even noncustodial parents. A system must be in place for ensuring that only authorized adults pick up children. In most programs for children under 5 and in some kindergartens, families must sign their children in and out. If an unfamiliar person arrives to pick up a child in your classroom, be certain to politely ask to see identification and then check the child's record to be sure the family has given this person permission to

pick up the child. Sometimes new teachers feel embarrassed or uncomfortable when asking for identification; however, in most cases adults will be appreciative of your attention to children's safety.

Prepare for Emergencies. Advance preparation can limit the number or the seriousness of injuries that occur as a result of an emergency. Following are steps you can take to prepare:

- Have available a well-stocked first aid kit and keep it in a visibly marked and accessible place.
- Maintain current first aid and CPR training certification.
- Learn how to use fire extinguishers and make sure they are checked regularly to be certain that they are charged.

TABLE 7.1 Teacher[1]-Child Ratios Within Group Size

Age Group	Group Size									
	6	8	10	12	14	16	18	20	22	24
Infants (birth to 15 months)[2]	1:3	1:4								
Toddler/Twos (12 to 36 months)[2]										
12–28 months	1:3	1:4	1:4[3]	1:4						
21–36 months		1:4	1:5	1:6						
Preschool[2]										
2.5-year-olds to 3-year-olds (30–48 months)				1:6	1:7	1:8	1:9			
4-year-olds						1:8	1:9	1:10		
5-year-olds						1:8	1:9	1:10		
Kindergarten								1:10	1:11	1:12

Notes: In a mixed-age preschool class of 2.5-year-olds to 5-year-olds, no more than four children between the ages of 2.5 years and 3 years may be enrolled. The ratios within group size for the predominant age group apply. If infants or toddlers are in a mixed-age group, the ratio for the youngest child applies.

Ratios are to be lowered when one or more children in the group need additional adult assistance to fully participate in the program:

a. because of ability, language fluency, developmental age or stage, or other factors or
b. to meet other requirements of NAEYC Accreditation.

A *group* or *classroom* refers to the number of children who are assigned for most of the day to a teacher or a team of teaching staff and who occupy an individual classroom or well-defined space that prevents intermingling of children from different groups within a larger room or area.

Group sizes as stated are ceilings, regardless of the number of staff.

Ratios and group sizes are always assessed during on-site visits for NAEYC Accreditation. They are not a required criterion. However, experience suggests that programs that exceed the recommended number of children for each teaching staff member and total group sizes will find it more difficult to meet each standard and achieve NAEYC Accreditation. The more these numbers are exceeded, the more difficult it will be to meet each standard.

[1]Includes teachers, assistant teachers/teacher aides.

[2]These age ranges purposefully overlap. Programs may identify the age group to be used for on-site assessment purposes for groups of children whose ages are included in multiple age groups.

[3]Group sizes of 10 for this age group would require an additional adult.

Source: NAEYC. 2007. *NAEYC Early Childhood Program Standards and Accreditation Criteria: The Mark of Quality in Early Childhood Education* (Table 2, p. 83). Washington, DC: Author. Reprinted with permission from the National Association for the Education of Young Children (NAEYC). www.naeyc.org.

- Have in place plans for:
  - what to do if someone (child or adult) needs emergency medical treatment.
  - supervision of children if someone must attend to an injured or ill child.
  - evacuation during emergencies; practice emergency evacuation with children.
- Post current telephone numbers for emergency services and poison control centers near the telephone.
- Keep emergency contact telephone numbers for children's family members and have a system for regularly updating contact information.

Though the most frequent first aid you will use with young children will involve soap, water, adhesive bandages, and ice packs, every early childhood educator needs to have basic training for giving first aid and infant and child CPR. In most states such training is mandatory. Along with learning how to give mouth-to-mouth resuscitation and how to clear a blocked airway, you will learn how to handle a bee sting and how and when to use universal precautions (i.e., safe practices for handling blood and other body fluids).

Your program should have a carefully developed disaster plan to ensure that both staff and families know what to do in the event of a disaster, such as a weather or a national defense emergency, and are prepared to deal with these in an, efficient way. Effective evacuation and emergency management plans include prior agreements about the roles and responsibilities of every staff member. Be certain you are familiar with this plan and share this information with families so they will know what will be done in these rare emergency situations.

Put Infants to Sleep Safely.   Sudden infant death syndrome (SIDS) is a tragedy that occurs when a seemingly healthy infant dies of no apparent cause while sleeping. No one knows exactly what causes SIDS, but research strongly supports the fact that SIDS deaths are significantly decreased when babies are put to sleep on their backs. You lessen the risk of SIDS when everyone caring for the infant follows a "safe sleep" policy. Guidelines are available from the American Academy of Pediatrics (AAP, 2008a, 2008b). Families need information about safe sleep for babies. There are a number of excellent brochures available. Check with a local health clinic or department of health, or download information from www.nichd.nih.gov/sids.

Help Children Learn to Be Safe

In order to help children learn to keep themselves safe, you need to view the world through children's eyes. You can help them to recognize risks and notice when activities may be dangerous. Children need information in unfamiliar situations and when new equipment, materials, or experiences are introduced. As you learn more about young children, you will become skilled at providing them information that they can remember, and teaching them safety skills that they can master through practice.

It is useful to teach them procedures for handling tools and materials safely. For example, we have discussed using a knife with 4-, 5-, and 6-year-olds in this way: "This is a knife. One side is sharp and the other side isn't. When you cut with a knife it's important to have the sharp side down and to make sure that your fingers aren't under the cutting blade. Hold onto the handle with one hand and use the other hand to push down—that way you won't accidentally get cut."

Reflect on childhood dangers

What do you recall from your childhood about things that were dangerous? How did adults teach you to deal with these risks? Think about children you know today. What are some risks that they encounter? What are some appropriate ways you can teach them to be safe?

Safety explanations for toddlers must be simple and accompanied with close supervision and physical protection: "The pot is hot. Let's just look until it cools down." Place the pot out of reach and place your body between the pot and the toddlers.

Young children learn about safety in the context of daily life. As you prepare for a field trip or a fire drill, children can help you to make up safety rules and procedures. Safety concepts can be integrated into activities that you are already doing. For example:

- Sing a song such as Woody Guthrie's "Riding in My Car," and add a verse about wearing a seat belt.
- Add a painted crosswalk to the trike path for practice.
- Place some obviously broken toys around the classroom and send children on a broken toy hunt as a way to teach them to always bring broken items to an adult.
- Include props and pictures of firefighters in full regalia in the dramatic play area to help children to be unafraid of them in a real emergency. (Young children have been known to hide during a real fire!)

You can also teach children about safety through planned curriculum on fire, home, and traffic safety and taking care of themselves. Help children become familiar with the people and procedures to follow in disasters (such as fires and tornadoes). Teach them to always come to an adult when they hear a siren or see something that may be dangerous.

It is tempting to teach safety as a series of warnings—don't play with matches, don't go near the water, don't run in the street, don't talk to strangers. It is more effective, however, to teach children things they *can* do and help them understand why they should do them. For example, always bring matches to a grown-up, walk across the street in the crosswalk, and only talk with people you know. Let children know that you are pleased to see their growing ability to care for themselves.

Protect Children from Abuse and Neglect

As an early childhood educator, you have legal and ethical responsibilities related to identifying and reporting child abuse and neglect. Your responsibilities include the following:

- To be aware of the indicators of abuse and neglect
- To report suspected cases to the appropriate agency so that the child and family can receive assistance
- To inform families of your reporting obligation as part of their orientation to the program
- To know about and use resources such as your local child protective service and the NAEYC Code of Ethical Conduct
- To know what is available in your community for educating families about how to interact with their children in constructive, non-abusive ways

A part of helping children to be safe includes teaching children some ways to avoid abuse and teaching them to get help if abuse does occur. How can you teach children to avoid abuse? When you show children that you appreciate them and respect their feelings, values, and culture, you lay the foundation that will enable them to build skills to protect themselves from abuse. Such relationships allow them to feel safe and to share concerns and feelings with trusted adults. Let children know that it is *never* okay for someone else to hurt them. You can teach them that it is OK for them to resist physical intrusion and to say "No, I don't want you to do that to me!" to other children and to adults. This requires that you respect children's feelings and invite their cooperation rather than insisting on their compliance. You show respect for children when you avoid using physical force (for example, picking children up and forcing them to be where they do not want to be) except in situations where a child's immediate safety is at stake.

It is impossible to "abuse-proof" very young children. No lesson, curriculum approach, or strategy will guarantee children's safety. Although several popular approaches are specifically designed to prevent child abuse by focusing on the concept of private parts, or the idea of good touches versus bad touches, or stranger danger, these tactics may mislead, alarm, or arouse the curiosity of children. They tend to place responsibility on the relatively powerless child instead of on the adult.

Effective child abuse prevention is an ongoing part of children's learning, not a onetime "inoculation." You can support this by applying the "Golden Rules for Helping Children Protect Themselves from Abuse" discussed in the accompanying box.

Reflect on your ethical responsibilities

You have a 6-year-old in your class who is frequently absent from school. When you ask her about her many absences, she tells you that she had to stay home to take care of her baby sister because her mom was sick or had to work. Using the guidelines on page 23, reflect on your ethical responsibilities in this situation.

GOLDEN RULES FOR HELPING CHILDREN PROTECT THEMSELVES FROM ABUSE

1. **Provide choices:** Offer children opportunities to make choices, including the choice to say no to an activity, food, or suggestion. This includes the right to reject physical contact. You offer choices by asking or alerting children before you touch or pick them up by saying things like "May I give you a hug?" "Would you like me to rub your back?" or "I'm going to pick you up and put you on the changing table," rather than doing so without warning.

2. **Develop body awareness and appreciation:** Provide many ways for children to appreciate their bodies through routines, games, songs, movement, and stories. Use correct names for body parts. Children who value their bodies are likely to avoid harming themselves or letting others harm them.

3. **Encourage children to express needs and feelings:** Help children understand feelings and encourage self-expression through words, stories, music, art, movement, and puppetry. Children who can express their ideas, needs, and feelings are better equipped to handle situations in which they are uncomfortable.

4. **Integrate safety education:** Integrate safety into classroom activities through discussion, role-playing, and dramatization so children learn things they can do to be safe in a variety of settings (such as crossing the street, riding in cars, playing at the beach, shopping at the mall, answering the phone, or being with a stranger or with a friend).

5. **Distinguish surprises from secrets:** Explore differences between secrets and surprises to help children understand that surprises are things you are waiting to share to make someone happy (like a birthday present), and secrets are things that someone wants you to hide that feels dangerous or wrong.

6. **Build positive self-esteem:** Help children feel good about themselves—their characteristics, abilities, and potential. Recognizing and valuing differences and affirming individuality through song, celebration, and activities help children to feel that they are worthy of protection.

Creating Healthy Places for Young Children

What could be more critical for children's overall welfare than being healthy? As a teacher, you will have many opportunities to involve children in regular routines that teach them to keep themselves healthy. You will also ensure that classroom environments are maintained in a manner that promotes health.

But what is health? According to the World Health Organization, "Health is a state of complete physical, mental and social well-being and not merely the absence of disease or infirmity" (1948). We keep children healthy when we provide for all aspects of their development and well-being—their mental health, their developing social abilities, their growing bodies and brains, and their intellectual development. Healthy People 2020, a national initiative of the U.S. Department of Health and Human Services (2010), stresses the important relationships between children's health and their ability to learn.

Part of your job as an early childhood teacher is to know and use practices that promote the health of each child. You will take precautions each day to limit the spread of disease. You will work to ensure that all children, including those with disabilities and those with chronic health conditions, have a healthy classroom. You will learn to identify health risks and to take precautions to limit them. With administrators and health care professionals, you can develop policies and procedures that address health routines and health emergencies. Equally important, you will develop curriculum that helps children learn to care for their bodies and engages them in daily exercise and healthy routines.

Understand How Illness Spreads

"She has a cold again! It seems like since Jasmine started school she is sick all the time."

Families and teachers alike are concerned about infectious diseases. Both want to ensure that early childhood programs are doing all they can to prevent and control the spread of illness. Learning to do this effectively will be an important part of your job. You control illness by eliminating *pathogens*—agents such as bacteria, viruses or parasites that cause infection or disease—and by limiting the ways that they can be transmitted. You also do this by helping to improve children's overall health. Good nutrition, exercise, and good psychological health all improve resistance and decrease susceptibility to disease.

The close contact that people have with one another in early childhood programs increases opportunities for pathogens to be transmitted. Respiratory diseases such as colds and flu are spread when secretions from the mouth, nose, eyes, and lungs pass from one person to the other. This can happen through direct touching; sharing of toys, objects, and food; or contact with droplets in the air when individuals cough or sneeze. Diarrhea and other diseases of the intestinal tract are caused by viruses, bacteria, or parasites that are spread through contact with fecal matter. This may occur when handwashing practices are inadequate or diapering practices unsanitary. Hepatitis B and HIV/AIDS are serious infections that are spread when the blood of an infected person comes in contact with a mucous membrane (lining of the mouth, eyes, nose, rectum, or genitals) or with a cut or break in the skin of another individual. Your attention to healthy routines can limit the spread of these diseases.

Follow Healthy Routines

In a healthy environment, routines established and maintained by the adults limit the spread of disease. Children are protected from many pathogens when sanitary handwashing, diapering, and toileting practices are followed.

Handwashing. The most effective measure for preventing the spread of disease in early childhood programs is frequent and thorough handwashing (Aronson, 2002; Marotz, 2012). All early childhood practitioners, particularly those who work with infants and toddlers, need to wash their hands many times a day. By doing so, they limit the spread of disease and protect their own health. It is recommended that you wash your hands at the following times:

- When you first enter the classroom
- Before and after handling food
- Before and after feeding children
- Before and after changing diapers or assisting a child with toileting
- After using the toilet yourself
- Before and after giving a child medication
- After any contact with body fluids
- After handling pets
- After playing or cleaning up sand or water play areas
- After cleaning or handling garbage

To make handwashing effective in preventing disease, you should use running water and liquid soap, rub your hands together vigorously for at least 30 seconds (Marotz, 2012), wash all over from fingertips to wrists, rinse thoroughly, dry hands on a disposable paper towel, and turn off the faucet using the towel to hold the faucet handle so as not to contaminate clean hands. Children also need to wash their hands, and younger children should be assisted with this task. Take time to teach children handwashing routines and insist that hands be washed thoroughly and regularly. Children can sing a song that lasts approximately 30 seconds, such as "Twinkle, Twinkle Little Star," or a handwashing song to help them to scrub for the appropriate length of time.

Diapering and Toileting. Because diapering and toileting are some of the most prevalent ways of spreading communicable ailments, great care must be taken in managing them. In order to protect yourself from contact with possible pathogens in feces, wear disposable vinyl or latex gloves when diapering or assisting a child who has had a toilet accident.

Healthy diapering procedures can be more easily followed if the changing area is well set up and maintained. A diapering area needs a changing table with a washable mat. Procedures for sanitary diapering should be posted at adult eye-level. Paper to cover the changing surface, plastic bags for soiled diapers, a pedal-operated lidded wastebasket, sanitizing solution, and each child's diapers and supplies need to be within easy reach. The sink used to wash hands after diapering needs to be separate from food preparation areas. Most programs require each family to bring a supply of disposable diapers for their child. Because children's skin may be sensitive to diaper wipes, creams, and lotions, use only those provided by the family. When the diaper change is complete, be sure to record information about the change on the child's daily record. If you work in a program in which children wear diapers, you need to receive training in how to diaper children in a caring and sanitary manner.

Toilet areas must be cleaned and sanitized daily and additional sanitizing may be necessary during the day. To encourage both independence and sanitary use of toilets and sinks, it is best if they are child-sized. Otherwise, stable stools or wooden platforms will be needed to make them accessible. Use of potty chairs in group care settings is prohibited in most states because they are difficult to use and maintain in a sanitary fashion. Toilet tissue, running water, soap, and paper towels need to be within the reach of the children. Staff should carefully supervise toddlers' and preschoolers' use of the toilet. Older children will want privacy but may occasionally need assistance in the event of an accident. In some cases, children with disabilities will require special assistance for toileting. Use gloves when you help children and when cleaning up after accidents. Clothing soiled with feces should be tightly bagged and sent home with the child's family for laundering.

Toothbrushing. If your program includes toothbrushing, a procedure needs to be developed to ensure that children brush their teeth in a sanitary manner. Children need to be taught how to brush teeth effectively and should be supervised during the toothbrushing. Toothbrushes require careful storage and sanitizing. Consult a health care professional about best practices for in-school toothbrushing.

Clean, Sanitize, and Disinfect. Regular cleaning, disinfecting, and sanitizing of classroom equipment and materials effectively limits the spread of illness in early childhood programs. Classrooms must be *clean*—free from dirt and debris. Classroom furnishings such as diaper change tables, countertops, door and cabinet handles, toilets, and rest mats must also be *disinfected*—treated with a solution that destroys or inactivates germs. Items that come in contact with food, such as countertops, cutting boards, and serving utensils as well as toys that children put into their mouths should be *sanitized*—treated with a product that reduces germs on inanimate surfaces to levels considered safe by public health regulations. See Table 7.2, Guidelines for Sanitizing and Disinfecting Toys and Furnishings in Early Childhood Classrooms.

If the staff in your program prefer not to use chlorine bleach, there are a number of acceptable sanitizing solutions available. Choose one with a label that notes that it is registered with the Environmental Protection Agency as a sanitizer or as a disinfectant. Always follow the label instructions regarding the length of time that the solution must be left on the surface and whether or not you need to rinse it off before contact by children. Most products require precleaning before the solution is applied (AAP, APHA, & NRC, 2011).

Caring for Our Children: National Health and Safety Performance Standards (2011) provides guidelines for developing an appropriate cleaning, sanitizing, and disinfecting schedule.

Personal items for each child such as bedding, clothing, and comfort objects should be stored in a separate storage unit, such as a cubby, locker, plastic tub, or box, labeled with the child's name. Bedding should be washed at least weekly, either in program facilities or family homes.

TABLE 7.2 Guidelines for Sanitizing and Disinfecting Toys and Furnishings in Early Childhood Classrooms

Purpose/Use	Type of Product Needed	Bleach Mixture and Application
Food contact surfaces such as dishes, utensils, cutting boards Toys that children place in their mouths Pacifiers	Sanitizer	1 tablespoon of bleach + 1 gallon of cool water Spray with a heavy spray, not a mist Let stand for 2 minutes or air dry. Mix a fresh solution daily.
Diaper-changing tables, countertops, door & cabinet handles, toilets & other bathroom fixtures (nonporous surfaces only)	Disinfectant	½–¾ cup of bleach + 1 gallon of cool water; or 1 to 3 tablespoons of bleach + 1 quart of cool water Apply as a spray or pour fresh solution; do not dip into a container with a cloth that has been in contact with a contaminated surface. Let stand for 2 minutes or air dry. Mix a fresh solution daily.

Source: Information from American Academy of Pediatrics, American Public Health Association, and National Resource Center for Health and Safety in Child Care and Early Education, *Caring for Our Children: National Health and Safety Performance Standards: Guidelines for Early Care and Education Programs,* 2011.

Use Universal Precautions. Always follow universal precautions (see Figure 7.1) when you have contact with blood. This includes when you clean a scrape or help a child with a bloody nose. Teach children not to touch sores, cuts, or bandages of others.

Safe Food Preparation and Storage. Attention to food preparation—both what is prepared and how it is prepared—is important to children's health. If you are involved in food preparation (even slicing apples for snack) you will have responsibility to make sure that surfaces, and utensils are kept scrupulously clean and sanitized. All trash must be disposed of in tightly covered containers that are emptied at least daily. Perishable foods must be refrigerated at or below 40 degrees and hot foods kept at 140 degrees until they are served. State department of health regulations require anyone who prepares and/or serves food to be free of communicable diseases and use frequent and thorough handwashing to reduce the spread of pathogens.

FIGURE 7.1 Universal Precautions for Handling Body Fluids

When handling body fluids (blood, saliva, vomit, feces):

- Wear disposable vinyl or latex gloves.
- Remove glove by grasping the inner cuff and pulling it off inside out.
- Wash hands thoroughly; lather for at least 30 seconds.
- Dispose of soiled clothing and bedding by securing in plastic bags to be laundered by families.
- Dispose of soiled diapers and other disposable items such as bloody Band-Aids by placing them in plastic bags and tying securely.
- Clean all contaminated surfaces with a disinfectant solution.

Source: Information from American Academy of Pediatrics, American Public Health Association, and National Resource Center for Health and Safety in Child Care and Early Education, *Caring for Our Children: National Health and Safety Performance Standards: Guidelines for Early Care and Education Programs,* 2011.

Reflect on your ethical responsibilities

A single mom drops her 4-year-old child off with you after he has been out of school for 2 days with a fever, constant runny nose, and cough. The mother reports that the child is feeling much better and that her boss has informed her that she will lose her job if she misses any more work this month. By 10:00 A.M. the child is running a fever of 101, coughing continuously, and complaining of a headache. He goes to the library corner and falls asleep. You do not have a school nurse in your program. Using the guidelines on page 23, reflect on your ethical responsibilities in this situation.

Follow Guidelines for Excluding Sick Children

Recognizing early signs of illness in children and having policies and procedures for exclusion also help to prevent the spread of infection. All programs need to have clearly written policies that address when children must be excluded due to illness and when they may return to the program. *Managing Infectious Diseases in Child Care and Schools: A Quick Reference Guide* (Aronson & Shope, 2008) gives useful information about symptoms of childhood illnesses and which ones require exclusion. In *Healthy Young Children* (2002), Susan Aronson notes: "Contrary to popular belief and practice, only a *few* illnesses require exclusion of sick children to ensure protection of other children and staff. *Children who have fever and are behaving normally do not need to be excluded. Neither do children with colds who are behaving normally*" [emphasis original]. This means that if children are able to engage in their usual play and classroom activities, they may remain in school even if they have an elevated temperature. Children with colds are most contagious before symptoms appear, so exclusion does little to limit the spread of this common illness. Children should not be in school, however, when they are not able to participate comfortably in school activities or when they need more care than the teacher or caregiver can provide while also caring for the other children in the group (Aronson, 2002). Most states have guidelines for when children should be excluded from schools and early childhood programs. Consult your local health agency or health care consultant if you have questions regarding an appropriate illness policy for your program.

It is important that you have basic training to learn about handling common symptoms of illness such as fevers and vomiting and when a child should be isolated from others for health reasons. In some schools a nurse or health aide will attend to health-related matters; in others, teachers or administrators will be responsible.

Work with a Health Care Professional

There are so many issues related to children's health needs that early childhood educators cannot possibly be knowledgeable about all of them. The *Caring for Our Children* health and safety standards (AAP, APHA, & NRC, 2011) and the NAEYC Early Childhood Accreditation Criteria (NAEYC, 2007) recommend that every program have a *health care consultant*—a licensed pediatric health professional or a health professional with specific training in health consultation for early childhood programs. Health care consultants can assist you with developing and implementing policies and procedures to promote children and adult health. Many states have received funding from the Healthy Child Care America campaign to support increased resources for health consultation for early childhood programs. You can visit the program's website (healthychildcare.org) to learn about resources in your state.

Conditions That Affect Health

There are many circumstances that affect children's health. Learning about these and ways to help children and families stay healthy is part of your job as an early childhood teacher.

Understanding and Preventing Childhood Obesity

According to the Centers for Disease Control and Prevention, childhood obesity has more than tripled in the past 30 years (2010). In fact, a recent report from the

FIGURE 7.2   Some Facts About Childhood Obesity

- Obesity rates among preschoolers ages 2 to 5 have doubled in the past four decades.
- 1 in 5 children are overweight or obese by the time they reach their sixth birthday.
- Over half of obese children first become overweight at or before age 2.
- Only 25% of children ages 2 to 11 years consume three servings of vegetables a day, and less than 50% consume two daily servings of fruit.
- Preschool children spend over 4 hours a day watching television and videos, including time in child care.
- 60% of children under the age of 5 are in some form of child care and spend an average of 29 hours per week in that child care setting.

Source: White House Task Force on Childhood Obesity: Report to the President (2010).

White House Task Force on Childhood Obesity found that 1 in every 5 children today will be overweight or obese by the time that they reach their sixth birthday (2010). This puts them at risk for developing significant health problems such as high blood pressure, heart disease, and type 2 diabetes.

Studies indicate that three trends in contemporary lifestyles have influenced the rapid increase in overweight children:

- Decreased opportunity for active play and a more sedentary lifestyle
- Increased "screen time," including television, video games, and computers
- Increased calorie consumption, including significantly more fast food and sugar-sweetened beverages

The *Let's Move Campaign* (letsmove.gov) was launched in 2011 through the combined efforts of private, nonprofit, and government groups. This initiative, supported by First Lady Michelle Obama, provides a variety of tools and educational strategies geared toward ending obesity within this generation. Most recently (June 2011) this initiative was expanded to include *Let's Move! Child Care* (healthykidshealthyfuture.org), which includes goals that early childhood programs can adopt as a focus for promoting children's health along a variety of other tools that teachers and programs can use. Figure 7.3 shows a checklist of healthy practices developed by the *Let's Move! Child Care* initiative.

Because young children spend a significant amount of time each week in early childhood care and education settings, you have many opportunities to influence their health through implementing the goals of the *Let's Move! Child Care* initiative.

FIGURE 7.3   Let's Move! Child Care Checklist

- Physical Activity: Provide 1–2 hours of physical activity throughout the day, including outside play when possible.
- Screen Time: No screen time for children under 2 years. For children age 2 and older, strive to limit screen time to no more than 30 minutes per week during child care, and work with parents and caregivers to ensure children have no more than 1–2 hours of quality screen time per day, the amount recommended by the American Academy of Pediatrics.
- Food: Serve fruits or vegetables at every meal, eat meals family style when possible, and no fried foods.
- Beverages: Provide access to water during meals and throughout the day, and do not serve sugary drinks. For children age 2 and older, serve low-fat (1%) or nonfat milk, and no more than one 4–6 ounce serving of 100% juice per day.
- Infant Feeding: For mothers who want to continue breastfeeding, provide their milk to their infants and welcome them to breastfeed during the child care day; and support all new parents in their decisions about infant feeding.

Source: www.whitehouse.gov

Lead Poisoning

Childhood lead poisoning is a serious health problem. The Centers for Disease Control and Prevention (CDC, 2011) estimates that there are 250,000 young children in the United States who have elevated lead levels (cdc.gov/nceh/lead). Children who ingest or inhale even small amounts of lead are at risk for decreased bone and muscle growth, developmental delays, and behavior and learning problems. Children who come in contact with lead from either paint or plumbing are at risk. Buildings constructed before 1978 may contain lead-based paint. If your classroom is in an older building, work with other staff and administrators to ensure that paint has been tested by a licensed inspector to determine whether lead is present. If it is, your program will need to follow local guidelines to remove lead-based paint from all surfaces or completely cover it with non-leaded paint. Older buildings may also have lead pipes. As with paint, ask your administration to consult your local health department to determine if you should have your water tested for possible lead contamination.

Research indicates that the incidence of lead poisoning is highest in children who live in low-income areas and who consume a nutrient deficient diet, which increases lead absorption (Marotz, 2012). If children in your program are at risk for exposure to lead in their homes, you can offer families information about the potential dangers from lead poisoning and encourage them to ask their health care providers to screen children for possible lead poisoning.

Food Allergies and Intolerances

Some children experience severe allergic reactions to certain foods—particularly to nuts and nut products, eggs, wheat, seafood, milk and milk products, citrus fruits, and berries. A severe allergic reaction to food (or other allergens such as bee stings) can cause *anaphylaxis*—swelling of the airway, serious breathing difficulty, a drop in blood pressure, loss of consciousness, and, in some cases, even death. Other children have food intolerances that cause stomach upset, rashes, or hives. The National Center for Health Statistics reported that in the 10 years between 1997 and 2007, food allergy rates increased significantly both among preschool age and older children, and that children under age 5 had higher rates of reported food allergies than did older children (Branum & Lukacs, 2008).

Children who have a history of severe allergic reactions may need to have an EpiPen kept at school. If you have a child in your class who may need this treatment, you will need to consult a health care provider about the proper way to administer this medication.

Most programs have systems in place to prevent teachers from accidently serving prohibited food to children with food allergies. Because of the increasing prevalence of nut allergies, many schools have adopted a "no-nuts" policy, which means that no one can bring to school any food containing nuts or nut oils. You should be familiar with and follow your school's policy for dealing with allergies.

Help Children Learn to Be Healthy

Young children are intrigued with learning about themselves and their bodies. If you make it interesting they will enjoy learning about the vital topics of health and nutrition. This will lay the foundation for habits that will promote health throughout their lives.

Children can learn good health habits in the context of classroom routines and during planned activities. When the day is scheduled to include periods of both planned and spontaneous movement activities, children learn to appreciate the value of being physically active. When they eat and help to plan healthy snacks and meals and when they participate in healthful routines, they begin to appreciate their bodies and to acquire important attitudes and skills. Carefully planned curriculum can help them to understand human growth and development, body parts and functions, and the value of cleanliness, medical and dental care, exercise, rest, and good nutrition. As they learn about these things they will come to appreciate their bodies and develop positive practices and habits

Promote Physical Activity and Movement

It is important that you make exercise and physical fitness an integral part of your daily curriculum. Most children enjoy movement and physical activity. You can support this natural inclination by helping them to understand and value physical activity as an important aspect of health.

The National Association for Sport and Physical Education (NASPE) recommends that "all children should engage in daily physical activity that promotes health-related fitness and movement skills." Further, the NASPE states that toddlers and preschool-age children *should not be sedentary for more than an hour* except when sleeping, and school-age children *should have not more than 2 hours of inactivity*. NASPE recommends that preschoolers and school-age children should accumulate at least 60 minutes each day of structured physical activity and toddlers should have up to 30. Additionally, all age groups need

GOLDEN RULES FOR SUPPORTING MOVEMENT

1. **Arrange the classroom flexibly to allow for movement.** Organize classrooms so that you have (or can easily move furniture to create) a space for active games and movement. If there are no open areas outdoors for running, jumping, rolling, and other active play, take children to nearby parks for part of each day.

2. **Select equipment with movement in mind.** Choose materials such as hoops, ropes, scarves, ribbon sticks, and balls of all sizes.

3. **Demonstrate enthusiasm for physical activity.** Children will learn from what you model for them. Show them that you enjoy being active. Make active play engaging and fun.

4. **Surprise children with new or unexpected movement activities.** Encourage everyone to run around the playground three times before coming inside. During choice time, ring a chime and have everyone jump in place for 3 minutes before resuming indoor play. Engage with them in a dance to lively music that you enjoy.

5. **Help children understand why movement is important.** Let children know why you are encouraging physical activities: "When you jumped like rabbits, that got your heart moving fast! Do you feel it? It's good for your heart to give it a workout like that sometimes."

6. **Offer children choices about movement activities.** Let them choose ones that they enjoy and acknowledge the pleasure they show as they engage in them. This lays a foundation for lifelong fitness.

Source: Pica, R. 2000. "Physical Fitness and the Early Childhood Curriculum." Young Children 61(3): 12–19. Adapted and reprinted with permission from the National Association for the Education of Young Children (NAEYC). www.naeyc.org.

What types of physical activity do you enjoy? How do you include physical activity in your life? Is being active is pleasurable for you? In what ways? How can you help children to enjoy being active?

at least 60 minutes and up to several hours per day of unstructured physical activity. NASPE recommends that children "participate each day in a variety of age-appropriate physical activities designed to achieve optimal health, wellness, fitness, and performance benefits" (2002).

These recommendations have important implications for scheduling and curriculum planning. You will need to find ways to plan structured movement activities and to design your schedule so that children are encouraged to be active. Follow the "Golden Rules for Supporting Movement" on the preceding page to help children become physically fit.

Encourage Healthy Food Choices

We know that a significant factor in overweight and obesity in childhood is children's food selections; both the types of foods selected and the amounts eaten. From infancy, children begin to make choices about food. They decide which foods they like. They learn about how much they should eat, when and where they will eat, which are foods are "treats," and which are good for them. A great many of children's food habits and preferences are established in early childhood. You can help children learn that their health is affected by the food they eat and that they can make food choices that will help them to grow and be healthy. You help them learn about nutrition and healthy eating when you follow the suggestions in the accompanying box, "Golden Rules for Supporting Children's Healthy Eating."

Help children learn the importance of choosing a variety of different foods each day. New recommendations from the U.S. Department of Agriculture (USDA, 2011), *Choose My Plate,* offer easy to follow suggestions for helping

GOLDEN RULES FOR SUPPORTING CHILDREN'S HEALTHY EATING

1. **Never use food as a reward or withhold food as a punishment.** This teaches children that food is about feeling good, not about nourishment, and can lead to later eating disorders. It may also teach that less-healthy treats like candy are better than healthier choices. All children have a basic right to food. When it is withheld, their trust in adults is compromised.

2. **Create a relaxed and pleasant eating environment.** Children thrive when meals are non-hurried times to enjoy food and the company of others. Plan so mealtimes are not rushed. Make tables attractive. Sit with children during meals and snacks.

3. **Model appreciation for a variety of healthful foods.** "Yum, these crunchy carrots are delicious," you can say as you enjoy a snack with the children. When a new, healthy food appears in the school lunch, express enthusiasm: "We never had this for lunch before—I'm looking forward to trying it."

4. **Encourage children to try new foods but never force them to eat.** You can invite them to taste, but never try to make them eat what they do not want.

5. **Give children many opportunities to try new or unfamiliar food.** As a class activity, serve a new food several times and in different ways—raw cauliflower chunks one day, lightly steamed and offered with a yogurt dip another day. Studies show that many young children need between 10 and 15 experiences with a new food before they enjoy eating it (Eliassen, 2011).

6. **Help children learn to listen to their bodies.** Encourage children to notice when they are hungry and when they are full. Never urge them to clean their plates.

7. **Whenever possible, offer children a choice of healthy snacks.** When children can choose between two healthy snack choices, they feel more control over what they are eating.

8. **Make cooking and food preparation a part of your curriculum.** Simple nutritious foods make rewarding "cooking" experiences for young children. Offer them opportunities to spread cream cheese on celery and to wash and tear lettuce for a salad. Plan opportunities for children to do simple cooking activities and try new recipes with children regularly.

9. **Allow children to serve themselves.** If possible, have "family-style" dining where children serve themselves. If this is not an option, offer snacks as a self-serve activity to encourage children's emerging competence.

10. **Involve children in meal setup and cleanup.** Children can help to set the table and arrange it attractively. They will be more likely to eat when they are involved

11. **Talk with children about food and nutrition.** Children are interested in talking about where food comes from, how it is prepared, and how it helps their bodies to grow. You can help develop these concepts by offering short informative statements like, "Milk has calcium in it. It helps your bones grow and be strong."

12. **Talks about "sometimes" foods versus "anytime" food.** Cake, cookies, chips, and ice cream are fun foods to enjoy sometimes, and children should know it is OK for them to have these foods occasionally. Fruit, vegetables, and whole grain foods are good to have whenever they feel hungry.

13. **Share resources with families about food and meal planning.** Include an article in your class newsletter about healthy snacks for children. Share recipes for easy and nutritious meal ideas. Include recipes that the children have enjoyed preparing at school. A list of websites to help families with meal planning is also useful; www.choosemyplate.gov and eatright.org are two we suggest.

both children and adults make healthy food choices. Refer to the website choosemyplate.gov.

Young children may not chew foods well and are therefore at risk for choking on some foods. Do not serve infants, toddlers, or young preschoolers (under age 4) the foods listed in Figure 7.4.

During the early childhood years, children can learn about the importance of health and nutrition and ways to make healthy choices. This foundation can help them to respect their bodies, take responsibility for their health, and develop positive practices and habits. The accompanying box, "Connecting with

FIGURE 7.4 Foods Commonly Linked to Childhood Choking

Raw carrots	Hot dogs, unsliced or cut into rounds (half rounds and smaller pieces are OK)	Popcorn
Fruit with seeds or pits		Marshmallows
Nuts and seeds		Chips
Spoonfuls of peanut butter	Dried fruit (raisins are OK)	
Gummy or hard candy	Grapes, whole	

CONNECTING WITH FAMILIES

About Nutrition

Busy families want to provide healthy and nutritious food for
their children but they may face some obstacles. It can be difficult for families to
provide food that meets guidelines for good nutrition because:

1. Fast food is easy and accessible; after a long day, the easiest way to feed a
   hungry child may be a stop at a fast-food restaurant.

2. Fresh food may not be easily available; in some neighborhoods it is a long way
   to a market that sells fresh foods. Families may use canned, boxed, and frozen
   quick meals because they are easier to get.

3. Fresh food may seem expensive; when you can buy a "kid's meal" for around
   $3.50, families may think this is a budget bargain.

4. Children tend to ask for and eat fast foods and boxed foods (such as macaroni
   and cheese); families may think getting some food into their children is better
   than nothing.

You can help families make better choices if you:

1. Offer a family night where people share ideas for quick, appealing, and healthy
   kid-friendly meals.

2. Invite a nutritionist to speak to families to offer them some suggestions.

3. Share a recipe or "quick-fix" idea in your newsletter.

4. Set up a coupon-swap where families can exchange coupons for foods.

5. Talk with children often about making healthy meal and snack choices.

Families About Nutrition," describes some challenges that families may face and
offers strategies to encourage them to offer nutritious foods.

Make Health a Part of the Curriculum

Leaning about health isn't a one-time experience—we don't "do health in February." Instead, we can include opportunities for children to learn about health on a
daily basis. Teaching children about health and how to care for themselves takes
different forms for different ages of children. Preschoolers learn about health
from stories, discussions, observation, hands-on explorations, and simple experiments. Kindergarten and school-age children can engage in more in-depth study
of how bodies work, what germs are, why fitness is important, and how disease
is spread. When you allow infants and toddlers to participate as much as possible
in diapering, dressing, and washing and you explain what you are doing and
why, you help them begin to learn about their bodies and how to care for them.

Young children are interested in their bodies and only gradually learn to feel
that physical functions are private or shameful. We were delighted on a recent
visit to a kindergarten classroom to find the children fully engaged in an exploration of digestion and elimination; one way they learned about these functions was
by squeezing prepared oatmeal (a model of digested food) out of an "intestine"
created from a stocking!

People who work with young children need to react to interest in body parts
and functions in supportive ways. All body parts and physiological processes
have names—shin, finger, knuckle, buttocks, knee, forehead, digestion, urina-
tion, saliva, and so on. Children can learn the names of body parts and functions

as part of learning about themselves. Treat their occasional "bathroom humor" matter-of-factly and give them the important message: "Your body is OK; it is safe to talk with adults about it." It is important that children have the words to describe their physical and psychological needs as well as symptoms of illness.

Use Personal Care Routines as Teaching Opportunities

Daily routines with children are good times to model good health practices and discuss the reasons for what you are doing. As you discuss and help them participate in self-care routines, children learn that:

- Handwashing can keep you from getting sick.
- Toothbrushing and regular dental checkups help to keep your teeth strong and healthy.
- Rest helps your body to calm down and gives you energy.
- Exercise make you feel good and helps your body stay healthy.

Well-Being

While ensuring children's physical safety and health is of primary importance, early childhood teachers and caregivers must also be attentive to children's need to be psychologically safe and healthy. Children whose needs for both physical and emotional care are met develop a sense of well-being. As Abraham Maslow's hierarchy of human needs reminds us, only when children's physical and psychological needs are well satisfied are they able to grow into loving, inquisitive, competent human beings (1968). When you build respectful relationships with each child and family, children experience psychological safety and a sense of overall well-being. When you provide physical and social environments where it is safe to experiment and to make mistakes, children feel secure and have the courage to explore and learn.

The Importance of Touch

Physical contact, such as gently rocking an infant or toddler or offering a pat on the back or appreciative hug to an older child, tells children they are safe and cared for. Babies come into the world needing to be handled and touched in order to survive and grow. Loving touch actively supports infants' brain development (Goodman-Bryan & Joyce, 2010). Throughout the early childhood years, touch continues to play a significant role in children's physical, social, emotional, and cognitive development. It is an essential part of forming positive bonds with caregivers and it contributes to children's social and emotional competence (Carlson, 2006). It is important that children are touched appropriately by their teachers and caregivers. In some programs, possibly in

response to allegations of child abuse in some settings, "no-touch" policies have been implemented. No-touch practices are not appropriate and actually deprive young children of the benefits derived from a hug, a snuggle, or a gentle pat. In a 1996 position paper, the National Association for the Education of Young Children states:

> No-touch policies are misguided efforts that fail to recognize the importance of touch to children's healthy development. Touch is especially important for infants and toddlers. Warm, responsive touches convey regard and concern for children of any age. Adults should be sensitive to ensuring that their touches (such as pats on the back, hugs, or ruffling the child's hair) are welcomed by the children and appropriate to their individual characteristics and cultural experience. Careful, open communication between the program and families about the value of touch in children's development can help to achieve consensus as to acceptable ways for adults to show their respect and support for children in the program.

Good Transitions Support Well-Being

Everyone experiences some transitions in their lives—times when significant changes happen. Young children may feel worried, insecure, or frightened during times of transitions. Early childhood teachers who pay attention to transitions promote children's sense of well-being.

Good Beginnings

Beginnings are times of change, excitement, and hope. They are also times of stress, fear, and anxiety. They are a time to say farewell to the security of the familiar and to go forward to meet new challenges. Life is composed of many beginnings; some are large and stressful, and others are small and easy to deal with. You can help guide children over the sometimes rocky paths of the transitions between home and classroom and the transitions within and between phases of the early childhood program.

The Transition from Home. Most of us can recall the anxious feelings that we had when separating from the familiar: leaving our childhood homes, starting college, moving to a new city, becoming a parent. When young children enter your program, they face an unfamiliar world filled with new people, noises,

objects, smells, and activities. They may have had little experience with being among many children or with being parted from their family members. It will be important to them and to their families that there are strategies in place that make their first days and weeks as safe and comfortable as possible.

Young children make the transition from home best when the introduction is gradual and when they have an opportunity to integrate familiar aspects of their homes into their new lives in an early childhood program. Classroom visits prior to the child's first day are a good way to help both children and family members feel comfortable in the new setting. In some programs, initial visits occur during the course of a regular day; the child and parent participate together in an hour or two of the program. In other places, a special orientation for one or several new children and families outside of regular program hours may precede the child's first day. Such initial visits are essential for infants, toddlers, and preschoolers. Kindergarten-age children also benefit from this type of orientation if it can be arranged. School-age children usually handle the transition to a new class or school with greater ease. However, an orientation visit still provides a valuable opportunity for them to get to know the teacher and the environment.

First Days and First Weeks.   On the first day, you can begin by helping each child feel welcome and comfortable. Expect that first days will be hard for some children—and for their families. Often a family member is asked to spend part or all of the first day, or of several days, with the child. In general, older infants, toddlers, and young preschoolers have a more difficult time making a transition to a new setting than do young infants or older children. The family of a toddler may spend a week or more gradually preparing to leave their child for a full day. A 4-year-old might pointedly ask a parent to go home at the end of the first hour. The individual temperaments and experiences of both the family members and the children will influence their responses to these transitions. We have found that the time and energy spent supporting individual transitions are well worth the effort.

The environment and the activities for first days should be simple to allow children to focus on a few new experiences at a time. Keep a relaxed pace to allow them to understand what is happening without being overwhelmed or fearful of doing the wrong thing. Some suggestions for helping first days go smoothly can be found in the accompanying box, "Golden Rules for Good Beginnings."

Almost all children experience anxiety the first time they are left at school. Some children overcome this easily; others will express it through tears, tantrums, or angry words; and still others withdraw, quietly sucking thumbs or holding comfort objects and resisting adult attempts to converse or make connection. Some may have toilet accidents or nightmares. Many will resist lying down for naptime. Some may angrily reject their parents when it's time to go home. A few will appear fine for a few days or a week and then will react as strongly as if it was the first day. It is helpful to reassure worried families that all of these responses are normal and that, in most cases, children will learn to separate happily within the first several months. When separation upset goes beyond this time frame or is very extreme, it may mean that the child needs a more gradual or a delayed entrance into the program. Remember that separation behaviors and processes of adaptation, like many other aspects of behavior, are unique to individuals.

Infants, toddlers, and most young preschoolers will need the reassurance of physical contact with you during their first days and weeks. If you work in a program where many children enter at the same time, you may sometimes feel like a mother opossum moving about the classroom with the small bodies of children clinging to you. As they become comfortable, most children will find more interesting things to do.

For many, a treasured blanket, stuffed animal, or piece of clothing (sometimes called a *transitional object*) is important in the separation process. Because they provide a sense of safety, it is important that children be allowed to keep them close, rather than being required to leave them in a cubby. With time, comfort objects may be needed only when a child is under stress or at nap times.

Reflect on a separation

Recall a change in your life that involved separation from friends and family or a familiar place. How did you feel? How did you cope with this transition? How might you apply this experience to working with children who are undergoing separation?

Reflect on your first day of school

Remember your first day of school or your first day in a new school or class. What stands out in your memory? What was most reassuring? What was most distressing? Why? What did this experience teach you about what is important to do for children on first days? What do you want to make sure *not* to do? Why?

GOLDEN RULES FOR GOOD BEGINNINGS

1. Have the child begin with a short first day.
   Children who have little experience in group settings may have absorbed all they can in an hour.

2. Encourage a parent or familiar caregiver to spend all or part of the first days with their child.

3. Help families establish a "good-bye ritual."
   For example, a father may read one story, give two hugs and one kiss, and then say good-bye and leave. This sequence can be repeated daily.

4. Let families know that they are welcome to stay and participate, but when they say good-bye, it is easiest for children if they leave promptly. Invite them to telephone to see how their child is doing.

5. Greet children and their family members by name each day as they arrive, and say good-bye as they depart. Keep families informed of how their child is adjusting.

6. Prepare a name-labeled cubby, locker, or other space for each child before the first day. Show them this safe place where they can store their belongings. If possible, include a photo of the child on the label.

7. Show children the location of the toilet and the water fountain and how they work and accompany them when they seem uncertain.

8. Stay close to children who need extra reassurance.
   Infants, toddlers, and young preschoolers may need to be held; older preschoolers and kindergartners may need a hand to hold or may want to stay close to you until they feel comfortable.

9. Encourage children to bring a special toy or comfort object to help provide a tangible bridge between home and school. A photograph of a family member comforts some children.

10. Allow children to borrow a book or toy from the classroom to provide a bridge when they return to their homes.

11. Provide an interesting but limited number of age-appropriate materials.

12. Provide soothing, open-ended materials like water, sand, and dough.

13. Provide time for independent exploration of materials.

14. Introduce a short group activity such as song or story to help preschoolers, kindergartners, and primary children feel that they are a part of a group. Sing songs or play simple games using each child's name.

15. Help children get to know their environment by taking small excursions to important places: the parent room, the play yard, other classes, the library, the office, and the kitchen.

16. In the first weeks avoid abrupt or major changes and excitement (fire drills, films, trips, room rearrangement).

A photo of their family comforts many children. Some classrooms display family photos on the walls at children's eye level or in standing frames atop shelves. A skilled teacher that we know takes a photo of the child and family on the child's first visit, glues it to tagboard and laminates it, then allows the child to carry it for as long as he or she chooses to do so.

During the initial weeks, children gradually adjust to their new setting. They become accustomed to the daily rhythm of activities, learn that they can care for many of their own needs, and discover that you will be there to help when needed. The most important tasks of this time are to develop trust, build relationships, and establish routines. These tasks are the curriculum. You should also ensure that children experience frequent successes.

As children become more comfortable, and as you become familiar with their individual skills and preferences, you can begin enriching the program with materials, activities, and trips that might have been overwhelming at first. By understanding and supporting children during first days and weeks, you help prepare them to be active and competent learners.

Good Endings

Just as beginnings and first days require thought and planning, endings also require special care. Children will experience times when they must change teachers, classrooms, or schools. Because children's relationships with both teachers and peers can be close ones, these times may be painful. For many children, it is the first time that an important connection has ended.

Changing Classes.   When children remain in a program for more than a year, they will usually experience at least one change of class or teacher. In programs that follow a 9-month or traditional elementary school calendar, the change will occur in the fall after a long summer vacation. In full-year programs, this change may occur when teachers feel that a child is ready for a new group or when space is needed in a classroom for younger children entering the program.

Many children are ready and eager to move on to a new class. Some may experiences feelings of anxiety comparable to those of the first days of school. Similar transition techniques are helpful. Moving to a new class is easier for young children when you and the children's family express confidence in the new group and teacher. It is also helpful when they can carry something familiar with them and when the transition is gradual.

Allow children in transition to make visits to their next class accompanied by you or a friend. Let them visit for an activity that they especially enjoy, perhaps choice time one day and outdoor time another day, so that they can discover new activities and companions. Help children locate their new personal space such as their locker or cubby and arrange their belongings. Going back to the old room to share lunch or nap or simply to visit for a few minutes can help the child feel secure.

When Adults Leave.   Like children, you will take vacations, become sick, and may eventually change jobs. These events sometimes take place in the middle of a school year. When you leave a group, either permanently or for an extended period of time, children experience feelings of loss. They may be sad that you are leaving and angry with you when you return. They may be fearful of the change and feel insecure until they build relationships with new staff.

In programs for young children that have a team of teachers in each class, the upsets of absences and departures are minimized. When children relate closely to two or more adults in the classroom, it is less traumatic when one of them goes on vacation or leaves the program, particularly when care is taken that neither is away or leaving at the same time.

Whatever the staffing, it is important that you let children know in advance if you will be leaving. If it is a vacation or other planned leave, explain to them what you will be doing and when you plan to return. Children age 4 and older can begin to use a calendar to understand the length of an absence. Younger children will not grasp time in this way but still need to hear from you that you will be leaving—and that even though it will seem long to them, you will be back. If possible, it is nice to send them a postcard or note during the time that you are away. If you are leaving the program, plan a celebration or other way to say good-bye to children and families.

Leave-taking is a natural part of relationships. Young children can accept these occasions more easily if adults do. When someone leaves, minimize changes in the environment and routines. Most importantly, help children understand that adults leave programs because of changes in their own lives and not in response to the actions of children or their families.

The Next School. Children often go on to other schools that are significantly different from their early childhood program. One of your jobs is to prepare the children in your group for the transition to the next school. Children generally anticipate starting their new schools with both interest and concern. You can aid in the transition by helping to strengthen their sense of themselves as competent, successful individuals. As you talk with them about the new school, acknowledge their growth and mention how the skills they have gained and the knowledge they have acquired will be useful in their new school. Say things like, "You know how to take care of your own lunch now, Hermie. You're going to be able to handle it all by yourself in kindergarten."

Research has confirmed and early childhood teachers have long known that children who experience successful transitions from preschool to elementary school are more likely to succeed in school (Pianta, Cox, Early, & Taylor, 1999). You can help children, families, and other teachers if you take time to build relationships with the schools that children from your classroom are likely to attend. Learn all you can about their program and their expectations for children. Gather information about dates and application requirements and share this information with families. Encourage families to become familiar with their child's new school and if possible to arrange for a tour or visit prior to the child's first day. You help both child and family when you present a positive and enthusiastic perspective about the child's transition to a new school. Let families know that you are excited about their child's growth and progression to a new program and that you will welcome them and their child back for visits.

Children's time in early childhood programs should be spent in experiences that are appropriate for the early years; they should not be training grounds for the next school. It is neither necessary nor useful to engage children in practices that are inappropriate for their age or stage because you wish to "get them ready" for school. However, during the last few weeks before a transition to a new school, it may be beneficial to help children learn a few skills they will need in the new setting. If they will be expected to change classes in response to a bell, stand in lines, do worksheets, or raise hands, you can help them learn these skills in a short time. We often practice these skills as large group dramatic play—"playing school." If you are in contact with the teachers in the next school, you may be able to get more specific information or even take the children to see their prospective school and meet the new teacher.

Everyone experiences some trepidation when anticipating change. Whether the children are moving to a new class or a new program, or you or a colleague are leaving a program, you can work to turn endings into beginnings filled with enthusiasm and hope.

Reflect on changing classes or changing schools

Remember changing to a new class or a new school. How did you feel? What did your teacher do? What made it easy or difficult? What does this experience suggest for you as an early childhood educator?

Supporting Children During Times of Crisis

In situations where children are threatened by major life upheavals or loss of loved ones, or when they live with ongoing fear of violence, teachers need to be particularly attentive to helping them develop a sense of safety and of hope.

Disaster and Loss

Natural disasters such as floods, tornadoes, hurricanes, tsunamis, or earthquakes can be extremely frightening for everyone, particularly young children. When homes and communities are severely damaged, normal life is disrupted. Families will be distressed, routines haphazard or nonexistent, and feelings of fear and loss intense. When families must relocate after their homes have been damaged, the resulting stress can feel overwhelming to adults as well as children. In situations of severe threats such as the World Trade Center attacks or the Oklahoma City bombing, everyone's lives are changed. Fear and uncertainty become the norm for everyone—not only for children. Because young children generally lack the verbal and conceptual skills necessary to understand or to deal with their strong feelings, they will look to adults for comfort and reassurance.

Teachers and caregivers can help children cope in the time immediately following a disaster by remaining calm and reassuring them that they will be all right. Separation is a major fear and special reassurance is needed for children who have lost family members, pets, or treasured possessions. Jim Greenman (2001) addressed this issue after the tragedy at the World Trade Center. He offered the following suggestions for supporting children in the aftermath of a traumatic event:

- Provide normal, predictable routines.
- Create lots of time for affectionate interactions that are appropriate for the individual child; hugs, laps, sitting together with a book, or an affectionate pat or touch are helpful.
- Provide verbal reassurance that you and they will be OK.
- Give them opportunities to express themselves with art materials such as clay or paint, as well as in conversation.
- Accept play that re-creates their concerns and fears.
- Listen carefully to their thoughts and ideas; answer their questions in simple ways.
- Gently and thoughtfully correct the erroneous idea that people who are different present a risk.
- Provide a curriculum and daily experiences that value differences.

Children may experience other types of trauma or upset while they are in your program. Serious illness or death of a parent or other family member, a divorce, or a long-term separation from a parent due to military deployment or job relocation are significant life changes for young children. Most children who experience these kinds of changes will feel anxiety and fear, many will experience anger, and some will feel despair and overwhelming sadness. Some common behaviors of young children experiencing loss are:

- Thumb sucking
- Bed-wetting
- Clinging to family members or teachers
- Sleep disturbances
- Loss of appetite
- Fear of the dark, of separation, or of change
- Regression to younger, "babyish" behaviors
- Withdrawal from friends and routines

Be aware that with help and support, children can move past negative feelings. Whatever the cause, children will need your understanding and acceptance as they struggle to overcome the feelings caused by these traumatic events.

Violence

Young children growing up in the 21st century are increasingly exposed to violence in their lives. All children are affected by the growing instances of violence that pervade our society, and as a result children's development and emotional health are affected. Research tells us that the younger the child, the greater the threat to healthy development from exposure to violence (NAEYC, 1993).

A fundamental "irreducible" need of every young child is the need for physical protection and safety (Brazelton & Greenspan, 2000). Exposure to violent situations, both directly and through television and other media, may compromise children's ability to feel safe and to build social and emotional competence. It is your responsibility as an early childhood educator to do all you can to ensure that children experience a sense of safety and protection from violence. Here are some strategies for helping children and families cope:

- Teach problem-solving and conflict resolution strategies and share these with families.
- Redirect play that focuses on repetitive violence re-created from television characters and encourage children to play in more imaginative and creative ways.
- Allow children to engage in dramatic play that helps them to deal with their feelings about lack of power and their fears of violence.
- Actively teach peace on a daily basis and include experiences that help children learn to be contributing members of a community.
- Encourage families to limit television viewing and to carefully supervise what young children watch. Share information with them about recommendations for television viewing and restrictions on screen time. The American Academy of Pediatrics (2011) recommends that children 2 and older have no more than 1–2 hours of "screen time" (television, video games, computers) per day and that adults encourage quality program selection. Screen time for children under age 2 is strongly discouraged. Research suggests that exposure to media violence leads children to see violence as a normal response to stress and as an acceptable means for resolving conflict. Children who are frequent viewers of violence on television are less likely to show empathy toward the pain and suffering of others and more likely to behave aggressively (NAEYC, 1993b).

Final Thoughts

Safe and healthy facilities, policies that promote health and safety, a curriculum that encourages children to participate in healthy activities and to learn about their bodies, attention to beginnings and endings, strategies to help children during times of crises—these are the crucial elements of a program that promotes children's well-being. When these are in place, teachers are able to meet children's basic needs in programs where children know that they are safe and valued. In such programs, children can direct their energy to exploring and learning. When you learn these skills and practice them in the classroom, you ensure that every child experiences a sense of overall health and wellness.

Learning Outcomes

When you read this chapter, and then thoughtfully complete selected assignments from the "To Learn More" section and prepare items from the "For Your Portfolio" section, you will be demonstrating progress in meeting **NAEYC Standard 1: Promoting Child Development and Learning** (NAEYC, 2009).

Key elements:

1a: Knowing and understanding young children's characteristics and needs

1b: Knowing and understanding the multiple influences on development and learning

1c: Using developmental knowledge to create healthy, respectful, supportive, and challenging learning environments

To Learn More

Use Health and Safety Checklists: Use the health and safety checklists found in Appendix B to evaluate an early childhood program. Report on what you found. Describe your thoughts about the safety and health provisions of this program and the ways in which the staff could make it a safer and healthier place for children.

Keep a Separation Journal: Observe a child and keep a journal on the child's behavior during his or her first days and weeks in school. Report on the child's responses to the school, the techniques used by the staff to support the child, and the family's reactions to the experience. Describe what you learned from your observation and its possible implications for you as an early childhood educator.

Plan and Carry Out a Cooking Activity: Plan a food preparation activity for a small group of children. Using pictures and simple words, create a recipe chart that they can follow. Do the activity with the children, paying attention to their engagement and what they seem to be learning. Describe what happened and what you learned.

Read a Book: Read one or more books about curriculum related to children's health and safety. Reflect on the book and decide on ways that you can use the information in your work with children. Some books to consider are:

Cook and Learn: Pictorial Single Portion Recipes (Veitch & Harms, Addison-Wesley).

The Cooking Book: Fostering Young Children's Learning and Delight (Colker, NAEYC).

Cup Cooking: Individual Child Portion Picture Recipes (Johnson & Plemons, Gryphon House).

Do Carrots Make You See Better? A Guide to Food and Nutrition in Early Childhood Programs (Appleton, McCrea, & Patterson, Gryphon House).

Everybody Has a Body: Science from Head to Toe (Rockwell, Williams, & Sherwood, Gryphon House).

Growing, Growing Strong: A Whole Health Curriculum for Young Children (Smith, Hendricks, & Bennet, Redleaf Press).

Here We Go . . . Watch Me Grow (Hendricks & Smith, ETR Associates).

Pretend Soup and Other Real Recipes: A Cookbook for Preschoolers & Up (Katzen & Henderson, Tricycle Press).

Investigate Related Websites:

Explore several of the websites listed below. Write a brief summary of what you found and how you might use it in the future. Share this information with classmates.

Action for Healthy Kids: actionforhealthykids.org

American Academy of Pediatrics: aap.org and aap.org/healthtopics/childcare.cfm

Centers for Disease Control and Prevention: cdc.gov

Child Health Alert: childhealthalert.com

Healthy Child Care America: healthychildcare.org

Healthy People 2020: healthypeople.gov

KidsHealth: kidshealth.org

Let's Move: letsmove.gov

National Resource Center for Health and Safety in Child Care and Early Education: nrckids.org

Prevent Child Abuse America: preventchildabuse.org

U.S. Consumer Product Safety Commission: cpsc.gov

USDA: choosemyplate.gov

For Your Portfolio

Improve Classroom Health and Safety: Use the health and safety checklists in Appendix B as a guide for examining the early childhood program in which you work or volunteer. Evaluate what you find and suggest some things that could be done to improve the health and safety provisions of the program. Describe what you propose and document your observations with photographs or illustrations. If you are able to implement changes document them with photos or illustrations. Write a paragraph explaining what you proposed and what you were able to implement. Explain the rationale for the changes. Place this documentation in your professional portfolio.

Plan and Implement Health and Safety Curriculum: Revisit the sections in the chapter titled "Help Children Learn to Be Safe" and "Help Children Learn to Be

Healthy." Based on your knowledge of the children in your classroom, select a safety or health concept or skill you feel is appropriate and important for them to learn. Plan an activity that will encourage the children to acquire this knowledge or skill. Implement the activity and document what happens. Place a description of the activity and your documentation (photographs, a written analysis, etc.) in your professional portfolio.

Build Your Recipe File: Review one or more of the children's cookbooks listed in the "Read a Book" section. Make a picture recipe that the children can follow, and then prepare the recipe with the children. Add the recipe to your file and place a copy of it along with a description and/or a photo of the children creating the recipe. Include discussion of what they learned from the activity as well as what you learned.

MyEducationLab

Go to Topic 8: DAP/Teaching Strategies in the MyEducationLab (myeducationlab.com) for *Who Am I in the Lives of Children?* where you can:

- Find learning outcomes for DAP/Teaching Strategies along with the national standards that connect to these outcomes.
- Complete Assignments and Activities that can help you more deeply understand the chapter content.
- Apply and practice your understanding of the core teaching skills identified in the chapter with the

Building Teaching Skills and Dispositions learning units.

- Listen to experts from the field in Professional Perspectives.
- Check your comprehension on the content covered in the chapter with the Study Plan. Here you will be able to take a chapter quiz, receive feedback on your answers, and then access Review, Practice, and Enrichment activities to enhance your understanding of chapter content

A wonderful place to be a child is a place where a child can fall
in love with the world.

ELIZABETH PRESCOTT

There is no behavior apart from environment.

ROBERT SOMMER

8

The Learning Environment

The learning environment speaks to children. When they enter your program, they will be able to tell whether it is a place for them and how you intend them to use it. A cozy corner with a rug, cushions, and books says, "Sit down here and look at books." A climbing structure with ladders, stairs, tunnels, ramps, slides, platforms, and a bridge suggests, "Climb up, find a way across, and come down a different way." An airy environment with light, color, warmth, and interesting materials to be explored sends a clear message: "We care—this is a place for children." In this chapter, we will talk about three interconnected aspects of the learning environment: space, equipment and materials, and time and the design of environments for different ages.

It is the first morning of a new school year. The teachers have carefully set up the indoor and outdoor environment. There are trikes to ride, easels with paint, tubs of water, sand, blocks, puzzles, building toys, picture books, a rabbit, pens and crayons, and a dramatic play area with dolls, clothes, and props including hats, shoes, fancy dresses, and lengths of cloth. Four-year-old Cordell and his mother enter the classroom and look around. Cordell makes a beeline for the dramatic play area, finds a construction hat, and puts it on. He slings a shiny beaded purse over his shoulder. He goes up to Kaito, who is wearing a cowboy hat, and says, "We're police guys, right?" He turns and smiles at his mom and then turns to play with his new friend.

Environments with space to move, comfortable child-sized furnishings, inviting materials, and an arrangement that suggests how materials can be used provide a feeling of comfort and security. Materials and images that reflect children, their families, their cultures, and their community let children and families

Chapter Eight

MyEducationLab

Visit the MyEducationLab for *Who Am I in the Lives of Children?* to enhance your understanding of chapter concepts with a personalized Study Plan. You'll also have the opportunity to hone your teaching skills through video-based Assignments and Activities, and Building Teaching Skills and Disposition lessons.

Reflect on the environment of your first school

Remember your first school (or any school that was important to you during your childhood). What about the environment stands out in your memory: the classroom, the playground, the equipment and materials, storage and distribution of materials? Was anything wonderful or magical for you? Why? How was the school similar to or different from your home? Did it reflect your culture and family in any way? What do you wish had been different? How do you think the environment affected your learning and relationships?

know that they belong. Soft lighting as well as natural and man-made items of beauty tell them that they are valued and that you care enough to provide an attractive place for them. Comfortable places for big and little people to sit tell them that they are welcome. A flexible schedule of activities, routines, and transitions is responsive to children's needs. All of these create an atmosphere of warmth and informality that meets the social-emotional needs of young children and enables them to interact with people and materials in ways that support their development and learning.

A unique characteristic of the field of early childhood education and care is the careful attention that teachers pay to designing learning environments. The philosophers and educators whose work forms the foundation of our field have long recognized the critical role of the environment in children's development. When you look at a well-designed environment for preschoolers or kindergarten children, you will see the following:

- Many opportunities for children to play, as suggested by Jan Amos Comenius
- Child-sized furniture and accessible and orderly shelves, as recommended by Maria Montessori
- Inviting hands-on materials like parquetry blocks and paper with scissors, based on the gifts and occupations of Friedrich Froebel
- Unit blocks designed by Caroline Pratt
- Daily opportunities for play outdoors with mud, sand, and water, as suggested by Margaret and Rachel McMillan
- Natural play materials, as described by Rudolph Steiner
- Environments filled with light and beauty, as suggested by Loris Malaguzzi

The learning environment that you establish should mirror your values for children as well as the values of the program and the children's families. It should confirm children's sense of identity, connection, and belonging. More than that, it should engage children in learning by awakening their senses, provoking curiosity and wonder, and stimulating their intellect.

Young children are learning all the time. In the eyes of the educators of Reggio Emilia, the environment is the children's "third teacher" (Edwards, Gandini, & Forman, 1998). The learning environment is both a powerful teaching tool and a visible sign to families that you are caring for and providing appropriate experiences for their children. Because it is so important, teachers of young children spend a great deal of time carefully arranging their learning environments.

Learning environments should meet the needs of children and support your educational values and developmental goals. The choices you make as you design the environment influence the quality of children's relationships with other people and learning materials. In making these choices, you need to ask yourself three very basic questions:

1. Is this environment appropriate for the age, stage, characteristics, community, families, and culture of these children? Does it reflect who the children are? Is it safe and healthy?
2. Does it engage these children physically, socially, emotionally, and intellectually? Does it include elements that develop a sense of wonder?
3. Does this environment support relationships between all the people here— between children, between adults and children, and between adults?

Jim Greenman, in his article "Places for Childhood in the 21st Century: A Conceptual Framework" (2005), suggests that there are nine overarching aspects of good early childhood learning environments. They are great places . . .

1. to **live**, where children feel welcomed, competent, and relaxed with a sense of familiarity and order.
2. of **beauty** that engage all of the senses through windows, lighting, acoustics, furnishings, and equipment.
3. that promote **strong families** of diverse kinds and encourage multiage sibling interaction.
4. for **caring communities** with spaces for gathering, places to be alone, and ways to see from place to place within the program.
5. for working **independently** and **with others**.
6. for **exploration** and **discovery** indoors and out, with room to move, filled with the hands-on exploration modeled on laboratories, studios, gardens, natural settings, libraries, gymnasiums and playgrounds.
7. that develop **responsibility, compassion, and community** by giving children access to resources and encouraging them to work together both in preparation and cleaning.
8. for **being connected** to the natural world, the larger community, and the world beyond.
9. **for staff** to learn and work with staff space Internet access, professional journals, and books.

Creating a Learning Environment

When you become a teacher you will have responsibility for creating a learning environment on your own or with a team of coworkers. You will arrange the space and select equipment and materials to facilitate all areas of development. You will design a schedule that ensures that the children's basic needs are met and that they have enough time for activities that support learning and their development. In fact, you are one of the most important aspects of the environment because you have control over—and responsibility for—the time, space, equipment, and materials. Your knowledge of children will help you design a program that provides opportunities to move, explore, represent, create, and manipulate.

Sally has been hired to teach a class of young 5-year-olds for a summer enrichment program in the basement of a neighborhood church. With little equipment or money she surveys the big room that will be home to 15 children for the next 6 weeks. In one corner she has draped a carton of hymnals with a pretty tablecloth. On it she has placed a small vase of flowers, a purple cup full of marking pens, and a basket of recycled paper. In a corner marked off by a low pew she has created a dramatic play corner with "housekeeping" furniture that she made out of cardboard boxes, her childhood dolls, and dress-up clothes from the rummage sale bin. She has posted a print of a mother and child painted by Mary Cassatt

from a calendar she saved. Dishpans and baskets with Lego bricks, wooden beads, and blocks gleaned from her friends' closets fill a board-and-brick shelf next to a small carpet. Sheltered by the piano, a library corner has been created with a pile of pillows re-covered with remnant fabrics and a basket full of books from the public library. Tables and chairs from the Sunday school and a garage sale easel complete the classroom. The park across the street with a play structure, sandbox, and swings will provide the outside play area. There's water in a portable cooler and a bathroom a few steps away. It's not ideal, but Sally feels sure that she can provide a good experience for children in this environment.

Space

The learning environment you create will be influenced by many things, but first by the building and the grounds that surround it. You may find yourself working in a space that is "purpose-built" to be an early childhood program. However, like Sally in the preceding vignette, you may find yourself in a building created for other purposes. Although these settings may not be ideal, they can be safe, workable, and even charming. We have known and loved classrooms in public schools, converted homes, church sanctuaries, basements, apartment units, offices, and storefronts.

Reflect on a place you like to be

Think of a place where you like to be. What do you do there? What do you like about it? Why? How could you add some of these things to the learning environment you create for children?

An appropriate environment for young children will be different for different ages, but some similarities cross the early childhood age span. All young children need a clearly defined "home" space for their group or class. They need secure, ongoing access to drinking water and toilets or diaper-changing space, and sinks for hand washing. They also need an outdoor play area with access to nature and space for active play that can be used year-round. Enough space indoors (at least 35 square feet usable space per child) and outdoors (a minimum of 75 square feet of outside play space for each child playing outside at any one time) is needed (AAP, APHA, & NRC, 2002).[1] A program also needs to provide access for individuals (children, family members, visitors, or staff) who use walkers or wheelchairs.

Self-Contained and Open-Design Classrooms

One type of early childhood program building has self-contained classrooms. Each class spends most of the time in "their" room. Another type of building has an open design constructed so that several classes are in one room most of the time. Designers of open-design buildings expect teachers to arrange interest centers throughout the room, with a large multifunction or large motor space in the middle. Facilities need not be used as they were designed. For example, in a school with self-contained classrooms, a team of teachers might decide to use their rooms together, giving each a particular function (e.g., one room may be the messy activity room for art and sensory activities). Open rooms are often turned into self-contained "classrooms" using dividers, furniture, and taped lines on the floor to suggest walls.

Self-contained classrooms offer a homelike atmosphere, a feeling of security and belonging. This is good for all children, especially very young children. However, very small classrooms might not provide enough space for children to move or allow you to provide a rich variety of learning experiences at all times. Large open-design classrooms offer space for movement and allow teachers to

---

[1] AAP, APHA, and NRC standards are identical to most states' and many countries' licensing standards and to NAEYC accreditation standards.

create more, and more diverse, learning centers. They are inevitably noisier and less homey. Smaller rooms and smaller group size have a positive effect on children. Large rooms with many children are less appropriate for young children and inappropriate for infants and toddlers, who thrive in environments that are more sheltered from stimulation and that are more like homes.

Principles for Arranging Space

Even though you will not design your building or construct your play yard you will have many choices in designing an environment that supports children's learning and well-being. It will be a reflection of who you are and who the children are. Though your environment will be unique, it should follow some basic principles. The following principles can be thought of as general guidelines or rules for action.

Arrange the Environment for Safety and Health. Every environment for young children must be safe and meet the health needs of their age and stage. Ensuring health and safety is the first principle of learning environment design. Your classroom and outdoor play space must be arranged so that areas can be easily supervised, cleaned, and maintained. In a program for infants and toddlers this means an adult must be able to see all of the children, all of the time. Drinking water, diapering, sinks, and sleep areas must be accessible and supervised whenever they are in use.

In a program for preschoolers you have greater latitude. If there are no environmental hazards, a preschooler may be safely playing in one area while you work with other children a few feet away, supervising all the children by sight and sound. While standing you should be able to see the whole preschool room or yard and all the children in it. Water to drink, toilets and sinks, and quiet places for resting must be accessible and easy to supervise throughout the day.

School-age children can safely have more independence. It is desirable, especially for kindergartners, to have toilets and drinking water in the classroom or yard. However, first and second graders can, and often must, walk to nearby bathrooms, drinking fountains, playground, or classrooms with minimal supervision.

Although health and safety considerations are important they should not overwhelm you. There is an unfortunate tendency in our society to worry about health and safety so much that we fail to take into account other concerns. Children need to run and play vigorously. They need to have opportunities for messy play. They need to take reasonable risks like rolling down a hill, climbing up a slide, or jumping off a low platform. Denying them these opportunities in the name of health or safety unnecessarily limits exploration and learning. A skinned knee or a stubbed toe can be an important part of the learning process.

Organize the Environment in Areas. Another principle for the design of the early childhood learning environment is to organize it in *areas, centers* (terms we use interchangeably to describe well-defined spaces in classrooms where a particular type of activity takes place), or *zones* (a term we use to describe larger, more flexibly defined parts of a room or yard). Anita Olds (2001) suggests thinking of a classroom for young children as having two "regions": a wet region (for activities like eating, art, and coming in with muddy boots) and a dry region for the remaining classroom activities, which she subdivides into active and quiet zones. The areas or zones that are included in an environment will vary with the age of the children and with the geographic locale of the program. Jim Greenman (2005) suggests thinking of serious work spaces (laboratories, artists, studios, gardens, parks, libraries, and gymnasiums) as models for the areas we provide for children.

Reflect on an early childhood classroom you have known

Think about an early childhood classroom you have observed. Was it a self-contained classroom or part of an open-design building? What advantages for children or teachers were evident to you in this kind of classroom? What were its drawbacks? If you were a teacher in this setting, how would you change the learning environment? Why?

Infants and toddlers need care or routine areas in which to be changed and washed and in which they can sleep, eat, and play. Preschoolers and kindergartners need areas for books, blocks, manipulative toys, sensory experiences, inquiry activities, art, writing, dramatic play, vigorous physical play and both small and large group gathering. Primary-age children need spaces to work on their own and with others, to work on and display projects, for play, and for whole-group meeting.

In geographic areas that have extreme weather conditions, you will also need an indoor area for active play. In mild climates you can use the outdoors for a wide variety of activities and may place some centers outside.

Place Areas with Special Requirements First. In both the indoor and outdoor environment some areas or zones have particular requirements that can only be accommodated in one or two places. Art, eating, sensory play, science, and diapering areas need to be near water and have an easy-to-clean uncarpeted floor. A library area requires good lighting. A science area, cooking area, or music center may need access to electricity. Wheeled vehicles like trikes and wagons require a hard surface such as asphalt or cement. If equipment needs to be stored at the end of the day, it's best to place those areas near the storage. Once you know where these special areas need to go, then you can plan the remaining centers or zones around them.

Equipment and Materials

The materials in early childhood programs are essential tools for learning. Harriet Cuffaro (1995) likens them to textbooks for older children: "Materials are the texts of the early childhood classroom. Unlike books filled with facts and printed words, materials are more like outlines. They offer openings or pathways by and through which children may enter the ordered knowledge of the adult world. Materials also become the tools with which children give form to and express their understanding of the world and of the meanings they have constructed" (p. 33). Equipment and materials suggest direction and provide raw material for children's exploration, development, and learning. Generally, *equipment* refers to furniture and other large and expensive items such as easels and climbing structures. The term *materials* usually refers to smaller, less expensive items such as puzzles, books, games, and toys. Consumables like paint, paper, glue, and tape are referred to as *supplies*.

Have you ever sat at a table that wobbled? Have you ever had a tool that broke when you tried to use it? It is frustrating and often unsafe to work with equipment and materials that are poorly made. Ensuring that the learning environment has safe equipment and materials is an important part of your job. Whenever possible, select good-quality, sturdy equipment and materials; discard those that are broken, unsafe, damaged, or that can't be fixed; maintain and fix the equipment and materials you have. Creatively recycle. And when you have money to spend, purchase materials that will last.

The furniture and equipment in an early childhood program should support classroom activities and respond to the needs of children. We favor wood because of its beauty and sturdiness and because it is easy to maintain. Appropriate furniture for young children fits their bodies and is stable, portable, and has rounded corners and edges. Infants need low, stable chairs that offer back and side support. Cube chairs that can double as stools for adults work well. Older children can be comfortable and can focus when seated at tables if their feet touch the floor and their elbows can rest on tabletops. Small tables provide greater flexibility than large tables and leave more space free for diverse activity.

Low, open shelves are good for storage of materials that children use independently. They allow children to make choices and make it easier for them to participate in cleanup. A shelf especially designed for books invites reading by displaying the books with their covers facing the children. Every child needs space for the storage of personal belongings. Cubbyholes (often shortened to cubbies) meet this need. Cubbies can be manufactured or improvised using such materials as dish tubs, sweater boxes, cardboard boxes, or commercial 5-gallon ice cream tubs. Where children come to school in coats and boots, hooks and storage shelves for these garments need to be provided.

Because teachers and parents also spend time in the classroom, it is important to have a comfortable places for an adult and child to sit together. This contributes to the homelike feeling that is so important for young children in group settings.

Good materials are attractive. They have sensory appeal and feel good to touch and hold. Because they are children's tools for learning, the materials in a classroom must be kept in good repair, work properly, and fit children's size, abilities, and interests. They must be nontoxic, clean, and free of hazards. They should be sturdy and not easily broken.

Every classroom should have enough appropriate materials for the number of children who work and play there to have several options. A classroom for 10 children might have 50 choices spread throughout eight centers, while a classroom for 20 children might have 100 choices. There is no precise formula—there should be enough choices in each area so that the number of children who play there can be actively engaged.

It is valuable to rotate materials on the shelves. The same materials left out week after week will lose their allure. A toy that has been put away in the cupboard for a few weeks will be more inviting and will encourage more creative play.

It is a basic principle of good learning environment design to remove broken toys, dolls with missing limbs, torn or scribbled-on books, tattered dress-up clothes, or puzzles and games with missing pieces. By leaving these in the classroom you give a message to children: We don't respect the toys and you don't have to either—it's OK to break or damage play materials here. Classrooms with damaged materials inevitably become home to even more damaged materials. They show children and parents that you don't care.

When a book is torn, a puzzle piece is missing, or a block is scribbled on, you can model respect for these resources by mending, refurbishing, or cleaning them. We like to do this with children, encouraging them to participate in the process (particularly if the children were party to the damage). Using broken toys, puzzle pieces, or children's books as the raw materials of art projects is not recycling to a young child. Instead it sends an unclear message that implies that it is acceptable to cut up books or glue puzzle pieces. Similarly, using a triangular block as a doorstop, or a hollow block as a stepstool in the bathroom, suggests that you do not respect these play materials and don't expect children to do so.

Reflect on a plaything

Think of a plaything you loved when you were a child. What did it look like? How did it feel when you held it? What could you do with it? Where is it today? Why do you remember it? Think about what makes a good toy. What good toys do you want to make sure you have in your classroom?

Outdoor Learning Environments

Every program for young children needs an outdoor play area. Inside, children are restricted—*walk slowly, talk softly, be careful, keep it clean.* But outside, the loud, active, enthusiastic play of children is safe, permitted, and encouraged. Just as the buildings that house programs vary, so do outdoor space designs.

Unfortunately, spacious *playscapes* (a term coined by landscape architects to join the idea of play with the concept of architectural landscapes) carefully designed for young children are the exception rather than the rule. In a large elementary school, the outside play area may consist of a jungle gym on the edge of the athletic field; in a school located in the business district of a big city, play space may be a rooftop or a paved parking lot. A suburban or rural setting is likely to have a grassy yard with some play equipment. Though none of these may be perfect outdoor learning environments, any can be enriched by creative and thoughtful teachers.

Because children are learning all the time, not just when they are in the classroom, outdoor space and equipment should support a range of developmental goals: physical, social, cognitive, and creative. The outdoors can be used for an endless variety of learning activities.

Outdoor Activity Zones

Like the indoor environment, you can think about your outdoor environment as having zones with distinct purposes. When you think of the outdoor environment in this way, it is easier to plan for the individual zones and thus easier to make improvements.

Transition Zone. The transition zone is where children enter and exit the playground. This area should allow children to see what is available and make choices. This is sometimes where equipment like balls, trikes, and wagons are waiting. It may be the place where other activities can be seen, considered, and chosen by the child entering the playground. In a transition zone it is important to make sure there is some place for children coming and going to wait or gather if necessary. Benches, large tires, steps, or the edge of a low wall make good places to wait.

Active Play Zone. Every outdoor environment needs space—to run, jump, skip, roll hoops, throw balls, and ride and pull wheeled vehicles. Big areas, grassy if possible, are needed for children to safely run and play games. Preschoolers and primary age children need a place to climb up high so they can see things from a different perspective and equipment for sliding and swinging to allow them to experience different sensations. The climbing or "super-structure" is the current evolution of what used to be called the "jungle gym." Super-structures often include platforms, slides, tunnels, nets, and ramps.

Although you will have little control over the size of the active play zone in your program or the fixed equipment it contains, one thing that you can do is to *create visual boundaries*. Visual boundaries help protect children's play, as well as their well-being (e.g., a child can be hurt walking through the space where another child is swinging or the base of a slide). Adding boundaries like a low border of used non-radial tires (available at a tire store) or potted plants can give a visual signal that keeps children safe.

School-age children benefit from greater challenge in the active play zone. They are able to climb and swing higher, jump farther, and learn new skills such as sliding down long poles, balancing along high balance beams, and turning on parallel bars. Primary-age children also make use of movable equipment such as hoops, bats, and balls for organized games, and hard surfaces for rope jumping and ball bouncing.

Natural Elements Zone. In many communities today young children spend most of their time indoors, so regularly scheduled experience with the natural world is vital. An outdoor environment needs plants, dirt, trees, grass, and the creatures that inhabit them. A large boulder is a nice addition to an outdoor space. If you have natural elements in your playground, nurture and protect them. This is a good place to plant a garden, put a bird feeder, or house a pet.

When the outside play area is a rooftop or parking lot, nature can be included by adding potted plants, garden boxes, pets, and sand tables (to fill with sand, water, or dirt). Mud and sand for digging and water for pouring are soothing and provide important learning experiences. Regular walks to parks can supplement but do not substitute for daily experience with nature in the playground.

Manipulative-Creative Zone. This zone is where table activities like art and woodworking may take place outdoors. Messy art materials such as clay and finger paint are especially well suited to outdoor use. Manipulative-creative activities are more often included in preschool than primary playgrounds. In some programs table games and books are brought into this zone.

Social-Dramatic Zone. Children create their own opportunities for social and dramatic play in the outdoor environment whether or not there is equipment provided. Their play is richer when there are playhouses, dress-up clothes and props, and "loose parts" like hollow blocks, sheets, small tires, planks, and other movable pieces that children can arrange. A social-dramatic zone can be placed near a vehicle path to extend dramatic play with the use of trikes, carts, and wagons to use as cars, delivery vans, buses, and garbage trucks.

An Outdoor Playscape for Infants and Toddlers

Have you ever seen a play yard designed just for infants and toddlers? The chances are good that you haven't. Outdoor learning environments for infants and toddlers have typically not received as much space, attention, and resources as outdoor environments for older children. This is unfortunate because the outside learning environment is important for youngest children and the design of a good outdoor playscape for infants and toddlers is somewhat different from one for older children. If you teach infants and toddlers, it is best if you have an area that is separate and different from the one for older children. Consider . . .

- **Safety**—Because they are more likely to sunburn, infants and toddlers need shade from the sun. Because they learn by putting things in their mouths, attention must be paid to removing potential hazards (small stones and sharp or toxic plants) and bringing out toys that can be safely mouthed. Because they crawl, there must be safe surfaces and knee protection for crawlers. Because they fall as they learn to walk, hard edges must be padded.
- **Movement**—Infants and toddlers need to move and they are learning new ways to move. They need different surfaces to crawl and walk on, low objects to crawl over and through, sturdy objects to pull up on, smooth surfaces for beginning walkers, rocking toys, low sling swings to use belly down, riding toys to push with their feet, and small slides that are safe to go down headfirst as well as feet first.

Using the Outdoor Environment

Almost every activity that happens indoors can come outside at least once in a while. In places where the climate is mild most of the year, it can be the primary location for sand and water play, pets, art activities, woodworking, and hollow blocks. In climates that are often cold, wet, or hot, there are still times when indoor activities can and should be taken outside.

Learning experiences take on new dimensions when they move outdoors. A story about trees, for example, read in the shade of an oak carries new meaning. Painting a picture with nature in view is different from painting in a classroom. Singing songs outside feels different from singing inside. Dressing up and pretending outside is more adventurous than doing so inside. We all enjoy a picnic now and again. For toddlers, just like older children, there are things done outside that feel different outside—a story, a song, a snack. Make sure there is space to dream, think, and relax. In the outdoor environment, just as in the indoor environment, children need a place to escape the noise and activity of the group. A playhouse, a secluded nook under the play structure, or a quiet place under a low tree can provide this kind of opportunity. If the landscaping and permanent equipment don't provide these kinds of places, you can add them temporarily with a wooden crate or a big cardboard appliance box. We recently visited a program where the teacher had created a "peace garden" in which she had placed many potted plants, a low bench, a birdbath, and a bird feeder around the base of a small tree.

Children need challenge. The outdoor environment is a good place to provide this. Once a challenge has been met, a new one must be found. Once a child has learned to climb up and slide down a slide, a new way to slide will be sought. There should be some things outdoors that take time and persistence to master. If your outdoor environment does not have challenges, children will invent their own. To make sure these are safe, you can add equipment and activities to fill this need. For example, a row of tires half-buried in the sand can create a balancing challenge. A pathway of cones on the sidewalk is a challenge for the driver of a tricycle. One of the important things that teachers can do is to think of new ways to create challenge in the outdoor environment.

Whether the equipment is purchased or improvised, your outdoor environment requires thoughtful evaluation, planning, and change on a regular basis. The accompanying box, "Golden Rules for Outdoor Playscapes," summarizes the guidelines presented here.

GOLDEN RULES FOR OUTDOOR PLAYSCAPES

1. Organize in zones.
2. Create visual boundaries for safety and to protect children's play.
3. Provide physical development challenges.
4. Include natural elements in the outdoor play area.
5. Make sure there is space to dream, think, and relax.
6. Take indoor activities outside at times.
7. Observe children and add new experiences and challenges regularly.

FIGURE 8.1   Simple Ways to Enhance an Outdoor Play Space

1. Add plants for sight and smell—make daily watering a classroom job
   - Bring in big sturdy pots of plants—position them so children can play near them
   - Create a garden bed and plant flowers to attract butterflies, beneficial bugs and humming-birds—marigold, cornflower, dill, hyssop, chives, zinnia, sage, viola, alyssum, basil, lavender
   - Create a sunflower house by planting a circle of sunflowers

2. Add animals
   - Hang bird feeders—make filling the bird feeder a classroom job
   - Add a birdbath
   - Make a home for a rabbit

3. Add sound
   - Hang wind chimes
   - Create a drumming stand with big, recycled, and cleaned plastic barrels
   - Hang pots and pan lids on the fence

4. Personalize it
   - Have children or families create concrete stepping stones (using ready-to-use concrete from the hardware store)
   - Let children paint the sidewalk or tires; or with administrator permission, invite them to create a temporary easel paint mural on the wall of the building or a storage shed

As a classroom teacher, you cannot independently create a wonderful play-scape for children. If you are fortunate you will have colleagues, administrators, and families who value the outdoor learning environment and together you can work to make it a wonderful place for children. If so, there are resources that will help you to think about how to do this (we recommend Keeler's *Natural Playscapes* and Elliott's *The Outdoor Playspace Naturally*). However, every teacher can plan for and work to enhance the outdoor environment that is available (see Figure 8.1).

Making the Environment Work

Designing a learning environment is not a onetime event; it is an ongoing process. Children's needs change as they grow and learn. Any setting can be modified and improved. The perfect arrangement for this year's class of children may not work as well for a new group. Plan on regularly reevaluating and changing the environment. When problems arise—for example, if children consistently fail to get involved in activities—you may want to look first at the environment to see whether it is part of the cause of the problem. Robert Sommer, a psychologist who has studied the effect of environment on behavior, has said, "There is no behavior apart from environment, even in utero" (Sommer, 1969, 19).

Before you finish arranging your indoor and outdoor space, and whenever you are about to change the environment, observe from the viewpoint of a child by sitting on the floor or the ground. From this perspective, observe from the entrance and each of the areas. Notice what you can see in each location, what is most attractive, and what is most distracting. This view may be quite different from what you perceive from your standing height and will help you to design an environment that works for children.

Consider Dimensions of Teaching-Learning Environments

Over the years, we have found it helpful to use specific dimensions or attributes described by Elizabeth Jones and Elizabeth Prescott in *Dimensions of Teaching-Learning Environments* (1984) as another kind of lens through which to observe and evaluate our environments (see Figure 8.2). Using a checklist like those in

FIGURE 8.2   Dimensions of Teaching-Learning Environments

- Hard–Soft: Comfortable furniture, pillows, rugs, grass, sand, furry animals, soft toys, sling and tire swings, dough, finger paint, clay, mud, water, and warm physical contact soften environments. Softness changes an environment, what happens, and how secure and comfortable people feel. Early childhood classrooms need to have soft furnishings, carpets, decorations, and lighting similar to homes. Hard environments, with indestructible materials like cement, unattractive colors, and harsh lighting are uncomfortable and indicate a lack of respect for children.
- Open–Closed (the degree to which the environment and materials restrict): Open materials inspire innovation. Materials that are closed can be rewarding when they provide appropriate challenge. Overly difficult materials cause frustration. Younger or less experienced children require more open materials. Older, more experienced children need and enjoy open materials but also enjoy closed challenges. When children appear bored or frustrated, the cause might be in the balance of open–closed experiences.
- Low mobility–High mobility: High mobility involves active motion. Low mobility involves sedentary activities. Both are important, both indoors and outdoors, throughout the day.
- Simple–Complex: Simple materials have one obvious use—they do not encourage children to manipulate or improvise. They include trikes, slides, puzzles, and concept games such as Chutes and Ladders. Complex materials allow children to use two different play materials together, making play less predictable and more interesting. They hold children's attention for a longer period of time—for example, a sandbox with tools, blocks with props, collage with paint. Super materials offer an even larger number of possibilities and hold children's attention much longer. They include sand with tools and water, or dramatic play areas equipped with furnishings, clothes, and props. Classrooms for inexperienced or less mature children need to be simple to help them focus and make choices. Older children can handle more complexity, which can be added by materials or people.
- Intrusion–Seclusion (who and what crosses boundaries between spaces): Intrusion adds novelty and stimulation that enrich learning—visitors, trips, and other experiences with the world outside the classroom. Seclusion from stimulation provides the opportunity to concentrate, think, and be alone. Tables or easels set up against walls provide partial seclusion; insulated spaces with protection on three sides allow privacy; hiding spaces, cozy closed places in crates, lofts, or under a table allow children to escape the stimulus of the classroom. When opportunities for seclusion do not exist, children often create their own seclusion by hiding or by withdrawing emotionally.

Source: From E. Jones & E. Prescott, *Dimensions of Teaching-Learning Environments*, 1984.

Appendix B or the Harms-Clifford Early Childhood Environment Rating Scale (2004), or the POEMS Preschool Outdoor Environment Measurement Scale (2005) can help you to take a systematic approach to the design of a learning environment.

Pay Attention to Organization and Aesthetics

At Children's Place Learning Center, visitors are struck by the difference between two classrooms. Lynn's room is cluttered—shelves are stuffed with toys stored in a miscellaneous assortment of cardboard boxes and dirty dish tubs. Children shout at one another over a loud recording of raucous music for children. The odor of Zippy, the rabbit, scents the air. The shelf tops are a jumble of paper for art products, recycled materials, stacks of books. Tattered posters adorn the walls.

In contrast, Summer's room is an oasis. The furniture has been arranged so chairs and tables color-coordinate; plants divide and define some learning centers. Shelves are filled with toys in baskets or on trays, and there is space between items. Most shelf tops are clear of clutter. The carpets, pillows, and window fabrics complement each other; art posters and children's art decorate the walls. Sammy, the guinea pig, is contentedly chewing his fresh bedding. Instrumental music plays softly, and the noise of children talking and laughing is the dominant sound.

We believe that children's environments should be beautiful places. This means looking for ways to make aspects of the classroom harmonious by paying attention to design, light, color, and texture in the selection and arrangement of furnishings, equipment, and materials. Aesthetics is often overlooked in early childhood classrooms and playgrounds. How do you create a well-organized and aesthetically pleasing environment? A few simple guidelines follow:

- **Choose soft, neutral colors.** Bright colors will dominate a room and may detract from art and natural beauty present. If you have a choice, select soft, light, neutral colors for walls and ceilings. If you don't have a choice, try to coordinate tablecloths, posters, curtains, and storage containers with the color of the walls. Color-coordinate within centers so that children begin to see them as wholes rather than as parts. Avoid having many different patterns in any one place because they can be overstimulating.
- **Group similar colors of furniture together.** Keep colors natural and neutral, to focus children's attention on the learning materials on the shelves. If you must paint furniture, use one neutral color for everything so that you have greater flexibility in moving it from space to space. Make sure that marks from crayons, paints, and markers are cleaned up right away. We like to give children brushes and warm soapy water and let them scrub the furniture on a sunny, warm day.
- **Display artwork.** Mount and display children's art and artists' prints and avoid cartoons, advertisements, and garish, stereotyped, faded, or tattered posters. Make sure that much of the artwork (both by children and adult artists) is displayed at children's eye-level. Use shelf tops sparingly for displaying sculpture, framed photos, plants, and items of natural beauty like shells, stones, and fish tanks.
- **Enhance the environment with natural objects and materials.** Look for ways to bring the beauty of natural materials and objects into your classroom and yard. Use plants, stone, wood, shells, and seeds as learning materials indoors. Outdoors, add small details like a planter box or a rock arrangement to show that the outdoors is also a place that deserves attention and care.
- **Make storage attractive and functional.** Storage areas can contribute to the smooth functioning of a program as well as to its aesthetic quality. Making storage functional, organized, and attractive is a principle of good design in early childhood programs just as it is in homes, kitchens, stores, and offices. A thoughtfully organized environment helps children to understand and maintain order and contributes to making your environment a pleasant place in which to spend time and work.
- **Store materials for children's use in sight and reach.** When children scan the environment they should be able to tell at a glance what materials are available to them. Things stored on low, open shelves tell children that they are available for their use. Items for adult use only should be stored out of children's reach and view. Cleaning supplies, files, first aid equipment, sharp tools, and staff personal belongings should be in locked or inaccessible storage.
- **Use attractive storage containers.** Baskets and wooden bowls are appealing choices. If you use plastic storage tubs, use the same kind and color on one shelf. If you use cardboard boxes, cover them with plain-colored paper or paint them. Avoid storing teachers' materials on the tops of shelves. If no other choice is possible, create a teacher "cubby" using a covered box or storage tub.

- **Avoid clutter** Crowded shelves look unattractive and are hard for children to maintain. Keep most shelf tops empty. Design your space so that everything has a place. Get into the habit of returning materials after each use and teach children to do the same.
- **Rotate materials regularly.** Rotate materials rather than having everything out at once. When you take something out, put something else away. The added benefit is that children have new and interesting things to try and familiar materials take on new life when they are brought out again.
- **Label shelves.** Children will be more self-sufficient if shelves and other storage areas are marked to indicate where to put things away. Even in rooms for infants and toddlers, it is helpful to the adults if shelves and containers are labeled with pictures of the contents. Some teachers code shelves and materials with self-adhesive colored dots to indicate the learning center in which they are stored (red dots for table toys, yellow dots for the writing area, and so on). Silhouettes of materials on shelves help children match an item to its proper place. Remember that your goal is to keep your environment functionally organized and pleasing to the eye.

Reflect the Children—Reflect the Place

We live in a diverse society and so early childhood learning environments need to reflect and honor that diversity. Select books, artwork, software, and dramatic play props that reflect differences in culture, gender, race, ability, language, and family structure. Choose materials that portray the specific culture, community, and locale of the children and families who attend your program. An early childhood program in rural South Carolina should look different from a program in Chicago, Alaska, or Delaware. Doing this is a tenet of *place-based education,* an education approach that is designed to connect children with their social and natural environment. You can reflect the children in your environment in many ways.

When children see photographs of themselves and their families in the classroom they know that it is a place that is for them. Use pictures of the children and the families to mark cubbies, make books, and create games. Families can be invited to share a family photo and a picture of their child. When you are selecting dolls, books, puzzles, and posters, be sure to look for those that resemble the children and their families.

Some of the ways that you can create an environment with a sense of place is to include natural materials and art from your local area and community. For example, in Hawai'i, teachers often use lauhala baskets for storage; pandanus seeds as brushes; Aloha shirts, lei, and muumuu for dress-up clothes; and dry coconuts for pounding nails. They also display the work of Hawai'i artists depicting Hawai'ian scenes on the walls. Similarly, we have seen programs in Alaska where the dramatic play area was turned into a fishing camp.

The "Golden Rules for Creating Indoor Learning Environments" box summarizes the important things to remember in creating a classroom for young children.

Avoid Being Cute

For many years we have opposed the pervasive tendency to make environments for young children cute. What do we mean by cute? Cute is not the naturally appealing qualities of children. Rather it is the affected, stereotyped falseness of an advertisement or a cartoon. What's wrong with cute? Jim Greenman speaks against what he calls the Unbearable Lightness of Cuteness: "Cuteness robs wonder of its evocative power, pasteurizing awe and delight into one-dimensional chuckles and fuzzy glows" (1998, 62).

GOLDEN RULES FOR CREATING INDOOR LEARNING ENVIRONMENTS

1. Arrange the environment so it can be easily supervised, cleaned, and maintained.
2. Make sure there is water to drink, toilets/diapering facilities, sinks, and quiet places for resting.
3. Choose child-sized furniture and include comfortable seating for adults.
4. Organize the classroom in areas.
5. Select safe, good-quality, sturdy equipment and materials and discard or repair broken, incomplete ones.
6. Store materials children can use at their eye-level on low, open, uncrowded shelves and store teacher materials out of reach.
7. Rotate play materials.
8. Regularly reevaluate and change the environment.
9. Add items of beauty to the environment.
10. Include materials that reflect the children, their families, and geographic location.

Overly cute materials are trivial. They suggest that because children are younger and less accomplished than adults, they also are less individual, less worthy of respect, and that their learning is neither serious nor important. It is overly cute to have posters of wide-eyed ladybugs instead of books about insects and opportunities to observe them. It is excessively cute when the walls of a school are covered with cartoon murals instead of displaying children's work.

Children are endearing, attractive, and charming. They are also human beings who are individual, strong, and worthy of our respect. They have intense, real feelings and desires. Appropriate early childhood learning environments and their contents are similarly endearing, attractive, and charming. They are also real. They are not cute.

Different Children—Different Places

Early childhood educators know that children at different ages and stages have different needs. This is as true in the environments we design as in the activities we provide.

Infant-Toddler Environments—A Place Like Home

Imagine a place that is made for babies and toddlers, a place where the floor is clean, the furniture low and soft, where everything within reach is for youngest children. Learning environments for infants and toddlers are designed differently from learning environments for older children. Infants and toddlers thrive in homes, so it is a principle of good infant-toddler environmental design to create the feeling of a home, rather than a school. What makes a place "like home"? Most homes have the qualities that we can use as design principles: They are comfortable, functional, and flexible.

Polly and Carol are teachers in a room for six infants ages 5 to 15 months. One Wednesday morning at 10:30 Polly is sitting on the carpeted floor looking at books with Shane, Lissa, and Guga. In the diapering area on one side of the room near the sink and cubbies, Carol is changing Olivia. In a corner in a rocking chair, Matthew's mom is nursing Matthew. And in the sleeping room just off the main activity area, Chris is sleeping in a crib.

Design for Comfort

An environment for infants or toddlers needs to be comfortable and calm so that both the children and their teachers are not stressed. A comfortable adult-sized chair or couch with soft cushions where adults can cuddle up with children is essential. A stable chair or couch also provides good climbing experiences and excellent handholds for beginning standers and walkers. Because most infants and toddlers are comforted by motion, a rocker (designed so that fingers cannot be pinched) or other chair that allows motion is important. Most activity in infant and toddler rooms takes place on the floor, so soft clean carpets are an essential ingredient of the classroom environment for youngest children.

Design for Routines

Indoor environments for infants and toddlers should be designed so that all of the important routines can happen safely in the available space. To accomplish this, most infant-toddler rooms include the following:

- **An arrival and departure area.** Here, family members sign in, bring in supplies, and read notes on their child's day. For toddlers it is a place to say good-bye. Separation can be hard for very young children, so it is important to make this a comfortable place for parents to spend a few minutes with their child. A good-bye window (a window at child level to watch a departing parent) is desirable in this area.
- **A diapering area.** Because diaper changing is a prominent feature of the daily program, a changing area with a sink and hot water must be close at hand and separate from eating and play areas. Infant-toddler environments require a sturdy changing table at a comfortable height for adults (we prefer tables with stairs that roll in and out to encourage toddler independence and save the backs of staff). Diapering is a time to interact, and the diapering area should be pleasant.

Toddlers may want to socialize with one another during diaper changing routines, so space should be available for a nearby friend. Because some toddlers and twos are beginning toilet learning, it is important there be an adjacent toileting area. Children have an easier time using toilets when fixtures are child-sized. Stable step stools or platforms that enable children to comfortably reach toilets and washbasins are essential if toilets and sinks are adult-sized.

- **An eating area.** There should be a low table with stable chairs for eating that is somewhat separate from the activity area.

In infant rooms it is also important to include these things:

- **A comfortable chair for sitting while bottle feeding babies.** This can also be used by mothers who come to nurse their children.
- **A food storage and preparation area.** The area should include a sink and counter, a refrigerator, equipment to warm food, and storage for food and utensils near the eating area but not within children's play areas.
- **A sleeping area.** This area should be shielded from stimulus of the play area but easily supervised.

Design for Flexibility

Homes are flexible, and programs for infants and toddlers need to provide this same kind of flexible space for the activities that take place each day. A sensible design principle is to center an infant or toddler room around an open, flexible activity zone/play area where materials and equipment can be moved in and out.

In an infant room, materials for play and exploration can be placed along the perimeter of this area so they are easy to find and bring into the larger space. Along the perimeter there should be several play spaces for mobile children and different levels on which they can crawl and climb. If the room includes both nonmobile and mobile infants, provide low barriers for protection for nonmobile infants.

In a toddlers room, the central activity area is a gathering place. Though structured group times are not appropriate for toddlers, it is not uncommon for a group to gather when you read or sing with them. This gathering place is also a good place for a movable climber or platform.

For an example of a program floor plan for infants, refer to Figure 8.3.

Design for Movement

A room for infants is defined by words like *safe, cozy, secure*—a small and beautiful space with light, color, and air and room for a small number of caring adults. But toddlers are movers. They run, jump, dance, and climb, so safe places to move indoors are a must. Short squat slides or small, low climbers are good for toddlers and twos. Risers and low ramps that allow children to view the world from a higher perspective are also worthwhile. It is essential to assume that anything that can be climbed will be climbed—therefore high and unstable shelves must be eliminated from toddler environments. Even relatively low shelves should be secured so that they do not tip. Avoid using shelves with wheels.

Around the perimeter of the gathering area you can position a few different areas including the following:

- **A toys area** for puzzles, table blocks, interlocking plastic blocks like Duplo, vehicles, nesting cups, pull toys, and animal figures. For infants and toddlers, toys and games must be large enough so they do not present a choking hazard, and sturdy enough to withstand frequent sanitizing. They must have safe, smooth edges and be large enough to be easily grasped, light enough to be lifted, soft enough not to hurt, and strong enough to be dropped, stepped on, or thrown. They can include homemade toys such as plastic bottles with clothespins to drop inside and commercially made equipment such as busy boxes. Duplicate toys placed side by side on the shelf will encourage parallel play and reduce conflicts. Infants and toddlers often interpret everyday objects as manipulative toys, so it is essential to keep unsafe or inappropriate items out of their reach. Two-year-olds can enjoy regular unit blocks and foam or cardboard large blocks.

FIGURE 8.3 Floor Plan for Infant Classroom

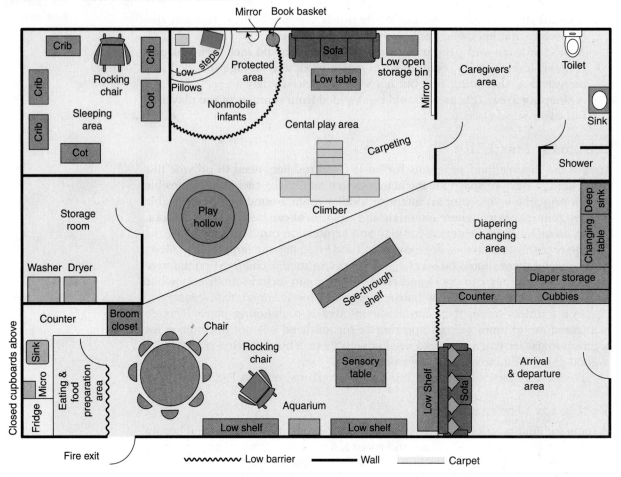

- **A table area** for eating, tasting and preparing food, and exploration of art materials like finger paint, play dough, and crayons. For infants and toddlers, art is primarily a sensory experience. They explore the raw materials of the artist through all their senses. Appropriate materials for toddlers include large, stubby crayons and watercolor markers with big pieces of paper, finger painting, paste and paper, and play dough. Toddlers and 2-year-olds can also enjoy easel painting with one or two colors at a time on an easel that has been adjusted to their size or on large sheets of paper hung on a wall or fence.

- **A book area** with baskets, low shelves, or wall pockets filled with high-quality, sturdy, appealing books and soft places to sit and enjoy them. In programs for infants, age-appropriate books can be provided in different places in the classroom. Small baskets provide accessible storage for sturdy board books. Book shelves, such as those found in most rooms for preschoolers, present a hazard in a toddler room because they invite climbing.

- **A pretending area** for make-believe play. Toddlers need simple, realistic, dramatic play materials. A good selection might contain hats, shoes, clothes with few fasteners, bags, baby dolls, plastic dishes, lightweight aluminum pots, and wooden or plastic stirring spoons. It is important to include duplicates of all items. Expect toddlers to bring blocks and other small toys to the pretend area and use them as part of their play.

- **A sensory table** for water, sand, and other safe materials such as bubbles. Natural materials are generally safe and are particularly satisfying for infants and toddlers. The younger the children, however, the more you will need to supervise. Because very young children are likely to put things in their mouths, you may wish to substitute dough for clay, and flour, cornmeal, oatmeal, or rice for sand.

For an example of a classroom floor plan and outdoor playscape for toddlers, refer to Figure 8.4.

FIGURE 8.4   Floor Plan for Toddler Classroom and Outdoor Playscape

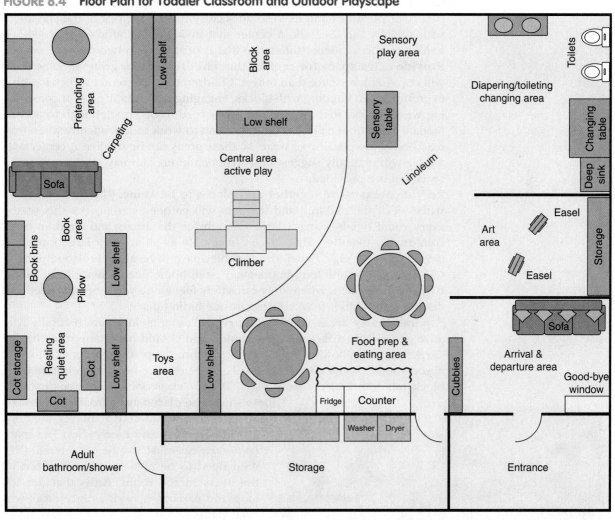

Outdoor Playscape for Infants and Toddlers

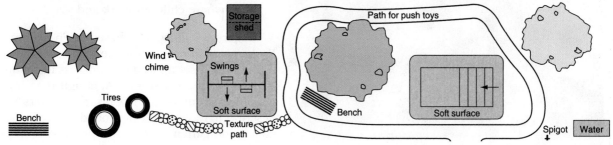

Preschool and Kindergarten Classrooms—A Child's Place

Envision a place where children are looking at books, building with blocks, painting at easels, playing with Lego, putting together puzzles, dressing up, and playing with dolls. You are imagining the learning environment of a preschool or kindergarten that is based on the interests and developmental stage of children. To design a classroom where all this (and more) happens with little conflict or confusion requires knowledge and skill. The following principles will help you design a functional and inviting learning environment:

- **Use partial seclusion.** Most learning centers in a preschool are devoted to particular purposes and need some seclusion from the rest of the classroom with shelves and dividers. A center that invites foot traffic on four sides is unlikely to be as successful as one that is protected on two or three sides.
- **Provide extra space for centers that children use in groups.** Some areas will require more space than others. Children naturally tend to work together in groups when building with blocks, engaging in dramatic play, or constructing with manipulative toys. These areas need to be large enough to accommodate a group of children. Children tend to work independently when they read books, do puzzles, or write, so these areas can be smaller. A center with a table will naturally suggest how many children can play by the number of seats that are provided.
- **Provide areas to be together and places to be alone.** There will be times when all of the children and teachers will gather together. For this reason every room needs a space large enough for the adults and children to sit comfortably together. This space can double as an area for large motor activities or block play. Quiet, comfortable space to be alone is also important. Children who spend long hours away from home need a place to be alone. By providing places where they can safely feel alone you meet this need and discourage children from creating unsafe hiding places.
- **Separate noisy areas from quiet areas.** Young children are naturally talkative and noisy—a fact that you cannot, and should not, attempt to change. Carpeting and pillows will provide a comfortable place to relax and help to absorb noise. Some areas necessarily involve more noise than others (e.g., block building and dramatic play). If your classroom is spacious enough, these should be placed away from areas that require quiet concentration (e.g., books, puzzles).
- **Avoid corridors and racetracks.** The space *between* areas must also be considered. Children need to be able to move between all the areas in the room. Paths that are too long and narrow, as well as racetracks (circular paths around shelves or tables), invite running. Avoid pathways that lead through areas where children work and play.

Figure 8.5 illustrates these design features. Each center in most preschool or kindergarten classrooms is set up as a more or less unchanging part of the classroom. Although there are many variations in classrooms, the centers we describe here are typically found in preschool and kindergarten (and some primary school)

FIGURE 8.5 Preschool/Kindergarten Floor Plan

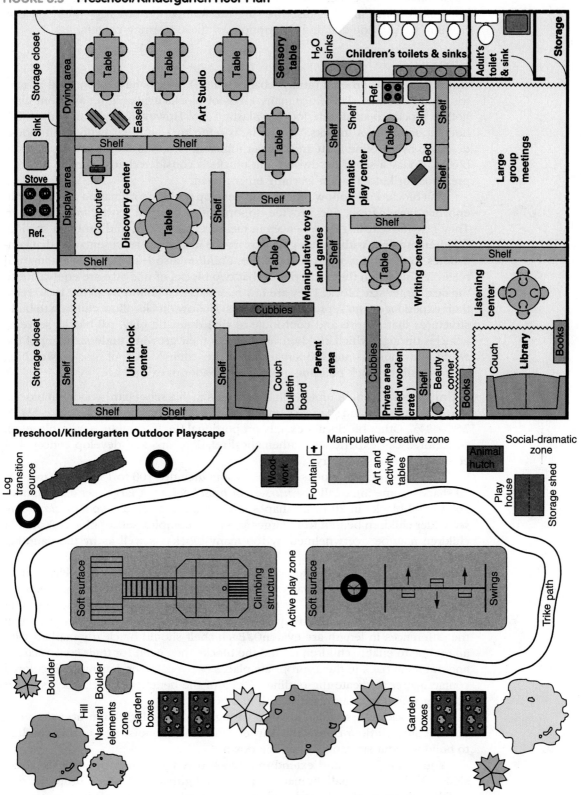

Preschool/Kindergarten Outdoor Playscape

classrooms. Because these centers are the most distinctive feature of early child-hood classrooms, and because they are the foundation of early childhood cur-riculum, we provide detailed descriptions of these learning centers.

Blocks

Since the time of Froebel (and probably before), blocks have been used as toys for young children. There are many kinds of blocks available today, from giant hollow blocks to small interlocking plastic Lego. However, when an early child-hood educator says "blocks," he or she is referring to the hardwood unit blocks designed by Caroline Pratt and Harriet Johnson, and their larger cousins, hollow blocks. Today a set of hardwood unit blocks is considered an essential part of a preschool or kindergarten learning environment.

Unit blocks and hollow blocks help develop motor coordination and strength, enhance imagination, and provide opportunities for children to work together. They provide learning experiences in measurement, ratio, and problem solving. Children building with blocks gain experience in abstract representation that con-tributes to the ability to read and write. Children also learn about mathematical relationships when they experience that two blocks of one size are equivalent to the next larger size block. They are raw materials that children can use to recreate their experiences and represent their ideas. Hollow blocks allow children to build structures that inspire and contribute to rich dramatic play. All blocks serve as vehicles through which children can express their growing understanding of the world. Preschoolers and kindergartners make extensive use of blocks. Watching as their skill in block building grows is a wonderful experience.

A Unit Block Area. A unit block area begins with a set of hardwood unit blocks. The different sizes and shapes of unit blocks are based on a unit block that is 5½″ × 2¾″ × 1⅜″. Other blocks are exactly proportional (½, ¼, double, quadruple, etc.), so children can experience mathematical relationships and develop concepts of equivalence and symmetry.

A basic set of unit blocks for a classroom includes 100 to 150 blocks in 14 to 20 shapes, sometimes called a *nursery* or *preschool set*. A larger set that includes 200 to 700 blocks in 20 to 25 shapes is sometimes called a *school* or *classroom set*. Older children benefit from larger and more complex sets of blocks. Younger children may be overwhelmed by too many blocks as well as by the daunting cleanup task they present.

Unit blocks should be stored on low, open shelves. Storage shelves should be spacious enough so that each type of block has its own individual place. Store blocks so that those with similar qualities are near each other. Place them so that children can easily see how they differ (e.g., lengthwise for long blocks so that the differences in length are evident). Each shelf should be clearly marked with an outline to enable children to find the blocks they need for their constructions and put them back in the appropriate places (we recommend using solid-colored contact paper to create the outline). Much of the benefit of block play is lost if they are stored without organization in a box or bin.

The block area should be large enough so several children at a time can build. A smooth floor or low-pile carpet will minimize noise and enable children to build without structures tumbling down.

You can enhance and extend unit block play by adding toy vehicles, street signs, dollhouses, small human and animal figures, and other props (carpet or fabric squares, stones, and sanded, smooth pieces of wood), and encourag-ing children to make their own props using materials available in the art area.

Provide storage baskets and separate labeled space on the shelves for props. Posters, photographs, and books about buildings can be displayed in the block area. Older preschoolers and kindergarten children will use paper, pens, and tape for sign making and writing stories about their creations if you make them available.

A Hollow Block Area. Hollow blocks are larger than unit blocks and include short and long boards for making roofs and platforms. They give children the opportunity to construct a world they can physically enter. A hollow block area should have enough blocks for a child to build a structure that can be climbed on or entered (a "starter set" is 17 big blocks). A larger collection (50+ blocks) promotes more extensive creative play.

Hollow blocks are expensive and require a good deal of space. When you set up a hollow block area, carpeting or other soft surfacing is essential to limit noise and to prevent damage to the blocks. Hollow blocks can be stored on shelves or can be stacked against a wall for storage. If you do not have indoor space for a hollow block area, it can be set up on a porch or in the play yard if sheltered storage is available.

We find that hollow blocks are used for more elaborate building and for more social-dramatic play if they are separated from unit blocks. If possible locate the hollow block area near the dramatic play area so that children can coordinate hollow block building with social-dramatic play. For instance, the firefighters in the hollow block area may be called to extinguish a fire in the dramatic play area, or the carpenters in the hollow block area may build an addition or a garage onto the house. Good props for hollow blocks include hats, sheets, and lengths of colorful chiffon or gauze, which you can store in bins, boxes, or baskets nearby.

Dramatic Play Area

Dramatic play is one of the most important activities for young children. Children imitate the actions of the important grown-ups in their lives and thus enact how different roles might feel. When they take on roles and use materials to pretend, they learn to symbolize and practice the skills of daily living. Manipulating the physical environment (e.g., putting on clothes with buttons and zippers) and managing relationships are skills learned in part through dramatic play.

A dramatic play area requires sheltered space and simple child-sized furniture typically including a pretend stove, and sink, and a table with chairs for two to four children. The addition of dress-up clothes motivates children to act out different roles. Dress-up clothes for both boys and girls should reflect different kinds of work and play, different cultures, and different ages. You may have to seek out props for the dramatic play area that reflect the families, cultures, and community of your children. Dolls representing a variety of racial backgrounds and common objects of daily life such as kitchenware, books, furnishings, and tools also form a part of the equipment of the dramatic play area. Open shelves with bins or baskets, or hooks on the wall, provide storage for dramatic play clothing and props. Arrange materials so they are easy to find. Make picture labels for the storage shelves for materials that are always available.

Dramatic play centers are frequently referred to as a "home" area, emphasizing domestic activity. The home theme relates to the most common and powerful experiences in children's lives, but children find new ways to vary this theme. In one classroom we observed children become a family of spiders when they spread a crocheted shawl between chairs to become a giant web. Dramatic play areas can be changed to present other options: a post office, hospital, store, bus, farm, camp, or restaurant. For this reason when we talk to children about this part of the classroom we call it the *pretend area*. Simple sturdy furniture that can be reconfigured to create different scenarios furthers this broader vision of a dramatic play area.

Because it is not possible or desirable to have all the props available at all times, it is a good idea to organize and rotate props in the dramatic play area. You can respond to children's dramatic play by adding appropriate materials when you observe a new interest developing or when you begin a new topic of study—for example, contributing fire hats, a rain slicker, boots, and a length of hose when the children are pretending to be firefighters. To prevent clutter, props can be stored in sturdy, attractive, lidded boxes organized by occupation, situation, or role.

Manipulative Toys and Games

Toys and games[2] (sometimes called *manipulative toys,* or just *manipulatives*) such as puzzles, beads, Lego Bristle Blocks, and pegboards give children practice in hand-eye coordination and help develop the small muscles of their fingers and hands. These experiences are important preparation for writing, and they expose children to such concepts as color, size, and shape, which help in the ability to recognize letters and words. In play with manipulative toys, children also have opportunities to create, cooperate, and solve problems.

There are several distinct types of manipulative toys, including these:

- Building/construction toys such as Lego, parquetry blocks, Cuisenaire rods, hexagonal builders, and interlocking cubes. These are open-ended, have many pieces, and usually are used by more than one child at a time.
- Puzzles and fit-together toys like stacking cups: These are closed-ended, designed to be taken apart and put together in one or two ways, and are usually used by one child alone.
- Collections of materials such as buttons, shells, seeds, bottle caps and lids, keys, or pebbles: Safe recycled materials are very appropriate. These are open-ended materials that children can use for a wide variety of purposes including sorting (a cognitive task), creating designs (an aesthetic activity), or pretending. We encourage you to include collectibles that reflect the children's cultures, community, and environment.
- Games, including those that are manufactured (such as pegboards, lottos, geoboards, and board games) and those made by the teacher, sometimes called *workjobs*. Games have simple rules. Older children will enjoy following the rules of the game while younger children are more likely to ignore the intended use and build or pretend with the game's pieces. Board games like checkers or Chutes and Ladders can be well used by children from age 5. We do not recommend battery-operated toys of any kind, even those that have an "educational" purpose, because these tend to prescribe and limit children's play.

If you have adequate space it is useful to have separate areas for the open-ended building toys that inspire noisier group play, and puzzles and games that require greater concentration and tend to be used by children alone or in pairs.

---

[2] Because the term *manipulative* is not very meaningful to young children, we refer to this area as the "toys and games" or "table toys" area when we work with children.

Because manipulative toys have many pieces that are easy to lose or mix up, storage in this area is especially important. An organized and clearly marked manipulative toy area invites children to play productively. Children can use the materials on tables or on a carpet. Attractive place mats or small carpet pieces can define individual workspaces. Labeled bins or boxes are essential for storage of loose pieces.

Sensory Play Center

Natural materials such as sand and water suit a wide range of developmental stages and abilities. They provide children with rich sensory experiences and an opportunity to learn about mathematical concepts like volume and measurement. Observation of almost any child will tell you that these are satisfying play materials. They are open-ended and can be used in many ways. Children learn about the properties of substances through pouring, feeling, and mixing. They may be soothed by the responsiveness of the materials and can safely vent strong emotions in their play with them. Cooperative and imaginative play is fostered as children work together with open-ended materials.

If you have room in your classroom, you can have a dedicated center for sensory play—otherwise these materials can be included in the art area and outdoors in good weather. The heart of a sensory center is a *sensory table,* often called a *water* or *sand table,* although it can hold much more (dirt, salt, aquarium gravel, sawdust, birdseed, dried used coffee grounds, soapy water, crushed ice, snow, cornstarch goop). Since play with these materials can be messy, the center needs space near a sink or on a porch with an easy-to-clean floor. Sensory tables are designed to hold materials that provide tactile experiences. If you do not have one, there are many workable alternatives: plastic dishpans or baby baths on a low table, children's wading pools, plastic or galvanized tubs (available from the hardware or garden supply store). Recycled feed troughs also work well. Along with the sensory table you will need props (bowls, cups, scoops, spoons, buckets, etc.), aprons, and plastic tablecloths or shower curtains to protect clothing and the floor. A place to hang smocks and a dedicated, labeled shelf for storage will also be needed.

To keep young children healthy when playing with water in a sensory table, special precautions need to be taken. Water should be emptied after each group is done playing, and the table and toys should be sanitized. Children with open cuts or sores should not participate in group water play (an individual tub makes a good alternative). Have children wash their hands before and after play in the sensory table.

Salt and flour dough, potter's clay, or other kinds of malleable materials (e.g., plasticine) are important sensory materials. A sturdy table and chairs, along with storage containers, aprons, mats, and tools, are needed for play with dough or clay.

Another kind of sensory exploration that you may wish to add is a light table. These are used in the classrooms of Reggio Emilia. A light table has a translucent surface with fluorescent light bulbs recessed underneath it. This provides a space for exploration of colored transparent materials, building with translucent manipulative toys, and exploring natural materials that are permeable to light. A light table can also be used for watercolor painting, tissue collage, and other art activities.

Art Area or Studio

The heart of the art curriculum in your classroom will be the art area. Teachers influenced by early childhood programs in the city of Reggio Emilia often call this area a studio or *atelier* (the French word for artist's studio). In the art area, children can work with materials that are developmentally appropriate, functional, and satisfying to use. Art materials provide opportunities for creative expression, problem solving, and physical and sensory development.

The location of the art area needs to be carefully thought out. A few built-in features will determine where you place your art area. Art is often messy, so the area should be in the "wet zone," near a sink if at all possible, on tile or linoleum that is easily cleaned. Choose an area in which there is good light from either natural (preferable) or artificial sources.

An art area requires worktables and easels that are sized to the children (they should be able to reach the top of the easel). We prefer children to stand at an easel so that they can utilize the full range of motion of their arms so we do not place chairs at easels. Old or secondhand furniture, smocks, and a good supply of plastic tablecloths minimize concerns about the inevitable paint and glue spills. Additionally, it will be helpful to have open shelves for supplies that children can use and closed storage for adults-only supplies. A place for drying finished work is important. A drying rack with wire shelves is best for this purpose, but a clothesline or clothes rack makes an acceptable substitute. Drying space for 3-dimensional work is also needed.

In addition to furniture, an art center needs good tools and supplies including the following:

- Different kinds of paint (tempera, cake and liquid watercolors, and finger paint or finger paint base)
- Brushes in a variety of widths and lengths (from narrow for painting fine lines, to short-handled and chubby) and other things to paint with, such as sponges, Q-tips, and feathers
- Lots of small containers to hold water and paint
- Paper in different sizes, colors, and weights (from tissue paper to cardboard)
- Things to draw with (crayons, markers, pencil crayons, chalk)
- Clay and dough to mold and model with, and tools like rollers and wooden or plastic tools for cutting
- Scissors
- Place mats and trays to define spaces and limit mess
- Glue and paste, and spreaders to use with them
- Assorted materials to glue together (wood, paper, magazines, natural items like shells and leaves, recycled items like ribbon and cloth scraps—one or two types at a time!)

Recycled materials can be used in art—old shirts for smocks, wrapping paper and ribbons, cloth scraps, old magazines, or paper that is too old for the copy machine. However, it is important to buy good-quality basic supplies, especially brushes, paint, markers, crayons, and scissors.

Art materials need to be stored so that staff and children can easily find them and put them away. Closed, well-marked storage for materials that only adults may access is especially important in the art area so that paints, glue, scissors, and bottles of food color or liquid water color are kept ordered and secure. Paying attention to organizing this well and returning it to order each day will make your job easier and more pleasant.

Young preschoolers explore and experiment with the materials and tools of art to discover what can be done with them. Older preschoolers and kindergarten children begin to develop definite forms and shapes and use art materials to represent their feelings, experiences, and ideas—but not always in ways that can be recognized by an adult. We suggest having a place in the art area where interesting objects (like a vase of flowers or a bowl with goldfish) can be placed temporarily to inspire observation and artistic endeavors.

Library

The best way to help children learn the joy of reading and become motivated to read is to have good books available and to read to children often. Every classroom for young children should have a large selection of books. Children need many opportunities to look at books, to hear stories, and to see adults using and enjoying books. Nothing is more important to support children in gaining literacy skills than to create the desire to read books. Having a good library area in your classroom is essential to creating this desire.

Children feel invited to use books when they are displayed with the covers visible on an uncrowded bookshelf at their eye-level. A book area that is comfortable, quiet, well lit, and stocked with a selection of quality children's books is an important part of a classroom. Locate the classroom library area in the best lit, quietest corner of the classroom and include soft pillows. An adult-sized chair or sofa will invite staff and parents to sit down and read to children. A library area can include decoration such as displays of book posters, alphabet posters, or laminated book covers. If there is room you can also include a listening center with books on tape, puppets, props, a flannelboard for storytelling, and a private area for one or two children to enjoy quiet time with a book.

Additionally, books can be integrated throughout the classroom. For example, science books might be kept in the science area, picture dictionaries in the writing center, and a cookbook, newspapers, and magazines might be located in the dramatic play area.

In a spacious classroom we like to combine the library with the writing center to create a *literacy center*. Besides books, storytelling, writing, and book-making materials, a literacy center can include literacy games.

A Story-Reading Place. A library area makes a cozy place to read to one or two children; however, most teachers read stories to a group of children at least once a day. Typically you will use an area of the classroom that serves another function, often the block center. A story-reading place has special requirements. It needs to have *good lighting* that shines on the page and not in children's eyes so children can see a book's pictures. Young children need to move when they listen to a story, so it's important for there to be *enough space* for wiggly children. It needs to be *sheltered from noise* so children can hear the words. It needs *comfortable seating* and *relatively few distractions* so that children remain attentive to the story. As you design your classroom, keep these needs in mind. To limit distractions and signal to children that an area has become the story-reading place, you might want to hang curtains over shelves or move dividers in front of shelves to keep tempting toys out of small hands. Some teachers set out mats, blankets, carpet squares, or pillows for children to establish boundaries and make sitting more comfortable.

Writing Center

Preschool and kindergarten classrooms need a writing center where children can explore, write messages and stories, and illustrate their writing. Children will be encouraged to write to communicate when writing supplies are available and when written words are available to look at and think about.

A writing center needs a table and chairs that are sized correctly for the children. Their feet should touch comfortably on the floor and their elbows should rest easily on the table. You will also need one or more low shelves to store materials and supplies. Supplies should be neatly organized so that it is easy for children to find what they need for their writing.

On the shelves you can place baskets or boxes to hold supplies—different types and sizes of paper, envelopes, note cards, paper notepads, pencils, erasers, markers of various widths, crayons, glue, staplers, string, and hole punches. Other useful materials include a children's dictionary, clipboards, chalkboards with chalk, carbon paper, collections of words on index cards (word banks), a letter-stamp set for printing, and a set of wood or plastic letters (both uppercase and lowercase) for constructing words and sentences and for tracing.

Older children will enjoy keeping journals in the writing center. A computer with a simple word-processing program designed for children is also valuable in this area and will, of course, require a child-sized computer desk and chairs.

Discovery Center

In preschool and kindergarten classrooms, discovery centers are laboratories for exploration. Teachers often call this area a *science center*. We prefer the term *discovery* since this suggests that the center is a laboratory where discoveries of many different kinds can occur and because the term *discovery* is one that children understand. What happened to the cereal that I ate? What does an earthworm need to survive? Where did the new child come from? Who is taller—Kane or Yoon Ki? Children solve problems based on observations and research, using tools and books you provide for science, math, or social studies. If you have space and an Internet connection in your classroom, the discovery center can be a good location for a computer that, like the books you provide, can be used to help children to research and discover the answers to questions.

Define the discovery center space with low, open shelves for storage and one or two low tables or counters for investigation. Chairs sized to the tables will also be needed. Set tables for displays against a taller shelf or wall.

Focus on Science. A discovery center is a home for science when you provide tools for exploration and for ongoing projects such as aquariums and terrariums, animal families, and plants. You can also include science games, collections of objects and pictures, and science reference books. Arrange your science area in a place in the classroom that has access to electricity and water. Set up a shelf with tools for investigation: sorting trays, plastic tubs and pitchers, aquariums, insect and animal cages, airtight containers for storage, balances, scales, measuring cups and spoons, and magnifying glasses. Select materials for investigation, sorting, collections (like buttons or rocks), machinery to investigate and disassemble, information books, and photographs and posters that illustrate science concepts.

Focus on Math. A discovery center is a home for math when it contains materials that encourage children to experiment and think about math-related experiences. You may also choose to place math discovery materials in the manipulatives area. In a math discovery center you might place math manipulatives like Unifix cubes, sorting and matching games, measurement tools like rulers, Montessori math and sensorial materials like number rods, math-oriented picture books like Pat Hutchins's *The Doorbell Rang*, and displays of math-related group work, such as graphs.

Focus on Social Studies. A discovery center is a home for social studies when it contains special displays and activities, bulletin boards, artifacts, learning games, maps and globes, and books that help children compare and contrast the attributes of the human and natural environments and how these affect people. Pictures, posters, and children's work relating to social studies can also be exhibited here. You might wish to use a single bulletin board or display area to attractively mount one type of work (for example, maps children have drawn) or set aside space for each child's work.

Woodworking

In an environment with adequate space and staffing, woodworking can be a wonderful addition to a program for preschool, kindergarten, and primary children. Woodworking contributes to the development of physical skills and problem-solving abilities. A woodworking area requires a specially built workbench. Make sure to have proper tools—*not* pretend, child-sized tools, which are usually of poor quality and therefore hazardous.

Though young children love to do woodworking, teachers are often uncomfortable with having a woodworking area in their program. If you feel uncomfortable, gaining comfort yourself is a must. You might begin by learning about woodworking—by reading *Woodworking for Young Children* (Garner, Skeen, & Cartwright, 1984), by taking a class, or by inviting someone who is familiar with woodworking materials into your program to teach you and the children how to use them. Like any other learning material, children will gain skills and use the materials more safely and productively if they have repeated opportunities to use them.

Primary Classrooms—A Place Called School

Do you remember your first-grade classroom? Did you sit in rows? Did you sit at tables? Was there a place to play? Did you have a pet? Did you have a desk? However it was structured, you probably remember it. It was your first experience of "real school."

Classrooms for primary-age children (first through third grade) can be quite similar to the preschool and kindergarten classrooms just described. However, they are more often more like classrooms for older children, with desks in rows and few interest centers. Available resources make a difference of course, but the most important variable is the philosophy of the teacher and the school. Although you can set up learning centers in any room (as Sally, the teacher in the example at the beginning of this chapter, did in a church basement), as a new teacher you may be unwilling to make your room too different from the classrooms that surround you. If you teach in an after-school program for primary children, you may not even have a classroom and may need to set up a temporary environment each day in a gym or all-purpose room.

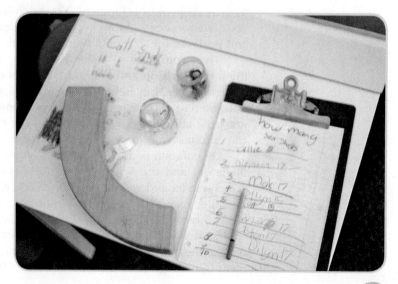

We started this chapter by saying that *the learning environment speaks to children*: What do you want your room to say to the primary-age children you teach? If you want it to say

"This is your room—you belong here—we make decisions together—we are on a learning adventure," you will do what you can to design a classroom that is quite a bit like a good preschool or kindergarten classroom. Instead of desks in rows there will be clusters of work tables, a place for group meetings, and comfortable learning centers for reading, exploring, experimenting, and playing (see Figure 8.6). You can have some of the same learning centers you might see in a preschool, but their size and proportion may be different. And to make them appropriate to these older children you will include some different things. Specifically:

- In the library, you will have more books to match a range of reading skills, and they can be shelved with only the spines showing.
- In the writing center, classroom computers take a more important role and are a boon to beginning authors.
- A dictionary and other reference books that match the children's reading level in the writing center as well as a computer for word processing and publishing.
- Discovery areas can hold more fragile artifacts (objects), reference books that match children's reading level, Internet access that children can use independently, maps, globes, and educational games geared to the ability level of the group.
- A shelf for toys and games can hold math manipulatives; more complex construction toys like K'NEX and Lincoln Logs; board games that require greater ability like Hi Ho! Cherry-O, Mouse Trap, and Monopoly Junior; and smaller, more complex jigsaw puzzles with 50 to 300 pieces.
- If you have space, blocks are a wonderful material for primary school classrooms. Primary-age children skillfully use blocks to reproduce structures they know. Blocks can be integrated into curriculum and used particularly to support social studies and math learning.

Computers and Other Technology in the Classroom

Technology is a part of our lives. We use technology when we drive a car, make toast, use a search engine, make a phone call—even when we hammer in a nail using a tool to augment our human strength. As in every aspect of the early childhood environment, you will provide children with technology that is appropriate to their stage of development. Young children are gaining technological skills in your environment when you help them learn to turn on the lights, use scissors, and push the buttons on a blender or a tape recorder.

When you think of technology you probably think of computers. You may think of television and video. Computers can be a great boon to you as a classroom teacher. They help you to communicate with families, create learning materials, do research, record your observations, and create documentation. We could not write and research this book without the Internet and computers. Television can entertain and inform us. It is present in virtually all homes.

Are computers and TV good for young children? The American Academy of Pediatrics and the White House Task Force on Childhood Obesity discourage screen media and screen time for children under 2 years of age and recommend limited screen time for older children (American Academy of Pediatrics, 2010; White House Task Force on Childhood Obesity, 2010). It is our strong belief, as well as that of many other educators, that computers supplement but must not replace the traditional play materials and activities of the early childhood environment (Campaign for a Commercial-Free Childhood, 2011).

FIGURE 8.6 School-Age Floor Plan

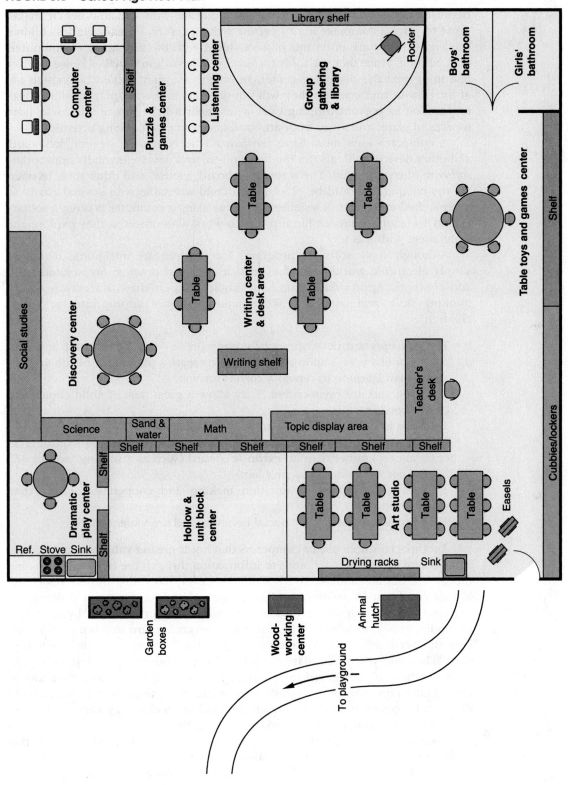

Computers

Because computers help people to communicate with one another, it makes sense to place a computer in or near the writing center. Primary grades children learning to write are often much more fluent with the assistance of computers than without. Since they are tools for gaining information it makes sense to place one in or near the discovery center. In either case they should be located out of the flow of traffic where they will not distract children at play; against a wall or partition to prevent tripping over wires; near a light source and away from sources of glare; and away from art, sand and water, or cooking activities.

A computer area must have *hardware* (the computer, printer, keyboard, and other devices) able to run the more recent and developmentally appropriate *software* (the programs). The screen, keyboard, mouse, and other tools to operate the computer should be placed on a child-size table with several chairs so several children can work together. Whereas using a computer is often a solitary activity for adults, many children prefer to work with others as they explore and experiment with this tool.

Although some software programs for children are intriguing, many are simply electronic workbooks that provide drill and practice on isolated skills and concepts. Appropriate programs should help children to develop critical thinking skills and creativity. What makes software appropriate for young children?

- The concepts are developmentally appropriate—that is, relevant and concrete. For example, children learn how to create a picture or initiate activity, rather than learning to repeat a correct answer.
- The programs are open-ended. They allow a great deal of child choice and child direction.
- The pace is set by the child, not by the program.
- The programs have an intrinsically appealing process (such as exploring an environment) rather than an extrinsic reward (such as a smiling face for giving the correct answer to a problem).
- They invite collaborative decision making and cooperation rather than competition.
- They provide models of prosocial behavior and are violence-free.

Another classroom use of computers that holds greater value, in our opinion, is the use of computers as portals to information through the Internet. Accessing the Web is not an "adults-only" activity. However, like using the encyclopedia, it does require adult assistance. Many preschool and kindergarten children understand that the Internet is a valuable source of information. Why does that caterpillar appear to have two heads? Why does cream turn into butter? Why are stop signs red? What do chameleons eat? What will the weather be like tomorrow? When and where did mastodons live? Young children are filled with questions. We have been pleased to observe teachers using the Internet as a tool to help children find the answers to their questions. This helps them to develop the desire to become scholars who understand and use technology well. And that is the real goal of using computers with young children.

Computer technology changes at a rapid pace. The skills and programs that children learn to use today may be obsolete tomorrow. To make appropriate use of the current computer technologies you need to know how to use them in ways that are consistent with our knowledge of how children learn.

Television and Video

Most children will spend far more time in their lives watching television than they will in school. A debate is ongoing about the negative effects of television. A study published in the journal *Pediatrics* (Christakis, Zimmerman, DiGuiseppe, & McCarty, 2004) recommends that children under the age of 2 not watch television because of its potentially damaging effects. The same study points to growing evidence suggesting that television viewing by preschoolers is linked to an increase in occurrence of attention deficit disorders. Whether television programs created for children are thoughtfully produced or merely marketing devices for toys appears to be irrelevant to television's harmful effects. For this reason we believe that television should never be used in programs for infants and toddlers and should be used rarely, if at all, in classrooms for preschoolers.

Used carefully as a tool with appropriate content and active teacher involvement, TV and video programs may be acceptable for kindergarten and primary school children if they meet the following criteria:

- It is shown to children in short (under 15-minute) segments that you have previewed.
- It contributes to educational goals.
- You sit and watch with a small group of children and talk with them about what they have viewed.
- It addresses children respectfully and is geared to their age.
- It is used infrequently as a supplement to more concrete activities and experiences.

Including Children with Disabilities

If your group includes children with disabilities, you are almost certain to need to make some adaptations in the arrangement of your environment. Sometimes such changes are obvious. Doors, pathways, centers, tables, climbing structures, and play materials must accommodate adaptive equipment such as wheelchairs and walkers. At other times adaptations may be subtler, such as creating additional alone spaces so a child with autism may have extra shelter from stimulation. Often small rearrangements of the furniture or schedule are enough to make your program a good place for all children.

It is important to adapt the outside environment, equipment, and activities so that children with physical challenges can also participate fully. Adaptations can be relatively simple. For example, creating conveyer-belt walkways across grass and sand (using recycled conveyer belts donated by airports or large stores) will extend the range of a child in a walker or wheelchair. A sling swing or hammock can be used by a child who does not have the upper body strength required to use a conventional swing. It is required by law that children with disabilities, like typically developing children, be provided with the access to playgrounds and equipment.

Including Adults

Though your program is first and foremost a place for children, it is important not to forget about adults when you design the environment (Greenman, 2007). This is especially important in a classroom for infants, where adults must cradle infants to help them to eat and sleep.

Create a place where you and other adults can sit comfortably. You may want to put this near the sign-in area or the library so parents feel invited to participate. Be sure to include an outdoor bench or chairs for family members who may be uncomfortable sitting on the ground. If you have space it is wonderful to include a family area in the classroom. Because you, too, spend long hours here away from your home, the environment contributes to how you feel about your work. You will also need a place where you can keep your own things safely, keep confidential records, and prepare materials.

Time

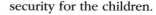

The final element to consider when planning a learning environment for young children is time. A typical day in any early childhood program is an artful blend of routines and learning experiences linked by smooth transitions. We think of the daily ebb and flow of learning activities and routines as being part of a larger experience of living and learning with children.

The Daily Schedule

A day for children in a good early childhood program has a relaxed and flexible pace. Children are not rushed from activity to activity. Perhaps this is why in some programs it is called *the flow of the day* rather than the schedule. Although there are many schedule differences depending on children's age and other factors, schedules in good early childhood programs share two similarities: Children are offered choices and large blocks of time in which to fully explore the chosen activities, and routines and transitions are thoughtfully planned. Nine-month-old Camille—delightedly crawling from shelf to shelf and exploring toys until she tires and crawls to her teacher for a cuddle—and 7-year-old Harrison—writing a story about tigers during learning center time over several days—are each making choices and governing their own use of time.

Both spontaneous and planned activities occur daily in a carefully prepared program for young children, although the amount of each varies. Your role as a teacher is to include time for engagement with the materials you have provided, routines that allow for increasing mastery, and rituals that bring a sense of security for the children.

Influences on the Flow of the Day

The structure of a program day is influenced by the needs and developmental stage of the children, your observations of individuals, and by your values and the values and concerns of parents, community, and the school administration. It is also influenced by the length of the program day, the physical setting, and the time of year.

Values and Goals. Your values and goals are among your most important considerations in planning your schedule. If you value creativity, independence, and the development of responsibility, you will allow large blocks of time (1 to 2 hours) during which children choose their own activities while you work with individuals and small groups. If you want to ensure that all children engage with all materials, you might have shorter play periods of assigned time in each area (for example, we have known programs with special art, block, and woodworking rooms where all children had assigned time each week).

Children's Needs and Developmental Stage.   Every teacher designing a schedule for a group of young children must include provisions for physical needs and take into account developmental differences. All children need time for rest, nourishment, and personal care. It is important to include periods of vigorous activity, quiet times, and daily times when choice is permitted to allow for individual interest and attention. The younger the children, the more flexible the schedule will be because younger children's needs vary greatly. During a 10:00 visit to a group of toddlers we saw Aimee lying down and drinking a bottle, Ian having a nap, Walden looking at books, Nadine cuddling on a teacher's lap, and Jonathan using the toilet. A rigid schedule could not meet such diverse needs and would inevitably lead to frustration for adults and children. A skilled infant teacher whom we know creates a written individual schedule for each child and posts it in the classroom. This allows everyone in the care setting to be aware of each child's routine. By reviewing these schedules weekly, caregivers ensure that they are adapting their routines and expectations to meet the needs of each child.

Typical schedules for different age groups have the following characteristics:

- **Infants:** Each child regulates him- or herself—meals, rests, toileting, active/quiet times.
- **Toddlers and young preschoolers:** Regular meals, snacks, and rest, with toileting and active/quiet times occurring in response to children's needs and interests.
- **Older preschoolers and kindergartners:** Scheduled eating, rest, group, activity, and outdoor times with some flexibility based on children's needs on any given day. As children mature, more structured plans for group and activity times are appropriate. A good way to start each day is with a group gathering to share news, sing a song, and map out the day's direction.
- **Primary children:** Similar to older preschoolers and kindergartners but with more structured group and activity times. A good way to finish each day is listening to a chapter from a book.

The Program Day.   Children in a full-day early childhood program spend up to 60% of their waking hours out of their home. This is a significant portion of a young child's life, and the program is like a second home. In full-day settings it is especially important to pay close attention to the quality of relationships, the design of the environment, and scheduling. For an example of scheduling, see Figure 8.7.

All early childhood programs must provide for the needs of children. A full-day program must offer lunch, a midday rest, and snack periods to avoid overstimulated, hungry children. Because their stomachs are relatively small, young children need to eat every 2 to 3 hours (Aronson, 2002), so schedules must be adjusted accordingly.

Children in full-day programs may stay 6 to 11 hours, but the staff in such programs generally remain for only 6 to 8 hours. So children may spend significant time with two separate groups of staff members. Care to coordinate the

FIGURE 8.7   Daily Schedule for a Full-Day Preschool

7:00–8:00	Arrival and child-chosen indoor activities
8:00–8:30	Breakfast—children may clean up their eating space and look at a book as they wait for the beginning of group meeting.
8:30–8:45	Group meeting—staff and children gather to sing songs, discuss the events of the prior day, and share plans for the day
8:45–10:30	Learning center time—indoor activities are available and small groups may meet for part of the time for project work or teacher-led activities
10:30–11:30	Outdoor activity time
11:30–12:15	Lunch—handwashing, setting of tables, family-style service, and individual cleanup as each child finishes eating
12:15–12:30	Nap preparation—children toilet, wash hands, brush teeth, take out their mats or place nap bedding on cots, and settle down with a book while others prepare for nap
12:30–1:00	Book time—an adult reads several books aloud to children who wish to join the group while others continue to remain on their mats with their own book
1:00–2:30	Nap time—the lights are dimmed, soft instrumental music plays, and the staff are available to pat backs (from 1:30 on snacks and quiet activities are available for children who wake up or who do not wish to rest longer)
2:30–4:30	Indoor/outdoor activities—children may select from a variety of activities indoors and outdoors with special activities and ongoing projects available
4:30–5:00	Closure—materials are put away, children. Wash up, settle down for songs, stories, and quiet activities as they wait for their families

transition between the shifts will help children to maintain the sense of trust they need to benefit from program experiences. Some educators hold the misperception is that anyone who cares for young children in the afternoon has a less important job than those who perform similar tasks in the morning. Children do not make this distinction. They learn and need nurturing throughout the day. Involving afternoon staff in planning and recognizing the vital tasks they accomplish is one way to maintain program quality throughout the day.

In part-day programs, it is likely that staff will remain consistent throughout the program day. Scheduled rest time is probably unnecessary, may meet with resistance, and is a waste of limited time. In a short program, a good blend of outdoor activity and indoor activities with a short snack break will provide for a pleasant, productive half-day experience.

Before- and after-school programs for kindergarten and primary children are designed to ensure children's well-being while parents are at work and to provide appropriate activities for children before and after school. Children need high-quality care and education throughout the day, and after-school programs should offer more than custodial care. However, children who are in structured school settings all day require a different, more relaxed program before and after school. Good after-school programs provide opportunities for play, socialization, and self-selected work. Although some homework can be incorporated, primary school children also need the opportunity to play in the second half of their days away from home.

The Physical Facility. The building in which the program is housed will influence how you structure the day. If it contains only your program and has sufficient space for younger children to be separated from older ones, it is relatively easy to schedule the day to meet the basic needs of all age groups. Where space is limited or facilities are shared, you may need to work out ways to accommodate different groups of children. If the bathroom or playground is located at a distance from the classroom, you will have to take this into account in planning.

Staff–Child Ratio and Group Size. The number of staff members in relation to the number of children is another factor of the physical setting that influences how you structure the day. Events, routines, and activities can be scheduled with more flexibility if there are lots of adults available to supervise. Teachers are free to be spontaneous and to plan for activities that have a variable time frame or that require more intense adult–child interaction. The size of the group will influence the flexibility of the daily schedule. Larger groups require more advance planning for the use of facilities, such as playgrounds, vans, and lunchrooms, and the daily schedule must be more tightly planned.

Time of Year. A program day may differ from the beginning of the year to the end. During the first days and weeks, your program must allow time to help children become accustomed to routines and new activities. As the year progresses, they will have mastered routines and become accustomed to program expectations. They will have developed new skills and abilities. Your schedule can be adjusted to recognize children's new competencies, cooperativeness, and skills. Group times may last longer as children come to enjoy group activities. Scheduled routines, such as toileting, may be omitted as children become independent and no longer require supervision.

Classroom Routines

Early childhood educators understand the importance of well-planned daily routines for young children. Carefully designed and implemented routines support the important goal of having young children to develop competence in independently meeting their physical and social needs. As an early childhood practitioner, you will want to give routines attention and thoughtful planning, just as you do the other aspects of the program. The accompanying box, "Golden Rules for a Good Day for Young Children," summarizes the information that follows.

Arrival. Arrival each day should be a friendly, predictable event. It is important to establish a routine in which every child is greeted. An arrival period during which you personally greet and talk briefly with families and children sets a relaxed tone. Arrival time may be one of the few regular contacts you will have with children's families, and it can be a good time for exchanging information. In some programs, one or two staff members greet families and help each child make the transition into the classroom.

Diapering and Toileting

Diapering is an important part of routine caregiving for infants and toddlers. While you will respond to individual infants' schedules, diapering will be a regular part of the daily schedule in a classroom for toddlers and 2-year-olds. Two-year-olds and young three-year-olds generally need a regular trip to the toilet in the daily schedule.

Mealtimes and Snacks. Some of the most pleasant times in an early childhood program occur when adults and children sit down and eat together. Most programs include a morning breakfast or snack as well as a midday meal. In full-day programs it will also have an afternoon snack. Some full-day programs also schedule an additional snack toward the end of the day. This extra snack helps children and families to have more pleasant departure times without the "arsenic hour" syndrome of tired parents and hungry, whining children.

Cleanup. Cleanup prepares the classroom for the next activity and is a natural and necessary part of living with others. Children begin to understand that they

sidebar
• • • • • • • • • •
The Learning Environment

Reflect on routines

What routines do you have in your own life? How do you feel when the rhythm of daily routines is disrupted? What do you like about your routines?

What routines have you observed or implemented in programs for young children? When did these routines seem to harmonize with the activity of the classroom? When did they seem to be a disruption?

**GOLDEN RULES FOR A GOOD DAY
FOR YOUNG CHILDREN**

1. Use large blocks of time (at least 1 hour long) for indoor and outdoor self-selected activities.
2. Alternate quiet sedentary activities with active play.
3. Keep structured group times short.
4. Include times for nourishment, rest, and personal care.
5. Maintain a relaxed pace. Avoid rushing children from activity to activity or area to area.
6. Use meaningful, enjoyable activities to create smooth transitions.
7. Allow children to govern their own use of time (how long to work, play, eat, nap, etc.) as much as possible.
8. Build rituals into the day (e.g., a morning song, a naptime story).

are members of a community and that they need to share in the responsibility for maintaining cleanliness and order. All adults who work with young children find themselves doing a good deal of tidying of toys and equipment. As you straighten and reorder the environment you are helping children to see learning possibilities. In doing so, you also help children to understand the process of maintaining order.

Rest Time. Rest time can be a positive experience if children are tired, if the environment is made restful, and if children feel secure. If they are fearful of the setting, they will be unable to relax. Most children under the age of 5, and many 5-year-olds, sleep if the environment is comfortable. Every child in a full-day preschool or kindergarten needs a mat or cot for sleeping. Infants need the protection of an individual crib or other sheltered sleeping space such as a mat surrounded by pillows. To create an atmosphere conducive to rest and sleep, dim the lights and allow children to cuddle personal comfort objects. We like to play quiet music for nap and there is research to suggest that the practice of playing quiet music helps children to fall asleep more quickly (Field, 1999).

The length of nap and rest periods should be based on children's needs. It may also provide a quiet period for teachers to collect themselves and do some planning or preparation—but it is not the primary purpose. The length of rest for nonsleeping children should be based on their ability to relax. We suggest that children who have not fallen asleep be allowed to get up and play after 30 or 40 minutes of quiet time. Five- to eight-year-olds also benefit from short quiet times in their day that may be combined with an opportunity for reading. Some kindergarten children who have not had a nap during the school day may need a time and place for napping or quiet resting in their after-school programs.

Transitions. Each time a scheduled activity or routine ends, it is followed by a *transition,* a time of gathering children or of movement into a new activity. Transitions can be smooth and relaxed if they are well planned and if children are prepared for them. Suggestions for meaningful and interesting activities that will help you to orchestrate smooth transitions can be found in Chapter 6, "Relationships and Guidance."

Departure. The end of the program day should provide a smooth transition back into life at home. If all the children leave at the same time, departure can be structured to provide closure. You may read a story, go over events of the day, and plan for tomorrow. If children leave at different times throughout the afternoon, you may complete these routines early in the afternoon and then provide open-ended activities that children can easily leave as they are picked up. In all programs a staff member should be available to share information with families and say farewell to children as they leave.

Final Thoughts

What do you want your environment to say to children and their families? How can you make it say "Welcome! I care. This is a place for you"? The environment is an essential part of children's learning experience in an early childhood program. It communicates your caring and competence to families. When you design a learning environment (the space, the equipment, and the time), you are creating a resource that helps you do your job, and you are creating your own work environment.

Your home changes as you change. It reflects your needs, tastes, activity, and lifestyle. It changes as your family changes. Creating an environment for children and making it work is also a process of change. It allows you to use your knowledge of children's development, your sensitivity in observation, and your creativity. As you gain more knowledge and skill, and as you devote time, energy, and resources to the environment, it will better meet children's needs. This kind of creation is a challenging and satisfying aspect of the work of a teacher of young children.

Learning Outcomes

When you read this chapter, and then thoughtfully complete selected assignments from the "To Learn More" section and prepare items from the "For Your Portfolio" section, you will be demonstrating progress in meeting **NAEYC Standard 1: Promoting Child Development and Learning** (NAEYC, 2009).

Key element:

1c: Using developmental knowledge to create healthy, respectful, supportive, and challenging learning environments

To Learn More

Take a Child's Eye View: Observe a classroom from a child's perspective by kneeling or sitting on a low chair. Observe from the entrance and the interest centers. Go back to each position and observe it again from your regular height. Reflect on how these are different and write about your experience. What did you learn about this classroom? What did you learn about the design of environments for children? What changes would you make in this classroom based on your experience?

Imagine a Dream Program: Pretend that you have the resources to create a perfect early childhood learning environment. Select the age and number of children for your class. Use the principles from this chapter to plan an ideal environment for them. Make a diagram of the indoor and outdoor space. Present your program to your classmates or a colleague. You may wish to create a shoebox model. Describe your environment and explain your decisions in terms of children's needs and your values and your goals. Explain how you will address the dimensions of teaching-learning environments in your environment.

Observe an Environment: Visit an early childhood program and observe the environment (classroom and outside play space) used by one class of children. Evaluate the environment using the Learning Environment Checklist in Appendix B. What is present and what is missing? Analyze the strength of the environment in supporting children's physical, creative, language, and cognitive development. Decide in what ways it is appropriate for the age and needs of the children. Share what you have observed and summarize your feelings about

the environment. Sketch a floor plan of the environment. You may wish to include a few photographs. Discuss your thoughts about the environment you observed and how you might change or modify it to better support children.

Compare Two Environments: Repeat the preceding assignment in another program or classroom for children of the same age. Compare and contrast the two.

Investigate Related Websites:

Alliance for Childhood—includes articles on playgrounds and computers: allianceforchildhood.org

Community Playthings: communityplaythings.com

Design Share—presents award-winning early childhood learning environments: designshare.com/index.php/awards/early-childhood

Early Childhood Australia—has excellent articles and links on a range of topics, including learning environments: earlychildhoodaustralia.org.au

 # For Your Portfolio

Create a Learning Center: In a classroom, play yard, or in your home, using materials you own or can borrow, create a specific learning center (e.g., a library, a writing center, a manipulatives center) for a particular age of children. Write a brief description of what you did and why. Invite a small group of children to use the center. Observe what they do and how they play. Make a video or photographic record of the children's use of the space. Use this documentation to demonstrate your skill in creating learning spaces for children.

Improve an Environment: Sketch a floor plan and take photographs of an existing classroom or outdoor play space in which you work or have a practicum assignment. Use the checklist located in Appendix B to evaluate the

learning environment. Decide how you might rearrange, change, or modify the environment to better support children's development. Implement some or all of the changes, take photographs, and sketch a new floor plan to show the changes—and then observe the effect on the children and program. Write about what happened, and place this documentation in your professional portfolio.

Create a Classroom and/or Playscape: If you are teaching or have been hired to teach, spend several days creating a classroom for children that follows the principles laid out in this chapter. Document your process with photographs and written reflections. Once children are in the environment observe and document how they use the environment.

MyEducationLab

Go to Topics 5: Program Models and 8: DAP/Teaching Strategies in the MyEducationLab (myeducationlab.com) for *Who Am I in the Lives of Children?* where you can:

- Find learning outcomes for Program Models and DAP/Teaching Strategies along with the national standards that connect to these outcomes.
- Complete Assignments and Activities that can help you more deeply understand the chapter content.
- Apply and practice your understanding of the core teaching skills identified in the chapter with the Building Teaching Skills and Dispositions learning units.
- Listen to experts from the field in Professional Perspectives.
- Check your comprehension on the content covered in the chapter with the Study Plan. Here you will be able to take a chapter quiz, receive feedback on your answers, and then access Review, Practice, and Enrichment activities to enhance your understanding of chapter content.

Through play, children learn what no one can teach them.

LAWRENCE FRANK

Play is a child's life and the means by which he comes
to understand the world he lives in.

SUSAN ISAACS

9

Understanding and Supporting Play

Do you remember the dizzy joy of rolling down a hill, the focused effort of building an elaborate structure with blocks, the satisfaction of learning to jump rope, or the concentration of pretending with friends? Whether rich or poor, in town or country, you played. Children all over the world play; they have always played.

Child development theory and the experience of practitioners tell us that children learn best through direct, hands-on experience. Play is the ultimate realization of the early childhood educator's maxim of "learning by doing." Since the field began, early childhood educators have sought to understand and support this most natural of activities. Today, as in the past, belief in the value of play is a distinguishing characteristic of early childhood education. It is a link to our past and a bond between early childhood professionals. As an early childhood educator, you will become knowledgeable about play—what it is, how it develops, its function in growth and learning, its role in early childhood education, and the role of the early childhood educator in supporting children's play.

As a teacher you will be frequently challenged to explain the value of play to families, educators of other age groups, and program administrators. This demand for explanations is reasonable in the current era in which the push for academic achievement continues to grow. You may occasionally hear the parental question "Why do they play all day? When are you going to start teaching them something?" Because play is essential for development, it is important that you know how to explain its value even before you are asked to do so.

Play serves all aspects of development, provides an avenue for children to practice emerging skills, confirms evolving concepts, and enables you to assess the developmental status of children. Because of the impressive power of play to lead the development of social, emotional, and cognitive competence, it is

MyEducationLab

Visit the MyEducationLab for *Who Am I in the Lives of Children?* to enhance your understanding of chapter concepts with a personalized Study Plan. You'll also have the opportunity to hone your teaching skills through video-based Assignments and Activities as well as Building Teaching Skills and Disposition lessons.

important that you have knowledge about how play has been viewed in the past, what is now known about it, and how this knowledge is relevant to what you do as an early childhood educator.

Because play is how children learn, it is the heart of a developmentally appropriate early childhood program, the center of the curriculum. Play is the way children develop and learn, the medium through which they express their understanding of the world, and an important means for early childhood educators to achieve their curriculum and learning goals.

Children's play provides a window into their lives. Through your observations of children at play you can learn a great deal about what they understand and can do. You also come to appreciate and know what they are like as individuals—what their interests and unique characteristics are.

Understanding Play

What is play? What is its significance? Why is play so compelling to children? Reflecting on the play of children and your own childhood play can help you to realize that many things can be play. As you observe a child at play, you may notice the characteristics of play. As you watch children of different ages, you will see that play changes as children grow. And as you observe boys and girls with different temperaments, experiences, and abilities, you will see some of the individual differences in children's play. The characteristics and stages of play described by theorists and researchers can help you to understand what you see.

Characteristics of Play

As the 4-year-olds gather, Ashley, the teacher, invites each child to select a center where he or she would like to begin the morning. Kaitlin, Bryce, and Ema select the dramatic play area. Kaitlin announces, "Let's play farm. I'm the lamb and Bryce you be the farmer." Ema protests, "You got to be the lamb last time. I get to be the lamb this time." Kaitlin concedes and claims the role of the mommy lamb as she puts a blanket in the doll bed to serve as a bed for her baby lamb. Bryce follows with a carton of eggs (large beads) and says, "I'm the mommy chicken and I'm making eggs." As he places the eggs in the doll bed, Kaitlin pushes him away proclaiming that chickens use nests, not beds. Ashley observes the interaction and responds by offering a shawl as nest material.

Ask adults how they can distinguish children at play and they will likely tell you "when they are having fun" or even "when I can't get their attention." Perhaps there is no single agreed-upon definition because no single activity is play. Is gardening play or work? Is running a joy or a punishment? Though no definition captures the essence of play, theorists, researchers, and educators have identified characteristics that distinguish play from other behaviors. These characteristics enable you to understand what play is—and what it is not. Knowing this can help you to make decisions and take actions that support children's play and avoid interrupting or misguiding it. Though the exact wording varies, specialists on play (Saracho & Spodek, 1998; Johnson, Christie, & Wardle, 2005; Brown & Vaughn, 2009) include the following characteristics as necessary for play:

- **It is intrinsically motivated.** Play is its own reward. Children play because it is satisfying, not because it meets a basic need or receives an external reward. It is the motivation, rather than the activity, that makes something play. Walking on a balance beam as you cross the playground is play; walking a balance beam as part of a gymnastics routine because your parents want you to win a prize is most likely work. The pleasure and focus that Kaitlin, Ema, and Bryce brought to play in the preceding example is a sign of this personal motivation. Had Ashley (the teacher in the example) rewarded them for playing farm it would have been work.
- **It is freely chosen.** Children choose play. The play opportunity beckons, and children decide to play. Ashley invited the children to play, but she could not have required children to pretend in this way. The moment compulsion enters it becomes work, not play.
- **It is pleasurable, enjoyable, and engaging.** Pleasurable, focused pursuit of an activity is a hallmark of play in children and adults. Although play can be seriously pursued and can include challenges, fears, and frustrations, it is the quality of joy that stands out when we think of play. Activity that is not enjoyable most of the time will not be chosen as play.
- **It is done for its own sake.** The play, rather than an end product, motivates. Children are more involved in discovery and creation (the process) than the eventual outcome. Play can have a product or goal, but this will be spontaneously decided by the players as part of play, and may change as the play progresses. Bryce, Ema, and Kaitlin were not putting on a lamb and chicken show—they were deeply involved in the process of pretending.
- **It is active.** Play requires physical, verbal, or mental engagement with people, objects, or ideas. Although we clearly recognize the rough-and-tumble actions of the young child as play, quieter activities such as drawing, molding play dough, or even daydreaming can be play, because the child is actively engaged.
- **It is self-oriented rather than object oriented.** In play the basic question is "What can *I* do with this object?" In contrast, when confronted with a new or unusual object, the first order of business for most children is to answer the basic question "What is this object and what can *it* do?" Play theorists and researchers call this *exploration* and distinguish it from play (Christie, & Wardle, 2005).
- **It is often nonliteral.** Many activities are playful, but it is nonliteral pretending, like the lamb and chicken scenario described in our example, that is the pinnacle of play. Children suspend and alter reality for make-believe. The external world is temporarily set aside for fuller exploration of internal imagining: *"Let's play farm—I'll be the mommy and you be the baby"* or (holding an egg carton full of beads) *"I'm the mommy chicken and I'm making eggs."*
- **It provides freedom from time.** Play creates a sense of timelessness and living in the moment. Mihaly Csikszentmihalyi, a professor of psychology noted for his study of happiness and creativity, calls this *flow*—complete and energized focus—and it is a characteristic of play (2008).

Reflect on your memories of play

When you were a child, how did you play? What made it play?

Children at play are powerful creators compelled by forces from within to create a world. Although the raw materials of their creations are life experiences, the shape of their creations is individual. Play is simultaneously an attachment to and a detachment from the world—a time during which children can act autonomously and freely and experience themselves and the world with intensity.

Scott Eberle, the vice president for interpretation at the Strong National Museum of Play in Rochester, New York, suggests that both children and adults go through a six-step process when they play: anticipation, surprise, pleasure, understanding, strength (or mastery), and poise (or grace and a sense of balance). When we experience all of these we are playing (Eberle, described in Brown, 2009).

Kinds of Play

Babies play in different ways from preschoolers. Children play in different ways from adults. Though play changes across the lifespan some types of play remain the same. As we consider play in early childhood it useful to remember that different types of play are not restricted to young children.

Body and Movement Play. Physical play is easy to identify. It is part of play from the first days of life. Whether you see a baby sucking his toes, a preschooler riding a trike, a kindergartner jumping rope, a fifth grader playing four-square, an adult dancing, or a kitten chasing a ball of yarn you know they are playing. Freely chosen body movement is innately pleasurable and playful.

Rough-and-Tumble Play. Play fighting without intent to harm, called rough-and-tumble play, is characteristic of almost all mammals. If you have ever watched a litter of puppies or a group of 4-year-old boys in a public playground, you have seen rough-and-tumble play. Despite its universality, allowing rough-and-tumble play in formal programs is controversial.

Object Play. Exploring and manipulating objects is another early-to-develop, easy-to-recognize form of play. We have a special word for play objects (toys), special industries that make them, and special stores that sell them. However, play objects can be as simple as a cup to bang or a box to climb in. They can be as complex as an old machine to take apart, or a new iPad with thousands of apps to explore.

Imaginative Play. Pretend, dramatic, or imaginative play involves the creation of a story or narrative. In imaginative play the players becomes immersed in acting out the story as they create it. A child dressed up in her mother's hat and shoes and an adult who is a knight in the Society for Creative Anachronism are both involved in imaginative play. Perhaps the most intellectually engaging form of play, imaginative play is considered by many to be the pinnacle of play, the play that is most important to master (Bodrova & Leong, 2003; Brown, 2009; Elkind, 2007; Smilansky & Shefatya, 1990).

Games. Structured play that has a goal, rules, and a distinct challenge is called a game. Games can be solitary but are more often interactive and involve competition. Games usually involve some kind of equipment (like board games and ball games). There are many different types of games ranging from individual and sedentary (like solitaire and most computer or video games) to active group games played in teams. Games cross the boundary between play and work when a player is employed or rewarded for play, as happens in professional sports.

Philosophers, theorists, educators, and psychologists have observed children at play for centuries and speculated about play's nature and purpose. Many of the philosophers and educators who have influenced early childhood education viewed play as worthy of serious consideration. Plato and Socrates wrote about play. John Locke suggested that it contributes to children's health, good spirits, and motivation. Friedrich Froebel, the "father of the kindergarten," believed that children learned through play, and created toys (gifts) and play activities (occupations) to be used in a play-based curriculum (Frost, Wortham, & Reifel, 2008).

During the 19th and early 20th centuries, a number of writers studied play and formulated explanations for the role of play in human development. In 1938, Johan Huizinga proposed that play was a special separate sphere of human activity that existed outside ordinary life and that it was necessary for the creation of culture (Huizinga, 1970). The *surplus energy theory* of play, introduced by British philosopher Herbert Spencer (1861), suggested that the purpose of play was to help human beings use energy they no longer needed for basic survival. Adults have work to do, but children need to expend their energy in play. G. Stanley Hall (1904) formulated the *recapitulation theory* of child development, which suggests that during childhood the history of evolution is relived. In Hall's theory, play serves to rid children of primitive and unnecessary instinctual traits carried over by heredity from past generations. Hall was the founder of the child study movement and influenced the creation of laboratory schools, where research could be done to form a scientific basis for teaching. John Dewey founded the Chicago laboratory school, an outgrowth of this movement. Dewey (1910) disagreed with Hall. He saw play as the way children construct understanding. *Instinct* or *practice theory,* developed by German philosopher and naturalist Karl Groos (1901), suggested that play was a natural instinct, necessary for children's growth and development. Groos argued that lower animals do not play but that more highly evolved species do. This theory suggested that play was practice for adulthood. Children at play practice the tasks and roles of adults. The *relaxation* or *recreation theory* of G. T. W. Patrick (1916) held that play was an essential mechanism to relieve tension and fatigue (Frost, Wortham, & Riefel, 2008; Hughes, 2009). Today we know that play is important to development of all kinds, and essential to brain development. It is one of the ways that neurons develop connections; in other words, how the brain builds itself (Brown, 2009; Elkind, 2007).

When we observe a group of children it is easy to see how these theories evolved. A group of energetic preschoolers cooped up on a rainy day certainly seem to have surplus energy. That same group, after an opportunity to run and yell outside, is much more relaxed when they come back in. A jungle gym full of climbing children is humorously reminiscent of our primate cousins and can seem to be replaying evolution. And it can be frighteningly apparent when we watch children playing house, school, or war that they are practicing adult roles.

Reflect on play in your life

Think of a way you play as an adult. What makes this activity play for you? How much and how often do you get to play? How important is play in your life? If you were being described by your friends or family, would they talk about the things you do as play? Why or why not?

Contemporary Theories of Play

There is still much to be learned, but recent theorists, researchers, and educators have expanded our understanding of why children play. We know that play is both a natural and an instinctive activity that helps children's development. Current theories of play strongly reflect the influence of Freud, Piaget, and Vygotsky.

Freud and his followers, particularly his daughter Anna Freud and Erik Erikson, felt that play provided a catharsis, an emotional cleansing, to help children deal with negative experiences. According to these theorists, in play children can feel more grown up and powerful, can exert some control over their environments, and can relieve anxiety created by real-life conflicts. Play therapy (psychotherapy for children) uses play and play materials in the diagnosis and treatment of children who have psychological conflicts and problems (Hughes, 1999).

Piaget and his followers believed that play is the medium through which children develop cognitively (Reifel & Sutterby, 2009). Based on his observations, Piaget described a set of stages in the development of children's play. Many of today's early childhood programs have a Piagetian orientation to play. Children are allowed time and materials to play, and their teachers trust that it will help them "construct" their own understanding of the world.

Theorist Lev Vygotsky also believed that play served as a vehicle for development. Unlike other theorists, Vygotsky thought play promoted several areas of development: cognitive, emotional, and social. He saw the special role of play as a bridge between what children already know and what they will soon be able to understand with assistance from other more experienced players or through independent replay. Vygotsky called this space between what the child knows and what she or he will soon comprehend the *zone of proximal development*. In Vygotsky's view, play provides an anchor between real objects and the ability to symbolize (Van Hoorn, Monighan Nourot, Scales, & Alward, 2007). He also believed that play facilitates the development of self-regulation, motivation, and decentration (the ability to consider multiple aspects of a stimulus or situation) (Bodrova & Leong, 2007).

Theorists have consistently confirmed the role of play in development. Recent research has recognized the ways that play helps children learn to self-regulate— to control their physical, emotional, social, and cognitive behaviors (Bodrova & Leong, 2003; Bronson, 2000). Current theory and research confirm the pivotal role of play in children's learning of some of the competencies and skills that lead to the development of competence, mastery, and self-control.

Stages of Play

As children grow and develop, they engage in different and increasingly complex types or stages of play. The ability to understand and identify the various stages of play is a valuable tool in your work with children of all ages. If you know that two 5-year-olds can play happily together building a road with blocks and sharing a single vehicle, but anticipate that two toddlers will play separately and each need his or her own truck, you will be able to make sensitive judgments of what behaviors are reasonable to expect from the children and you will know how to provide developmentally appropriate opportunities for each child in your setting.

Stages of play have been described from several perspectives by developmental theorists. Parten studied the social dimensions of play and identified types that typified different age groups. Piaget and Smilansky focused on the cognitive aspects of play. Elkonin, a student of Lev Vygotsky, identified levels of make-believe play.

Parten: Stages of Social Play

In the early 1930s, Mildred Parten developed categories of play that described the nature of the relationships among the players (Parten, 1932). Her categories of play continue to be used by early childhood educators. Parten identified six stages of social play that can be viewed along a continuum from minimal to maximal social involvement. The first two (unoccupied behavior and onlooker) are periods of observation preceding the venture into a new situation. The four remaining stages each dominate a particular age (although they occur at other ages as well), with children tending toward more and more social play as they get older. These four stages are as follows:

- **Solitary play** (dominates in infancy). During solitary play, children play alone and independently with objects. Other children playing nearby go unnoticed. Although solitary play is dominant in infancy and is more typical in younger children, older children also select and benefit from solitary play.
- **Parallel play** (typical of toddlers). In parallel play, children play side by side but still are engaged with their own play objects. Little interpersonal interaction occurs, but each may be aware of and pleased by the company of a nearby companion engaged in similar activity.
- **Associative play** (seen most in young preschool-age children). Parten identified two forms of group play. The first, associative play involves pairs and groups of children playing in the same area and sharing materials. Interaction may be brisk, but true cooperation and negotiation are rare. Two children each building a zoo in the block area, sharing animal props, and talking about their zoo, but *not* creating a joint zoo or negotiating what will happen at their zoo, are involved in associative play.
- **Cooperative play** (characteristic of older preschool and kindergarten/primary-age children). In this most social form of group play, children work together to create sustained play episodes with joint themes. They plan, negotiate, and share responsibility and leadership. For example, a group of children pretending to go on a picnic might cooperatively decide what food to take, who should attend the event, how to get there, who will drive, and what joys and catastrophes await them on their outing.

Piaget and Smilansky: Cognitive Stages of Play

Unlike Parten, who was concerned with the social aspects of play, Jean Piaget (1962) looked at how play supports cognitive development. He developed a framework with three stages of play development that are parallel to his stages of cognitive development. Sara Smilansky adapted Piaget's stages of play, based on her observations of young children from diverse cultural and economic backgrounds (Smilansky & Shefatya, 1990). She categorized play into four types, similar to those of Piaget, and added an additional type—constructive play. Piaget's and Smilansky's stages provide only slightly different ways of looking at similar play behaviors. Smilansky's work can be seen as building on Piaget's. Here is a summary that combines their cognitive play stages:

- **Practice or functional play (infancy to 2 years of age).** In practice or functional play, children explore the sensory qualities of objects and practice motor skills. This stage parallels Piaget's sensorimotor stage of development. Children who are engaged in functional play repeat actions over and over again, as if practicing them. A baby who repeatedly drops a toy over the side of the crib for you to pick up and a toddler who dumps and refills a coffee can over and over are each engaged in practice play. These actions are viewed as explorations to learn about objects. Although this type of play is most common in the first 2 years, it does not disappear. A preschooler repeatedly pouring water from one container to another and a teenager repeatedly combing his already perfect coiffure in front of the mirror are both involved in practice play.

- **Symbolic play (2 to 7 years of age).** In symbolic play, children use one object to represent another object and use make-believe actions and roles to represent familiar or imagined situations. Symbolic play emerges during the preoperational period as the child begins to be able to use mental symbols or imagery.

  The different forms of symbolic play are further separated by Smilansky into two categories: *constructive play,* in which the child uses real objects to build a representation of something according to a plan (e.g., creating a bird's nest with play dough), and *dramatic and sociodramatic play,* in which children create imaginary roles and interactions where they pretend to be someone or something (mommy, doctor, dog, etc.) and use actions, objects, or words to represent things or situations (a block for an iron, arm movements for steering a truck, or "woof woof" for the bark of a dog).

- **Games with rules (7 to 11 years).** In games with rules, children recognize and follow preset rules in the interest of sustaining solitary or group play that conforms to the expectations and goals of the games. During this period, children's play is typified by games with rules, though such games may also be enjoyed by younger children. The ability to agree on and negotiate rules is viewed as growing from the cooperation and negotiation developed in cooperative play. Chutes and Ladders, dominoes, kickball, jump rope, and perhaps even peek-a-boo are examples of games with rules.

Vygotsky and Elkonin: Levels of Make-Believe Play

Vygotsky saw make-believe play as the basic mechanism for the development of higher mental functioning (such as goal setting, de-centering, and symbolizing). Vygotsky believed that in order for play to do this it must involve a play scenario, roles, and a set of rules that evolve with the roles. He viewed the development of imagination as the result of make-believe play rather than the prerequisite for it.

Daniel Elkonin, a student of Vygotsky, extended Vygotsky's theories by describing levels of make-believe play (Bodrova & Leong, cited in Rogers, 2011). Elkonin's levels of play resemble Smilansky's stages in some ways but are more detailed and focus only on sociodramatic play. Elkonin described but did not name the middle levels.

Level 1 (Object Centered). In level 1 play children do not name their roles. Their actions are object centered, stereotyped, and are repeated often without any particular order (e.g., the child pretending to be a baby crawls on the floor and cries throughout the play). Children do not insist that their play partners follow any particular "rules" in acting out their roles.

Level 2. In level 2 play roles are named and specific actions are associated with the roles. Events are sequenced as they might be in real life (e.g., the child pretending to be a waiter takes the order and brings the food; he does not sit down at the table). When a child violates the sequence, other players in the group tell him that he must resume the role and there is no negotiation or argument.

Level 3. In level 3 play children name their roles before the play begins. They use a special kind of role speech with words and intonation determined by the role. If a child acts in a way that is inconsistent with the role, other children point out the mistake. Then the errant player will attempt to correct or explain the error.

Level 4 (Fully Developed Mature Play). In level 4 play roles are well defined. Children plan the action and stay in character consistently and logically

throughout the play scenario. The relationships between players become the content of the play (e.g., the "mother" feeds the baby, gives him a bath, and puts him to bed, and the "baby" cries, eats, and sleeps, and says, "I wuv you, Mommy"). When a player acts inconsistently with his or her role, other players explain not only the rule for that role but also the reason for the rule.

In Elkonin's view it is only when children reach the fourth and highest level of make-believe play that the higher mental functioning can develop. Research tends to support the view that children who reach level 4 are more cognitively capable. Disturbingly, it is less common today than in was in the 1940s for young children to reach the level of fully developed mature play out of which higher-level thinking evolves (Bodrova & Leong in Rogers, 2011). The reasons for this are not clear but may be related to increased media exposure or the "shrinking" of time available for sustained play.

Understanding the Stages of Play

Understanding the stages of play helps you to appreciate children's play behavior. An awareness of Parten's stages makes it more likely that you will understand rather than be irritated by the infant whose solitary play takes the form of repeatedly banging a rattle on a tray and who never seems to tire of dumping objects on the floor. You will appreciate the movement toward social competence represented by the toddler who engages in parallel play by carrying the basket of cubes to the block rug to build beside a friend. You will understand that 2-year-olds might enjoy a game, such as ring-around-the-rosy, led by a teacher. You will realize that they are just beginning to be involved in associative play on their own and would be unlikely to initiate such a group game. Likewise, you may be somewhat concerned about a 4-year-old who rarely engages in the associative or cooperative play typical of her age, such as building a block tower with a friend, and never uses materials to pretend. You might worry about a 5-year-old who is not able to take on a role and sustain the character throughout a play period. This child may require encouragement or play training from you, discussed later in this chapter. Knowledge of the stages and levels of play enables you to plan a program appropriate for the children in your class and gives you some important clues to use in observing the developmental progress of each child.

Because the different play stages tend to parallel the stages of cognitive and social development, the play of individual children can serve as assessment (see Table 9.1). However, the stages of play and the milestones of cognitive and social development are different in that the appearance or dominance of one stage of play does not signal the extinction of the previous play stage. For example, a child will continue to enjoy sensorimotor experiences (for example, playing with water and sand) typical of the practice play of an early stage even after cooperative play of older preschool-age children has become their dominant form of play. Indeed, we think of the companionable silence of sitting and reading a book near a friend as a grown-up version of the parallel play of the typical toddler.

Dramatic and Sociodramatic Play. In her work concerning the nature and importance of dramatic and sociodramatic play, Smilansky points out that dramatic play represents a different and potentially higher level of play behavior than any other kind: "Dramatic and sociodramatic play differs from the three other types of play in that it is person-oriented and not material and/or object-oriented" (Smilansky & Shefatya, 1990, 3). *Dramatic play* is acting out human relationships using symbols ("when I put on the big boots and hat, I'm the daddy"). It may be carried out individually or with another child. *Sociodramatic play* involves acting out complex interactions in cooperation with others. A story line is created, roles are assigned, and changes are negotiated as the play proceeds ("I put on the big boots and the hat, and you can be the little boy and get in the car and I'll drive you to the zoo"). "Sociodramatic play allows the child to be an actor, observer and interactor simultaneously, using his abilities in a common enterprise with other children" (Smilansky & Shefatya, 1990, 3).

Smilansky identified the important elements of dramatic and sociodramatic play as follows:

- **Imitative role play.** The child undertakes a make-believe role and expresses it in imitative action and/or verbalization. (Miriam shows that she's a puppy by getting down on all fours and barking to ask for supper.)
- **Make-believe with regard to objects.** Toys, nonstructured materials, movements, or verbal declarations are substituted for real objects. (Miriam uses a block as a pretend bone.)
- **Make-believe with regard to actions and situations.** Verbal descriptions are substituted for actions and situations. (Miriam acts out being scared of another child who she says is a mean lady who wants to steal puppies.)
- **Persistence.** The child continues playing in a specific episode for at least 10 minutes. (Even though activity time is over, Miriam continues in the role of puppy and comes to circle time on all fours. She barks for the first song.)
- **Interaction.** At least two players respond to each other in the context of a play episode. (Miriam and Rivera both are pets, but Rivera is a kitty. They play together and meow, hiss, whine, purr, and bark to one another.)
- **Verbal communication.** Some of the verbal interaction relates to the play episode. (Periodically, Rivera gives Miriam directions on the next event in the play such as, "It's nighttime and the puppies and kitties have to go to sleep for 100 minutes.")

These elements of play can be used as a basis for evaluating the play skills of individual children. When a particular play skill is not seen, play skill training can be used to teach it to the child. (See the sample sociodramatic play checklist in Figure 9.3 later in the chapter.)

TABLE 9.1 Stages of Play and Stages of Development

	Piaget's Stages of Cognitive Development	Erikson's Stages of Social-Emotional Development	Parten's Stages of Play	Piaget's Stages of Play	Smilansky's Stages of Play	Vygotsky/Elkonin's Levels of Make-Believe Play
Infants (birth through 15–18 months)	**Sensorimotor Stage** (Birth–2 years)	**Trust vs. Mistrust**	**Solitary play** Children play alone with toys; if other children are nearby, they go unnoticed.	**Practice play** Children explore the sensory qualities of objects and practice motor skills.	**Functional play** Children engage in sensory and motor exploration of toys, materials, and people in order to learn about them.	
Toddlers (15 months through 30–35 months)	**Preoperational Stage** (2–7 years)	**Autonomy vs. Shame and Doubt**	**Parallel play** Children play side-by-side with little interaction, engaged with their own toys, aware of and pleased by the company of others.	**Symbolic play** Children use objects, actions, and roles to represent reality and familiar or imagined situations.	**Constructive play** Children manipulate objects in order to create something.	**Level 1 Object Centered** Roles not named. Actions object centered, stereotyped, and repeated without any particular order. No "rules" in acting out roles.
Young Preschool Children (30 months–4 years)		**Initiative vs. Guilt**	**Associative play** Pairs and groups of children play together and share materials but cooperation and negotiation rare.		**Dramatic play** Children pretend to be other than what they are and use actions, objects, or words to represent things or situations.	**Level 2** Roles named during play, actions sequenced as in real life. No negotiation or argument.
Older Preschool and Kindergarten Children (4–6 years)			**Cooperative play** Groups of children engage in sustained play episodes in which they plan, negotiate, and share responsibility and leadership.			**Level 3** Roles named before play. Role speech used. Inconsistent roles pointed out.
Primary School Children (6–8 years)	**Concrete Operational Stage** (7–11 years)	**Industry vs. Inferiority**		**Games with rules** In solitary or group play children recognize and follow rules that conform to the expectations and goals of the game.	**Games with rules** Children behave according to rules in order to sustain play.	**Level 4 Mature Play** Roles well-defined. Action planned. Children stay in character consistently and logically. Focus on relationships. Rules for roles explained.

The Role of Play in Development

Play isn't the enemy of learning, it's learning's partner. Play is like fertilizer for brain growth. It's crazy not to use it.

Stuart Brown

Children need to play. Play supports the development of the *whole child*—a person able to sense, move, think, relate to others, communicate, and create. Play is important to healthy brain development (Brown, 2009; Shonkoff & Phillips, 2000; Frost, 1998). The importance of play was recognized by the United Nations General Assembly in November 1989, which approved the Convention on the Rights of the Child, which asserts that every child has the right to play and must have the opportunity to do so.

> The States party to the present convention . . . recognize the right of the child . . . to engage in play . . . appropriate to the age of the child. (Article 31, United Nations Convention on the Rights of the Child)

Early childhood educators have long been able to justify play's value in supporting physical, social, and emotional development. In recent decades they have met with ever-increasing pressure to justify play in terms of how it contributes to cognitive and language development. It is of particular interest that researchers have found positive relationships between the play abilities of children and their subsequent academic achievement and school adjustment (Brown, 2010). Play researchers continue to discover how play facilitates all areas of development.

The Role of Play in Physical Development

Play contributes to physical development and health throughout life. Children at play develop physical competence efficiently and comprehensively. The vigorous activity of children's own spontaneous play builds the strength, stamina, and skills they need to succeed as learners. Children learn best when they have bodies that are strong, healthy, flexible, and coordinated and when all of their senses are operating. From infancy on, children display an innate drive to gain physical control of their arms and legs as they strive to reach for and eventually grasp and manipulate objects (Bodrova & Leong, 2003; Bronson, 2000).

Children have an innate drive to explore, discover, and master skills. The concentrated play of childhood leads naturally to the physical mastery that was probably essential to our survival as a species. Running, jumping, climbing, throwing balls, riding bikes—the activities we most commonly think of as play—are of prime importance in the development of *perceptual-motor coordination* (the ability to use sensory information to direct motor activity) and in the attainment and maintenance of good health.

The Role of Play in Emotional Development

Therapists and educators have long appreciated the rich emotional value of play. Freud and his followers identified play as a primary avenue through which children express and deal with their fears, anxieties, and desires. Contemporary therapists still use play as the medium for helping children deal with the feelings associated with traumatic events and disturbing situations in their lives.

Children at play devise and confront challenges and anticipate changes. In the process they master their fears; resolve internal conflicts; act out anger, hostility, and frustration; and resolve personal problems for which the "real" world offers no apparent solutions. It is no wonder children are motivated to play all day.

Children at play feel they are in control of their world, practicing important skills that lead them to a sense of mastery over their environment and themselves. They discover ways to express emotions and to communicate their inner state that enable them to maintain the self-control necessary for a cooperative relationship with other players.

The Role of Play in Social Development

From birth, children are enmeshed in a social environment. They need to develop ways of expressing emotions and develop behaviors that enable them to create positive relationships with others (Bronson, 2000). Survival depends on adult care from the moment of birth. Caregivers *play* with infants in a way that is unlike anything adults do in any other life situation. You will hear a grown-up addressing questions to the infant and then taking the infant's part to answer: "Now, don't you have about the most beautiful eyes in the whole world?" "Well, of course I do, I got them from my daddy." An ordinarily dignified adult will make undignified noises and facial expressions ("ZZZZZZZZZZZZ Gotcha!") and respond with the greatest joy when the baby laughs aloud for the first time. Infant-adult play progresses to games like pat-a-cake and this-little-piggy (which have their equivalents in every culture).

This type of social play leads to increased social interaction skills. Children learn how to initiate play with relatives, family friends, and peers. In early play encounters, children learn awareness of others, cooperation, turn-taking, and social language. They become aware of group membership, develop a social identity, and learn a lot about the rules and values governing the family, community, and culture. The play becomes increasingly complex and is sustained for greater periods of time. By the time children reach their second birthday, most are making attempts to portray social relationships through dramatic play; for example, pretending to feed a favorite doll or toy animal. By age 4 or 5 most will have learned the things they need to know to enact complex social relationships with their peers in sociodramatic play; for example, pretending to be customers and workers in an ice-cream store. Soon after, they become able to play rule-governed games like tag. Through this play, social concepts such as fairness, justice, and cooperation evolve and influence play behavior and other social relationships.

The social competence developed in sociodramatic play leads to the development of cooperative attitudes and behaviors. Most peers, families, and educators prize the sharing, helpful, and cooperative behaviors associated with high levels of social competence developed through this kind of play.

The Role of Play in Cognitive Development

A major task of the early childhood years is the development of skills for learning and problem solving. In play children learn to set goals, plan how to proceed, develop the ability to focus, and create ways to organize their approach to cognitive tasks (Bronson, 2000). Play is the primary medium through which young children make sense of their experiences and construct ideas about how the physical and social world works. The functional play that begins in infancy and

persists through life is basic to the process of learning about the properties of objects and how things work.

Constructive play, typical of the toddler, is the mode we use throughout life for discovering and practicing how to use unfamiliar tools and materials (for example, learning to use a computer or a map). The dramatic (pretend) play of preschool children has a critical role in the development of representational or symbolic thought and the eventual ability to think abstractly. In sociodramatic play, children develop understanding of the world by reenacting with playmates experiences they have had or observed (e.g., a trip to the grocery store). They alter their understanding based on the response and ideas of their friends ("I'm the store man and you have to give me 50 dollars for that orange. Oranges cost lots of money!"), and then use the new meaning as they again experience the real world ("Mom, do we have enough money for oranges?"). This circular process is one in which information is constantly being gathered, organized, and used. It is one of the primary ways in which children come to understand the world. The following description of children's dramatic play clarifies its significance:

> The familiarity of life's scripts is what makes the daily life of adults efficient. . . . We are free to think about other things. . . . We recognize this only when we find ourselves in an unfamiliar setting—driving a borrowed car . . . placing a phone call in a foreign country. Young children . . . play in order to find their way around in what is for them the foreign country of adults, to master its daily scripts. (Jones & Reynolds, 1992, 10)

Sociodramatic play is of particular interest to play researchers and educators because of its significance in cognitive development. Sociodramatic play involves symbols, and the ability to use and manipulate symbols is the foundation for later learning. In their book *Facilitating Play: A Medium for Promoting Cognitive, Socio-Emotional, and Academic Development in Young Children* (1990), Sara Smilansky and Leah Shefatya describe many studies in which competence at sociodramatic play is highly correlated with cognitive maturity, creative, and social abilities.

The Role of Play in Integrating Development

Authentic play comes from deep down inside us. . . . [T]hat's part of the adaptive power of play: with a pinch of pleasure, it integrates our deep physiological, emotional, and cognitive capacities. And quite without knowing it, we grow.

Stuart Brown

Throughout this book, we refer to the development of the *whole child*. At play, more than at any other time, children engage all aspects of themselves and most fully express who they are, what they are able to do, and what they know and feel. Blocks, dramatic play props, construction toys, art materials, books, puzzles, climbing structures, sand, and water—the play equipment and materials found in almost every early childhood program—are rich in their potential for supporting all aspects of development.

> *Ethan, Sienna, and Isaac are constructing a tower in a block area. Ethan, the oldest, tallest, and strongest child, directs the group: "Get some triangles. We need more big blocks!" Sienna interrupts: "What about the windows?" Ethan carries floor boards to the building site. Isaac totes the double unit blocks that hold up the corners. Sienna brings a pile of unit blocks. They work together, sometimes talking, sometimes building. The tower gets higher and higher. It has five stories. Ethan places a series of cylinders and triangles along the top. Isaac places a row of bears on the second story. Sienna adds dollhouse people to each floor.*

- **Physical development.** Coordination and strength are enhanced as each child lifts, carries, and stacks blocks; small muscles are developed as they decorate the building; and sensory awareness is gained as they handle the blocks, feel the texture, and note the grain of the wood.

> *Tommy, a younger child prone to knocking over block structures, approaches the group with three little cars. "Go away, Tommy!" Isaac says. Tommy's lips quiver and his eyes fill with tears. Ethan intervenes: "Put the cars in the car place here," motioning to the second floor. "No!" says Isaac, "Cars go in the basement." Sienna points to the bottom floor: "This is the basement. Put the cars here. But don't knock it down!" Tommy places his cars and Sienna adds a dollhouse person to the car floor and directs Tommy, saying, "Go get a blue one." Tommy smiles and returns with the basket of vehicles and begins to park them all on the bottom floor.*

- **Social development.** Cooperation and negotiation skills are practiced as the children work out how to use the cars in the building; interpersonal sensitivity and concepts of justice are used as the group includes a younger, less skillful child.

> *The children sit back and look at their building. Ethan calls the teacher over: "Hey, Steve, we made a cool tower!"*

- **Emotional development.** Initiative is used as the children plan and build the tower. A sense of competence is gained as the children create the building and accomplish the task in cooperation with friends.
- **Cognitive development.** Problem-solving skills are developed as the children solve the problems of balance and symmetry inherent in construction. And they plan and communicate as they build.

Reflect on more memories of play

Reflect on a time when you developed or improved a skill or learned through play. Did the activity take energy and work? Was it still play?

Explaining Play's Role

As an early childhood educator whose program provides opportunities for children to play, you are likely to have many occasions in which you will need to understand and explain the role of play in children's development. Figure 9.1 provides you with a summary of some of the things that children develop through play and its relationship to academic success. You may find it useful to keep a copy of *Play in the Early Years: Key to School Success* available to share. You can download it from the website of the Alliance for Childhood, at allianceforchildhood.org.

FIGURE 9.1 **What Children Develop Through Play**

- Representational competence: The ability to represent objects, people, and ideas. This provides the foundation for reading and math.
- Oral language competence and narrative understanding: The ability to understand and use language to talk to others and to think in stories. These skills are necessary for reading and to understand subjects like history and science.
- Positive approaches to learning: Curiosity, motivation, and a sense of mastery—attitudes that are key to school success.
- Skills in logic: Concepts of cause and effect, as well as the ability to classify, quantify, order, and solve problems. These form the basis for higher-order thinking in math, science, and other subjects.
- Self-regulation and social negotiation: The ability to negotiate, cooperate, advocate, listen, handle frustration, and empathize. This has been shown to contribute to emotional health and school success.

Source: Information from J. Tepperman, *Play in the Early Years. Key to School Success*, 2007.

CONNECTING WITH FAMILIES

About Play

Families care about what their children do at school (that's their job!). But the value and power of play is not obvious to many families. Make it visible to them in many ways so that they come to understand why play is a part of your programs. Here are some ideas for how you might do this.

- Create a documentation panel with photographs or create a slide show that shows children learning through play.
- Plan a "play night" where families get to experience play activities and reflect on why they are fun and how they help children learn.
- Create a "guided tour" with posters or handouts to help a visiting family member to see how the play they observe is contributing to development. Use descriptions from your college textbooks or online resources (allianceforchildhood.org, ipausa.org, acei.org) to help you write the content.
- Feature a type of play and its importance in each issue of your newsletter.
- Create play backpacks for weekend borrowing. Each backpack can include play materials and a laminated sheet that explains how the activity supports development and suggests ways that a parent might use the materials with children.
- Involve families in the creation of play spaces and play materials for children. As they participate in creating play opportunities they will gain insight into and appreciation for play.

Facilitating Play

It is a happy talent to know how to play.

Ralph Waldo Emerson

You are learning about play and have come to understand it as a natural and powerful way for children to develop. As an early childhood educator you have a significant role in children's play. By your attitudes and your actions you can support or discourage play. What you do will influence the nature of children's play. Your next step is to learn a variety of techniques to support development through play.

Supportive Attitudes

When you understand play's role in children's development and learning, you approach children at play with an attitude of respect and appreciation. When you understand that you have an important role to play in facilitating children's play, you approach it with an attitude of serious attention. You see play as your ally and the support of play as an important part of your job.

Some practitioners in early childhood education and care accept play as part of the "care" aspect of their work but fail to trust it as a primary process in their "educator" role. These individuals might feel uncomfortable when children play in the educational part of the program and may try to intervene in play to make it seem more like "school." They don't understand play's role in children's development.

Your view of play will be influenced by your professional setting. Those who work with infants and toddlers generally receive support and approval for giving play an important role in their programs. The same is true for many, though not all, who work with 3- to 5-year-olds. If you teach in an elementary school you may find that play is not understood or supported by your colleagues or the families of the children you teach. In this case, your appreciation for play must be coupled with information that supports its importance.

Supportive Roles

> *Mirah and Aiden are in the dramatic play area playing with the dishes. Granette, the teacher, enters, sits down, and asks, "Is this the House of Dragon restaurant?" (naming a recently visited restaurant). "Can I have some noodles with black beans?" Mirah looks quickly around the area then says to Granette, "Can we get the restaurant stuff?" Granette smiles and nods as she lifts the restaurant kit from the nearby storage cabinet.*

Children play regardless of the circumstances. What you do before and during their play can make a vital difference in the quality of play and in what children gain in the process. Appreciation for children's play brings with it the realization that in play, children—not adults—are the stars. You can, however, fulfill many supporting roles that facilitate their play. Your role begins by setting the stage but continues throughout all the roles.

Stage Manager

The essential elements of play are *time, space, equipment,* and *materials.* Your first supporting role in children's play is providing these elements. Elizabeth Jones and Gretchen Reynolds (1992) refer to this important role as that of *stage manager.* Being a stage manager involves more than simply setting out materials for play. It includes selecting and organizing materials, space, and equipment so that they suggest play that is meaningful to the children. Children of all ages must have time to play. Early childhood educators who value play are flexible about time. They view children's play as more important than strict adherence to a schedule.

Part of the role of the stage manager is the artful arrangement of equipment and materials. This assists children in what Jones and Reynolds refer to as distinguishing figure-ground relationships—in other words, distinguishing what you are looking at from the background (Jones & Reynolds, 1992). If your classroom has too much equipment, or if what you have is disorganized, it may be overwhelming or confusing to children and inhibit play. The cycle of setting up, playing, and reordering the environment is an ongoing process in early childhood settings. When you understand it and participate in it willingly, you communicate that you value play.

Observer

Another important role you will have in children's play is that of observer. When you observe carefully and assess what you see based on what you know about child development and play, you are better able to understand what is happening for children, what children might need, and how you can support them in play.

> *Emily filled several buckets with sand and water. She sat them in the sand and then went to get more water. Kenese and Sage sat down and began to play with the bucket of sand and water. Emily turned around and yelled, "Hey! That's my lab. I don't want anyone to work in my lab."*

If you have observed that Emily still functions best in a parallel play mode you might offer Kenese and Sage additional buckets and a space to play near her. Or, if you have observed that Emily is ready to move into cooperative play, you could provide her with additional containers and suggest that she give them to the scientists in the next-door laboratory.

Structured observation records can yield important insight about play. Checklists or scales have been developed for looking at play behavior. These tools can be used to increase your understanding of play. The social-cognitive play scale (see Figure 9.2) codes play on its social and cognitive dimensions and enables you to get a quick look at a child's stage of play development.

To develop a profile on the play behavior of each child in your class, you can use a sampling system over a period of several days. To begin, you make a gridded sheet like the one in Figure 9.3 for each child in the class, shuffle the sheets so they will have a random order, start your sample with the top sheet, observe the child, and then place it on the bottom of the pile to be used for subsequent samples on the same day. Observe the child for approximately 15 seconds, mark the play behavior on the sheet, then move on to the next child. You can sample three children each minute, so if you had a group of 15 you could take six samples of each child in a half-hour. After 4 or 5 days you would have enough material to see typical patterns of play behavior for each child. In a classroom of infants you would probably find more play occurrences marked in the solitary-functional grid. If you were to shadow an 8-year-old for a day, many of the play behaviors would likely fall in the lower right-hand corner, indicating games played with groups of peers. This information is useful to you in making decisions about what intervention might be needed to support the play of individual children.

Mediator and Protector

Children's play is most productive when they feel safe from harm and relatively free from interference. Because group play has the potential for disorder and disruption, you will sometimes take the role of play protector and play mediator. As opposed to limit setter, disciplinarian, or rule enforcer, a *mediator* collaborates with children. As a mediator you help individuals to work out conflicts and concerns when a neutral third party is needed. A mediator does not intervene when the participants can handle a problem. Children's conflicts in play can give you

FIGURE 9.2   Social-Cognitive Play Scale

Name _____   Observation _____

	SOCIAL LEVEL		
	Solitary	Parallel	Group
C O G N I T I V E L E V E L Functional			
Constructive			
Dramatic			
Games			

Source: Information from J. E. Johnson, J. F. Christie, & T. D. Yawkay, *Play and Early Childhood Development* (2nd ed.), 1999.

an opportunity to teach peaceful conflict resolution skills that will assist children in handling problems on their own.

As a play *protector,* you maintain the delicate balance between guidelines that support and sustain play and excessive control that interferes with play. It's important to encourage play but not let it get dangerous or uncontrolled. The way you enter children's play to ensure safety and order needs to be respectful of the play ("Excuse me, birds, would you like me to help you move your nest here under the table? I'm afraid it might fall out of the tree and the eggs will crack."), rather than intrusive and thus interrupting the play ("Get down from the table. Tables are not for playing on; someone might get hurt.").

Dramatic play episodes that are prolonged and engrossing often attract late-comers who wish to join in. In this situation the play protector and mediator can observe carefully and assist shy or anxious children in entering the play. Delicacy is the order of the day. It is best if you can unobtrusively help the child find a role. For example, in a camp scene you might say, "Would you like to get wood for the campfire? I think I know where we can find some." If the entering child is disruptive, you may help by setting the child a task that makes use of high energy in the scene, such as chopping the wood.

The hallmark of highly developed dramatic play is that the children use objects to represent things: A bowl becomes a hat, a plate becomes a steering wheel, and a block becomes a telephone. Therefore play can be a disorderly process, as play materials for one type of activity are transformed in children's

FIGURE 9.3 Sociodramatic Play Checklist

Instructions: Select children who have shown infrequent engagement in group-dramatic play on the social-cognitive play scale. Observe these children closely over several days in a variety of settings (indoors in the dramatic play area, blocks, etc., and outdoors). Check the appropriate column when you observe the play elements being used by the child. Refer to page 314 for a description of each of the elements.

Name	Imitative Role-Play	Make-Believe w/Objects	Make-Believe w/Actions	Persistence in Role-Playing	Interactions w/Others	Verbal Communication

Source: Information from S. Smilansky & L. Shefatya, *Facilitating Play: A Medium for Promoting Cognitive, Socio-Emotional, and Academic Development in Young Children,* 1990.

imaginative pretending. This tendency can present a dilemma. If you are overly concerned about the proper use of equipment, you may curtail play and important learning; if you provide no limits, the resulting disorder can be overwhelming for both you and the children. Deciding on the best course requires sensitivity. It can help to see what children are doing with the materials; if they are being used in a way that is important to extending a play episode, it is best not to discourage the activity. For example, in a classroom we know, when manipulative toys were consistently being used as "food" in the nearby dramatic play area, the teachers moved the manipulative toy area and added materials to dramatic play to use as food. Sometimes you might decide to allow play that would normally be restricted, as happened in a classroom we visited once when a child was dealing with a family move. When the child began to move dramatic play area materials across the room, the teacher observed and asked questions and then made moving a legitimate activity, explaining to the children: "We're pretend moving today, so the library is going to be our new pretend area, for a while."

Participant

The conventional wisdom in early childhood education was once that teachers should not become directly involved in the play of children. Play was seen as the arena in which children were to be left free to work out their inner conflicts and exercise power over their environment. It was regarded as the duty of an adult to keep out of the child's play world so as not to interfere with important psychological development. The only valid roles allocated to the adult were those of stage manager and observer. In recent decades, however, research has pointed to reasons for joining in children's play as a *participant*.

Why should adults play with children? When adults play they lend support to the amount and quality of the play. Your participation gives children a strong message that play is a valuable activity in its own right, so they play longer and learn new play behaviors from observing you. It also builds rapport with the children. As you learn more about their interests, and characteristics you are better able to interact with them. When you participate, play may last longer and become more elaborate.

Of course, your participation must harmonize with the play of the children or else it will disrupt or end the play. When you play with children, take your cues from them and allow them to maintain control of the play. Limit your role to actions and comments that extend and enrich the play. When you join in, it is important that you do so in a way that supports ongoing play. Sometimes children offer a role to an adult. "Would you like a cup of coffee?" is an invitation to join a restaurant scene being enacted. If not invited, you might observe and then approach the player who seems to be taking leadership and ask to be seated as a customer and in this way gain entry into the play. As a customer you might inquire about the price of a cup of coffee, ask for cream to put in it, and praise the chef for the delicious pancakes she prepared. By asking questions, requesting service, and responding to things children have done, you introduce new elements into the play without taking over.

Sometimes teachers think they should intervene in children's play to teach concepts or vocabulary. We once observed a teacher stepping into a play scenario to question children

about the colors and shapes of the food being consumed at a pretend picnic. Just as this interjection might interrupt the conversational flow at a real picnic, the interruption did not lead to a meaningful discussion of colors and shapes, and it stopped two players having a lively interchange on the merits of feeding hamburgers to the pretend dog. It is possible to help children to be aware of new ideas in play, but it takes skill to do so without manipulating and diverting the activity. For example, when joining the group at a pretend picnic, it would be possible to comment "Could you please pass me that red apple? It looks very tasty," rather than "What color is this apple?"

Why play with children? Perhaps the best reason is because it is a way to share their world, to demonstrate your respect, and to renew your appreciation of the complexities and importance of children's play.

Tutor

Although children play naturally, not all children have fully developed play skills. Children who have been deprived of opportunities to play, whose families do not value play, or who are traumatized may need the help of a *tutor* in learning to play.

A study conducted by Smilansky (1968) in Israel found that children from low-income families in which parents lacked a high school education engaged less often in dramatic and sociodramatic play than did children from more affluent families. Since then, other researchers have found the same pattern in other countries. Intervention strategies have been designed to teach the play skills that a child lacks. In this play tutoring, you demonstrate or model a missing skill until the child begins to use the skill in spontaneous play situations. For example, if a child is dependent on realistic props you might offer substitution ideas—"Let's pretend that these jar lids are our plates" or "Let's pretend that the sand is salt"—until the child begins to do so independently. It is important to note that

---

GOLDEN RULES FOR SUPPORTING CHILDREN'S PLAY

1. Provide enough time—45 minutes to 1 hour of uninterrupted play time several times a day, both indoors and outdoors whenever possible, even if the weather is less than perfect.
2. Choose play materials to meet needs and interests of the particular children.
3. Observe children as they play—to learn, to support, and to enjoy.
4. Add materials or equipment to support play as it happens.
5. Help children who have difficulty entering play by assisting them to find a role in play (e.g., "It looks like you need a fire dog in your fire station. Joe is good at barking—can he be the fire dog?")
6. Participate in children's play, but let children take the lead.
7. Observe and think twice before stopping play, unless a child is in danger.
8. Be playful and child oriented when you guide or participate in children's play.
9. Avoid interjecting adult concepts or judgments into children's play (e.g., "How many are there? Was that nice?").
10. Redirect play (when necessary) in a way that supports rather than stops it.

the goal of play tutoring is to teach play skills in the context of the spontaneous play episode. The adult should not change the content of the play by taking a directing role. Play tutoring has proven effective in improving the dramatic and sociodramatic play skills of children, which in turn has brought about gains in cognitive and social development.

Just as some children lack play skills because they are deprived of a safe physical and emotional environment in which to play, other children do not develop play skills because they are deprived of time to play. They are compelled to conform to adult standards of behavior, to excel academically at an early age, and to master skills typically developed by older children. To them, play time is something they must "steal" from their busy schedule of dance lessons, soccer practice, math practice, and full-day school (Elkind, 1981).

The Special Role of Outdoor Play

**Reflect on playing
in school**

Reflect on a time when you played in school. Where did you play? Who supported your play? How much time did you have for play? What do you think your teachers thought about play? Why do you still remember this play today?

It is likely that some of your most poignant memories of play involve playing out-doors. Why? While all play is important, there is something special about playing out-of-doors. Perhaps it is the freedom to run, to yell, and to discover the limits of your physical abilities. Maybe it's the challenge of learning to use equipment like trikes, swings, and wagons, or the excitement of overcoming your fear at the top of a slide. Perhaps it is the opportunity to experience the adventure of nature. It might be feeling the joy of play that is not as bound by adult rules. Whatever the reason, outdoor play has a special role in programs for young children and deserves special consideration.

What is different about outdoor play? It is obvious that the outdoors affords children the opportunity for a wider range of large-motor activity than a class-room can. Similarly, it is the place where children can engage in messy, sensory play with water, dirt, and sand without the mess-avoiding precautions needed indoors. And, of course, the outdoors is the best place to explore and learn about the natural world and its animals, plants, and weather.

There are additional, less obvious, reasons that outdoor play is important. Young children's social development is enhanced when they play outside. Away from the density of play materials and the restrictions of the classroom, children out-of-doors have more space to develop friendships. They learn to be leaders, learn to be a part of a group, and learn to be alone. Children play differently outdoors than they do indoors. As well as involving more gross motor play, they engage in play that is more complex, filled with language, and less stereotyped by gender (Frost, Wortham, & Reifel, 2008).

Children's lives and children's play in the 21st century are generally more restricted than they were in the past. Because of this, the children in your care may have few opportunities to play outdoors in their home lives. Knowing this, it is important to advocate for young children, whatever their age and wherever they live, to have time each day to play outdoors.

Issues in Play

At the beginning of the 21st century, a number of issues affect children's play in the United States. Because play is the cornerstone of early childhood curriculum, these issues will affect your work and it is important that you are aware of them.

Diversity and Play

Drew, a 4-year-old African American child, enters the big playground run-
ning and calls to his Caucasian friend Jason, "Come on!" They both scramble
up the big climbing structure and slide down the fireman's pole then crawl
into the tunnel made of tires. Siow Ping, whose family emigrated from Asia,
sits in the shade of a tree. She has collected all the pebbles she can find and
has lined them up from biggest to smallest. As she observes them, their teacher,
Dena is aware that the children are each playing in their preferred ways.

Play researchers and practitioners have studied play in a variety of settings
and found that cultural background, social class, and gender are factors, along
with stage of development, that interact in dynamic ways to influence the types,
amount, and quality of play that children engage in. In the preceding vignette, the
differences in play preferences and activity level could be attributed to cultural
or gender differences or to a combination of both.

Understanding that there are different play preferences, abilities, and styles
among children will increase your sensitivity to individuals and help you be more
supportive of the play of all children. It is wise to assume that all children want
to and can play. Given that assumption you can use your ability to observe, your
understanding of individual children, your ability to create environments, and
your skill in supporting play to help each child to engage in productive play.

Culture, Social Class, and Play

In Euro-American culture, play is often seen as the means by which children learn
about the physical and social world and develop language. In some cultures it is
valued as entertainment, and in still others it is seen as a needless distraction from
work in which children are expected to participate. The value a culture places on
play influences how much support the adults provide. Where play is assumed to
contribute to learning, the adults are more likely to make available the materials, settings, and time for play. If it is seen as relief from boredom or a waste of
time, children may be left on their own to improvise times, places, and materials
for play. Whichever the case, children in all cultures play (Johnson, Christie, &
Yawkey, 1999; Rogers, 2011).

It is important to provide play props and other materials that represent the
experience and cultural background of the children. Children from different
cultures may not respond to the play props found in the typical early childhood
program designed for middle-class American children. When the play props relate more closely to their life experiences, their play is likely to become richer
and more complex.

How can toys and props represent cultural diversity? The makers of educational equipment strive to do this by selling elaborate ethnic costumes, musical
instruments, and plastic food. Many of these props may be as exotic to young
children as they are to you. When selecting dramatic play materials it's important to know the families in your program and what their lives and cultures are
like. For example, some cultural groups (Native American, African American,
Mexican, and Asian, to name a few) value the extended family, and elders play
a significant role. So props that represent the elders of the family (hats, bags,
shawls, scarves, jackets, books, cooking utensils) might increase dramatic play
by children from these cultures (Trawick-Smith, 1994). How do the families of
children in your classroom dress? What do they carry? If children's parents and
grandparents dress like the rest of the population, it is unlikely that adding a
happi coat or dashiki will contribute to richer, more meaningful play. As you

communicate with family members and pay attention to the ways in which their daily lives are influenced by their culture, you will be able to bring this information into the play environment. For example, in Hawai'i, where lei are given for most major events, it makes sense to have lei in the dramatic play area. The same prop in Minnesota or New Brunswick would be decorative rather than meaningful for most of the children.

Cultures differ in their approach to relationships among people and these differences can affect the play abilities of children. A child whose cultural background emphasizes cooperation and inclusiveness may be intimidated by children who have been taught to be competitive and exclusive. As an educator you may need to assist such a child to learn how to enter a play situation dominated by children who may exclude others or not think to include them in their play ("Ask them if they need someone to hold the firefighters' hose"). And similarly, you may need to support the child from the more competitive culture in finding ways to be more inclusive of others ("Firefighters always need a crew to put out fires. Ask firefighter David to be part of the crew").

Early research on play and development often identified play deficits and linked them to cultural background or the deprivations of poverty. More recent work has uncovered bias in the prior work (Johnson, Christie, & Wardle, 2005). When children of different cultural and social class backgrounds are observed at play in settings and with materials with which they are familiar, they too display rich, complex play behaviors (Johnson, Christie, & Wardle, 2005). Your job as an early childhood educator is to find ways to bridge the differences between your classroom and the children's home environments. You can do this by thinking beyond the usual middle-class housekeeping material found in the dramatic play area. As you come to know the children in your group you can introduce play materials and props throughout your program that relate to their life experiences.

Disabilities and Play

Like all children, children with disabilities benefit from play because it makes such important contributions to development. However, for children with disabilities it may be even more critical. Play can build on their strengths and provide feelings of success and a sense of independence that may not be as easily gained in other school activities.

Disabilities may interfere with children's ability to play. Some educators and parents of children with disabilities may not trust that play is a worthwhile learning experience for these children and so may limit their play opportunities. Programs for young children with disabilities often use "direct instruction" rather than a play-based curriculum. And children with disabilities may be segregated from their typically developing peers and so have fewer play partners and models. In addition to all of this, of course, some disabilities interfere directly with play or with the ability to interact with peers. We advocate for inclusion of children with special needs in programs with their typically developing peers in part because it puts them in settings where play is valued and where peers provide play models.

The ways in which you help young children with disabilities to engage in play will vary based on the disability. Parents, occupational therapists, and special educators can provide you with ideas for ways to help individual children with disabilities to play—by modifying the furniture, equipment, materials, teaching techniques, or the schedule. First and foremost, however, you must understand that children with disabilities can, want, and need to play. With that in mind you will be able to facilitate the play of all children.

Gender-Stereotyped Play

Although the play of all children has many similarities, particularly during the first 3 years of life, differences exist in the play behavior and characteristics of boys and girls. It is difficult to determine the source of these characteristics. Evidence exists for a biological basis for more aggressive play in males, but the social environment also influences the expression of these characteristics (Schickedanz, Schickedanz, & Forsythe, 1993). We were fascinated to learn that research on juvenile rhesus monkeys (Hassett, Siebert, & Wallen, 2008) shows that the sex differences in play and toy preferences that are observed in children are also visible in monkeys. Young male monkeys, like boys, show consistent and strong preferences for wheeled toys, while young female monkeys, like girls, showed greater variability in preferences. The similarities suggest that nature rather than nurture lies behind at least some of the gender play differences that you are likely to see.

Other gender differences in play may be attributed to gender stereotyping. From birth, adults tend to describe girl babies as little, soft, and pretty and boy babies as big, strong, and active—even when identical in size and activity level. Differences are magnified by the manufacturers of products for children—T-shirts, toys, lunch bags, books, sheets and towels, even disposable diapers come emblazoned with gender-stereotyped decorations. These give children a clear message beyond pink is for girls and blue is for boys. They say that boys should be active and aggressive while girls should be passive and pretty. They suggest that play must conform to the expectations of society, that there is a preferred way to be a boy or a girl, and that happiness comes from owning the right (gender-specific) stuff. Instead of enhancing imagination and possibilities, these products limit it.

Gender-related play characteristics may be influenced by environment and inheritance, but it is difficult to assign primary influence to one or the other. Although the causes remain a mystery, boys at all ages engage in active rough-and-tumble play, use the outdoors, and play in groups more than girls do. Girls begin to prefer same-sex playmates earlier than boys, but both do so between 2 and 5 years of age. By age 5, girls begin to be interested in cross-sex play, but boys tend to persist in their same-sex preference throughout the elementary years. Girls generally prefer art materials, dolls, and small constructive toys and play with them in quieter ways. Boys generally prefer blocks and wheeled vehicles and play with them more noisily and repetitiously. Girls play with toys regardless of the gender category generally assigned to an item; boys avoid "girls' toys." Boys appear to prefer larger groups of playmates from preschool age through the primary years, while girls show a marked preference for small groups (Johnson, Christie, & Yawkey, 1999).

All of us know individual children who do not conform to these gender-related play behaviors. Averages or norms are not individuals—all girls are active at times, and all boys engage in quiet play at times. It is important to remember that both girls and boys explore, build, and pretend and need our support in fully realizing their play potential. The similarities are more important than the differences.

We believe it is reasonable for early childhood educators to take steps to avoid gender stereotyping in the materials offered to girls and boys—to make certain that both males and females are offered a wide range of play materials.

Similarly, the environment can be arranged to encourage all children to participate in the same play activities. One way to encourage more diverse play for both boys and girls is to integrate block areas (particularly areas for large hollow blocks) and dramatic play areas. The building and dramatic play then naturally merge together. If you wanted to encourage Drew and Jason (described in the vignette at the beginning of this section on diversity) to engage in some art and literacy activities, an easel set up in a corner of the playground or a blanket beneath a tree stocked with books might attract them as a quiet break from more rambunctious play episodes. The same setup might entice Siow Ping and her friends to the playground, where they may discover some more vigorous activities to enjoy.

Another important way to overcome gender-stereotyped play is through your expectations and behavior. As you practice ball skills with girls and involve boys in domestic dramatic play episodes, you are taking small, important steps toward breaking down gender stereotypes that limit the choices of children in our culture.

Violent Dramatic Play

Children's play reflects their experience. As of this writing, the children in our care live in a country that is at war. They are exposed to violent television programming, some of which is aimed at children. Many live in communities where violence or fear of violence is a part of daily life. This makes it almost certain that in any group some children will introduce violence and war play into dramatic play. Although early childhood educators generally encourage children's spontaneous dramatic play, it is common for gunplay to be forbidden. The proscription of gun and war play is a response to the fact that it tends to dominate otherwise peaceful classrooms. Additionally, in violent dramatic play children tend to imitate the stereotypic behavior of media characters and the violent action of the programs they see. Imitation and repetition replace imagination and creativity (Levin & Carlsson-Paige, 2006).

This dilemma requires a decision. Should you prohibit children's violent dramatic play, or allow children to play out any drama they choose? In deciding whether and how to intervene, it helps to understand some of the reasons that children are so attracted to violent dramatic play:

- Young children are fascinated by heroes, weapons, and machines. In a world where they are virtually powerless, they are drawn to power.
- Dramatic play about violence provides a safe way to work through a fear.
- Violent dramatic play involves fast action and a thrilling chase. Adults find this exciting, and so do children.
- Today's toy weapons and accessories are often realistic. This realism is tantalizing and often creates a strong response in other children and adults.
- Intense interest may be evoked by sophisticated marketing aimed at children through television.

Several strategies can be used in coping with violent dramatic play:

- Come to some basic agreements with your coworkers over the limits that you will place on violent dramatic play in your setting. Even if you disagree, it's important for there to be consistency in how teachers respond to this kind of play. Whatever your decisions, it is never acceptable to allow children to hurt or bully one another.
- Observe the play to help you understand what it means to the children.
- Participate in children's play by asking questions to increase empathy—such as, "How does the bad guy feel? Who does he play with when he goes home? What does he do on his birthday?" In doing so, it is possible to help children to think beyond stereotypes.
- Guide children in choosing times, places, and behaviors that do not interfere with the play of the group. For example, just as yelling and shouting disturbs

Reflect on your ethical responsibilities

You disagree with the other teachers in your school over whether or not to allow children to engage in violent pretend play. As a staff you have decided that all forms of pretend guns and fighting are forbidden. A child in your class often pretends to shoot other children. You know this child has gone through some rough times and you feel this play is important to him. Using the guidelines on page 23, reflect on your ethical responsibilities in this situation.

others indoors, shooting and crashing is also disruptive. Ask children to think of where and when this kind of play will not disturb other people.

In a society where violence is prevalent we cannot eliminate children's fascination with violence. We can provide children with alternatives (ask the bad guys why they want to shoot you up), and help them learn to be responsible and thoughtful members of their community.

Rough-and-Tumble Play

Physically vigorous play that involves actions such as chasing, jumping, and play-fighting accompanied by positive affect from the players toward one another is known as rough-and-tumble play (Pellegrini, 1995). As we have previously noted, rough-and-tumble play is nearly universal in young human males and amongst the young of other mammals, particularly primates (Brown, 2009). If this is true, and because we generally support children's natural play behaviors, you may wonder why we have placed rough-and-tumble play with play issues.

Rough-and-tumble play is often discouraged or banned in programs for young children because educators have many fears about it. Teachers fear that play-fighting is the same as or will lead to real fighting. They worry that rough-and-tumble play will dominate and overshadow other kinds of play. And most of all they fear that a child may be hurt during rough-and-tumble play. We share some of these concerns. We have seen an inadvertent poke during play-fighting turn into a real fight. We have witnessed children so entranced by rough-and-tumble play that they do little else. And we have seen children bruised as they play.

So why would you allow rough-and-tumble play in your program? Play researchers point to a number of benefits (Pellis & Pellis, 2007). By its very nature rough-and-tumble play is physically active so it builds health as well as providing a way for children to meet their needs for touch. Perhaps more importantly, children (especially boys) learn the give-and-take of social interactions in rough-and-tumble play. They learn to detect and read social signals and to alternate and change roles as we do in other social interactions. So it may be that by forbidding this natural avenue for social learning we deny it to the very children who need it most. This dichotomy makes rough-and-tumble play an issue, and whether or not to allow it a dilemma.

Should you choose to allow rough-and-tumble play in your classroom (and we do not advocate that you do) you will need to be prepared to justify it to parents, other staff, and administrators and gain their support. Those who support rough-and-tumble play suggest that you learn to differentiate it from real fighting (in play-fighting children smile and laugh, join the play readily and eagerly, and keep returning for more). Finally you must ensure children's safety and well-being by providing an appropriate environment (enough space, padded surfaces, no tripping hazards), guidelines (e.g., no kicking, choking, hair-pulling; listen to others' bodies and words), teaching (e.g., "Tell him, 'That hurts. Please let go.'"), and supervision. If these requirements are possible in your setting, you can safely allow this natural form of play. If they are not possible, then you will need to explain to children that rough-and-tumble play is not safe at school.

Exclusion—You Can't Say You Can't Play

Exclusion is another issue that arises in early childhood classrooms. Exclusion takes a number of forms. Children may overtly exclude one another because of gender (girls only), age (you're too little), or visible differences like race or ability (you don't know how to climb so you can't play). More subtle exclusion may occur when one child is obviously not welcomed into play. What should a teacher do?

Some educators believe no child should be excluded from the play of other children. They think that it is important to have a rule like the one phrased by Vivien Paley (1993), "You can't say you can't play." Such a rule is designed to ensure equity and build empathy as children are asked to consider the feelings of children who are excluded. Others feel that this is interfering in the natural play choices of children and thus in the development of social skills. While there is no definitive way of handling exclusion in early childhood programs, there are some things you can do when children are being excluded from play.

- Be clear and unambiguous about exclusion that is unacceptable and create scripts that match your beliefs and values. For example: *This classroom (material, area) is for everyone in our class. Boys get to play and girls get to play. Everyone gets a turn.*
- Help children to include others in the play: *Tell Lydia how to be a space alien so that she can play too. Show her how to get in your spaceship without knocking it down.*
- If one child is regularly excluded, find ways to give that child particularly desirable responsibilities: *I need someone to help me get the lunch from the kitchen. Ethan, can you come with me and can you choose one friend to go with us?*
- Teach excluded children to handle disappointments and find alternatives: *Cielo and Jasmine are friends. Right now they don't want to play with anyone else. That makes you sad but there are other things for you to do. Would you like to draw with me and Soullee or help Baylor with his block structure?*

Shrinking Opportunities for Play

When you think of the play you engaged in during your childhood, you might remember hours spent climbing, sliding, pretending, swinging, running, and riding bikes. But the quantity and quality of play available to children today has changed. Factors that have limited or changed young children's play include families' hurried lifestyles, changes in family structure, changes in the availability and characteristics of play environments, increased focus on academics and enrichment activities at the expense of play, the substitution of TV and video games for active play (Ginsberg, 2007) as well as a prevalent fear of children being harmed in communities in which neighbors no longer know one another.

Children play less today because there are safety issues. In many communities, particularly in areas that are unsafe because of violence or other environmental dangers, children cannot play safely outside of the home unless they are under close adult supervision and protection.

Children play less because there are fewer places for them to play. In

Reflect on play you've observed

Think about a classroom you recently observed. How did the children play? How did the adults facilitate play? What seemed to be their attitudes toward play? Did you observe violent dramatic play or gender-stereotyped play? How did it make you feel? How did the adults respond? How did this affect children?

333

1981 concerns with safety and liability in public places resulted in standards for public playground safety (Frost, Wortham, & Reifel, 2008). While guidelines can help to create safe and wonderful playgrounds, implementing guidelines can be costly. In some communities, play structures were removed rather than improved.

Children play less because they tend to spend their time being passively entertained through television or computer/video games. Children spend an average of 6 hours 32 minutes per day watching television and videotapes or playing video games (American Academy of Pediatrics, 2001).

Time spent in front of a television or computer screen, time spent in organized enrichment, and time spent preparing for tests and on other academics leaves little time for the active and creative play that contributes to children's development. The increase in childhood obesity may be one result of less time for play. Data from two National Health and Nutrition Examination surveys (1976–1980 and 2003–2004) show that childhood obesity is increasing (Centers for Disease Control, 2007). The issue of childhood obesity provides a strong argument for the inclusion of active play in the curriculum, particularly outdoor play.

Reflect on your ethical responsibilities

The principal of your school has decided that with the importance of testing mandates, it is essential to devote more time to preparing children. To this end, recess and physical education have been eliminated. You believe that this is inappropriate and harmful. Using the guidelines on page 23, reflect on your ethical responsibilities in this situation.

Final Thoughts

Realizing the learning potential of play ensures that you will value it in its own right and make full use of it in your work with children. It is important not to lose sight of the exuberant, joyful, and nonsensical aspects of play. Treasure the creativity in fantasy and see worlds open up as children pretend. Appreciate the bravery, joy, and exhilaration as children take risks, laugh hysterically, run, fall, tumble, and roll without restraint. The uninhibited, imaginative quality of play distinguishes child from adult, and play from all other activities. Teachers who appreciate and understand the power of play can help children realize their human potential.

You may need to become an advocate for children and play. This role can be hard if other educators and children's families don't understand its value. We urge you to continue to learn about play and help others to understand play's importance, not only in learning and health but also as an inoculation against the pressures that society imposes on children. The children in your care need the opportunity to play now. You can speak to support them, and safeguard this right. When you do, you give them a precious gift.

Learning Outcomes

When you read this chapter, and then thoughtfully complete selected assignments from the "To Learn More" section and prepare items from the "For Your Portfolio" section, you will be demonstrating progress in meeting **NAEYC Standard 1: Promoting Child Development and Learning** (NAEYC, 2009).

Key elements:

1a: Knowing and understanding young children's characteristics and needs

1b: Knowing and understanding the multiple influences on development and learning

1c: Using developmental knowledge to create healthy, respectful, supportive, and challenging learning environments

To Learn More

Observe the Play of Two Groups of Children: **Observe** two groups of different-age children for an hour of self-selected play in each group. Compare them and report on the following:

- The types of play in which the children engage
- The stages of play shown in each group
- What the adults' attitudes toward and beliefs about play seem to be
- What the adults do to facilitate play in their programs

Interview Two Educators: Ask the educators about how they view play and report on their responses regarding the following:

- The role of play in their classrooms and in the development of the ages they teach
- What they do to support play in their program
- How they handle the issues of war play and gender-stereotyped play in their program

Observe a Child and Support His/Her Play: **Observe** a child during an outdoor and an indoor play period. Note his/her stage of play and preferred kinds of play. Write a brief description recounting what you observed, and this child's play strengths or needs. Go back a day or two later and with a plan to support the child's play. Write a brief description of what happened and reflect on what you might do with regard to play for this child if you were the teacher.

Use a Structured Play Observation: Use one of the structured play observation forms (Figure 9.3) to observe a group of children at play. Describe your findings and suggest some actions that you might take if you were the teacher in this group.

Read a Related Book:

Play: How It Shapes the Brain, Opens the Imagination, and Invigorates the Soul, by Stuart Brown with Christopher Vaughn

The Power of Play: Learning What Comes Naturally, by David Elkind

The Play's the Thing: Teachers' Roles in Children's Play, by Elizabeth Jones & Gretchen Reynolds

The War Play Dilemma: What Every Parent and Teacher Needs to Know, by Diane Levin & Nancy Carlsson-Paige

A Child's Work: The Importance of Fantasy Play, by Vivian Paley

Investigate Related Websites:

Alliance for Childhood—includes links and articles on play, playgrounds, and play policy: allianceforchildhood.org

IPA—International Play Association: ipausa.org and ipaworld.org

National Institute for Play: http://nifplay.org

Additionally, most early childhood professional associations have information, position statements, and publications on play.

Association for Childhood Education International: acei.org

National Association for the Education of Young Children: naeyc.org

Southern Early Childhood Association: southernearlychildhood.org

Zero to Three: National Center for Infants, Toddlers, and Their Families: zerotothree.org

For Your Portfolio

Write an Article: Write an article for a school or classroom newsletter addressed to a group of families who have questions about the role of play in the early childhood program. Explain your rationale for making play an important part of early childhood education in your program.

Create a Poster or Brochure: **Design** a poster or brochure to educate others about the value of play. Choose a play material (for example, play dough), a type of play (for example, dramatic play), or a play experience (for example, jumping rope). Your goal is to help a noneducator (such as a parent) understand how this kind of play experience contributes to young children's development.

Support a Play Interaction: **Describe** a play interaction during which you played one or more of the supportive roles—stage manager, observer, protector/mediator, participant, or tutor. Describe how the children responded to you and how the play episode worked, how long it lasted, and what elements of play were used by the children.

MyEducationLab

Go to Topic 2: Child Development/Theories in the MyEducationLab (myeducationlab.com) for *Who Am I in the Lives of Children?* where you can:

- Find learning outcomes for Child Development/Theories along with the national standards that connect to these outcomes.
- Complete Assignments and Activities that can help you more deeply understand the chapter content.
- Apply and practice your understanding of the core teaching skills identified in the chapter with the Building Teaching Skills and Dispositions learning units.
- Check your comprehension on the content covered in the chapter with the Study Plan. Here you will be able to take a chapter quiz, receive feedback on your answers, and then access Review, Practice, and Enrichment activities to enhance your understanding of chapter content.

The universe is the child's curriculum.

MARIA MONTESSORI

All genuine education comes about through experience . . . but not all experiences are genuinely or equally educative.

JOHN DEWEY

10

The Curriculum

Because you want to teach young children, you are studying early childhood education. As an early childhood teacher you will create a safe and nurturing place for learning, relate to children, and support their play. Another critical part of your work is planning and implementing learning experiences, or *curriculum*—in other words, teaching.

Another word for the art and science of teaching is *pedagogy*. Because of the broad scope of their responsibilities, early childhood educators, particularly those who teach children younger than 5, must pay attention to all aspects of children's development. This responsibility can be so demanding that early childhood teachers sometimes fail to attend seriously to pedagogy, to being professionals who teach. Yet nothing so clearly distinguishes you as a professional early childhood educator as your knowledge of what young children can learn in the early years and your ability to help them learn in ways that preserve their zest for school and learning.

Developing the necessary skills and knowledge to teach young children is complex. Good teachers continue to learn about it throughout their careers. This chapter gives you an introduction to the content of the early childhood curriculum. In it we do not attempt to include all of the content you will teach. Instead we give a framework so that you can think about curriculum and how children might best learn it. We cannot do more here than give you a taste of early childhood curriculum, but we hope you enjoy that taste and are inspired to learn more. In each curriculum content section we provide a list of easy-to-find books and useful websites[1] that you may use if you wish to learn more.

What Is Curriculum?

Different early childhood educators have distinct, but related, ideas when they speak of curriculum. Some mean something very broad: everything the child experiences both in and out of school, called the *umbrella curriculum* (Colbert, 2003). Others have in mind a curriculum approach or model (e.g., the *Reggio Emilia approach* or the *High/Scope model*). Still others mean a document or kit that is published and designed by a curriculum specialist, something that addresses the whole early education program (e.g., the *Creative Curriculum*) or a specific content area (e.g., Scholastic's *Building Language for Literacy* curriculum, or the *Second Step* curriculum for social development). This is sometimes called *packaged* or *commercial curriculum*. Another common definition, and the one we will use in this chapter, is the intentional learning experiences designed by a teacher, or team of teachers, in response to what they know and observe about children. We call this the *planned curriculum*.

Where Does Curriculum Come From?

Curriculum is based on a vision of society, values, a philosophy, a particular view of learners and teachers, and the ways educators translate this vision into learning experiences. It can originate from three broad sources: (1) beliefs about what is worth knowing, (2) knowledge of learners and their development, and (3) knowledge of subject matter.

Curriculum in early childhood programs is significantly different from curriculum for older children because early childhood educators believe that all areas of children's development are important. They believe that planned learning experiences need to engage children and be responsive to individual interests, needs, and learning styles. They understand the critical connection between children's learning, family, and culture. They know that teachers must design environments and experiences that support children's learning. They understand how play, child-choice, and cooperative relationships are an important part of the serious business of learning, and a part of the curriculum. These understandings and beliefs are the underpinning of what is called *developmentally appropriate curriculum* (DAP). For a brief outline of the tenets of DAP see Figure 10.1.

---

[1] Internet resources can change quickly. The ones included in this chapter may have changed since the time of writing. Also, it is important to critically evaluate Internet resources. Do not assume that because it is on the Internet (or in a book) that it ensures good practice.

FIGURE 10.1 Developmentally Appropriate Practice

The concept of developmentally appropriate practice was created to counteract the growing trend to use age-inappropriate practices with young children. The core considerations of DAP are

- **Age/Developmental appropriateness**—anticipating and responding to the age/developmental characteristics of children likely to influence the validity of assessment methods.

- **Individual appropriateness**—making curriculum choices and adaptations of assessment methods to provide optimal learning experiences for a particular child.

- **Cultural appropriateness**—considering what will make sense to a child given his or her linguistic and cultural background, as well as interpreting a child's behavior in light of the social and cultural contexts in which he or she lives.

- **Intentionality**—continuously adjusting, changing, and planning for experiences that will promote children's learning and development.

In terms of curriculum this means that teachers should . . .

- Meet children where they are—know them well—and enable them to reach goals that are both challenging and achievable.

- Engage in teaching practices that are appropriate to children's age and developmental status, be attuned to them as unique individuals and responsive to the social and cultural contexts in which they live.

- Ensure that goals and experiences are suited to children's learning and development, and challenge them enough to promote progress and interest—not make things "easy."

- Base practice on knowledge—not on assumptions—of how children learn and develop.

Source: Information from C. Copple & S. Bredekamp, *Developmentally Appropriate Practice in Early Childhood Programs*, 2009.

Curriculum is also a product of its time. Educational values and practices are influenced by social and political forces. For example, in the early years of the 20th century, when many immigrants were arriving in the United States, a strong curricular emphasis was placed on the acquisition of American language, culture, and values. In the years following World War II, curriculum reflected the value that society placed on nuclear families. Today's curriculum mirrors the cultural diversity that is prevalent and more valued today than in the past. It also echoes our society's increasing concerns with violence, values, young children's readiness for school, standards, and the acquisition of basic content, especially literacy. Tomorrow's curriculum will address these and new concerns in ways that we may not anticipate today.

We can think of these changes as an "educational pendulum" that swings between emphasis on the nature and interests of the learner and emphasis on the subject matter to be taught. Each swing reflects a reaction of people to perceptions of the shortcomings of the current educational approach. Early childhood educators have long been committed to providing experiences that are meaningful, that engage children, that develop their curiosity, and that support positive attitudes about learning and school. They embrace the idea that learning should be a joyful and meaningful experience for children, and this makes them different from many other educators.

The swinging pendulum of popular opinion has some important implications for you as a beginning early childhood educator. One implication is that you must be aware that there will be ongoing shifts in accepted views of curriculum and teaching during your career. For example, during the last years of the 20th century early childhood educators' views of developmentally appropriate practice had an impact on education, as part of a movement to focus school programs on the needs and interests of children. And predictably, in the early years of the 21st century the pendulum has swung the other way, to shift focus back toward content standards, accountability, test scores, and less child-sensitive practice. We are happy to say that as we write, we sense another shift about to move back toward child-centered practice. Just remember—if you find yourself disagreeing with today's outlook on education, you are likely to find yourself agreeing with the views that will be favored in another 5 or 10 years (and vice versa, of course).

Knowledge is powerful. When you know about arts, sciences, and humanities and you understand how young children learn, then you are able to make more informed assessments of new views of early childhood curriculum. We urge you to keep an open mind so that you can learn, but to have a healthy sense of skepticism. You can rely on the combination of what research tells us about how children learn and your own observations. Your own stance will then be firm enough to withstand the inevitable shifts of popular opinion.

The second implication of the swinging pendulum of society's views on curriculum is the realization that early childhood education stands somewhat apart from vacillating popular opinion. Respect for the individual, a belief in the value of play, and a vision of education as helping children to become self-directed and creative are consistent beliefs that have guided early childhood educators over time. You can hear this view in the words of the historical founders of our field:

> *The proper education of the young does not consist in stuffing their heads with a mass of words, sentences, and ideas dragged together out of various authors, but in opening up their understanding to the outer world, so that a living stream may flow from their own minds, just as leaves, flowers, and fruit spring from the bud on a tree.*
>
> *John Amos Comenius,* Didactica Magna (The Great Didactic)

> *Play is the highest expression of human development in childhood for it alone is the free expression of what is in a child's soul.*
>
> *Friedrich Froebel,* The Education of Man, *1885*

> *While devoted deeply to the growth of ideas and concepts, you have similarly consistently shown that education must plan equally for physical, social, and emotional growth.*
>
> *James Hymes,* speech to National Association for Nursery Education, *1947*

Our goal is to help you learn to design curriculum that reflects these views. As you develop your own educational philosophy, we hope that you will see yourself as part of a long line of educators who put children first.

Reflect on the curriculum of the schools you attended

What was taught in the schools of your childhood? What do you remember most about the curriculum? When were you motivated to learn more? Do any of these experiences influence you today? What are the implications of these experiences for you as an early childhood educator?

How Children Learn

Early childhood teachers need to know about young children and how they learn in order to design and implement meaningful and appropriate learning experiences for them. They need to understand that all aspects of development are interdependent. This means that curriculum subjects are not distinct entities, but rather natural parts of the life of the child. A few basic principles that guide early childhood teaching are outlined in Figure 10.2.

FIGURE 10.2   Principles of Early Childhood Teaching

> **Principle #1: Children learn by doing**—through play and through concrete, sensory experience. Concepts are learned best when they are directly experienced.
>
> **Principle #2: Children learn best when they have many direct experiences with the world around them.** Real experience through trips, visitors, and real-world activities are essential for learning.
>
> **Principle #3: Children need to reflect on their actions and experiences** by playing, painting, building, singing, dancing, and discussing their observations and experiences. This is how they *reconstruct* their experiences and *construct* concepts (see Figure 10.3).
>
> **Principle #4: Children formulate concepts over time and through repeated experiences.** Teachers who understand how children learn are careful to plan so that children can repeat experiences many times.
>
> **Principle #5: Each child learns in a unique way and at an individual pace,** so we must teach them in diverse ways. Children learn best when they can choose activities that are appropriate and meaningful to them.
>
> **Principle #6: Children learn best when adults provide support** to help them become more capable. Your job as a teacher is to know many ways to provide support, observe with an open mind and heart, and provide the support needed for each individual child.
>
> **Principle #7: Children learn best when there is communication and consistency between home and school.** When you involve families in the curriculum, you make it meaningful.

Source: Information from E. Moravcik, S. Nolte, & S. Feeney, *Meaningful Curriculum for Young Children*, 2013.

Curriculum in Early Childhood Education

Young children are learning all the time, from all their experiences, both in and out of school. Early childhood educators need to ask themselves, "How, when, and in what ways do I want to participate in this natural process?" Because children are so interested in the world around them, the choices about the curriculum you provide in an early childhood program are almost infinite. Nevertheless, your choices must be thoughtful and appropriate for the children with whom you work.

What do early childhood educators teach? Every functioning adult knows more about the world than a young child. You have physical skills; you know how to take care of yourself and relate to others; you can read, write, and compute; you know things about science and nature, the structure of society, and the arts. You know how to find out the answers to questions. These things will help you to teach—but you need to know more than these basics to be an early childhood educator. You need to be educated. All early childhood college programs require that you study arts, sciences, and humanities because you need this broad education to effectively teach young children. You also need to know about children and how they learn so that you can design and implement meaningful and appropriate learning experiences. And you definitely need to understand curriculum content.

States and national organizations have created "content standards." These provide guidelines for selecting curriculum. Standards are almost universally available for teachers in K–12 programs and are also available for teachers in programs for 4-year-olds. Content standards can be controversial. However,

FIGURE 10.3   Flying Cockroach with Golden Wings (tissue paper collage)

they can provide important information to help you in the complex task of designing curriculum. In each section that follows we provide you with the addresses for the websites of some of the organizations that have created content standards. Because preschool content standards (often called early learning guidelines) vary from state to state, we provide you with a link to the National Child Care Information and Technical Assistance Center, which maintains a page to link to the guidelines for your state (nccic.acf.hhs.gov/resource/state-early-learning-guidelines). These content standards reflect what early childhood educators believe to be essential content for young children.

We are living at a time when standards drive much of what we do in education. When thoughtfully constructed and written well, standards can be useful at helping to identify what content is most useful and important to children at a particular age and stage of learning. However, it is valuable to remember that there are many things content standards do not address. All aspects of development are interdependent; curriculum areas are not distinct entities but natural parts of the life of the child. We agree with Lilian Katz, who suggests that a more appropriate approach would be to look at *standards of experience*. Katz suggests that we should ask ourselves if young children have frequent opportunities to experience things such as intellectual engagement, absorbing and challenging activities, taking initiative and accepting responsibilities, experiencing the satisfaction of overcoming obstacles and solving problems, and applying literacy and numeracy skills in purposeful ways (Katz, 2007).

> *The 4-year-old class took a trip to the zoo yesterday. Today Kurt, Shauna, Max, and Kauri go to the block area. Their teacher suggests that they might build the zoo. They create enclosures around the animals and make a path on which several dollhouse people are placed. Shauna picks up a zebra and puts it in with the lions and Kauri says, "NO! The lions will bite the zebras!" The two argue about the placement of the zebras. The teacher asks the children to think of some ways to put the lions and the zebras together so the zebras won't get hurt. The girls build a nearby enclosure for zebras. Kurt and Max create a wall of blocks that encircles the entire block area. Another child stumbles over it. Max and Kurt yell and the teacher asks, "What could you do so people would know that they should be more careful?" Max goes to the writing center and makes a sign that says ZU! STP! He tapes it to the wall and the teacher suggests that he tell the other children about the sign and what it means.*

These children were engaged in a planned inquiry activity designed to help them build an awareness of a social studies concept. But they were also engaged in a satisfying creative endeavor during which they were building motor coordination, using language, developing social problem-solving abilities, and gaining literacy skills.

> *On a hot, sunny day on the toddler playground, Georgia, the teacher, brings a bucket full of crushed ice and dumps it in the water table. Immediately Sango, Noah, and two other children rush to the table. Noah plunges his hands into the mountain of ice. His eyes widen. Georgia, who is crouched near the children, says, "It's really cold!" As the group plays, Sango stands hesitantly a foot away. Georgia says, "You can touch it, Sango." Noah finds a cup that Georgia has placed nearby and scoops the ice and dumps it into a pail also conveniently set nearby. He scoops and scoops until the pail is*

full. Sango picks up a tiny scrap of ice and holds it in her hands. In a few seconds it is nothing but a drop of water. Sango looks at Georgia, who says, "What happened to the ice?" Sango says, "Wada." "Your ice melted into water," Georgia expands. Meanwhile Noah is placing little hills of ice on the sidewalk that quickly melt away.

Just like the 4-year-olds, these toddlers were engaged in a planned discovery activity. They were using their senses, building physical coordination, and learning concepts about the world. Their learning was skillfully guided by a teacher who knows about how toddlers learn. In addition, they were developing language, confidence, and a sense of self-reliance.

It is morning work time in the kindergarten class. Five children are working on their hundredth day collections (making trays with 100 things on them). Four more are constructing a block model of the path from their classroom to the cafeteria. Two sit on pillows in the library corner, reading books. Two more are finishing their morning journal assignment. One is painting using watercolors. Kit and Sierra are examining Checkers, a tortoise that was recently added to the classroom discovery center. They are looking at a book on tortoises. They ask Ms. Narvaez, their teacher, "Can Checkers eat hamburger?" She says, "That's a good question. I see you have the tortoise book. What did you find out?" The children continue searching with some guidance from Ms. Narvaez. When the book fails to answer the question, she asks them to write their question on a chart hanging in the discovery area. The class will try to find out the answer in some other way.

The skillful design of curriculum includes ensuring that in addition to planned activities there will be time, space, and interesting things to explore. Ms. Narvaez clearly knows that children can be self-directed learners. She has structured the environment, the time, the relationships, and the planned learning experiences to help these 5- and 6-year-olds to develop knowledge and skills in math, science, social studies, language, literacy, and art. Perhaps more important, she is helping them to become active, collaborative learners with a disposition to inquire.

Curriculum includes opportunities for learning that you will provide as choices in your program. It also includes the guided activities that you will implement with individual children and the whole group to help them learn. The planned curriculum can address all domains of development and it can be designed to help children develop understanding and skill in one or more subject areas (e.g., math, literature, art). Each subject area in the early childhood curriculum can contribute to all domains of the child's development but can be seen as primarily emphasizing one or two areas as illustrated in Figure 10.4. In this chapter we will talk about subject areas in clusters that relate to each domain of development.

Each curriculum area is a specialty in itself that takes study to master. You may have an area that is your forte, in which you have particular talent or skill, and other areas in which you feel less sure teaching. This should not stop you from planning and teaching every curriculum area, because each has value for children. Each early childhood teacher is, of necessity, a "general practitioner" in the art and science of teaching. You can use your skill in one area to teach content with which you are less comfortable. An excellent storyteller with a math

FIGURE 10.4 **Curriculum Contributions to Development**

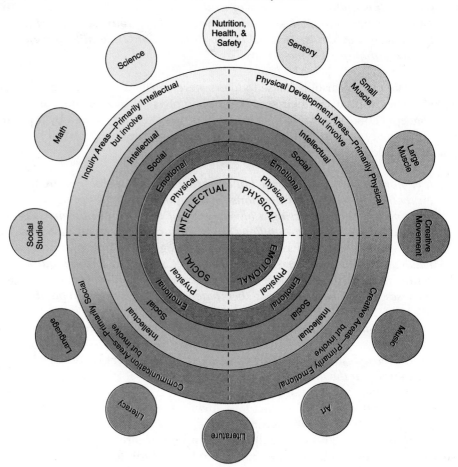

phobia, for example, might teach children, and overcome his or her own fears, by finding ways to incorporate math in storytelling!

Throughout this chapter we provide you with lists of practical, "teacher-friendly" books and websites that have articles, position statements, links, and practical information on each broad area of curriculum. (See Figure 10.5.)

CONNECTING WITH FAMILIES

About Curriculum

Families can contribute to the curriculum. They can be your partners. Invite families to participate in the curriculum. Survey incoming families to find out their skills and interests. Then invite them to come as honored guests to cook a dish, tell a story, teach a song, or demonstrate a skill. Those who prefer to work behind the scenes can make play dough, borrow books from the library, and sew pillows for the book corner. Find ways to regularly and meaningfully involve them in their children's learning.

FIGURE 10.5 **Teacher-Friendly Curriculum Books and Useful Websites**

BOOKS

Basics of Developmentally Appropriate Practice, by Carol Copple & Sue Bredekamp (NAEYC)

The Creative Curriculum for Preschool (5th ed.) and *The Creative Curriculum for Infants and Toddlers* (2nd ed.), by Diane Dodge et al. (Teaching Strategies)

Developmentally Appropriate Practice in Early Childhood Programs (3rd ed.), by Sue Bredekamp & Carol Copple (eds.) (NAEYC)

Explorations with Young Children, by Ann Mitchell & Judy David (eds.) (Gryphon House)

Learning Together with Young Children: A Curriculum Framework for Reflective Teachers, by Deb Curtis & Margie Carter (Redleaf Press)

Enthusiastic and Engaged Learners: Approaches to Learning in the Early Childhood Classroom, by Marylou Hyson (Teachers College Press)

The Intentional Teacher: Choosing the Best Strategies for Young Children's Learning, by Ann Epstein (NAEYC)

Meaningful Curriculum for Young Children, by Eva Moravcik, Sherry Nolte, & Stephanie Feeney (Pearson)

A Practical Guide to Early Childhood Curriculum, by Claudia Eliason & Loa Jenkins (Pearson)

Tools of the Mind: The Vygotskian Approach to Early Childhood Education, by Elena Bodrova & Deborah Leong (Pearson)

WEBSITES

Association for Childhood Education International—for teachers of children birth through early adolescence, with a focus on primary school children: www.acei.org

National Association for the Education of Young Children—includes an online interactive magazine for teachers; has reliable information in keeping with best practices: www.naeyc.org

Southern Early Childhood Association—includes teacher tips and curriculum ideas: www.southernearlychildhood.org

Thinkfinity.org—has free, comprehensive, standards-based K–12 lesson plans, materials, tools, and reference materials reviewed by education organizations (AAAS, IRA, NCTE, NCTM, NCEE, etc.): www.thinkfinity.org

British Association for Early Childhood Education: www.early-education.org.uk

Canadian Child Care Federation: www.cccf-fcsge.ca

Early Childhood Australia: www.earlychildhoodaustralia.org.au

New Zealand Child Care Association (Te Tari Puna Ora o Aotearoa): www.nzchildcare.ac.nz

Early childhood educators of other nations also have associations with online curriculum resources. Here are a few you may wish to explore:

Association for Early Childhood Educators (Singapore): aeces.org

European Early Childhood Education Research Association (EECERA): eecera.org

Learning and Teaching Scotland: ltscotland.org.uk

The Physical Development Curriculum

And look at your body . . . what a wonder it is! Your legs, your arms, your cunning fingers, the way they move.

Pablo Casals

The body is a young child's connection to the world. Sensory and motor development are prerequisite to many areas of competence. To learn to read and write, children must first develop the ability to make fine visual and auditory discriminations. To play an instrument or use a computer requires fine motor skill that emerges from practice in the control of the muscles of the fingers and hands. To discover that blue and yellow paint mix together to make green requires eyes that see, and fingers that respond. To discover that you can see the ocean from the top of a nearby hill may require a hike and strength and stamina. To appreciate the order and beauty of the world, children must be able to experience it with their senses.

The ways in which you provide the physical curriculum will have distinctive qualities and challenges depending on the age of the children, the place where you work, and the culture and values of the families.

Large Motor Curriculum

Movement is central to the lives of young children. The large muscle (or gross motor) curriculum—the part of the program concerned with the development of arms, legs, and torso—helps children gain and maintain physical skills and abilities as they work and play. It is also an intrinsic part of every other domain of development. Children must learn to move, and must also move in order to learn.

Physical activity is essential for lifelong health. In the past it was assumed that physical inactivity and its attendant health problems—obesity, diabetes, high blood pressure, cancer—were of concern only in adults. Today these are also problems in children, including children under the age of 6 (Ogden & Carroll, 2010). Attention span and concentration increase as children use their bodies in challenging physical movement. Exercise helps to release tension and promotes relaxation. Children's early physical development experiences influence how competent they feel and whether they will enjoy physical activity throughout their lives. Large muscle curriculum activities help children develop greater strength and endurance, retain flexibility, and develop coordination and agility.

There are predictable patterns in children's development of large muscle skill. *Strength* and *stamina* (the capacity for the sustained use of strength) increase with age. Older children generally are stronger and have greater endurance. *Flexibility* (ease and range of movement) lessens with age as the muscle system becomes less elastic. Infants easily bring toes to mouth, but this flexibility wanes as children get older. *Coordination*—the ability to move body parts in relation to one another—grows with experience. *Agility*—the ability to move with control

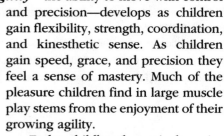

and precision—develops as children gain flexibility, strength, coordination, and kinesthetic sense. As children gain speed, grace, and precision they feel a sense of mastery. Much of the pleasure children find in large muscle play stems from the enjoyment of their growing agility.

Early childhood curriculum includes helping children develop fundamental or basic movement skills. Movement skills to transport a child from one place to another are called *locomotor*. Movement skills that involve bending, balancing, and twisting while staying in one spot are called *non-locomotor*. Another category of large motor skills developed during

early childhood years involves the use of arms, hands, and feet to move objects like balls. These are called *object control skills*.

It used to be considered sufficient physical development curriculum to send young children outside to play and occasionally organize a game of Duck, Duck, Goose. Today we know we can do much more to help young children become physically fit and competent individuals who have a positive attitude toward physical activity. Children need time for large motor play several times a day. They need optimal challenge—equipment, materials, and activities that provide the right degree of difficulty—to develop the skill that is just within their reach. The National Association for Sport and Physical Education (NASPE) recommends that preschoolers engage in unstructured physical activity whenever possible, (NASPE, 2004). The Council on Physical Education for Children (COPEC) recommends 30 to 60 minutes daily. We believe that preschool children should have significant blocks of time (45 minutes to an hour) daily for vigorous physical activity, in both the morning and the afternoon, and not be sedentary for more than one hour at a time. In addition to providing time for unstructured large motor play, all programs for young children should include guided large motor activity. NASPE recommends daily structured physical activity for preschool children and suggests structured physical education totaling 150 minutes per week for elementary age children (NASPE, 2004).

As a teacher in a preschool or kindergarten you will have a good deal of responsibility for planning and providing these opportunities. As a teacher in a primary school you may have less control and responsibility. Eliminating recess—as is being done in some elementary schools to create more time for "work"—deprives children of needed opportunities for physical activity. In a nation in which obesity and inactivity are epidemic, even among children, this trend is foolish.

Many children develop physical competence from their self-directed play, but others need encouragement and support. All direct physical training and intervention needs to be carried out in pleasurable play situations so that the child's attitude will be positive and physical activity will be gratifying. Children may be discouraged if you are overly concerned about safety. If children are willing to attempt using a piece of equipment, they can usually manage it if you are prepared to provide careful supervision and occasional assistance and instruction.

Teaching young children to develop large muscle skills does not mean physical education as you remember it. Instead, children need teachers who know to place a toy just out of reach when they are learning to crawl; hold their hands as they struggle to take their first steps; sing as they play ring-around-the-rosy; follow as they play Follow the Leader; explain the rules of Red Rover; toss a ball as they learn to bat; and share their triumph as they learn to climb a rope or use a hula hoop. By encouraging and playing *with* children, you support their activity and provide a model of an adult who is physically active—a powerful demonstration that being active is natural and pleasurable. Adult-led activities like creative movement, simple yoga, group games, and exercises provide focused practice in developing physical competencies. All children, not just those who are physically competent, will participate if you minimize competition and win-lose situations in games and other physical activities. Cooperative games that do not focus on winners and losers are particularly appropriate for young children and encourage children who are reluctant to participate for fear of losing.

Fine Motor Curriculum

Learning to coordinate the hands and fingers begins when babies in their cribs reach out to feel, grasp, and manipulate. Those initial impulses will eventually

Reflect on your school experiences with physical education

Remember a time when you were a child in a physical education class in school. Why do you remember this experience? How did the teacher encourage or discourage you? Did you feel successful in physical education or unsuccessful? What physical activity do you do as an adult? Did your childhood experience influence this in any way?

lead to the competent use of tools such as spoons, crayons, hammers, pens and pencils, and keyboards. Fine motor skills are the ability to control fingers, hands, and arms. These skills include reaching, grasping, manipulating objects, and using different tools like crayons and scissors. Fine motor (or small muscle) curriculum involves activities that build control, agility, strength, and coordination of the hands, fingers, wrists, and arms. Fine motor skills work in concert with brain development. As fine motor skills develop, neural pathways spread, making the brain more complex and flexible. There is research to suggest that children's fine motor skills relate to cognitive skills and can predict reading, mathematics and general school achievement (West, Denton, & Germino-Hausken, 2000).

Time, practice, and many experiences are required to develop fine motor competence. These skills involve sensory and muscular interplay—hand-eye coordination and coordination of the two hands. Children growing up with normal abilities and opportunities to use their hands develop the strength, coordination, and agility required to do most small muscle activities.

The fine motor curriculum is a part of many other curriculum areas that require the controlled use of hands and fingers. It can be helpful to think about some categories of activities and skills in order to plan specifically for small muscle development.

As with every other area of curriculum, teachers support fine motor development when they understand development, observe children, and are sensitive to individual differences. They interpret each child's level of development and provide materials and activities that present optimal challenge. Fine motor skills include the development of grasp, eye-hand coordination, finger dexterity (quickly moving fingers to pick up small objects, press, or tap), in-hand manipulation (positioning and moving an object within one hand), and hand or bilateral coordination (moving both hands together). Three aspects of fine motor development are often given consideration in fine motor curriculum for hand preference, the ability to use a pencil (called "pencil grasp"), and the ability to use scissors. Figure 10.6 describes these.

It is essential that children have materials and adequate time to engage with them using their small muscles. Puzzles, manipulative toys, table games, drawing and painting, sensory activities like playing with play dough, woodworking, blocks, and daily living activities all help children develop small motor skills. Primary school children continue to enjoy manipulative toys but may be more motivated by more productive, grown-up, fine motor activities like cooking, crafts, and woodworking.

If a child becomes frustrated or bored with a small muscle activity you can support his or her continued involvement by offering assistance, encouragement, or a different challenge. For example, if a child is having trouble cutting, you might say, "I see that paper is hard to cut. Would you like to use construction paper? Maybe it won't flop so much." You might also be sure to stock the shelf with a variety of different weights of paper and see whether more functional scissors are needed.

It is important to design experiences that will build prerequisite skills for more challenging small motor tasks such as cutting. The child who hasn't yet mastered scissors needs plenty of grasping, tension/release, coordination, and strength-building experiences. Providing dough and clay to build strength and tools such as tongs, hole punches, tweezers, and staplers that require similar

Reflect on your fine motor skills

What is your most highly developed fine motor skill? Is it something you do for work (like using a computer keyboard), for pleasure (like knitting), or for daily living (like cooking)? How did you develop the fine motor coordination for doing this? Trace your fine motor history back to the experiences in your childhood that led to your development of this ability.

FIGURE 10.6 Three Fine Motor Abilities

Hand Preference: Around 2 years of age hand preference emerges, though children frequently alternate hands. By 3, one hand will often lead activities and the other hand will assist. Though some switching will continue, by age 4 a strong preference for a lead and dominant hand is clear. Between 4 and 6 years, hand preference will be consistent and the roles of lead and assist hands established. The skill of the dominant hand will exceed the nondominant hand.

Grasp: By 4 months babies gain control over their arms and progress from reaching with both hands to reaching with one hand. They become capable of grasping and holding objects and can squeeze and hold objects in a closed fist. By 6 months they can pick up small items and by 12 months can hold small objects between their thumbs and index fingers, transfer objects from one hand to the other, and release objects voluntarily. At 12 months babies can make marks with crayons and markers, stack toys, turn pages, and roll a ball. Between 1 and 2 years they begin to move fingers independently and can poke and point. When using crayons they use whole-arm movements and hold a crayon in a closed fist with thumb pointing up. By 2 years of age coloring progresses from circular scribbles to horizontal or vertical scribbles and a crayon or pencil is held with fingers pointing toward the paper—called a *pronated grasp*. Between 3 and 4 years children hold a crayon in their lead hand while the assist hand stabilizes the paper. By 4 years of age, many children hold crayons pinched between thumb and index fingers, resting on their middle finger like most adults—called a *tripod*, *mature*, or *efficient pencil grasp*.

Scissors: At 2 years children use both hands to open and close scissors. By 3 years most can snip paper with the scissors in one hand and can cut a piece of paper into two pieces, but cannot cut along a line. By age 4 children typically move the scissors in a forward direction and can cut along a straight line and along simple curves with the assist hand turning the paper. By 5 years most children make smaller, more precise cuts and are be able to cut out simple straight-edged shapes. When they cut, they hold the scissors in a thumbs-up position perpendicular to the floor. By age 6 most children hold scissors in a mature fashion.

Source: Summarized from Skill Builders Pediatric Occupational Therapy, *Fine Motor Development 0 to 6 Years*, 2008. Used with permission.

motor action will contribute to this emerging skill. You may sometimes need to demonstrate and instruct to help children learn complex fine motor skills.

Sensory Development Curriculum

Learning depends on sensory input—hearing, smelling, seeing, touching, moving, and tasting. We are not born with the ability to fully discriminate sensations but must learn to distinguish them. If a child's ability to receive and use sensory input is impeded, normal development may be delayed. In addition to helping children learn, the senses are the source of appreciation and pleasure. For all of these reasons, early childhood programs should include a strong sensory component.

Two related processes are needed for receiving and organizing sensory data. The first is *sensation*, that is, stimulation of the sensory receptors—eyes, ears, skin, etc. The second is *perception*, the process of attending to, discriminating, and interpreting sensation based on past experiences. The brain then *integrates* the information that comes from the senses and uses it in a wide array of physical and cognitive tasks.

The sense we most commonly associate with learning is *sight*, and like other senses it requires opportunities for practice. In the early years children learn to see details (*acuity*), follow (*track*) and recognize objects at different angles (*constancy*) and in three dimensions (*spatial orientation*), judge distance (*depth perception*), distinguish an object from its background (*figure-ground perception*), and visually direct movement (*visual motor coordination*). The auditory sense, *hearing*, involves learning to screen and attend—to exclude irrelevant sounds and pay attention to what is meaningful. In addition children learn to tell where sound is coming from (*localization*), and hear differences between sounds (*discrimination*). The *kinesthetic* sense is an internal awareness of movement and position, which children develop as they learn to crawl, walk, jump, climb, and establish and maintain balance. It includes the ability to detect differences in weight, force, distance, and speed (*discrimination*), as well as *body, spatial,* and *directional awareness*. The sense of *touch* is a primary mode of learning as well as a dominant aspect of our lives. *Localization* (identifying where a touch occurs on the body) and *discrimination* (differentiating stimulation) are two tactile abilities that young children acquire. We make many decisions based on the sense of *smell;* even newborns are highly sensitive to some smells. The sense of *taste* provides information about a few qualities: sweet, salty, sour, bitter, and *umami* or savory. The sense of taste, combined with smell, provides a critical guide to the edibility of food (poisonous plants are bitter; fruit is sweet; salt is appealing).

To support the development of the senses, make sure that you regularly provide experiences that use and develop each one. However, it is important to realize that senses are integrated, not isolated.

> The "Elephant Groovers" (a group of 3-year-olds) are involved in making banana pancakes. Sheyden touches the flour and salt as he pours it in. Torie smells the banana as she peels it. Emily experiences resistance when she stirs the batter. Keila comments on the bubbles she sees forming as air is beaten in. Their teacher, Jackie, says, "Listen to the sizzle as batter is poured in the pan." And all of the Elephant Groovers eat the finished product with gusto, commenting on its warmth and delicious taste.

Which sense was being developed? To separate these individual sensations would be difficult and unnecessary. The children learned from the entire experience.

Children are developing their senses as they paint; manipulate clay and dough; play in sand, water, and mud; feel the shape, weight, and texture of blocks; observe fish in the aquarium; feel the rabbit's fur and its heart beating; listen to stories; move to music; sort objects by shape, color, and size; and cook, taste, and discuss what they have made. The play activities that abound in good early childhood classrooms offer many opportunities for sensory development. You can provide space and materials that can be fully explored and help children focus on sensory experiences (see Figure 10.7). For example, you might help children to notice the sensory qualities of the pancake batter by saying things like "How does it smell as it cooks?" "What do you notice when you mash the banana?" and "Can you think of something else that tastes like this?"

Although sensory development is vital to children's learning it is not often addressed in content standards for older children. In early learning guidelines it is included either in physical development or science standards.

Figure 10.8 lists some books and websites that can help you learn more about the physical development curriculum.

To understand how the physical development curriculum is addressed in standards check out your state's early learning guidelines (accessible through nccic.acf.hhs.gov/resource/state-early-learning-guidelines) or the National Standards for Physical Education for K–3 (aahperd.org/naspe/standards).

FIGURE 10.7 **Materials to Explore and Pour in Sensory Table**

- Sand—dry or wet
- Water—plain or with added color, aroma, soap
- Ice—blocks, crushed, with salt

- Mud
- Whipped soap or shaving cream
- Aquarium gravel (inappropriate for infants and toddlers)

- Birdseed
- Recycled dried coffee grounds
- Cornstarch and water
- Flour, rice, or beans*

Other activities with a strong sensory component:

- Finger painting
- Collage
- Play dough
- Claywork
- Using musical instruments
- Cooking

- Tasting—compare different varieties of one thing such as cheese, apples, bread, vegetables
- Gardening
- Almost any field trips but especially to natural environments (e.g., a field, the beach, forest)

* The use of food as a sensory exploration material is controversial. It is accepted practice in some programs and with some families. It is banned and highly offensive to others. It is inappropriate in any program in which families struggle financially to put food on the table or where any family feels it violates their values.

FIGURE 10.8 **Books and Websites on Physical Development Curriculum**

BOOKS

Active for Life: Developmentally Appropriate Movement Programs for Young Children, by Stephen W. Sanders (NAEYC)

Active Start: A Statement of Physical Activity Guidelines for Children Birth to Five Years, by the National Association for Sport and Physical Education (Author)

Essential Touch: Meeting the Needs of Young Children, by Frances M. Carlson (NAEYC)

Follow Me Too: A Handbook of Movement Activities for Three- to Five-Year-Olds, by Marianne Torbert & Lynne B. Schneider (NAEYC)

Jump, Wiggle, Twirl & Giggle!, by Roberta Altman (Bank St. College and Scholastic Books)

Movement-Based Learning: Academic Concepts and Physical Activity for Ages Three through Eight, by Rhonda L. Clements & Sharon L. Schneider (National Association for Sport and Physical Education)

Mud, Sand, and Water (rev. ed.), by Dorothy M. Hill (NAEYC)

The Outside Play and Learning Book: Activities for Young Children, by Karen Miller (Gryphon House)

Developmental Physical Education for All Children, by D.L. Gallahue & F.C. Donnelly (Human Kinetics)

Experiences in Movement, by Rae Pica (Delmar)

Hand Function in the Child: Foundations for Remediation, by A. Henderson & C. Pehoski (Mosby)

Lifelong Motor Development (4th ed.), by C. P. Gabbard (Benjamin Cummings/Pearson Education)

More Than Graham Crackers, by N. Wanamaker, K. Hearn, & S. Richarz (NAEYC)

Woodworking for Young Children, by Patsy Skeen et al. (NAEYC)

WEBSITES

American Alliance for Health, Physical Education, Recreation and Dance: www.aahperd.org/naspe

Skill Builders Pediatric Occupational Therapy: www.skillbuildersonline.com

Appropriate Practices in Movement Programs for Young Children Ages 3–5 Recreation & Dance: cahperd.org/cms-assets/documents/ToolKit/NASPE_ApprroPrac/5286-668190.children3to5approprac.pdf

Occupational Therapy—Kids Health Information: In-Hand Manipulation: www.rch.org.au/emplibrary/ot/InfoSheet_D.

The Smell Report, an Overview of Facts and Findings: sirc.org/publik/smell.pdf

Taste, Our Body's Gustatory Gatekeeper: dana.org/news/cerebrum/detail.aspx?id=788

Teaching Left-Handers How to Write. Handedness Research Institute Papers: handedness.org/action/leftwrite.html

The Communication Curriculum

Talking with one another is loving one another.

African proverb

To understand the world and function in it, we need to be able to communicate with others. Learning language is one of the characteristics that unites people and one of our most important challenges. *Language* (both talking and listening) is of primary importance in the communication curriculum. *Literacy* (the developmental process of learning to write and read) is the tool that extends language over distance and time. *Literature* is the art form that uses language. All are dependent on language.

The goal of the communication curriculum is to help children become enthusiastic, competent users of spoken and written language. Your job is to provide relationships that are filled with language in all its forms. As you speak to children honestly and respectfully and listen to them attentively, you will encourage language use. As you use language to mediate problems, communicate information, and share feelings and ideas, you will demonstrate the usefulness and value of oral language. As you sing songs, tell jokes, recite rhymes and poems, and play verbal games with children, you help them to find joy in talking. In a similar way the value of written language is demonstrated to children as you write a note, a grocery list, or a thank-you letter, or read a recipe, story, poem, or book. And as you introduce children to many wonderful children's books you will give them a gift and an appreciation that they will carry throughout their lives.

States have developed language arts early learning guidelines (links at nccic.acf.hhs.gov/resource/state-early-learning-guidelines) and there are Common Core Standards in the language arts for kindergarten through twelfth grade (corestandards.org/the-standards/english-language-arts-standards).

Reflect on communicating as a child

Remember yourself as a young child. Was it easy for you to talk to other people, or did you feel shy or uncomfortable? When, where, and with whom did you feel most comfortable expressing yourself? Why? How did your family or teachers support you or discourage you from communicating?

Language Curriculum

Learning to understand and use language is one of the most significant accomplishments of early childhood. Almost all children acquire language at about the same age and in about the same way, whatever their language or culture, without any formal teaching. It is a skill that appears to be "caught, not taught." As they forge their language, children develop an inseparable part of themselves, as well as a tool for communication, self-expression, and learning.

Both the developmental stage and the desire to communicate influence language learning. Children learn the complex structure, rules, and meanings of language and develop the ability to create speech through processes that are still not completely understood. Young children learn customs for language in their homes and communities. They learn to select appropriate speech for different settings and people: in the classroom; on the playground; to a friend, parent, or teacher. Very early they learn to include nonverbal features (gestures, facial expressions, intonation) in speaking. They come to understand the expectations and signals for turn-taking in conversations. These unspoken ways of communicating are highly dependent on culture. Some of the children you teach will come from families for whom English is not the home language; they are referred to as *English language learners* (ELLs), English as a second language students (ESLs), or emergent bilinguals (EBs).

In a culturally diverse society young children in a group may have different nonverbal customs, such as whether to make eye contact during conversations with adults. Part of your role requires sensitivity to and respect for these kinds of communication differences. Hesitant or shy children, those who have less home language experience, or those who speak a different language at home than at school may require a longer time to become full participants in the language life of the classroom. It is important to be sensitive to these differences and give these children time and lots of opportunities to speak.

In early childhood programs, language is taught in both incidental and planned activities. It is primarily taught through language-rich relationships. When you have conversations with young children you are teaching language. When you play with children, listen to their ideas, lead games, sing songs, tell stories, and recite poems, you are teaching language. Language learning is also part of structured group activities such as discussions that are included in most preschool, kindergarten, and primary school programs.

As you teach young children, you help them to unconsciously master five aspects of language: (1) *syntax* or *grammar,* the "rules" of language; (2) *morphology,* the structure of words and adding suffixes and prefixes; (3) *semantics,* the meaning of words; (4) *phonology,* the sounds of words; and (5) *pragmatics*, the social conventions of language. Children learn language by hearing you speak clear, grammatically correct, rich language and by talking with you and with one another—not from drill or correction. As children hear language, they internalize rules and apply them in their speech. Mistakes like *knowed* and *eated* show that they understand rules about past tense and can apply them. When you speak clearly, they hear the distinct sounds of words. As they encounter new words, they add them to their vocabulary. As they engage with you and other children, they learn the many ways to use language in social settings and learn the pragmatics of school language.

You will not actually instruct children in a subject called "language" (a discipline studied by linguists and other scholars). Instead you will help children develop language by **modeling** and **interacting** as well as in **planned activities**. Children need a chance to express their ideas, to tell about the things they know and that are important to them. This helps them to learn to talk and to make sense of their experiences. You do this when you ask questions, listen carefully to what children say, and take time to respond their questions. They acquire and build language in **conversations**. What is a conversation? It is an exchange of ideas, a dialogue. Because there are more children and fewer adults, there are fewer opportunities for conversation in early childhood programs than in most homes. In language-rich homes, conversations are complex and are related to the child's life. By contrast, conversations in most schools tend to be brief, less complex, and more adult-oriented. It is important to know *how* to have conversations with children, and to *do so* regularly with every child. Like all conversations, a dialog with a young child involves mutual interests and requires you have a topic and take turns. It is different because of experience, size, status, and skills. It is an art that you will develop with experience. (See the accompanying "Golden Rules for Having a Conversation with a Young Child.") As you have conversations with children you will help them learn to **use abstract language** or *decontextualized* speech: talking about ideas and experiences that are not present—people,

GOLDEN RULES FOR HAVING A CONVERSATION WITH A YOUNG CHILD

1. **Crouch or sit at the child's eye level.** This minimizes both the physical and social differences between an adult and child.
2. **Show attention physically as well as verbally.** Use eye contact, smiles, nods, a gentle hand on a shoulder or back.
3. **Take turns and participate.** Otherwise it's not a conversation.
4. **Read nonverbal communication.** Notice and put into words what you think the child is feeling and thinking: "It sounds like you're really happy." "That's very exciting." "It's a little scary."
5. **Respect the child's language.** Don't correct the child's speech or ideas. Don't hurry or interrupt. If you don't understand, say: "Show me." "Tell me more about that."
6. **Listen.** Focus on what the child says. Remember this is about the child, not about you. Ask clarifying questions. Help the child to extend: "What did your mom do when the eggs all spilled on the floor?"
7. **Select what to say carefully.** Make it brief and to the point—a child cannot concentrate for as long as an adult. Use a vocabulary that is simple but with a few words that are new and interesting.
8. **Remember, it's not a quiz or a lecture.** Questions can be conversation stoppers. Say simple things: "I like to do that too." "I didn't know that."

places, and events of past or future, imagined and actual.

As you plan for language, remember that all children have language facility you can nurture. Talk to them. Listen to them. Trust them. They need and want to communicate.

Literacy Curriculum

Reading and writing are facets of communication, tools to unlock ideas, and adventures. In everyday speech literacy means *the state of being able to read and write*. When educators talk about early literacy, they mean *the skills that are the foundation for reading and writing. Emergent literacy* is the evolving process by which children become literate. The period of emergent literacy encompasses the span "between birth and the time when children read and write in conventional ways" (Teale & Sulzby, 1986, 1).

Children who live in a print-filled world have early awareness of written language and develop concepts about it from an early age. Learning about reading and writing does not wait for children to be declared officially "ready." The foundations for making sense of written language start long before they receive formal teaching about it.

Unfortunately, many children do not learn to read with comfort and fluency. The Children's Defense Fund reports that 68% of the nation's fourth graders read below grade level (Children's Defense Fund, 2010), and a child who cannot read well by the end of third grade will be seriously disadvantaged throughout life. Early literacy experiences are critical. By providing children with thoughtfully planned language and literacy opportunities before first grade we are helping to prevent later reading problems. The accompanying box, "Golden Rules for Helping Children Develop Concepts About Print," offers some suggestions.

The stages of emergent literacy, like the stages of language development, occur in a predictable order and unfold according to an individual timetable. The phrase *literacy begins at birth* illuminates the idea that experiences in infancy with language, books, and reading are important parts of the process of becoming literate. Each child learns to read and write as an individual, putting together ideas in ways that make sense. The curriculum for literacy must be similarly individualized.

Your approach to teaching literacy will vary with children's developmental needs, family, and interests. The skills and knowledge that are foundational for reading and writing include ***oral language*** (ability to talk), ***vocabulary*** (knowledge of words), ***phonological awareness*** (realization that the sounds of words can be manipulated; e.g., initial sounds, rhyming words), ***alphabetic knowledge*** (familiarity with the shapes and sounds of letters and awareness that there is a relationship between letters and sounds), ***print knowledge*** (understanding rules about using print; e.g., we read from left to right, and that print is permanent, it always says the same thing), and ***book knowledge*** (how to use books). This knowledge is built through meaningful experiences, relevant to children's interests and experiences, and presented in ways that are engaging. Having children participate in word and letter drills, nonrelevant worksheets, and repetitive alphabet exercises usually lessens literacy learning rather than enhances it (Neuman & Roskos, 2005).

There is strong evidence to suggest that children who have lots of real-world experiences coupled with rich and varied language are more likely to become readers (Bowman, 2003). Experiences with functional print—using reading and writing as a tool and for pleasure is also important for literacy success. These experiences are sometimes referred to as "predictors" of reading success.

Children show their developing awareness of written language in many different ways. Some begin to take an interest in favorite storybooks as they read along, point to the print, or retell the story. Familiar books may be "read" to a group by a child who pretends to be the "teacher." Other children recognize or discuss the meanings of the signs or labels all around them—traffic signs, logos for products on packages, and in television advertising. Children's first interest is often in their own names, which they recognize and may wish to write, or they may print their initial. All of these provide you with evidence that print has been noticed and is being explored.

To support children in becoming literate requires a watchful eye and sensitive ear. Whatever the age of children you work with, it is also important that you visibly enjoy reading and writing yourself. Write and read in front of children often and comment on your use of books and writing as resources: "I wonder what ingredients we'll need for the lasagna. I'm going to look it up here in my cookbook. Oh, mozzarella cheese. I'd better write that down on our shopping list." Share your writing with children so they will begin to understand adult purposes for writing.

Every classroom needs many appealing books. Every child needs to be read to. Planned and spontaneous reading aloud to individuals, to a small group, and to the whole class is an essential part of every early childhood teacher's day.

Reflect on your ethical responsibilities

The administrator of your school has decided that the children in second grade will no longer be allowed to read picture books because she believes picture books do not promote reading skills. You believe this is inappropriate and will damage children's motivation to learn to read. Using the Guidelines for Ethical Reflection on page 23, reflect on your ethical responsibilities in this situation and think about an ethical response that you might make.

A program for even the youngest children should have books and words throughout. Your appreciation of children's literature and your visible enjoyment is one of the most important ways you demonstrate that reading is a worthwhile experience. The box "Golden Rules for Helping Children Develop Concepts About Print" includes ideas for how to put literacy into your daily life with children.

Literature Curriculum

Children who love books come to love reading. Children who have many positive experiences with literature come to love books. Literature is not merely the carrot with which we motivate children to read; in a real way, it is the most important reason for learning to read. Through good literature, children experience both language

GOLDEN RULES FOR HELPING CHILDREN DEVELOP CONCEPTS ABOUT PRINT

Read books joyfully, frequently, to the group, to individuals, every day, as often as you can.

1. Be bountiful. Fill the room with books, books, and more books—in the library and in other places that make sense.
2. Have favorites. Reread children's favorite stories over and over.
3. Let children help—once in a while let a child read the title, turn the page, read the story.
4. Show and talk about print in books, read the name of the author, comment on the style of the print, the words used, the parts of the book, even the punctuation.
5. Be playful—do silly things—turn the book upside down and talk about why it can't be read like that.

Use print often for authentic, practical reasons.

6. Communicate with print in front of children—to children, to parents, to other teachers, to people far away—write notes, write letters, make signs.
7. Remember with print. Model for the children—write lists, create recipes, write what you recall.
8. Learn with print in the presence of children—read directions, look things up, go to the encyclopedia, a cookbook, an informational book, or the Internet to read the answers to real questions.
9. Label the room—label shelves and containers, puzzles and games, charts and posters. Make signs that are permanent (The Block Area) and signs that are temporary (Bailey's Blocks—Please Don't Knock Them Down).

Encourage creativity with print.

10. Let them play—provide time, space and materials for writing. Make a writing center with lots of print to copy, cut, and play with.
11. Help them write—As individuals or as a group, write or dictate stories to illustrate and bind for the classroom library.
12. Appreciate their efforts, including scribble writing, pretend writing, and inventive spelling.

and art and learn about the world, themselves, and other people. It can provide information and motivate exploration, a concern for others, and a love of reading.

Young children are not able to purchase books or use the library on their own, so it is up to adults to present a range of quality literature from which children can make choices. As children's literature has become an accepted product, it has also become a vehicle for marketing. Most grocery stores, variety stores, and even bookstores have a shelf of children's books that accompany television shows and movies. These are advertisements, not literature, and do not belong in early childhood programs.

The sense of adventure that accompanies making a choice and opening a new book is what creates active, eager readers. All books for young children must respect childhood and children's lives. Every classroom needs a variety of different kinds of books that change regularly. The different kinds of books are called the *genres* of children's literature. These genres include fiction, informational books, mood and concept books, and collections of rhymes and poetry. Although it is certainly possible to read other kinds of books (especially to children in second and third grade), in the early childhood years we rely on picture books and oral literature.

Fiction, which includes fantasy, folklore, and realistic fiction, should create memorable, believable characters and the illusion of reality in time and place (even in a fantasy). The plot should encourage children to understand reasons behind events. The point of a good story need not be heavy-handed; stories that preach or devalue their experience will not appeal to children. To make all children feel included and support children's appreciation of the common humanity they share with others, provide books that include a range of diverse characters.

Fantasy has its own logic and rules that remain true for the story. An example of a great fantasy picture book is *Where the Wild Things Are* by Maurice Sendak. *Folklore* touches on themes and questions that have universal appeal and universal similarity—magic, good and evil, joy and sorrow, the origins of the world, and the people and animals that inhabit it. *Anansi the Spider* by Gerald McDermott is an example of folklore. *Realistic fiction* should have an affectionate, unsentimental voice. *When Sophie Gets Angry . . . Really, Really Angry* by Molly Bang is a good example of realistic fiction.

Informational books can broaden children's understanding of the world. To be appealing without being inaccurate is the great challenge of informational books for young children. To teach they must be factual. To enhance interest they must be well paced and skillful in their presentation. Illustrations help to convey more than the words alone can. *An Egg Is Quiet* by Dianna Hutts Aston and Sylvia Long is a lovely example of a good informational book for young children.

Mood and concept books sensitize children to ideas, feelings, and awareness. They include wordless books and books that use organizing concepts such as the alphabet. These books encourage children to think and use language. Concept books are most valuable when they provide a sense of joy and wonder in the world and are not used to drill children. *And Here's to You* by David Elliott and Randy Cecil is a good example of a concept book.

Collections of rhymes and poetry (like *My Very First Mother Goose* by Iona Opie and Rosemary Wells) and picture books that feature a single poem (like *The Owl and the Pussycat* by Edward Lear, illustrated by Jan Brett) belong in every program. Nursery rhymes and poetry present mood and melody in language in a natural and unforced manner. They help to enhance children's understanding of the world and develop their sensitivity to language. This heightened awareness of the sounds of language is an important precursor of literacy.

Good children's literature has the following qualities:

- It shows respect for the reader (is not condescending; does not stereotype by gender, race, culture, etc.).
- It is written and illustrated with care and craftsmanship. The language and illustrations are created with artistry and are appropriate to the content.
- It has integrity (honesty and truthfulness within the context of the story).
- It teaches by example—does not preach or moralize.
- It helps the reader to understand and feel more deeply.
- It interests and delights children—the children want you to read it again.
- It is not based on movies, TV shows, or other products—the purpose of these books is to promote a product and sell to children.

A literature-rich classroom has an extensive collection of high-quality books located throughout. Books may be presented in ways that make a connection to a topic (e.g., a set of books on friendship might be presented together). Time and space for children to interact with books is built into the environment and schedule. Daily story reading is a prominent part of the day in a literature-rich classroom.

In the past, children's literature failed to include minorities, individuals with disabilities, and other groups. If we are to lead all children to a love of reading, we need to include people who are like them. To help children appreciate the humanity they share with people who are different, they need books that include diversity. Make sure that the books you choose represent diverse ethnicities, lifestyles, cultures, appearances, race, ages, and activities.

Good programs provide large blocks of time each day during which children and teachers can read as well as a scheduled 10- to 20-minute story time at least twice in a full day. It is important to learn to read to children with skill and responsiveness and to design experiences to expand on literature. If you work with

GOLDEN RULES FOR READING A STORY TO A GROUP

1. Practice so that you know the story well and can pronounce all the words.
2. Sit close to the children on a low stool or chair so the children can see the book.
3. Focus the group with a song or finger-play or by showing the cover of the book and talking about it.
4. Have an alternative activity for young children or children with disabilities so they can leave if they get restless.
5. Use a natural voice and make sure to speak clearly and loud enough for the group to hear.
6. Be expressive—match your voice, volume, tempo, facial expression, pauses, and gestures to the content of the story.
7. Stick to the story—avoid asking many questions or interrupting with too many comments.
8. Pay attention to the children—make eye contact with them, notice their faces and bodies—have children move if they are restless—then continue reading.
9. Leave them wanting more—quit before children are tired, bored, and restless.

children younger than 3, it is best to read stories to individuals or groups of two or three. This is also usually the most comfortable when you first begin to read stories, even to older children. Reading a story to a group requires skill you will develop only through practice (see the accompanying "Golden Rules for Reading a Story to a Group").

Although reading is the most common way to share literature, a number of other techniques engage children and help them to build understanding of literature: telling a story without a book or using a prop such as a puppet or flannelboard story, having children act out stories, and listening to recordings of stories and poems. *Literature extensions*—for example, cooking oatmeal and waiting for it to cool after reading *Goldilocks and the Three Bears*—also help children understand a story.

Although children's literature can be expanded into many other areas of classroom life, it is important not to turn literature into reading texts or use it as a basis for worksheets and tests. When children's literature is "basalized" in this way, children's inherent love of books is in danger of being squelched.

Figure 10.9 (see page 362) lists some books and websites that will help you learn about the communication curriculum.

The Creative Arts Curriculum

Every child is an artist. The problem is how to remain an artist . . .

Pablo Picasso

The arts are vital in the development of children who can feel as well as think and who are sensitive and creative. Art, music, and creative movement help children to express their feelings, communicate ideas in new forms, and develop their senses. Creativity, or originality, is not restricted to artists or to people who have great talent or high intelligence. All people are creative when they put together what they know and produce an idea, process, or product that is new *to them*. Creativity in early childhood programs occurs as children engage with the arts. It also occurs in activities such as building with blocks and dramatic play. Through arts experiences, children come to:

- Feel good about themselves as individuals
- Develop the ability to observe and respond sensitively
- Develop creativity along with art, music, and movement skills
- Develop a beginning understanding of the arts disciplines
- Become appreciative of music, art, and dance from their own and other cultures, times, and places
- Construct understanding and communicate what they know
- Develop a way to express feelings and ideas

Understanding how young children develop helps you to provide a

FIGURE 10.9 **Books and Websites on Communication Curriculum**

BOOKS

Language

Learning to Listen and Listening to Learn, by Mary Jalongo (NAEYC)

Learning Language and Loving It, by Elaine Weitzman & Janice Greenberg (Hanen Centre)

One Child, Two Languages: A Guide for Early Childhood Educators of Children Learning English as a Second Language (2nd ed.), by Patton O. Tabors (Brookes)

Learning to Talk and Listen by the National Institute for Literacy: http://lincs.ed.gov/publications/pdf/LearningtoTalkandListen.pdf

Literacy

The Living Classroom: Writing, Reading, and Beyond, by David Armington (NAEYC)

Let's Begin Reading Right: A Developmental Approach to Emergent Literacy (6th ed.), by Marjorie V. Fields, Lois Groth, & Katherine L. Spangler (Pearson)

Much More Than the ABC's, by Judith Schickedanz (NAEYC)

Literacy and the Youngest Learner: Best Practices for Educators of Children from Birth to Five, by V. Susan Bennett-Armistead et al. (Scholastic)

Writing in Preschool: Learning to Orchestrate Meaning and Marks, by Judith Schickedanz (NAEYC)

Literature

The Important Books: Children's Picture Books as Art and Literature, by Joseph Stanton (Scarecrow Press)

Young Children and Picture Books, by Mary Renck Jalongo (NAEYC)

The Read Aloud Handbook, by Jim Trelease (Penguin)

Story Stretchers (3 versions: infants and toddlers, preschoolers, and primary); also *More Story Stretchers,* by S. Raines & R. J. Canaday (Gryphon House)

WEBSITES

ReadWriteThink: www.readwritethink.org

International Reading Association: www.reading.org

Children's Literature Network: childrensliteraturenetwork.org/index.php

Children's Literature Web Guide: people.ucalgary.ca/~dkbrown/index.html

Guide to Research in Children's and Young Adult Literature: library.illinois.edu/edx/edkclass.html

Vandergrift's Children's Literature Page: comminfo.rutgers.edu/professional-development/childlit/ChildrenLit

climate that supports creativity, imagination, and self-expression. Satisfying experiences with the arts occur when you understand what you can reasonably expect of children and when you provide activities that match their needs and abilities. When children's unique expressions are acknowledged, they become aware of their value as individuals, and their self-concept is enhanced.

> *Two-year-old Katie comes to the children's center with her mom for the first time. She is attracted to the easel and the brilliant colors of paint. Katie takes a brush full of magenta and paints a large blotch of color. A brush full of deep blue follows, then one of yellow and another of black. The dripping colors glisten wet and intense on the paper. Katie steps back, turns, then grins at her mom.*

For very young children like Katie, the most important aspects of the arts are the development of awareness, new skills, and feelings of self-worth. Your role is to provide an environment, materials, and experiences that support creative development and aesthetic appreciation. A classroom that provides for all of these needs has a creative climate—an atmosphere where expression is nurtured and where creativity can flourish.

It is not necessary for you to be an artist, dancer, or musician yourself to teach the arts to young children. It is necessary, however, to believe that experiences with and participation in art are valuable. It is also important to have a basic understanding of arts disciplines—that is, to understand the elements that make up each of the arts and to have a beginning understanding of the techniques that young children can learn. Because creative expression is an outgrowth of life, another aspect of your role is to provide experiences that heighten awareness and provide inspiration.

Creative expression is also stimulated by exposure to the arts. When children have opportunities to view artwork in public places, listen to music, and attend dance and drama productions, they begin to understand the appeal of the arts.

Through their artwork, children can disclose their ways of perceiving. They can risk this expression only if they feel safe, and encouraged. You support creativity by accepting *all* of the feelings and ideas that children create, whether or not they are "nice" or "pretty" by adult standards. Things that move children and adults are not always the most pleasant aspects of their lives. Nevertheless, if they have the power to evoke strong feelings, they are important parts of life and a part of their creative expression. For an example, see Figure 10.10.

To understand how arts curriculum is addressed in standards, check out your state's early learning guidelines (find a link at nccic.acf.hhs.gov/resource/state-early-learning-guidelines) or the Consortium of National Arts Education Associations Content Standards: K–4 (artsedge.kennedy-center.org/educators/standards.aspx)

Reflect on your experiences with the arts in school

Remember an experience with the arts that you had in school. How did your teacher support or discourage your creativity and individuality? How did this influence your feelings about yourself as an artist, musician, or dancer?

FIGURE 10.10   **My Mommy Is Mad at Me (drawing by a 4-year-old)**

FIGURE 10.11 **Crown Flowers with Caterpillars (ink and watercolor wash by a 4-year-old)**

Visual Art Curriculum

The visual art curriculum is the curriculum designed to help children gain a sense of themselves as artists and art appreciators. Art is a way to express feelings and understanding; it provides opportunities for children to explore and manipulate. It is a medium of learning and a medium of communication. Its sensory and physical nature makes art a form of play. As they mature, children use art to express ideas, but they continue to enjoy the satisfaction of "messing about" with materials. For very young children, *process* is the whole of the art experience and *product* is not important. Toddlers are unconcerned with their artwork after they are done. As children grow older, they use art as a process both to create meaning, and to express what they know and feel. They also may begin to be more self-critical of the quality of their creations and want to destroy work that does not meet their standards and share the work that does with others.

As children use art media they reap other educational benefits. They develop motor control and perceptual discrimination. They use language and learn new vocabulary. They learn about materials and develop problem-solving strategies. Developing aesthetic awareness and appreciation are important benefits of art experiences (see Figure 10.11). The work of John Dewey and the example of the preprimary schools of Reggio Emilia help us to understand that art is also a primary way to construct and communicate understanding.

One day at school, a new pet arrives—Kea, a gray and white cockatiel. The children crowd around the new addition to their classroom. They watch it as it hops from perch to perch in the large birdcage. Five-year-old Jonah asks the teacher for a piece of brown paper. He takes black and white crayons from the shelf. He sits down, studies, and painstakingly draws the cockatiel. Looking up every few seconds as he draws, gray and white feathers, a crest, pink three-toed feet, a long tail, and a pointy beak emerge. He draws a pattern of crisscross black lines above and below the bird. The teacher says, "Tell me about your drawing." And Jonah explains that he has drawn Kea. "Tell me about this part," the teacher says, indicating the black lines. "Those are the wires," Jonah explains, pointing to the mesh of the cage.

You can see Jonah's drawing of a cockatiel in Figure 10.12.

Three approaches to teaching art to young children have developed over time: child centered, teacher centered, and art centered (Dixon & Tarr, 1988). A *child-centered approach* reflects the view that art for young children should be open ended and process oriented. Adult intervention is avoided because it "is seen as an impediment for artistic development" (Mulcahey, 2009). Children are given free access to art materials and little instruction. Until recently, this viewpoint has been predominant in early childhood education. In a *teacher-centered approach*, there is a focus on pattern art (often called *craft*). In this approach, children copy an adult-made model, or cut out or color "patterns" with little creativity or artistic expression. This approach has been predominant in some preschools and many primary schools. An *art-centered approach* focuses on art production and art appreciation (Dixon & Tarr, 1988). It encourages aesthetic development and art appreciation in addition to developing children's skill in using art media. The teacher provides some instruction and modeling of techniques and also helps children learn about art and society by viewing and discussing fine artwork. The goal is to nurture children's creativity and aesthetic development. The teacher's job is to support children in developing the ability to express ideas and feelings, not dictate what they draw, paint, or sculpt. We advocate this approach because it supports artistic development, exposes children to beauty, and allows them to explore the world through art.

FIGURE 10.12   Jonah's Drawing of a Cockatiel

Art for young children includes five basic processes: *drawing* (sometimes referred to as graphic art), *painting*, *print-making* (making an image by stamping or burnishing), *collage and construction* (creating a work of art by affixing flat materials to a flat surface or three-dimensional materials to one another), and *modeling and sculpting* (fashioning three-dimensional art out of a soft malleable material like clay or by carving a moderately hard material like soap or plaster with a safe tool). Every work of art is composed of visual, graphic, and other sensory *art elements:* line, color, shape, space, and design. Much of the creative process of art for young children is exploration of the elements of art. You will help children to think about art by talking with them about these elements. Table 10.1 describes some aspects of the art elements.

TABLE 10.1   The Elements of Art

Art Element		Words to Use in Talking About the Art Element
Line	*That line is . . .*	straight, curved, heavy, light, wide, thin, wandering, wiggling, jagged, broken, zigzag, long, short
	It goes . . .	up and down, diagonally, from side-to-side
	Those are . . .	crossed, separate, parallel lines
Color	*You used . . .*	pure or primary colors (red, yellow, blue), mixed or secondary colors (orange, green, purple), or tertiary colors (magenta, turquoise, chartreuse)
	The color is . . .	cool (blue end of the spectrum), warm (red end of the spectrum)
	The colors are . . .	intense, saturated, luminous, bright, dusky, shadowy light, dark
Shape	*Those shapes are . . .*	open, closed, irregular, regular (rectangle, circle, triangle, trapezoid, hexagon, octagon, oval, square, etc.), filled, empty, connected, overlapping, enclosed
	That shape is . . .	
Space	*You used the . . .*	center, top, bottom, side, corner, inside, near, far part of the paper
	It is . . .	crowded, full, sparse, empty, balanced/unbalanced, included/excluded
Design	*I see how you . . .*	organized, repeated, made some texture, used the idea of . . ., varied the . . ., made it symmetrical, balanced the . . ., alternated the . . .

Reflect on talking with children about art elements

Look at the artwork in Figure 10.13. How do you respond to it? What do you think you might say to a child about it? Now notice the way the child used color, shape, space, and design in the work. Think of some other things you might say to encourage the child and develop awareness of art elements.

Young children do not become artists simply because art media are available. They pass recognizable landmarks on the path to artistic maturity but need time, space, materials, and the support of adults in order to become artistically competent. Much of the creative process of art for young children is exploration rather than an attempt to represent something. Realizing this distinction can help you appreciate children's early artwork. Your most critical task is to understand and value the art of young children. It has worth in and of itself—not for what it may become when children gain more skill, but for what it is now.

The way you talk to young children can support their artistic development. As they work it is best, at first, to offer only minimal input. Avoid asking *what* they have created. They may have had nothing particular in mind and the question implies that they should have. Instead ask them if they wish to tell you about what they have done and accept it if they do not. You can comment on aspects such as the following:

Effort—"You worked on your clay for a long time today."

Innovation—"When you used the side of the crayon, it made a different kind of mark than drawing with the tip."

Technique—"There are lots and lots of dots on your painting."

You can also comment on children's use of art elements:

Color—"The green looks really vibrant next to the red."

Line—"You used thick and thin lines in your painting."

Shape—"What a lot of circular objects you chose for your collage."

Space—"Your box collage is almost as tall as the top of the shelf."

Design—"The top of your paper has lots of little prints and the bottom has lots of big prints."

Some children may not seem interested in art. A period of disinterest or observation may precede participation. Others may simply be more interested in different activities or other ways of being creative. Still others may not want to attempt art activities because they feel they cannot measure up to their teacher's or parents' expectations. Easily accessible, plentiful supplies, encouragement without pressure, and acceptance and appreciation for the child's work will give the child confidence to engage in art activities.

Today we know that children's artistic development is closely related to the culture in which they live. The work of young children in Asia and in the preprimary programs of Reggio Emilia in Italy show a high level of aesthetic awareness and skill in artistic production. Studying the way art is taught in other cultures is leading to a growing understanding that teachers can support young children's artistic abilities by providing frequent opportunities to be involved in art; giving careful attention to the quality and presentation of art materials; providing appropriate tasks; talking with children about their intent and efforts; instructing children in technique; providing lots of time to explore and revisit methods; and beautifully displaying children's work. The children's art that you see in this book (Figures 10.3, 10.10, 10.11, 10.12, 10.13, 10.14, 10.16, 10.19, 10.20, and 10.21) are examples of work produced by children who were

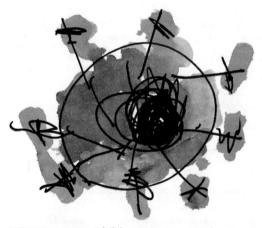

FIGURE 10.13 **Child's Painting:** *Hala Seed Growing in a Pot*

given this kind of support, and whose work was truly valued and respected by their teachers.

At times teachers will make a distinction between work they call "craft" and other work they call "art." Often the "craft" activities consist of look-alike patterns. What is craft? The dictionary defines *craft* as something such as a piece of pottery or carving produced skillfully by hand, especially in a traditional manner. The handwork that we give children to do—claywork, woodwork, stitchery, paper folding, and cutting—can legitimately be called craft and are worthwhile activities for young children. They are especially appropriate for primary-age children who have the fine motor coordination required to learn a craftsman's technique. True craft is a far cry from look-alike coloring books or identical snowmen made with cotton balls. Creative expression should be a reflection of the child's ideas and abilities—not patterns from a teacher's magazine or book. Coloring books and prepared patterns to be copied by children have nothing to do with the development of creativity—in fact they can be destructive to children's feelings of competence and self-worth. These activities take up valuable time that children should be using to develop other skills and ideas. They are not used in good early childhood programs.

FIGURE 10.14 **Tissue Paper Collage:** *Yellow Sunflower*

Music Curriculum

Music is pervasive and has been called a universal language. In the heart of a city we experience the "song" of traffic, footsteps, and voices. In the solitude of the country we listen to the harmony of birds, wind, and water. Even before we are born, we experience the music of a heartbeat. It can make us happy or sad, calm or excited—and can evoke feelings of patriotism, sanctity, love, and empathy.

All young children need music. The most important reasons to provide music to children are that listening to and making music brings pleasure; it provides a powerful and direct link to emotions; and because sharing music with others is an important way to be a part of your culture. Of course, it is also the way children begin to learn about music as a subject, start to develop the skills of a musician, and the ability to listen. Music can also be a path to many other kinds of learning. It can be a vehicle for language ("The song says that Aiken Drum played upon a ladle—have you ever seen a ladle?"), it helps to build literacy skills related to phonemic awareness (*"Willowby wallaby woo"*), and even for remembering facts that might not otherwise be easy to recall (e.g., singing the ABC song to remember whether Q comes before R). There is research that demonstrates that listening to music has a positive impact on learning (Campbell, 2000) and that children's musical skills (e.g., being able to keep the beat in a song) are linked to school success (Weikart, 2003).

Musical *elements* (rhythm, tone, and form) are the raw materials out of which every piece of music is made. The organization of these elements is what distinguishes music from noise. As children engage in music they experience these elements. Table 10.2 explains these music elements and describes some aspects of them that you can help children to notice.

The music curriculum that you provide should help children acquire musicianship skills to the degree that is appropriate for their age: singing, playing instruments, composing and improvising, listening to and appreciating music, and performing. *Singing* offers opportunities for children to experience music and to develop musical skills. Children have an easier time learning songs that are relatively short and simple and have a distinct rhythm. All early childhood educators

TABLE 10.2 The Elements of Music

Music Element	Some Aspects to Help Children Notice
Rhythm (characteristics of music that relate to movement and time)	Beat: the musical pulse Melodic rhythm: the rhythm of the melody or words Tempo: the speed of the music Rests: the silences in music
Tone (characteristics of the notes)	Pitch: high or low Melody or tune: the arrangement of notes in a singable sequence Tone color of timbre: the characteristic sound of an instrument Dynamics: loudness or softness
Form (structure of a piece of music)	Phrase: short but complete musical ideas in a piece of music Repetition: when identical phrases recur in a piece of music Variation: when similar phrases occur in a piece of music Contrast: when very different phrases occur in a piece of music

need a repertoire of singable songs with different moods, subjects, tempos, and styles. *Playing instruments* helps young children to acquire musical skills. Simple rhythm instruments provide excellent first experiences. *Composing and improvising* represent the creative use of musical skills. Young children who have had many musical experiences spontaneously improvise songs to accompany their play. You help children to improvise when you ask them to think of new words for a song. Composing requires creating and preserving a new composition with a recorder or musical notation. *Listening to* and *appreciating music* made by others is an important part of music education. Recordings can provide experiences with diverse styles of music and music from different cultures. When you play instruments and sing in the classroom or have musicians visit, you help children to understand that recorded music is made by real people. *Performing* by singing, moving to music, or playing instruments for others is another musical skill. Because the goal of music education is to help children to become comfortable with musical expression, performance is the least important part of the music curriculum for young children. The MENC (National Association for Music Education) position statement asserts: "[Young] Children should not be encumbered with the need to meet performance goals" (1991). Though it can be motivating and enjoyable for older children, it is generally not appropriate in early childhood.

Every young child's day should include music. It should be a component of the program environment, a segment in the daily schedule, and a part of your interactions with children. Of course, it should also be a part of your planning. When you share music with young children, be enthusiastic! Show you like music by clapping, tapping your feet, and dancing as you sing or listen to music. Include diverse styles of music as well as music from many cultures. Sing with children every day—individually in spontaneous activities, during transitions, and during group times. Choose simple songs with singable melodies and lyrics. Sing in a comfortable range for children (approximately middle C to E an octave above). Vary the lyrics of songs to sing about the children and their activities and interests. During group music times, sit with children on the floor or on a low stool or chair. Add movement to music to enhance children's interest. Regularly use simple rhythm instruments in guided activity. Take good care of these instruments and avoid leaving them out to be damaged or turned into noisemakers. Learn to play a simple chorded instrument (e.g., guitar, autoharp, ukulele, omnichord) to accompany music activities.

When music making is a part of their lives, children become spontaneous music makers. You can help children to be comfortable with music by bringing it informally into the classroom and by formal planned music experiences during a special time each day.

Creative Movement Curriculum

Another way that children can express themselves is through creative movement. When is movement creative? When ideas and feelings are expressed in imaginative ways through movement. It is different from, and not a substitute for, games or large muscle activities on the playground. It is the forerunner of dance and theater but differs from them. Dance and theater are more formal and prescribed than creative movement.

In creative movement, children interpret and follow suggestions and are encouraged to find their own innovative ways of moving. They express ideas with their bodies and develop a repertoire of movement possibilities. Creative movement offers challenges and new ways to practice developing physical skills. As children participate in creative movement they experience the elements of movement: body awareness and control, space, time and form. Table 10.3 discusses these elements and gives some examples of how you might use them in movement activities with young children.

Successful creative movement activities take thoughtful planning. Basic rules for safety (no pushing or bumping, and so on) and an attitude of respect for individual interpretations and skill levels need to be established. We find it useful to have a written plan to use as a "map" to guide us as we lead children in creative movement activities. With a group of very young children, creative movement might be as simple as jumping and stopping to the beat of a drum. As children become more experienced they can be given more complex movement tasks, such as moving a single body part in isolation ("Show you're happy with your foot!") or representing something ("As I play my drum, slowly grow toward the sun and blossom like a flower"). Older preschoolers and primary-age children enjoy choreographing a song or story.

As children develop confidence and movement skills, they will become able to express their ideas with little direction. In the beginning, however, you will need to provide guidance. (See the accompanying "Golden Rules for Creative Movement with Young Children.") Most children are delighted to participate in creative movement, but a few will hesitate. Children should never be forced to participate in these activities or be criticized for the way they move.

Aesthetics Curriculum

Every human being has the potential to develop sensitivity to beauty and the heritage of the arts. You can help young children develop this potential. *Aesthetics* refers to the love of beauty, to the cultural criteria for judging beauty, and to individual taste. Malcolm Ross says:

> Aesthetic perception involves the capacity to respond to the uniqueness, the singular quality of things—to value individual integrity and to reject the cliché and the stereotype. (Ross, 1981, 158)

TABLE 10.3   The Elements of Creative Movement

Movement Element	Aspects of the Element	Examples of Using the Element
Body awareness (awareness and control of body)	Location: where you are in space Locomotor movement (actions): the ways you can move from one place to another Nonlocomotor movement: the ways you can move while staying in one place Body isolation: moving part of the body without moving the rest	"Look at who's in front of you, who's behind you, what's above you." "Walk, jump, hop, run, skip." "Keep your feet planted on the ground and make your arms stretch." "Wave good-bye with your elbow."
Space (how area is used)	personal space (occupied just by you) vs. general space (used by the whole group) Level: high/low/middle Boundaries: inside/outside	"Imagine yourself inside a bubble." "Make your head float to the sky." "Put one body part inside the hoop."
Time (tempo or speed)	Slow or fast Steady or changing	"Flap your eagle wings slowly, then soar across the sky." "March, march, march to the drumbeat."
Force (energy)	Heavy or light Relaxed or tense Smooth or jerky	"Tromp like an elephant across the room." "Float like a butterfly." "Pretend your legs are made of boards and can't bend." "Walk like a machine."

GOLDEN RULES FOR CREATIVE MOVEMENT WITH YOUNG CHILDREN

1. Begin movement sessions sitting down or standing still before inviting children to move freely around the room.
2. Establish a signal (like a hard drumbeat) to tell the children to freeze. Practice stopping to this signal as a game until they understand it as an integral part of every movement activity.
3. Include all children. If children are not yet comfortable enough to participate, ask them to be the audience and watch and clap at the end.
4. Alternate vigorous and quiet movement. Start low, small, slow, and light; gradually build to high, big, heavy, and quick—then slowly work down to slow and small again.
5. Quit while you're ahead—when it's going well and you have reached a natural ending place.
6. End with movement in a way that provides a transition to the next activity: "Tiptoe to the playground when I touch you on the shoulder."

You can support young children's aesthetic development. First of all, be aware of beauty in your environment and talk about it with children. Secondly add beauty to your classroom and create an island of calm by including beautiful natural objects, flowers, sculpture, and representations of the work of fine artists (available in museum and gallery shops). Beautiful music can be played for activities and routines. For preschoolers and older children, you can make games in which children sort and classify artwork by subject matter, technique, color, or personal preference. When introducing children to art, it is important to guide them in a way that helps the art to be more personally meaningful. For example, you might ask children to talk about what they see in the different parts of the picture and what the artist might have been thinking and feeling when she or he created the work. Beautifully illustrated children's literature can be used to discuss aesthetic impact and preferences in art.

Help children to reflect on colors, patterns, and textures found in nature as you go on walks and other trips into the natural world. Take trips to view works of art in your community (e.g., to see a sculpture that adorns a public building) and to galleries, studios, and performances make worthwhile activities for young children. Children need exposure to beauty and time to reflect on it with a caring and thoughtful adult. The early years may be the optimal time to lay the foundation for a lifetime of pleasure and enjoyment. The national arts content standards incorporate aesthetic appreciation as a part of each arts area.

You have many gifts to give children. Being able to create and appreciate art, music, and dance and to express ideas and feelings through the arts is a gift. Figure 10.15 lists some books and websites that can help you learn more about the creative arts and aesthetic curriculum.

The Inquiry Curriculum

It is little short of a miracle that modern methods of instruction have not already completely strangled the holy curiosity of inquiry, because what this delicate little plant needs most, apart from initial stimulation, is freedom; without that it is surely destroyed.

Albert Einstein

Young children have a compelling curiosity to figure out why and how the world works. They learn by doing. From their earliest months they observe, discover relationships, search for answers, and communicate their discoveries. They construct understanding as they explore, and act upon their environment. Children *inquire* (seek information) and develop concepts as they play and as they participate in curriculum activities. Experiences in mathematics, science, and social studies are uniquely suited to the development of thinking and problem solving and are the areas of the curriculum in which inquiry is a primary emphasis.

If you remember math, science, and social studies education as memorizing facts to recall for a test, you may question whether these subjects are appropriate for young children. If so, you will be pleased to know that learning "facts" is not the purpose of the inquiry curriculum in early childhood education. Instead, the goals are to support children's natural curiosity and sense of wonder, to help them to learn to think flexibly, to inquire and solve problems, and to gain greater understanding of the world. Giving children information is not your primary role in the inquiry curriculum (indeed, it is not your primary role in early childhood education). Instead, you help children construct understanding by providing the necessary raw materials: time, space, equipment, and experiences. You encourage and support them in discovering for themselves.

FIGURE 10.15   **Books and Websites on Creative Arts and Aesthetic Curriculum**

BOOKS

Art

Don't Move the Muffin Tins: A Hands-Off Guide to Art for the Young Child, by Bev Bos (Turn the Page Press)

In the Spirit of the Studio: Learning from the Atelier of Reggio Emilia, by Lella Gandini, Lynn T. Hill, Louise Boyd Cadwell, & Charles Schwall (NAEYC)

The Art of Teaching Art to Children: In School and at Home, by Nancy Beal (Farrar, Straus & Giroux)

Art: Basic for Young Children, by Lila Lasky & Rose Mukerji-Bergeson (NAEYC)

Experience and Art: Teaching Children to Paint (2nd ed.), by Nancy Smith, Carolee Fucigna, Margaret Kennedy, & Lois Lord (Teachers College Press)

The Language of Art: Inquiry-Based Studio Practices in Early Childhood Settings, by Ann Pelo (Redleaf Press)

Young at Art: Teaching Toddlers Self-Expression, Problem-Solving Skills, and an Appreciation for Art, by S. Striker (Henry Holt and Company)

Music

Music and Movement: A Way of Life for the Young Child (7th ed.), by Linda Carol Edwards (Pearson)

Music in Our Lives: The Early Years, by Dorothy T. McDonald (NAEYC)

TIPS: Music Activities in Early Childhood, by John M. Feierabend (Rowman & Littlefield Education)

First Steps in Music for Preschool and Beyond, by John M. Feierabend (GIA Publications, Inc.)

Creative Movement

Hello Toes: Movement Games for Children, Ages 1–5, by Anne Lief Barlin & Nurit Kalev (Princeton Book Company Publishers)

Feeling Strong, Feeling Free: Movement Exploration for Young Children, by Molly Sullivan (NAEYC)

A Moving Experience: Dance for Lovers of Children and the Child Within, by T. Benzwie (Zephyr Press)

Creative Experiences for Young Children, by Mimi Brodsky Chenfeld (Heinemann)

Experiences in Music & Movement: Birth to Age 8, by Rae Pica (Wadsworth)

Teaching Children Dance: Becoming a Master, by T. Purcell (Human Kinetics)

Aesthetics

Aesthetics for Young People, by Ronald Moore (ed.) (National Art Education Association)

Designs for Living and Learning: Transforming Early Childhood Environments, by Deb Curtis & Margie Carter (Redleaf Press)

WEBSITES

ArtsEdge—the National Arts and Education Network: http://artsedge.kennedy-center.org/teach

National Art Education Association: naea-reston.org

National Association for Music Education: menc.org

Creative Dance Center: creativedance.org

Children's Music Network: cmnonline.org/index.htm

Children's Music Web: childrensmusic.org

Children's Museum of the Arts: http://cmany.org/intro.php?pn=home

KPR (Kids Public Radio): kidspublicradio.org

National Dance Education Organization (NDEO): ndeo.org

Young at Art Children's Museum: youngatartmuseum.org

Inquiry does not mean learning right answers. It means to ask, to find out, to think, to take risks, to make mistakes, and to learn from them. Facts pronounced by adults deprive children of the opportunity to learn through inquiry and develop higher-level thinking skills. Children need to understand that it is desirable to think creatively about problems, acceptable not to have an answer, and OK to give the "wrong" answers.

The processes a child uses to learn about the world and construct concepts are called *inquiry processes*. Inquiry for a young child involves the organization of experiences through exploration. An inquiring child uses the senses to gain information that will contribute to the development of concepts. Figure 10.17 provides a list of inquiry processes that best apply to young children.

Talking with children as they explore is one of the most important things you will do to help them learn to think. Skilled educators target their questions, and activities to support the natural curiosity of children. Supportive comments about children's discoveries encourage further inquiry and model an inquiring mind. They help children to form concepts but do not hand them preformed ideas.

Children are encouraged to think when they are asked *open-ended questions*. Open questions can be answered in a number of different ways and have more than one correct answer (see Figure 10.18). *Closed questions* have only one correct or acceptable answer—for example, "What color is it?" Even though closed questions do not stimulate inquiry, they can help you to learn whether children have acquired a piece of information. For this reason, in most classrooms, educators use a mixture of open and closed questions.

FIGURE 10.16 **Sunflower with Roots (annotated work sample)**

Annotation: After transplanting flowers in the garden during outside time, Alex went to the art area. He drew a flower with a marker then painted over his drawing with liquid water color. Afterward he said to the teacher, *These are the roots for the flower to drink water.*

Comment: Alex observes, makes inferences, and demonstrates knowledge—he drew and painted to express what he knows about plants.

Math Curriculum

Mathematics is a way to structure experience to form ideas about the quantitative, logical, and spatial relationships. Young children are natural mathematicians who are genuinely curious and unafraid of mathematical processes. During the early childhood years, young children come to think of themselves as part of a

FIGURE 10.17 **Inquiry Processes That Best Apply to Young Children**

- **Exploring:** Using the senses to observe, investigate, and manipulate
- **Identifying:** Naming and describing what is experienced
- **Classifying:** Grouping objects or experiences by their common characteristics
- **Comparing and contrasting:** Observing similarities and differences between objects or experiences
- **Hypothesizing:** Using the data from experiences to make guesses (hypotheses) about what might happen
- **Generalizing:** Applying previous experience to new events

community of people who use numbers to order and communicate about their world. In the same way that young children will pretend to write and read, they will label distance and ages with numbers: "My doll is twenteen." "It's thirty-fifty miles."

The conceptual underpinnings of adult skills are based on many years of concrete experiences that may not seem to relate to mathematics. You may be surprised to learn that math curriculum for young children is far more than numbers, equations, counting and measuring. In fact, although numbers are useful symbols, much of math is not about numbers. Instead, math can be viewed as a way of thinking, the science of patterns. Concepts such as more and fewer, far and near, similar and different, short and tall, now and later, first and last, and over and under precede later mastery of complex mathematical concepts. Young children develop concepts that provide the foundation that helps them to make sense of the physical and social world and to master abstract mathematical concepts later in their school careers (see Table 10.4). These form the math curriculum for young children.

As you plan for math experiences, it is important to be aware of when and how mathematics is meaningful to children. A child who is comparing and arranging the dishes in the dramatic play area and setting the table for the other children is using ideas of one-to-one correspondence, classification, and quantity. A child who is building a block tower is using concepts of proportion and symmetry, shape and proximity. Based on your observations of children, you can add additional activities and ask stimulating questions that will provide more opportunities for them to learn.

Children learn about math when you ask questions that encourage mathematical thinking: "What shall we put next in our pattern?" "How could we find out who's tallest?"—but be prepared to forgo questioning when children do not appear interested. Providing children with many opportunities to manipulate

FIGURE 10.18 Asking Open-Ended Questions

Open questions can be answered in a number of different ways and have more than one correct answer. If you wish to stimulate children to inquire, you will ask many open-ended questions and allow children time to think and answer.

Ask questions and make statements that help children to:

- *Reason:* "What do you suppose?" "How do you know?" "What would happen if?" "How could we find out?"

- *Notice details:* "What do you see (hear, feel, smell)?" "I wonder why clouds are moving so quickly?" "The baskets all nest together, the little ones inside the big ones." "I can feel the rabbit's heart is beating quickly and hard."

- *Make comparisons:* "How are they the same (different)?" "Look how different each shell is."

- *Come to conclusions:* "What would happen if . . . ?" "Why do you suppose that's happening?"

TABLE 10.4   Math Concepts Learned by Young Children

Concept	What It Is	What a Child Might Do That Demonstrates Understanding
Matching	The foundational skill for understanding one-to-one correspondence. There are several kinds of matching tasks—matching identical items, different items, and matching groups or "sets" of identical items	Put together matched pairs of shoes. Place one napkin at each place at the table. Place a cup on each saucer.
Sorting and Classifying	Sorting or grouping by shared characteristics	Put all the beads in a basket and all the buttons in a box.
Ordering and Seriation	Sequencing based on a difference in the degree of some quality such as size, weight, texture, or shading	Arrange balls from smallest to largest.
Number • **One-to-one correspondence** • **Quantity or cardinal number** • **Order or ordinal number** • **Numerals**	Quantity and order • Matching objects one for one • "Many-ness"—the amount or number of different objects • The order of objects—first, second, third • Symbols that stand for certain quantities or order (i.e., 1-2-3)	Pass out one bell to each child (see matching). Note that there are three bears and three chairs. Note who arrives first in at school and who is second. Place three items by the numeral 3.
Operations	Actions or procedures that produce a number value	
• **Counting**	• Adding one more to a series—a sequence of number names always used in the same order	Count 3 to 5 objects.
• **Part-part-whole relationships**	• Understanding that a number of objects includes smaller groups of objects	Say "I have two red beads and three green beads," "I have five beads."
Patterns	Ordering based on repetition	Create a bead necklace with alternating colors, sing the chorus after every verse of a song.
Measurement	Comparing size, volume, weight, or quantity to a standard	Find out how many blocks cover the table top, compare the heights of friends.
Geometry and Spatial Sense	Properties of objects and the way objects relate to one another based on position, direction, proximity, arrangement, and distance	Place long blocks on the bottom shelf and the short on the shelf above; drive a tricycle forward and then backward; kick a ball to child who is near.

(continued)

TABLE 10.4 Math Concepts Learned by Young Children *(continued)*

Concept	What It Is	What a Child Might Do That Demonstrates Understanding
Shape	2- and 3-dimensional objects and their properties. Regularity and irregularity; whether open or closed; how appearance changes based on position; and how shapes can be manipulated while retaining their characteristics	Hold and show objects from different angles. Flatten a ball of dough into a circle.
Data Analysis	The collection, organization, and representation of information (e.g., a chart comparing who has a cat and who does not have a cat—you are collecting, organizing, and representing data; a graph of how many pockets are in our clothes)	Create a picture showing how many are needed.
Probability	How likely it is that an event will occur	Talk about likely and unlikely events— "Maybe it will rain"—"It probably won't be a tornado."

objects—including those made as math teaching equipment (like Unifix cubes or Cuisenaire rods) and other materials (like blocks and button collections)—supports the development of math concepts. Children learn about math as they handle the routines of the day. When each child has one cracker and rests on one mat, one-to-one correspondence is experienced. As they learn the sequence of the daily schedule, learn to pour half a glass of milk, or cut their apples in two parts, they are using math.

Because many teachers of young children have "math anxiety" (a common fear of math similar to stage fright), they are afraid to provide math experiences to young children. If you have math anxiety, it may help if you consider all the ways you use ideas of pattern, measurement, reasoning, estimation, classification, and order in your life. As you do so, you may realize that you are probably much better at math than you think. You *can* teach math. In fact, here are six ideas for ways to teach math in the early childhood classroom that don't seem like math:

1. Sing songs with mathematical ideas—like "Eency Weency Spider" (geometry and spatial awareness), "Old MacDonald Had a Farm" (pattern), and "Five Little Monkeys Jumping on the Bed" (number and operations).
2. Read books that showcase math—like *The Doorbell Rang* by Pat Hutchins and *Ten, Nine, Eight* by Molly Bang (number and operations), *Guess How Much I Love You* by Sam McBratney (measurement), *The Secret Birthday Message* by Eric Carle (space), *The Three Bears* by Paul Galdone (seriation), *The Very Hungry Caterpillar* by Eric Carle (pattern, number, and operations), and *Bread Bread Bread* by Ann Morris (displaying and analyzing data).
3. Build with blocks with children and use words like half-unit, unit, quadruple-unit, big, little, tall, short, wide (geometry and spatial awareness, number and operations, seriation, pattern, measurement).
4. Play with sand and water—provide scoops and containers of different sizes (number and operations, geometry and spatial awareness, measurement).

5. Cook good things to eat—follow recipes that are written out and visible to children (number and operations, measurement, time, geometry and spatial awareness, seriation).

6. Use routines—have children set the table (number and operations), clean up (classification, geometry, and spatial awareness), take roll (number and operations), feed pets (measurement), vote for activities/names (number and operations, displaying and analyzing data).

To understand how math curriculum is addressed in standards check out your state's early learning guidelines (find a link at nccic.acf.hhs.gov/resource/state-early-learning-guidelines) or the National Governors Association Center for Best Practices (NGA Center) and the Council of Chief State School Officers (CCSSO) as part of the common core state standards for kindergarten through twelfth grade (corestandards.org/the-standards/mathematics).

Science Curriculum

Young children are natural scientists. Their play is full of scientific exploration. It is true for an infant who is learning about physiology as she first discovers her toes, and about physics as she drops a bottle from a high chair. It is also true for a third grader who is carefully observing and drawing a cricket (see figure 10.19).

For some adults science involves a collection of facts and concepts learned by rote from a teacher or a textbook. For others it is specific information that must be communicated to children. Some teachers believe because young children don't learn through formal instruction, "playing around" is sufficient science curriculum in the early years. We know today that science education for young children must not only be "hands-on" but must also be "minds-on"—in other words, intentional. You can see by the drawings and paintings of plants and bugs done by 3-, 4-, and 5-year-olds included in this chapter (see Figures 10.3, 10.11, 10.12, 10.13, 10.14, 10.16, 10.19, 10.20, and 10.21) and throughout this edition of the text that young children can be careful observers of the world. Scientists—and educators who have maintained their own playfulness and enthusiasm for science—view it as a process of exploration and experimentation through which they find out about the world. It is this view that we want to share with children.

Science is a large field, encompassing many aspects of life. What do you teach young children about science? The most important thing you do is to build children's ability and disposition to inquire. The first of the National Science Education Standards for young children is that all children *should develop abilities to do scientific inquiry*. Doing science depends on sensory input—hearing, smelling, seeing, touching, moving, tasting. Therefore, sensory experience should be at the core of the early

Reflect on your feelings about math

How do you feel when you think about teaching math? What experiences in your life contribute to your feeling positive or negative about it? How might you communicate your feelings to children? What do you want to communicate?

FIGURE 10.19 **Cricket (annotated work sample)**

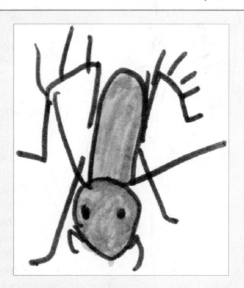

Annotation: Tyler observed the crickets in the bug box for about 3 minutes before picking up markers and drawing the cricket. He looked up frequently as he drew. He took a magnifying glass and looked at the cricket then added hair to the legs.

Comment: Tyler demonstrates inquiry skills—he observes to gain information and records data in meaningful ways.

childhood science curriculum. To do scientific inquiry children need to be able to the following:

- Ask questions about objects, organisms, and events in the environment
- Plan and conduct a simple investigation
- Employ simple equipment and tools to gather data and extend the senses
- Use data to construct a reasonable explanation
- Communicate investigations and explanations (National Research Council, 1996)

You may find it useful to think about three broad categories: life science, physical science, and earth science.

Life science (the study of the structures, origins, growth, and reproduction of plants and animals) is inherently interesting to children. Where did the butterfly come from? How did the bean grow into a plant? How did the bulging mother mouse get the babies inside her? Why does a dog have four legs and a spider eight? Life science involves the structures, origins, growth, and reproduction of plants and animals (see Figures 10.20 and 10.21). Interest in their own growth can lead children to explore and learn about physiology. Children's fascination with their own bodies and with animals can be the springboard to further discovery

Physical science (the study of objects, materials, and energy and the interactions between them) is learned when children explore and observe the properties of substances—reactions to temperature and force and interactions. When children explore objects and act to create or alter speed, leverage, and balance, they are experiencing physics (energy, motion, and force). When they act to make substances change by combining, heating, or cooling, they experience chemistry (the composition, properties, and transformation of matter). An unbalanced pile of blocks collapsing, play dough disintegrating in the water play table, or an ice cube melting in the sun are children's first science experiments. Physical science activities are uniquely appropriate to young children because they involve action and observation of everyday things that are experienced in play and daily life.

Earth science (the study of the earth, sky, and oceans) involves children as they observe and wonder about the common features of the earth, sky, and oceans. Basic concepts of earth science are explored by young children in the course of daily activity. As they walk over hills, look at layers of rock formations, or pound sandstone into bits, they are experiencing *geology*. When they observe the moon hanging in the sky above the playground in the morning, they are observing phenomena related to *astronomy*. When they guess that dark clouds hold rain, they are making predictions that are a part of *meteorology*. Young children's concepts of earth science are limited to what they can see and experience. Children will be curious about these phenomena, and in school they can talk, draw, write, and read about them.

Your main role in science education is the preservation and encouragement of the natural curiosity of children. To maintain children's attitude of playfulness toward science, you need to view their questions as an

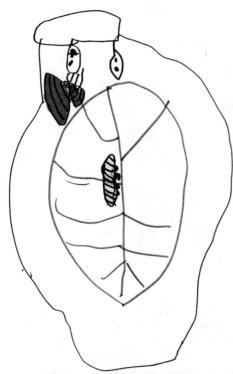

FIGURE 10.20 Butterfly Emerging from a Chrysalis (life drawing with felt pens)

opportunity to model the attitudes of the scientist—curiosity, questioning, openness to exploration, and problem solving. In science activities, you can guide children's curiosity and help turn a pleasant experience into one that has deeper learning. For example, a small group of children looking at a squirmy family of baby mice will be delighted by their tiny size and their mother's care. They may not spontaneously realize that the babies are seeking milk, that their eyes are closed, or that these babies are like many other babies, including human infants, in some ways. You can encourage thinking and concept development by asking children questions: "Why do you suppose the baby mice were squirming?" "What do you think will happen if their mother goes and runs on the wheel?" "What do the babies remind you of?" Part of your role is to find resources (books, people, or media) to expand their knowledge. As you model an inquiring and respectful attitude toward the world, you help children to think like scientists. Science is everyday, accessible, infinitely interesting, and definitely worth knowing.

To understand how science curriculum is addressed in standards check out your state's early learning guidelines (find a link at nccic.acf.hhs.gov/resource/state-early-learning-guidelines) or the K–4 science standards developed by the National Committee on Science Education, a branch of the National Research Council (nap.edu/openbook.php?record_id=4962.)

(harvesting taro)

(tadpoles in the lo'i, or taro patch)

FIGURE 10.21 Drawings Made by 4-Year-Olds Following a Trip to a Taro Patch

Social Studies Curriculum

Social studies concerns relationships among people and between people and the world in which they live. It is an umbrella term that includes many fields. In an early childhood program it can include aspects of ***psychology*** (emotions and behavior), ***sociology*** (society, its development, and organization), ***cultural anthropology*** (the way people live in different cultures), ***economics*** (how people consume, produce, and deliver goods and services), ***political science*** (how people are governed and use power to make and enforce decisions), ***geography*** (the earth, its features, and the effects of human activity), and ***history*** (the events that make up the past).

You may remember school social studies as dull and unrelated to the real world, requiring memorization of dates, names, and places. You may have other memories of interesting and exciting social studies experiences taught in pleasant and memorable ways such as taking trips or cooking food from another culture.

Young children are social scientists; they are interested in other people. They study the behavior, customs, interactions, power, and work of the people who share their homes, schools, and communities. They experience the geography of their homes. They do not wait to learn social studies until they are old enough

to read a textbook about it. When appropriately taught to young children, social studies has a great deal of important content that is worth knowing. It can help children to:

* Appreciate and respect themselves, other people, their culture, and their environment
* Deal with important issues in their lives
* Develop a sense of belonging to and responsibility for their family, community, and environment
* Recognize some of the significant patterns that shape people's lives and the world
* Explore, understand, and experience aspects of the world that lay the foundation for later comprehension of the social sciences
* Develop skills in a range of subject areas

Virtually any curriculum activity can be geared to social studies learning. Art, music, cooking, graphing, story telling, and creative dramatics can be integrated with social studies. Because social studies is so broad and can be approached in so many different ways, it is one of the two best subjects (the other is science) for organizing and integrating curriculum. Food preparation, visits from resource people, songs, dances, artifacts (from a family, culture, or place), books, and trips related to a topic all contribute to concept development in the social sciences (see Figure 10.22). Follow-up activities can occur in every area of the curriculum. Children gain deeper understanding when they re-create and re-experience concepts in blocks, dramatic play, art work, graphs, child-authored books, songs, and games.

Some, but not all, states have preschool social studies standards. To understand how social studies curriculum is addressed in your state's preschool programs look at the early learning guidelines (a link can be found at nccic.acf.hhs.gov/resource/state-early-learning-guidelines). The National Council for the Social Studies has identified 10 themes that belong in education for children from kindergarten on. You can find these at socialstudies.org/standards/strands.

Figure 10.23 lists some books and websites that can help you learn more about the inquiry curriculum.

FIGURE 10.22 **Five Activities That Are Primarily Social Studies**

Learning Trips—"field work" (the most important social studies activity). Children are social scientists going into the community to learn.

Using and Making Maps—(representations from a bird's-eye perspective) are valuable when they are concrete and of high interest, such as body-tracing (a life-size map), mapping with blocks, and mapping a familiar place like the playground.

Resource Visitors—to serve as a subject to be learned about (a pregnant mom who allows children to feel the baby kick), to demonstrate a skill or artifact (a cultural representative who teaches a song and demonstrates making a special food), or to share information (a trainer with an assistance dog)

Block Building and Dramatic Play—enable children to recreate their experiences and build social studies concepts.

Source: Information from E. Moravcik, S. Nolte, & S. Feeney, *Meaningful Curriculum for Young Children*, 2013.

FIGURE 10.23   Books and Websites on Inquiry Curriculum

BOOKS

Math

Mathematics in the Early Years and *The Young Child and Mathematics*, by Juanita V. Copley (NAEYC)

Spotlight on Young Children and Math, by Derry G. Koralek (NAEYC)

Active Experiences for Active Children: Mathematics, by Carol Seefeldt & Alice Galper (Pearson)

Early Childhood Mathematics, by Susan Smith (Pearson)

Young Mathematicians at Work: Constructing Number Sense, Addition, and Subtraction, by Catherine Twomey Fosnot (Heinemann)

Science

Science with Young Children (rev. ed.), by Bess-Gene Holt (NAEYC)

Science Experiences for the Early Childhood Years: An Integrated Affective Approach (10th ed.), by Jean D. Harlan & Mary S. Rivkin (Pearson)

Active Experiences for Active Children: Science (3rd ed.), by Carol Seefeldt, Alice Galper, & Ithel Jones (Pearson)

Worms, Shadows, and Whirlpools: Science in the Early Childhood Classroom, by Karen Worth & Sharon Grollman (Redleaf Press)

Discovering Nature with Young Children, by Ingrid Chaulfour and Karen Worth (Redleaf Press)

Social Studies

Explorations with Young Children, by Anne Mitchell & Judy David (Gryphon House)

Active Experiences for Active Children: Social Studies (2nd ed.), by Carol Seefeldt & Alice Galper (Pearson)

Alike and Different: Exploring Our Humanity with Young Children, by Bonnie Neugebauer (Exchange Press)

Roots and Wings: Affirming Culture in Early Childhood Programs, by Stacey York (Redleaf Press)

WEBSITES

National Council of Teachers of Mathematics: nctm.org

National Science Teachers Association: nsta.org

National Council for the Social Studies: ncss.org

The National Council of Teachers of Mathematics: nctm.org

Illuminations NCTM Lesson Plans: illuminations.nctm.org

Montessori Mathematics Introduction: infomontessori.com/mathematics/introduction

NAEYC Position Statement on Early Childhood Mathematics: Promoting Good Beginnings: naeyc.org/positionstatements/mathematics

Final Thoughts

Young children learn by doing, observing, and interacting. They construct and order knowledge through play. You will guide them on this voyage of discovery and help them to understand the world in which they live. As you do so, you support their natural curiosity, develop their love of learning, and help them to be the thinkers and problem-solvers of the future.

There are many ways to organize curriculum to ensure that you provide a full range of appropriate activities for the children in your program. No single "right way" prescribes how to think about or teach a particular subject to young children (though some ways are "wrong" because they do not reflect what we know about how children learn).

As you learn to be an early childhood educator you will have opportunities to learn much more about curriculum. In creating this chapter we wanted to give you an overview of the kinds of learning experiences that are developmentally appropriate and meaningful to young children—a framework onto which you could add the practical details you will need to actually teach. We applaud you as you begin this adventure.

 Learning Outcomes

When you read this chapter, and then thoughtfully complete activities from the "To Learn More" section and prepare items from the "For Your Portfolio" section, you will be making progress in meeting **NAEYC Standards for Early Childhood Professional Preparation Programs** (NAEYC, 2009).

Standard 1. Promoting Child Development and Learning
Key elements:

1a: Knowing and understanding young children's characteristics and needs

1c: Using developmental knowledge to create healthy, respectful, supportive, and challenging learning environments

Standard 4. Using Developmentally Effective Approaches to Connect with Children and Families
Key elements:

4a: Understanding positive relationships and supportive interactions as the foundation of their work with children

4b: Knowing and understanding effective strategies and tools for early education

4c: Using a broad repertoire of developmentally appropriate teaching/learning approaches

4d: Reflecting on their own practice to promote positive outcomes for each child

Standard 5. Using Content Knowledge to Build Meaningful Curriculum
Key elements:

5a: Understanding content knowledge and resources in academic disciplines

5b: Knowing and using the central concepts, inquiry tools, and structures of content areas or academic disciplines

5c: Using their own knowledge, appropriate early learning standards, and other resources to design, implement, and evaluate meaningful, challenging curricula for each child.

 To Learn More

Observe a Program: For a morning, observe a program and see how the staff structures the environment and program to support children's development in one of the curriculum areas: physical development, creative arts, communication, or inquiry. Look at the plans and see how the planning reflects what you observed. Interview a teacher to learn how he or she thinks about this area of curriculum.

Observe a Child: For a morning observe a child in a classroom, with a focus on the child's activity in one of the curriculum areas. Notice how the child engages with the experiences offered and how the child constructs his or her own opportunities for learning. Notice the extent to which the child's learning experiences and the planned curriculum seem to match. Observe to see how staff support the child's learning in this area.

Observe a "Master Teacher": Spend a morning with an early childhood educator who is experienced and has a curriculum leadership role in a program. (This teacher may be called the "lead," "head," or "mentor" teacher.) Then interview the educator about how he or she plans for and provides curriculum.

Observe an Activity: Observe a teacher teaching a planned activity. Using this chapter, identify the curriculum content area and the specific learning that occurs. Interview the teacher to find out the objectives for the activity. Reflect on any differences between what you saw and the focus of the plan.

Compare Two Programs: Observe two early childhood programs in one of the curriculum areas. Compare the ways that the two address the area—their similarities and differences. Reflect on which program seems to best support children's learning and why. What implications does this comparison have for your future work with young children?

Compare Two Ages: Observe two classrooms—one preschool and one for either infants and toddlers or primary-age children. Report on how each enhances children's development in one of the areas of development. Talk to the staff about how they make their curriculum choices in this area. Notice how the stage of development influences curriculum choices.

 ## For Your Portfolio

Plan an Activity: Write and implement an activity plan in one of the subject areas, using the activity-planning format described in the next chapter (Figure 11.2). Reflect on how children responded and how you felt about what you did. What worked? What might you do differently next time? How might you expand on this experience for children? For your portfolio include the plan, a work sample or photograph, and a reflection on what you learned about yourself, children, planning, and teaching.

Create a Learning Material: Design and make a learning material to support the development of a particular child or group of children in one of the subject areas. Introduce it to the child or children and observe how it is used. Reflect on how the children responded and how you felt about what you did. What worked? What might you do differently next time? How might you expand on this experience for children? For your portfolio include a photograph of a child using the material and a reflection on what you learned about yourself, children, learning materials, and teaching.

MyEducationLab

Go to Topic 7: Curriculum/Content Areas in the MyEducationLab (myeducationlab.com) for *Who Am I in the Lives of Children?* where you can:

- Find learning outcomes for Curriculum/Content Areas along with the national standards that connect to these outcomes.
- Complete Assignments and Activities that can help you more deeply understand the chapter content.
- Apply and practice your understanding of the core teaching skills identified in the chapter with the

Building Teaching Skills and Dispositions learning units.
- Examine challenging situations and cases presented in the IRIS Center Resources.
- Check your comprehension on the content covered in the chapter with the Study Plan. Here you will be able to take a chapter quiz, receive feedback on your answers, and then access Review, Practice, and Enrichment activities to enhance your understanding of chapter content.

Lively intellectual curiosities turn the world into an exciting laboratory and keep one ever a learner.

LUCY SPRAGUE MITCHELL

Awareness of alternatives and the bases of choices distinguishes the competent teacher from the merely intuitive one.

ELIZABETH BRADY

11

Curriculum Planning

Worthwhile curriculum contributes to all aspects of development and provides opportunities for children to learn about the world. As an early childhood teacher, one of your tasks is to involve the children with whom you work in a variety of challenging and engaging experiences that will help them to understand the world, develop the skills they need, and acquire attitudes that will lead them to become caring and productive human beings.

Curriculum is the intentional learning experiences designed by a teacher, or team of teachers, in response to what they know and observe about children as well as program goals and standards. Being *intentional* means using your knowledge, judgment, and expertise to organize learning experiences purposefully to respond to unexpected situations as teaching opportunities. Keeping specific goals in mind for children's development and learning enables you to integrate and promote meaningful learning in all domains of development. Meaningful curriculum includes three interconnected elements: the learner (*who*), the *content* or subject matter (*what*), and the process or kinds of planned learning opportunities (*how*). Your study of child development teaches you about the *who*. Classes on curriculum teach you about the *what*. In this chapter we explore the *how*—the selection and organization of curriculum content.

Planning Considerations

What is a plan? In everyday life, jotting your appointments in a calendar is a plan ("Meet Shauna at the mall at 9:00 A.M."). But in working with young children, a plan means a detailed map for teaching. Virtually all teachers create some form

Reflect on something you planned

Think of a time when you planned something for yourself, your family, or your community—a trip, a party, a project. Reflect on what you did and how you went about organizing the event or activity. What did you do? How did you know that you had succeeded? How did planning or lack of planning impact how it turned out?

of written plans. They plan in order to make sure they know what they're doing and that they have everything they need. They plan as a guide for teaching.

Whether you are designing an integrated study or outlining a specific activity, every educational plan includes some essential elements: purpose, content, methods, and assessment. Statements of purpose—what you are trying to accomplish—can be called *goals* or *objectives*. Although you may see these words used interchangeably, a distinction can be made between them. Goals are broad statements of desired ends toward which teaching is directed (e.g., a goal of the preschool curriculum is to help children become active learners). More specific and immediate intended outcomes of curriculum activities are called *objectives* (e.g., at the end of this activity children will demonstrate that they understand that all birds have feathers and lay eggs).

Many strategies or *methods* can be used to accomplish your purpose. One of the pleasures of teaching young children is that there are many ways to teach. For example, to teach children about birds, you might take a trip to the zoo to see different kinds of birds, cook dishes made with eggs, read books about birds, sing a song about birds that fly home to their nest, paint using feathers, play a game matching feathers from different birds, set up a bird feeder in the yard, hatch eggs in an incubator, or study the habitats of birds in different places. One of the challenges of teaching young children is selecting methods that both engage children and help them learn things that are meaningful about the world.

How do you know whether you have accomplished your purpose—whether children have learned what you intended to teach? *Assessment* of what children have learned is a part of planned curriculum. In early childhood settings this is most often done by observing children's acquisition of concepts and skills and documenting what you have observed in written anecdotal records, photographs or video, or by collecting work samples that demonstrate their abilities and understanding.

Purpose, content, methods, and assessment interact with one another. To achieve a particular purpose (e.g., to learn about the characteristics of birds), you select the content and methods (observing and drawing a bird). The methods will determine how you assess (collect the children's drawings). What you assess depends on your purpose (do the drawings include birds with feathers and eggs?).

Influences on Curriculum Choices

As you plan curriculum for children, you will choose the content to be taught, how to organize it, and how to present it to children. These decisions will be based on your values and beliefs about children and education (and those of the program in which you teach); your assessment of children and knowledge of their families, culture, and community; and your appraisal of whether the content is worthwhile for young children to learn.

Values and Beliefs

Your choices about teaching are the way you touch the future. Barbara Biber of Bank Street College has pointed out that programs for young children are a powerful force in influencing the intellect, and more:

> . . . the school is a mighty force not only [for] the excellence of intellect but in shaping the feelings, the attitudes, the values, the sense of self and the dreaming

of what is to be, the images of good and evil in the world about and the visions of what the life of man with man might be. (Biber, 1969, p. 8)

What you teach and how you teach reflects your values for society. The children you teach today are potential doctors, politicians, caregivers, artists, teachers, parents—people who will one day make the decisions and do the work that will affect the lives of others (including your own). What do you want the people of the future to be like? What knowledge and skills will the children you teach need to be productive citizens in society as it exists now, and as it will exist tomorrow? Your answers to these questions will help you to determine your *aims* as an educator. Aims are inspirational ideals based on philosophy and values that frame the program as a whole (e.g., an aim of my program is to help create a society of participatory citizens).

What do you believe about how children learn and what they should be learning? Do you believe children are self-motivated and self-directed learners who will naturally choose what they need to learn? Do you believe that selecting what children will be taught is the responsibility of adults who have more experience and knowledge? Your beliefs about children's motivation and ability to choose worthwhile learning will influence on what you teach.

Teachers' beliefs about how children learn and what they should be learning fall along a continuum that ranges from the belief that children are capable of making choices that will help them acquire needed knowledge and skills (i.e., the process of learning is more important than the specific content) to a belief that young children will not naturally learn without direction (i.e., the content—the acquisition of specific knowledge and skills—is more important than the process). Most teachers' beliefs fall somewhere in the middle. Early childhood educators have typically believed in children's inherent ability to learn and in the importance of process. We, the authors, believe that all areas of children's development are important; we trust children to create many opportunities for their own learning; and believe play, child-choice, and cooperative relationships are essential parts of the child's educational experience. We value the individuality and dignity of children and families, and appreciate that they are part of a culture and community. We also believe that adults have a responsibility to select rich and diverse educational experiences for children. Our beliefs fall in the middle of the continuum, but nearer to the end that addresses process. In this chapter we will describe a way of planning curriculum that is consistent with this philosophy.

Values and beliefs are not restricted to individuals. Programs are founded on values and a view of children and learning, usually stated in the program's philosophy and mission statement. The views of the program in which you work will also influence your curriculum choices. Many early childhood programs are based on a view of children as capable learners and have a mission to foster the development of the whole child and

Reflect on the role of education in shaping the future

What do you want the world to be like in the future? What would people need to be like in order for the world you envision to exist? What do children need to learn and experience in school in order to become these people?

create lifelong learners. Others are designed to impart the values of a religious or cultural group. Some, particularly in public schools and in schools for older children, are founded on the belief that the primary goal of education is the acquisition of academic skills and knowledge.

Knowledge of Children

Early childhood education program practice is based on knowledge of children. This knowledge enables educators to plan for children at the appropriate level for their age and for their individual needs, backgrounds, and interests. This is part of *developmentally appropriate practice* (DAP). According to NAEYC's *Developmentally Appropriate Practice in Early Childhood Programs* (Copple & Bredekamp, 2009), two of the core considerations of DAP are:

Age/developmental appropriateness—anticipating and responding to the age/developmental characteristics of children.

Individual appropriateness—making curriculum choices to provide optimal learning experiences for a particular child.

Your knowledge of children's *developmental characteristics* provides a framework from which you will prepare the learning environment, select teaching practices, and plan appropriate experiences to benefit all the children of a particular age and stage of development. Your knowledge of *the strengths, interests, and needs of each individual child* allows you to be responsive to each child's individual pattern and timing of growth as well as his or her unique personality and learning style. Both the curriculum and adults' interactions with children should be responsive to individual differences in interest, style, and ability.

Just as educational experiences for individual children within a group will differ, planning for the range of age groups is markedly different. The younger the children, the more child-centered and family-sensitive the curriculum must be. For infants and young toddlers, you develop very broad goals that are applicable to all children in this stage of development. Their basic needs are intense and must be met quickly. They need warm physical contact with a few affectionate adults. They are developing a sense of themselves. They are growing and developing new skills with amazing rapidity. They are embedded in families with individual child-rearing practices that must be taken into consideration. The curriculum for infants and toddlers consists of opportunities for spontaneous exploration, with individualized activities for particular children. Planning will be flexible and done on a short-term basis.

Curriculum will be more elaborate for preschoolers and kindergartners. Planning should take into consideration the predictable characteristics of this age group. Three- to five-year-olds learn by doing, by actively exploring. They are beginning to use language effectively. They enjoy playing with one another but have some difficulty working as a group. They eagerly seek new stimulation and have a low tolerance for inactivity. They benefit from planned learning experiences based on carefully chosen topics that supplement their play and exploration. You need to plan for short-term activities, and also further in advance, to make sure that more complex activities (such as trips and projects) can occur.

For primary-age children, curriculum can be more subject-related, project-oriented, and structured. School-age children, like preschoolers, learn best by active, hands-on experiences, but they are able to think more abstractly than preschoolers. They represent ideas symbolically and are increasingly able to read and write about what they are learning. Curriculum in primary school can take advantage of these abilities by pairing experiences in which children learn about the world with many opportunities to represent what they have learned.

If you teach in a public primary school, you will be tasked with addressing academic standards and readying children for standardized tests. These mandates should not prevent you from making every effort to provide meaningful learning experiences that are developmentally appropriate.

Family, Culture, and Community

Young children live in families. Though individual themselves, children's families reflect the characteristics and values of their culture and community. Developmentally appropriate practice means considering what will make sense to a child given his or her linguistic and cultural background, as well as interpreting a child's behavior in light of the family and community in which he or she lives. Your understanding of *the social and cultural context in which children live* will help you to ensure that planned learning experiences are meaningful, relevant, and respectful for children and their families. As you plan curriculum, ask yourself: What do *these* families believe is important for children to learn? Are there subjects or activities with which the families or members of the community might be uncomfortable? How can the families and this community serve as resources for curriculum?

Events in the families and community and locale will influence your curriculum. Think about what curriculum you might plan if several families in your class are having new babies, if a cultural celebration is taking place in your community, if the city is installing wheelchair access ramps at the street corner by your school, if a nearby field or garden is ready for harvest, or if heavy rains caused a flood. Skillful teachers use the life of the families and the community as opportunities for discovery. They know that real events like these lead to powerful learning.

What's Worth Knowing?

What is worth knowing when you are a young child? Curriculum has little value if the content isn't worthwhile to the learner. Children want to know many things about the world in which they live. They want to know about themselves, about how to get along with others and care for their own needs, about their families and communities, and about the natural and physical aspects of their world. You can see this as you observe a 1-year-old's fascination with water, a 2-year-old's triumphant "Me do it!", a 4-year-old's passion for firefighters, or a 6-year-old's enthrallment with horses.

We find ourselves endlessly fascinated when we listen to young children's questions and conversations. They show observation skills, curiosity, and intellectual engagement, as these quotes from 4-year-olds demonstrate:

"There's two caterpillars, that's why they have antenna on both sides."

"The little pickle is light green and the big cucumber is dark green."

"There are eleven-hundred-thousand and thirty-one kids in the whole wide world."

"Not everything on TV is true. I watch TV and not everything on TV is true."

"Do you know how much is in here? (shaking a container) Ten! That's why it sounds so many."

"God made a big boom that started the world turning—but that was a long time ago."

Reflect on something you wanted to know when you were a child

Remember a time in your childhood when you were intensely interested in learning something. What did you want to know about? Why was it important to you? What did you do to find out? What did you learn? How was this similar to or different from what you did in school?

"Bees like this kind of flower. They get honey from it."

"Oh, look, the moon! The moon is out. It's half a moon."

"Where's the praying mantis to sit on the praying mantis egg?"

"This is my computer to see where Megan's blood goes. See, here is where it goes."

"There's two helicopters! I think they're finding the airport!"

When we ask our students to reflect on what they wanted to know when they were young children, their memories are rich and sometimes surprising. They wanted to know about birth and death, the moon and the stars, the nature of God and the nature of sand, divorce and conflict, power and authority, the workings of the plumbing and the workings of the mind, the structure of their bodies and the structure of a worm. With few exceptions, they sought the answers outside of school.

Children want and need to know complex things about complex topics. But schools often limit curriculum for young children to simple facts to recite: shapes and colors, the alphabet and numbers. We maintain that for curriculum to be *of worth* to young children it must be based on the genuine investigation of a topic that has intellectual meaning—in other words, something that is real, that requires genuine investigation and thought. In this chapter we will give you an example of one such investigation: a study of birds.

What about shapes, colors, numbers, the alphabet, and so on? There is certainly value in knowing these things. And it is our responsibility to help children learn them. But they can be learned as children pursue tasks and learn about things that are interesting and meaningful to them rather than as isolated fragments divorced from context and meaning. In isolation, they have little significance or relevance to children's lives.

Content Standards

Teachers today are required to be *accountable* for their teaching. That means they need to know what they are supposed to be teaching and to teach those things. As an early childhood educator in the 21st century, you need to know about *early learning guidelines,* also known as *content standards*, which describe either (1) what young children need to know, understand, and be able to do in a variety of learning domains or (2) the learning opportunities that should be provided in early care and education programs. States and professional associations (e.g., National Association for Sport & Physical Education and the National Council of Teachers of Mathematics) have written K–12 standards for most curriculum areas. Head Start and almost all states have early learning guidelines for most curriculum areas. You can find guidelines for almost every state online. The National Child Care Information and Technical Assistance Center (NCCIC) has links to all state early learning guidelines at http://nccic.acf.hhs.gov/resource/state-early-learning-guidelines. Availability of standards for other countries vary, but the United Kingdom, Sweden, Singapore, Finland, and New Zealand (among others) have national curriculum standards (in English) that you can view online. Australia and Canada have standards by state or province. Your program's goals may be based on your state's standards or they may have been developed independently by the staff or a curriculum specialist. These standards help you to know the broad expectations for both for the content that children are expected to acquire and how you are expected to teach it.

Early learning guidelines have become more and more influential in the design of early childhood curriculum. When they are written with knowledge of young children and how they learn, they help you to identify how the activities you provide help children to acquire skills, knowledge, and dispositions (habits of mind, sometimes called attitudes). They can provide you with important information to help you in the complex task of designing curriculum. However, content standards should not be a substitute for thoughtfully considering what is "worth knowing" for a group of children. Good early childhood practices such as creating a rich play environment and providing appropriate teacher-led activities help you to meet standards.

Accountability does not come about simply because you are following good practice. It involves demonstrating how the curriculum experiences you plan for children address the required standards. One way to do this is to identify the standards relevant for your plans. We recommend that you keep a copy of your state or program standards close at hand as you plan.

Organizing Curriculum

Curriculum can be organized in different ways. How you choose to organize the curriculum reflects your values and beliefs. The organizational approaches most often used are *learner-centered, subject-centered*, or *integrated*.

Learner-Centered Organization

When curriculum organization is based on the developmental stage, needs, and interests of children, it is called learner-centered. In a learner-centered curriculum design, teachers provide few preplanned activities and instead ensure that children have large blocks of time to play and explore in a planned environment. They make changes in the environment in response to their observations of children. Advocates of this approach believe that all planned learning experiences should emerge from observations of children and be based on children's interests. They feel that imposing activities that originate from outside sources is counterproductive because children will fail to engage with the content. For this reason this approach is often called *emergent curriculum.*

A learner-centered organization is the best way to plan for infants, toddlers, and young preschoolers. It can also be used with older preschoolers, kindergartners, and primary-age children. But because it is limited by what children bring to the educational experience, it may not be sufficient to provide intellectual challenge and stimulation as children get older.

Subject-Area Organization

Organization by subject areas (e.g., math, science, social studies, reading) reflects the view that education is about the attainment of knowledge. Teaching is generally organized into blocks of time (e.g., reading 9:00 to 9:45, math 10:00 to 10:30). Sometimes two or more disciplines—for example, math and science—are combined for instruction. In this type of organization the role of the teacher is usually to impart knowledge. You will sometimes hear this approach referred to as *direct instruction.*

Although organization by subjects ensures that a variety of content areas are given attention, it does not help children understand relationships that exist between subjects. It also fails to take into account children's different interests and different strengths. This approach is often used in classrooms for older children, adolescents, and adults, but it is not appropriate for young children who best learn and understand when information is presented in more holistic ways—involving senses, body, and mind working together.

Integrated Organization

Integrated organization refers to an educational approach in which a topic of study provides a focus for the curriculum. The topic serves as an umbrella under which different developmental and subject areas are integrated. In an integrated study, children investigate a topic in depth over a period of time. The topic forms the hub for curriculum in many different subject areas. Children's interests or the teacher's ideas about what children would enjoy or benefit from can be sources of the topic. You have experienced integrated curriculum formally and informally in your life. You experienced integrated curriculum in school if you studied a country and made traditional food (using math, science, and nutrition concepts), learned a dance (developing physical skill while learning about music), read their folklore (developing reading skills, vocabulary, and understanding of literature), and made maps of the country. That was a social studies integrated study. You experienced an informal integrated study if you went on a trip and experienced the climate and landscape of a new place (social studies), saw the plants and animals that lived there (science), learned phrases local people used (language), bought a souvenir and calculated how much you had to spend on it (math), visited a gallery (art), and listened to the local radio station (music).

An integrated approach reflects that children learn holistically. It is mindful of the idea of multiple intelligences—that is, that individuals learn best through their particular strengths or intelligences. Good integrated curriculum provides many different avenues for learning about a topic. A study can be tailored to fit the learning styles of a group of children and of individual children in the group.

Advocates of integrated curriculum believe that it is appropriate and effective, especially for children 4 years and older. We have seen it used effectively with much younger children when the topic was carefully selected, with activities matched to their stage of development. For example, in a toddler classroom we know, the children's activities for several weeks were focused on water. Children *experienced* water in many forms—for washing, playing, drinking. It was a wonderful and appropriate exploration of the nature of water, quite different from a study of water in a kindergarten or 4-year-old class.

An integrated study of a topic contributes simultaneously to children's growing awareness, skill, and understanding in many areas. It provides opportunities for children to learn by doing and have many direct experiences with the world. Used well and thoughtfully, it helps children to understand that learning is connected to life. For these reasons we think that integrated planning is the most effective way to plan curriculum for older preschool, kindergarten, and primary school children. In our experience, it also makes teaching more interesting and satisfying.

Content and Methods

Young children are learning all the time, from all of their experiences. Much of what they learn comes through the routines, relationships, and incidental encounters that they have with people, places, and objects. They learn through their own self-directed play. For infants and young toddlers these are the only ways that they learn: routines, learning environments, and relationships *are* the curriculum. In fact, routines, learning environments, and relationships are the foundation of curriculum for all young children. Whatever the planned curriculum, it is the life of the classroom that is most important—the snack, play time, the teacher, friends, and toys.

Routines, relationships, and spontaneous play remain important curriculum activities throughout the early childhood years. As children get older, however, teachers plan a variety of activities to present curriculum content. The art of planning involves selecting content and teaching strategies that are right for the children (individuals with particular interests, cultures, and abilities) and for the information or skill being acquired. Four categories of teaching strategies form the foundation of early childhood pedagogy (see Table 11.1). These can be thought of as existing on a continuum from most **child initiated** (i.e., activities that are selected and directed by a child) to most **teacher directed** (i.e., selected and guided by the teacher).

1. **Play**—child-selected and child-directed activities that are explored independently in an environment designed for purposeful play and learning
2. **Scaffolded activities**—involve one or two children with a teacher. The teacher responds to the child and may shape the direction of the activity.
3. **Small-group activities**—are focused, planned, and directed by the teacher for 3–10 children. Because the group is small, the teacher can be flexible and responsive to children.
4. **Large-group activities**—are teacher-directed, whole-class activities with 10 or more children. Because the group is larger, the teacher must be more directive and in control

TABLE 11.1 Four Categories of Teaching Strategies

Play	Scaffolded Activities	Small-Group Activities	Large-Group Activities
Child selects	Child selects	Teacher plans	Teacher plans
Child plays independently or with peers	1 or 2 children with a teacher	3–10 children	Whole-class—10 or more children
Child directs	Child and teacher direct in a play/learning dialogue	Teacher plans and directs, taking cues from children	Teacher plans and directs
Teacher plans and arranges environment and supervises purposefully to support play	Teacher responds to the child and may guide the direction of the activity	Teacher responds flexibly to children	Teacher more directive and in control; responds to the group to maintain order and positive learning

Play

Early childhood teachers have historically placed play above all other teaching strategies. Through their exploration and self-initiated play in a planned learning environment, children develop skills and knowledge of many kinds simultaneously. At the same time, they enjoy themselves and become motivated to keep exploring and learning.

Young children need many opportunities for play each day. How and when do you plan for play? Play is the most appropriate learning medium when you want children to explore and discover for themselves. When you purposefully provide play opportunities that support the curriculum you have chosen, you are planning for play. For example, to support a child's fine motor development you might plan for play opportunities with clay, dough, or stringing beads. To support the development of the understanding of concepts of volume and measurement you might plan for open-ended play activities with water, sand, and containers of different sizes. To develop understanding of people you ensure that children have lots of time to play with one another. If you are planning play opportunities while using an integrated curriculum study, you might plan to add dramatic play props related to the topic. For example, in the study of birds that we use as an example in this chapter, teachers added puppets, toy birds, and cloth hoods colored and shaped like the crests of birds to the dramatic play and block areas to encourage children to reenact their developing understanding of birds. And while children are playing you can be teaching (see Figure 11.1).

Scaffolded Activities

Do you remember learning to drive a car? It's unlikely that you would have developed driving skill by playing with a car. You also probably would not have learned if you had attended a lecture class on driving. Instead, you learned when you were ready and interested with the guidance from someone more competent than yourself. New abilities are first developed in collaboration with an adult or more competent peer in what Vygotsky called the *zone of proximal development* or ZPD (Berk & Winsler, 1995).

FIGURE 11.1   Some Strategies for Teaching While Children Play

- **Intentionally wait.** Purposefully allow children time for purposeful play, mindful struggle, and independent discovery.

- **Observe** and make notes while children are playing to inform your planning.

- **Play** with children to build relationships and help them develop play skills. *Model* how to play (how to use toys, take on roles, support other players). Sensitively join the play without taking it over or interfering.

- **Acknowledge and encourage** children who are working on a skill. Physically or verbally acknowledge them and encourage them to persevere.

- **Scaffold** (support) children as they develop a skill or concept during play by physically or verbally helping them *only as much as they need*. As a child acquires a skill or concept, gradually withdraw assistance until the child is able to be independent.

- **Adjust the challenge.** Be alert to the signs that a child needs a different (harder or easier) challenge. If a toy is misused, if children destroy or walk away from their work, or if a child finishes a project without thought or attention, it may be that the level is wrong.

Source: Information from E. Moravcik, S. Nolte, & S. Feeney, *Meaningful Curriculum for Young Children*, 2013.

When you want to help a child acquire a specific concept or skill in his or her zone of proximal development, you may want to plan a scaffolded activity with that child. This kind of planned activity enables you to concentrate on a particular child's learning process in a learning dialogue. As you work together, you observe and assess a child's knowledge and skill and modify what you do based on the child's response. You can plan to support the development of skills, and concepts for the individual child, for skills that you want all the children to develop or to support development of the major understandings of a topic of study. For example, in the study of birds that we describe later in this chapter, the teachers prepared several *workjobs* (simple teacher-made games that help children to learn concepts and develop skills) that were introduced to children individually: One involved counting birds in fine art postcards, another involved matching photographs of different birds that inhabited the playground, and another involved sequencing the stages of a bird's development from hatching to fledgling.

Group size, teacher–child ratio, and the way you organize both time and the physical environment will influence the extent to which you can engage in teacher-child activities. The smaller the group and the more that self-selected independent activities are supported, the more you will be able to engage in one-on-one activities with children. This is why low teacher–child ratios and smaller group sizes are hallmarks of quality in early childhood settings (Phillips, Mekos, Scarr, McCartney, & Abbott–Shim, 2000).

Small-Group Activities

When you work with a few children at a time, it is called a *small group*. The size of a small group varies with the age of the children. For toddlers, a small group is 2 to 4 children. With preschoolers, a small group may be 5 to 10 children, though fewer is better, especially for 3-year-olds. And with kindergarten and primary school children, 8 to 12 children is a small group—though again, fewer is better.

A small group size helps you to present concepts, facilitate conversations between children, and have meaningful personal contact with each child. It is probably the most effective teaching strategy for preschool and primary children. This approach reduces waiting time and allows for activities that involve turn-taking, guided peer interaction, manipulation of materials, and quite a lot of teacher assistance.

In a small group you are able to attend to the way children respond and can evaluate and modify what you do. When you have children with diverse developmental needs (as you do in any mixed-age classroom), you can tailor the length of the small-group time and the kind of activity to match the children. For example, a planned process for naming groups in a class of children aged 2½ through 5 took place in two small groups divided by age. The younger group spent 10 minutes thinking of and naming their group (the Flowers). The older group spent three 15-minute group times on subsequent days brainstorming, negotiating, and voting for their small-group name (the Cloud-Airplanes).

If you need to discuss an activity with the children while it is happening, then a small group is the best choice. Activities such as I Spy, discussions, acting out stories, creative movement, cooking, and walks work best in small groups.

Small groups that meet together on a regular basis develop an identity of their own. They help children to develop some important skills including the ability to listen and converse in a group, solve problems and make decisions democratically, take leader and follower roles, and accept responsibility for the outcomes of their decisions.

Large-Group Activities

Large-group activities (planned for a whole class of more than 12 children) are generally the least effective for teaching and the hardest for teachers to implement successfully. This may account for the fact that they are often named by children as their least favorite activities in school (Wiltz & Klein, 2001).

In most classrooms children gather together at least once a day for a meeting or circle time. These gatherings can be valuable when they allow children to share a common experience and build a sense of community. In preschool they are appropriate only when children can all be active (e.g., by singing a song or engaging in creative movement). Older children can benefit more from large-group activities but they are not appropriate if the activity requires a great deal of passive listening while the teacher attends to individual responses (e.g., show and tell) or when children must wait a long time for a short turn (e.g., in cooking). They can be effective for story time, singing and for group games like dodge ball. In general, the younger the children the less you plan for large-group experiences.

Selecting the Activity

There are many hundreds of different activities that can make up curriculum in early childhood programs. You will select those that best meet your purpose, and those that you can present effectively in your program with your children and the resources available to you.

The relative balance of child-initiated exploration of the planned learning environment and teacher-guided experiences will vary based on the characteristics of the children as well as on the characteristics of the program. Both processes have advantages and disadvantages and are most appropriate for different kinds of content. For example, it is unlikely that a 5-year-old would spontaneously learn to read a clock or tie shoelaces without individual help from a teacher. Similarly, it is unlikely that any amount of planned activity would teach that same 5-year-old to climb a rope, although she might learn to do so in focused, self-initiated play.

Infants, toddlers, and young preschoolers can learn little through direct instruction. Both you and the child will feel frustrated if you try. But as children get older they will learn more from direct teaching when they are interested and motivated. Every educator will seek an optimal balance between child-chosen and adult-directed activity. As you plan, you need to ask yourself which approach best meets the developmental characteristics of the children and your educational purposes. The answer to this question will help you find the right balance for your group.

Choose Appropriate Methods. We know that young children learn at varying rates, that they are active learners, that they learn through play, and that they need many opportunities to practice skills as they are acquired (Copple & Bredekamp, 2009). They learn through active engagement and concrete experiences. Because we know these things, we also know that young children do not benefit from abstract methods of teaching such as worksheets, lectures, and drill on isolated skills.

Observe a young child who is required to sit still and listen to an adult try to teach a fact out of context. Chances are, you will see a child who is inattentive, or disruptive. In addition to knowing what methods are appropriate for young children, you also need to be able to identify and avoid inappropriate methods. These methods do not build understanding and, because they are often aversive, can lead to negative feelings toward schooling. They do not belong in programs for preschool and kindergarten children. They have limited utility in programs for primary

Reflect on presenting curriculum

Think of an early childhood program that you know. What did you see children doing? How could you tell the children were learning? During what kinds of activities did you sense the children were most engaged?

school children. The picture is very different when you observe a child who is actively engaged in a hands-on learning experience relating to a topic of interest.

Basing Plans on What You Observe

In most programs for children 5 and younger, the focus for planning will come from what you observe about the children in your group. You will plan to accomplish a purpose (goals and objectives) and choose an appropriate activity for that purpose. This will relate to values and beliefs, the characteristics of children and families, and curriculum standards. But perhaps most important, your plans should depend on what you have *observed* about the children. As an early childhood student, you are developing observation skills. The purpose

of learning these skills is to help you be a more skillful teacher. When you plan, you use what you learn from observation to help you teach. When you base your plans on what you observe, you are much more likely to plan appropriate, successful activities.

Observe Individuals

Zoe, Tyler, Aidan, and Kaitlin (all 4-year-olds) are playing in the dramatic play area. Zoe wears an apron and directs Kaitlin and Aidan: "You be the mom. You be the baby. Have dinner at the Spaghetti House." Tyler gives them a piece of paper and asks, "What do you want to eat?" Kaitlin looks at the paper and then says, "Peanut butter." Tyler explains—"It's a spaghetti restaurant; you have to have spaghetti." He scribbles on a pad of paper, picks up a phone, and says to Zoe—"Make spaghetti for the mom and milk for the baby." Aidan sits quietly and watches the others.

Intentional teachers observe children all the time. They purposefully observe individual children looking for a number of things so they can consciously support children's development through curriculum. You will observe children to learn about their:

- **Strengths**—What a child is able to do well gives you ideas for what and how to teach. New knowledge and skills can be built on the foundation of each child's abilities.
- **Interests**—Children learn best doing the things they *like* to do. Let their interests guide you so that a child will *want* to learn.
- **Needs**—All children have strengths; all children have needs. While it is important to consider children's needs, avoid basing plans on what a child cannot do or does not know. It is far more engaging to start with interests and abilities as a base from which to learn new things.

If you happened to observe the restaurant dramatic play described above you might decide to create a literacy activity that would build on Tyler's obvious understanding of the purposes of reading and writing. You might plan a cooking activity to support Zoe's interest in food, and you might add some props that encourage cooperative interactions (e.g., another small table and chair) to invite Aidan to engage as another a customer in the restaurant.

Observe the Group

Good teachers observe their children as a community. Every class has a group identity and a group personality with friendships, relationships, and rivalries. Sometimes, a group is mature with many life experiences and skills. At other times, the group will seem much younger and be less experienced. The curriculum will be planned differently for each.

For example, when you observed the restaurant play described above you would have noticed that the children had interest in restaurants. You might notice that Tyler and Zoe are leaders who direct others. You would see that Kaitlin and Aidan do not seem to know as much. As a result you might read a book about a restaurant to build on these interests and to give all of the children some background knowledge.

Observe with a Focus

If you are planning intentionally, with a purpose in mind, you will also observe intentionally, with a focus. For example, if want to plan for social studies, then you would observe the dramatic play episode just described with a social studies focus. You might ask yourself *what do these children understand about how people in communities work to meet one another's needs?* You might use their interest as a springboard for an integrated study of your local community and the different ways people make, buy, and sell food.

Writing Plans

All educators plan. As a teacher, you will choose what to plan, in what detail, and how far in advance. When early childhood educators use the word *plan*, they mean different things. Sometimes they are referring a detailed written outline for a specific learning activity, called an *activity plan* or *lesson plan*. At other times, they mean a calendar of activities to be done at different times over a week, which in some settings called a *weekly plan*. They may also mean a plan for several weeks of activities, in many different content areas, based on a topic, called an *integrated plan*.

Teachers of infants and young toddlers usually plan for individual children and for ways to modify the environment. Preschool and primary teachers often write a weekly calendar to share with others and keep track of what happens next. In kindergartens and primary schools, teachers often write detailed plans with purpose statements and objectives for many activities in a day or week. Many teachers plan activities for specific children in their group, particularly if the group includes children with disabilities or other special needs.

Activity or Lesson Plans

A detailed written design for a single curriculum event is usually called an *activity plan* in preschools and a *lesson plan* in elementary schools and special education settings. These plans specify objectives, list needed materials, describe teaching procedures, and outline ways to assess success in achieving the objectives. To be useful, a plan should be brief, specific, and complete. You can think of an activity or lesson plan as a recipe for teaching. Like a recipe, it outlines each essential step but assumes that you know the basics.

Carefully thinking through and writing an activity helps to ensure success. When your planning is good, you will be clear in your communication to children and feel more comfortable in teaching. Because this process is so valuable, you will practice writing many detailed plans during your preparation to become an early childhood educator. We give our students a basic outline to use in planning activities (see Figure 11.2). It describes a typical sequence for planning, but the way you actually write your plans may be different. As long as you think through all the pieces eventually, it doesn't really matter which part you write down first.

Decide What

The beginning of a written activity/lesson plan is a brief explanation that sets the stage and helps you to think through what you are going to do with children and why. The first thing you have to do is decide what you are going to plan. To do that, you need to think about your particular circumstances—the children, the setting, the families, and the standards and expectations of the school.

Activity name and description—Every teaching activity has a name you use to talk about it. It can be classified by type—is it a game, a group discussion, a book? If you are writing plans to share with others (colleagues, families, your college professor), elaborate by briefly describing it.

Primary curriculum area—Good early childhood teaching activities address a number of curriculum areas. Although young children learn in integrated ways, identifying the curriculum area that is going to be the primary focus is helpful for a number of reasons, especially when you are learning to plan. When you are clear about the curriculum area you are primarily addressing, you are more likely to accomplish your purpose. For example, children engaged in a finger painting activity are developing sensory awareness and fine motor control (physical development), learning about color mixing (science), expressing feelings and ideas through art media (art), and having rich conversations (language). If your primary curriculum area and purpose is to help children express feelings and ideas using art media you will call this an art activity. And you will want to use good-quality paint and paper in order to preserve children's efforts. You will focus your teaching and comments on children's awareness of how their work expresses a feeling or idea ("Your swirls of gray remind me of a stormy cloud"). If your primary curriculum area and purpose is to enhance children's awareness of texture, you will call this a sensory activity. You might use colored shaving cream on a tray that can be easily hosed off and that leaves no lasting documentation. Again, your comments and teaching will be targeted: "How does the paint feel against your fingers? Is it slick or sticky? Sniff it. What does it remind you of?"

Who it's for: The children—You are planning for specific children at a specific time in a specific place. When you write a plan it is valuable to note on the plan the name of the group, age, and number of children for whom you are planning.

FIGURE 11.2   Activity Plan Format—Detailed

WHAT is it?
Activity name and **brief description:**
Primary curriculum area:
WHO is it for?
The children: Particular children, or group for whom you are planning:
Age:
Number of children (at a time):
WHY this activity?
Rationale: What you have observed or know about the children that explains why you have chosen this activity for these children at this time
Objectives: Skills, knowledge/concepts/understanding, dispositions/attitudes you want children to acquire or expand. "By participating in this activity the children will . . . "
Standards: State or national content standard(s) addressed
WHAT do you need?
Materials, equipment, space, time required
How to prepare and set up
Things to consider (risks you must supervise and other important points to remember)
WHAT do you do?
Teaching procedures: What you will do and say, in what order
Introduction: How to begin so children will be interested and know what to do
Teaching steps: What to do and say step-by-step to provide the experiences that will teach children the concepts, develop the skills, or build the attitudes or dispositions described in the objectives
Closure: What you will do or say to reinforce/support what children have learned and help them make a transition to another activity
HOW will you assess?
What to look for to identify if the objectives were met and how to document it

Objectives	Evidence of learning	How to document the evidence
Objectives from the first part of the plan	Things a child might do or say during the activity if objectives are met Things a child might do or say later during play, routines, or other activities if objectives are met	Observations, work samples, photographs, etc.

Explain Why

What you observed provides the **rationale**, or *reason,* for your plan. We believe that writing a statement of rationale is one of the most useful things you can do to help yourself become an intentional teacher. We ask our college students to write a rationale statement that answers the question, "Why have you chosen this activity for this child/these children, at this time?" This is different from a statement of objectives. Your answer (*"I have chosen this activity for the Elephant Groovers because I observed that they enjoy and are interested* *in sensory activities"*) helps you make sure that what you are doing has some meaningful connection to the children.

Objectives. Every written activity has specific objectives: the attitudes, skills, knowledge, and experiences you want to help children acquire. Because family members and parents often cannot perceive the educational content of the play activities that form such a large part of the early childhood curriculum, an important part of your professional role is articulating the area of learning and the purpose of every activity you do with children (whether or not you have written a plan for it). Being able to do so distinguishes you as a professional teacher. It is rare for a single activity to "teach" a skill, understanding, or attitude for all time. Instead think of objectives as drops of rain contributing to filling a pool.

Another category of objective for which we often plan is the acquisition of "dispositions," what Lilian Katz calls "habits of mind" (Katz, 1993). Curiosity is an example of a disposition that we want children to acquire. There are many other dispositions that we wish to encourage—a disposition to read, a disposition to be kind, a disposition to be resourceful, or to ask questions. When you plan curriculum activities for children, it is valuable to remember that these dispositions are important objectives.

A plan's objectives describe its intended outcomes in terms of the abilities, knowledge, experiences, and dispositions that you want children to gain. For example, for a music activity you might write the following objectives:

By participating in this activity, children will:

- *Learn the term* tempo—*understand that tempo means the speed at which a song is played or sung*
- *Develop beginning ability to play simple rhythm instruments with care*
- *Hear and begin to appreciate music from another culture*
- *Understand how to use music to express feelings and develop a disposition to do so*

The age group of children and the program in which you work will determine the kinds of objectives you address. Objectives for preschool programs may be broader than those for elementary schools and may include involvement, awareness, and appreciation as well as concepts, understandings, and skills to be acquired. The objectives should match the overall purpose and rationale. They should be reasonable for the scope of the activity. It is reasonable for a music activity to help children begin to *hear and begin to appreciate music from another culture*. It is not reasonable to expect that same music activity to help children to be accepting of people who are different from themselves.

Objectives can be thought of as progressing from simple to complex (see Table 11.2). Simple objectives involve recalling and identifying. More complex objectives involve making connections, understanding relationships, solving problems by combining what is known, and evaluating (Bloom, Mesia, & Krathwohl, 1964). As you write objectives it is useful to consider whether your objectives and your activities are helping children to acquire more complex skills. For example, in the objectives for the music activity just described, the first objective (*Learn the term* tempo) is a simple objective—recall; the second objective involves application (*beginning ability to play simple rhythm instruments with care*); and the fourth (*Understand how to use music to express feelings and develop a disposition to do so*) is more complex and involves evaluation.

TABLE 11.2   Bloom's Taxonomy of Educational Objectives

	Level	What It Is
Least complex ↓ **Most complex**	Recall	The ability to repeat or recognize a concept or skill
	Comprehension	Understanding and the ability to explain what is known
	Application	The ability to use what is known
	Analysis	The ability to make connections, see patterns, or understand interrelationships
	Synthesis	The ability to integrate and recombine
	Evaluation	The ability to assess, critique, or appraise based on specific criteria

Source: Summarized from B. S. Bloom, B. B. Mesia, & D. Krathwohl, *Taxonomy of Educational Objectives*, 1964.

TABLE 11.3   Examples of Beginnings for Objectives

Knowledge	Skill	Attitude	Experience
Learn about . . .	Practice . . .	Develop awareness of . . .	Try . . .
Gain understanding of . . .	Develop skill in . . .	Enjoy . . .	Hear . . .
Describe . . .	Begin to be able to . . .	Develop a disposition to . . .	See . . .
Recognize . . .	Demonstrate . . .	Be sensitive to . . .	Taste . . .
Sort . . .	Show . . .	Be respectful of . . .	Feel . . .
Identify . . .	Differentiate . . .	Appreciate . . .	Smell . . .

When you begin to write plans, you may find that writing objectives is not easy. There are many things to consider. Our college students find it helpful to look at a number of beginnings to objectives to get started (see Table 11.3).

Objectives that precisely describe a behavior are called *measurable* or *behavioral objectives*. They describe specific behaviors, the conditions under which they take place, and the criteria for success ("When presented with five sheets of paper with lines drawn down the center, the child will cut at least one sheet of paper along the line"). There are different points of view regarding how specific and measurable objectives ought to be. For example, we think it is reasonable for a music activity to help children begin to develop a disposition to use music to express feelings. However, since this disposition is not measurable, some educators might reject this objective.

Behavioral objectives leave little room for individual choice, require all children to be at the same place at the end of a lesson, and do not allow for spontaneity or creativity. They are often used in special education where teaching is often quite prescriptive. They are not consistent with the belief that children must construct knowledge from their own active involvement with materials and experiences. Because they sometimes focus on trivial though achievable goals, they can lead teachers to emphasize less important aspects of activities and lose track of important learning that isn't observable or measurable.

Measurable objectives can help you demonstrate that your teaching has had an effect. When you are required to write them, it is important to learn how to do so in ways that have integrity.

Standards. To show *how* you are teaching to meet your state early learning guidelines, we recommend identifying the relevant standards for activity/lesson plans along with the objectives. Many teachers find it helpful to have a copy of their state or program standards close at hand as they write plans. Since most of these are available online, they can simplify the process of writing plans.

Identify What You Need

Once you have selected what you are going to do and have identified your objectives, the next step in writing a plan is to begin to think through what you will need for your activity. Just like with a recipe, you need to have all the ingredients to make your plan work. Often the difference between a plan's success or failure is having the right materials, equipment, space, and time. Make a list of the *materials* that you need to prepare, borrow, or buy so that you have them nearby ahead of time. Think about the *space* and *equipment* you need, the best *time* in the schedule for the activity, and how much time to allow. Think about what else is needed. Does anyone need to be called or alerted? Do you need to cut paper or cover the table with newspaper? Plan for it.

As you think through the steps of the activity and write down the procedures, you may discover that there are additional things you need. You will go back and add these to your activity plan.

Plan the Teaching: What You Do

Teaching procedures spell out what you will do and say, and in what order. They are the heart of a plan for teaching. Teaching procedures generally include at least three sections—an introduction, steps to teach the content, and closure.

The ***introduction*** describes how you will get children's attention, engage their interest, and let them know what to do. For many activities the introduction can be very simple: "I brought a new game to share with you today. It's this box. There is something soft inside. You can to put your hand in here and guess what it is."

If the activity involves an unfamiliar word, concept, or skill, you may need to introduce it in advance. If the activity involves an item that is novel or highly attractive to the children, you will want to plan a way for them to get acquainted with it before you begin teaching ("Each person will get a turn to pat the puppet before I tell you the puppet story"). Skilled teachers know that it is important to give children lots of time for a new experience. In fact, simply introducing an item may be an entire activity. One of the most common mistakes of novice teachers is to introduce many intriguing and exciting objects at one time ("Here are three new puppets, a cape to wear, and a magic wand to use in our story"). They are then surprised when children focus on the "things" rather than the content they were planning to teach.

Teaching steps describe what you will do and say to accomplish your objectives. The steps should match the objectives you wrote and should be appropriate for the children. The amount of detail can vary. You need at least an outline of the basic steps, simply described with enough information so that you (or a colleague) will be able to use the plan again at a later date. Beginning teachers, and anyone planning an activity that is particularly complex, should map out what to say and questions to ask to support the objectives. As you gain experience, you will not plan in as much detail. But while you are learning, detailed planning is more than a class assignment—it will help you learn to think like a teacher.

The *closure* of an activity sums up the learning in some way that makes sense for children. It may be a statement you make ("You really knew a lot about birds") or it may be a way for children to show something that they know and make a *transition* ("Think of a bird and fly like your bird to the playground"). A well-thought-out closure and a smooth transition help you to focus children on what they know and are able to do (see Figure 11.3).

Plan for Assessment

What children do and say during and following an activity gives evidence of what they have learned. The last part of a written activity plan describes what you will look for that indicates that children have gained the knowledge, skills, or attitudes in the objectives.

In our earlier example, we looked for whether children were attentive to the music and asked questions about it, or asked to have it repeated; whether they moved to the music; whether they played the instruments in ways that made sound and were rhythmic; and whether they began to recognize and use the names of the instruments. This growth could be documented through anecdotal records, through video or audio recordings, or even through work samples—children's drawings and journals. We like to use an anecdotal record form like the sample included in Figure 11.4 to record children's responses.

Implementing the Plan

Although a good plan helps you teach in the same way that a good recipe helps you cook, children are not as predictable as flour and salt. The best planned activity can fail miserably if you are not responsive to the children. If you went to a lot of trouble to write a plan, you may feel committed to using it just the way it's written. Just as a cook must adjust to the tastes of the diners, the characteristics of the ingredients, and the available equipment, a teacher must adjust to the children and the circumstances. Experienced teachers know that they need to make modifications in response to children's interests and needs. Their teaching resembles a dance in which the children are their partners. They observe and respond to the children—and the children respond to them.

Inexperienced teachers often find it difficult to be flexible in implementing a plan. For example, we observed a student attempting to lead a group of 4-year-olds in a movement activity (walking as a group like a centipede with many legs). The children had many things to say about centipedes and did not attend to the well-planned activity. The novice teacher became flustered by the children's inattention and was unable to find a way to incorporate their ideas and move forward with the activity. With more confidence and attention to the children, the discussion could have contributed to the activity instead of detracting from it.

Assessing and Documenting Learning

The measure of your success as a planner is whether children learned what you intended to teach. If you observe children carefully, you will see evidence

FIGURE 11.3 **Detailed Activity/Lesson Plan Example**

Curriculum Planning

WHAT is it?

Activity name and brief description: *The Names of the Birds Workjob*—Matching photographs of birds with printed name to photographs and names

Primary curriculum area: Literacy

WHO is it for?

The children: The Scary Monsters

Age: 4–5 yr. olds

Number of children: 9

WHY this activity?

Rationale: The children are highly aware of the different birds in the yard and what they are called. Megan, Jonah, Janae, and Edwin are particularly intrigued by letters and words.

OBJECTIVES:

By participating in this activity the children will . . .

1. understand print has meaning

2. begin to connect sounds to letters

3. build vocabulary (beak, crest, tail, talons, vented, waxbill, whiskered, wings, bulbul, cardinal, dove, egret, finch, golden, heron, java, mannikin, mejiro, northern, plover, saffron, sparrow)

Standards: **HPCS** Domain III (Communication)

Standard 7:   Acquire concepts of print.

Standard 8:   Acquire emergent literacy skills while exploring print in books and the environment.

(Note: For purposes of this example, we have used the Hawaii Preschool Content Standards.)

WHAT do you need?

Materials: Workjob in a box

Equipment: Table with chairs

Space: Manipulative Toys and Games area

Time: Introduce at small group and make available at activity time

How to prepare and set up:

• Download bird photographs. Make picture same size (2.5"x2.5").

• Print 2 copies each with name of birds underneath.

• Print birds' names separately.

• Laminate pieces.

• Put in a box with 3 sections. Decorate box with pictures and title.

Things to consider (risks you must supervise and other important points to remember)

WHAT do you do?

Introduction: Show the game. Spread out sets of cards. Pick up one card with familiar bird. Invite children to look and name bird. Tell them the name is written underneath.

(continued)

FIGURE 11.3 Detailed Activity/Lesson Plan Example *(continued)*

Explain: *There is a matching picture for this bird. Ask: Can you find it? When found say: There's something even trickier. There's a word that matches without a picture. Can you find it?* Once word has been found, explain that the game will be available to play with during activity time. Say: *You can play this on your own or with a friend.*

Teaching steps: As children play the game, observe and help.

Extend learning by saying things like: *That one says RED CRESTED CARDINAL. Can you find another bird with RED in its name? Or: That one is a Mmmmmmmejiro—I wonder what its name starts with.*

Encourage more able children to help those who have difficulty: *I saw Megan find the northern cardinal's name. Ask her if she can help you.*

If a child has difficulty, suggest the child just match the pictures. If a child is having an easy time, invite the child to match the word to the word.

Closure: Based on children's ability, play a putting-away version, saying something like: *You tell me one to put away and then I'll tell you one to put away.* Comment on the skill and competence: *Wow, you know which one is the Northern Cardinal. I wonder if I'll be able to get the next one. Or: You know 10 different birds!*

HOW will you assess?

Objectives	Evidence of Learning	How to document the evidence
For child to . . . 1. understand print has meaning 2. connect sounds to letters 3. build vocabulary	**child might . . .** • match words and pictures • create images of birds and ask the teacher to write about the bird on their work • create images of birds and attempt to write on their work • use bird names and vocabulary	Anecdotal Records Word samples

that they have or have not gained the knowledge, skill, or attitudes described in the objectives. In the example in Figure 11.3 the teacher would watch to see if children matched words and pictures in the game, created images of birds using art media and asked the teacher to write about the bird or attempted to themselves, or if the children used bird-related vocabulary. This growth could be documented through anecdotal records like those in Figure 11.4, or work samples that could be annotated (see Figure 11.5) to provide documentation of children's learning.

While it is valuable to document children's learning, it is important to make sure that the documentation authentically shows what children have actually learned. A photograph of a child posing for the camera rarely provides evidence of learning.

Evaluating the Plan: What Worked and What Didn't Work

Whether you plan an activity with children or a party for your friends, you evaluate your plan. Did it go well? Could it have gone better? Is it worth doing again? Did it accomplish what I intended? After you have written and implemented

FIGURE 11.4 **Anecdotal Records**

Curriculum Planning

Activity: The Names of the Birds Workjob

Child: *Megan*

Played game first. Matched all pictures, then matched half the words. Said words as she worked: myna, mejiro, cardinal. Later went to writing table and drew a Brazilian cardinal and wrote letter B and K (see work sample).

Objective demonstrated: OB 1, 2, & 3
Comment: *First inventive spelling?*

Child: *Jonah*

Wanted teacher to play with him. When teacher had "difficulty" finding pieces J laughed aloud—found pieces, said name of bird, said: I am very good at this.

Objective demonstrated: OB 1
Comment: *Seems confident; likes the idea of reading.*

Child: *Janae*

Did about half the game matching pictures and words. Asked: Which one is the mommy bird, how does she lay her eggs? Then went to writing center and drew a picture of mother bird with eggs and asked the teacher to write explanation (see work sample).

Objective demonstrated: OB 1, 2, & 3
Comment: *Ready to use reference materials?*

Child: *Keila*

Looked and matched the cardinal pictures then left—did not put pieces away.

Objective demonstrated: OB 1
Comment: *Didn't seem very interested.*

Child: *Edwin*

Took out each set (pictures and words, pictures only, words only) and lined up. Matched all. Did not interact with other child during activity. Wrote bird names in writing center using cards as model (see work sample).

Objective demonstrated: OB 1 & 2
Comment: *Very serious!*

Child: *Brandy*

Smiled a lot during intro. Made several comments—egret does not come to bird feeder, there are two kinds of sparrows—Did not try the game.

Objective demonstrated: OB 3
Comment:

a plan, take a few moments (that's probably all you'll have!) to reflect on what you did and how children responded. This reflection ensures that the learning experience you planned for children also becomes a learning experience for you. Evaluating your planning and implementation is different from assessing whether the children acquired the objectives for the activity, as you can see in Figure 11.6.

Sometimes an apparent planning disaster may be the result of overstimulating materials, timing mistakes (not allowing enough time for children to explore materials, or asking them to wait and listen when they need to move and do), poor room arrangement, insufficient opportunities for physical activity, or expectations that are too challenging or not challenging enough for the children. Modified and tried again, the plan may prove sound. But if you don't reflect on what happened you will never be able to figure out what went wrong and make the changes.

It may actually be even harder to evaluate a success. Were the children engaged in the activity because the materials were interesting, because you were responsive to the children, or because Jon was absent today? Evaluate your successes as well as your failures.

To help you remember, it is worthwhile to make a note of anything you would add or do differently on the plan. Reflecting in this way is usually a requirement for students, but it is good practice for all teachers. Then, when you go back to your plans, you will remember what happened last time. Reflecting and evaluating closes the planning circle.

FIGURE 11.5   Annotated Work Sample

The Mama bird makes eggs with baby birds inside.
They come out right there under her tail.

Child: Janae

Following playing the "Name of the Birds Workjob," Janae went to writing center and drew the above picture. She asked the teacher to write her words: *The Mama bird makes eggs with baby birds inside. They come out right there under her butt.* When the teacher read the words back to her Janae asked the teacher to change it: *The Mama bird makes eggs with baby birds inside. They come out right there under her tail.*

Objective demonstrated: OB 1, 2, & 3

Comment: Janae demonstrated growing understanding of both science and literacy.

FIGURE 11.6   Evaluation

Evaluation, Comments, What to Do Next:

The activity went fairly well. It was interesting to most kids. Too many pictures, too small—next time limit the number of pictures when introducing game, add a set of pet bird pictures and words.

Reflect on planning for children

Think about a time when you planned an activity to do with children. What happened? How did having a plan help you? What happened that surprised you? Would you use your plan again? What would you do differently?

Writing Activity/Lesson Plans in the Real World

When you become a teacher, will you write plans for every activity? It would be impossible and a little silly to spend hours writing plans for everything you do with children. Written plans are useful and may be necessary when clarity and sequence are crucial or where procedure or content is complex or unfamiliar. An activity such as reading a simple, familiar story will be included in a weekly plan but generally does not call for a detailed written plan. Locating the book, reviewing it, and spending a few moments thinking about questions to ask and how to structure discussion may be enough preparation. However, you should be *able* to write a clear plan for even a simple activity.

As you gain experience, you may want to use a simplified format such as the one in Figure 11.7 when you write activity plans. We like to keep these so that they can be easily retrieved and used again—in a digital file, in a notebook, or on 5-by-8 cards in file boxes or on metal rings. Digital storage allows you to easily retrieve and revise your plans, but because technology changes, you may find digital versions unreadable in a few years, so it is wise always to keep a hard copy.

FIGURE 11.7   Simple Format Activity Plan

Curriculum Planning

Activity name	The Names of the Birds Workjob
Curriculum area	Literacy
Objectives	To help children . . . 1. understand print has meaning 2. connect sounds to letters 3. build vocabulary
Standards	HPCS Communication 7 & 8
Needs	Workjob in a box
What you do	1. Show game at small group. Explain. Invite children to play in game center. 2. At center extend learning. Encourage more able children to help those who have difficulty. 3. Play a putting-away game, taking turns.

Weekly Plans

Experienced teachers almost always plan for each week by writing down the names of the activities, when they will be implemented, and noting what will be needed (see the example in Figure 11.8). They identify objectives for the activities, though not all teachers write these down. These few notes may guide them through most activities.

Writing a weekly plan helps you think through what you will do and stay organized. It also helps to keep the teaching team on track. Many teachers post their weekly plans so that families know what's coming up too.

For most preschool teachers and many kindergarten teachers the schedule of regular daily activities (e.g., story, small group, circle, and outdoor play), and special weekly events (e.g., cooking and field trips) provide a structure for weekly plans. Many also include the ways they will modify learning centers each week.

Primary school teachers often use subject areas in lieu of daily "events" to structure the weekly plan. It is common to plan for daily reading, math, and spelling, along with "special" activities that may happen only once a week, like art and PE. They frequently use a published curriculum.

As you plan for a week, you will keep in mind the skills and concepts that you want all the children to develop, as well as plans for specific children. You will include routines that are a feature of the week (e.g., cooking or a weekly visit from an adopted grandparent) and activities related to a curriculum focus (e.g., trips, visitors). You will also consider the impact of events in the school, among families, or in the community (e.g., holidays, elections, seasonal activities, bake sales, open house). In addition to planning the activities you will provide, you can also write a short statement of objectives for the week.

Weekly plans vary in the amount of detail included for each activity. Some teachers include an objective or purpose statement for each activity. Some include a list of materials to prepare or things to do. An example of a preschool weekly plan (Figure 11.8) is included here. When the week is over a brief assessment can be written directly on it and kept for future reference.

FIGURE 11.8 Preschool Weekly Plan

A Study of Birds • Week 4

Objectives for the week: To help children to . . .

- build understanding of the habits, needs and habitats of birds
- build skill in representing ideas and feelings symbolically
- acquire greater ability to cooperate as members of a community

	Monday	Tuesday	Wednesday	Thursday	Friday
Story8:50	*One Crow*—Aylesworth	*What Makes a Bird a Bird?*—Garelick	*Do Like a Duck Does*—Hindley and Bates		*Tough Boris*—Mem Fox
Outdoor Activity 9:00–10:00 Activity purposes: *to help children to . . .*	**Parachute Play** • develop large motor coordination • work cooperatively with others	**Build a Waffle Blocks Structure** • build large motor coordination • work together cooperatively	**Woodworking: Making a Brooder House** • use measurement tools • acquire concepts of shape and space		**Bubbles in the Water Table** • develop sensory awareness • learn about cause and effect
Small Group 10:00–10:20 (4–5 years) *Scary Monsters* Activity purposes: *to help children to . . .*	**Bird Clay Sculpture Lesson/Demonstration** • learn art techniques (modeling and sculpting) • explore shapes and gain awareness of birds' bodies	**Clay Sculpture** • practice art techniques (modeling and sculpting) • explore shape and space	**Trip Prediction—*What Might We See at the Audubon Nature Park?*** • prepare for field trip • develop the ability to hypothesize	**Learning Trip to Audubon Nature Park** *Trip Purpose—to give children experience with diverse birds and help them understand birds' needs, habits, and habitats*	**Write and Illustrate a Book About the Audubon Nature Park Trip** • understand the purpose of print • reconstruct understanding of birds' needs, habits, and habitats
10:00–10:10 (3–4 years) *Elephant Groovers* Activity purposes: *to help children to . . .*	**Move Like a Bird** • express ideas through movement • develop awareness of birds • increase large motor coordination	**Move Like a Bird** • express ideas through movement • develop awareness of birds • increase large motor coordination	**Trip Discussion—*What Might We See at the Audubon Nature Park?*** • prepare for field trip • develop the ability to hypothesize		**Look at Pictures of the Audubon Nature Park Trip** • develop understanding of birds' needs, habits, and habitats

Indoor Special Activity 10:20–11:30 Activity purposes: to help children to . . .	Clay Sculpture Using Tools	Clay Sculpture Using Tools	Feather Collage (also clay for two)	Reminders:	Play Dough Collage
	• practice art techniques (modeling and sculpting) • explore shape and space	• practice art techniques (modeling and sculpting) • explore shape and space	• learn about art elements of color, texture, and design • create and express ideas using a variety of art media	• Bring a sack lunch that does not require refrigeration. • Wear secure shoes. • Apply bug repellant before school, if desired. **Please be here by 8:00—the bus will leave at 8:15.** **Families are welcome to come on this trip.** **We will be back by 1:30.**	• build fine motor control • use art elements of color and design
Circle Time 11:30–11:45 Activity purposes: to help children to . . .	Manu Lai Titi (Pretty Little Birdie) Song and Movement	Manu Lai Titi (Pretty Little Birdie) Song and Movement	Los Pollitos (Baby Chicks) Song and Movement		Los Pollitos (Baby Chicks) Song and Movement
	• express ideas through music and movement • develop awareness of birds • develop awareness of language and cultural diversity	• express ideas through music and movement • develop awareness of birds • develop awareness of language and cultural diversity	• express ideas through music and movement • develop awareness of birds • develop awareness of language and cultural diversity		• express ideas through music and movement • develop awareness of birds • develop awareness of language and cultural diversity
Changes for Indoor Learning Centers	Block area—add bird figures, tree blocks.	Pretend area—add bird hoods and bird puppets.	Manipulatives area—add new bird puzzle.	Writing area—bird word cards.	Discovery area—visiting birds: zebra finches.
Changes for Outdoor Zones	Social-dramatic zone—add boots and hats.	Active play zone—add rickshaw trikes.	Natural elements zone—sand in the sensory table.	Manipulative-creative zone—palette painting at the easel.	

How It Went—What We Changed: Clay sculpture was surprisingly successful. Children consulted pictures of birds as well as the visiting finches as models. The trip was wonderful! Following the trip we added a new suet feeder to the yard.

Assessment of Objectives: Children talked about the birds and what they needed and showed their understanding in the book.

Planning an Integrated Study

As we have said, we believe that integrated planning is the most effective way to plan curriculum for older preschool, kindergarten, or primary school children as well as an interesting and satisfying experience for teachers. In a well-chosen and well-designed integrated study, children have many real experiences with a topic. These real experiences are the foundation of the plan. Children then read about, reflect on, represent, and re-create the real experiences through dramatic play, block building, discussions, writing, drawing, art, music, movement, measuring, graphing, and mapping. Through their investigation of a topic, children develop skills in sensing and moving, thinking and problem solving, communicating, creating, and working and playing with others.

An effective integrated study starts with the investigation of something that is important to young children. It needs to be based on experiences and ideas that are interesting and complex enough to engage both children and adults, because the study will last several weeks to several months. It is created in a dynamic process that involves initial planning, providing experiences, observing children, and then planning additional opportunities for learning. When you are planning such a study, it is important to stay open to possibilities that emerge from children's ideas and interests. A kindergarten teacher we know once planned an integrated study of gardening for her class. A swarm of bees settled in the children's play structure causing much fear. After thoughtful deliberation, the teacher abandoned her gardening plan and embarked on a study of bees. The children's fear of the bees gave way to fascination as they learned about the social structure of the hive

---

CONNECTING WITH FAMILIES

Using Weekly Plans

Families want to know what their children do each day, and they want to know why you teach the way you do. You can let them know and help them to be more involved by sharing your weekly calendar. Doing this encourages families to talk with their children about school! There are several ways to do this:

1. Post the weekly plan by the entrance so that families can read it when they drop off and pick up their children.

2. Send a copy of the plan home each week so that families can post and refer to it.

3. E-mail a copy to families each week.

and the production of honey and watched a beekeeper relocate the hive to a site farther removed from the classroom.

Though integrated planning is widely accepted among early childhood educators, it has sometimes come under fire. These criticisms are typically aimed at the *way* in which the integrated curriculum is approached. Specifically, integrated curriculum is criticized:

- When it is short lived (a week or two for a plan) so children can't explore a topic in depth
- When it is planned far in advance and repeated each year without thinking about its relevance to the group of children or changes that could be made to improve it
- When the topic cannot be experienced in real ways (e.g., pirates, outer space, dinosaurs)
- When the topic is "cute" but not actually worthy of serious study (e.g., Mickey Mouse's birthday, Teddy Bears' Picnic)
- When it is used in a shallow way without developing understanding (e.g., playing with plastic bugs and making ants on a log without looking at what insects are actually like)
- When children do not have open-ended materials to reconstruct or represent their understanding
- When it is used inflexibly and teachers go on with the plan despite children's changing interests

This kind of superficial planning is often associated with the words *unit* and *theme,* and for this reason we now refer to them as studies. Good integrated planning helps children investigate meaningful ideas. It is appropriate to the individuals and group, flexible, and meaningful. See Figure 11.9 (page 414) for comparison of different approaches to integrated curriculum.

Select a Topic of Study

The first step in integrated planning is the choice of a topic of study. Meaningful thematic curriculum based on a well-chosen topic helps children make connections. Children's lives and their environment—their families, cultures, community, or elements of the local environment—are good sources. Exploration of these kinds of topics can contribute to children's understanding of the world and themselves, as well as heightening their sense of uniqueness and pride in their families and community. While these larger goals are being realized, children are exploring, experimenting, discussing experiences, creating art, building with blocks, manipulating materials, writing, and cooking.

We have found from our teaching and observation over the years that some topics are better than others for the purpose of integrating curriculum. When you have chosen well there is an almost magical quality. Children are focused, energized, and intensely engaged in the business of learning. In order for this to happen, the topic must meet several criteria:

- First, it must be of *interest* to children, teachers, and families. For example, when the teacher as well as several mothers of children in a 4-year-old class became pregnant, a curriculum study of babies and birth was a natural focus. The teacher brought in many books, made a sequencing game of fetal development, helped the children compose a simple lullaby, had babies and puppies visit, and took the children on a trip to the local hospital to view the nursery. The children built a hospital in the block area, created a nursery in the dramatic play area,

413

FIGURE 11.9   Comparison of Integrated Approaches to Planning

Developmental Interaction—Curriculum is integrated around the study of a social studies topic selected by the teacher based on knowledge of the children and the learning potential of the topic. The topic is investigated in depth over several weeks through real experiences (learning trips, etc.) and follow-up opportunities to represent learning through play and planned activities (blocks, dramatic play, writing, art, etc.). The community of the classroom is emphasized. A culminating activity ends the study.

Reggio Emilia—The teacher and children select an in-depth project that is highly motivating to the children. Many modes or "languages" are used for children to express their growing knowledge symbolically. Strong emphasis is placed on the arts and the learning environment. Less emphasis is placed on ensuring that every area of curriculum is addressed as part of the project. Teachers collect and prepare documentation of children's projects to share with families and the community.

Project—The teacher and children select a learning project that is highly motivating to the particular group. Completing the project requires research to answer questions posed by the children and/or teacher. The project has three distinct phases: (1) introduction/initial assessment of knowledge, (2) research and representation of learning, and (3) culmination and sharing. The project continues until the children reach a point of completion.

Emergent Curriculum—A child or group of children explores a particular interest. It may be quite small (e.g., Band-Aids) and fleeting (a day, a week), but more typically lasts for several weeks. The teacher webs ideas for activities, and then designs experiences to expand on children's interest.

"Deep" Unit/Theme—A study is selected by the teacher based on knowledge of the children and the learning potential of the topic. The topic is investigated over 1–3 months through real experiences (learning trips, etc.) and follow-up opportunities to represent learning (blocks, dramatic play, writing, art, etc.). The process for creating the study is not established, but plans are created by the teacher.

We use the word *deep* to contrast with *shallow* thematic planning in which a topic is selected by the teacher or program administrator based on the calendar, tradition, or whim. In a *shallow unit* the topic is only an organizing motif for a brief 1–2 week period during which few (if any) real experiences are provided. Because the activities are often abstract and unconnected activities (e.g., worksheets, songs, games) these units/themes do not serve children, teachers, or our field well and bring integrated curriculum under fire for lacking intellectual integrity.

Source: Information from E. Moravcik, S. Nolte, and S. Feeney, *Meaningful Curriculum for Young Children*, 2013.

and painted and drew many pictures and wrote many stories about babies. All the children—not just the new big brothers and sisters—learned a great deal about how babies develop and the ways that families care for infants. They were simultaneously developing fine motor and hand-eye coordination; understanding of letters and numbers; discrimination of size, shape, and color; and a myriad of other skills and understandings.

• Next, a topic of study must be *accessible*—you should be able to give children direct and frequent hands-on experience with the topic. If direct experience is not available, the topic—no matter how interesting—will not lead to genuine understanding. This is especially important for younger children. But it is true for all young children because real experiences are the best way for them to learn.

• Third, a topic should be *important,* worth knowing about. A good integrated study requires time, effort, and intellectual engagement on the part of children and teachers. It's not worth your time, or children's time, to study something that is trivial and not worthy of intellectual engagement.

• Finally, you should consider whether the topic of study you choose is the *right size* for children's age and stage of development: *simple* enough to be understood but *complex* and interesting enough to be explored in some depth. It should involve concepts and skills that provide the right level of challenge. We call this the "three bears" principle (not too easy, not too hard, "just right").

Many topics are interesting, accessible, worth knowing and the right size and can be used for successful integration of subject areas. We have seen teachers of preschoolers plan successful integrated studies of topics such as water, food, trees, animals, insects, family, self, rain, gardens, and farms. Artwork throughout this text and many examples used in Chapter 10 grew out of preschoolers' integrated curriculum studies. We have seen teachers of older children investigate these same topics with more depth, and also more complex topics such as life cycles, the ocean, harbors, grocery stores, hospitals, and bakeries. The accompanying Golden Rules Box provides you with some criteria to help you to choose a topic of integrated study.

When you have selected a topic, write down the reasons for your choice. These reasons are your statement of *rationale*. Having a brief written statement of rationale will help you to explain your curriculum to others and will help you to document your work. In this chapter we are using a study of birds as an example of integrated curriculum. The teachers of the 3- and 4-year-olds at the Leeward Community College Children's Center, along with Eva and her college students, selected this topic for the following reasons:

• They had observed children's interest in the abundant bird life that visited the school playground and the surrounding community.

GOLDEN RULES FOR SELECTING A TOPIC FOR AN INTEGRATED CURRICULUM STUDY

1. Choose a topic that is *interesting*—to the children and to the teachers.
2. Choose a topic that is *accessible*—you can provide real, frequent hands-on experience.
3. Choose a topic that is *important*—worth knowing about to a young child.
4. Choose a topic that is the *right size*—not too big and complex, not too small and trivial.
5. Choose a topic that is *consistent* with program philosophy and goals.
6. Choose a topic that can be taught through *direct experiences*.
7. Choose a topic that *builds understanding* and appreciation—of self, others, and the world.
8. Choose a topic that can *integrate*—experience, subjects, and development.
9. Choose a topic that is *realistic*—in terms of resources available.
10. Choose a topic that can have lots of ways to *involve families* and encourage family input and participation.

- A nest of baby birds had fallen into their yard and the class was caring for them.
- They had pet chickens, which were an ongoing source of interest to the children.
- The staff themselves were interested in birds, and both teachers had pet birds.
- Four families in the class raised birds or had birds as pets.

The topic of birds was clearly interesting, was appropriate for the community and families, and came with abundant resources. It also met all the other criteria that are described in the "Golden Rules for an Integrated Curriculum Topic." The statement of rationale for the study was as follows:

In considering what is important for the 3- to 5-year-olds in our class to learn, we selected the topic Birds. *We made this choice because we observed children's interest in the many birds in our environment; there are many resources available in our community to support a study of birds; and it will serve to further our goals of helping children to become active, creative learners who appreciate and respect their environment.*

Not all topics are effective for generating meaningful learning experiences. A topic can give a surface appearance of connecting ideas but do nothing to enhance children's understanding. We once observed 3-year-olds "studying" the letter M by making *magazine* collages, baking *muffins,* and coloring a picture of a *monkey.* When we asked the children what they had been learning, they responded that they had been gluing, cooking, and coloring. Their teacher corrected them, saying that they had been studying M. This approach failed to integrate children's learning because it focused on an abstract symbol that was not of real interest to an inquisitive group of 3-year-olds.

Similarly, just because children "like" or are fascinated by something does not necessarily make it a good topic. For example, after viewing a movie about pirates, children may seem to like and be interested in pirates. It might even have historical relevance if your program is located near a coastline where piracy frequently occurred. However, the reality of piracy, a serious crime at any time in history, is quite chilling and has little to do with the swashbuckling fiction seen in movies and on television. It would be impossible to provide curriculum on pirates that had integrity (honesty) and that was appropriate for young children.

A good topic allows children to develop real understanding and mastery. A child might delight in red flowers, and enjoy mixing red and yellow while finger painting, but this does not make "red" a good topic of study. However, it might lead you to design an integrated study around the topic of flowers or kaleidoscopes. Remember not to confuse a subject area (e.g., math), an important way of learning (e.g., reading books), or an attribute that is related to many different topics (e.g., color) with a topic that is appropriate for in-depth study.

Often holidays are used as the basis for integrated curriculum. Some holidays have an impact on children's lives and can be studied in terms of culture, the joys of family celebrations, and their impact on children. Others have little or no appropriate content for young children. Even meaningful holidays used as topics are often made trivial and inappropriate when are reduced to look-alike crafts and commercial symbols. The study of holidays that are based on religious content in public schools is likely to have little real meaning because the religious content has to be excised based on the necessity of separating church and state.

An integrated study should be a source of genuine learning and not a way to sugarcoat academic activities. Worksheets covered with dinosaurs or bees used as part of a "theme" are not even distantly related to meaningful learning or good integrated planning. When we encounter colleagues who dismiss thematic planning or unit planning as superficial or inappropriate, we are quite sure that this is the kind of plan they have in mind.

Look at Your Purpose

Why have you selected a study? What is your purpose? The goals (broad statements of desired ends toward which teaching is directed) of all curriculum for young children include helping them to acquire knowledge, skills, and positive attitudes toward themselves, learning, and other people. As you consider the topic you have chosen, you will identify goals for your study. For instance, consider these goals for a integrated study of birds:

To help children to develop:

- Increased knowledge of birds, their characteristics, and habits
- A disposition to be curious and inquiring about the birds in their environment
- An attitude of respect for, and disposition to be kind and humane to, birds and other living creatures
- Skills in language, literacy, inquiry, physical coordination, and creative expression

Identify Major Understandings

Once you have selected a topic and spelled out the goals of the study, you will gather resources, read and reflect, then identify the *major understandings* (which we also call *big ideas*) that you wish children to acquire. Major understandings are the important concepts, related to the topic, that the activities in an integrated study are designed to help children acquire. They give direction to the study and help you to be clear about what you want children to learn.

The first thing to do once you have selected a topic is to take some time to read about and reflect on it. This is a critical part of the planning process. Teachers often assume that because they are older and more experienced than children, they already know enough about a topic to teach it. Background reading is often overlooked in the excitement of generating lots of activities. While you do not need to know everything about a topic in order to plan, it is necessary to learn something, particularly if the topic is outside your areas of expertise. Children deserve to have accurate information given to them. Even if the topic is something "simple" such as studying "me," you will need to gather information on the children and their families. In our own work in researching topics for integrated curriculum we make use of the information readily available on the Internet. Online encyclopedias, such as Wikipedia, provide instant access to basic facts and help us identify sources for finding out more. The public library and your school library are other important resources that you should not overlook.

Once you have acquired some basic information you can begin to identify the important understandings or "big ideas" that you want children to acquire through the study. These will give you a guide for planning and will help you to decide if the activities you are designing are actually contributing to

Reflect on an integrated study in your childhood

Remember a time when you experienced an integrated study in school What did you learn about? What do you remember most about the study? How was it different from other ways of learning? What did you enjoy? Is there anything you wish your teachers had done differently?

children's understanding of the topic. We have developed a sorting process that we use have used with college students and staff to identify the major understandings for an integrated study. Here is an example from the program that Eva directs: after researching birds on the Web and reading informational books about birds (including Mae Garelick's *What Makes a Bird a Bird*, the National Audubon Society's *First Field Guide to Birds*, the Hawaii Audubon Society's *Hawaii's Birds*, and the Dorling Kindersley *Introduction to Birds*), the teachers and students at the Children's Center wrote down all the words they could think of about birds on slips of paper. Their work looked something like this:

aviaries, baby birds, bird feeders, by the freeway, cardinals, chickens, cliffs, colors, conures, crowing, ducks, egg farm, eggs, egrets, endangered birds, farms, feathers, flying, frittatas, guano, Hawai'i birds, homes, hopping, incubator, mainland birds, migrating, mynah birds, nene goose, nests, omelets, parakeets, parrots, peacocks, pets, playground, seabirds, singing, state bird, swans, swimming, talking, Thanksgiving turkey, trees, walking

They then sorted the words into five piles and assigned a category to each pile. The papers were sorted several different ways and the content was considered. These were the results:

- Different kinds of birds: *chickens, egrets, parakeets, parrots, conures, peacocks, endangered birds, ducks, swans, mainland birds, Hawai'i birds, cardinals, nene goose, mynah birds, crowing, singing*
- Special things about birds: *flying, feathers, eggs, colors, nests, baby birds, incubators*
- Where birds live: *sea birds, cliffs, homes, aviaries, trees, farms, playground, by the freeway*
- How birds move: *flying, hopping, swimming, walking, migrating*
- Birds in our lives: *pets, Thanksgiving turkey, feathers, guano, chicken manure, omelets, bird feeders, egg farm, state bird*

After they identified the categories, the staff thought about what they wanted children to know abouteach category and wrote a statement of major understandings:

"Big Ideas" for a curriculum study of birds:

- There are lots of different birds with many colors, sizes, and shapes.
- All birds have feathers and lay eggs to create baby birds.
- Birds move in different ways—most fly, some hop, some walk, some swim.
- Birds are part of people's lives—some can be pets, some give us food and feathers, some help the plants to grow.
- Birds live in different places where they can find food, be safe, and raise their young.

We write "big ideas" in simple language such as a child might use or understand. The point of this activity is not to think of words that are *taught*—instead, they should help you to help children to *construct* understanding of the big ideas for themselves.

Generate Ideas for Activities

The next step is to generate ideas for activities that will help children to develop the major understandings. For many years we have used a system called *mind-mapping* to begin our planning. In a mind-map you place a topic in a circle in the center of a piece of chart paper, off of which numerous lines are drawn to map ideas related to the topic. You will see similar charts referred to as *webs* or *curriculum maps*. The process of mind-mapping or webbing is useful because it allows you to add ideas as they arise without being concerned about their order or organization. When the map is completed you can examine each item to see how it fits in the whole plan.

In our own planning we begin by selecting trips and resource visitors because these may determine the direction of other experiences that we will offer. If trips require reservations it is also the time to make contact and set up the trip(s), making sure to plan an initial trip early in the study. Ideas for other activities that support the major understandings are then webbed. This is also a time to make a list of some of the new vocabulary, especially "rare words" that will be introduced and used during the study. Make sure to identify some activities that help children to acquire each of the understandings (see Figure 11.10).

The value of different activities should be assessed with consideration of the goals, the extent to which the activities support the major understandings, and the resources and time required. If you find that there is a big idea for which you can think of no age-appropriate activities or if you think of good activities that do not seem to fit within your big ideas, it means you need to go back and add or omit big ideas.

Your initial web is the starting place. As you explore the topic you are likely to get good ideas for additional activities from by the children, and, some of the activities you generated at the beginning may seem less viable when you get involved in the study.

FIGURE 11.10 Initial Curriculum Activity Brainstorming Web

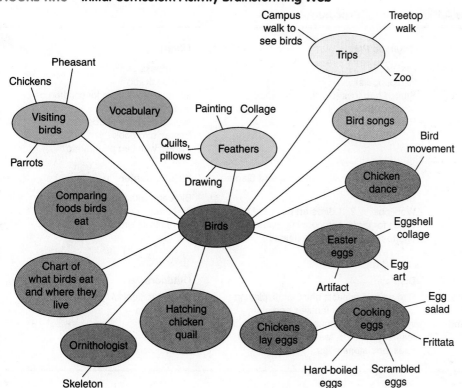

Enrich the Environment

Following the initial planning process, you will begin to gather and create the resources you need to teach. This is the time when you will reassess the pictures, puppets, dramatic play and block props, games, puzzles, and toys that are available and select some that will help children make connections to the topic. You will make a trip to the library to gather good children's literature on the topic. Be sure to ask a librarian to help you to find good books. Tell families about the study and invite them to participate by sharing resources that they have or know about. Your local museum or art gallery may have prints, posters, or artifacts that can be borrowed to enrich the environment. Schedule trips and resource people and begin to plot activities for the first weekly plans.

A good curriculum study will be visible in almost every classroom center. For example, in the bird curriculum the teachers at the LCC Children's Center added the items in Figure 11.11 to the environment.

Make the Plan

Once you have goals, major understandings, and a list of activities you have generated, you are ready to plan for teaching. Think about ways to bring real experience into the study right away (a trip; a visit from a resource person; making or cooking something; bringing in real animals, plants, or other artifacts). Think about an activity that will make a good beginning to introduce the topic to children and families. Think about activities that will help children build understanding to use in the middle of the study. Consider which activities will help children express and generalize their understanding at the end. Plan ways to involve families throughout the study.

FIGURE 11.11   Environment Additions for a Curriculum on Birds

Blocks	*Dramatic Play*	*Library*
Bird figures (wooden and plastic)	Bird hoods	Storybooks on birds
Stuffed bird toys (shared with	Bird puppets	(see book list)
dramatic play)	Stuffed bird toys (shared with blocks)	Informational books for children on birds
Art prints of birds in a nest	Mobile with origami cranes	and eggs
Wooden flying goose mobile	Plastic eggs	Nature guides on birds
	Art prints of birds	Poster: bird book
		Pillows with bird print fabric
Science Center	**Manipulative Toys, Puzzles, and Games**	**Writing Center**
Egg poster	Bird puzzles	Birdcage with visiting birds to observe
Egg and feather artifacts and	Workjobs: *1, 2, 3 Birds* art postcard games;	and draw
magnifying glass	words for birds; egg counting game;	Art prints of birds
Bird nests	egg-to-fledgling seriation game	
Brooder house for baby chicks		
Art Area	**Display**	**Outdoors**
Feathers for painting and collage	Bird art and artifacts shelf for displaying	Cards for identifying birds
Eggshells for collage	objects brought by families and staff,	Bird feeders
Bird visitors for life drawing and	including bird figurines, ostrich egg,	Birdhouse
collage	feather hatbands, feather fans, painted	Chickens
Art prints including birds	eggs, and stone eggs	Binoculars

CONNECTING WITH FAMILIES

Involving Them in Integrated Curriculum

Any integrated curriculum study will be better when you involve children's families. They can make many contributions, and in any class there will be many who welcome the opportunity to do so. They can:

1. Find resources in your community
2. Create games and props
3. Modify the environment on a work day
4. Loan and donate materials
5. Come on trips
6. Share expertise with you
7. Come as resource visitors for the children.

Because creating an integrated study plan is a big job, it's a good idea to begin to write a simple guide to refer to as you work. The outline for an integrated study plan in Figure 11.12 suggests some things to include.

FIGURE 11.12   Outline for an Integrated Thematic Study

1. **Topic:** focus of the study

2. **Children:** age and characteristics for whom you are planning

3. **Rationale:** why this topic was chosen for these children at this time

4. **Goals:** 3–6 board statements of desired ends—the attitudes, skills, abilities, and experiences that children are intended to gain by participating in this study

5. **Major understandings:** 4–6 important ideas you intend children to construct by participating in this study, worded as children might understand them, not as objectives

6. **Resources:** books, articles, and other resources that you used to guide your development of the study

7. **Environment additions:** a list of materials to add to each learning center to support awareness of the topic and the development of the big ideas; be sure include ideas for blocks, dramatic play, manipulative toys, puzzles and games, art, writing center, library, science area, and outdoors

8. **Trips:** a list of learning trips to give children real experience related to the topic

9. **Activities:**
   a. Introductory activities: how you will introduce the study to children, including the activities that will build *awareness* of the topic.
   b. Activities to build *understanding:* a list of activities to encourage exploration, support the development of the major understanding, and build skills
   c. Culminating activities: activities to help children *express* and *generalize* what they have learned, including how you will bring closure to the study

10. **Assessment:** activities and work that will demonstrate children's understanding of the big ideas and ideas for documentation through observation, photography, or the collection of work samples

Note: Items 6–10 will not be completed until you near the end of the study.

Remember that you will continue to observe children and plan for each week and day as you go along. The children's responses, teacher's new insights, families' input, and the serendipitous opportunities that you discover will be added to the integrated plan. You will not finish writing your integrated plan until close to the end—when you do it, may look something like the plan in Figure 11.12.

Implement the Study

Once the initial plans are in place and you have begun to bring the topic into the learning environment, you will start to implement activities. The first activities provide an introduction to the topic. Introductory activities give children awareness of the topic through real experience and books. They provide the raw material for that children's developing understanding of the topic.

Some teachers begin the curriculum by interviewing the children, asking them questions such as: "What do you know about the topic? What would you like to learn?" This activity is also often used as a culminating activity for an integrated study (called K/W/L, which stands for "What do you KNOW? What do you WANT to learn? What have you LEARNED?").

Teachers in elementary schools often use this process to guide the design of a study. Though it is a good starting place for planning, it must be supplemented with observation of children, reflection, and research. As you can see from the example in Table 11.4, preschoolers are more able to identify what they know than to identify questions for investigation. Inquiry questions will emerge as they investigate a topic.

In preschool we usually select a more hands-on introduction to a topic. In the study of birds we have been describing, teachers introduced the study by bringing pet birds into the classroom and by asking the children what they knew about birds and what they wanted to learn about birds. They took a walk to look for birds in the trees and lawns around the school. During the first weeks, they enriched the environment with fine art prints that included birds, puzzles and workjobs featuring birds, bird toys and puppets for the dramatic play and block areas, and many books about birds. They constructed and put up bird feeders in the yard and added bird feeding (wild and pet) to the jobs that children did each day. During the third week, they went on a trip to the local zoo, which had an extensive bird collection.

After the initial input, activities to help children build and demonstrate their understanding are implemented. Blocks, art media, dramatic play, music, and book making are all excellent ways for children to demonstrate what they are learning. This is a good time for children to discuss their ideas about the topic.

While you are implementing the middle section of the plan it is important to remain open to changes in children's interests and to fortuitous events. For example, the interest that the children showed in birds laying eggs and nesting (see the annotated work sample in Figure 11.5) convinced the teachers to begin a project that involved incubating and raising quails.

The activities in a good integrated study can address every (or most) curriculum area and help you to teach many content standards. However, they are not the only thing that happens in your classroom. Children will continue to read books, sing songs, create art, engage in physical activities, and learn about many things other than your subject. As you can see from the week's plan in

TABLE 11.4 Example of a K/W/L Chart Made with 4- and 5-Year-Olds

What do you KNOW about birds?	What do you WANT to learn about birds?	What have you LEARNED about birds?
Humming birds fly really fast and eat from flowers.	How do peacocks eat?	Peacocks can fly up into the trees.
Some birds have sharp claws that scratch your arm.	What do peacocks look like?	Hombills eat mice.
Birds peck branches.	How do birds lay eggs? How do eggs become baby birds?	Chickens eat chicken scratch and bread.
Birds drink water.		Baby birds have pink skin.
Birds use their beaks to eat. Cardinals use the tips of their beaks to eat.		Birds have sharp claws to hold onto branches.
Lovebirds sometimes bite you.		Peacocks make their tails big.
A little bird is called a chick.		Some birds can swim.
Baby birds can't fly but they can when they're older.		Baby birds have to peck on the eggs to get out.
Mama birds and daddy birds make nests with hay and sticks—they sit on the eggs to keep them warm.		Big birds have big nests and iittle birds have little nests.
Some birds chase tractors—they like the bugs.		Cardinals eat papayas.
		Baby birds get real hungry. Their mamas bring them food.
		Some people have pet birds.

Figure 11.8, not all the planned activities during the bird study were about birds. Trying to fit every activity into a study topic is unnecessary.

Early in the study the teachers invited families to participate. Over the 3-month course of the study, families brought in pet birds, sewed bird hoods for dramatic play, went on trips to the zoo and a nature preserve, donated a pet cockatiel, made bird feeders with the children, came in to read stories, and loaned artifacts from their cultures, including Japanese origami cranes, a German toy goose, Samoan feather fans, an Italian rooster-shaped pitcher, Hawai'ian feather lei, a French porcelain Chanticleer (a rooster), a Chinese platter depicting a peacock, a Haida (Northwest Coast tribe) raven, and a Czech turkey toothpick holder.

An integrated study has a life span of its own. You may find that children's interest in the topic deepens, as we saw in the study of birds that we are using as an example. The initial plan for 8 weeks of study extended to the end of the school year—3 months. You may find that the study links to another topic, as we saw when a study of water led to a study of the ocean.

Eventually you will draw your study to a close. When you are ready to move on to a new topic it is important to plan closure for the children, families, and the teachers. A class book or newsletter explaining what was learned, a documentation panel, a scrapbook or video that shows the outcome of the study, or a social event during which children's work and learning are shared with others are good ways to both assess the study and bring it to an end. The study of birds was brought to an end by inviting families to the school for an evening walk to see the birds settling down for the evening, followed by a potluck, a reading of class-made books about birds, and a sing-along of all the songs learned about birds during the study. During the evening children's work and documentation panels of the study were displayed and videos of the children engaged in the many activities were shown.

For our own documentation when we are teaching children, we create a sunburst, a graphic expansion of the original mind-map to show everything that was planned during the unit (see Figure 11.13) and put together all the plans, songs, finger-plays, newsletters, and so on that we created during the study. We make this an assignment for students in our college classes in which they are studying integrated curriculum. Students then share these with one another as valuable resources for their future teaching.

Evaluate the Integrated Study

As you implement, remember to assess children's learning and evaluate the study. To evaluate whether children have acquired the major understandings you have targeted, you can observe their play as it pertains to the study or have children discuss the topic, dictate stories, or write in their journals. Children who make representational drawings may spontaneously, or upon request, draw pictures that demonstrate their understanding. For example, during the study of birds the 3- to 5-year-old children were provided with many different kinds of art media. Their drawings, sculptures, and collages provided visible proof of the internalization of concepts relating to birds (see Figure 11.14).

Photographs and video of the children engaged in learning activities also provide valuable evidence of the learning that is occurring. Photographs, work samples, and observations can be put together into documentation panels (posters with photos and work samples). These document children's learning and make it visible to families and community members.

When you are finished teaching, put the plans and materials you have created especially for this study in a resource box so you can easily store and retrieve them. Cardboard banker's boxes or lidded plastic storage boxes work well for this purpose. It may be some time before you use the resource box again, but when you do the materials will be there. If and when you decide to revisit the topic, you will make changes based on new ideas, interests, materials, children, and families, but you will not have to start over from scratch.

FIGURE 11.13   Bird Sunburst

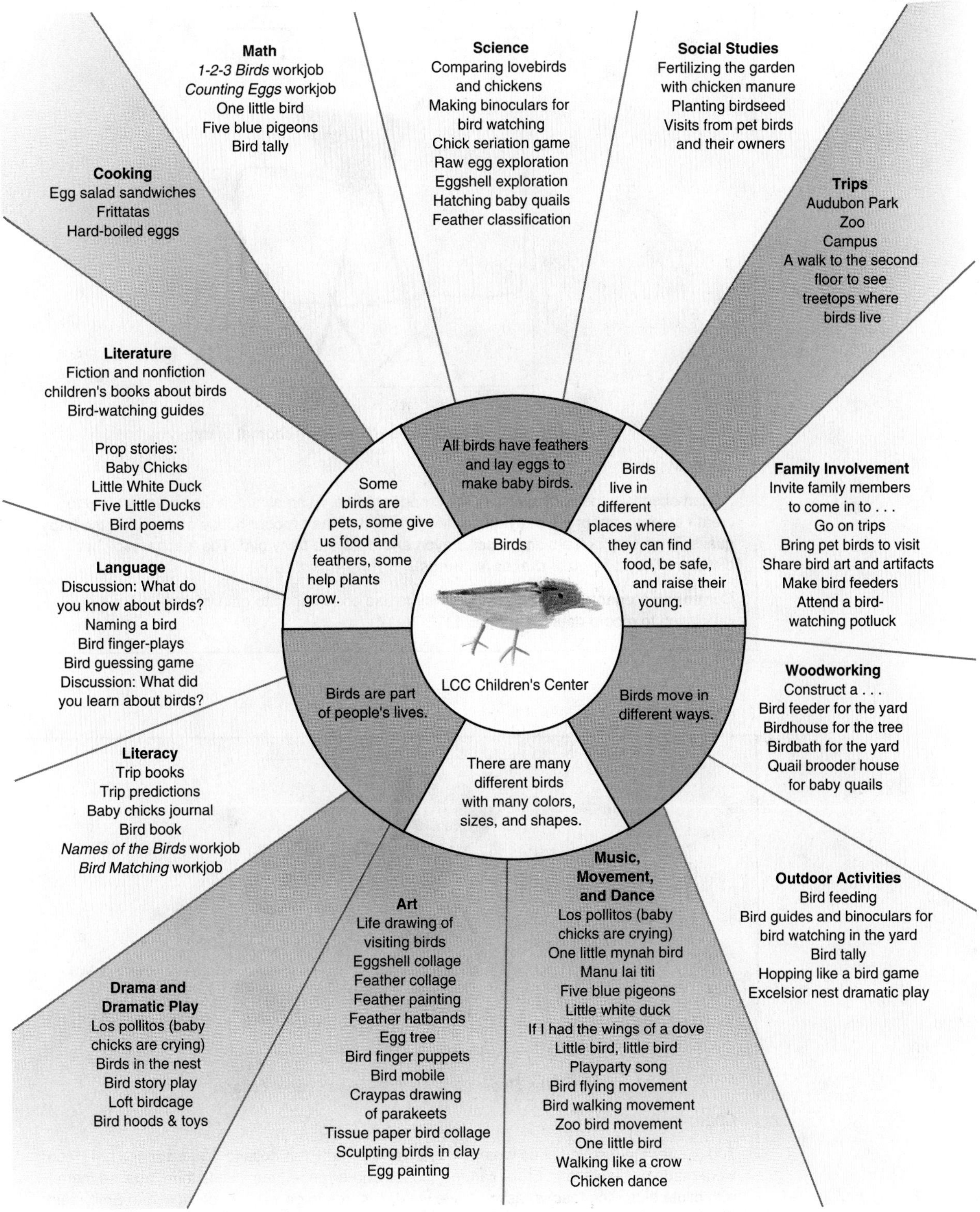

Math
1-2-3 Birds workjob
Counting Eggs workjob
One little bird
Five blue pigeons
Bird tally

Science
Comparing lovebirds
and chickens
Making binoculars for
bird watching
Chick seriation game
Raw egg exploration
Eggshell exploration
Hatching baby quails
Feather classification

Social Studies
Fertilizing the garden
with chicken manure
Planting birdseed
Visits from pet birds
and their owners

Cooking
Egg salad sandwiches
Frittatas
Hard-boiled eggs

Trips
Audubon Park
Zoo
Campus
A walk to the second
floor to see
treetops where
birds live

Literature
Fiction and nonfiction
children's books about birds
Bird-watching guides

Prop stories:
Baby Chicks
Little White Duck
Five Little Ducks
Bird poems

Language
Discussion: What do
you know about birds?
Naming a bird
Bird finger-plays
Bird guessing game
Discussion: What did
you learn about birds?

Literacy
Trip books
Trip predictions
Baby chicks journal
Bird book
Names of the Birds workjob
Bird Matching workjob

Family Involvement
Invite family members
to come in to . . .
Go on trips
Bring pet birds to visit
Share bird art and artifacts
Make bird feeders
Attend a bird-
watching potluck

Woodworking
Construct a . . .
Bird feeder for the yard
Birdhouse for the tree
Birdbath for the yard
Quail brooder house
for baby quails

Outdoor Activities
Bird feeding
Bird guides and binoculars for
bird watching in the yard
Bird tally
Hopping like a bird game
Excelsior nest dramatic play

**Drama and
Dramatic Play**
Los pollitos (baby
chicks are crying)
Birds in the nest
Bird story play
Loft birdcage
Bird hoods & toys

Art
Life drawing of
visiting birds
Eggshell collage
Feather collage
Feather painting
Feather hatbands
Egg tree
Bird finger puppets
Bird mobile
Craypas drawing
of parakeets
Tissue paper bird collage
Sculpting birds in clay
Egg painting

**Music,
Movement,
and Dance**
Los pollitos (baby
chicks are crying)
One little mynah bird
Manu lai titi
Five blue pigeons
Little white duck
If I had the wings of a dove
Little bird, little bird
Playparty song
Bird flying movement
Bird walking movement
Zoo bird movement
One little bird
Walking like a crow
Chicken dance

Inner ring:
All birds have feathers and lay eggs to make baby birds.
Birds live in different places where they can find food, be safe, and raise their young.
Birds move in different ways.
There are many different birds with many colors, sizes, and shapes.
Birds are part of people's lives.
Some birds are pets, some give us food and feathers, some help plants grow.

Center:
Birds
LCC Children's Center

425

FIGURE 11.14 **Children's Artwork Demonstrating Their Understanding of Birds**

The Baby Quail Shakes His Wings—Journal entry

Child: Megan

Megan observed the baby quails in the brooder house. At small group time when invited to create an entry about the baby quails, Megan went to the brooder house and studied the baby quails. Then she took a black pencil crayon and drew the baby bird. The teacher took her dictation: *The baby quail shakes his wings.*

Comment: Megan demonstrates the ability to use observation to gain information and illustration to record data. SCIENCE, LITERACY

The Birdie Flies Away!—Tissue paper collage

Child: Emily

Today after the rescued birds were released, Emily made this collage. Varied shapes of pieces were made available, and Emily carefully chose and arranged the pieces then brushed them with dilute glue. The teacher asked if she wanted words to go with her collage, and Emily said, *The birdie flies away!*

Comment: Emily uses art materials with skill to express ideas. Fine motor control well-developed. ART, FINE MOTOR, LANGUAGE

A Red Parrot—Felt marker drawing

Child: Jonah

After Kaitlin's father brought in red and gray parrots, Jonah used felt markers to draw the red parrot. He explained that the feet had claws to hold on tight to Kaitlin's daddy's arm.

Comment: Jonah was able to accurately capture details of the parrot, including the black beak and eye ring, the yellow 3-toed feet, and the blue feather on the wing. Clearly observing a great deal of detail. SCIENCE, ART

Final Thoughts

The curriculum you plan should reflect your vision for children, for society, and for the future. It should be intellectually engaging for children and for teachers. The choices you make as you select what to teach and how you will teach it impact children's lives, your own life, and possibly the larger world. If you take this responsibility seriously, you will be thoughtful and thorough in your planning. Your plans will help you to support all areas of children's development. They will increase children's understanding of the world, build their love of learning, and help them to be curious, creative, active problem-solvers. It will help them to become the kind of adults that our society needs.

Learning Outcomes

When you read this chapter, and then thoughtfully complete selected assignments from the "To Learn More" section and prepare items from the "For Your Portfolio" section, you will be demonstrating progress in meeting **NAEYC Standards for Early Childhood Professional Preparation Program** (NAEYC, 2009).

Standard 2. Building Family and Community Relationships

Key element:

2c: Involving families and communities in their children's development and learning

Standard 3. Observing, Documenting, and Assessing to Support Young Children and Families

   Key element:

   3b: Knowing about and using observation, documentation, and other appropriate assessment tools and approaches

Standard 4. Using Developmentally Effective Approaches to Connect with Children and Families

   Key elements:

   4b: Knowing and understanding effective strategies and tools for early education

   4c: Using a broad repertoire of developmentally appropriate teaching/learning approaches

Standard 5. Using Content Knowledge to Build Meaningful Curriculum

   Key elements:

   5a: Understanding content knowledge and resources in academic disciplines

   5b: Knowing and using the central concepts, inquiry tools, and structures of content areas or academic disciplines

   5c: Using their own knowledge, appropriate early learning standards, and other resources to design, implement, and evaluate meaningful, challenging curricula for each child.

 # To Learn More

Plan an Activity: Use the Activity Plan Format—Detailed found in Figure 11.2 to plan an activity and implement it with children. Assess whether you were successful in accomplishing your goals. Reflect and write about what contributed to the success or failure of the activity.

Research and Begin to Write a Plan for an Integrated Study: On your own or with a partner select an appropriate topic for an integrated study with young children. Research the topic and begin to write the plan using the integrated study plan outline in Figure 11.12. Write the goals and big ideas, brainstorm activities, gather and make materials, and implement all or part of the plan in a program with children. Assess whether you were successful in accomplishing your goals. Reflect and write about what you learned.

Observe a Classroom: Observe a classroom in which teacher-directed and child-chosen activities are planned. Notice how children respond to both kinds of learning. Reflect and write about what you think the goals and objectives of the activities might be, how the activities contribute to accomplishing the goals you have identified, and whether the activities are successful in accomplishing the teacher's purpose.

Interview a Teacher: Interview a teacher about his or her program goals and their influence on curriculum planning. Ask about how these goals are modified or influenced by the community, the interests of children, the concerns of parents, the school administration, and educational trends. Ask the teacher to describe some ways that the goals impact the day-to-day curriculum. Reflect and write about how this affects children's experiences. Reflect on what you learned that might be helpful to you as a future teacher.

Interview Two Teachers: Interview two teachers about the kinds of planning they do regularly, how much time it takes, how important it is in program success, and so on. Compare their responses. Reflect and write about what you learned.

Investigate Related Websites:

ARTSEDGE (the National Arts and Education Network)—has free, standards-based teaching materials, professional development resources, student materials, and guidelines for arts-based instruction and assessment: http://artsedge.kennedy-center.org

Investigate Websites Related to Integrated Curriculum Models:

For example:

Developmental Interaction Approach
Bank Street: bankstreet.edu/theory-practice

Reggio Emilia Approach
The Reggio Emilia Approach to Education: reggioemiliaapproach.net

North American Reggio Emilia Alliance: reggioalliance.org

Project Approach
The Project Approach: projectapproach.org
Illinois Projects in Practice: illinoispip.org

 **For Your Portfolio**

Write Your Philosophy (Viewpoint) on Curriculum and Curriculum Planning: Identify your curriculum aims and values by asking yourself: As an educator, what am I trying to accomplish—for children and for society? What does that mean for the content of the curriculum I want to teach and how I want to present it? Write a one-page statement of philosophy to put in your portfolio.

Document Your Competence in Planning an Activity: Write a plan for an activity for children using the planning format found in this chapter. Implement your plan with children. Write anecdotal records on children's responses, reflect on what happened and what you learned, and evaluate your work. Put the plan and records in your portfolio to document your competence as a planner. Eva, I think you have something like this in Ch. 10. Maybe it is better here ok.

Document Your Competence in Integrated Planning: Develop and implement an integrated plan using the guidelines found in this chapter. Create a sunburst for the plan. Document children's learning by collecting work samples, writing anecdotal records, and taking photographs. Put the sunburst and a select sampling of the documentation in your portfolio.

MyEducationLab

Go to Topics 6: Curriculum Planning and 8: DAP/Teaching Strategies in the MyEducationLab (myeducationlab .com) for *Who Am I in the Lives of Children?* where you can:

- Find learning outcomes for Curriculum Planning and DAP/Teaching Strategies along with the national standards that connect to these outcomes.
- Complete Assignments and Activities that can help you more deeply understand the chapter content.
- Apply and practice your understanding of the core teaching skills identified in the chapter with the

Building Teaching Skills and Dispositions learning units.
- Listen to experts from the field in Professional Perspectives.
- Check your comprehension on the content covered in the chapter with the Study Plan. Here you will be able to take a chapter quiz, receive feedback on your answers, and then access Review, Practice, and Enrichment activities to enhance your understanding of chapter content.

We all have different gifts, so we all have different ways
of saying to the world who we are.

FRED ROGERS

12

Including Diverse Learners

On their first day of kindergarten, cousins Maya and Rashana are excited about school. They will finally be together in the same classroom. Maya has an infectious smile, doesn't speak very clearly, and seldom remembers where she puts her glasses, but she likes to dance and laugh. Rashana is tall for her age, doesn't like vegetables, can write her name, and loves to sing and climb trees. They have been best friends all their lives. They play with their dolls, chase each other around the yard and draw rainbows endlessly. Maya, who has Down syndrome, has been in a preschool classroom for children with special needs while Rashana attended her church preschool program. This year they are attending an inclusive program at their neighborhood elementary school.

These cousins are more alike than different, but Maya's exceptional needs require somewhat different instructional approaches than those that are effective for Rashana. Every young child has different gifts and different needs—the child who is unusually active, learns with difficulty, is emotionally insecure, is exceptionally verbal, speaks another language, learns like a 3-year-old but has the feelings of a 6-year-old (or vice versa), has advanced spatial ability, is fearful of loud noises, comes from a single-parent family, stutters, and many others. In every early childhood program, you will find as many distinctive needs as there are children, and every child requires individual attention.

Some children, like Maya, arrive with a clear determination of their disability and you can plan for their participation in your program with the help of specialists who know and understand their particular needs. You may also find yourself working with children who do not have a disability but who have other special needs such as those who have been abused or neglected, who are gifted or talented, or who have chronic physical or mental health conditions. And you will find that other children require special attention, too. Jimmy needs to sit near you in order to pay attention. Jeremiah always seems to bump into things. Josie sparkles when you provide her with activities that keep her moving. Teachers of young children need to be responsive to the needs of all children—those who have been evaluated or identified as having disabilities before coming to a program and all of the others. In this chapter we will focus primarily on children who have identified disabilities. These are children who are delayed in reaching developmental milestones in one or more areas, or have conditions that make it difficult for them to learn and function at the same rate as a typically developing child.

You may be surprised to learn that you will be teaching children with special needs, but all teachers work with a wide range of abilities. A child may have chronic asthma, wear glasses, be very verbal, or seldom speak. Another may speak another language, cry easily, have poor motor skills, or learn much faster than other children. Working effectively with all children requires the same knowledge and skills that characterize all competent early childhood educators— the ability to reflect on your own feelings and reactions, understanding of child development, skill in guiding behavior, and knowledge of how to design a learning environment and plan curriculum. In addition to these basics, you may need some specific information and additional skills to provide support for children with diverse abilities. You will benefit from being in touch with knowledgeable professionals in your community who work in the field of early childhood special education.

Because it is increasingly common for children with a range of abilities to be included in regular classrooms, it is very likely that at some time in your career you will work with children who have special needs. The Centers for Disease Control recently published a study that indicated that families of 1 in 6 children had been told that their child had a developmental delay (Boyle et al., 2011). Children identified with a developmental delay are those who a professional has determined do not meet developmental milestones in one or more domains—physical, cognitive, language, social, emotional, or adaptive. Autism, attention deficit/hyperactivity disorder (ADHD), and similar developmental disorders are more frequently identified today than in the past and account for much of the rise in identification of developmental delay. In publicly funded programs such as Head Start, public school, or a state-funded preschool program, you are *mandated* (required by law) to serve all children. In states where there are no state-funded programs for children under 5, you may also be asked to include a child with identified disabilities or other special needs in your class.

"Promoting development and belonging for every child is a widely held value among early childhood educators. . . . Early childhood inclusion is the term used to reflect these values and societal views" (DEC/NAEYC, 2009). Inclusion is not just about a place. It is about children belonging, being valued, and having choices. It is about accepting and appreciating human diversity. And it is about providing the necessary support to children, teachers, schools, and families so that *all* children and their families can participate in the programs of their choice (Allen & Schwartz, 1996). As described in the box "Benefits of Inclusion," everyone involved is positively influenced when children with disabilities and typically developing children are enrolled in full inclusion classrooms.

Benefits of Inclusion

When Children with Disabilities Attend School with Their Typically
Developing Peers

- **Children with disabilities benefit.** They develop friendships and are able to
  observe and learn from their peers who are typically developing. They learn to
  cope with everyday expectations and problems, and they practice new skills in
  the real world of the classroom.

- **Children without disabilities benefit.** They learn that children who look different
  or learn differently are like them in many ways, can be their friends, and make
  worthwhile contributions to the classroom. They witness perseverance and the
  value of struggling to accomplish something. They have the opportunity to be
  a coach, a helper, or a tutor to another child. Early childhood educators report
  time and again that the caring relationships developed among the children are
  an overwhelmingly positive outcome of inclusion.

- **Teachers benefit.** They broaden their professional understanding and gain
  a sense of satisfaction as the child with disabilities or other special needs
  successfully learns and functions in the classroom. It also gives them a valuable
  opportunity to teach things they could not teach or teach in different ways than
  if the child with disabilities or special needs was not a part of the group.

- **Families benefit.** They feel their child is accepted and they feel part of a community
  of families and children. They gain support that helps them to better meet their
  child's needs.

People-First Language

You may notice that we refer to children *with* special needs or children *with*
disabilities throughout this book as opposed to referring to them as disabled or
handicapped children. The terms *children with a disability* and *children with
special needs* are often used interchangeably, although children with a disability
can be described as having special needs while children with special needs may
not have a disability as defined by the rules governing special education services.
Diverse learners is a term used to indicate that we are committed to the belief that
all children can learn although they learn in different ways. Accepted terminology for describing children who are diverse learners has changed over the years
as educators have attempted to emphasize the commonalities among all children
rather than their differences. Defining people as disabled or handicapped promotes stereotypes that devalue and disrespect children as individuals. Today we
recognize that individuals with disabilities are *people* first and *people with disabilities* second. This view has shaped the language we use (Snow, 2009). The
newer language emphasizes that it is important to see the whole child, including
areas of strength and abilities.

A good guideline is to speak of the child first and the disability second
(e.g., "a child with Down syndrome," rather than "a retarded child"). Usually,
we should refer to a child by his or her name and mention the disability *only*
when that information is relevant in a particular situation, typically for medical,
educational, or legal reasons. It is also important to use language that acknowledges the benefit, rather than the burden, of support. For example, saying a
person *uses* a wheelchair; rather than that they are *confined* to a wheelchair.

**Reflect on your
own abilities
and challenges**

Think about your own
abilities and challenges.
What things were most
difficult for you when
you were a child? How
have these difficulties
affected your life? How
did they influence your
childhood experiences?
What do you wish your
teachers had known?
What are the implications
of these experiences for
your work with young
children?

Similarly, we might say that a child uses a communication device rather than stating that he or she can't talk. When we use "people-first" language, we are acknowledging that the child is more important than the disability.

Inclusion and the Law

Inclusion of children with disabilities in their natural environments (the places where children are naturally learning, such as preschools, playgrounds, and family outings) is recommended by federal legislation (IDEA, 2004) and by early childhood professional groups (NAEYC, DEC). Inclusion is beneficial to children and it is also the law. The purpose of the Individuals with Disabilities Education Act (IDEA) is to enable children with disabilities to learn with their typically developing peers. The law requires that all children with disabilities have access

to a *free, appropriate public education,* often referred to as FAPE. It also calls for young children with disabilities to participate in what is referred to as the *least restrictive environment* (LRE). This means that, rather than self-contained special education classes, children should participate in regular education classrooms to the greatest extent possible and experience the same curriculum that is provided for all children. Children with disabilities are best served in the same learning environments as their peers—a practice called *inclusion.* Providing inclusive services is based on the belief that all children benefit when children with a range of abilities learn together in the classroom.

In order to participate in the least restrictive environment, preschool children with disabilities may attend community preschools, Head Start, public school preschool, kindergarten, and primary grade classrooms. If you work in a community preschool, you may not realize that the Americans with Disabilities Act (ADA) mandates that you provide access to children with disabilities when it is reasonable to do so. While it does not impose undue hardship on a program, it may require you to add a ramp for a wheelchair or rearrange the furniture. It may necessitate accepting a child in diapers even though your school policy generally prohibits this.

IDEA makes funding available to states to provide early intervention services for infants and toddlers who have or are at risk of developing disabilities. These services are provided to the family, usually in the child's natural environment, typically their home or child care setting. Services are designed to minimize the potential for developmental delays, reduce the need for special education services when the child reaches preschool, and enhance the family's capacity to meet the child's needs.

Reflect on your experiences with people with disabilities

Recall a relationship or an interaction that you have had as an adult with a child or adult with a disability. Was it positive or negative? Why? How did you feel? Did it change your ideas about people with disabilities? How?

Preparing Yourself for Inclusion

Kindergarten and primary schools are increasingly adopting inclusive practices, so you may very well have a child or several children with disabilities placed in your classroom. Your first reaction to learning that there will be a child with a disability in your class may not be positive. You didn't choose to be a special education teacher, and you may be afraid that you are not prepared. However, inclusion is consistent with what you are already doing in your classrooms to welcome, support, and nurture the development and learning of typically developing children with diverse abilities.

If children have been identified as having disabilities, special assistance should be available to support the teacher who works with them. Your training in early childhood education will have prepared you to view each child as an individual and to focus on children's skills, interests, and needs. You have also learned to be aware of your own feelings, reactions, and biases and to monitor them so that they do not have negative effects on children. These skills and dispositions will serve you well when a child with a special need is included in your classroom.

The first thing you can do when you know that a child with a disability is going to enter your classroom is to reflect on your attitudes. Children with disabilities need teachers who value acceptance and equality. When you believe that learning in a classroom with peers is a right of all children, not a privilege granted to a few, you will be able to support inclusion. Self-reflection may be necessary to ensure that you are seeing each child as a unique, worthwhile individual. Sometimes teachers make assumptions or generalizations. Check yourself to be sure that you do not assume that children who live in poverty or drug-affected homes are more likely to be slow learners or have behavioral problems. Remember that when a family does not read bedtime stories it does not mean that they don't care about their child's education. Consider whether you assume that a child who cannot speak is not able to learn or think or communicate. Think about whether you tend to blame parents for children's disabilities. Consider whether you engage in stereotyped thinking (for example, that canes and hearing aids are for old people).

The next thing you will do to prepare for inclusion of children with diverse needs and abilities is to draw on what you already know how to do—incorporate principles of developmentally appropriate practice into your classroom. You will use best practices that include activity/play-based learning, child- and family-centered policies, and culturally relevant instruction. Your teaching will be based on your knowledge of child development and be flexible enough to met the diverse needs of the children in your care. You will use *differentiated instruction*—a strategy in which a teacher tailors learning activities to the needs of each child, those with learning disabilities, those who qualify as gifted, and all other children as well.

You know that teaching children begins with relationships, so you take the time to develop trusting, caring relationships with the children and their families. You have taken advantage of opportunities to learn about typical development for children so that you can recognize circumstances that call for additional support. You make efforts to learn more about the cultures of children in your care and encourage and welcome families into your program. As a good early childhood educator, you will value differences and foster respect and opportunities for all children to work together.

Identifying Children with Special Needs

You know that the early years of life are critical for development and learning. This is the period of maximum opportunity to promote children's growth in every area—social, emotional, cognitive, and physical. "If their special needs are recognized and met during these years, children with disabilities will have a much better chance of succeeding and becoming independent adults" (Hull, Goldhaber, & Capone, 2002, 162).

Observe and Document

As a teacher you will come to know every child in your group in the natural context of daily routines and activities. Because of this you may be the first person to recognize that a child needs additional support. Knowledge of child development and your observation skills will prepare you to recognize a child whose development differs in significant ways from other children in your group. Early identification coupled with appropriate intervention (education and services) can sometimes help avoid developmental problems that will be more difficult to remediate when the child gets older. For example, a teacher we know observed that a child in her class often seemed to drift off in daydreams and was not making progress comparable to that of the other children. She decided that the problem needed to be explored. A full evaluation led to the conclusion that the child suffered from a form of epilepsy. The daydreaming episodes were actually *petit mal* seizures, and the child's developmental lags were caused by this undiagnosed condition. Medical intervention was needed.

In order to get help in a timely fashion, teachers need to observe children carefully and know the signs of physical, emotional, or cognitive disabilities. Remember, however, that although you should be alert to physical and behavioral characteristics that suggest the need for further screening or evaluation, it is not your role to diagnose a disability.

> *Fifteen eager 4-year-olds are eating their morning snack. It is the middle of the school year, and they have all learned how to cooperate to make snack time pleasant—except Jeremy. He cruises the edges of the room, stopping briefly to dump a puzzle from a shelf and run his hands through the pieces, only to be distracted by the morning's paintings drying nearby. As he passes a table of children, his attention is again deflected. He tries to squeeze his body onto a chair occupied by another child.*

Jeremy's behavior consistently precipitates conflicts with children and adults. He is unable to engage for any length of time in meaningful activity. Many young children are easily distractible at age 4, but if you were Jeremy's teacher you might find his behavior was extreme. The first thing you might do under these circumstances would be to try to understand what is causing his behavior. Careful observation of his actions and talking with the family are good places to start. Then you might try modifying your learning environment, schedule, and curriculum to better meet his needs. If none of these things proved to be helpful, you might conclude that Jeremy needed additional help to cope with the demands of a preschool classroom. At that point you might initiate steps to have him evaluated and to find help for him, so he can learn to function in more positive ways.

If your first teaching position is in a setting with typically developing children, a situation similar to this one may be your first encounter with a child who has a disability—a child whose condition has not been formally identified and who is not yet receiving specialized services or supports. The behavior of a child like Jeremy may perplex and frustrate you. Your observations are your cue to a possible problem. Many developmental or psychological issues are first detected when a child enters an early childhood program. As a classroom teacher, you will be in a position to notice that a child might benefit from evaluation and special services and after consultation with his family, you may initiate the process of getting help.

What steps do you take when you believe a child in your care has a condition that may require special attention? Start by observing the child in a variety of situations. Note the child's strengths and the ways she or he is functioning appropriately and similarly to other children. Then pinpoint the ways in which the child's behavior and skills seem atypical or cause concern. Make written anecdotal records, being careful to make objective statements about what you observe the child doing and when it occurs. You can also learn more by conducting time samples or event samples. In what situations is the child unable to participate like the other children? Does the child's behavior meet some developmental expectations? Is there a cultural or language difference that might be related? Once you have documented the child's behavior and reviewed your observations, you can decide on the next step.

You might want to share your observations and concerns with a coworker, director, or supervisor. As you do this, be careful not to come to conclusions too quickly or to label or blame the child. Colleagues can often offer insights from a more objective point of view that will help you sort out your reactions. You might ask one of them to make an independent observation of the child. Sometimes adult expectations for children's behavior are "developmentally inappropriate."

For example, we have known teachers who were surprised when they encountered a 2-year-old who didn't talk in school, or a 5-year-old who did not follow directions well. These behaviors are quite likely to be a function of individual differences that are the result of the child's life experiences and not disabilities.

Response to Intervention

A second step that is becoming more common in the early primary grades is called Response to Intervention (RTI). RTI is a program that provides *evidence-based interventions* (what we call best practices) and relies on frequent assessment of progress to determine how effective each intervention is for an individual child. Although this is a general education program, it is often funded by special education funds and, at its best, is a partnership between special education and general education teachers (Allington, 2009).

RTI proponents agree that a high-quality, developmentally appropriate classroom with well-trained teachers provides the impetus for development that benefits all children. However, up to 20 percent of children in kindergarten and first grade may require more intense support to reach their academic goals, such as recognizing rhyming sounds or developing fine motor skills. Additional practice on targeted skills is usually provided in smaller groups of children and is always based on research on effective teaching. At this point, many children are able to "catch up" with their peers. The few who need even more focused intervention are given one-to-one support by skilled classroom teachers. Only when assessment data show that this level of support is insufficient, is a child referred for evaluation for special education eligibility. The intent is not to delay needed services, but rather to encourage earlier identification of those children who need help and to reduce the need for special education services (Buysse & Wesley, 2006).

While RTI may not translate exactly to the preschool setting, early childhood principles already support the idea of prevention and providing individualized support for each child. Helpful tools for identifying preschool children who may be at risk for later problems, tools for monitoring progress over time, and research-based effective practices are being developed by the Center for RTI in Early Childhood, the RTI Action Network, the Frank Porter Graham (FPG) Child Development Institute, the National Center for Learning Disabilities, and others.

IDEA specifies that children may not be classified as having a learning disability due to lack of appropriate reading or math instruction or limited English proficiency. RTI is planned to ensure that every child has appropriate instruction before being considered for special education referral. It is a part of what you are already doing to meet the individual needs of the children in your care.

Eligibility for Special Education Services

Occasionally, despite your best efforts, the help of support staff, and ongoing communication with the family, you may be convinced that a child truly does have a problem that calls for additional action beyond what you are able to provide. At this point, you will discuss it with your director, supervisor, or principal and you or the administrator will ask the family for consent to make a referral for evaluation with the goal of identifying the problem and providing appropriate assistance for the child if it is called for. In some cases the family might not be ready to accept that their child may have a problem. When this occurs, you will work with the child to the greatest extent possible and gather more data. Talk to your program administrator about other ways to approach the family. In some cases, the family may be urged to come into the classroom and observe, or to discuss the concerns with their pediatrician. During this process, it is important that you continue to do everything you can to meet the child's needs in your classroom.

Enlist the support of your colleagues and program administrator. Use resources available in your community. Both public and private agencies provide screening for groups of children and evaluation and consultation for children with disabilities and other special needs. If you teach in a preschool or child development center, a nearby elementary school may be able to provide such services, or help may be available through a state or county department of health, human services, or education. Private agencies such as the Association for Children and Adults with Learning Disabilities and children's hospitals may also be able to provide assistance. If you work in a public school system, check with your administrator about what policies are in place for making referrals. Most school districts have specialists on their staff whose job it is to help you to evaluate the needs of a child.

Because development varies so greatly between individuals, in the early years the distinction between children who have a disability and those who are typically developing is often not clear. You already know that early childhood educators have children with a wide range of developmental levels in every group. The Individuals with Disabilities Education Act (IDEA) defines more than a dozen categories of disabilities—including mental retardation, hearing impairment, speech or language impairments, visual impairment, serious emotional disturbance, orthopedic impairments, autism, traumatic brain injury, other health impairments, specific learning disability, and developmental delay. These are conditions that significantly interfere with a child's learning and development.

Marjorie Kostelnik and her colleagues (2002) suggest that there are both positive and negative aspects to identifying and labeling disabilities. On the positive side, a label is necessary in order for a child to receive special education services, and it can help adults to know where to look for more information about a child's condition. The negative aspects are that the label focuses on only one dimension of a child rather than giving a full picture. Teachers may then focus on the disability rather than the child's interests and strengths. Although it has shortcomings, the practice of identifying children by disability is still in use and is likely to continue until a better system is found.

Determining Educational Needs

Standardized assessments are generally used by those specially trained to identify whether a child is eligible to participate in special education services. This is usually coordinated by a Department of Education when the child is age 3 and older. Early intervention assessments for children under the age of 3 are offered through various government agencies such as the Departments of Health, Human Services, or Families and Children.

If it is determined that a child needs special education services in order to meet his or her educational potential, a team that includes the teacher, family members, educational specialists, and others with relevant expertise work together to develop an Individualized Education Program (IEP) or Individualized Family Service Plan (IFSP) for children younger than 3. In addition to standardized tests, the process of developing the plan includes the use of authentic assessments such as observations of the child in natural settings, like the home or preschool classroom, and includes information gathered from family members and others familiar with the child (DEC, 2007).

The specific services to be provided to a child with an identified disability are outlined in the IEP. It also includes developmental goals for the child and identifies any accommodations and/or modifications that the teacher may need to make to help the child participate more fully in the program. It is desirable to base an IEP on the philosophy and goals of the family and the instructional practices of the regular classroom staff. It should also reflect the philosophy of the early childhood program and current views about the ways that young children learn. It is the collaboration of the family, special education staff, and the child's teacher that makes this document possible. IEPs can be written to focus on the whole child, linking evaluation and assessment information with developmentally appropriate instructional practices (Edmiaston, Dolezal, Doolittle, Erickson, & Merritt, 2000; McCormick & Feeney, 1995).

The document specifies who will be responsible for each goal or accommodation and the frequency of the intervention. For example, Maya's IEP might say that she will meet with a speech therapist twice a week to increase articulation, and the classroom teacher will make two attempts daily to teach social conventions by encouraging her to say hello and goodbye at appropriate times. An occupational therapist may come to the classroom weekly to assist Maya in learning to button and zip her clothing. Each person on the team will make regular assessments of her progress in the course of their work with her. The IEP team meets at least once a year to discuss, update, and revise each child's IEP. In addition to the goals stated in the IEP, you will provide any other accommodations or strategies that you feel are needed to ensure access and participation by every child. When a child has an IEP, the team has decided on the next steps the child should reach. These goals should be accompanied by resources and support for the teacher. Figure 12.1 provides an example of an Individualized Education Plan.

An individualized family services plan (IFSP) is required by IDEA for children under the age of 3 who have been found eligible to receive early intervention services. Family members and service providers, who work as a team, write the IFSP. The family is asked to identify the outcomes they want for their child and a written plan is created based on their input. This team plans the child's program, implements it, and then evaluates its effectiveness. The IFSP is reviewed regularly and revised as needed to best support the child's development (Dunlap, 2009). As a caregiver for an infant or toddler with a disability, you will have responsibility for carrying out some of the recommendations in the child's IFSP.

Implementing Inclusion

As you are with all children, when a child with a disability enters your room you will be welcoming—help the child to feel like part of the classroom community. You do not need to become an expert on the causes, symptoms, and nature of a disability to be an effective teacher in an inclusion classroom. But you may need specialized information or training to guide you in providing appropriate education and services. Sometimes this will be fairly simple, like learning what to do for a child who has seizures. Sometimes it may require special training, like learning some sign language to communicate with a child with a hearing disorder.

Preparation

While young children tend to be very accepting of differences, you will want to consider some things you can do to help the children in your class understand

FIGURE 12.1 Example of an Individualized Education Plan (IEP)

INDIVIDUALIZED EDUCATION PROGRAM (IEP)

NAME OF CHILD: Maya Child
BIRTHDATE: 12/08/2005
GRADE: Kindergarten

AGE: 5 Yrs. 11 Mos.

DATE: 11/10/2011

STUDENT PROFILE

Maya is a 5-year-old girl with Down syndrome, developmental delays, motor and speech delays. She lives with her mother, father, 2 older brothers, an aunt, and her 5-year-old cousin. She reached developmental milestones, including speech and motor skills, later than typical. She attended a self-contained preschool program for 2 years, and this is her first placement in an inclusion setting.

Her teacher indicated that Maya has slightly limited receptive language and considerable delay in expressive language. As a result, she has trouble expressing her wants and needs. This is interfering with her ability to participate in group activities and to interact with the other children, although she likes to play alongside her peers. When she is not included or cannot accomplish a task, she sometimes reacts by hitting, crying, and kicking. Additionally, her fine motor development prevents her from performing some tasks, such as dressing and manipulating writing and drawing tools.

The family indicated that Maya is difficult to understand and prefers to play with her cousin Rahsana, who will be in the same classroom. She is typically happy and cooperative although she often seems to "not pay attention" when given directions. When frustrated, she tantrums by lying on the floor, crying, and kicking.

CLASSROOM ACCOMMODATIONS

Self-Help: Provide assistance with toileting, dressing, and eating.

Social/Emotional: Practice Positive Behavioral Support to decrease causes of frustration and tantrums.

Provide peer buddy for role modeling: Plan structured opportunities for turn taking, cooperative play, and peer interaction.

Physical arrangements: Have Maya seated near a teacher at group time to help her focus on the activity.

Plan for her to sit near peers, who will model behaviors for her. Provide a visual schedule to help Maya learn the routine of each day.

Materials: Provide extra large crayons and other materials for creative expression and writing.

Supply duplicates of favored materials so she can use them alongside other children.

Communication: Use picture/word communication book, simplified commands, visual cues, pictures, and gestures.

Annual Goals: Practice goals (self-help, vocabulary, social, behavioral, cognitive, physical) in the course of regular classroom activities.

MEASURABLE GOALS

AREA: Language/Literacy

PRESENT LEVEL OF ACADEMIC ACHIEVEMENT AND FUNCTIONAL PERFORMANCE:
Standardized testing indicates that Maya has an expressive vocabulary of at least 20 words and uses basic single-word utterances. She expresses her wants and needs on a limited basis through one-word requests or pointing and/or gesturing. Her limited verbalizations adversely affect her ability to communicate with peers and adults. Receptive vocabulary testing revealed that she can point to common objects.

MEASURABLE ANNUAL GOAL related to meeting the student's needs:
By May 2012, Maya will respond appropriately to greetings (hello, good-bye, how are you?) in 8/10 trials.

AREA: Physical Development (Fine motor)

PRESENT LEVEL OF ACADEMIC ACHIEVEMENT AND FUNCTIONAL PERFORMANCE:
According to teacher and parent observations, Maya is able to grasp large objects in her hands but has fine motor delays that impact her ability to dress herself when it involves buttons, zippers, or other fasteners.

MEASURABLE ANNUAL GOAL related to meeting the student's needs:
By May 2012, Maya will fasten and unfasten all buttons and zippers on the front of her clothing with 90% accuracy.

(continued)

FIGURE 12.1 Example of an Individualized Education Plan (IEP) *(continued)*

SPECIAL EDUCATION AND RELATED SERVICE(S)				
Type of Service(s)	Frequency of Service(s)	Amount of time	Beginning/ Ending Date	Location of Service(s)
Related Services Speech therapist (ST) will introduce vocabulary, articulation	2 times weekly	30 min.	1/12/12 to 05/20/12	Preschool classroom
Related Services Occupational and Physical Therapists (OT, PT) will consult with ECSE and preschool teachers.	weekly	30 min.	1/10/12 to 5/20/12	Preschool classroom Playground
Special Education Early childhood special education (ECSE) teacher will provide small-group instruction, incorporating instructions provided by OT and PT.	3 times weekly	60 min.	1/10/12 to 5/20/12	Preschool classroom
Supplementary Aids and Services Preschool teacher will introduce and reinforce new vocabulary, incorporating instructions provided by ST.	daily	30 min.	1/10/12 to 5/20/12	Preschool classroom

and accept the new child. Think about the words you will use if children ask questions or want more information about the child. A simple explanation of the specific disability or condition with some personally meaningful examples is a good approach. For example, for a child who has difficulty with expressive language, you might say, "Mark has trouble saying what he wants to say sometimes. Do you ever want to tell someone something and the words come out all mixed up?"

Answer children's questions as honestly and directly as you can. Help them understand any differences they notice. You could say, "Rose wears a hearing aid so that she can hear us when we talk to her." If they seem interested you might bring in some hearing aids for children to try and to learn about how they work.

You may need to assure other children that a disability isn't "catching." Some children (especially those of elementary age) may initially laugh at or ridicule any child who looks or learns differently. Remember that this response may be fueled by embarrassment. It provides you with an opportunity to talk about the wide range of differences among people and the value of respectful relationships. Your warm, accepting attitude will provide a powerful model for the development of these relationships.

In *Children with Special Needs: Lessons for Early Childhood Professionals,* Marjorie Kostelnik and her coauthors recommend that when a child with special needs is first enrolled in your class, you gather information about the child based on your observations and what you learn about her or him from others. They suggest that you find out the following:

- How the child reacts to sensations
- How the child processes information (his or her preferred way to learn)
- How the child approaches problems, makes plans, and takes action
- The child's style of emotional, social, and intellectual functioning
- How the child communicates with others
- How the child typically interacts with peers and adults
- What the family is like and their typical routines (Kostelnik, Onaga, Rohde, & Whiren, 2002, p. 4)

As you observe, you will find out about the child's likes and dislikes, abilities, interests, and areas in which he or she needs assistance. Remember that knowledge about a disability may help you deal with your anxiety, but it will not help you to know the child. No two children with the same disability are alike. A disability is only one characteristic of a person. When a child who wears a brace on her leg works a puzzle or paints at an easel, your first response will be the strategies she uses for completing the puzzle or the colors of the painting. When she is on the playground and cannot run or climb like the other children, you may need to provide physical assistance or help her find alternative activities.

An essential source of information about any child will be his or her family. Pediatricians, therapists, special education teachers, early intervention specialists, as well as workshops and classes will also be able to help you to understand and work with a child who has disabilities. When you get to know the child with a disability as a person, you will be better able to build a good relationship with the child and meet his or her needs in your program.

You will want to give the child the opportunity to participate as fully as possible in the daily events of the classroom and support his or her developing a sense of competence (see Figure 12.2). This will be facilitated if you do not demand uniform participation from any of the children. If each child is able to contribute in her or his own way, the participation of the child with the disability will not seem very different. Avoid overprotecting—this might single out the child as less competent. Other children may then become overprotective or may exclude the child.

You can help the children in your class understand that no one can do everything equally well and that all of us have strengths and weaknesses. You may also help children in the group find specific ways to include a child with a disability in their play. For example, you might show them how to help a child with a visual impairment feel the shape of a block structure and then to give verbal guidance so that the child can place blocks in the structure.

You may find that at first you are uncomfortable about including a child with a disability. You may feel unsure of your ability to manage or feel that it should not be your responsibility. Yet it is important that teachers be positive and supportive, for we know that a supportive emotional environment is a basic requirement for children to develop to their fullest. One way to feel more confident is to learn as much as possible about inclusion. Your own program may provide you with professional development and many communities offer regular training

FIGURE 12.2   Including a Child with Disabilities or Other Special Needs

- Learn about the child by talking with his or her family members. They will be your best source of information about the child's strengths, needs, and challenges. Be sure to listen carefully to family members and others who know the child.
- Consult with the child's doctor, therapists, and former teachers for additional information. Find out whether the child is taking medication and any side effects that might be an issue. Ask what special classes or therapy services the child participates in and find out any precautions, limitations, or requirements you should know about.
- Maintain regular communication with the family and other specialists who are working with the child.
- Find out what services will be available to support your work with the child.
- Brainstorm with the experts and consultants on how you can best support the child's development.
- Be careful not to make judgments based on first impressions. Get to know the child and be sure to look for strengths and abilities.
- Ask yourself: "How can I make classroom routines and activities relevant to this child and also meet the needs of the other children?"
- Be patient—some children may need to be told or shown many times.
- Be flexible and open to learning new things about children and about yourself.

Reflect on how you might feel as the parent of a child with special needs

If you were the parent of a child with a disability, what kind of educational program would you want for your child? How would you like your child to be treated? How would you like early childhood professionals to treat you?

opportunities. The Office of Head Start in particular has made available many resources online that are intended to support their longstanding commitment to effective inclusion, and their SpecialQuest training library is available to everyone. The Head Start Center for Inclusion also has easy-to-use materials designed to address any barriers to inclusion and to develop confident and competent teachers of children with special needs.

Program Modifications

Both policy and recommended practice identify positive benefits for children with and without disabilities and with a variety of diverse needs who attend high-quality inclusive early childhood programs. However, merely placing children in the same room is not sufficient. Children's individual needs must be addressed.

Your knowledge of child development and what is developmentally appropriate for young children in general will guide your planning as you decide what materials, activities, and teaching strategies to use for the child with special needs in your classroom. As in teaching any child, you will observe this child's strengths, interests, and preferences to help him or her engage productively in learning experiences. Just as you support other children's learning, you will model desired behavior, demonstrate sequences in an activity, and play with the child. Remember to let the child take the lead when possible, provide encouragement and contact, and stay nearby so you can offer support when it is needed. Allen and Schwartz (1996) remind us to keep in mind the ways that children with disabilities are like other children instead of concentrating on remediation of deficits and delays.

You will make your classroom a good place for a child with disabilities or other special needs by making some fairly simple modifications in the curriculum, materials, and learning environment. The general goals you have for children with disabilities will be the same as those you have for children who are developing typically. Begin by thinking about the learning experiences you are providing for children. Keep in mind that all children, particularly those with disabilities or other special needs, need to have opportunities that will help them develop confidence; to explore; to plan what they want to do and implement their plans; to practice self control, communication, and cooperation; and to develop relationships with their peers.

Think, too, about whether a child with disabilities will have access to all of the learning opportunities available in your classroom. This process of reflection will help you to decide the kinds of modifications you can make in your program to assist the child with special needs. Susan Sandall and Ilene Schwartz offer helpful guidance for this process in their book *Building Blocks for Teaching Preschoolers with Special Needs*. They define *curriculum modification* as a change to the ongoing classroom activity or materials in order to facilitate or maximize a child's participation and assert that modifications should be easy-to-implement changes that require some planning, but most do not require additional resources (Sandall & Schwartz, 2002, 45).

Successful inclusion means that children have access to all learning opportunities, are able to enjoy full participation in activities with their peers, and have the supports needed to be successful (DEC/NAEYC, 2009). Providing access includes removing physical barriers, providing a wide range of activities, and creating exciting opportunities for each child to learn and develop. Participating with the other children is an important part of early childhood education. Participation is increased when we provide children with embedded learning opportunities (ELOs). These are experiences that address learning goals in the context of everyday routines, such as the activities in which all children participate. The activities provided for children with disabilities may have a slightly different focus but should be the same activity that others are pursuing. For example, when some children are stacking blocks, others may be encouraged to count them or identify the shapes. While we will describe modifications that can be made to help achieve inclusion goals, it is important to remember that the fewer modifications and changes the better.

Sandall and Schwartz describe six types of curriculum modifications that can help children with special needs participate in the daily program as fully as possible. These offer a good framework for thinking about what you might do in a classroom.

Environmental Support

Environmental support involves modifying parts of the environment to make it responsive to the needs of children. Remember that the learning environment includes the routines and schedules as well as the physical setting and the emotional climate of the classroom. If a child has trouble with mobility, you may need to widen pathways between areas. If a child has a verbal processing problem, you can provide a picture of the activity or area he or she is to go to next. If a child is having trouble attending in a group, it might be helpful to review your schedule. Circle times are often too long for typically developing children, let alone those who have additional challenges. So watch the children carefully at circle time to make sure that everyone is involved. When attention lags, add some movement or singing or go on to the next activity. Be sure to arrange the learning environment (including materials and activities) in ways that promote the child's interactions with peers.

Materials Adaptations

Materials adaptations are modifications of classroom toys and other tools to support the child's participation. An occupational or physical therapist can help you figure out simple adaptations that make a big difference. It will be easier for a child with motor difficulties to be a full participant in the classroom if you wrap tape or yarn around the handles of brushes, sew handles on stuffed animals, provide short-handled eating utensils, lower the easel, tape pieces of wood to the pedals of the bike, and use nonslip materials to keep toys from sliding. You may already have a supply of puzzles and manipulatives with various levels of difficulty. If not, adding these is a simple modification.

Simplification of Activities

Simplify activities for children who are having difficulties with complex tasks. Breaking down a complex task into its component parts and teaching them separately as a series of sub-skills (called *task analysis*) is a useful tool. Tasks such as putting on clothes and brushing teeth can be practiced in components for a time as preparation for carrying out the whole task. If you have ever taught a toddler to pull up his or her pants, you have some practical experience with this process. Reading, or taking a special education class or workshop, can help you learn about task analysis. You can also do things like give the child materials one at a time, design an activity to have fewer steps, and make photo cards that show the steps in a sequence.

Use of Adaptive Devices

Adaptive devices (specially designed furniture and equipment) can be employed to assist a child's involvement. An occupational or physical therapist or a special education resource person can recommend equipment and other adaptations. These specialists can help you to arrange for furniture and materials like a special table to help a child in a wheelchair or brace get near an activity, adaptive scissors to assist a child who has fine motor difficulties, or footrests and back props on a chair for a child with large motor difficulties. Assistive technology is also available to help a child to express ideas and show what they know and can do. Professionals who are experts in the design and provision of assistive technology can help you in identifying what the child needs and how to provide it (Bowe, 2000; Mulligan, 2003).

Support from Peers

Peer support can be very helpful for a child with disabilities. Peers are good models. It may work well to pair the child who has special needs with one who knows the activities and routines and will be supportive. You could suggest that children invite the child with special needs to join them in play or share a discovery.

Invisible Support

Invisible support involves arranging activities in less obvious ways to support the child's participation. This might include making sure that the child with special needs has a chance to see how other children are doing an activity, letting the child pour last so the pitcher isn't too full, providing more movement activities during circle time so the child is able to attend longer, or having the child with special needs go first to ensure that he or she has enough time to complete an activity.

Having children with disabilities in your classroom does not mean you will need to do everything differently, or make time-consuming individual plans for one child. It means being observant and responsive to every child's needs and continuing to provide engaging opportunities so children will achieve their optimal development. Your ongoing assessment will give you an idea of what is next on the developmental continuum for a child and you can plan accordingly.

Reflect on your experiences with children with special needs

Think about the ways in which children with disabilities were, or were not, a part of your early school experiences. How do you think your teachers felt about these children? How did you feel? What implications do these reflections have for you as a future teacher?

Inclusion and Developmentally Appropriate Practice

Inclusion is supported in NAEYC's position statement on developmentally appropriate practice (DAP), which states that teachers should be prepared to meet the identified special needs of individual children, including those with disabilities (Copple & Bredekamp, 2009).

Play is the primary vehicle for learning for all young children and an important hallmark of appropriate practice. It is important that teachers who work with children who have disabilities and other special needs not become so concerned with remediation or individualized instruction that they forget that *all* children need opportunities to play. Engaging in play is particularly important for children with disabilities, as it offers unique opportunities for them to experience feelings of mastery, resourcefulness, and competence so crucial to the development of a positive sense of self.

The guidance you provide may be particularly important for supporting the play of children with disabilities. You may need to do some direct teaching of play skills and take an active role in helping a child build these. Children with disabilities and special needs, like all children, need opportunities to engage with a variety of both open-ended and specific-purpose play materials.

Collaboration

When you have children with disabilities and other special needs in your classroom, you will be called on to collaborate with other professionals. This will involve working with special education teachers, consultants, and professionals from different disciplines. In the past, specialists in different areas tended to work in isolation. For example, the child attended speech therapy outside of school and the teacher and speech therapist never spoke to one another. Collaboration is advocated today so that teams can address the needs of children and families in a more integrated and systematic way. It is also a benefit to you as a classroom teacher because these others often have specialized knowledge about the disabilities that you are addressing in your program so they can provide resources and support. In turn, you can share the natural ways that you embed learning opportunities in children's play experiences.

Working with others to provide the best possible experience for a child with a disability can be gratifying. It can also be challenging. Working with a team involves crossing discipline boundaries and may require some new behaviors. It is not unusual for early childhood educators to be focused on learning processes while those trained in special education are more focused on learning outcomes. In order to serve children effectively, team members need to have a commitment to smooth relationships, work on building trusting relationships, respect the contributions of others, and have good communication skills (Sandall & Schwartz, 2002; Turnbull, Turnbull, Shank, & Smith, 2004; Wolery & Wilbers, 1994). Collaboration enables a team of educators, specialists, and family members to share their resources and strengths to help children and address issues in creative and responsive ways.

Characteristics and Strategies for Working with Young Children with Disabilities

The following pages contain brief descriptions of some of the kinds of disabilities that you may encounter in early childhood settings and some suggestions for how you might work effectively with children who have these disabilities. Keep

in mind that a category does not give you a full picture of a child. Characteristics observed in children in one category are often similar to those of children in other categories. Children with a similar condition often differ from each other as much as they differ from children in other categories. And children who have been identified as having different disabilities may behave in similar ways.

Children with Orthopedic Impairments

Children who have *orthopedic impairments* have difficulty controlling or easily moving their bodies. Consult with the family and the physical or occupational therapist to help you design changes. Talk to the family and therapist to learn about activities the child enjoys that could be used with the whole group. For example, body awareness activities will be helpful in improving all children's appreciation for their bodies.

Young children are often fascinated by special equipment, like walkers or wheelchairs. Check with the family—they may be willing for the other children to satisfy their curiosity by trying out the equipment. You might also invite an adult with an orthopedic impairment to visit with the children and answer their questions.

Following are suggestions for adaptations that will assist the positive functioning of children with orthopedic impairments in your classroom:

- Rearrange furniture to make it easier for the child to move from one area to another.
- Adjust table and easel heights.
- Relocate supplies and toys to make them more accessible.
- Adapt standard equipment, like tricycles.
- Let the child discover his or her own abilities and limitations by trying activities.
- Encourage independence by teaching self-help skills, like dressing and eating.

Children with Cognitive Delays

Although all children learn at different rates, some learn significantly more slowly than their peers. Cognitive disorders and intellectual disabilities can arise before, during, or after birth. One of the leading causes of cognitive delay is a genetic abnormality called *Down syndrome*. During the preschool years children with cognitive delays appear much younger than their chronological age and may have difficulty learning skills and developing concepts. They may be unable to remember things, or may be unable to use information to solve problems. They may also have trouble using language or may encounter difficulties playing cooperatively, initiating activities or interactions, or learning to function independently.

Children who have mild cognitive delays may not seem much different from the youngest children in an age group. Children who have moderate cognitive deficits will have greater difficulties in self-help skills, motor development, social skills, and language development. Children with significant cognitive delays will have trouble functioning in most areas of development.

Following are suggestions for adaptations that will assist the positive functioning of children with cognitive delays in your classroom:

- Break down directions, giving them more slowly.
- Provide many opportunities for the child to successfully practice a new skill.
- Simplify routines, and allow more time for transitions.
- Do not assume what the child can do and can't do. Encourage the child to try.
- Use shorter sentences and a simpler vocabulary than you might with the other children.
- Spend more time and use a multisensory approach when you teach a new activity.
- Focus on contrast and give lots of real-life examples when helping the child learn a concept.

Children with Learning Disabilities

The term *learning disabilities* refers to a variety of problems exhibited by children with normal intelligence but below age-level academic functioning. Children with learning disabilities can be extremely uneven in their development. For example, a child may have advanced verbal abilities and find it very difficult to learn how to read.

Learning disabilities in preschool children may not have much impact on daily functioning. In school-age children, however, the inconsistency between ability in one area of development and disability in another often leads to their being blamed for not trying hard enough or of being lazy or stubborn.

When you work with a child with learning disabilities, be sure to focus on strengths and provide lots of encouragement for successes. The strategies are largely the same as what you do with other children, but they are more critical. Following are suggestions that will assist the positive functioning of children with learning disabilities in your classroom:

- Use several sensory modalities so that the child can learn in the way he or she learns best.
- Allow the child to touch and manipulate materials.
- Be well organized and keep activities short.
- Keep transitions and large-group times short to avoid situations where the child is waiting with nothing to do.
- Allow adequate time and opportunities for the child to practice new concepts and skills.
- Avoid overstimulation to help the child concentrate.
- Simplify activities so that the child experiences success.
- If needed, add more deliberate attention-getting strategies such as using words like *look, listen,* or *watch me.*

Children with Communication Disorders

It is typical for young children to have problems with communication and language. Lack of fluency is part of normal speech development; so are errors in articulation. You should be concerned about a child's language development if he or she does not talk by age 2, is not speaking in two- or three-word sentences by age 3, is very difficult to understand after age 3, or uses poor sentence structure or stutters after age 5. Preschool children exhibit many normal articulation errors such as saying *wif* for *with*. When these differences persist beyond the age of 5, or if unusual pitch, volume, or voice quality characterizes a child's speech, an evaluation by a speech therapist is in order.

Children with *receptive language problems* have difficulty understanding the meaning of words or the way words are put together. Children with *auditory processing problems* may be unable to tell the difference between speech sounds (auditory discrimination) and may be unable to isolate the sounds from a noisy background. Children with *speech problems* are difficult to understand. When children have *expressive language problems* they have difficulty verbalizing ideas, selecting appropriate words, or using correct grammatical structures. When children cannot communicate, they have difficulty learning, and social interactions are hindered when it is difficult for others to understand them.

These strategies are effective when you work with a child who has speech or language problems:

- Converse with the child regularly and encourage conversation among all the children.
- Be careful not to interrupt, rush, or pressure the child.
- Model correct language and expand the child's own comments.
- Use simple constructions and vocabulary.
- Provide many opportunities for all children to enjoy language in activities.
- Incorporate songs, rhymes, and chants into daily routines.
- Encourage the child to talk about his or her feelings during times of stress, frustration, or excitement.
- Redirect the communication to another child: "Could you tell Willie what you just told me?"

Children with Sensory Impairments
Visual

A child whose inability to see interferes with participation in daily activities is considered *visually impaired*. A child with partial sight may have a visual acuity problem that is correctable with glasses. Few children are completely unable to see. Many can see light and dark areas, broad shapes but not details, or have peripheral (side) rather than frontal vision.

The development of children whose visual impairment occurred after birth generally resembles that of other children, but the development of children who were blind at birth tends to be much slower. Because they may not be able to see well enough to imitate the actions of peers and because movement may be perceived as dangerous and therefore curtailed, these children may be somewhat slower in physical development than their peers. Social development may also lag behind because they may not see facial expressions that provide social cues and are a necessary part of social interaction.

Following are suggestions for adaptations that will assist the positive functioning of children with visual impairments in your classroom:

- Provide good overall lighting. Avoid glare or deep contrasts between light and shade.
- Keep the room arrangement and traffic patterns simple and uncluttered—and when a change is needed, have the child with the visual impairment participate in making the change.
- Use detailed description to accompany your actions when you introduce an activity or game.

- Keep a child with visual impairment close to you for group activities so that you can provide physical cues for participation.
- Provide larger toys and add different textures or sounds to materials when possible.
- Teach the child to look in the direction of the person speaking.

Hearing

Children have a hearing impairment when they have difficulty understanding and responding to speech or sounds. A hearing impairment may involve volume or clarity of sound. When children cannot hear, even with the use of a hearing aid, they are said to be deaf. Those who have a permanent but less severe hearing loss may be assisted by the use of a hearing aid.

When children cannot hear well, their spoken words may be unclear and difficult to understand. The rhythm and voice quality of their speech may be unusual. Social interactions are hindered when it is difficult for others to understand them. Cognitive skills may be slower to develop if hearing loss has resulted in a language delay.

Hearing problems are often first noticed in school. If a child has trouble paying attention, especially in group activities, doesn't answer when called, seems confused by directions or questions, or often gives the wrong answer, you should suspect a hearing problem and initiate investigation. Sometimes hearing loss is only temporary, caused by a middle ear infection, but because frequent infections can lead to permanent hearing loss it is important to urge families to seek treatment.

Following are suggestions for adaptations that will assist the positive functioning of children with hearing impairments in your classroom:

- Place yourself at the child's eye-level and in a well-lit place when speaking to the child.
- In a group activity, have children sit in a circle, so all faces are visible.
- If the child uses a hearing aid, ask the family to teach you how it works and how to care for it. Find out what to look for to make sure it is working
- If the child seems not to understand, rephrase your sentence instead of simply repeating it.
- Use visual clues and gestures to aid understanding.
- Encourage participation in activities like dramatic play that involve lots of language.

Sensory Integration

Sensory integration (SI) is the process by which the brain assembles a picture of the environment using information from the senses. The importance of this process was introduced in the 1960s by occupational therapist Jean Ayres. In most children sensory integration occurs naturally, but in others the brain isn't able to effectively integrate information from one or more of the senses (e.g., visual, auditory, kinesthetic). Children who have sensory integration difficulties may receive too much or too little sensory input, which can result in difficulty organizing and interpreting sensory information. This disorder may make it difficult for the child to focus on learning.

Ayres and others have developed approaches to intervention that involve a wide variety of tactile experiences such as swinging, deep pressure touch, tactile stimulation, and soothing sensory experiences like playing with shaving cream and play dough that appear to support better sensory integration in children. At present there is no consensus about the most effective intervention strategies to use for helping children who have sensory integration problems. Because the situation is in flux, it is best for teachers who want to know how to work with a child who has this disorder to consult with an occupational therapist or another professional who has specialized training in working with this condition. Strategies that may be considered include play-based activities in a sensory-rich environment and participation in activities involving swinging, tactile, visual, auditory, and tasting opportunities. The primary goal is to help children improve their ability to regulate motor and behavioral responses to sensory stimuli. Positive outcomes include increasing appropriate attention to people and activities, developing modified responses to sensory input, and the ability to complete daily tasks such as dressing, eating, sleeping, and conversing with others.

Children with Attention Deficit/Hyperactivity Disorder

Children who show an inability to focus and stay on task may have *attention deficit disorder* (ADD). When they also exhibit impulsive, out-of-control behavior beyond what seems to be typical, it is called *attention deficit/hyperactivity disorder* (ADHD). Children with ADHD are easily excitable, have trouble waiting for explanations or taking turns, and can seldom pause long enough to relax, watch, or listen. Jeremy, the child in the example earlier in this chapter, may experience this disorder. Children with ADHD may struggle to learn because they have difficulty focusing. They frequently have trouble developing social skills and often misunderstand the responses of others to their behavior.

Following are suggestions for adaptations that will assist the positive functioning of children with ADHD in your classroom:

- Simplify surroundings and reduce visual/auditory stimulation to help the child focus.
- Clearly define the child's work or play area.
- Position yourself near the child so you can offer assistance or encouragement.
- Acknowledge constructive and appropriate behavior.

Not every active young child has an attention deficit/hyperactivity disorder. Children with this diagnosis are identifiable due to the extremes of their behavior. A child must exhibit several characteristics (e.g., impulsiveness, short attention span, distractibility, inability to focus on a task, constant motion, and difficulty following through) to be identified as having ADHD. Children with attention deficit/hyperactivity disorders are sometimes disruptive in the classroom, so you may need a professional evaluation to determine the best course of action. Be careful not to label children as hyperactive; high activity level may simply be a characteristic of a child's temperament. After careful observation, if you think the child might have ADHD, suggest an evaluation.

Children with Emotional Disorders

Children with emotional problems may be more aggressive, unhappy, anxious, or withdrawn than their peers. Those with severe problems are extreme in their reactions and may require specialized care. Withdrawal, anxiety, or aggression may characterize their behavior. They may also exhibit unusual behaviors such as self-mutilation, rocking, running with arms flapping, extreme fearfulness, withdrawal, or total loss of self-control. Emotional problems interfere with relationships, with learning, and with the development of a positive sense of self.

A child with emotional problems may be difficult for you to handle, not only because the child is intense but also because even the experts disagree about the causes, classification, and treatment of these conditions. You may want to consult with a mental health professional to help you understand and work with the child. You may also need to be persistent in finding appropriate assistance for these children and their families.

Following are suggestions for adaptations that will assist the positive functioning of children with emotional difficulties in your classroom:

- Make sure that daily routines are consistent and predictable.
- Provide soothing activities like water play.
- Make an effort to build a supportive relationship with the child. Start by finding the things you like about the child and telling them to yourself and to the child.
- Give the child extra support and nurture.
- Be sensitive in comforting the child—one child may love being hugged while another may shrink away from physical contact.
- Find an activity or interest that you can talk about with the child. Make an effort to incorporate this into the environment or curriculum.

Children with Autism Spectrum Disorders

Autism is a developmental disability that significantly affects a child's ability to communicate, to play, and to interact with others. Autism is described as a *spectrum* of behaviors because individuals with autism vary in the degree of severity of their symptoms and the characteristic ways they behave, develop, and learn. At present our best understanding is that it is a neurological disorder that results from some abnormality in brain development.

A child is considered to have an autism spectrum disorder when a formal assessment determines that he or she meets some of the following criteria (Hall, 2009, 3):

- Impairment in social interaction in areas such as the use of nonverbal behaviors, eye contact, development of peer relationships, sharing with others, and social or emotional reciprocity.
- Impairments in communication, such as delay in or lack of spoken language, inability to have a conversation with another person, repetitive use of language, or lack of make-believe play appropriate to the child's developmental level.
- Restricted, repetitive, and stereotyped patterns of behavior. For example, rigid following of nonfunctional routines or rituals, motor mannerisms like hand or finger flapping.

Temple Grandin, a writer who has eloquently described her experiences as a child with autism, explains that she was almost unbearably sensitive to things like the rubbing of new clothing on her body and that she was unable to modulate noise. She says that she "had to shut it all out and withdraw or let it all in like a freight train" (Turnbull, Turnbull, & Shank & Smith, 2004, 288).

Autism is typically identified in the first 3 years of life and is four times more common in boys than in girls. Data from the Centers for Disease Control (cited in Hall, 2009) suggest that 1 child in every 150 shows symptoms of autism.

Asperger syndrome (AS) is a disorder considered to be part of the autism spectrum. This disorder can range from mild to severe and is characterized by tendencies toward social isolation, communication difficulties, and eccentric behavior. Individuals who have this syndrome fall within the normal intelligence range, do not have delays in language, and can communicate normally. They often exhibit exceptional skill or talent in a specific area (Dunlap, 2009).

Reflect on working with children with disabilities

Think about working with children with disabilities. Does the idea make you feel excited and comfortable, or anxious and uncomfortable? Why? What implications does this reflection have for you as a teacher? What might help you prepare for this challenge?

Following are suggestions for adaptations that will assist the positive functioning of children with autism spectrum disorders in your classroom:

- Provide consistent and predictable schedules and routines in order not to trigger anxiety.
- Alert the child well in advance if there are going to be changes in the schedule or routines.
- Make classroom expectations very clear and consistent.
- Use a variety of strategies in teaching—demonstrate, give visual cues, give consistent directions.
- Limit extraneous stimulation by providing the child with a quiet and protected place to work.

Children with Challenging Behaviors

Some children have serious behavior problems that interfere with their own learning and development and the experiences of others in the classroom. These are often among the most challenging children for teachers to work with. They engender feelings of frustration and failure on the part of the teacher, rather than satisfaction and accomplishment that can be a large part of teaching in an inclusion setting. In today's society, with its lack of adequate support for families and increased societal violence, more children with behavioral problems are part of early childhood programs. Children who have been exposed to repeated violence learn to use violence to cope with their own feelings and needs.

Sometimes behavior concerns are associated with another category of disability. The angry outbursts of a child with a hearing loss may be the result of frustration at being unable to find ways to have his or her needs met. Children with learning disabilities may have low self-esteem from frequent failures, causing either withdrawal or aggression. Children with physical disabilities may have never been asked to be independent because families have been overprotective in their efforts to help their child. When expected to help with cleanup, they are confused and even outraged.

In some cases, the behavior is a symptom of the disability itself. This is especially true of children with ADHD and autism. Their out-of-bounds behavior is more likely to cause teachers to feel angry than to feel eager to support them. A behavior disorder is the only disability that we sometimes view as intentional. It is important to see the ability to function in a classroom as another skill that a child has not mastered. A child with ADHD who constantly disrupts circle time is not choosing to be "naughty" or looking for attention. He or she may think that others are enjoying the behavior and be surprised at the strong response that results. An inability to read the reactions of others is a characteristic of ADHD. This leads peers to avoid the child with ADHD, and the resultant isolation decreases opportunities for the child to learn prosocial behaviors. When a child with autism throws blocks repeatedly at the wall, it is not an act of willful disobedience. Instead, the child is likely to be concentrating on the sensations of the throwing behavior and have little awareness of how others use the blocks. Children with autism are often more in touch with the characteristics of objects, like the blocks, than they are with the people around them.

It takes skill to help children develop to their fullest when they have any type of special needs, and behavioral needs are no different. Try not to take the behaviors personally or feel that they are intended to hurt you or others. Coursework and training on challenging behaviors may provide helpful guidance. Using consistent, caring, and firm guidance is beneficial for all children and a necessity for children who are struggling to learn positive social behaviors. Just as when you work with children with other disabilities, you should ask for help to understand behavioral disorders. Public schools usually have staff trained to work with children with behavior problems and training opportunities are available in many communities. Online resources such as challengingbehavior.org offer a wealth of information and many free materials to support you in your work.

Other Special Needs

In addition to knowledge about children with disabilities, you will need information and skills needed to deal with children who have other special needs. They may have been abused or neglected, have chronic health problems, speak a different language, or be gifted and talented.

Children Who Have Been Abused or Neglected

Like all children with special needs, those who have been abused or neglected can benefit from relationships with caring adults in a thoughtfully planned program. To rebuild a healthy self-concept and the ability to trust adults, extra time and attention must be devoted to the child. If it is possible, one person on a team should be designated as the child's primary contact, responsible for being physically and emotionally available to meet needs for positive attention, care, comfort, and positive discipline. The consistency of loving firmness can help the child realize that adults can be trustworthy, predictable in their reactions, and in control of themselves and the environment. It will also be helpful to the child if you structure a safe, predictable, and comforting environment; keep the child physically safe; and provide predictable routines to give him or her a sense of security.

The child's experience of daily activities and expectations should be carefully structured to promote feelings of mastery, security, and control. A caring adult can participate with the child in sensory activities, such as play dough and water play—first as a way to foster the nurturing relationship, and then as a bridge to encourage normal interest in play activities and socialization with other children and adults. It is also important that teachers refrain from criticizing the child's family or otherwise expressing disapproval of them.

Children with Acute or Chronic Health Conditions

Children with acute or chronic health conditions also require special assistance. These children may have any of a wide variety of ailments including respiratory conditions, diabetes, severe allergies, asthma, cancer, or many other health issues.

Health problems may have an impact on the child's ability to function in a school setting. Children who have been ill may lag in the development of motor skills. They may tire easily and need extra time or support for participation in class activities. Some may be more dependent on adults than is typical of children their age. In dealing with a child who has a chronic health problem, as in all of the other situations we discuss in this chapter, you will need to know the strengths, interests, and needs of the child, to provide support and encouragement that will let the child function as much as possible like others in the group.

A child's need for support from the teacher and program will vary with the nature and seriousness of the health condition. A child with a serious allergy, for example, might need only protection from the dangerous allergen and a teacher trained to administer emergency first aid, while a child with epilepsy or a feeding tube might need regular assistance.

The child's pediatrician, the child's family, and the health department in your state will be able to help you plan for inclusion of a child with health problems. When a child who has a severe chronic health condition enters your program, you will need to be involved in planning and collaboration with health professionals. A team including school personnel, a nurse from the school or a community agency, the child's family members, and others can be convened to develop an Individualized Health Care Plan (IHCP). This plan will address routine health care procedures, identify who is responsible for addressing needs, and establish communication networks among the members of the team. Health care specialists will handle many of the provisions of the IHCP, but teachers may be trained to deal with some procedures like giving the child medication (French, 2004).

Children with Special Gifts and Talents

Children who have unusual strengths, abilities, or talents are often called *gifted*. No single measure can identify giftedness in children. There may be a single unusual strength or ability, such as a child who has a phenomenal ability to remember, to read, or to perform music at a very young age. Or a child may have both a "gift" and a disability, as did the son of a friend of ours who had unusual verbal and artistic ability *and* a learning disability. It is important to keep in mind that the child who is gifted or talented has the same social and emotional needs as other young children.

Children who are gifted may exhibit intense curiosity, ask many questions, conduct investigations into how things work, develop a passionate interest in a particular topic (or topics), demonstrate the capacity for abstract thinking and the use of symbol systems at an early age, be highly independent, be unusually perceptive, have extraordinary memory, show great persistence in self-chosen tasks, or have advanced language ability and the ability to use and appreciate verbal humor.

If you have a child in your program who appears to be unusually advanced in one or more areas of development, you can provide encouragement by offering many opportunities for the child to develop and extend his or her interests. The child will benefit from learning materials that are open-ended, and from self-directed activities that require active involvement and problem solving. Find out what the child really wants to know or do, and then find the materials that will support his or her desire to learn. You may have to find materials designed for children older than the ones in your group. The child who is gifted may have less need for structure than most other children and may work quite independently. Large blocks of time for exploration will give the child the opportunity to concentrate and to work in depth. You can support his or her learning by providing a variety of materials and by being available as a resource.

Dual Language Learners

High-quality instruction is beneficial for all young language learners but it is not enough for children who are learning English while they are still developing their first language. Because these young children are learning two languages at the same time, we refer to them as dual language learners (DLL) rather than second language learners or simply English language learners. While it may seem that our responsibility is to teach these children English, we must also ensure that they maintain and develop their first language and culture. Families should be involved as strategic planners in their children's learning and their goals for their children discussed.

You may need to encourage families to continue to support the primary language at home, since many families feel their children will learn English faster if they hear and speak only English in school. There are many advantages to children becoming bilingual, including personal, social, economic, and cognitive benefits (U.S. Department of Health and Human Services, 2008). In addition, concepts of language that develop in the first language are easier to transfer to a second language.

An early introduction to English in a preschool setting is very beneficial to children's success in later grades. When immigrant children enter the K–5 setting as newcomers to the U.S. school system, they need to learn the social and academic rules of the school as well as the culture of a new country. English language learning may not start until they have become acclimated to the new expectations, causing them to fall behind their peers from the beginning.

Several considerations must be taken into account when planning for the inclusion of dual language learners. First, because all teaching and learning occurs in the context of trusting relationships, you may want to use the first language to develop positive interactions. While this is not always possible, learning to speak a few words in the child's primary language will be appreciated. A few "feeling words" in the first language are especially useful for providing comfort and supporting emotional development. When the teacher does not speak a child's home language, having others on staff who do helps children realize that both languages are valued at school. Sharing even a wordless experience such as making a classroom snack with a child can help to establish important feelings of commonality and trust. Next, it is important to know that each home environment brings different culturally determined uses of language. Do not make assumptions about a child's culture. Get to know the families and the ways they use language. For example, some cultures may not support the reading of bedtime stories to their young children; however, they may tell their children family history stories that are rich opportunities for understanding vocabulary, and other components of language. These stories may be taped by an adult or retold and illustrated for retelling by the children to build oral language.

The following are effective strategies for supporting dual language learners:

- Slower, expanded, simplified, and repetitive speech
- Gestures, body language and expressive communication
- Frequent comprehension checks
- Repetition through routines such as a welcome and greeting song to begin each day
- One-step directions
- Using features of first language and culture to illustrate English principles, such as the way plurals are formed in each language
- Visual clues such as pointing and picture cards with directions
- Charts with words and pictures for songs, poems, instructions
- Longer wait times to allow for mental processing
- New vocabulary in context; for example, names of foods at snack time
- New concepts and ideas presented in first language
- Children's literature that authentically depicts the cultures present in your classroom
- Using words in the primary language to hold conversations and build relationships.

All these strategies should be presented in context of appropriate play activities and classroom routines.

Working with Families of Children with Disabilities

Your relationship with the families of children with disabilities will be in most ways like your relationship with families of all the children in your care. When you have concerns about a child, like Jeremy, described earlier in this chapter, you will schedule a conference with the family after you have collected observational data and researched community resources. We do not advise approaching the family by saying, "I want to talk with you about Jeremy," or "Jeremy has a problem." This kind of statement may arouse their anxiety to such a degree that open communication becomes difficult, if not impossible. Instead, make a simple statement about the problem: "I'd like to talk with you about what we're trying at school to help Jeremy get involved in play activities and see what works for you at home. Can we get together some afternoon this week to talk about it?"

When you meet with a family to discuss a concern, begin on a positive note. Parents appreciate hearing what you especially enjoy about their child, so begin with positive comments. Tell them what you see as their child's strengths and capabilities. Then share the recorded observations that caused your concern. Work to build an alliance with the family by asking them if they have observed similar behavior and how they handled it. Offer to work with them to clarify the problem and seek assistance for the child. If you think they need some time to think over what you have talked about, you might want to schedule a second meeting to discuss it further.

Often parents have had concerns about their child but have not known where to turn for help. They may be relieved to learn that you are committed to supporting them and working together to find answers to your mutual questions. The information and insight you offer may prompt them to arrange a referral for evaluation of the child, or they may ask the school to arrange for the referral. On the other hand you may be the first professional who has suggested that there might be a problem and a family may react defensively and reject the possibility that something could be "wrong" with their child. They may prefer to believe it is something the child will outgrow. In this situation you will want to explore other avenues for getting help and support while you continue working with the child and family. All families need to be reassured that a concern about a child does not mean that you or your program is going to reject the child and family. This can be challenging for a beginning teacher and you may want to get some help from an experienced colleague or administrator when this occurs.

The family of a child with disabilities faces some difficult challenges: accepting the fact that their child has a disability, finding help for the child, providing special care, and interacting with professionals who are working with them and the child. Like all families, they need your respect and support. Keep in mind that they have their own culture and unique set of strengths, values, skills, expectations, and needs. They need acceptance, open communication, and to be treated as part of a team working on behalf of the child.

The family of a child with disabilities has both the right and the responsibility to play a primary role in determining the nature and extent of services provided for them and their child. They should always be involved in decisions and give their consent to any special services their child receives in addition to those provided for all children in the program. You can help by being a bridge between the family and other professionals, working to ensure that communication is clear between home, school, and other professionals.

Confidentiality is an important issue. How much is appropriate to reveal to others? If you have a child with a disability in your class, ask the family what they would like you to say to other families and the children in your group about the disability. Explain to other families when they ask that you are not able to give them details about the child's condition, and that you have an ethical obligation to not share confidential information about any child. It may be helpful to assure them, without violating confidentiality, that the disability is not "catching." They need to know that children rarely adopt any developmentally inappropriate behavior displayed by a child with a disability. You can offer general reassurance, emphasizing the benefits of children learning to accept differences and to be caring and respectful in relationships with all people. Encourage families to get to know one another. This may alleviate some of the social isolation that accompanies having a child with a disability. Your own attitude will provide a positive model.

Including Diverse Learners

Reflect on your ethical responsibilities

A parent volunteer in your class often asks questions about which children have disabilities, the kinds of disabilities they have, and how they are being treated. Using the "Guidelines for Ethical Reflection," reflect on your ethical responsibilities in this situation and think about an ethical response that you might make.

Final Thoughts

We wrote this book to help you learn to work effectively with a wide range of children. What you know about being a caring and competent early childhood educator will help you a great deal in dealing with all children. We believe that the most important thing you can do is to provide children with disabilities and other special needs the opportunity to feel a sense of belonging and to interact with their peers. The current commitment in the early childhood field to providing inclusive opportunities for children is a positive movement and marks the recognition of the common humanity in all children. Working with a child who has a disability or special need also has the potential to be an unprecedented learning experience in your own development as an educator. You will learn about the child and the family, you will develop skills in collaboration, and you will see the child benefiting from your efforts. You will also be learning about the wide spectrum of human differences.

Learning Outcomes

When you read this chapter, and then thoughtfully complete selected assignments from the "To Learn More" section and prepare items from the "For Your Portfolio" section, you will be demonstrating progress in meeting **NAEYC Standards for Early Childhood Professional Preparation Program** (NAEYC, 2009).

Standard 1: Promoting Child Development and Learning

Key elements:

1a: Knowing and understanding young children's characteristics and needs

1c: Using developmental knowledge to create healthy, respectful, supportive, and challenging learning environments

Standard 2: Building Family and Community Relationships

Key elements:

2a: Knowing about and understanding diverse family and community characteristics

2c: Involving families and communities in their children's development and learning

Standard 3: Observing, Documenting, and Assessing to Support Young Children and Families

Key elements:

3a: Understanding the goals, benefits, and uses of assessment

3c: Understanding and practicing responsible assessment to promote positive outcomes for each child

3d: Knowing about assessment partnerships with families and with professional colleagues

Standard 4: Using Developmentally Effective Approaches to Connect with Children and Families

Key elements:

4a: Understanding positive relationships and supportive interactions as the foundation for one's work with children

4c: Using a broad repertoire of developmentally appropriate teaching/learning approaches

 # To Learn More

Observe a Program: Observe an early childhood program that includes a child with a disability or other special need. Report on how the staff works to meet the child's needs. How do they appear to feel about the child? Reflect and then comment on the effect that this child has on children and staff in the program. What did you learn from this observation?

Interview a Teacher: Interview a teacher of a child with a disability—a child who was evaluated and placed in a regular early childhood classroom—to find out what procedures were followed in identifying and planning for his or her educational experience. Describe this process, your reactions to it, and the implications for your future practice.

Observe a Child I: For at least an hour, observe and "put yourself in the shoes" of a child who has been identified or is suspected of having a disability. Describe what you think the child's experience might be. Based on this experience, discuss how well the program appears to be meeting this child's needs and how it might do so more effectively.

Observe a Child II: Observe a child with a disability who is included in an infant-toddler, preschool, or K–3 school setting. Report on what you would do if you were going to have a conference with the child's parents. What would you tell them? What questions would you ask? How would you create a climate of safety and trust within the conference?

Research Resources I: Find out what services are offered in your community for children with disabilities who are between birth and age 8 (these might be housed in departments of education, health, and/or social services). Write a pamphlet for teachers that explains this information. Include a brief description of the services, who is eligible, phone numbers, and names of contact persons.

Research Resources II: Contact your local school district and see who is eligible for IDEA services. How long does it take for an assessment to be done? What services are available for infants and toddlers? Preschool children? Elementary children?

Research Resources III: Contact the child welfare agency serving your area to find out how child abuse and neglect reports are handled. How are abuse and neglect defined? What kind of services are available to families who are at risk of abuse or have already abused their children?

Investigate Related Websites:

American Speech-Language-Hearing Association (ASHA): asha.org

Autism Society of America: autism-society.org

Center on the Social and Emotional Foundations for Early Learning: vanderbilt.edu/csefel

Children and Adults with Attention Deficit/Hyperactivity Disorder (CHADD): chadd.org

Council for Exceptional Children: cec.sped.org

Division for Early Childhood (DEC): dec-sped.org

National Dissemination Center for Children with Disabilities: research.nichcy.org

National Early Childhood Technical Assistance Center (NECTAC): nectac.org

United Cerebral Palsy: ucp.org

U.S. Department of Education, Office of Special Education and Rehabilitative Services: ed.gov/about/offices/list/osers/osep/index.html

 # For Your Portfolio

Write a Community Resources Pamphlet: Research and write a pamphlet on resources for children with special needs and available resources for teachers in your community.

Document Work with a Child: For a semester, work with a child who has a special need and document the things you did to meet the child's needs and what you learned.

Adapt a Toy or Material: Identify a toy or a material that could be changed or adapted to make it more suitable for use by a child with disabilities. Photograph the toy, then make the identified adaptations. Photograph the adapted material. Use the materials with a child and document what you learned. Place the documentation and photos in your portfolio.

Adapt or Simplify an Activity Plan: Identify an activity that is difficult for a child with a disability to complete successfully. Create a plan to simplify the activity and/or break it down into manageable steps. Implement the activity with the child and document what you learned. Place the plan and documentation in your portfolio.

MyEducationLab

Go to Topics 10: Cultural & Linguistic Diversity and 11: Special Needs/Inclusion in the MyEducationLab (myeducationlab.com) for *Who Am I in the Lives of Children?* where you can:

- Find learning outcomes for Cultural & Linguistic Diversity and Special Needs/Inclusion along with the national standards that connect to these outcomes.
- Complete Assignments and Activities that can help you more deeply understand the chapter content.
- Apply and practice your understanding of the core teaching skills identified in the chapter with the Building Teaching Skills and Dispositions learning units.

- Examine challenging situations and cases presented in the IRIS Center Resources.
- Access video clips of CCSSO National Teachers of the Year award winners responding to the question, "Why Do I Teach?" in the Teacher Talk section.
- Listen to experts from the field in Professional Perspectives.
- Check your comprehension on the content covered in the chapter with the Study Plan. Here you will be able to take a chapter quiz, receive feedback on your answers, and then access Review, Practice, and Enrichment activities to enhance your understanding of chapter content.

Parents are like shuttles on a loom. They join the threads of the past with the threads of the future and leave their own bright patterns as they go, providing continuity to succeeding ages.

FRED ROGERS

13

Partnerships
with Families

Children come to school wrapped in the values, attitudes, and behaviors of their families. As a future early childhood educator, you need to be aware that each child is a part of a unique family whose members play a critical role in his or her life and are the child's first and most important teachers. Because of this, your relationships with families are of the utmost importance.

You probably entered the field of early childhood because you wanted to work with young children and you may not have realized that working with families is a pivotal part of your role. The awareness and sensitivity that you are developing as you work with children are also important to your work with families. Members of children's families need relationships in which they feel safe and respected, just like their children. Families differ in their individual needs, interests, knowledge, and skill, but many similarities can be found among them. All families are concerned with the welfare of their children. They want the best for them and want to be kept informed of the important events of their lives away from home. As a teacher, you share this wish. The basis for your relationships with families is your joint commitment to providing support for the development of their children. You will have the opportunity to be part of their journeys and to partner with them as they raise their young children. This shared commitment can be the foundation for creating healthy partnerships with families—partnerships that serve children and offer each of them opportunities to grow into confident, healthy adults. Being a participant in this process is an honor. Though it has challenges, partnering with families can be a joy and is an important aspect of your role as an early childhood educator.

Families today take a variety of forms that often include adults other than parents. Stepparents, siblings, grandparents and other relatives, foster parents, or friends may assume parental roles. To simplify the wording of this chapter, we will most often use the term *family* and in doing so we are speaking of the entire cast of adults who play a significant role in a child's life. When we speak of *parenting,* we are discussing the nurturing done by all of the important adults who take on a parental role.

Preparing to Work with Families

There are two aspects to preparing yourself to work with families. First, you need to learn some things about families—what they are like, the kinds of issues they encounter in their lives, and some knowledge of theory related to families (called *Family Systems Theory*). Second, you need to understand some things about yourself in relationship to working with families. You need to reflect on your attitudes and experiences and how these influence the ways you approach families. It will also be helpful for you to gain some insight into the expectations and responsibilities attached to your role as a teacher, and your stage of development in terms of your relationship with families.

Understanding Families

Parenting young children is both a delight and a challenge. It is a complex task that brings most families great joy. Many parents say that their years of raising young children, while sometimes sleep-deprived and frustrating, were among the happiest and most rewarding periods of their lives.

Being sympathetic and supportive is easier when you realize that parenting is a complicated task. It involves a total, day-in, day-out responsibility that cannot be ignored or avoided. It comes with moments of great tenderness, joy, and humor and with times of stress, concern, and exhaustion. The stresses may sometimes overshadow the pleasures. The particular circumstances of each family's life will influence their ability to nurture and care for their children. As an early childhood teacher, increasing your awareness of the many aspects of parenting—the joys as well as the struggles—will help you relate to families effectively.

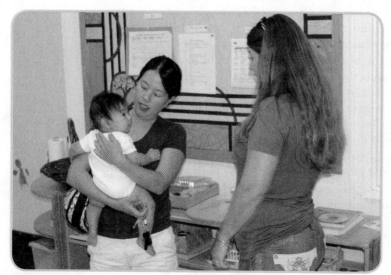

Stages of Parenting

People enter into child rearing with many kinds of expectations. The reality is almost always different from what was anticipated. As parents develop, they seem to follow a relatively predictable sequence. Ellen Galinsky (1981) describes the early childhood years as the time in their child's life when parents learn to be nurturers and define themselves as authority figures in the family. Assuming this role can be stressful as parents learn to balance the competing responsibilities of child care, relationships with partners and other family members, home, and work. As you become aware of the circumstances of individual families, your abilities to understand their actions and to work in harmony with them will be enhanced.

The Role of the Family Today

During the last century, the family's role has enlarged from ensuring children's physical well-being (food, shelter, clothing, health, and safety) to include the more abstract tasks of providing psychological security and skills for dealing with an increasingly complicated world. Families may be unsure of what skills and knowledge will be important for their children to master in a rapidly changing society. With torrents of information and opinions available from all types of media, families may feel bombarded, confused, and concerned about what parenting strategies to use or what types of education will best serve their children in the future.

Additionally, families are increasingly aware of the importance of the early years in children's development and learning. Some families feel they must hurry their children into activities that are supposed to ensure success—academic tutoring; music, dance, and athletic lessons; team sports; and entrance into the "best" preschool to ensure access to the best primary school, high school, and even college. The current trend toward high-stakes testing and the recurring pressure to meet academic standards may contribute to a family's sense that they must press schools and teachers to focus on academics at the expense of other activities.

Families Are Diverse

Families come into your program from a wide variety of backgrounds and circumstances. Their experiences, along with their values and beliefs about children and education, may be quite different both from one another and from those of your family and culture.

> *Sasha, a teacher in a 3-year-old class, welcomes the children and families as they enter. In the first half hour she greets Leah and her grandma Carol; Maré, her mother, Selina, and baby brother Sol; Tara and her stepdad, Will; Emily and her "nang-nang" (great-grandmother); Emma and her half-brother, Suli; Cole and his mom, Trudy; and Noah and his mom's boyfriend, Sam.*

There is great diversity in family structure in the United States, and this has been true for many years. According to the Census Bureau (2008), 67% of children in the United States live in two-parent families. Many live in families with single parents (27%), stepparents (16%), or foster parents. Some live in "blended" families that include children of parents' current and former relationships. Some live in extended families with grandparents and other related and unrelated adults. In some families, parents are not present and grandparents or other family members are serving as parents. Families with gay, lesbian, and transgendered parents are increasingly common. All of these configurations can provide loving, healthy, and secure relationships for children.

The 2008 census confirms growing diversity in the United States. This data indicates that by the middle of this century, "minorities"—nonwhites—will be the majority in the United States. This means that you will work with children whose families are from a variety of races and ethnicities. They will bring parenting practices and values about child rearing that are influenced by their cultures and families, their neighborhoods, religions, socioeconomic status, education, and individual circumstances. The challenge for you as a future early childhood educator is to understand and respect this diversity.

In a 1995 position statement, *Responding to Linguistic and Cultural Diversity: Recommendations for Effective Early Childhood Education*, NAEYC makes the following recommendations for working with diverse families:

* Actively involve families in the early learning program and setting.
* Encourage and assist families in becoming knowledgeable about the value for children of knowing more than one language and provide them with strategies to support, maintain, and preserve home-language learning.
* Recognize that families must rely on caregivers and educators to honor and support their children in the cultural values and norms of the home.

Family Systems Theory

Family systems theory describes the ways that interconnected family members influence one another in predictable and recurring ways. It focuses on the roles and patterns of behavior of individual families and the ways that these influence adults' and children's relationships, both to one another and to people outside of the family. It identifies the connections between family members as well as the predictable ways in which they relate to one another (Christian, 2006).

Knowing about family systems theory can be helpful to you for understanding the dynamics of families and how you can be supportive to children from different kinds of families. Understanding how the family works as an interrelated system can help you build partnerships and offers insights into the needs and preferences of diverse families. Six of the dimensions described in this theory (discussed below) are particularly relevant to those who work with young children. Some of these occur on a continuum; where families fall on those continua influences their interaction patterns.

Boundaries—*the expectation for togetherness or separateness and understanding about who is in or out of the family.* Families' boundaries fall along a continuum, with families at one end valuing separateness, independence, and autonomy and those at the other emphasizing togetherness, conformity, control, and connectedness. In families with very strong boundaries, a low performance on a reading test or misbehavior at circle time may be viewed as a negative reflection on the entire family. Strong family boundaries may mean that decisions about discipline, self-help skills, and children's social connections are determined by the family unit and that input from others is considered intrusive. Families with strong boundaries are likely to attend school events *en masse,* so teachers must be prepared and welcoming. On the other end of the continuum are families who value independence and openness to ideas of others who are not in the family unit. They may seem disconnected to children's school experiences and/or may let children make many independent decisions. Their focus on autonomy may appear to be disinterest when not understood by teachers. Remember that neither of these is better or worse than the other—just a different family dynamic.

Roles—*the parts that individual family members play in their relationship to others.* In all families, each member has one or several important roles. This includes children as well as adults. Some members may be the peacemakers in their family, expected to always assist with resolving conflicts. Others may be the clown, the victim, the problem-solver, the caretaker. These roles will carry over into the school setting, influencing how both children and grown-ups behave. Your careful attention to these roles will help you to understand children better and to communicate effectively with their families.

Rules—*the standards and procedures that give directions about how to behave and relate to others.* All families have rules, both spoken and unspoken, about how to act in particular situations and with particular individuals. Some families have many and very stringent rules; others have fewer rules and/or are more relaxed about applying them. Passing rules from one generation to the next is a primary function of culture, therefore rules are culturally determined to a greater or lesser extent. In some cases family rules may be different from those at school; for instance, some family rules require that children "stand up for themselves" and behave aggressively when they feel threatened. Certain school experiences such as welcoming both boys and girls to play dress-up may be counter to family rules about gender behavior and expectations. You will need to learn about the families' beliefs in order to help children negotiate these differences and to discuss them sensitively and respectfully with families.

Hierarchy—*the determination of which members have decision-making power within the family.* In some families decision-making is shared by two partners; in others one partner may hold this role; other families have a respected elder who makes most of the significant decisions. Understanding a family's hierarchy helps you understand some important things about how they communicate and relate to one another, to their children, and to you. Hierarchy may be determined by age, gender, or status within the family. It is important for teachers to address concerns and questions to the members of the family who have the role of decision makers without leaving out other family members.

Climate—*the emotional and physical environment of the family.* This dimension includes the extent to which families are warm and supportive or distant and detached Families can provide warm and supportive relationships in a variety of circumstances, even those where fiscal resources are limited or the surrounding physical environment is harsh or threatening. Conversely, affluent families sometimes offer limited emotional safety and support to individual members. Teachers who create supportive classroom climates support all children, particularly those from families with challenging emotional or physical environments.

Equilibrium—*the amount of stability or consistency offered by the family.* Families on one end of this continuum experience a great deal of stability and lack of change in their circumstances; on the other end are families where there is a great deal of inconsistency and imbalance. Most families fall somewhere in the middle. Negative circumstances such as illness, unemployment, death, or mental illness decrease equilibrium as do other changes such as a move, a new baby, or a job promotion. Understanding individual family circumstances will increase your understanding of their relationships and how these affect the child. When you provide a consistent school setting, you help children deal with disequilibrium at home.

Understanding Yourself and Your Role

Effective teachers of young children are aware of their personal values and beliefs about parenting as well as their beliefs about the roles teachers and families should assume in young children's lives. Throughout this book we have encouraged you to examine your values and attitudes about working with children. In order to build successful partnerships with families, it is helpful to take time to explore some of your own attitudes about the role of parents and what you believe are the characteristics of good parenting.

Your Values and Beliefs Related to Child Rearing

Four-year-old Kayla comes to school dressed in shiny white shoes and a crisply ironed dress, with her hair carefully combed, braided, and decorated with barrettes. Her friend Toni arrives in sneakers, old shorts, a clean T-shirt, and disheveled hair. By the end of the day Kayla's shoes are scuffed, her dress is painted, and her barrettes are missing. Her mother scolds her, "You wrecked your new dress! I can't afford to buy you new clothes every week!" Toni's shirt is covered with paint and she has torn her shorts. Her dad says, "Looks like you had fun today!" and gives her a hug.

You will work with diverse families who have a variety of approaches to child rearing and a range of views about education. Some of their views and beliefs will be congruent with yours; others will be quite different. It is important to be prepared to deal with these differences in constructive ways—without assuming the role of "expert" or assigning blame. In the vignette above, which parent's viewpoint was closest to yours? Did you react strongly to either child's dress or either parent's behavior? It is typical for people to view differences as "wrong" rather than different. By becoming an early childhood educator, you are making a commitment to learning about and being open to the range of families you will encounter and the ways they care for and raise their children. When you find that you are reacting intensely to a family's child-rearing beliefs or practices, it is a sign that you need to look more deeply at your own.

It is useful to be aware that when you encounter differences in ideas about how children "should" be cared for, what you may be experiencing is a cultural difference. Remember that cultural differences are reflected not only in differences in skin color, language, religion, and country of origin. Cultural differences may be found between families that are racially similar but come from different socioeconomic backgrounds, between families with the same ethnic backgrounds whose families immigrated in different generations, and between those who came from different parts of the same country, including our own.

Some of the biggest areas of miscommunication with between teachers and families concern the things each may take for granted because of cultures. With insight and awareness that many differences are cultural, you will find yourself more open and more ready to accept and appreciate all families. In order for this to happen you must be aware that your own views of what constitutes good parenting comes from your own culture and experience.

It is beyond the scope of this book to provide you with information on the multitude of ways that culture can influence families and their views of children and education. The accompanying box, "How Culture Influences Child Rearing," describes some common differences you are likely to encounter. As you read it, consider your own values and beliefs and reflect on them.

How Culture Influences Child Rearing

- **Toileting,** the age at which families expect children to be toilet trained, and the process they use to teach children how to use the toilet.

- **Food and feeding,** when different foods are introduced; what foods are considered appropriate and inappropriate; how much food children are expected to eat; who feeds children and until what age; where and with whom the child should eat; table manners; and when children should be fed.

- **Nursing, bottles, and pacifiers,** whether children should be nursed, until what age and in what circumstances; whether infants are fed on demand or on a schedule; at what age bottle-fed babies are expected to give up the bottle; and whether pacifiers are given and when they should no longer be offered.

- **Sleeping arrangements** for children, with whom the child sleeps; when, where, and how the child is put to sleep; whether the child takes regular naps and, if so, for how long.

- **Bathing and grooming,** how often the child is bathed; time and attention given to creating and maintaining neat hair, nails, and clean teeth; and the extent to which children are expected/allowed to get messy.

- **Personal care and independence,** when children should be expected to complete self-help tasks independently; whether children should be carried after they can walk; and how much assistance children should be offered when completing tasks.

- **Ways children demonstrate respect/disrespect** for adults, whether or not children are expected to make eye contact as a sign of respect; whether children are expected to ask adults questions, engage in dialog, or make jokes with adults; and the names adults are called by children.

- **Role of the child in the family,** whether children or adults are central in the household and family; the extent to which children's activities influence the household and where children's belongings are located in the home; and whether children are included or excluded from important family events such as weddings and funerals

- **Responsibilities of children,** whether children are expected to perform household tasks and the age at which serious responsibility such as caring for younger siblings is given to children.

- **Relative value placed on play and academics,** whether play is viewed as an important task or a distraction and whether academics are viewed as the most significant type of learning.

- **Definitions of safe and healthy,** whether children should be protected from health and safety risks like getting cold or climbing high or whether they should be exposed to risks to build strength and skill.

- **Appropriate dress for school and other situations,** whether the child is dressed in specially purchased school clothes that the child is expected to keep clean or is sent to school in play clothes that can get dirty.

- **Gender roles,** whether the child is expected to play and behave in ways designated by gender (e.g., playing with dolls versus roughhousing) and whether adults are expected to adhere to traditional gender roles.

- **Modesty,** what body parts should be covered; what types of clothing and adornment are considered appropriate/inappropriate for young children and adults.

- **Appropriate knowledge for children,** whether and at what age children are exposed to such things as the proper names of body parts, sexuality, birth, illness, disability, death, and violence.

- **Attitudes toward emerging sexuality,** whether children are expected to be innocent and ignorant of sexuality and whether adults think some exploration of sexuality is appropriate

Choose two or three of the practices described in the box, "How Culture Influences Child Rearing." Think about how these were handled in your home when you were a child. Do you have some strong views about how they should be done? How might your feelings about these practices impact your relationship with families of children with whom you will work?

Because of your commitment to children, it may be hard to accept parents whose expectations and attitudes toward their children are significantly different from your own. This will be especially true if you perceive those differences to be uncaring or harsh. You may even find it difficult to decide if the treatment of a child is simply a difference in values and expectations or abuse, which you should report.

To support diverse families, it is best to avoid making assumptions. Remember that families do not all celebrate the same holidays, eat the same foods, see the role of child and parent in the same way, have the same ways of caring for children, believe in the same (or any) god, or share the same view of death and what happens after death. To avoid making assumptions, ask families to help you to support their child by explaining their perspectives, values, and beliefs. One way to begin this kind of dialogue is to ask families to tell you about if and how they celebrate holidays and birthdays (see Figure 13.1). In subsequent sections of this chapter, we will describe additional ways to learn about families' values and their preferences.

Your Role—Differences Between Being a Teacher and Being a Parent

As you begin to work with families, it is helpful to recognize some of the differences between the role of a teacher and that of a parent. Although important similarities characterize these roles, we have found that the distinctions described by Lilian Katz in "Mothering and Teaching—Some Significant Distinctions" (1980) to be very helpful for beginning teachers. Katz talks about how parents' and teachers' roles are different and how they can complement one another in helping the child grow and learn.

Parents and teachers need to be quite different in their attachment to a child. Teachers need to appreciate children realistically. They need to keep enough distance to observe and evaluate children objectively and balance the requirements of the individual with the welfare of the group. Parents need to be their children's most passionate advocates and fans. They care about their children for the child's whole life, while educators care about children for the time that they are involved with them. Do not expect families to have an educator's perspective—their job is to be their child's champion. And, though you are committed to each child's learning, your relationship to the child is much different from those of their family.

Your Stage of Development in Relating to Families

Another lens for viewing teachers' relationships to families is to become familiar with the three stages many teachers go through in their relationships with families (Gonzalez-Mena & Eyer, 2009; Keyser, 2006). Knowing about these stages can put your reactions to families and approaches to dealing with them in a broader perspective.

Beginning teachers often wish to become a savior to children; they see their role as rescuing children from their family members. In this stage teachers distance themselves from families and assume that their knowledge makes them superior to children's families. If you find yourself thinking you would like to take a child home with you because you could make his or her life so much better, you are probably in this initial stage.

With experience and reflection, teachers usually move into stage 2—understanding that families are the predominant force in children's lives, the ones who have the most influence on them. In this stage, teachers might work to change or "fix" the family to make them better for the child. If you find yourself

FIGURE 13.1 **Celebration Survey Form**

Partnerships
with Families

CELEBRATION SURVEY

Most people have special days that they celebrate, that are part of their cultural and family traditions. We want to be respectful of your family's beliefs and would like to recognize your family's celebrations in our program. In order to be as inclusive as possible we would like to find out about celebrations in your family. Please let us know by completing the following survey. If, for religious or philosophical reasons, you prefer that your children not participate in celebrations or activities, we want to know that, too. We're beginning with the fall celebrations that are coming up but would like to know about any celebrations or holidays that are important in your family. Thanks for your help.

Family name: _____

Are there any holidays, celebrations, or celebration activities that you prefer we avoid while your child is enrolled? Please describe:

Please tell us about what you celebrate in your family and how you celebrate.

Holiday	How you celebrate it in your family	Would you like to share your celebration at school in some way? How?
Birthdays		
Fall		
Halloween		
Day of the Dead		
Rosh Hashanah		
Other fall celebrations		
Winter		
Christmas		
Kwanzaa		
New Year's Day		
Valentine's Day		
Lunar (Chinese) New Year		
Other winter celebrations		
Spring		
Ramadan		
Girls Day		
St. Patrick's Day		
Mother's Day		
Other spring celebrations		
Summer		
Father's Day		
4th of July		
Other summer celebrations		

wishing you could give a family more skills and knowledge for interacting with their children, you are most likely in this second stage.

In the final stage teachers understand their role as a partner to the family. In stage 3 they understand that each child is with them for a relatively brief period and that the teacher's role is to support the family in their permanent relationship with their child. When you are able to reach out to form true partnerships with families, honoring their expertise and sharing your own, you will have moved into this final stage.

Building Relationships with Families

The most effective programs we know are ones in which teachers genuinely value families and strive to build relationships, create policies, and make decisions that support the child as a member of a family. Teachers and administrators in these programs relate to families in ways that increase each family's sense of competence and their enjoyment of their children.

Sometimes referred to as *family-centered practice*, this approach is built on meaningful and trusting relationships between teachers and families (Keyser, 2006). While family-centered practice is valuable for all children and families, it is especially beneficial for families whose children have disabilities. In a family-centered program, teachers regularly and respectfully communicate with each family. This takes both practice and intention—to be a family-centered teacher, you must decide that communicating with families is important, and worth the time and effort it takes. You may need to switch your perspective from thinking that programs should be focused on children to considering the merits of programs with a focus on families.

Getting Started

Once a family has chosen your program, other avenues open for continuing and expanding this new relationship. When a child begins school, the family should receive an orientation to the program and to your classroom. At the beginning of a year or when a number of new children enter, some programs invite families to participate in an initial meeting where goals and policies of the program are introduced and families are invited to ask questions. Other programs do this for one family at a time

It is important for you to talk with family members to learn about their child's growth, development, and family situation; to listen to their perspective on their child as a person; and to get insight into their methods of child rearing. In an initial meeting you can engage the family in dialogue to learn about their goals for their child and their expectations of the program. This is a good time to ask them to tell you how they would like to be involved in the program. You may also ask the family to complete a written questionnaire that provides information about their child's habits, preferences, needs, strengths and skills. It is helpful to include questions that invite family members to share both their perceptions about their children and their goals, wishes, hopes, and dreams for them. We like to use both a written form and an initial meeting to begin our relationship with new families in our programs.

Home Visits

Some programs use home visits as a way for families, children, and teachers to become acquainted and comfortable with each other. Teachers set up a convenient time to visit each child's home prior to or soon after the beginning of a new school year. In Head Start programs, home visits may be scheduled more frequently. These visits usually last between 30 to 45 minutes and are at time when teachers and families can get to know one another. Some children will be very excited to show their special toys or pets to their new teacher; others will feel shy.

While many teachers and families feel that home visits are a valuable tool in for fostering positive communication, be aware that they can be stressful for families. Some feel uncomfortable about the appearance of their homes and worry about being negatively judged. Others feel that their personal space has been invaded. They may think of it as an inspection of their parenting. We find it helpful to tell families of the purpose of a home visit—to encourage families, children, and teachers get to know each other, and help children know that their families and teachers trust one another—and to offer them the choice of whether or not to have a teacher visit them at home.

Establishing Rapport

Relationships are fostered in an atmosphere of concern, respect, acceptance, and individual attention. The things that you do to build good relationships with the families in your program are usually small, easy to overlook, and as simple as common courtesy. These relationships begin when families feel welcome—when you greet them warmly when they enter the school and take a few moments to speak with them—and they grow as you find frequent times for relaxed and informal conversations. As you talk with families, you can learn about what they are interested in, what they do, and what they care about. Remember what they have told you and ask about it in a subsequent conversation. "How did it work out when you took the puppy to the vet yesterday?" "What color paint did you decide on for the baby's nursery?" Such follow-up lets the person know you are interested and were paying attention to their concerns and activities.

Regular informal conversation helps you to know one another and establishes a sense of shared confidence. Tell families stories about happenings in their child's school day—almost every parent wants to know about important moments missed while away from his or her child. "Jeremy was so excited today when he completed all the steps for the yeast experiment and recorded them in his science notebook. He was pleased that he accomplished such a grown-up task and can't wait to share some of his new 'scientist vocabulary' with you!" Or "Lila spent 20 minutes today going up and down the steps. She's so intent on mastering that climbing skill!"

Acknowledge events and transitions in the child's school life and in the family's life at home. Recognize and share a family's joys and sorrows. "It would be wonderful if you could bring Ira's new baby sister in and introduce her to the class; Ira would be so excited and we'd love to meet her!"

It is also appropriate to let families get to know you as a person with particular enthusiasms and skills—"I made that great lasagna from the school cookbook last night; my family really loved it!"—though it is not appropriate to share *your* personal problems. Remember to be scrupulous about maintaining confidentiality, even in casual conversation. Nothing destroys trust faster than idle gossip and broken confidences.

Making Families Feel Welcome

Whether it is the first or fortieth time they enter your classroom, it is important always to make family members feel that they are welcome in your program.

It is the middle of the morning during the first month of school. Jackie, the 3-year-olds' teacher, is making cinnamon toast with the children. Madison's mom comes through the door. "Hi, Tara!" Jackie says, looking up and smiling. "Would you like to join us?"

In the 4-year-old classroom across the hall, Matt's mom, Amanda, enters. Wendy, Matt's teacher, is reading a story. Wendy looks up, her brows knit, and she frowns. Amanda stands by the classroom door for about 10 minutes without acknowledgment from Wendy. Finally, Amanda signs Matt out and leaves without having talked to a teacher.

The ways that these family members were treated gave very different messages about whether they were welcome in the classroom. What makes a person feel welcome? It is welcoming when teachers greet family members by name and use the form of address that they prefer. Some adults prefer to be called by their first names; it feels friendly to them. Others prefer to be called by a formal title (Mr., Mrs., etc.) and see this as a sign of respect. It is welcoming when you have an "open door" policy—meaning family members can visit at any time and they are treated like valued guests, not intruders.

You can make family members feel welcome every day. If possible, be available to greet them and answer their questions. Learn their names as soon as you can. Remember what they tell you about their child and family and ask how they are doing. Invite them to come into the classroom, and be understanding when they don't have time to stay. Give them meaningful ways to help out at school and at home. When you do these simple things you are building relationships that will support the family, the child, and the program.

Another way to make families feel welcome and included is for a program to have a "family corner." This area might have a comfortable adult chair or a couch, reading material, access to coffee or tea, photographs of the children at play, or even a simple video presentation about the program. Family members may enjoy talking to one another in this area, and bonds between families can be promoted. In infant programs, a comfortable, private space for a nursing mother supports mother-child attachment and healthy infant nutrition, and lets the family know that you value their special relationship with their babies.

Communicating

Your work with families involves communication. Some of this is social, establishing and maintaining rapport, some involves exchanging information. Both families and you possess information that you each need for the child's well-being. Families bring knowledge and experience of their child as an individual, and you bring your knowledge of children in general and awareness of current best practices in working with young children. Both types of information are vital if you are to create the optimal experience for each child.

In order for families to understand your goals and how the program contributes to their child's growth and learning, you need to be able to communicate your knowledge of child development and early childhood education in ways that are meaningful. This means translating professional jargon into language that is clear to families. For example, saying that you *provide opportunities for motor development* is not as valuable as letting a family know that *swinging, sliding, trike riding, and climbing help your child develop strength, and coordination. And it may not be nearly as meaningful as letting them know that physical skill and confidence contribute to social and academic success.*

Communication Skills

You can apply the communication skills you are learning as you study child guidance to communication with adults. Active listening and I-messages are useful when interacting both with children and with adults. Active listening means paying attention not only to family members' words but to their nonverbal cues. Let them know you are listening by reflecting back to them the messages you believe you hear. "It sounds like you are worried that Emma is not getting the skills she will need to be successful in kindergarten," or "I think you are telling me that you are worried that Carlyle will catch cold if he plays in the water table." This type of communication helps families feel that you are attentive to their concerns.

Practice sharing your ideas clearly with respect: "I provide many hands-on experiences for children in my classroom because I believe it helps them to develop important skills for learning," or "I have noticed that Becca seems reluctant to engage in art activities, and I wonder if this is because she is afraid of getting her clothes dirty." These types of statements describe your thoughts accurately but in a nonconfrontational manner.

Remember that you and the family both have worthwhile ideas and that neither of you is infallible. Be sure to share information in a dialogue, not a lecture. While you must be respectful of families, you also need to act on your best professional judgment. If a family's requests violate what you know to be best for children, you have an ethical responsibility to do what is right for children—but you will need to consider carefully and explain the reasons clearly and with courtesy.

Daily Communication

Good daily communication with families requires flexibility and planning. In most preschools, families enter the program each day to drop off and pick up their children. When they do, you have an opportunity to share what you have observed about their children.

> *"Sidney worked very hard on math today. He was persistent and figured out how to group math cubes into different sets. He was so excited when he explained to me the different ways he had organized his groups."*

> *"Courtney had a kind of hard day. She was unhappy when LeShan wouldn't play with her. Then her bunny got buried in the sand and we couldn't find it at nap time and she couldn't sleep for a long time. She finally slept a little and felt better this afternoon, especially after we found Bunny."*

Daily contact should always include positive points and anecdotes about what the child did well and enjoyed. When a child has difficulties, it is important that you find ways to share this information with the family. However, avoid having this be the sole or even the main focus of your daily interactions. We sadly recall a mom sharing with us that she dreaded picking up her child because of the litany of "bad behavior" stories she knew she would hear. When you share information about concerns, be certain to do so in a tactful manner. If you have ongoing concerns, schedule a time to sit and talk with the parent privately.

Written Communication

Every teacher needs to communicate with families in writing. Whether you share information through bulletin boards, notes, newsletters, or e-mail you need to have a system for regular written communication.

In many infant-toddler programs, a written daily report such as the one in Figure 13.2 is given to families each day. This informs families of important care information such as what and when the child ate, slept, and eliminated. A brief description of something special about the day helps families feel included.

Schools for children under 5 need a family communication center—a place where families can get a quick update on what's happening in their child's classroom. It is a good idea to create a message center where each family has a mailbox or message pocket near the sign-in sheet at the entrance to the classroom. A nearby bulletin board can be used to post announcements about upcoming events, exciting happenings of the day and other brief messages you wish to share. Hang the week's plan nearby so that families can be informed of each week's activities and your goals for children's learning.

FIGURE 13.2 Daily Information Form for Families of Infants or Toddlers

Daily Information

Date: _____   Child's Name: _____

Family Section:
When you check in, please give us some information to help us meet your child's needs today.

Feedings: _____

Sleep: _____

Diapers/toileting: _____

What else do you want to share with us today? _____
_____
_____

Teacher Section:
Dear Family: Here's some information about your child's day. Please talk with us for more information.

Feeding/eating: _____

Sleeping: _____

Diapers/toileting: _____

Other information about today: _____
_____
_____

In programs that run longer than 8 hours, teachers are not available to talk with families every day. In these cases, we have found it effective to keep a communication log (in a notebook or folder) for each family near the sign-in sheet to serve as a substitute for face-to-face communication. Staff and family members read and write in it frequently to share information about the child.

A communication center is also desirable in kindergarten or primary classrooms when parents drop off and pick up their children in the room. However, in most elementary schools and in some preschools, family members do not drop off and pick up their children in the classroom. If you teach in such a school, you may rarely have an opportunity to talk with families. When this is the case, it is important to devise alternative ways to keep in touch. A weekly newsletter, a log that goes home with the child and is returned each day, or short, frequent e-mails can help you maintain communication. Some teachers communicate via an e-mail listserv or a regularly updated class blog.

School websites and newsletters offer opportunities to provide information of general interest, to explain aspects of the program in greater detail, to solicit assistance from families, and to provide information about child development and other topics of interest. These are most successful when they are attractive, short, and easy to read. Some programs use telephone hotlines, from which families can receive prerecorded information about children's homework and other relevant messages.

Regardless of their age, when children live in two families it is important to find ways to share written materials with both households. If families do not speak or read English, written materials will need to be translated. And of course, all written materials, whether a quick note or an end-of-term progress summary, need to be prepared carefully and with attention to grammar, spelling, and punctuation. If this is a challenge for you ask a colleague to proofread your writing before sending it to families.

Family Conferences

A regular feature of your life as a teacher will be to hold conferences with family members. A conference provides time for each of you to share information and insights. It allows for in-depth and personal exchange of information that is not possible in other ways.

A central purpose of a conference is to form an alliance with the family that will support the child's development. Regular conferences help you build relationships with families. If conferences are held rarely or only in the event of a problem, they will be more stressful both for you and for the family, as well as less productive.

Family members may be apprehensive about attending a conference. They may have bad memories of their own school experiences and may only associate a parent conference with the telling of bad news. Be certain to explain the conference's purpose when you invite families to attend, and make a clear distinction between a regularly scheduled conference to share progress and information and one planned to discuss a particular concern.

Plan carefully to ensure that you have time and space for an unpressured and productive meeting. You may have to come in early or stay late to make sure that you have enough time. Prepare by looking over anecdotal observations and other assessments, review other records you have on the child, and gather any photographs, videos, or samples of the child's work that will illustrate the child's development and learning. Many teachers create a portfolio, write a developmental summary, or fill out a checklist to document the child's progress.

Some teachers find it helpful to prepare a written conference plan using a format such as the one described in Figure 13.3. This helps them to feel more relaxed about the conference, knowing that they have organized their ideas and are less likely to forget important points they wish to share with the family. The written plan also serves as a reminder to encourage the family's contributions as an important part of the conference.

FIGURE 13.3 **Family Conference Planning Form**

Family Conference Form

Child: _____   Date: _____

Family member(s): _____

Teacher(s): _____

Topics to Discuss

Ideas for supporting the child's growth at school:

Ideas for supporting the child's growth at home:

Resources requested by family at the conference:

Questions or concerns raised at the conference:

Follow-up plan:

Family's plan for child's future (next school, etc.):

At a first conference, you will want to begin by explaining that conferences are regularly scheduled times for parents and teachers to share information and get to know one another better. Assure them that you welcome their ideas and questions and that the conference is a joint process. You may use the conference as an opportunity to set common goals for the child which you will revisit during subsequent meetings.

As you share your perceptions of the child in school, try to describe what the child *does* rather than saying what he or she *is*: "Lucas usually watches the others use a new piece of equipment before he tries it. He seems to like to have a quiet space and a long period of time." Do not say, "Lucas is very shy." It is best to discuss the child's strengths and skills and look at other aspects in terms of areas for growth. Invite parents to contrast your observations and perceptions to what they know from their experience of the child. Ask them to tell you about what they have observed and to share their suggestions for activities and strategies that will meet their child's needs appropriately.

In many elementary schools and a few preschools the child participates in the conference and takes the lead in describing classroom activities and sharing his or her work. Teachers who have done this kind of conference are very pleased with how effectively it involves the family and communicates the child's school experience.

When it is necessary to discuss a problem—for example, when you are working with a parent to identify ways to help a child find alternatives to hurting others—assume that family members have good intentions and that solutions can be found. You can use conference time to clarify the issues, agree on goals, develop a plan of action for home and for the program, and decide when you will meet again to evaluate what you have done. We recommend writing down what you agree on with families and providing a copy for each of you.

Addressing Questions and Concerns

When Jules's grandmother comes to pick him up, he is sitting alone at the snack table, finishing a cracker and the last sips of his milk. "Why do you leave him all alone like that?" she asks his teacher in an angry tone.

Because families are so deeply concerned about their children, it is inevitable that questions and concerns will arise regarding things that are happening in your program. It is valuable to remind yourself that not only is it a *right* of family members to ask questions, it is their *responsibility*. Parents who are doing their job want to know what you are doing and why you are doing it. Such questioning can lead to an open exchange of information that can help you to better understand the family and their relationship to their children. You need to be prepared to respond to questions without being defensive and in ways that keep the lines of communication open.

Families frequently ask about:

- The purpose of play and its value in their child's academic progress
- The care of their child's possessions and clothing
- The child's health and safety in the program

These issues relate to their expectations about children and school and may relate to their culture.

Rose, the mother of 4-year-old Peter, came into her son's class one morning and said to Gary, the teacher, "I don't think you're offering Peter enough challenge. He will write his ABC's when I sit down with him at home. But all he does here is play with blocks and ride trikes. He's going to go to kindergarten in the fall, you know."

What could Gary have said? If he answered defensively—"We told you when Peter started here at our center that we had a play-based program, because research tells us that children learn through play"—he would not have demonstrated that he had understood or cared about what Rose said. Similarly, if Gary had not taken responsibility—"Well, a lot of the children are interested in letters but Peter just doesn't seem to unless we force him"—he would not have addressed her concern.

When families question you about the curriculum, it is essential that you take their concerns seriously and not dismiss them. When they look at your program they may not see activities that they associate with academic learning. They may have had little recent experience with hands-on learning activities that are a main feature of your program. As you talk with them you can help them understand that young children learn in ways that are significantly different from adults, and that the development of motor and perceptual skills form the base of later, more abstract learning. You can remind them of the things that they learned by doing—cooking, driving a car, bathing a baby, using a computer—and that *doing* is an important way of learning. Explain the sequence of development in concrete terms: "Children first have to learn to tell the difference between more obvious things like round blue beads and square purple beads before they can tell the difference between less distinctive things like numbers and letters." Specific examples will help adults to see the purpose of the activities that you do with children.

Gary, in the previous example, might have had a dialogue with Rose that sounded something like this:

Gary: Thank you for telling me about what you've been doing and what you're worrying about. I've noticed that Peter can write the alphabet. But it doesn't seem to be what he's most interested in at school. Does he enjoy writing the alphabet at home?

Rose: Well, not unless I sit him down. But he knows he has to do his work.

Gary: What I've noticed is that Peter loves to look at books and listen to stories. That's a really important first step in learning to love reading. Another thing I've noticed is that he likes playing with rhyming words. That's another important part of learning to read.

Rose: What about teaching letters and words? I bought a workbook for him last week, and that's his homework—just like his big brother. Why aren't you teaching him anything like that?

Gary: What I have been doing is to create a word bank for each of the children. Here's Peter's file of "special words." He has five words—all the members of his family. I've also been introducing more print into the room. You know, back at the beginning of the year I put up some labels on different things in the classroom, like the box of bristle blocks, and recently I've added some more labels as well as some signs. Peter's also been enjoying a "hunt the letter" game we've been playing. What seems to work best for him is when I make letter activities personal and active.

Rose: Yeah, he really does like to move.

Gary: I want him to keep on liking school, so I want to make learning about reading fun and meaningful. His whole group is going to kindergarten in the fall and we are planning more letter activities for the rest of the year. I'll be sure to let you know how Peter responds to them. Does that sound good to you?

Rose: Oh, yes!

Many a parent is distressed to return at the end of a long work day and find that the clean clothes they helped the child to put on in the morning are dirty or stained. The messes inherent in the sensory activities, art, and science curricula are frequent topics of concern. Sometimes families feel better about this once they understand the purpose of these activities. Some families are willing to send their children to school in clothes that can get dirty. For others, this is not comfortable—they want their child to look good and they want people to know they take good care of the child. Some families prefer to keep play clothes at school and have their child change into clean clothes before going home at the end of the day.

Some adults may be astonished and alarmed by the physical challenges that children undertake in early childhood education and care settings. They may never have allowed their children to climb to the top of a climbing structure or to use functional saws, scissors, or knives. They may not understand why you do. They may not be aware of what young children can safely do with close supervision. We find it helpful to let family members know that we share their regard for safety and then go on to talk about the value of the activity and the safeguards that we take. You can let families know that you won't allow children to attempt activities that are beyond their capacities; then describe the ways that you safely provide opportunities for exploration that contribute to development.

Families whose children have disabilities may question how well you are helping their child to meet identified goals and milestones and/or whether their child is being accepted by others and given equal opportunities for participation. Take time to answer these concerns thoughtfully using specific examples. Often your explanations will help families to see the many ways that their child is similar to other children and to know that the child is experiencing daily successes and interactions with others.

In each of these situations it is important to discuss family concerns openly, work for a mutually acceptable solution, and avoid judging families if their opinions are different from yours. Parents who feel heard are much more likely to be supportive of your program. They are also much more likely to hear your answers and explanations when they have concerns.

The "Golden Rules for Building Strong Relationships with Families" box offers a summary of some strategies for relating to families.

**Reflect on
your ethical
responsibilities**

A mother has requested that her daughter stay indoors every time there is any suspicion of a slight illness beginning. This would require that a staff member remain indoors with the child, creating a much higher child-to-staff ratio on the playground than is safe.

Using the "Guidelines for Ethical Reflection" on page 23, reflect on your ethical responsibilities in this situation.

GOLDEN RULES FOR BUILDING STRONG RELATIONSHIPS WITH FAMILIES

1. Listen more than you talk.
2. Communicate with all families; use a variety of strategies.
3. Smile and greet families as they enter the classroom or playground.
4. Include positive points in every communication.
5. Help families identify and articulate their goals, hopes, and dreams for their children.
6. Keep all information about families strictly confidential.
7. Create comfortable places for families in classrooms.
8. Offer a wide variety of opportunities for families to be part of the program.
9. Encourage families to know and support one another.
10. Let families know that you enjoy and appreciate their child.

Family involvement in early childhood programs can run the gamut from including families in all aspects of the program to contacting parents only when a problem needs to be addressed. Different levels of involvement reflect the lives and needs of different families and the preferences of different educators.

Classroom Involvement

When family members participate in your classroom, it can be a wonderful asset! Involved family members can work with the children during activities, orient other families to classroom participation, provide input into program policy, build supportive social relationships, and strengthen the connection of the program to the community. They bring knowledge and resources that might not be available to you from other sources. When family members participate as volunteers in the classroom, they can enrich your program and enable you to do more. Family members support children's experience when they work with individuals and small groups in the classroom and accompany you as you take children on learning trips outside of the program site.

When family members volunteer, everyone can benefit: the families, the staff, and the children. When they participate in the classroom, *family members*:

- Have an opportunity to learn about new ways of guiding growth and development
- Gain insight about their children as they watch them participate in an out-of-home setting
- Develop increased understanding about the curriculum that they may be able to apply at home
- Feel more proficient as a teacher for their own children
- Build a sense of competence and a feeling of being needed as they contribute to the program

When family members participate in the program, the *children:*

- Have a chance to see their family members in a different role
- Become acquainted with adults who have skills, feelings, and ways of relating that are different from their own family members and teachers
- See familiar adults interacting with one another in respectful, meaningful, and productive ways
- Have more individualized attention available to them
- Experience a richer curriculum

When family members participate in the program, the *teachers:*

- Have a chance to expand their program because of the improved child-adult ratio
- Gain knowledge and expertise from what families bring and share

- Have an opportunity to observe the relationship between the child and members of the family
- Increase their understanding of individual families, their values, preferences, and styles
- Have a chance to develop a more meaningful relationship with individual family members
- Have more opportunity to interact with individual children

It takes a while for families to become comfortable with classroom involvement, so begin simply. Have available a wide variety of ways that family members can make a genuine contribution to their child's school experience. When a family first enrolls, it is a good time to find out how they want to be involved. The family involvement survey in Figure 13.4 is a good place to start.

A traditional form of family involvement is to provide opportunities for family members to work with you and the children in the classroom. This works well if a family member is not working outside the home. But do not assume that working family members are unable to participate. They may work on weekends or at night and so have time during the week that they wish to spend with their child in school, or they may have a vacation day when your program is open. Retired grandparents may enjoy an opportunity to read, bake, or garden with the children. Don't forget to extend invitations to noncustodial parents to share in school events and activities.

To ensure successful classroom participation, have family members begin with a simple task such as joining you on a walk, reading a story to two or three children, or assisting you as you set up activities. It is important to allow them to participate in ways that feel comfortable and natural to them and to offer them support in developing skills. As they become more comfortable, some may take a more active part in the program by planning with you and possibly sharing their unique abilities or special knowledge.

Plan activities to work with family schedules. It is easy to invite family members to visit, observe their child, and help in the classroom. Those with flexible schedules can come during the school day to read a story, go on a trip, or be a special resource visitor for your curriculum. Some will be able to attend a special breakfast, and others can attend an occasion planned for the end of the day. With advance notice they may be able to come for special occasions such as a birthday or a special luncheon.

You need to make an effort to ensure that men as well as women participate, because men may feel that early childhood classrooms, particularly those for very young children, are not their natural province and they may not feel that they have anything to contribute. In fact, many men will be perfectly comfortable doing the activities just described. They may require a special invitation from you to feel assured that they are welcome. Alternatively, some may feel more at ease if you begin by asking them to lend their expertise in a realm in which they already feel competent, such as repairing a broken tricycle or helping children plant a garden.

Remember that when family members participate, you have the additional responsibility of supervising them. An informal orientation to learn policies, routines, and procedures will help family members to feel prepared and ensure that they understand program expectations so that quality is maintained. A satisfying classroom experience is enhanced when you can find time to cooperatively plan activities and talk at the end of the school day to discuss experiences and give each other feedback.

A card file containing information about activities and jobs that need to be done is useful for letting family members know what kind of participation is needed and will be welcomed. Posting written statements in each area of the

FIGURE 13.4 Family Involvement Survey Form

Family Involvement Survey

Family members are important people at our center. We welcome your involvement in all aspects of the program . . . both little and big. Participating in your child's early childhood program is a great way to share in your child's experiences. It helps the teachers, shows your child you care about his or her education, and it can be fun, too! There are lots of ways for you to participate depending on your time and interests. We know that not everyone will want or be able to do everything. To help us help you get involved, please fill out this survey and return it with your enrollment forms.

Your name: _____ Phone number: _____ E-mail: _____

The Program for Children

_____ I'd like to come and have lunch with the children at school.

_____ I'd like to come on a field trip and assist.

_____ I'd like to help out in the classroom.

_____ I'd like to help plan an event for the children (a trip, a party, etc.).

_____ I'd like to bring in an activity to do with the children such as cook, share a story, work in the garden, teach a song. I'd like to:

Best days and times for me:

The Program for Families

_____ I'd like to attend a parent social event such as a potluck, campout, or a picnic.

_____ I'd like to meet with other parents for a parent support group.

_____ I'd like to attend a parent education event (about guidance or child development and learning, etc.). Topics that interest me are:

_____ I'd like to join the *Parents & Friends Club* and participate in their activities.

_____ I'd like to work with other parents on fund-raising or planning events for families and children. Specifically I'd like to help with:

Improving and Maintaining the Environment

_____ I'd like to send in plastic bags or other recyclables that we use (ask first please).

_____ I'd like to help out on a work day, on a weekend, or school break.

_____ I'd like to borrow/return library books, or do shopping.

_____ I'd like to make or mend something for the classroom (we have lots of projects for someone who's handy: make a new batch of play dough, sew or mend dress-up clothes, make pillows, put together a game or scrapbook). Specifically I'd like to:

Managing or Promoting the Program

_____ I'd like to sit on a committee/board to give input into how the school is run.

_____ I'd like to be part of a hiring committee.

_____ I'd like to review the policy handbooks and make recommendations for changes.

_____ I'd like to help out in the office.

_____ I'd like to speak as a parent representative to legislators or community groups.

_____ I'd like to organize a display in the community to educate others about the program.

Other ideas that staff haven't thought of:

---

classroom describing the purpose of the activities and how adults can interact with children is another good technique for supporting participation.

Thought and preparation are required to enable those who cannot come into the classroom to be involved. Many will make an effort to come to a class potluck, an open house, or a special curriculum-related event in the evening. You can prepare book, art, or nature packs with activities for families to sign out and do at home with their children. You can also ask family members to create something at home for the class. This will be more successful if you prepare materials for parents to use (e.g., all the ingredients or materials needed plus instructions to make play dough, a game, smocks for the class).

Program Involvement

As families become involved in the program, they often become your greatest allies. Some may plan social events that help other families to become a part of the school community, some may offer to help in finding resources through fundraising events or grant-writing. Others may be willing to join with the staff to do renovation, repair, or cleanup projects.

Many programs periodically hold work days at which families and staff spend a day cleaning or doing repairs. Work days are better attended when families have had some say in the tasks to be done and can choose jobs based on their skills and interests. In addition, the staff and families must gather the required equipment and materials, arrange for food, and make sure that the jobs can be done in the designated time. Work days can include children but responsible adults must be selected to monitor their safety while staff and parents are working. Events like hands-on workshops and family work days can contribute to creating a sense of community among families in your school.

Many families of young children feel isolated from others. This may be particularly true for families who have recently moved to a new community and those whose children have disabilities. Opportunities to work alongside of others will help them build support networks and share the joys and stresses of parenting young children.

Family members can also be included as members of advisory councils, policy boards, and hiring committees. When families are members of decision-making bodies, they become genuine collaborators with staff in creating programs that are family centered and that accurately reflect the interests and needs of the families involved. Family members who participate in policy-making feel that the program truly belongs to them and their children. They are willing to expend more of their energy and resources because of their greater commitment. These parents become valuable advocates for your program.

Family members want to know about their child's experiences in their early childhood program. Many also appreciate ways to be part of the program. Be sensitive to the needs of different families and offer a variety of ways to encourage them to engage with their children and with the program. The "Connecting with Families: About Program Involvement" box summarizes the strategies discussed above.

Partnerships
with Families

Reflect on the ways your family was involved in your education

Recall the ways your family participated in your educational experiences. How did the school encourage family participation? What do you remember about the impact of this participation on you and on your family?

CONNECTING WITH FAMILIES

About Program Involvement

Families are encouraged to become involved when you offer them:

1. **Information:** Share fliers, handouts, and articles about parenting, child development, child guidance, and ways to support children's growth and learning. Connect families with information about community resources.

2. **Volunteer opportunities:** Provide a variety of ways for families to volunteer their time and expertise both in and out of the classroom.

3. **Suggestions for contributions:** Let families know that you welcome both material contributions as well as ideas and suggestions about the program. Be sure to give them opportunities to participate in program decision making.

4. **Strategies for encouraging children's learning:** Share ideas about ways that families can provide activities and experiences at home that support children's learning.

Family Education

Traditionally, programs for young children have included family education activities. Family education can focus on a broad range of topics: those related to children's development, parenting skills, and other interests of family members. You provide family education informally in your regular interactions with families and as you model positive interaction strategies in your classroom. When you find that a number of family members share areas of interest, you can offer more structured opportunities to provide them with appropriate information such as a newsletter article, a family discussion night, a workshop, or a class. If a topic is beyond your skills and expertise, you can draw on others in your school and community.

Families and community members who have been involved in your program may have resources for a family education program. We have experienced topics as diverse as a workshop on allergies conducted by a pediatrician parent and a workshop on scrapbooking presented by a young, creative mom with scrapbooking skills. Family members who understand the values and goals of the program will often be willing to share their special skills and knowledge and even invite their friends to contribute.

Like other aspects of the early childhood program, a family education program requires planning. It is valuable to survey the families to find out what they most wish to learn about and what times and settings will work best for them. Participation in family education events will increase if you provide child care and offer children and families a meal or hearty snack before, during, or after the presentation. Lively, interactive sessions are usually the most effective, and families are most likely to be engaged in the presentation when the presenter is informed in advance about the knowledge level and learning style of the participants.

Another way to provide parenting education is to develop a library of books and magazines for families to borrow. You may fund such a library by asking a local business or foundation to make a contribution or by having a fund-raiser run by parents. Sometimes families will donate books or magazines that they have found helpful. An area in the classroom or near the school office can be designated for the library. It is effective to set up an attractive display to entice parents to look at and borrow books.

Reflect on family involvement you have seen

Think about a program that you have observed or worked in. What kinds of family participation did you observe? What appeared to be the attitudes of the school staff toward family involvement? How do you think families felt about what was done?

Supporting Families

All families must deal with a variety of tasks required to care for young children and must handle an array of difficulties that occur in the course of daily parenting. However, some families face circumstances that require additional support. One of your tasks as a teacher of young children will be to recognize these challenges and offer appropriate kinds of support.

Helping in Times of Stress

Everyone experiences stress. Some stress is relatively minor, the result of juggling the responsibilities of a busy life. Other stresses are more serious, such as a when family structure changes, as with a new baby, death, divorce, deployment, or remarriage, or when there is a loss of a job or home. The trusting relationships that you initially establish with families help to ensure that they will feel comfortable letting you know when there is stress in their lives and letting you offer support to them when such stress occurs.

Even though you are not a counselor, you will find it helpful to know about and have strategies for supporting families during difficult times. There are several ways that you can do this. The first is by being there and doing your job. Children and families are supported when you are present, attentive, and professional. When you are not, it adds to their stress.

One of the simplest ways you can help is by being aware and keeping a child's school life as stable as possible during periods of stress. These are not times to move a child to a new group or make major changes in the schedule or room arrangement. A second way is to help families find needed assistance. To do this you need to know how resources such as medical clinics, family counseling, legal aid, mental health services, family violence shelters, family mediation organizations, fiscal support such as WIC and food stamps can be accessed. We find it helpful to keep a resource list of program names and services, hours of operation, and contact information. Families will appreciate it if you can give them specific information that makes it simple for them to contact the appropriate agency or program.

It is almost inevitable that at some time you will be asked to play a supportive role for one or both parents in divorce or child custody conflicts. A clear statement explaining your program's policies and procedures in these situations (often found in the parent handbook) can help the parents to understand what you can and can't do and that your primary commitment is to the child's welfare. One way to offer support to families going through a divorce or separation is to communicate to families that such problems are by no means unique or a sign of failure. When a divorce or custody battle does take place, it can be tempting to express your preference for one parent or the other. Keep in mind that you serve a child better by maintaining neutrality unless the child appears to be endangered. In cases where family members are in conflict, the NAEYC Code of Ethical Conduct states, in section P-2.14, "In cases where family members are in conflict with one another, we shall work openly, sharing our observations of the child, to help all parties involved make informed decisions. We shall refrain from becoming an advocate for one party" (see Appendix A).

Strengthening Families

Because of your important role in the lives of children and families, you can play a key part in preventing—not just reporting—child abuse and neglect. Your work helps reduce children's risk of abuse and neglect by supporting and strengthening families (NAEYC, 2004). The Center for the Study of Social Policy has identified five factors that protect children from child abuse and neglect. For adults, these factors are (1) parental resilience, (2) social connections, (3) knowledge of parenting and child development, and (4) concrete support in times of need. For children, the key factor is healthy social and emotional development (CCSP, 2004).

As an early childhood teacher, your work with families supports the development of each of these factors. When you put into place many of the strategies discussed in this chapter, you are taking steps to help families acquire the knowledge and skills that they need to relate positively to their young children.

NAEYC's Supporting Teachers, Strengthening Families initiative encourages teachers to learn about and use a family-strengthening approach in their early childhood programs. Figure 13.5 shows the framework for this approach.

Supporting Families of Children with Disabilities

Families of children with disabilities should be a welcome part of the ongoing life of your program. One way you can support them is to make sure they can participate like the families of typically developing children. Invite them to help at

FIGURE 13.5 The Family Strengthening Approach to Abuse Prevention

Early childhood teachers support and strengthen families and reduce the risk of child abuse and neglect when they:

1. Provide quality care and education through developmentally appropriate practices.

2. Develop reciprocal relationships with families.

3. Recognize situations that may place children at risk of abuse, and signs of abuse, and provide families with appropriate support.

4. Understand, and help families to understand and handle, children's challenging behaviors.

5. Build on child and family strengths.

6. Inform themselves about their professional responsibilities.

Sources: Information from M. Olson, "Strengthening Families: Community Strategies That Work," *Young Children* 62(2), 2007; NAEYC, *Building Circles, Breaking Cycles—Preventing Child Abuse and Neglect: The Early Childhood Education Role*, 2004.

Reflect on your strengths and challenges in supporting families

What do you see as your potential strengths in communicating with families and supporting them when they are dealing with stressful situations? What might be challenging for you? What experiences, understandings, and skills do you have that may help you? What understandings and skills do you need to work on?

a work day or provide field trip assistance just as you would with any other family. When planning family events, be sure the child care provided will meet the needs of all children. Help them to meet other families. For example, at a family event or when they drop off or pick up their child you might say something like, "Mrs. Brown, I'd like you to meet Mrs. Nishimoto. Her daughter Lisa was Nicole's partner on our field trip today."

Just like families of typically developing children, families of children with disabilities need regular communication and sharing of positive information. Another way to provide support is to be sure that the family has access to you in several different ways (e.g., phone calls, written logs, e-mail). Having a communication log for each child may make it easier for some family members who are more comfortable sharing a concern in writing rather than speaking to you directly. Conferences should feel "safe" so family members can hear information about their child without feeling it is prejudiced or judgmental. The anecdotal records you keep on the child can serve as the basis for a dialogue between you and family members. Make a special effort to collect data on children with disabilities, because the more data you have, the easier it will be to see progress that you can share with the family.

If the family has been in your program for a while before their child is identified as having a disability, you may need to increase the frequency of communication to ensure that the child and family get needed services. Make a special effort to keep the family involved in ordinary events as well. Even if they can't participate much while they are adjusting to this new dimension of their lives, later they will appreciate being kept informed.

Understanding Legal and Ethical Responsibilities

Thus far in this chapter we have described your role and responsibilities to the families of the children with whom you will work as a professional early childhood educator. In addition to these, every teacher also has ethical and legal obligations.

Confidentiality

Maintaining confidentiality is an ethical obligation of every teacher and one whose importance we cannot stress strongly enough. Confidentiality with regard to families means sharing information about them and their children only when there is legitimate need to do so. Even a "cute" story told to a friend that identifies a child in your classroom is a violation of confidentiality.

A related legal responsibility has to do with children's records. Generally, the only individuals who legally may have access to a child's file (apart from the child's teachers and program administrative staff) are parents or guardians and those professionals who have been identified as needing to have the information to serve the best interests of the child. The Family Education Rights and Privacy Act (FERPA) grants families the right to examine their child's official records and protects the privacy of the records. In most programs, official files are stored in a locked file cabinet.

Reporting Child Abuse and Neglect

As an early childhood educator, you have an ethical and legal responsibility to report suspected cases of child abuse or neglect. Just like a doctor, you are a "mandated reporter." Every state has its own laws and regulations pertaining to child abuse reporting in early childhood education programs. Compliance is often the obligation of program administrators; however, it is important for you to be aware of your specific responsibilities. You can learn more about legal mandates from the agency that regulates early childhood programs in your state. Families should be notified upon entering a program that early childhood educators are "mandated reporters" and that the staff's goal is to work with family members to educate and to protect their children.

Every program should have written policies that describe the program's and the staff's obligation to report child abuse and neglect and of policies designed to protect children. Information about these should be given to you as part of your orientation to a new job. Ask if these are not given to you. So that you know what to do, become familiar with the reporting procedures of your program and your state as well as the resources that are available in your community to prevent child abuse and neglect.

Most schools and child care centers have a person, often the principal or director, who will provide guidance and help you in documenting your concerns and reporting cases of abuse. It is also your responsibility to be aware of the indicators of abuse and neglect. A discussion of these indicators can be found in Chapter 7, "Health, Safety, and Well-Being," in this text.

When you suspect child abuse or neglect, you, a colleague, or administrator needs to confer with the family to develop a plan for addressing the situation, provide consultation and parent education as appropriate, and make referrals to agencies that might help the family. If you find yourself in this situation, make every effort to maintain a good relationship and work with the family as cooperatively as possible. Focus on positive aspects of the child in discussions and take care to notice and comment on the family's attempts to handle the child in a constructive way. Do all you can to suspend judgments about the family and let them know that your goal is to support them and help them cope. Avoid communications that might make the parent feel inadequate or incompetent and try to reassure them that they continue to have your respect. Neither child nor parent should be labeled as "abused" or "abuser," and confidentiality should be rigorously kept. Remember that families suspected of abuse or neglect are living in stressful circumstances and may need additional support and assistance in their efforts to nurture their children.

**Reflect on
your ethical
responsibilities**

Jeremy's mother tells you early in the school year that he can be "wild" and that she and her boyfriend are taking steps to discipline him to prevent this behavior. She asks that you always let her know when he misbehaves at school. One day Jeremy throws sand at another child, then strikes her with a shovel. When you approach, Jeremy begins to sob and shake, asking you over and over, "Please don't tell Ma; please don't tell Paul."

Using the guidelines on page 23, reflect on your ethical responsibilities in this situation.

Final Thoughts

Families and early childhood professionals can become partners who share a common goal—to educate and care for children in ways that support optimal development. Early childhood teachers know that when they care for children, they are also caring for and caring about families. As a member of this field, you will play an important role in the lives of many families. You will be part of the network of people who will lend support to the families' efforts to function in a complex society and provide their children with the protection and nurture they need.

Learning Outcomes

When you read this chapter, and then thoughtfully complete selected assignments from the "To Learn More" section and prepare items from the "For Your Portfolio" section, you will be demonstrating progress in meeting **NAEYC Standard 2: Building Family and Community Relationships** (NAEYC, 2009).

Key elements:

2a: Knowing about and understanding diverse family and community characteristics
2b: Supporting and engaging families and communities through respectful, reciprocal relationships
2c: Involving families and communities in their children's development and learning

To Learn More

Interview and Observe in a Program: Choose an early childhood program. Interview the director or family involvement coordinator to discover the kinds of family involvement available, the program's philosophy regarding family involvement, and the ways the program communicates with families. Observe the school environment and note efforts to communicate with families (e.g., family bulletin boards). Notice what is done to include different cultures, abilities, languages, and family constellations. Discuss what you learned from your exploration either with classmates or in a paper and reflect on the implications for you as an early childhood educator.

Compare Two Programs: Repeat the preceding activity with a second program and write a paper that compares and contrasts the two.

Review the NAEYC Code of Ethical Conduct: Review Section II of the Code of Ethics. Reflect on how the things you observed during your school visits and interviews meet or do not meet the Ideals and Principles listed in Section II and write about your conclusions.

Compare Family Materials: Choose two early childhood programs. Collect a sample of the materials that each program gives to families: brochure, application, handbook, newsletter, policy statements, and so forth. Compare and evaluate the materials based on the ideas presented in this chapter and write about how the programs appear to differ in their philosophy and attitudes toward families, and what you learned from this experience that may be helpful to you as an early childhood educator.

Interview Family Members: Interview one or two family members of children in early childhood programs. Ask them to talk about the day-to-day experience of parenting a young child. Ask what they expect from their child's program in terms of participation, information, and support. Find out how well they think the program is doing in providing these things. Write about what you learned and its implications for you as an early childhood educator.

Interview Your Family: Interview your own parents or guardians. Ask them to recall what it was like to parent you as a young child and what kinds of support they got from your schools. If possible, look at the "artifacts" that they have (report cards, school newsletters, parent handbook). Ask them to describe the ways they were involved in programs you attended as a child. Reflect and write about what you learned and its implications for you as an early childhood educator.

Investigate Related Websites:

Building Circles; Breaking Cycles: Preventing Child Abuse & Neglect: The Early Childhood Educator's Role: http://nccic.acf.hhs.gov/node/28654

Center on School, Family, and Community Partnerships: csos.jhu.edu/P2000/center.htm

Especially for Parents: ed.gov/parents

Families and Work Institute: familiesandwork.org

Family Support America: familysupportamerica.org

National Coalition for Parent Involvement in Education: ncpie.org

National Network of Partnership Schools: partnershipschools.org

National Parenting Center: tnpc.com

Parents as Teachers: parentsasteachers.org

 **For Your Portfolio**

Write a Newsletter for Families: Write a newsletter article aimed at helping family members of children in an early childhood program to understand children's development and learning. Select an area of development, write the article, and distribute it to families. Ask families for feedback. Put a copy of the article, a summary of the feedback, and a reflection of what you learned from the experience in your portfolio.

Make a Classroom Family-Friendly: Assess a classroom for young children and find ways to make it more family-friendly. For example, add an adult-sized chair, create a parent area, make a family bulletin board, or create information for family members and post it in the interest centers. Write about, photograph, and include samples in your portfolio to show how you made the room more family-friendly.

Involve Families in an Early Childhood Program: Help involve families in an early childhood program. Meet with a teacher and one or two family members and create a list of ways for family members to get involved. Include

on-site involvement (like volunteering in the classroom or on learning trips) and at-home involvement (like sewing pillows or doing laundry). Share the list with families and invite them to participate. In your portfolio, include the list, a description of how families responded to it, and a reflection of what you learned from the experience.

Create a Family Event: Plan and implement a family event such as an open house, potluck, or workshop. In your portfolio include the poster or newsletter in which the event is announced as well as a description of what happened, photos if you have them, and a reflection on whether it was effective in involving families in the program and what you learned from the experience.

Develop a Resource Directory for Families: Research agencies in your community that provide services to families with young children and community resources and events that might be interesting to families. Give contact information, referral procedures, and a brief description of each one.

MyEducationLab

Go to Topic 3: Family/Community in the MyEducationLab (myeducationlab.com) for *Who Am I in the Lives of Children?* where you can:

- Find learning outcomes for Family/Community along with the national standards that connect to these outcomes.
- Complete Assignments and Activities that can help you more deeply understand the chapter content.
- Apply and practice your understanding of the core teaching skills identified in the chapter with the

Building Teaching Skills and Dispositions learning units.
- Check your comprehension on the content covered in the chapter with the Study Plan. Here you will be able to take a chapter quiz, receive feedback on your answers, and then access Review, Practice, and Enrichment activities to enhance your understanding of chapter content.

Those of us who are in this world to educate—to care for—
young children have a special calling: a calling that has very
little to do with the collection of expensive possessions but
has a lot to do with the worth inside of hearts and heads.
In fact, that's our domain: the heads and hearts of the next
generation, the thoughts and feelings of the future.

FRED ROGERS

14

Becoming an Early Childhood Professional

When you began your journey through this book, we asked you to reflect on what you saw in your imagination when you thought of an early childhood teacher. Your ideas may have been quite simple—our students often envision a nice person who reads stories, teaches the ABC's, and puts on Band-Aids. As you reach this last chapter, you have realized that teaching young children is a much more complex and demanding task. In fact, as Mister Rogers says in the quote on the previous page, it is a calling—an inwardly felt dedication. Do you hear early childhood education calling to you? If so, you may be wondering what's next. You may be questioning what a commitment to educating young children entails. And you may be thinking about what it would be like to be an early childhood educator and what you would need to do to be successful at it.

We have written this chapter to help you think about these things. We want to encourage you to make a commitment to early childhood education and care because young children, families, and society need you. Now it is time to think about the path you might take to becoming a professional early childhood educator (someone who has received training and who uses personal skills and abilities to serve society through realizing commitments to children). We will offer a map with some directions for your journey. We will describe some things you may need to assist you as you travel. We want you to know that there may be challenges along the road that will require you to stand firm in what you know is best for children. Finally, we want to let you know that the joys and the burdens you will carry on your journey will be shared by mentors and colleagues who are traveling with you.

Make a Commitment to Children

I am persuaded that good teachers, first of all, must hold strong commitments and convictions from which their practices flow.

James Hymes

Your first, most important, and ultimate commitment as an early childhood educator is your allegiance to children. When you choose to work with young children, you are choosing the most important job in the world. Tomorrow's adults, in their most vulnerable stage of life, will be in your hands. Today's young children need to be protected, so tomorrow's adults will be healthy and strong. They need nurturing, so tomorrow's adults will be sensitive and care about others. They need experiences that will help them to delight in learning, so tomorrow's adults will be knowledgeable, creative thinkers, discoverers, and problem-solvers. Today's children will have many problems to solve. They need guidance, so tomorrow's adults will appreciate and care for the fragile world in which we live. Today's young children need to learn to cooperate, so tomorrow's adults will be peacemakers at home and in the world. To adequately meet the needs of the young children you will teach, you need a philosophical base, knowledge and skill, and a commitment to ethical behavior.

Develop a Philosophy

You came into the field of early care and education with some ideas about children and how they should be taught, and some vision of who you wished to be in their lives. You have read and studied and your knowledge expanded and some of your thoughts may have changed and expanded. As you begin to work in the field, reflect on your practice, and learn more, these ideas will coalesce into a philosophy—an organized group of principles and beliefs that guide your practice. This philosophy is an important part of your identity as an early childhood educator—it will continue to evolve throughout your career.

We suggested in Chapter 1 that you start a professional portfolio and write about what you believe and value for young children. Now is a good time to go back to what you wrote and reflect on whether or not it still represents what you believe, who you are, and who you want to be in the lives of children. As you revisit it, you can use it to write a statement that can become your "working educational philosophy."

Know About Children and Best Practice

At the center of your knowledge as an early childhood educator is your appreciation for, and understanding of, children. Observing children is the first and usually most lasting activity of a professional early childhood educator—and because children are complex and theory is ever changing, it is something you will continue to learn about throughout your career.

When you hear new ideas about curriculum, guidance, and children's development, they may sometimes conflict with what you have been taught or what you believe to be true. Keep an open mind when you hear these ideas so that you can make use of the new information. But don't blindly accept everything that "experts" tell you, particularly if they have something to sell. Trust what you know from your own observations. Sometimes a new idea will resonate and you will respond with, "Yes! That makes sense. I really see that in the children I know." At other times you may find yourself wondering if the writer or researcher ever spent time with real children. The dissonance you experience may reflect cultural or community differences or the views about childhood and learning of the author or researcher. Use your own experience and observations of children to help you distinguish between what makes sense and what is just a passing fad.

Remember, only a few years ago some of today's accepted practices (e.g., putting up a poster of the alphabet, allowing mildly ill children to come to school, integrating children with disabilities into classrooms with typically developing children) were considered poor or unnecessary practices. At the same time, now-discredited practices (e.g., lengthy group times for toddlers, time-out, changing diapers without gloves, and placing playground equipment over hard surfacing) were considered perfectly fine. There is danger both in blindly accepting new trends and in being stubbornly attached to old ways. What seems certain is that while many ideas will change, respect for children and childhood is not a passing fad.

Understand and Use a Code of Ethics

We hope that you will find the NAEYC Code of Ethical Conduct and the core values upon which the code rests (included in Appendix A and also available online at naeyc.org/positionstatements/ethical_conduct) or the ethical code that is used in your program helpful in guiding you to act on the shared ethical responsibilities of all early childhood educators. These are an important part of your professional commitment to children and families. Understanding your ethical responsibilities will help you to resist the temptation to do what is easy or what will make you popular, at the expense of doing what is right. When you choose to do something because it is easy or expedient but it violates your ethical obligations (e.g., taking personal phone calls while you are on duty with children, requiring children to finish their lunch before getting milk because a coteacher requires it), it cannot be morally justified. You have an ethical responsibility to give children your full attention and to provide healthy experiences for them. It is important to remember that neither personal convenience nor social comfort are professional values.

The code delineates your ethical responsibilities, and it gives you guidance about what to do when you encounter an *ethical dilemma* (a professional predicament for which there is more than one justifiable solution). In a dilemma, the good of one group or individual to whom you owe professional allegiance is in conflict with the good of another group or individual to whom you also have a professional responsibility. The "Reflect on Your Ethical Responsibilities" boxes included in this text have described some ethical dilemmas.

Reflect and Set Goals

You know that it is important to know yourself and be able to reflect on your actions. Reflective teachers take time to think about what has happened and

Reflect on who you want to be in the lives of children

Reflect on what you value about young children and childhood. As you read each question jot down a few words to capture your thoughts. What do you believe young children need in an early childhood program? What do you know about how young children learn, and what do you believe that means to you as a teacher? What do you think early childhood programs should be like? What role do you want to play in the life of a child and a family? Who do you want to be in the lives of children?

Use your reflections and jottings as the basis of your written educational philosophy.

Reflect on a time when you changed

Think about a time when you learned something that changed the way you did something you had always done (the way you write papers, travel to a destination, cook, do a household routine). Did you make the change all at once, try it, and then go back to your old way, or think about it for a long time and then change? Do you enjoy change or resist it? What do you hope to do when you are asked to make a change in your work with children?

wonder about how their decisions and actions have influenced children, families, and colleagues. We have encouraged you to practice this skill as you thought about the questions in the Reflection boxes throughout this book. Ann Epstein reminds us of the importance of *intentional teaching*—acting with specific outcomes and goals in mind for children's development. In order to ensure that the practices and strategies we select meet these goals, we must take time to "reflect on and change teaching strategies based on children's responses" (2007). In our experience, teachers who have developed the habit of ongoing reflection tend to be those who continue to be excited about their work and who grow and adapt appropriately as new knowledge comes to light.

Make a Commitment to Yourself

Throughout this book we have emphasized the importance of personal reflection and self-understanding. We began by asking you to reflect on yourself as a person, because that is the foundation of who you will be as a teacher. Now we ask you to make a commitment to yourself as a person and a professional.

No book, toy, video, or computer program can substitute for *you,* a human being who knows about and cares about young children. *You* are the vital ingredient. *You* will set the goals and make plans to address them. What you have to give is yourself—your caring, your energy, your knowledge and skills, and your commitment.

Take Care of Yourself

Anyone who has never made a mistake has never tried anything new.

Albert Einstein

In order to accomplish the demanding task of providing care and education for young children, you need to be in good physical and emotional health. Take care of your body by paying attention to nutrition, exercise, rest and relaxation. Nurture your mind, so you stay excited and motivated as a learner. Stay connected to others, so you feel meaningfully involved and intellectually stimulated. Nurture your spirit by taking time for quiet reflection, for enjoying beauty, and for creative pursuits.

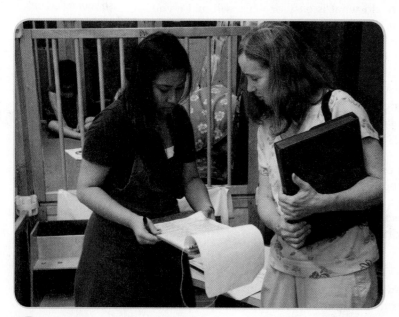

As a new practitioner, it is important that you set realistic goals for yourself, that you find your strengths and build on them, and that you acknowledge your mistakes and learn from them. It is also important not to expect to be able to do everything perfectly, especially in your first year or two of teaching. In order to accomplish the many tasks involved in working with young children, you need to be satisfied with doing a "good enough" job. Putting children first is a good beginning. You will have many years to develop a more "perfect" classroom and curriculum.

Connect with Colleagues

Another way to take care of yourself as you begin your career is to build good relationships with colleagues. Your colleagues are more than coworkers. They are the people who share your work life and your commitments. If you are fortunate, they will share your philosophy and your passion, understand your joys and sorrows, and give you a sympathetic ear, a pat on the back, honest feedback, and words of encouragement. They give you an opportunity to engage in collaborative learning. Cooperative learning is exciting and powerful. It helps you to improve your practice and also increases your professional satisfaction.

Good relationships with your coworkers will enhance the program for children and make your work easier and more pleasant. Using the communication skills you learn as a part of your training to be an early childhood teacher can help you to develop good relationships with adults as well as with children. People will regard you as a good colleague if you make every effort to be pleasant and fair and if you make sure that you do your share (and even a little more than your share) of the work. Be sensitive to and respectful of the cultural expectations, values, and interaction styles of those with whom you work. Be sure that you are aware of your ethical responsibilities to your coworkers and your employer. These are spelled out in the Code of Ethical Conduct.

Plan Your Career Path

Work is love made visible. And if you can't work with love but only with distaste, it is better that you should leave your work and sit at the gate of the temple and take alms of the people who work with joy.

Kahlil Gibran

You have learned many important things and have begun to develop the skills that you need to be a caring and competent early childhood educator. And you have many choices to make as you join the field. They are personal choices, value choices, and career choices. There are some things that you can think about that will help you make the career choices.

The first question to ask yourself is: *What age of children am I drawn to as a teacher?* Each stage in early childhood has its charms and needs teachers who love its particular joys and challenges. Some teachers are drawn to infants and toddlers, some to preschoolers, some to kindergartners, and others to primary-age children. Still others can find joy working with more than one of these ages. Which one are you? You will be happier in your career choice, and children will be better off, if you select the right age(s). You do no service to yourself or children if you teach in inappropriate ways because you'd really prefer to work with a different age group.

The next question to consider is: *What teaching role do I want as I begin my career?* Do you want to teach alone most of the time or do you want to be part of a teaching team in which decisions are shared? Do you want to be in charge or would you prefer to start out assisting someone else who shoulders more of the responsibility? Often, after they have completed a practicum placement and realized the scope of a teacher's work, our students decide that they prefer to start out as assistant teachers.

Reflect on your future career

What kind of setting and what kind of children would you like to work with as you begin your career? What would the perfect job for you in early childhood education and care be like? Why does it appeal to you? What training is needed for this job?

Other questions to ask yourself are: *How much independence do I desire?* and *Do I want to work within the constraints and benefits of a large bureaucracy?* Everyone wants to make a decent salary, and everyone wants to be allowed the freedom to do what they believe is best. There is usually some trade-off, however, between having freedom to teach in ways you feel are best and having the stability along with the better salary and benefits of working within a larger system.

No job is perfect. Do you prefer working with younger children? Do you like being part of a team? Would you prefer not having many dictates about how and what to teach? Then you probably will be happier working in a preschool or infant-toddler program. Do you prefer to work with older children with less teamwork? Do you need better salary and are you comfortable with curriculum and assessment specified by the school or district? Then you may be happier teaching in a kindergarten or primary classroom in a public elementary school. Reflecting on these questions will help you make choices about your educational path.

If you are just starting out, another thing to think about is the kind of teacher training program that would be best for you. Should you be in a program that prepares you to work with children younger than 5, one that will enable you to teach in elementary schools, or one that will allow you the flexibility to do either? It is important to be aware of the implications of this choice. We have had students who were very surprised to discover that with an associate's degree they would need several more years of school and another degree in order to teach in a public school. And we know teachers who were shocked to discover that despite a teaching credential and a master's degree, they had to go back to school to get the specialized training required for working with infants and toddlers.

Career decisions are not set in concrete and don't have to last forever. As you grow and change, so do your needs for professional fulfillment. The more experience you have in working with children of different ages in a variety of settings, the sooner it will become clear whether working with young children is the right choice for you and what kinds of positions will suit you best.

Many kinds of work offer opportunities for you to act on your commitment to children. Not everyone who gets a degree in early childhood education spends her or his entire career working in directly with young children. Some decide to move into other professional roles and find that their knowledge of child development and early learning provides a good foundation for these endeavors. What is most important is that you learn about yourself and about the field and make a decision that will be good for you and for children and their families.

Make a Commitment to Your Profession

We live in a world in which we need to share responsibility. It is easy to say "It's not my child, not my community, not my world, not my problem." Then there are those who see the need and respond. I consider those people my heroes.

Fred Rogers

Educating and caring for young children is caring for the future. You are caring for the future by making a commitment to your profession. Your initial commitments will evolve as you gain experience and mature as a professional. When you join a professional organization, help parents understand how children learn, share your knowledge at a workshop or conference, collaborate with other professionals to meet a child's or family's needs, mentor a new teacher, speak to a friend or legislator on behalf of children, or take a stand based on a code of ethics, you are caring for the profession and the future of us all.

Behave Like a True Professional

You make a commitment to children, yourself, and your profession when you commit to behaving like a professional. We have all heard someone called a "true professional." That term is generally meant as a high form of praise. Being a true professional means that in dealing with children, families, and society you:

- Take pride in the important work you do
- Learn about and live by a code of ethics
- Commit yourself to supporting children's development and families in their task of child rearing
- Are objective in viewing children and families and rational in your dealings with them
- Are honest in dealing with children and families and take care not to exaggerate your knowledge, training, or skills
- Build relationships with families and colleagues based on trust
- Are trustworthy—honest and scrupulous in upholding confidentiality, resisting the urge to gossip even though the temptation is strong
- Follow through on commitments and keep your promises, being careful not to promise what you can't deliver
- Commit yourself to being a good colleague and a good employee
- Collaborate with other professionals (therapists, educators, licensing workers, etc.) to serve children and families
- Seek out opportunities to continue to learn and grow as a professional
- Carry yourself with dignity
- Are a good model for children and families
- Advocate for children, families, and program practices that meet their needs

By choosing to behave according to the highest professional standards, you fulfill your commitment to children. Behaving according to the ideals of professionalism will make you feel good about yourself; will earn you the respect of families, colleagues, and community members; and will help the field of early childhood education gain more professional recognition.

Continue to Learn and Grow

One of the trademarks of a professional is the desire to learn and grow. Like children, you need resources, time, and encouragement to explore, experiment, and learn. The length of time you have been teaching and your experiences as a teacher will to a large extent determine the type of ongoing professional development that will nurture your continued growth. See Table 14.1, "Stages of Teacher Development," for descriptions of the types of professional development activities that are likely to be appropriate for each stage. Elizabeth Jones and Gretchen Reynolds suggest that educators can regard their intellectual interests and concerns as a form of play (Jones & Reynolds, 1992). You can pursue topics that are interesting and fun and make decisions about what *you* want to learn and skills you want to develop.

Join a Professional Organization

You may wonder why your college instructors, and the authors of this text, are always promoting professional organizations. You are likely to have been given a brochure or been encouraged to spend a sum of money to become a member of one or more professional groups.

Why is membership in an organization so highly valued? One reason will be clear as you browse through the bibliographies at the end of this book. You will notice that professional organizations publish books and journals that further the knowledge base of the field. Another reason is that professional organizations do important work on behalf of children, practitioners, and the profession. They gather the research, provide information, create position statements, develop standards, advocate for children, and provide a collective voice for the field.

Joining a professional organization gives you the opportunity for growth and participation with the community of your peers. Organizations provide their members with a sense of common purpose and support in the form of publications, conferences, and community events. Find an organization that is active in your area and get involved in it. Not only will you gain valuable information but you will get to spend time with others who do the same work you do, who care

TABLE 14.1 Stages of Teacher Development

Teacher Stage	Hallmark	Appropriate Professional Support/Education
Stage 1: Survival Year 1	Applying what you have learned	Connection with colleagues; practical suggestions and advice
Stage 2: Consolidation Years 2 Up to 5	Bringing together what you know; creating your own style and approach to teaching	On-site assistance, consultants, coaching, and mentoring
Stage 3: Renewal Between 3 and 5 Years	Growing confidence may lead to boredom and a need for rekindling professional enthusiasm	Visits to other programs, professional reading, conferences, classes, doing action research, and joining professional associations
Stage 4: Maturity After 5 or More Years	Increasing interest in the values, theories, issues, and philosophy that underlie your work	Seminars, work toward advanced degrees, and theoretical professional reading

Source: Information from L. G. Katz, "The Developmental Stages of Teachers," *Talks with Teachers of Young Children*, 1995.

about some of the same things, and who may have similar concerns. Sharing with colleagues is one of the great joys of being an early childhood educator.

A professional organization can represent you only if you are a part of it. You should join a professional organization for more than the journal, a membership card, reduced conference fees, or lowered insurance rates. You should join to declare yourself a member of a profession and to support it. Figure 14.1 provides website information for a number of different early childhood professional organizations. You cannot join them all, but as a committed early childhood professional you will find one (or more) that best represents your interests. If you reside in a country outside of the United States, there are likely to be early childhood professional organizations there that you can join. We have included a few of them in Figure 14.1, and you can find others in your geographic area by searching the Internet.

Advocate

Another of your professional commitments is *advocacy*. What does advocacy mean? It means giving support to a policy or cause that you believe to be right. The idea of advocacy may seem quite alien to you. You have chosen a career that involves very personal relationships and in which you are encouraged to be warm, accepting, and nurturing. Advocacy seems to require the opposite

FIGURE 14.1   Website Information for Early Childhood Professional Organizations

U.S. Early Childhood Professional Organizations

American Montessori Society
www.amshq.org

Association for Childhood Education International (ACEI)
www.acei.org

Association for Supervision and Curriculum Development
E-mail: member@ascd.org
www.ascd.org

National Association for the Education of Young Children (NAEYC)
www.naeyc.org

Southern Early Childhood Association (SECA)
www.southernearlychildhood.org

U.S. Professional Organizations Representing Subsections of Early Childhood Education and Care

Council for Exceptional Children
www.cec.sped.org

National Association for Family Child Care
E-mail: nafcc@nafcc
www.nafcc.org

National Association of Child Care Resource and Referral Agencies
www.naccrra.org

National Coalition for Campus Children's Centers (NCCCC)
E-mail: ncccc@smtp.bmai.com
www.campuschildren.org

ECE Professional Organizations Outside the United States

Organization Mondiale pour l'Education Préscolaire (OMEP)
www.omep.org.gu.se

U.S. National Committee
www.omep-usnc.org

Association for Early Childhood Educators (Singapore)
www.aeces.org

Association Montessori International
E-mail: info@montessori-ami.org
www.montessori-ami.org

The British Association for Early Childhood Education
www.early-education.org.uk

The Canadian Child Care Federation
E-mail: info@cccf-fcsge.ca
www.cccf-fcsge.ca

The Canadian Association for Young Children (CAYC) Membership Service
E-mail: caycmeb@cayc.ca
www.cayc.ca

Early Childhood Australia Inc., formerly the Australian Early Childhood Association
E-mail: eca@earlychildhood.org.au
www.aeca.org.au

Pacific Early Childhood Education Research Association—
Japan
www.org.kobe-u.ac.jp/pecera-japan
Hong Kong
www.pecera.org.hk

Te Tari Puna Ora O Aotearoa/ New Zealand Childcare Association
www.nzchildcare.ac.nz

traits. Some advocacy for children is very public and involves speaking out in assertive ways to policy makers. But it can also be personal and cordial. When you make a careful display of children's art that demonstrates your belief in its beauty and worth, you are advocating for children. When you treat children with dignity and respect in your classroom and ask others to do so, you are advocating for children. When, at a staff meeting, you suggest a change in the time snack is served because you have observed that children are hungry, you are advocating for children. As you grow, you may find that your confidence builds and that you are increasingly able to speak out for children in more public arenas.

Why should you be an advocate? Though you may not believe it now, you are an influential person. You are influential with your family and friends. They know and trust you and what you tell them about early childhood education and care may be more powerful for them than what they read in the newspaper or see on television. You are influential in your community. The people on your street, in your neighborhood, in your town know you. You are *their* expert on early childhood education, and they trust you. You are influential in your local government. You know the friends, families, and associates of the members of your local school board, your municipal council, and your state legislature. You represent the opinions and votes of those who elected them. You are as important, or more important, to them than any expert.

Early childhood educators are increasingly committed to advocacy. We are slowly trying to change our image from one of "nice ladies" to effective advocates for children. We are becoming more sophisticated about political process and are forming alliances with others who have similar concerns in order to heighten community awareness and influence public attitudes and legislation on behalf of young children and their families. When you become informed about the political process; when you stay informed about community, state, and national efforts to improve programs and services for children; and when you express your views and share your knowledge with members of your community, the media, or government leaders, you are advocating for young children.

Each time you join with other early childhood educators, each time you influence another person, you strengthen the voice of the field. In a large and diverse country such as ours, it is easy to feel hopeless about influencing government policy. You are just one person, probably a young person, and you are not yet an acknowledged expert in your field. But you are a citizen, you are a voter, and you influence other citizens and other voters. As a growing professional, you will learn ways to make your voice one that speaks effectively for children.

Stand Firm in What Is Right for Children

You have learned that young children learn best through the natural activities of childhood: play, hands-on exploration, and individualized interaction with a teacher who is a sensitive observer. You know that you must consider each child in the context of family, culture, and community. But, while these views are strongly held by early childhood educators, they are certainly not the prevalent beliefs in American education today. You may encounter family members, teachers, administrators, and policy makers who do not share your knowledge of child development or your ideas about desirable practices for teaching young children. You may encounter decisions made by school districts, administrators, or teachers that you don't think are in the best interests of children. It is possible that some time in your career you will be:

- Asked to eliminate play, art, nap, recess, or snack so that children can spend more time on academic tasks
- Asked to teach children skills or content that are not appropriate to their age and ability
- Required to give children paper-and-pencil tests that may be beyond their ability, cause them stress and/or be used to determine their future educational experiences
- Directed to use a system of discipline that you think is harsh and does not help children learn inner control

When those kinds of things occur, what can you do? If you don't want to ignore demands or run away, you could do what Mister Rogers (2003) suggests: *"Be a grain of sand in an oyster."*

To be the grain of sand that forms the core of the pearl, you must learn the gentle art of using disagreement about educational practice to your advantage. You may hear dismissive comments when you talk about how young children learn and their need for appropriate curriculum and assessment. You do not have to acquiesce to what others think. When pushed to focus on academic content because it is deemed important, you can agree that the early years *are* a critical time for laying academic foundations. You can also maintain that because the early years are so critical, it *is* crucial that we provide educational experiences that actually work.

You will be better able to withstand pressures to follow practices that are not in the best interests of children if you are able to articulate your knowledge and beliefs when others challenge your views. You can explain how play and other forms of appropriate instruction help children to be academically prepared. To be effective, you will want to be able to do more than say "children learn through play." Your ongoing study will help you to explain to others what research tells us about how children learn. As you become skilled at observing and documenting children's learning, you will be able to make it visible to their parents, to administrators, and to policy makers in ways that have meaning to them. Be sure to stay connected to early childhood educators and other concerned professionals so that you have colleagues and supporters: You can't do this alone. Offer support to all who are champions for children—the ones who stand up for us all.

It is important to choose when to stand firm and when not to. Not every issue is worth fighting; not every battle can be won. As an ethical professional, you may have hard choices to make. We urge you to stand up for children and to make their well-being your primary concern; to say no when asked to do what is wrong; to insist on speaking what you know to be true; to risk making yourself unpopular; and to give others the courage to do the same. It's a lot to ask. But it's the right thing to do, and children need you to do it.

Final Thoughts

Who will you be in the lives of children? Who will you be as an early childhood educator? Becoming a professional in early childhood education takes time and experience, caring and commitment, and a willingness to keep on learning. It can be difficult and challenging. But it brings with it the joy and the satisfaction of being with young children and the knowledge that you are helping to shape the future. As your colleagues, we welcome you.

Learning Outcomes

When you read this chapter, and then thoughtfully complete selected assignments from the "To Learn More" section and prepare items from the "For Your Portfolio" section, you will be demonstrating progress in meeting **NAEYC Standard 6: Becoming a Professional** (NAEYC, 2009).

Key elements:

6a: Identifying and involving oneself with the early childhood field

6b: Knowing about and upholding ethical guidelines and other professional standards

6c: Engaging in continuous, collaborative learning to inform practice

6d: Integrating knowledgeable, reflective, and critical perspectives on early education

6e: Engaging in informed advocacy for children and the profession

To Learn More

Join a Local Professional Association: Find out what professional associations have active chapters in your community (there may even be one on your college campus). Attend a meeting and join the association. Reflect on what you learn.

Create a 5-Year Plan: Consider your professional goals and create a 5-year plan for your career. Show it to a friend and/or a family member and talk to them about your plan. Take it to a college counselor and find out what kind of financial resources might be available to help make your plan a reality. Document what you have done.

Create a Professional Pledge: Read the section in this chapter on becoming a true professional and the NAEYC Statement of Commitment at the end of the Code of Ethical Conduct in Appendix A. Write your own professional pledge. Post it by your mirror or on your bulletin board and put it in your professional portfolio.

Read a Professional Journal or Publication: Read an issue of one or more of the professional publications listed below.

Child Care Information Exchange: ccie.com
Childhood Education: acei.org/childhood-education
Early Childhood Research and Practice: ecrp.uiuc.edu
Early Childhood Research Quarterly: naeyc.org/publications/ecrq
Journal of Early Intervention: jei.sagepub.com
Scholastic Early Childhood Today: http://teacher.scholastic.com/products/ect
Teaching Young Children naeyc.org/tyc
Young Children: journal.naeyc.org
Young Exceptional Children: yec.sagepub.com

Investigate Related Websites:

Alliance for Childhood: allianceforchildhood.org

Canadian Coalition for the Rights of Children: rightsofchildren.ca

Center for the Future of Children: futureofchildren.org

Child Rights Information Network: crin.org

Child Welfare League of America: cwla.org

Children Now: childrennow.org

Children's Defense Fund: childrensdefense.org

The Children's Foundation: childrensfoundation.inc.com

Prevent Child Abuse America: preventchildabuse.org

Save the Children: savethechildren.org

 **For Your Portfolio**

Clarify Your Position: Read and revise your autobiography, personal mission statement, and educational philosophy. Include the revised version in your portfolio.

Join Your Local Professional Association: Attend a meeting. Reflect on what you have done and what you learned for the professionalism section of your portfolio.

Document an Act of Advocacy: Write about a visit to a legislator, a public display of children's work, a letter to the editor, or some other advocacy of your choice.

MyEducationLab

Go to Topic 12: Professionalism/Ethics in the MyEducationLab (myeducationlab.com) for *Who Am I in the Lives of Children?* where you can:

- Find learning outcomes for Professionalism/Ethics along with the national standards that connect to these outcomes.
- Complete Assignments and Activities that can help you more deeply understand the chapter content.
- Apply and practice your understanding of the core teaching skills identified in the chapter with the Building Teaching Skills and Dispositions learning units.

- Access video clips of CCSSO National Teachers of the Year award winners responding to the question, "Why Do I Teach?" in the Teacher Talk section.
- Listen to experts from the field in Professional Perspectives.
- Check your comprehension on the content covered in the chapter with the Study Plan. Here you will be able to take a chapter quiz, receive feedback on your answers, and then access Review, Practice, and Enrichment activities to enhance your understanding of chapter content.

NAEYC Code of Ethical Conduct and Statement of Commitment

**A position statement
of the National Association
for the Education of Young Children**

Revised April 2005,
Reaffirmed and Updated May 2011

Endorsed by the Association for Childhood Education International

Adopted by the National Association for Family Child Care

Preamble

NAEYC recognizes that those who work with young children face many daily decisions that have moral and ethical implications. The **NAEYC Code of Ethical Conduct** offers guidelines for responsible behavior and sets forth a common basis for resolving the principal ethical dilemmas encountered in early childhood care and education. The **Statement of Commitment** is not part of the Code but is a personal acknowledgement of an individual's willingness to embrace the distinctive values and moral obligations of the field of early childhood care and education.

The primary focus of the Code is on daily practice with children and their families in programs for children from birth through 8 years of age, such as infant/toddler programs, preschool and prekindergarten programs, child care centers, hospital and child life settings, family child care homes, kindergartens, and primary classrooms. When the issues involve young children, then these provisions also apply to specialists who do not work directly with children, including program administrators, parent educators, early childhood adult educators, and officials with responsibility for program monitoring and licensing. (Note: See also the "Code of Ethical Conduct: Supplement for Early Childhood Adult Educators," online at www.naeyc.org/about/positions/pdf/ethics04.pdf and the "Code of Ethical Conduct: Supplement for Early Childhood Program Administrators," online at http://www.naeyc.org/files/naeyc/file/positions/PSETH05_supp.pdf)

Core values

Standards of ethical behavior in early childhood care and education are based on commitment to the following core values that are deeply rooted in the history of the field of early childhood care and education. We have made a commitment to

- Appreciate childhood as a unique and valuable stage of the human life cycle
- Base our work on knowledge of how children develop and learn
- Appreciate and support the bond between the child and family
- Recognize that children are best understood and supported in the context of family, culture,* community, and society
- Respect the dignity, worth, and uniqueness of each individual (child, family member, and colleague)
- Respect diversity in children, families, and colleagues
- Recognize that children and adults achieve their full potential in the context of relationships that are based on trust and respect

Conceptual framework

The Code sets forth a framework of professional responsibilities in four sections. Each section addresses an area of professional relationships: (1) with children, (2) with families, (3) among colleagues, and (4) with the community and society. Each section includes an

---

*The term *culture* includes ethnicity, racial identity, economic level, family structure, language, and religious and political beliefs, which profoundly influence each child's development and relationship to the world.

introduction to the primary responsibilities of the early childhood practitioner in that context. The introduction is followed by a set of ideals (I) that reflect exemplary professional practice and by a set of principles (P) describing practices that are required, prohibited, or permitted.

The **ideals** reflect the aspirations of practitioners. The **principles** guide conduct and assist practitioners in resolving ethical dilemmas.* Both ideals and principles are intended to direct practitioners to those questions which, when responsibly answered, can provide the basis for conscientious decision making. While the Code provides specific direction for addressing some ethical dilemmas, many others will require the practitioner to combine the guidance of the Code with professional judgment.

The ideals and principles in this Code present a shared framework of professional responsibility that affirms our commitment to the core values of our field. The Code publicly acknowledges the responsibilities that we in the field have assumed, and in so doing supports ethical behavior in our work. Practitioners who face situations with ethical dimensions are urged to seek guidance in the applicable parts of this Code and in the spirit that informs the whole.

Often "the right answer"—the best ethical course of action to take—is not obvious. There may be no readily apparent, positive way to handle a situation. When one important value contradicts another, we face an ethical dilemma. When we face a dilemma, it is our professional responsibility to consult the Code and all relevant parties to find the most ethical resolution.

Section I

Ethical Responsibilities to Children

Childhood is a unique and valuable stage in the human life cycle. Our paramount responsibility is to provide care and education in settings that are safe, healthy, nurturing, and responsive for each child. We are committed to supporting children's development and learning; respecting individual differences; and helping children learn to live, play, and work cooperatively. We are also committed to promoting children's self-awareness, competence, self-worth, resiliency, and physical well-being.

Ideals

I-1.1-To be familiar with the knowledge base of early childhood care and education and to stay informed through continuing education and training.

I-1.2-To base program practices upon current knowledge and research in the field of early childhood education, child development, and related disciplines, as well as on particular knowledge of each child.

I-1.3-To recognize and respect the unique qualities, abilities, and potential of each child.

I-1.4-To appreciate the vulnerability of children and their dependence on adults.

I-1.5-To create and maintain safe and healthy settings that foster children's social, emotional, cognitive, and physical development and that respect their dignity and their contributions.

I-1.6-To use assessment instruments and strategies that are appropriate for the children to be assessed, that are used only for the purposes for which they were designed, and that have the potential to benefit children.

I-1.7-To use assessment information to understand and support children's development and learning, to support instruction, and to identify children who may need additional services.

I-1.8-To support the right of each child to play and learn in an inclusive environment that meets the needs of children with and without disabilities.

I-1.9-To advocate for and ensure that all children, including those with special needs, have access to the support services needed to be successful.

I-1.10-To ensure that each child's culture, language, ethnicity, and family structure are recognized and valued in the program.

I-1.11-To provide all children with experiences in a language that they know, as well as support children in maintaining the use of their home language and in learning English.

I-1.12-To work with families to provide a safe and smooth transition as children and families move from one program to the next.

Principles

P-1.1-**Above all, we shall not harm children. We shall not participate in practices that are emotionally damaging, physically harmful, disrespectful, degrading, dangerous, exploitative, or intimidating to children. *This principle has precedence over all others in this Code.***

P-1.2-We shall care for and educate children in positive emotional and social environments that are cognitively stimulating and that support each child's culture, language, ethnicity, and family structure.

P-1.3-We shall not participate in practices that discriminate against children by denying benefits, giving special advantages, or excluding them from programs or activities on the basis of their sex, race, national origin, immigration status, preferred home language, religious beliefs, medical condition, disability, or the marital status/family structure, sexual orientation, or religious beliefs or other affiliations of their families. (Aspects of this principle do not apply in programs that have a lawful mandate to provide services to a particular population of children.)

---

*There is not necessarily a corresponding principle for each ideal.

P-1.4-We shall use two-way communications to involve all those with relevant knowledge (including families and staff) in decisions concerning a child, as appropriate, ensuring confidentiality of sensitive information. (See also P-2.4.)

P-1.5-We shall use appropriate assessment systems, which include multiple sources of information, to provide information on children's learning and development.

P-1.6-We shall strive to ensure that decisions such as those related to enrollment, retention, or assignment to special education services, will be based on multiple sources of information and will never be based on a single assessment, such as a test score or a single observation.

P-1.7-We shall strive to build individual relationships with each child; make individualized adaptations in teaching strategies, learning environments, and curricula; and consult with the family so that each child benefits from the program. If after such efforts have been exhausted, the current placement does not meet a child's needs, or the child is seriously jeopardizing the ability of other children to benefit from the program, we shall collaborate with the child's family and appropriate specialists to determine the additional services needed and/or the placement option(s) most likely to ensure the child's success. (Aspects of this principle may not apply in programs that have a lawful mandate to provide services to a particular population of children.)

P-1.8-We shall be familiar with the risk factors for and symptoms of child abuse and neglect, including physical, sexual, verbal, and emotional abuse and physical, emotional, educational, and medical neglect. We shall know and follow state laws and community procedures that protect children against abuse and neglect.

P-1.9-When we have reasonable cause to suspect child abuse or neglect, we shall report it to the appropriate community agency and follow up to ensure that appropriate action has been taken. When appropriate, parents or guardians will be informed that the referral will be or has been made.

P-1.10-When another person tells us of his or her suspicion that a child is being abused or neglected, we shall assist that person in taking appropriate action in order to protect the child.

P-1.11-When we become aware of a practice or situation that endangers the health, safety, or well-being of children, we have an ethical responsibility to protect children or inform parents and/or others who can.

Section II
Ethical Responsibilities to Families

Families* are of primary importance in children's development. Because the family and the early childhood practitioner have a common interest in the child's well-being, we acknowledge a primary responsibility to bring about communication, cooperation, and collaboration between the home and early childhood program in ways that enhance the child's development.

Ideals

I-2.1-To be familiar with the knowledge base related to working effectively with families and to stay informed through continuing education and training.

I-2.2-To develop relationships of mutual trust and create partnerships with the families we serve.

I-2.3-To welcome all family members and encourage them to participate in the program, including involvement in shared decision making.

I-2.4-To listen to families, acknowledge and build upon their strengths and competencies, and learn from families as we support them in their task of nurturing children.

I-2.5-To respect the dignity and preferences of each family and to make an effort to learn about its structure, culture, language, customs, and beliefs to ensure a culturally consistent environment for all children and families.

I-2.6-To acknowledge families' childrearing values and their right to make decisions for their children.

I-2.7-To share information about each child's education and development with families and to help them understand and appreciate the current knowledge base of the early childhood profession.

I-2.8-To help family members enhance their understanding of their children, as staff are enhancing their understanding of each child through communications with families, and support family members in the continuing development of their skills as parents.

I-2.9-To foster families' efforts to build support networks and, when needed, participate in building networks for families by providing them with opportunities to interact with program staff, other families, community resources, and professional services.

Principles

P-2.1-We shall not deny family members access to their child's classroom or program setting unless access is denied by court order or other legal restriction.

---

*The term *family* may include those adults, besides parents, with the responsibility of being involved in educating, nurturing, and advocating for the child.

P-2.2-We shall inform families of program philosophy, policies, curriculum, assessment system, cultural practices, and personnel qualifications, and explain why we teach as we do—which should be in accordance with our ethical responsibilities to children (see Section I).

P-2.3-We shall inform families of and, when appropriate, involve them in policy decisions. (See also I-2.3.)

P-2.4-We shall ensure that the family is involved in significant decisions affecting their child. (See also P-1.4.)

P-2.5-We shall make every effort to communicate effectively with all families in a language that they understand. We shall use community resources for translation and interpretation when we do not have sufficient resources in our own programs.

P-2.6-As families share information with us about their children and families, we shall ensure that families' input is an important contribution to the planning and implementation of the program.

P-2.7-We shall inform families about the nature and purpose of the program's child assessments and how data about their child will be used.

P-2.8-We shall treat child assessment information confidentially and share this information only when there is a legitimate need for it.

P-2.9-We shall inform the family of injuries and incidents involving their child, of risks such as exposures to communicable diseases that might result in infection, and of occurrences that might result in emotional stress.

P-2.10-Families shall be fully informed of any proposed research projects involving their children and shall have the opportunity to give or withhold consent without penalty. We shall not permit or participate in research that could in any way hinder the education, development, or well-being of children.

P-2.11-We shall not engage in or support exploitation of families. We shall not use our relationship with a family for private advantage or personal gain, or enter into relationships with family members that might impair our effectiveness working with their children.

P-2.12-We shall develop written policies for the protection of confidentiality and the disclosure of children's records. These policy documents shall be made available to all program personnel and families. Disclosure of children's records beyond family members, program personnel, and consultants having an obligation of confidentiality shall require familial consent (except in cases of abuse or neglect).

P-2.13-We shall maintain confidentiality and shall respect the family's right to privacy, refraining from disclosure of confidential information and intrusion into family life. However, when we have reason to believe that a child's welfare is at risk, it is permissible to share confidential information with agencies, as well as with individuals who have legal responsibility for intervening in the child's interest.

P-2.14-In cases where family members are in conflict with one another, we shall work openly, sharing our observations of the child, to help all parties involved make informed decisions. We shall refrain from becoming an advocate for one party.

P-2.15-We shall be familiar with and appropriately refer families to community resources and professional support services. After a referral has been made, we shall follow up to ensure that services have been appropriately provided.

Section III
Ethical Responsibilities to Colleagues

In a caring, cooperative workplace, human dignity is respected, professional satisfaction is promoted, and positive relationships are developed and sustained. Based upon our core values, our primary responsibility to colleagues is to establish and maintain settings and relationships that support productive work and meet professional needs. The same ideals that apply to children also apply as we interact with adults in the workplace. (Note: Section III includes responsibilities to co-workers and to employers. See the "Code of Ethical Conduct: Supplement for Early Childhood Program Administrators" for responsibilities to personnel (*employees* in the original 2005 Code revision), online at http://www.naeyc.org/files/naeyc/file/positions/PSETH05_supp.pdf.)

A—Responsibilities to co-workers
Ideals

I-3A.1-To establish and maintain relationships of respect, trust, confidentiality, collaboration, and cooperation with co-workers.

I-3A.2-To share resources with co-workers, collaborating to ensure that the best possible early childhood care and education program is provided.

I-3A.3-To support co-workers in meeting their professional needs and in their professional development.

I-3A.4-To accord co-workers due recognition of professional achievement.

Principles

P-3A.1-We shall recognize the contributions of colleagues to our program and not participate in practices that diminish their reputations or impair their effectiveness in working with children and families.

P-3A.2-When we have concerns about the professional behavior of a co-worker, we shall first let that person know of our concern in a way that shows respect for personal dignity and for the diversity to be found among staff members, and then attempt to resolve the matter collegially and in a confidential manner.

P-3A.3-We shall exercise care in expressing views regarding the personal attributes or professional conduct of co-workers. Statements should be based on firsthand knowledge, not hearsay, and relevant to the interests of children and programs.

P-3A.4-We shall not participate in practices that discriminate against a co-worker because of sex, race, national origin, religious beliefs or other affiliations, age, marital status/family structure, disability, or sexual orientation.

B—Responsibilities to employers

Ideals

I-3B.1-To assist the program in providing the highest quality of service.

I-3B.2-To do nothing that diminishes the reputation of the program in which we work unless it is violating laws and regulations designed to protect children or is violating the provisions of this Code.

Principles

P-3B.1-We shall follow all program policies. When we do not agree with program policies, we shall attempt to effect change through constructive action within the organization.

P-3B.2-We shall speak or act on behalf of an organization only when authorized. We shall take care to acknowledge when we are speaking for the organization and when we are expressing a personal judgment.

P-3B.3-We shall not violate laws or regulations designed to protect children and shall take appropriate action consistent with this Code when aware of such violations.

P-3B.4-If we have concerns about a colleague's behavior, and children's well-being is not at risk, we may address the concern with that individual. If children are at risk or the situation does not improve after it has been brought to the colleague's attention, we shall report the colleague's unethical or incompetent behavior to an appropriate authority.

P-3B.5-When we have a concern about circumstances or conditions that impact the quality of care and education within the program, we shall inform the program's administration or, when necessary, other appropriate authorities.

Section IV
Ethical Responsibilities to Community and Society

Early childhood programs operate within the context of their immediate community made up of families and other institutions concerned with children's welfare. Our responsibilities to the community are to provide programs that meet the diverse needs of families, to cooperate with agencies and professions that share the responsibility for children, to assist families in gaining access to those agencies and allied professionals, and to assist in the development of community programs that are needed but not currently available.

As individuals, we acknowledge our responsibility to provide the best possible programs of care and education for children and to conduct ourselves with honesty and integrity. Because of our specialized expertise in early childhood development and education and because the larger society shares responsibility for the welfare and protection of young children, we acknowledge a collective obligation to advocate for the best interests of children within early childhood programs and in the larger community and to serve as a voice for young children everywhere.

The ideals and principles in this section are presented to distinguish between those that pertain to the work of the individual early childhood educator and those that more typically are engaged in collectively on behalf of the best interests of children—with the understanding that individual early childhood educators have a shared responsibility for addressing the ideals and principles that are identified as "collective."

Ideal (Individual)

1-4.1-To provide the community with high-quality early childhood care and education programs and services.

Ideals (Collective)

I-4.2-To promote cooperation among professionals and agencies and interdisciplinary collaboration among professions concerned with addressing issues in the health, education, and well-being of young children, their families, and their early childhood educators.

I-4.3-To work through education, research, and advocacy toward an environmentally safe world in which all children receive health care, food, and shelter; are nurtured; and live free from violence in their home and their communities.

I-4.4-To work through education, research, and advocacy toward a society in which all young children have access to high-quality early care and education programs.

I-4.5-To work to ensure that appropriate assessment systems, which include multiple sources of information, are used for purposes that benefit children.

I-4.6-To promote knowledge and understanding of young children and their needs. To work toward greater societal acknowledgment of children's rights and greater social acceptance of responsibility for the well-being of all children.

I-4.7-To support policies and laws that promote the well-being of children and families, and to work to change those that impair their well-being. To participate in developing policies and laws that are needed, and to cooperate with families and other individuals and groups in these efforts.

I-4.8-To further the professional development of the field of early childhood care and education and to strengthen its commitment to realizing its core values as reflected in this Code.

Principles (Individual)

P-4.1-We shall communicate openly and truthfully about the nature and extent of services that we provide.

P-4.2-We shall apply for, accept, and work in positions for which we are personally well-suited and professionally qualified. We shall not offer services that we do not have the competence, qualifications, or resources to provide.

P-4.3-We shall carefully check references and shall not hire or recommend for employment any person whose competence, qualifications, or character makes him or her unsuited for the position.

P-4.4-We shall be objective and accurate in reporting the knowledge upon which we base our program practices.

P-4.5-We shall be knowledgeable about the appropriate use of assessment strategies and instruments and interpret results accurately to families.

P-4.6-We shall be familiar with laws and regulations that serve to protect the children in our programs and be vigilant in ensuring that these laws and regulations are followed.

P-4.7-When we become aware of a practice or situation that endangers the health, safety, or well-being of children, we have an ethical responsibility to protect children or inform parents and/or others who can.

P-4.8-We shall not participate in practices that are in violation of laws and regulations that protect the children in our programs.

P-4.9-When we have evidence that an early childhood program is violating laws or regulations protecting children, we shall report the violation to appropriate authorities who can be expected to remedy the situation.

P-4.10-When a program violates or requires its employees to violate this Code, it is permissible, after fair assessment of the evidence, to disclose the identity of that program.

Principles (Collective)

P-4.11-When policies are enacted for purposes that do not benefit children, we have a collective responsibility to work to change these policies.

P-4.12-When we have evidence that an agency that provides services intended to ensure children's well-being is failing to meet its obligations, we acknowledge a collective ethical responsibility to report the problem to appropriate authorities or to the public.

We shall be vigilant in our follow-up until the situation is resolved.

P-4.13-When a child protection agency fails to provide adequate protection for abused or neglected children, we acknowledge a collective ethical responsibility to work toward the improvement of these services.

Statement of Commitment*

As an individual who works with young children, I commit myself to furthering the values of early childhood education as they are reflected in the ideals and principles of the NAEYC Code of Ethical Conduct. To the best of my ability I will

Never harm children.

Ensure that programs for young children are based on current knowledge and research of child development and early childhood education.

Respect and support families in their task of nurturing children.

Respect colleagues in early childhood care and education and support them in maintaining the NAEYC Code of Ethical Conduct.

Serve as an advocate for children, their families, and their teachers in community and society.

Stay informed of and maintain high standards of professional conduct.

Engage in an ongoing process of self-reflection, realizing that personal characteristics, biases, and beliefs have an impact on children and families.

Be open to new ideas and be willing to learn from the suggestions of others.

Continue to learn, grow, and contribute as a professional.

Honor the ideals and principles of the NAEYC Code of Ethical Conduct.

---

*This Statement of Commitment is not part of the Code but is a personal acknowledgment of the individual's willingness to embrace the distinctive values and moral obligations of the field of early childhood care and education. It is recognition of the moral obligations that lead to an individual becoming part of the profession.

Glossary of Terms Related to Ethics

Code of Ethics — Defines the core values of the field and provides guidance for what professionals should do when they encounter conflicting obligations or responsibilities in their work.

Values — Qualities or principles that individuals believe to be desirable or worthwhile and that they prize for themselves, for others, and for the world in which they live.

Core Values — Commitments held by a profession that are consciously and knowingly embraced by its practitioners because they make a contribution to society. There is a difference between personal values and the core values of a profession.

Morality — Peoples' views of what is good, right, and proper; their beliefs about their obligations; and their ideas about how they should behave.

Ethics — The study of right and wrong, or duty and obligation, that involves critical reflection on morality and the ability to make choices between values and the examination of the moral dimensions of relationships.

Professional Ethics — The moral commitments of a profession that involve moral reflection that extends and enhances the personal morality practitioners bring to their work, that concern actions of right and wrong in the workplace, and that help individuals resolve moral dilemmas they encounter in their work.

Ethical Responsibilities — Behaviors that one must or must not engage in. Ethical responsibilities are clear-cut and are spelled out in the Code of Ethical Conduct (for example, early childhood educators should never share confidential information about a child or family with a person who has no legitimate need for knowing).

Ethical Dilemma — A moral conflict that involves determining appropriate conduct when an individual faces conflicting professional values and responsibilities.

Sources for Glossary Terms and Definitions

Feeney, S., & N. Freeman. 2005. *Ethics and the early childhood educator: Using the NAEYC code.* Washington, DC: NAEYC.

Kidder, R. M. 1995. *How good people make tough choices: Resolving the dilemmas of ethical living.* New York: Fireside.

Kipnis, K. 1987. How to discuss professional ethics. *Young Children* 42(4): 26–30.

Environment Checklists

Safety Checklist

This checklist can be used to evaluate the safety of an existing environment for children or to plan an environment.

Program _____ Date _____

Number of staff _____ Number of children _____ Age of children _____

Use the following code as appropriate: ✓ = yes/adequate, − = no/inadequate

General

_____ Program is licensed or meets licensing standards.

_____ Children are appropriately supervised at all times.

　　_____ Infants and toddlers are never left unattended, are always visible and within easy physical reach.

　　_____ Preschoolars are never left unattended and supervised by sight and sound.

　　_____ School-age children may work independently for brief periods if supervised by sight or sound.

_____ Building and equipment are structurally sound, free of rust, peeling paint, and splinters.

_____ Bolts and rough edges on equipment and furniture are recessed or covered.

_____ Entrances and yard are secure. Staff monitor anyone entering the facility.

_____ Arrival and departure procedures ensure children are safe from traffic and from leaving with unauthorized persons.

_____ Sign-in/out procedure is followed and well known to staff and families.

_____ Inside and outside are free of debris and standing water.

_____ Sharp tools and utensils, glass items, and bleach spray are out of children's reach.

_____ Medicines, cleansers, pesticides, aerosol sprays, and other poisonous items are locked out of children's reach.

_____ Stairs, ramps, lofts, decks, and platforms above 20″ have stable guard railings.

_____ Stairs, ramps, lofts, and platforms are kept free of toys and clutter.

_____ Equipment is free of entrapment hazards (openings are less than 3.5″ in width or more than 9″).

_____ Equipment and furniture are appropriately sized for the children enrolled.

_____ Pathways between play areas (both indoors and outdoors) are kept clear of toys and equipment to prevent tripping.

_____ Kitchen, storage closets, gardening sheds, adult bathrooms, and other areas with hazardous materials are secured from children.

_____ A procedure for regularly surveying and maintaining program safety is in place.

_____ Shooting or projectile toys are not permitted.

_____ Plastic bags are kept out of children's reach; balloons are not allowed at any time.

Emergency Prevention and Preparation

___ A telephone is accessible with emergency numbers posted nearby; the address and phone number of the facility is posted.

___ A staff member with current training in pediatric first aid and CPR is always on-site when children are present.

___ There is a procedure for handling first aid emergencies and staff are familiar with it.

___ A first aid kit is adequately stocked, easily available, and marked for visibility.

___ A first aid kit is carried on trips.

___ A first aid handbook is available.

___ Injury reports are written and an injury log is kept.

___ A plan for handling medical emergencies is in place and is known to all staff.

___ Emergency exits are clearly marked and free of clutter.

___ An emergency evacuation plan is posted. The fire department has evaluated it.

___ Emergency evacuation procedures are practiced monthly.

___ Emergency procedures include a plan for children with special needs.

___ A plan for civil defense emergencies exists and is known by staff and families.

___ Smoke detectors are installed and functional.

___ A fire extinguisher is available in each room, is annually tested, and staff know how to use it.

___ A plan exists for safe classroom coverage in case a child or teacher must be taken to the hospital.

___ When children are transported by the program they are appropriately, legally, and safely restrained in vehicles.

Inside

___ Environment is arranged so all areas can be easily supervised.

___ Furniture is stable.

___ AV equipment and equipment carts are secured so that they cannot be tipped over. They are put away when not in use.

___ Equipment is unbroken and in good working order.

___ Low windows, doors, and mirrors have safety glass or Plexiglas.

___ Glass doors and floor-level windows have stickers to ensure that people do not walk into them.

___ Heaters, radiators, pipes, and hot-water tanks are inaccessible to children.

___ Hot-water taps are turned off or are below 120°F so that hot water does not scald.

___ Stable, nonskid stools are provided if children must use high toilets, sinks, or water fountains.

___ Furniture is stable; high, unsecured shelves are not used.

___ Unused electric outlets are covered in programs for children under the age of 5.

___ Electric cords do not cross pathways or run under rugs.

___ Rugs are secured or backed with nonskid material and edges do not create a tripping hazard.

___ Floors where water is used and entrances have nonskid surfaces.

Outside

___ Outdoor play area is protected by fences and has childproof gates.

___ No poisonous plants grow in the yard.

___ A well-stocked first aid kit is available in the outdoor area.

___ Permanent outdoor equipment is securely anchored and movable equipment is stable.

___ There is manufactured rubberized surfacing in good condition or approximately 12″ of noncompacted sand, wood chips, or pea gravel beneath all climbing, swinging, and sliding equipment extending through fall zones.

___ Slides and climbing structures do not exceed safe height limitations (2 × the height of the average child).

___ Swings are attached with closed fasteners, not open S hooks.

___ Swing seats are constructed of soft or lightweight material.

___ Swings are away from pathways, and barriers prevent children from walking into the path of a swing.

___ Metal slides are located so that they are shaded or facing away from the midday sun to prevent burns.

___ Equipment has no places where pinching or crushing of fingers can occur.

Special Precautions in Infant-Toddler Programs

____ Cribs and gates have slats less than 2⅜" apart.

____ Cribs and childgates have locking devices that work.

____ Cribs meet 2011 CPSC Standards.

____ Furniture that can be climbed is securely anchored.

____ Furniture has rounded edges or edges are cushioned.

____ Mattresses fit snugly in cribs.

____ Dangling strings do not hang from cribs, playpens, curtains, etc.

____ There are no dangling appliance cords.

____ Strollers and carriages are stable, have workable restraining straps, and have adequate brakes.

____ Toys are at least 1½" in diameter.

____ Stairway gates are locked when children are present.

____ Separate space is set aside for nonmobile infants.

____ An adult keeps at least one hand on a child on a changing table at all times.

____ Infants and toddlers are visually supervised by adults when sleeping.

Health Checklist

This checklist can be used to evaluate the healthfulness of an existing environment for children or to plan an environment.

Program _____ Date _____

Number of staff _____ Number of children _____ Age of children _____

Use the following code as appropriate: ✓ = yes/adequate, − = no/inadequate

Policies and Procedures

____ Program is licensed or meets licensing standards.
____ Health records:
    ____ are on file for every child and are well-organized and accessible.
    ____ document current immunizations, screenings, and health examinations.
    ____ when appropriate, contain instructions for meeting special health needs or chronic health conditions.
    ____ include current contact information for emergencies including the child's health care provider.
____ Families complete a health history prior to enrollment.
____ The program has a written agreement with a health consultant who is either a licensed pediatric health professional or a health professional with specific training in health consultation for early childhood programs.
____ A basic manual of childhood health and disease is available.
____ Program has written health policies, developed in collaboration with a health care professional, which are given to staff and parents.
____ There is a written policy describing when children must be excluded from the program because of illness; this policy is available to families and staff.
____ A policy and procedure exists for isolating sick children within the setting; a comfortable space is available for ill children where they can be supervised by staff.

The Environment

____ Clean drinking water is available to children at all times.
____ Toilet facilities are clean and easily accessible to children at all times.
____ Tissue, soap, paper towels, and toilet paper are available where children can reach them.
____ A sign showing proper handwashing procedures is posted at every adult sink.
____ Classroom areas and materials are cleaned and sanitized in accordance with the guidelines described in Table 7.2 on page 243.
____ Windows and doors are opened regularly to let out pollutants.
____ Room temperature and humidity are maintained at a comfortable level.
____ Air conditioners, air filters, humidifiers, and dehumidifiers are cleaned often to minimize pollutants.
____ Animal cages are cleaned frequently and regularly as needed.
____ The building has been assessed for lead, radon, and asbestos, and if warranted action has been taken to prevent children and adults for coming in contact with these substances.
____ The facility and outdoor play areas are entirely smoke-free.

Health Practices

____ Handwashing procedures are known and practiced by adults and children.

____ Children are instructed in handwashing procedures and assisted as necessary.

____ Children and adults wash their hands after toileting and before handling food.

____ Children's clothes are changed as necessary. There are extra clean clothes kept for children.

____ Soiled clothes are stored in closed plastic bags away from children's play areas.

____ Toys are washed and sanitized every time they are soiled or mouthed.

____ Nutritious foods are chosen for meals, snacks, and cooking activities.

____ Staff do not offer children younger than 4 years these foods: hot dogs, whole or sliced into rounds; whole grapes; nuts; popcorn; marshmallows, gummy candy; spoonfuls of peanut butter; or chunks of raw carrots, apples, or meat larger than can be swallowed whole.

____ Food is not withheld as punishment or used as a reward.

____ Tables are cleaned and sanitized prior to meals, snack, and food preparation.

____ Children brush their teeth after meals.

____ Toothbrushes are stored hygienically.

____ Clean, individual napping arrangements are available for each child.

____ Trash cans are lined, kept covered, and emptied daily.

____ Children wear clothing that is dry and layered for warmth in cold weather.

____ Children have the opportunity to play in the shade. When in the sun, they wear sun-protective clothing, applied sunscreen, or both.

Practices Specific to Infant-Toddler Programs

____ Healthful diapering procedures are known and practiced.

____ Changing tables are covered with paper during use and cleaned with disinfecting solution after each use.

____ Bottles are kept refrigerated.

____ Pedal-opening trash cans are available for diaper disposal.

____ Daily records are kept on children's food intake, elimination, and other health concerns. This information is shared with parents.

____ Breast-feeding is supported: a comfortable place for breast-feeding is provided; human milk is stored and served in a manner that preserves its nutrients.

____ Infants unable to sit are held for bottle-feeding. All others sit or are held to be fed. Infants and toddlers/twos do not have bottles while in a crib or bed and do not eat from propped bottles at any time. Toddlers/twos do not carry bottles, sippy cups, or regular cups with them while crawling or walking.

____ Each child has individual sleeping arrangements and bedding; linens are changed at least weekly or when necessary.

____ Infants are placed on their backs to sleep on a firm surface; pillows, quilts, comforters, sheepskins, stuffed toys, and other soft items are not allowed in cribs or rest equipment for infants younger than 8 months.

____ After each feeding, infants' teeth and gums are wiped with a disposable tissue or individual clean soft cloth.

Infant-Toddler Learning Environment Checklist

Use this checklist to evaluate an existing environment for a group of infants or toddlers or to plan one. No program will have everything, but the * items are essential and are found in most high-quality programs.

Program _____ Date _____

Number of staff _____ Number of children _____ Age of children _____

Use the following code as appropriate: ✓ = yes/adequate, – = no/inadequate

Indoor Environment

Space

____ clearly defined "home" space separate from other groups/classes*

____ 35 square feet per child*

____ arrangement of space allows one adult to see all of the children, all of the time*

____ drinking water, sinks, and toilets accessible*

____ sheltered from outside noise and stimulus*

____ ventilated and temperature controlled as needed*

____ well lit with natural light if possible*

____ "wet regions" (entrances, eating areas) have waterproof, easy-to-clean, uncarpeted floors

____ "dry regions" (e.g., sleeping and play areas) have clean, comfortable floor coverings

____ access for individuals (children, family members, visitors, or staff) who use walkers or wheelchairs

Areas

____ changing and dressing area away from eating and play areas*

____ sleeping /quiet area*

____ food preparation/eating area*

____ arrival and departure area where families enter and exit*

____ flexible central area*

For infant rooms

____ protected area for nonmobile infants*

____ play areas for mobile children

For toddlers and twos rooms

____ toys area

____ table area

____ book area

____ pretending area

____ sensory play area

Indoor Equipment and Materials

Arrival and Departure Area

____ child-safe gates/doors*

____ bulletin boards and mailboxes for communication between families and staff*

____ clock and sign-in

____ cubby shelf labeled with children's names and pictures*

____ adult-sized chair or sofa nearby

____ good-bye window—place where children can watch family depart

Food Preparation/Eating Area*

____ adult-height counter/table for preparing food*

____ cabinets or shelves for equipment and supplies labeled to facilitate cleanup

____ sink for washing hands and rinsing dishes* (dishwasher or triple sink if dishes washed)

____ appliances (refrigerator, stove, or microwave)*

____ at least one child-safe locked cupboard

____ clipboard or notebook to record eating

____ dishes, pots, pans, etc.*

____ cleanup equipment such as sponges, brooms, mops, etc.*

For infant rooms

____ adult seating for comfortably holding and feeding/nursing children*

For toddlers and twos rooms

____ toddler-sized tables and chairs

Sleeping Area*

____ mirrors, pictures, mobiles, etc., where children can see them*
____ labeled storage for shelves/bins for bedding and toys from home
____ rocking chair*
____ clipboard or notebook to record sleeping

For infant rooms

____ cribs or other safe, culturally appropriate sleeping arrangements for infants*

For toddlers and twos rooms

____ mats or cots

Diapering/Changing/Toileting Area*

____ sturdy adult-height counter or changing table* with stairs that roll in and out
____ shelf above or beside changing table for easy organization for ointments, etc.*
____ adult-height sinks, with warm water for handwashing
____ large/deep sink for bathing children
____ paper towel dispenser that can be used with one hand
____ labeled boxes or bins for each child's diapers and clothes*
____ plastic bags for soiled diapers and clothes*
____ lidded garbage can for soiled diapers*
____ clipboard or notebook to record diapering/toileting*
____ area clean and pleasant*

For toddlers and twos rooms

____ low toilets and sinks for toddlers or stable step stools to make toilets and sinks accessible*
____ place for another child to sit/watch nearby.

Flexible Central Play Area

____ clean carpeted floors
____ steps, stable sofas, cruise bars, platforms, or climbers*
____ dumping containers (baskets, buckets)
____ clean cages or aquariums for pets*
____ plants/animals fed, watered, protected*
____ unbreakable mirrors*
____ toys are:
    ____ large enough to be easily grasped
    ____ light enough to be lifted
    ____ soft enough not to hurt
    ____ strong enough to be dropped, stepped on, or thrown

For infant rooms

____ materials for play and exploration placed along the perimeter to bring into the larger space
____ several play spaces for mobile children
____ low barriers for protection for nonmobile infants if room includes both nonmobile and mobile infants
____ couches or low tables that provide handholds

For toddlers and twos rooms

____ movable climber or platform
____ no high and unstable shelves
____ shelves secured so they do not tip

Sensory Play Area*

____ table and chairs for messy play
____ toddler-sized water table
____ sand/water play with lots of containers*
____ rhythm instruments
____ clay and dough
____ paint
____ soap and goop

Toys*

____ "peek-a-boo" toys
____ animal figures
____ boxes with lids
____ busy boxes
____ complete puzzles with 1–8 pieces*
____ homemade toys
____ interlocking blocks like Duplos
____ jack-in-the-box
____ jumbo wooden beads with strings
____ large snap beads
____ mobiles
____ music boxes
____ nesting containers (plastic bowls, cups)
____ pegboards and pegs (jumbo size)
____ pop-up toys
____ pull toys
____ rattles and bells
____ shape-sorting boxes
____ simple one-piece knobbed puzzles
____ simple-to-put-together toys
____ squeeze toys
____ stacking toys
____ table blocks
____ texture balls
____ toys for sucking and teething
____ toy vehicles
____ low, open shelves for storage of materials*

Books*

____ cloth or cardboard picture books*
____ picture collections (mounted and covered)
____ a variety of styles of illustration*
____ homemade books with photographs of the children and things they know*
____ new and classic books
____ baskets or wall pockets to hold books
____ simple stories with plots
____ multiethnic and multiage nonstereotyped characters*
____ not based on commercial products
____ nursery rhymes
____ wordless books and books with text
____ mood and concept books*
____ sturdy books that are not board books
____ clean pillows and carpets
____ soft, large chairs/couch for adults and children to sit together

Active Play*

____ push and pull toys
____ small climber with slide
____ tunnel (purchased or homemade)
____ large boxes to crawl through
____ cars and trucks
____ wagons and buggies to push and pull
____ soft balls of various sizes
____ soft pillows to climb on
____ duplicates of toys and several choices (2–3) per child

Additional Areas for Older Toddlers and Twos

These areas can be separate for older toddlers and twos or may be incorporated into the play zones as for younger toddlers.

Block area

____ posters or photographs of buildings
____ low, open shelves where blocks can be stored*
____ low napped carpet or clean floor*
____ unit blocks (100 blocks in 5–10 shapes)
____ large figures (animals/people) and vehicles
____ table blocks
____ large soft blocks

____ if space allows, 20+ cardboard, plastic, or light wood hollow blocks
____ blocks clean and unsplintered

Art area

____ painting surfaces—table, wall, or easel (toddler-sized)
____ low tables and chairs*
____ nontoxic, washable paints in at least primary colors (red, yellow, blue), black, and white*
____ brushes in a variety of sizes: wide and narrow with short handles*
____ base or paint for finger painting*
____ dough boards and tools*
____ large paper for easel painting*
____ white paper, clean on one side*
____ recycled materials (card, Styrofoam, paper, ribbons, fabric, plastic jars and lids)*
____ large nontoxic unwrapped crayons and felt pens
____ bowls, spoons, and measuring tools
____ collection of textured materials (fabrics, etc.)
____ yarn, string, ribbons
____ smocks or old shirts (to protect clothing)*
____ clay boards and clay tools*
____ special papers (construction, tissue)
____ trays and plastic cups or containers*
____ potter's clay
____ play dough*
____ white glue and paste*

Pretending area

____ child-sized table and chairs*
____ area "bed" or crib mattress for a child and dolls
____ open shelves for storage*
____ small open cupboard without doors that pinch fingers
____ full-length unbreakable mirror
____ cloths and props that reflect children's families*
____ uniforms, clothes, and props that reflect a variety of cultures, jobs, and fantasy roles*
____ two telephones*
____ pots and pans
____ unbreakable dishes
____ large wooden or plastic utensils
____ pictures depicting family life and other scenes

Indoor Organization and Aesthetics

____ orderly and attractive*
____ neutral color walls
____ shelves close to play areas*
____ sets of toys stored separately, not jumbled*
____ toys and books are in good condition*
____ toys and books are neat and orderly*

____ shelves labeled with pictures
____ floor and table coverings (plastic or old tablecloths) available
____ clutter minimized*
____ duplicates of items and several choices (2–3) per child

____ extra materials stored and rotated
____ patterns, colors, and storage coordinate
____ no promotional or media products or characters
____ items of beauty such as flowers, plants, or sculpture
____ pictures and displays at infant and toddler eye-level*

____ wall hangings (textured and touchable)
____ areas decorated with art prints, photographs, children's work, book covers, and displays
____ pictures reflect culture and characteristics of children and families
____ record/tape player and recordings* appropriate (e.g., soothing music for nap)

Outdoor Environment

Space

____ fenced for protection*
____ 75 square feet of outside play space for each child playing outside at any one time
____ gates with child-safe locks*
____ located near indoor environment
____ access to toilets and sinks*
____ natural features (e.g. boulders, hills, and trees)
____ shelter from sun, wind, rain*
____ hard surface for vehicles away from other play
____ levels and textures to touch, crawl, climb on*
____ comfortable places to sit and lie*
____ access to water for drinking and play*

Outside play space for infants

____ designated outdoor play space for infants separate from areas for older children*
____ separation for nonmobile children*
____ shaded

Outside play environment for infants and toddlers

____ designated outdoor play space for toddlers separate from areas for older children

Outdoor Equipment and Materials

____ equipment scaled to children
____ equipment for climbing, sliding, swinging with safe surfacing underneath

____ large playground balls that bounce*
____ water play toys (cups/spoons, basters, funnels, pitchers, tubing, water wheels, etc.)
____ sand toys (cups/spoons, pots, cars, buckets, trowels, etc.)
____ wading pool

For infants

____ blankets to lie on
____ light catchers and wind chimes hung in trees

For toddlers and twos

____ tables for outdoor table activities
____ space for art
____ a line/rack to hang clothes and artwork
____ a covered sandbox or alternative
____ wagons and buggies to push and pull
____ toddler-height sand/water table or tub
____ shed or other secure storage for outdoor supplies
____ natural or manufactured balance beams
____ mud toys (shovels, pots, pans, buckets, trowels)
____ riding toys to propel by feet
____ storage for vehicles
____ wheeled pushing, pulling, and child-sized riding vehicles

Outdoor Organization and Aesthetics

____ water, sand, mud toys separate from one another
____ storage near the sand, water, mud areas for toys*

____ toys arranged in an orderly and attractive manner

Time

____ daily opportunity to play outside (weather permitting)*
____ infants regulate their own schedule*

____ toddlers' schedules flexible with general times for predictable routines*

Preschool/Kindergarten Learning Environment Checklist

Use this checklist to evaluate an existing environment for a group of preschoolers or kindergartners or to plan one. No program will have everything, but the * items are essential and are found in most high-quality preschool and kindergarten programs.

Program _____ Date _____

Number of staff _____ Number of children _____ Age of children _____

Use the following code as appropriate: ✓ = yes/adequate, − = no/inadequate

Indoor Environment

Space

_____ clearly defined "home" space*
_____ 35 square feet per child*
_____ arranged in learning centers* using partial seclusion with shelves and dividers
_____ arranged for easy supervision (one adult can supervise children by sight and sound)*
_____ noisy and quiet areas are separate
_____ paths do not lead through centers*
_____ extra space for centers that children use in groups—blocks, dramatic play, manipulative toys
_____ all areas useful (no "dead" space)*
_____ sheltered from outside noise and stimulus
_____ well lit* with natural light if possible
_____ ventilated* and temperature controlled
_____ drinking water, sinks, and toilets accessible*
_____ no corridors (long and narrow paths) or racetracks (circular paths around shelves or tables)
_____ "wet regions" (entrances, art, eating) have waterproof, easy-to-clean, uncarpeted floors
_____ "dry regions" (e.g., blocks, dramatic play) have clean, comfortable floor coverings
_____ access for individuals (children, family members, visitors, or staff) who use walkers or wheelchairs

Learning Centers/Areas Include . . .

_____ arrival/departure
_____ unit blocks*
_____ hollow blocks
_____ library*
_____ dramatic play*
_____ toys and games*
_____ art*
_____ writing*
_____ discovery (science, math, social studies)
_____ woodworking (may be outdoors)
_____ private area for children
_____ outside play environment*
_____ space for large group gathering*
_____ indoor space for messy activities* where climate requires*
_____ indoor space for active play where climate requires*
_____ space for eating snacks/meals*
_____ space for resting (* in full-day programs)
_____ shelf tops uncluttered
_____ space for small group gathering*

Indoor Equipment and Materials

Arrival and Departure Area

_____ child-safe gates/doors*
_____ bulletin boards and mailboxes for communication between families and staff*
_____ clock and sign-in
_____ cubby shelf for children's things labeled with names and pictures*
_____ adult-sized chair or sofa nearby

Pretend (Dramatic Play) Area*

_____ located near hollow block area if possible
_____ child-sized table and 2–4 chairs*

_____ small cupboard with doors
_____ pretend stove/sink unit or alternative that can serve different functions*
_____ open shelves with bins or baskets, or hooks to hang clothes on the wall
_____ containers/shelves for materials that are always out, labeled with words and pictures
_____ full-length unbreakable mirror
_____ dress-up clothes and props for both boys and girls*
_____ uniforms, clothes, and props reflecting families, cultures, jobs, and fantasy roles*

_____ clothes and props reflect the families, cultures, community and locale of children
_____ common objects of daily life such as kitchenware, books, furnishings, and tools
_____ two telephones*
_____ multiracial dolls
_____ sturdy "bed" to hold a child and dolls
_____ pictures depicting family life and other scenes
_____ extra props stored in sturdy, attractive, lidded boxes organized by occupation, situation, or role and rotated with children's interests and topics of study

Manipulative Toys and Games Area*

_____ space for at least 4 children to play, building toys separate from table games if possible
_____ trays, mats, or table space for work
_____ low, open shelves for storage close to work space*
_____ comfortable carpet or low tables and chairs*
_____ building toys, such as Legos, hexagonal builders, Tinkertoys—sets stored separately
_____ math manipulatives like parquetry blocks, Cuisenaire rods, and interlocking cubes—sets stored separately
_____ complete puzzles with 8–25 pieces*
_____ collection such as buttons or caps
_____ complete concept games/workjobs— manufactured or teacher-made
_____ no battery-operated toys of any kind
_____ containers/shelves labeled with words and pictures
_____ trays or space where children can save and display completed work

Unit Block Area*

_____ space for at least 4 children to build*
_____ 100–150 clean and unsplintered hardwood unit blocks* for 3- to 4-year-olds; 200–700 for 5- to 6-year-olds
_____ 14–25 block shapes
_____ low, open shelves for storage of blocks*
_____ low-napped carpet or clean floor*
_____ blocks stored so that each type of block has its own individual place* clearly marked with an outline
_____ blocks with similar qualities are near each other, placed so that the ways blocks differ is easily seen
_____ posters or photographs and books about buildings
_____ toy vehicles, street signs, dollhouses, small human and animal figures, tree blocks, and other props
_____ special storage baskets and separate labeled space on the shelves for props*

Hollow Block Area

_____ space for at least 4 children to build inside, on a covered porch, or outside in a sheltered location
_____ located near dramatic play area if inside
_____ at least 17 clean and unsplintered hollow blocks* and 6 planks
_____ low-napped carpet or soft surfacing to limit noise and prevent damage to the blocks*
_____ stacking space for all blocks* on the floor or on shelves
_____ hats, sheets, and lengths of fabric as props*

Art Area*

_____ closed or covered storage for materials available to adults
_____ shelves for materials available to children
_____ an easel adjusted so the smallest child can reach the top of one side*
_____ low tables and chairs* that may be dirtied or are easily cleaned
_____ different kinds of paint including: easel paints in at least primary colors, black, and white;* liquid and cake watercolors; finger paint
_____ brushes in a variety of sizes*
_____ wide-weave fabric
_____ clay boards and clay tools
_____ for drawing: nontoxic felt pens,* unwrapped nontoxic crayons,* chalk
_____ play dough
_____ large paper for easel painting*
_____ scissors that can be easily used by children in either hand*
_____ dough boards and tools
_____ recycled materials (cardboard, Styrofoam, wrapping paper, fabric, plastic jars and lids)*
_____ collectiion of textured materials and fabric
_____ yarn, string, ribbons
_____ smocks or old shirts (to protect clothing)
_____ base or paint for finger painting*
_____ food color
_____ potter's clay*
_____ white glue and paste*
_____ white paper, clean on one side*
_____ trays and plastic cups or containers*
_____ bowls, spoons, and measuring tools
_____ special papers (construction, tissue)
_____ items of beauty to inspire
_____ floor/table coverings available

Library*

____ separate, quiet area*

____ comfortable, clean pillows and carpets or chairs where children can sit and read*

____ low bookshelf that displays covers*

____ big, comfortable chair or couch where an adult can sit with a child and read

____ even lighting*

____ many books* . . .

    ____ appropriate for developmental stage*

    ____ a variety of styles of illustration*

    ____ multiethnic and multiage characters in nonstereotyped roles*

    ____ females and males in various roles*

    ____ not based on commercial products

    ____ fiction: realistic and fantasy*

    ____ informataional books*

    ____ mood and concept books*

    ____ poetry*

    ____ new and classic books*

    ____ child-authored books

    ____ listening center with book-tape sets

    ____ big books and a big-book shelf

____ books in good condition* or repaired

____ decorated with book jackets/posters and reading-related art prints

____ listening center with books on tape

____ puppets, props, and flannelboard for storytelling

Writing Center*

____ even lighting*

____ child-sized table and chairs*

____ storage shelf close to table*

____ peeled crayons*

____ nontoxic felt marking pens*

____ hole punch

____ rulers, protractors

____ sharpened primary pencils*

____ paper cut in uniform sizes*

____ yarn

____ recycled envelopes

____ baskets, jars, cans for pens, crayons, etc.*

Discovery Center*

____ located near window*

____ located near sink

____ low table or counter*

____ tables and chairs

____ water/sand table* (may be found outside or in sensory play area—tubs/basins may be used instead)

____ plastic tubs and pitchers*

____ measuring cups/spoons

____ balance and scale

____ photographs and posters to illustrate concepts

____ information books* (may be in library)

____ sorting collections (buttons, rocks, etc.)

____ materials with sequence and proportion

____ math manipulatives (may be in manipulative toys/games) attribute beads or blocks, Cuisenaire rods, colored cubes, etc.

____ concept games and puzzles (may be in manipulative toys/games)

____ globes and maps

____ magnifying glass*

____ trays*

____ machinery to investigate and disassemble

____ aquariums and animal cages

____ airtight containers for storage

____ probes

____ photographs and posters that illustrate concepts

Sensory Play Area*

____ located near sink or outside*

____ sand/water table

____ light table

____ low, open shelves for storage of materials*

____ table and chairs

____ basins or tubs*

____ bowls, cups, and buckets

____ ladles, measuring cups, and pitchers

____ funnels, basters, whisks, and eggbeaters

____ eyedroppers and translucent ice-cube trays for light table

____ aprons or waterproof smocks*

____ plastic tablecloths or shower curtains

____ water*

____ natural materials: sand, dirt, mud*

____ modeling materials*: dough, clay (may be in art area)

____ dry materials: sawdust and aquarium gravel if appropriate; rice, beans, macaroni, oatmeal

____ mixtures: cornstarch and water, "super sand" and "flubber"

____ food color

____ dishwashing liquid

____ clear colored toys for light table

____ tablemats or trays for modeling work

Woodworking Area

____ sturdy workbench and platform for shorter children to stand on*

____ sawing table children can kneel on

____ storage rack for tools close to table,* with tools arranged in an orderly manner (e.g., a storage rack labeled with pictures and words)*

____ 3 pairs of safety glasses* (1 for teacher, 2 for children) with adjustable nonelastic strap

____ tools:

    ____ C clamps or small bar clamp

    ____ 2 lightweight hammers

____ 1 regular adult hammer*

____ hacksaw and extra blades

____ small crosscut saw

____ 2 bit braces and drill bits, auger bits, and Phillips bits

____ flat-head screwdriver

____ 2 Phillips screwdrivers

____ rasp and file

____ 25″ tape measure

____ a speed square

____ supplies:

    ____ screws, nails, and glue

    ____ sandpaper

    ____ percils

    ____ soft untreated wood such as pine or fir (not particle board)*

____ storage boxes for wood pieces*

Indoor Organization and Aesthetics

____ room is orderly and attractive*

____ clutter minimized*

____ neutral color walls

____ patterns, colors, and storage coordinate

____ each center has equipment/materials complete, working, and in good condition

____ animals are fed, have water, and are protected in clean cages or aquariums*

____ plants are cared for*

____ shelves, floors, and carpeting are clean

____ high or closed secure storage for staff personal items*

____ locked cabinet for hazardous materials*

____ shelves labeled with pictures

____ sets of toys stored separately, not jumbled*

____ toys and books are in good condition*

____ toys and books are neat and orderly*

____ areas decorated with art prints, photographs, children's work, book covers, and displays

____ some pictures reflect culture and characteristics of children and families

____ most pictures and displays at child's eye-level*

____ items of beauty such as flowers, plants, or sculpture

____ provision of appropriate music (e.g., soothing music for naps)

____ no promotional or media products or characters

____ floor and table coverings (plastic or old tablecloths) available

____ extra materials stored and rotated

Outdoor Environment

Space

____ fenced for protection*

____ 75 square feet of outside play space for each child playing outside at any one time

____ gates with child-safe locks*

____ located near indoor environment

____ access to toilets and sinks*

____ large grassy areas for running

____ natural features (e.g., plants, grass, boulders, hills, and trees)

____ shelter from sun, wind, rain*

____ hard surface for vehicles away from other play

____ levels and textures to touch, crawl, climb on*

____ comfortable places to sit and lie*

____ access to water for drinking and play*

Zones/Areas Include . . .

____ transition*

____ manipulative-creative

____ physical/active play*

____ natural elements*

____ social-dramatic

Outdoor Equipment and Materials

Transition Zone

_____ benches, tires, steps, or the edge of a wall for children to wait, gather, or see what is available and make choices*

_____ parking area for trikes, scooters, and wagons; vehicles near the entrance to the riding area

_____ storage for trikes and wagons* (may be in physical/active play zone)

Manipulative-Creative Zone

_____ tables and chairs for outdoor table activities*

_____ easels*

_____ woodworking table

_____ a line/rack to hang clothes and artwork*

Physical/Active Play Zone

_____ climbing or "super-structure*" for climbing, sliding

_____ swings

_____ surfacing underneath and to 6″ beyond structures (10″ sand, wood chips, etc., or 2″ rubber matting)*

_____ portable equipment for building and climbing

_____ natural or manufactured balance beams*

_____ materials to encourage active play: hoops, parachutes, rope

_____ trikes and wagons sized for the children*

_____ varied sizes of balls that bounce*

_____ baskets and bags or other containers for ball storage

Natural Elements Zone

_____ logs, smooth boulders

_____ bench or other place to sit

_____ a covered sandbox or appropriate alternative*

_____ sand/water table or large tub*

_____ clean sand in plentiful supply*

_____ clean water in plentiful supply*

_____ dirt/mud for digging*

_____ a place to garden

_____ a bird feeder, bird bath

_____ pets—if weather permits

_____ sand toys (cups/spoons, pots, cars, buckets, trowels, etc.)*

_____ water play toys (cups/spoons, basters, funnels, pitchers, tubing, water wheels, etc.)*

_____ mud toys (shovels, pots and pans, buckets, trowels)

_____ water, sand, mud toys kept separate from one another

_____ hoses and big buckets*

_____ kits for bubble play

Social-Dramatic Play Zone

_____ playhouse or alternative

_____ dress-up clothes and props

_____ "loose parts" (hollow blocks, sheets, small tires, planks, and other movable items)

_____ a vehicle path

Outdoor Organization and Aesthetics

_____ yard is orderly and attractive*

_____ clutter minimized*

_____ equipment/materials complete, working, and in good condition

_____ animals are fed, have water, and are protected in clean cages or aquariums*

_____ plants are cared for*

_____ locked storage for hazardous materials*

_____ storage labeled with pictures

_____ toys stored in an organized manner*

_____ toys and books in good condition*

_____ items of beauty such as flowers, plants, or sculpture

_____ no promotional or media products or characters

Time

_____ daily opportunity to play outside (weather permitting) at least 1 hour in morning and afternoon*

_____ large blocks of time for child-selected activity indoors and outside (at least 1 hour in morning and afternoon)*

_____ quiet, sedentary activities alternated with active play

_____ structured group times are short (10–20 minutes based on age and ability of the group)*

_____ times for nourishment, rest, and personal care scheduled*

_____ children govern their own use of time (how long to work, play, eat, nap, etc.) as much as possible

_____ there are daily rituals* (e.g., a morning song, a nap-time story)

Primary Grades Learning Environment Additions

Primary grades classrooms can be quite similar to the preschool and kindergarten environments. They are more often more like classrooms for older children with desks in rows. In an after-school program for primary children, you may need to set up a temporary environment each day in a gym or all-purpose room. If the classroom you are assessing or setting up is a learning center classroom, use the Preschool/Kindergarten Checklist and add the items on this checklist when possible.

Program/grade(s) _____ Date _____

Number of staff _____ Number of children _____

Use the following code as appropriate: ✓ = yes/adequate, − = no/inadequate

Block Area Additions

____ shelves labeled with pictures and words
____ paper and pens for writing signs available nearby

Dramatic Play Area Additions

____ prop boxes accessible to children
____ shelves and racks labeled with pictures and words
____ boxes, platforms, etc., for children to create stage sets

Toy/Game Area Additions

____ jigsaw puzzles with 25–100 pieces
____ large sets of construction toys with wheels, gears, etc.
____ direction and patterns to use with construction toys
____ simple board games (e.g., Candyland, Chutes and Ladders, Monopoly Junior, Don't Break the Ice)
____ simple card games (e.g., Go Fish, Old Maid, Uno)

Discovery/Sensory Area Additions

____ measuring tools
____ waterwheels
____ tubing/pipes

Art Area Additions

____ pencil crayons
____ brushes clean and stored upright
____ containers and shelves labeled
____ oil-base modeling clay

Writing Center Additions

____ pencil and thin wax crayons
____ dictionary or word file
____ lined paper
____ staplers
____ computer with simple word processing/page processing/drawing programs

Discovery Area Additions

____ tools like knives and scissors
____ artifact collections
____ globes and maps
____ children's encyclopedia and other library resources (e.g., atlas)
____ computer with Internet connection

Outdoor Additions

____ cargo nets and ropes
____ bikes and scooters
____ equipment for organized games
____ hard surfaces for hopscotch, jump rope, etc.

BIBLIOGRAPHY

Chapter 1

Barnett, W. S. (2004). Better teachers, better preschools: Student achievement linked to teacher qualifications. *NIEER Preschool Policy Matters, 2*(1–11).

Bellm, D. (n. d.) Establishing teacher competencies in early care and education: A review of current models and options for California. Policy brief for Building California's preschool for all workforce. Berkeley, CA: Center for the Study of Child Care Employment.

Biber, B., & Snyder, A. (1948). How do we know a good teacher? *Childhood Education, 24*(6), 281–285.

Bredekamp, S. (1992). Composing a profession. *Young Children, 47*(2), 52–54.

Bredekamp, S. (2011). *Effective practices in early childhood education: Building a foundation.* Upper Saddle River, NJ: Pearson.

Bredekamp, S., & Copple, C. (Eds.). (2009). *Developmentally appropriate practice in early childhood programs* (3rd ed.). Washington, DC: NAEYC.

Burks, J., & Rubenstein, M. (1979). *Temperament styles in adult interaction.* New York: Brunner/Mazel.

Cartwright, S. (1999). What makes good early childhood teachers? *Young Children, 54*(6), 4–7.

Colker, L. J. (2008, March). Twelve characteristics of effective early childhood teachers. *Beyond the Journal.* Available online from NAEYC. Retrieved from http://journal.naeyc.org/btj/200803/BTJColker.asp

Council for Exceptional Children. (n. d.). *CEC standards for professional practice.* Retrieved from www.cec.sped.org/content/navigationmenu/professional-development/professionalstandards/

Council for Professional Recognition. (2011). *National Competency standards for CDA credential.* Retrieved from www.cdacouncil.org/the-cda-credential/about-the-cda/cda-competency-standards

Derman-Sparks, L. (1989). *Anti-bias curriculum: Tools for empowering young children.* Washington, DC: NAEYC.

Early, D. M., Maxwell, K. L., Burchinal, M., Alva, S., Bender, R. H., Bryant, D., . . . Zill, N. (2007). Teacher's education, classroom quality, and young children's academic skills: Results from seven studies of preschool programs. *Child Development, 78,* 558–580.

Epstein, A. S. (2007). *The intentional teacher: Choosing the best strategies for young children's learning.* Washington, DC: NAEYC.

Feeney, S., & Chun, R. (1985). Effective teachers of young children. *Young Children, 41*(1), 47–52.

Gardner, H. (1983). *Frames of mind.* New York: Basic Books.

Jersild, A. (1955). *When teachers face themselves.* New York: Teachers College Press.

Katz, L. G. (1993, April). Dispositions: Definitions and implications for early childhood practices. Retrieved from http://ceep.crc.uiuc.edu/eecearchive/books/disposit.html

Katz, L. G. (1995). The developmental stages of teachers. In *Talks with teachers of young children.* Norwood, NJ: Ablex.

Kidder, R. (1995). *How good people make tough choices.* New York: Simon & Schuster.

Kipnis, K. (1987). How to discuss professional ethics. *Young Children, 42*(4), 26–33.

Kontos, S., & Wilcox-Herzog, A. (2001). How do education and experience affect teachers of young children? *Young Children, 56*(4), 85–91.

National Association for the Education of Young Children (NAEYC). (2005). *Code of ethical conduct and statement of commitment* (Rev. ed.). Washington, DC: NAEYC.

National Association for the Education of Young Children (NAEYC). (2009). *NAEYC standards for early childhood professional preparation programs: Position statement.* Washington, DC: Author. Retrieved from www.naeyc.org/files/naeyc/file/positions/ProfPrepStandards09.pdf

National Board for Professional Teaching Standards (NBPTS). (2001). *Early childhood generalist standards* (2nd ed.). Retrieved from www.nbpts.org/userfiles/File/ec_gen_standards.pdf

Thomas, A., & Chess, S. (1977). *Temperament and development.* New York: Brunner/Mazel.

Chapter 2

Ackerman, D. J., & Barnett, W. S. (2009). Does preschool education policy impact infant/toddler care? Preschool Policy Brief, National Institute for Early Education Research. Rutgers, NJ. Retrieved from http://nieer.org/resources/policybriefs/21.pdf

Administration for Children & Families. Early Childhood Learning & Knowledge Center. (2011). Head Start performance standards and other regulations. Retrieved from http://eclkc.ohs.acf.hhs.gov/hslc/Head Start Program/Program Design and Management/Head Start Requirements/Head Start Requirements

Administration for Children & Families. (n. d.). ARRA—Child Care and Development Block Grant. Retrieved from www.cfda.gov/index?s=program&mode=form&tab=step1&id=43a6d927e2c8c46904d85a06d0d11543

Administration for Children & Families, Office of Head Start. Head Start Program Fact Sheet. Fiscal Year 2010. Retrieved from www.acf.hhs.gov/programs/ohs/about/fy2010.html

Administration for Children, Youth, and Families. (2001). Head Start FACES, Chapter 5. Retrieved from www.acf.hhs.gov/programs/opre/hs/faces/reports/perform_3rd_rep/meas_99_title.html

Administration for Children, Youth, and Families. (2003). Head Start FACES, progress report. Retrieved from www.acf.hhs.gov/programs/opre/hs/faces00/reports/perform_4thprogress/faces00_title.html

Administration for Children, Youth, and Families. (2006). Head Start FACES, progress report. Retrieved from www.acf.hhs.gov/programs/opre/hs/faces/reports/research _2003_title.html

Alliance for Childhood. (2011). Policy brief, Why we object to the K–3 Core Standards. Retrieved from www.allianceforchildhood.org

Barnett, W. S. (1995). Long-term effects of early childhood programs on cognitive and school outcomes. *The Future of Children; Long-Term Outcomes of Early Childhood Programs, 5*(3). Los Altos, CA: Center for the Future of Children, The David and Lucile Packard Foundation.

Barnett, W. S. (2004). Better teachers, better preschools: Student achievement linked to teacher qualifications. *Preschool Policy Matters, 2.* New Brunswick, NJ: National Institute for Early Education Research, Rutgers University.

Barnett, W. S., Epstein, D. J., Carolan, M. E., Fitzgerald, J., Ackerman, D. J., & Friedman, A. H. (2010). State preschool yearbook: The state of preschool 2010. Retrieved from the website of the National Institute for Early Education Research, http://nieer.org/yearbook

Barnett, W.S., Hustedt, J.T., Friedman, A.H., Stevenson Boyd, J., & Ainsworth, P. (2007). State preschool yearbook: The state of preschool 2007. Retrieved from the website of the National Institute for Early Education Research, http://nieer.org/yearbook

Belsky, J. (2001). Emanuel Miller lecture, Developmental risks (still) associated with early child care. *Journal of Child Psychology and Psychiatry, 42*(7), 845–859.

BUILD Initiative. (2009). Early childhood systems working group. Retrieved from www.buildinitiative.org/content/early-childhood-systems-working-group-ecswg

Burchinal, M. R., Cryer, D., Clifford, R. M., & Howes, C. (2002). Caregiver training and classroom quality in child care centers. *Applied Developmental Science, 6,* 2–11.

CLASP (Center for Law and Social Policy). (2008). Retrieved from www.clasp.org/publications/ehs_pir_2009.pdf

CLASP (Center for Law and Social Policy). (2010a). Head Start by the numbers: 2009 PIR profile. Retrieved from www.clasp.org/admin/site/publications/fil es/hsdata2009us.pdf

CLASP (Center for Law and Social Policy). 2010b. Early Head Start participants, programs, families, and staff. (2009). Retrieved from www.clasp.org/publications/ehs_pir_2009.pdf

Common Core Standards Initiative. (2010). Core standards. Retrieved from www.corestandards.org

Cryer, D. (2003). Defining and assessing early childhood program quality. *Annals of the American Academy of Political and Social Science, 563,* 39–55.

Department of Defense. (2008). Overview of the military child development system. Retrieved from www.militaryhomefront.dod.mil/portal/page/mhf//MHF/MHF _DETAIL_1?id=20.80.500.95.0.0.0.0.0& current_id=20.80.500.95.500.30.30.0.0

Early, D. M., Maxwell, K. L., Burchinal, M., Bender, R. H., Bryant, D., Cai, K., . . . Zill, N. (2007). Teacher's education, classroom quality, and young children's academic skills: Results from seven studies of preschool programs. *Child Development, 78,* 558–580.

Foundation for Child Development. (2008). How can we improve the education of America's children? New York: Foundation for Child Development Newsletter. Retrieved from www.fcdus.org/issues/issues_show.htm?doc _id=447076

Frank Porter Graham Center. (1999, October). *Early learning, later success: The Abecedarian Study.* Chapel Hill, NC: Frank Porter Graham Child Development Center, University of North Carolina.

Gomby, D. S., Larner, M. B., Stevenson, C. S., Lewit, E. M., & Behrman, R. E. (1995, Winter). Long-term outcomes of early childhood programs: Analysis and recommendations. In R. E. Behrman (Ed.), Long-term outcomes of early childhood programs. *The Future of Children, 5*(3). Los Altos, CA: Center for the Future of Children, The David and Lucile Packard Foundation.

Graves, D. H. (2002). *Testing is not teaching: What should count in education.* Portsmouth, NH: Heinemann.

Haring, N. G., McCormick, L., & Haring, T. G. (1994). *Exceptional children and youth: An introduction to special education* (6th ed.). Upper Saddle River, NJ: Pearson.

Head Start Bureau. Administration for Children and Families. (2004). Head Start fact sheet. Retrieved from www.acf.hhs.gov/programs/ohs/about/fy2004.html

Hruska, K. (2009). Your updated guide to military child care. *Military Money,* Spring 2009. Retrieved from www.militarymoney.com/spouse/militarychildren/tabid/128/itemId/2216/Default.aspx

Hyson, M. (2003). Introducing NAEYC's Early Learning Standards: Creating the conditions for success. *Young Children, 58*(1), 66–68.

Iruka, I. U., & Carver, P. R. (2006). *Initial results from the 2005 NHES Early Childhood Program Participation survey.* Washington, DC: U.S. Department of Education, National Center for Education Statistics. Retrieved from http://nces.ed.gov/pubs2006/earlychild/index.asp

Kagan, S. L., & Kauerz, K. (2007). Reaching for the whole: Integration and alignment in early education policy. In R. C. Pianta, M. J. Cox, & K. Snow (Eds.), *School readiness and the transition to kindergarten in the era of accountability* (pp. 11–30). Baltimore: Brookes.

Kagan, S. L., Scott-Little, C., & Stebbins Frelow, V. (2003). Early learning standards for young children: A survey of the states. *Young Children, 58*(5), 58–64.

Karoly, L. A., Greenwood, P. W., Everingham, S. S., Hoube, J., Kilburn, M. R., Rydell, C. P., . . . Chiesa, J. R. (1998). *Investing in our children: What we know and don't know about the costs and benefits of early childhood interventions.* Santa Monica, CA: Rand Corporation.

Kauerz, K. (2005, March). State kindergarten policies: Straddling early learning and early elementary school. *Young Children: Beyond the Journal.* Retrieved from http://journal.naeyc.org/btj/200503/01Kauerz.asp

Klein, J. (2011, July 07). Time to ax public programs that don't yield results. *Time, 178,* 3.

Kohn, A. (2000). *The case against standardized tests: Raising the scores, ruining the schools.* Portsmouth, NH: Heinemann.

Lazar, I., & R. Darlington. (1983). *As the twig is bent: Lasting effects of preschool programs.* Hillsdale, NJ: Erlbaum.

Lewit, E. M., & Baker, L. (1995, Summer–Fall). School readiness. *The Future of Children, 5*(2), 128–139.

McKey, R. H., (Ed.). (1985). Project Head Start, a national evaluation: Summary of the study. In D. G. Hayes (Ed.)

Britannia Review of American Education (pp. 235–243). Chicago: Encyclopedia Britannica.

Morgan, G. G. (2003). Regulatory policy. In D. Cryer & R. M. Clifford (Eds.), *Early childhood education and care in the United States* (pp. 65–85). Baltimore: Brookes.

National Association of Child Care Resource and Referral Agencies (NACCRRA). (2007). Parents and the high price of child care: 2007 update. Retrieved from www.naccrra.org/docs/press/price_report.pdf

National Association of Child Care Resource and Referral Agencies (NACCRRA). (2008). Child care in America: 2008 state fact sheets. Retrieved from www.naccrra.org/policy/docs/ChildCareinAmerica.pdf

National Association of Child Care Resource and Referral Agencies (NACCRRA). (2011). Number of children potentially needing child care. Retrieved from www.naccrra.org/randd/docs/Children-Under-Age-6-Potentially-Needing-Care.pdf

National Association for the Education of Young Children. (1993). *Position statement on school readiness*. Washington, DC: NAEYC.

National Association for the Education of Young Children. (1997). NAEYC position statement on licensing and public regulation of early childhood. *Young Children, 53*(1), 43–50.

National Association for the Education of Young Children. (2003). *Early learning standards: Creating the conditions for success*. Joint position statement of NAEYC and the National Association of Early Childhood Specialists in State Departments of Education. Executive Summary. *Young Children, 58*(1), 69–70.

National Association for the Education of Young Children Academy. (2009). Accreditation of programs for young children. Retrieved from www.naeyc.org/academy/accreditation/search

National Center for Education Statistics (NCES). (2011). *Digest of education statistics, 2010*. Washington, DC: Department of Education, Office of Educational Research and Improvement. Retrieved from http://nces.ed.gov/pubs2011/2011015.pdf

National Commission on Excellence in Education. (1983). *Nation at risk: The imperative for educational reform*. Washington, DC: U.S. Government Printing Office.

National Education Goals Panel. (1997). *National Education Goals report: Building a nation of learners*. Available from the University of Illinois at Urbana-Champaign at its ReadyWeb website http://readyweb.crc.uiuc.edu/virtual-library/1997/goals/contents.html

NICHD Early Child Care Research Network. (1997). The effects of infant child care on infant-mother attachment security. *Child Development, 68,* 860–879.

NICHD Early Child Care Research Network. (1999). Child outcomes when child care center classes meet recommended standards for quality. *American Journal of Public Health, 89*(7), 1072–1077.

Padak, N., & Rasinski, T. (2003, April). Family literacy programs: Who benefits? Columbus Ohio: Ohio Literacy Resource Center, Kent State University. Retrieved from http://literacy.kent.edu/Oasis/Pubs/WhoBenefits2003.pdf

QRIS National Learning Network. (2009). Quality, rating and improvement systems. Retrieved from http://qrisnetwork.org/

Ray, B. D. (2006, July). Research facts on homeschooling. National Home Education Research Institute (NHERI). Retrieved from www.nheri.org/Research-Facts-on-Homeschooling.html

Schulman, K. (2000). The high cost of child care puts quality care out of reach for many families. Issue brief. Washington, DC: Children's Defense Fund.

Schweinhardt, L. J., & D. P. Weikart. (1997) *Lasting differences: The High/Scope preschool curriculum comparison study through age 23*. Ypsilanti, MI: High/Scope Press.

Scott-Little, C., Lesko, J., Martella, J., & Milburn, P. (2007). Early learning standards: Results from a national survey to document trends in state-level policies and practices. *Early Childhood Research and Practice, 9*(1). Retrieved from http://ecrp.uiuc.edu/v9n1/little.html

Thorman, A. & Kauerz, K. (2011). QRIS and P-3: Creating synergy across systems to close achievement gaps and improve opportunities for young children. Early Childhood Systems Reform brief. Retrieved from www.buildinitiative.org/files/QRIS_P-3brief.pdf

U.S. Census Bureau. (2005). Who's minding the kids? Child care arrangements: Spring 2005, detailed tables. Retrieved from www.census.gov/population/www/socdemo/child/ppl-2005.html

U.S. Charter Schools. (n. d.). Overview. Retrieved from www.uscharterschools.org/pub/uscs_docs/o/index.htm

U.S. Department of Health and Human Services. Administration for Children and Families. (2010). News release. Formation of policy board on early learning. Retrieved from www.hhs.gov/news/press/2010pres/08/20100803a.html

U.S. Department of Health and Human Services. Administration for Children and Families (2011). Press release. Obama Administration announces $500 million for Race to the Top Early Learning Challenge. Retrieved from www.hhs.gov/news/press/2011pres/05/20110525a.html

Whitebook, M., Howes, C., & Phillips, D. (1998). *Worthy works, unlivable wages: The national child care staffing study, 1988–1997*. Washington, DC: Center for the Child Care Workforce.

Whitebook, M., Howes, C., & Phillips, D. (1990). *Who cares? Child care teachers and the quality of care in America: Executive summary*. Washington, DC: National Center for the Early Childhood Workforce.

Zero to Three. (2008). Early learning guidelines for infants and toddlers: Recommendations for states. Washington, DC: Zero to Three. Retrieved from www.zerotothree.org/site/DocServer/Early_Learning_Guidelines_for_Infants_and_Toddlers.pdf?docID=4961

Chapter 3

Antler, J. (1987). *Lucy Sprague Mitchell: The making of a modern woman*. New Haven: Yale University Press.

Auleta, M. S. (1969). *Foundations of early childhood education*. New York: Random House.

Beatty, B. (1995). *Preschool education in America: The culture of young children from the colonial era to the present*. New Haven and London: Yale University Press.

Braun, S. J., & Edwards, E. P. (1972). *History and theory of early childhood education*. Belmont, CA: Wadsworth.

Brosterman, N. (1997). *Inventing kindergarten*. New York: Abrams.

Byers, L. (1972). *Origins and early history of the parent cooperative nursery school movement in America.* ERIC Document Reproduction Service No. ED091063

Cleverley, J., & Phillips, D. C. (1986). *Visions of childhood: Influential models from Locke to Spock* (Rev. ed.). New York: Teachers College Press.

Colville, D. (2011). Froebelian kindergarten and association school. *The UCL Bloomsbury project.* London, UK: University College London. Retrieved from www.ucl.ac.uk/bloomsbury-project/articles/individuals/ronges.htm

Coontz, E.K. (n.d.). *Best-kept secret: Cooperative preschool programs.* Davis, CA: University of California.

Cuffaro, H. K. (1995). *Experimenting with the world: John Dewey and the early childhood classroom.* New York: Teachers College Press.

Cunningham, H. (1995). *Children and childhood in Western society since 1500.* London and New York: Longman.

Deasey, D. (1978). *Education under six.* New York: St. Martin's Press.

Dewey, J. (1961). *The school and society.* Chicago: University of Chicago Press. (Original work published 1899.)

Dewey, J. (1972). *Experience and education.* New York: Collier Books.

Education Commission of the States. (2011). *Access to kindergarten: Age issues in state statutes.* Retrieved from http://mb2.ecs.org/reports/Report.aspx?id=32

Edwards, C. P. (2002, Spring). Three approaches from Europe: Waldorf, Montessori, and Reggio Emilia. *Early Childhood Research and Practice, 4*(1). Retrieved from http://ecrp.uiuc.edu/v4n1/edwards.html

Edwards, C., Gandini, L., & Forman, G. (Eds.). (1998). *The hundred languages of children.* Norwood, NJ: Ablex.

Goetz, H. W. (1993). *Life in the Middle Ages from the seventh to the thirteenth century.* Notre Dame, IN: University of Notre Dame Press.

Goffin, S. G., & Wilson, C. (2001). *Curriculum models and early childhood education: Appraising the relationship* (2nd ed.). Upper Saddle River, NJ: Pearson.

Grubb, W. N., & Lazerson, A. M. W. (1988). *Broken promises: How Americans fail their children* (Rev. ed.). Chicago: University of Chicago Press.

Gutek, G. L. (1994). *A history of the Western educational experience* (2nd ed.). Longrove, IL: Waveland Press.

Haas, L. (1998). *The Renaissance man and his children: Childhood and early childhood in Florence 1300–1600.* New York: St. Martin's Press.

Hartley, D. (1993). *Understanding the nursery school.* London: Cassel.

High/Scope Education Research Foundation. (1989). *The High/Scope K–3 curriculum: An introduction.* Ypsilanti, MI: High/Scope Press.

Hohmann, M., & Weikart, D. P. (2002). *Educating young children: Active learning practices for preschool and child care programs* (2nd ed.). Ypsilanti, MI: High/Scope Press.

Hymes, J. L. (1996). Industrial day care's roots in America. In K. M. Paciorek & J. H. Munro (Eds.), *Sources: Notable selections in early childhood education* (2nd ed.). Guilford, CT: Dushkin/McGraw-Hill.

Kramer, R. (1988). *Maria Montessori: A biography.* Reading, MA: Addison-Wesley.

Lascarides, V. C., & Hinitz, B. F. (2000). *History of early childhood education.* New York and London: Falmer.

McMillan, M. (1919). *The nursery school.* New York: Dutton.

Michel, S. (1999). *Children's interest/mothers' rights: The shaping of America's child care policy.* New Haven: Yale University Press.

Mitchell, A., & David, J. (Eds.). (1992). *Explorations with young children.* Mt. Rainier, MD: Gryphon House.

Montessori, M. (1965). *Dr. Montessori's own handbook.* New York: Schocken.

Montessori, M. (1967). *The absorbent mind.* New York: Holt, Rinehart & Winston.

Nager, N., & Shapiro, E. (Eds.). (2000). *Revisiting progressive pedagogy: The Developmental Interaction Approach.* Albany: SUNY Press.

Orme, N. (200)3. *Medieval children.* New Haven, CT: Yale University Press.

Osborn, D. K. (1991). *Early childhood education in historical perspective* (3rd ed.). Athens, GA: Education Associates.

Paciorek, K. M., & Munro, J. H. (Eds.). (1996). *Sources: Notable selections in early childhood education.* Guilford, CT: Dushkin.

Paciorek, K. M., & Munro, J. H. (Eds.). (1999). *Sources: Notable selections in early childhood education* (2nd ed.). Guilford, CT: Dushkin/McGraw-Hill.

Prochner, L. (2009). *A history of early childhood education in Canada, Australia, and New Zealand.* Vancouver, BC: University of British Columbia Press.

Schweinhart, L. J., Barnes, H. V., & Weikart, D. P. (1993). Significant benefits: The High/Scope Perry Preschool Study through age 27. *Monographs of the High/Scope Educational Research Foundation, 10.* Ypsilanti, MI: High/Scope Press.

Shapiro, M. S. (1983). *Child's garden: The kindergarten movement from Fröebel to Dewey.* University Park: Pennsylvania State University Press.

Silber, K. (1965). *Pestalozzi: The man and his work.* New York: Schocken.

Smith, T. E. & Knapp, C. E. (Eds). (2010). *Sourcebook of experiential education: Key thinkers and their contributions.* New York: Routledge Publications.

Standing, E. M. (1959). *Maria Montessori: Her life and work.* Fresno, CA: Academy Library Guild.

Steiner, G. Y. (1976). *The children's cause.* Washington, DC: Brookings Institution.

Steinfels, M. O. (1973). *Who's minding the children?* New York: Simon & Schuster.

Weber, E. (1969). *The kindergarten: Its encounter with educational thought in America.* New York: Teachers College Press.

Weber, E. (1984). *Ideas influencing early childhood education: A theoretical analysis.* New York: Teachers College Press.

Williams, C. L., & Johnson, J. E. (2005). The Waldorf approach to early childhood education. In J. L. Roopnarine & J. E. Johnson (Eds.), *Approaches to early childhood education* (4th ed., pp. 336–362). Upper Saddle River, NJ: Pearson.

Williams, L. R. (1993). Historical and philosophical roots of early childhood practice. *Encyclopedia of Early Childhood Education.* New York: Garland.

Wolfe, J. (2002). *Learning from the past: Historical voices in early childhood education* (2nd ed.). Mayerthorpe, Alberta, Canada: Piney Branch Press.

Wortham, S. C. (1992). *Childhood, 1892–1992.* Wheaton, MD: Association for Childhood Education International.

Chapter 4

Ainsworth, M. (1979). *Patterns of attachment*. New York: Halsted Press.

Bailey, D. B., Jr., Bruer, J. T., Symons, F. J., & Lichtman, J. W. (Eds.). (2001). *Critical thinking about critical periods*. Baltimore: Brookes.

Berk, L. E. (2008). *Infants and children: Prenatal through middle childhood* (8th ed.). Needham Heights, MA: Allyn & Bacon.

Berk, L. E. (2009). *Child development* (6th ed.). Upper Saddle River, NJ: Pearson.

Berk, L. E., & Winsler, A. (1995). *Scaffolding children's learning: Vygotsky and early childhood education*. Washington, DC: NAEYC.

Bodrova, E., & Leong, D. (2007). *Tools of the mind: The Vygotskian approach to early childhood education* (2nd ed.). Upper Saddle River, NJ: Pearson.

Bowlby, J. (1969). *Attachment and loss*. New York: Basic Books.

Breslin, D. (2005). Children's capacity to develop resiliency: How to nurture it. *Young Children, 60*(1), 47–52.

Bruer, J. T., & Greenough, W. T. (2001). The subtle science of how experience affects the brain. In D. B. Bailey, Jr., J. T. Bruer, F. J. Symons, & J. W. Lichtman (Eds.). *Critical thinking about critical periods*. Baltimore: Brookes.

Chess, S., & Thomas, A. (1996). *Temperament: Theory and practice*. New York: Brunner/Mazel.

Copple, C., & Bredekamp, S. (2006). *Basics of developmentally appropriate practice: An introduction for teachers of children 3 to 6*. Washington, DC: NAEYC.

Copple, C., & Bredekamp, S. (Eds.). (2009). *Developmentally appropriate practice in early childhood programs serving children from birth through age 8* (3rd ed.). Washington, DC: NAEYC.

Damon, W. (1988). *The moral child*. New York: Free Press.

Dennis, W. (1973). *Children of the creche*. New York: Appleton-Century-Crofts.

Edwards, C. P. (1986). *Promoting social and moral development in young children*. New York: Teachers College Press.

Eisenberg, N. (1992). *The caring child*. Cambridge, MA: Harvard University Press.

Erikson, E. (1963). *Childhood and society* (Rev. ed.). New York: Norton.

Frager, R. D., & Fadiman, J. (Eds.). (1987). *Motivation and personality* (3rd ed.). Upper Saddle River, NJ: Pearson.

Galinsky, E. (2010). *Mind in the making: The seven essential life skillsevery child needs*. New York: Harper Collins.

Gardner, H. (1983). *Frames of mind*. New York: Basic Books.

Gardner, H. (1991). *The unschooled mind*. New York: Basic Books.

Gardner, H. (1993). *Multiple intelligences: The theory in practice*. New York: Basic Books.

Gerber, M. (Ed.). (1997). *The RIE manual for parents and professionals*. Los Angeles: Resources for Infant Educators.

Gesell, A. (1940). *The first five years of life*. New York: Harper & Row.

Gesell, A., & Ilg, F. L. (1974). *The child from five to ten* (Rev. ed.). New York: Harper & Row.

Gilligan, C. (1982). *In a different voice*. Cambridge, MA: Harvard University Press.

Gonzalez-Mena, J., & Eyer, D. W. (2009). *Infants, toddlers, and caregivers* (8th ed.). New York: McGraw-Hill.

Hawley, T. (2000). *Starting smart: How early experiences affect brain development*. Washington, DC: Ounce of Prevention Fund and Chicago: Zero to Three.

Healy, J. M. (1990). *Endangered minds*. New York: Simon & Schuster.

Hunt, J. M. (1961). *Intelligence and experience*. New York: Ronald Press.

Kagan, J. (1984). *The nature of the child*. New York: Basic Books.

Kagan, J., Arcus, D., Snidman, N., Feng, W., Hendler, J., & Green, S. (1994). Reactivity in infants: A cross national comparison. *Developmental Psychology, 60*, 342–345.

Kaiser, B., & Rasminsky, J. (2012). *Challenging behavior in young children: Understanding, preventing, and responding effectively* (3rd ed.). Upper Saddle River, NJ: Pearson.

Kamii, C., & DeVries, R. (1993). *Physical knowledge in preschool education*. New York: Teachers College Press.

Kersey, K., & Malley, C. (2005). Helping children develop resiliency: Providing supportive relationships. *Young Children, 60*(1), 53–58.

Kohlberg, L. (Ed.). (1981). *The philosophy of moral development: Moral stages and the idea of justice*. San Francisco: Harper & Row

Kohlberg, L. (1984). *The psychology of moral development: The nature and validity of moral stages*. New York: Harper & Row.

Kostelnik, M. J., Whiren, A., Soderman, A. K., Gregory, K., & Stein, L. C. (2002). *Guiding children's social development* (3rd ed.). Albany, NY: Delmar.

Lewis, M., Ramsay, D., & Kawakami, K. (1993). Differences between Japanese infants and Caucasian American infants in behavioral and cortisol response to inoculation. *Child Development, 64*, 1722–1731.

Lickona, T., Geis, G., & Kolhberg, L. (Eds.). (1976). *Moral development and behavior: Theory, research, and social issues*. New York: Holt, Rinehart & Winston.

Lin, H. L., Lawrence, F. R., & Gorrell, J. (2003). Kindergarten teachers' views of children's readiness for school. *Early Childhood Research Quarterly, 18*(2), 225–236.

Lalley, R. J. (2009) The science and psychology of infant–toddler care: How an understanding of early learning has transformed child care. *Zero to Three, 30*(3), 47–53.

Maslow, A. H. (1968). *Toward a psychology of being*. Princeton, NJ: Van Nostrand.

Maslow, A. (1970). *Motivation and personality* (2nd ed.). New York: Harper & Row.

McCall, S. G., & Plemons, B. (2001). The concept of critical periods and their implications for early childhood services. In D. B. Bailey, Jr., J. T. Bruer, F. J. Symons, & J. W. Lichtman (Eds.). *Critical thinking about critical periods*. Baltimore: Brookes.

McDevitt, T. M., & Ormrod, J. E. (2010). *Child development and education* (4th ed.). Upper Saddle River, NJ: Pearson.

Mooney, C. G. (2000). *Theories of childhood: An introduction to Dewey, Montessori, Erickson, Piaget, and Vygotsky*. St. Paul, MN: Redleaf Press.

National Center for Learning Disabilities (NCLD). (2010). *What is executive function?* Retrieved from www.ncld.org/ld-basics/ld-aamp-executive-functioning/basic-ef-facts/what-is-executive-function#top

National Institute of Child Health and Human Development (NICHD). (2006). *The NICHD study of early child care and youth development (SECCYD): Findings for children up to age 4 1/2 years*. Retrieved from www.nichd.nih.gov/publications/pubs_details.cfm?from=&pubs_id=5047

Piaget, J. (1965). *The moral judgment of the child*. New York: Free Press. (Original work published 1932.)

Piaget, J. (1966). *The origins of intelligence in children* (2nd ed.). New York: International Universities Press.

Ramey, C., Campbell, F., & Blair, C. (1998). Enhancing the life course for high-risk children. In J. Crane (Ed.), *Social programs that work* (pp. 184–199). New York: Russell Sage Foundation.

Reynolds, A., & Ou, S. (2011). Paths of effects from preschool to adult well-being: A confirmatory analysis of the child-parent center program. *Child Development, 82*(2), 555–582.

Rothbart, M. K., Ahadi, B. A., & Evans, D. E. (2000). Temperament and personality: Origins and outcomes. *Journal of Personality and Social Psychology, 78*, 122–135.

Santrock, J. W. (2009). *Child development* (11th ed.). New York: McGraw-Hill.

Shonkoff, J., & Phillips, D. (Eds.). (2000). *From neurons to neighborhoods: The science of early childhood development*. Washington, DC: National Academy Press.

Shore, R. (1997). *Rethinking the brain*. New York: Families and Work Institute.

Skeels, H. M. (1966). Adult status of children with contrasting early life experiences. *Monographs of the Society for Research in Child Development, 31* (Serial No. 105).

Smetana, J. G., Killen, M., & Turiel, E. (1991). Children's reasoning about interpersonal and moral conflicts. *Child Development, 62*, 629–644.

Sylwester, R. (1995). *A celebration of neurons: An educator's guide to the human brain*. Alexandria, VA: Association for Supervision and Curriculum Development.

Tabors, P. O. (2008). *One child, two languages: A guide for early childhood educators of children learning English as a second language*. Baltimore: Brookes.

Thomas, A., & Chess, S. (1977). *Temperament and development*. New York: Brunner/Mazel.

Thomas, A., Chess, S., & Birch, H. G. (1970). The origin of personality. *Scientific American, 223*, 102–109.

Vygotsky, L. S. (1962). *Thought and language*. Cambridge, MA: MIT Press.

Vygotsky, L. S. (1978). *Mind in society: The development of higher psychological processes*. Cambridge, MA: Harvard University Press.

Walker, L. J. (1995). Sexism in Kohlberg's moral psychology? In W. M. Kurtines & J. L. Gewirtz (Eds.), *Moral development: An introduction*. Boston: Allyn & Bacon.

Werner, E. E., Bierman, J. M., & French, F. E. (1971). *The children of Kauai: A longitudinal study from the prenatal period to age ten*. Honolulu: University of Hawaii Press.

Werner, E. E., & Smith, R. S. (1992). *Overcoming the odds: High-risk children from birth to adulthood*. Ithaca, NY: Cornell University Press.

Woolfolk, A., & Perry, N. (2012). *Child and adolescent development*. Upper Saddle River, NJ: Pearson.

Youngquist, J., & Martinez-Griego, B. (2009). Learning in English, learning in Spanish: A Head Start program changes its approach. *Young Children, 64*(4), 92–98.

Chapter 5

Bentzen, W. R. (2008). *Seeing young children: A guide to observing and recording behavior* (6th ed.). Albany, NY: Delmar.

Cryan, J. R. (1986). Evaluation: Plague or promise? *Childhood Education, 62*(5), 344–350.

Curtis, D., & Carter, M. (2000). *The art of awareness: How observation can transform your teaching*. St. Paul, MN: Redleaf Press.

Daniels, D. H., Beaumont, L. J., & Doolin, C. A. (2007). *Understanding children: An interview and observation guide for educators* (2nd ed). New York, NY: McGraw-Hill Higher Education.

Dichtelmiller, M., Jablon, J. R., Dorfman, A. B., Marsden, D. B., & Meisels, S. J. (2001). *The work sampling system: Work sampling in the classroom (a teacher's manual)*. San Antonio, TX: Pearson.

Dodge, D. T., Colker, L. J., & Heroman, C. (2010). *The creative curriculum for preschool* (5th ed.). Washington, DC: Teaching Strategies.

Dodge, D. T., Rudick, S., & Berke, K. (2006). *The creative curriculum for infants, toddlers, and twos* (2nd ed.). Washington, DC: Teaching Strategies.

Epstein, A. S., Schweinhart, L. J., DeBruin-Parecki, A., & Robin, K. B. (2004, July). Preschool assessment: A guide to developing a balanced approach. *Preschool Policy Matters*. New Brunswick, NJ: National Institute for Early Education Research.

Forman, G., & Hall, E. (2005). Wondering with children: The importance of observation in early education. In *Early Childhood Research & Practice* (ECRP) 7(2). Retrieved from www.ecrp.uiuc.edu/v7n2/forman.html

Friedman, D. L. (2012). *Creating and presenting an early childhood portfolio: A reflective approach*. Belmont, CA: Wadsworth.

Galper, A. R., & Seefeldt, C. (2009). Assessing young children. In S. Feeney, A. Galper, & C. Seefeldt (Eds.), *Continuing issues in early childhood education* (3rd ed., pp. 329–345). Upper Saddle River, NJ: Pearson.

Graves, D. H. (2002). *Testing is not teaching: What should count in education*. Portsmouth, NH: Heinemann.

Gronlund, G., & Engel, B. (2001). *Focused portfolios: A complete assessment for the young child*. St. Paul, MN: Redleaf Press.

Guddemi, M. P. (2003). The important role of quality assessment in young children ages 3–8. In Gullo, D. F. (2005). *Understanding assessment and evaluation in early childhood education* (2nd ed.). New York: Teachers College Press.

Helm, J., Beneke, S., & Steinheimer, K. (2008). *Windows on learning: Documenting young children's work* (2nd ed.). New York: Teachers College Press.

High/Scope. (2003). *High/Scope preschool child observation record*. Florence, KY: Wadsworth.

Hughes, K., & Gullo, D. (2010). Joyful learning and assessment in kindergarten. *Young Children, 65*(3), 57–59.

Jones, J. (2004). Framing the assessment discussion. In D. Koralek (Ed.), *Spotlight on young children and assessment*. Washington, DC: NAEYC.

Koralek, D. (Ed.). (2004). *Spotlight on young children and assessment*. Washington, DC: NAEYC.

Losardo, A., & Notari-Syverson, A. (2011). *Alternative approaches to assessing young children* (2nd ed.). Baltimore: Brookes.

Marion, M. (2004). *Using observation in early childhood education*. Upper Saddle River, NJ: Pearson.

Maxwell, K. L., & Clifford, R. M. (2004, January). Research in review: School readiness assessment. *Young Children: Beyond the Journal*. Available from NAEYC at www.journal.naeyc.org/btj/200401/maxwell.asp

McAfee, O., & Leong, D. J. (2010). *Assessing and guiding young children's development and learning* (5th ed.). Upper Saddle River, NJ: Pearson.

McAfee, O., Leong, D., & Bodrova, E. (2004). *Basics of assessment: A primer for early childhood educators.* Washington, DC: NAEYC.

Meisels, S. J. (2006). *Accountability in early childhood: No easy answers.* Occasional Paper, No. 6. Chicago: Erikson Institute Herr Research Center for Children and Social Policy.

Meisels, S. J., & Atkins-Burnett, S. (2005). *Developmental screening in early childhood: A guide* (5th ed.). Washington, DC: NAEYC.

Meisels, S. J., Dombro, A. L., Marsden, D. B., Weston, D., & Jewkes, A. M. (2003). *The Ounce Scale: An observational assessment for infants, toddlers, and families.* New York: Pearson Early Learning.

National Association for the Education of Young Children (NAEYC) & National Association of Early Childhood Specialists in State Departments of Education (NAECS/SDE). (2003). Joint Position Statement. *Early childhood curriculum, assessment, and program evaluation: Building an effective, accountable system in programs for children birth through age 8.* Retrieved from www.naeyc.org/about/positions/pdf/CAPEexpand.pdf.

Puckett, M. B., & Black, J. K. (2008). *Meaningful assessment of the young child: Celebrating development and learning* (3rd ed.). Upper Saddle River, NJ: Pearson.

Seitz, H. (2008, March). The power of documentation in the early childhood classroom. *Young Children, 63*(2), 83–92.

Shillady, A. L. (2004, January). Choosing an appropriate assessment system. *Young Children: Beyond the Journal.* Retrieved from www.journal.naeyc.org/btj/200401/shillady.ASP.

Shores, E. F., & Grace, C. (2005). *The portfolio book.* Upper Saddle River, NJ: Pearson.

Wortham, S. C. (2011). *Assessment in early childhood education* (6th ed.). Upper Saddle River, NJ: Pearson.

Chapter 6

American Academy of Pediatrics. (2009). Discipline and your child. *Healthy children.* Retrieved from www.healthychildren.org/English/family-life/family-dynamics/communication-discipline

Bilmes, J. (2004). *Beyond behavior management: The six life skills children need to thrive in today's world.* St. Paul, MN: Redleaf Press.

Bowlby, J. (1982). *Attachment and loss: Vol. 1. Attachment.* London: Hogarth.

Brazelton, T. B., & Greenspan, S. I. (2000). *The irreducible needs of children: What every child must have to grow, learn, and flourish.* New York: Perseus.

Breslin, D. (2005). Children's capacity to develop resiliency: How to nurture it. *Young Children, 60*(1), 47–52.

Bronson, M. (2000). Recognizing and supporting the development of self-regulation in young children. *Young Children, 55*(2), 32–37.

CASEL Forum Report. (2011, April 13–14). *Expanding social and emotional learning nationwide: Let's go!* Collaborative for Academic, Social, and Emotional Learning (2011). Retrieved from http://casel.org/wp-content/uploads/2011-Forum-Report.pdf

Copple, C., & Bredekamp, S. (Eds.). (2009). *Developmentally appropriate practices in early childhood programs* (3rd ed.). Washington, DC: NAEYC.

Durlak, J., Weissberg, R., Dymnicki, A., Taylor, R., & Schellinger, K. (2011). The impact of enhancing students' social and emotional learning: A meta-analysis of school-based universal interventions. *Child Development, 82*(1), 405–432.

Dreikurs, R. (1969). *Psychology in the classroom.* New York: Harper & Row.

Fields, M. V., Perry, N. J., & Fields, D. M. (2010). *Constructive guidance and discipline: Preschool and primary education* (5th ed.). Upper Saddle River, NJ: Pearson.

Fox, L., Dunlap, G., Hemmeter, M. L., Joseph, G. E., & Strain, P. S. (2003). The teaching pyramid: A model for supporting social competence and preventing challenging behavior in young children. *Young Children, 58*(4), 48–52.

Fox, L., Carta, J., Strain, P., Dunlap, G., & Hemmeter, M. L. (2009). Response to intervention and the pyramid model. Tampa, FL: University of South Florida Technical Assistance Center on Social Emotional Intervention for Young Children; www.challengingbehavior.org

Gartrell, D. (1987). Punishment or guidance? *Young Children, 42*(2), 55–61.

Gartrell, D. (1995). Misbehavior or mistaken behavior? *Young Children, 50*(5), 27–34.

Gartrell, D. (2001). Replacing time-out: Part One—Using guidance to build an encouraging classroom. *Young Children, 56*(6), 8–16.

Gartrell, D. (2002). Replacing time-out: Part Two—Using guidance to maintain an encouraging classroom. *Young Children, 57*(2), 36–43.

Gartrell, D. (2004). *The power of guidance: Teaching social-emotional skills in early childhood classrooms.* Clifton Park, NY: Delmar; and Washington, DC: NAEYC.

Gilliam, W. (2005). Prekindergarteners left behind: Expulsion rates in state prekindergarten programs. *FCD Policy Brief Series No. 3.* NY: Foundation for Child Development.

Ginott, H. (1972). *Teacher and child: A book for parents and teachers.* New York: Macmillan.

Gonzalez-Mena, J. (2011). *Foundations: Early childhood education in a diverse society* (5th ed.). Boston: McGraw-Hill.

Gonzalez-Mena, J., & Eyer, D. W. (2009). *Infants, toddlers, and caregivers* (8th ed.). Boston: McGraw-Hill.

Gordon, T., with Burch, N. (2003). *Teacher effectiveness training: The program proven to help teachers bring out the best in students of all ages.* New York: Three Rivers Press.

Hemmeter, M. L. (July/August, 2007). We are all in this together. Supporting children's social emotional development and addressing challenging behavior. *Exchange.*

Hitz, R., & Driscoll, A. (1998). Praise or encouragement: New insights into praise. *Young Children, 43*(5), 6–13.

Honig, A. S. (1985). Compliance, control, and discipline. *Young Children, 40*(3), 47–52.

Howes, C., & Ritchie, S. (2002). *A matter of trust: Connecting teachers and learners in the early childhood classroom.* New York: Teachers College Press.

Hyson, M. (2002). Emotional development and school readiness. *Young Children, 57*(6), 76–78.

Kaiser, B., & Rasminsky, J. S. (2012). *Challenging behavior in young children: Understanding, preventing, and responding effectively.* Upper Saddle River, NJ: Pearson.

Katz, L. G. (1984). The professional early childhood teacher. *Young Children, 39*(5), 3–10.

Kersey, K. C., & Malley, C. R. (2005). Helping children develop resiliency: Providing supportive relationships. *Young Children, 60*(1), 53–58.

Kohn, A. (2001). Five reasons to stop saying "Good job!" *Young Children, 56*(5), 24–28.

Kostelnik, M., Whiren, A., Soderman, A., Stein, L., & Gregory, K. (2003). *Guiding children's social development* (4th ed.). Belmont, CA: Cengage Wadsworth.

Livergood, N. D. (n. d.). *Social intelligence: A new definition of human intelligence*. Retrieved from www.hermes-press.com/socint4.htm

Marshall, H. (2001). Cultural influences on the development of self-concept: Updating our thinking. *Young Children, 56*(6), 19–25.

Meece, D., & Soderman, A. K. (2010). Positive verbal environments: Setting the stage for young children's social development. *Young Children, 65*(5), 81–86.

Pizzolongo, P., & Hunter, A. (2011). I am safe and secure: Promoting resilience in young children. *Young Children, 66*(2), 67–69.

Rogers, F. (2003). *The world according to Mister Rogers: Important things to remember*. New York: Hyperion.

Schreiber, M. E. (1999). Time-outs for toddlers: Is our goal punishment or education? *Young Children, 54*(4), 22–25.

Straus, M. A., Sugarman, D. B., & Giles-Sims, J. (1997). Spanking by parents and subsequent antisocial behavior of children. *Archives of Pediatric and Adolescent Medicine, 151*(8), 761–767.

Sugai, G., Horner, R. H., Dunlap, G., Hieneman, M., Lewis, T. J., Nelson, C. M., . . . Ruef, M. (2000). Applying positive behavioral support and functional behavioral assessment in schools. *Journal of Positive Behavior Interventions 2*(3), 131–143.

Vance, E., & Weaver, P. J. (2002). *Class meetings: Young children solving problems together*. Washington, DC: NAEYC.

Willis, C., & Schiller, P. (2011). Preschoolers' social skills steer life success. *Young Children, 66*(1), 42–49.

Chapter 7

American Academy of Pediatrics Committee on Public Education. (2001). Children, adolescents, and television. *Pediatrics, 10*(2), 423–426).

American Academy of Pediatrics (AAP), American Public Health Association (APHA), & National Resource Center for Health and Safety in Child Care and Early Education (NRC). (2011). *Caring for our children: National health and safety performance standards: Guidelines for early care and education programs* (3rd ed.). Elk Grove Village, IL: American Academy of Pediatrics; Washington, DC: American Public Health Association. Also available at http://nrckids.org.

American Academy of Pediatrics (AAP). (2008a). *A child care provider's guide to safe sleep*. Retrieved from healthychildcare.org/pdf/SIDSchildcaresafesleep.pdf

American Academy of Pediatrics (AAP). (2008b). *A parents' guide to safe sleep*. Retrieved from healthychildcare.org/pdf/SIDSparentsafesleep.pdf

Aronson, S. (Ed.), with Spahr, P. M. (2002). *Healthy young children: A manual for programs*. Washington, DC: NAEYC.

Aronson, S., & Shope, T. (Eds.). (2008). *Managing infectious diseases in child care and schools: A quick reference guide*. Elk Grove Village, IL: American Academy of Pediatrics.

Branum, A., & Lukacs, S. (2008). *Food allergy among U.S. children: Trends in prevalence and hospitalizations*. NCHS data brief, no. 10. Hyattsville, MD: National Center for Health Statistics.

Brazelton, T., & Greenspan, S. (2000). *The irreducible needs of children: What every child must have to grow, learn and flourish*. Cambridge, MA: Perseus.

Copple, C., & Bredekamp, S. (Eds.). (2009). *Developmentally appropriate practices in early childhood programs* (3rd ed.). Washington, DC: NAEYC.

Carlson, F. (2006). *Essential touch: Meeting the needs of young children*. Washington, DC: NAEYC.

Centers for Disease Control & Prevention (CDC). (2011). *Lead*. Retrieved from cdc.gov/nceh/lead

Consumer Product Safety Commission (CPSC). (2008). *Nursery product-related injuries and deaths among children under age five*. Washington, DC: U.S. Government Printing Office.

Consumer Product Safety Commission (CPSC). (2010). *Public playground safety handbook*. CPSC Document #325. Retrieved from www.cpsc.gov/cpscpub/pubs/325.pdf

Eliassen, E. (2011). The impact of teachers and families on young children's eating behaviors. *Young Children, 66*(2), 84–89.

Galinsky, E. (1971a). *School beginnings: The first day*. New York: Bank Street College of Education.

Galinsky, E. (1971b). *School beginnings: The first weeks*. New York: Bank Street College of Education.

Goodman-Bryan, M., & Joyce, C. (2010). Touch is a form of communication. *The Urban Child Institute*. Retrieved from www.urbanchildinstitute.org

Greenman, J. (2001). *What happened to the world? Helping children cope in turbulent times*. New York: Bright Horizons.

Greenman, J. (2007). *Caring spaces, learning places: Children's environments that work*. Redmond, WA: Exchange Press.

Hirsch, E. [n.d.]. *Transition periods: Stumbling blocks of education*. New York: Early Childhood Education Council of New York.

Holland, M. (2004). "That food makes me sick!" Managing food allergies and intolerances in early childhood settings. *Young Children, 59*(2), 42–46.

Huettig, C., Sanborn, C., DiMarco, N., Popejoy, A., & Rich, S. (2004). The O generation: Our youngest children are at risk for obesity. *Young Children, 59*(2), 50–55.

Jacobs, N. L. (1992). Unhappy endings. *Young Children, 47*(3), 23–27.

Jordan, N. H. (1993). Sexual abuse prevention programs in early childhood education: A caveat. *Young Children, 48*(6), 76–79.

Marotz, L. (2012). *Health, safety, and nutrition for the young child*. Belmont, CA: Wadsworth Cengage Learning.

Maslow, A. (1968). *Toward a psychology of being*. New York: Van Nostrand Reinhold.

National Association for the Education of Young Children (NAEYC). (1993). *Violence in the lives of children*. Position Statement. Washington, DC: NAEYC.

National Association for the Education of Young Children (NAEYC). (1996). *Prevention of child abuse in early childhood programs and the responsibilities of early childhood professionals to prevent child abuse*. Position Statement. Washington, DC: NAEYC.

National Association for the Education of Young Children (NAEYC). (2005/2011). *Code of ethical conduct and statement of commitment* (Rev. ed.). Washington, DC: NAEYC.

National Association for the Education of Young Children (NAEYC). (2007). *NAEYC early childhood program standards and accreditation criteria: The mark of quality in early childhood education.* Washington, DC: NAEYC. Retrieved from www.naeyc.org/academy/standards

National Association for the Education of Young Children (NAEYC). (2009). *NAEYC standards for early childhood professional preparation programs.* Washington, DC: NAEYC.

National Association of Child Care Resource and Referral Agencies (NACCRRA). (2010). *Child care in America: 2010 fact sheets.* Arlington, VA: NACCRRA.

National Association for Sport and Physical Education (NASPE). (2002). *Active start: A statement of physical activity guidelines for children birth to five years.* Reston, VA: NASPE.

Pianta, R. C., Cox, M. J., Early, D., & Taylor, L. (1999). Kindergarten teachers' practices related to the transition to school: Results of a national survey. *Elementary School Journal, 100*(1), 71–86.

Pica, R. (2006). Physical fitness and the early childhood curriculum. *Young Children, 61*(3), 12–18.

Sanders, S. (2002). *Active for life: Developmentally appropriate movement programs for young children.* Washington, DC: NAEYC.

Sicherer, S., Muñoz-Furlong, A., & Sampson, H. (2003). Prevalence of peanut and tree nut allergy in the United States determined by means of a random digit dial telephone survey: A 5-year follow-up study. *Journal of Allergy and Clinical Immunology, 112*(6), 1203–1207.

Sorte, J., & Daeschel, I. (2006). Health in action: A program approach to fighting obesity in young children. *Young Children, 61*(3), 40–48.

U.S. Department of Agriculture. (2011). *My Plate.* Retrieved from www.choose myplate.gov

U.S. Department of Health and Human Services. (2003a). *Easing the transition from preschool to kindergarten: A guide for early childhood teachers and administrators.* Retrieved from head-startinfo.org/recruitment/trans_hs.htm

U.S. Department of Health and Human Services, Office of Disease Prevention and Health Promotion. (2006). *Healthy people 2010.* Retrieved from healthypeople.gov

White House Task Force on Childhood Obesity: Report to the President. (2010). *Solving the problem of childhood obesity within a generation.* Executive Office of the President of the United States. Retrieved from www.letsmove.gov/sites/letsmove.gov/files/TaskForce_on_Childhood_Obesity_May2010_FullReport.pdf

WHO. (1948, June). Preamble to the Constitution of the World Health Organization as adopted by the International Health Conference, New York.

Chapter 8

American Academy of Pediatrics (AAP), American Public Health Association (APHA), & National Resource Center for Health and Safety in Child Care and Early Education (NRC). (2002). *Caring for our children: National health and safety performance standards: Guidelines for out-of-home child care programs* (2nd ed.). Elk Grove Village, IL: AAP; and Washington, DC: APHA. Also available at the NRC website, http://nrckids.org/CFOC/index.html

American Academy of Pediatrics (AAP), Committee on Public Education. (2001). Children, adolescents, and television. *Pediatrics, 107*(2), 423–426.

American Academy of Pediatrics, American Public Health Association, & National Resource Center for Health and Safety in Child Care and Early Education. (2010). Preventing childhood obesity in early care and education programs, p. 58. Retrieved from http://nrckids.org/CFOC3/PREVENTING_OBESITY/index.htm

American Academy of Pediatrics. (2010). Policy statement—media education. *Pediatrics, 126*(5). Retrieved from http://pediatrics.aappublications.org/content/early/2010/09/27/peds.2010-1636

Aronson, S. (Ed.), with Spahr, P. M. (2002). *Healthy young children: A manual for programs.* Washington, DC: NAEYC.

Bergman, R., & Gainer, S. (2002, September–October). Home-like environments. *Child Care Information Exchange, 50–52.*

Berry, P. (2001). *Playgrounds that work.* Baulkham Hills, NSW, Australia: Pademelon Press.

Bredekamp, S., & Copple, C. (Eds.). (2009). *Developmentally appropriate practice in early childhood programs* (3rd ed.). Washington, DC: NAEYC.

Bronson, M. B. (1996). *The right stuff for children birth to 8: Selecting play materials to support development.* Washington, DC: NAEYC.

Bullard, J. (2010). *Creating environments for learning: Birth to age eight.* Upper Saddle River, NJ: Pearson.

Bunnett, R., & Kroll, D. (2000, January–February). Transforming spaces: Rethinking the possibilities—Turning design challenges into opportunities. *Child Care Information Exchange, 26–29.*

Campaign for a Commercial-Free Childhood. (2011). May 31, 2011 response to NAEYC's draft statement, "Technology in early childhood programs serving children from birth through age 8." Retrieved from www.commercialfree childhood.org/pdf/naeycreply

Chandler, P. A. (1994). *A place for me: Including children with special needs in early care and education settings.* Washington, DC: NAEYC.

Christakis, D. A., Zimmerman, F. J., DiGiuseppe, D. L., & McCarty, C. A. (2004). Early television exposure and subsequent attentional problems in children. *Pediatrics, 113*(4), 708–713.

Consumer Product Safety Commission (CPSC). (2008). *Public playground safety handbook.* CPSC Document #325. Retrieved from www.cpsc.gov/cpscpub/pubs/325.pdf

Cordes, C., & Miller, E. (Eds.). (2000). *Fool's gold: A critical look at computers in childhood.* College Park, MD: Alliance for Childhood.

Cuffaro, H. K. (1995). *Experimenting with the world: John Dewey and the early childhood classroom.* New York: Teachers College Press.

Curtis, D., & Carter, M. (2003). *Designs for living and learning: Transforming early childhood environments.* St. Paul, MN: Redleaf Press.

DeBord, K., Hestenes, L. L., Moore, R. C., Cosco, N. G., & McGinnis, J. R. (2005). *Preschool Outdoor Environment Measurement Scale-POEMS.* Winston Salem, NC: Kaplan.

Dodge, D. T., Ruddik, S., & Berke, K. (2006). *Creative curriculum for infants and toddlers* (2nd ed.). Washington, DC: Teaching Strategies.

Edwards, C., Gandini, L., & Forman, G. (eds.). 1998. *The hundred languages of children.* 2nd ed. Norwood, NJ: Ablex.

Elliott, S. (Ed.). (2008). *The outdoor play-space naturally.* Castle Hills, NSW, AU: Pademelon Press.

Feeney, S., & Moravcik, E. (1987). A thing of beauty: Aesthetic development in young children. *Young Children, 42*(6), 7–15.

Field, T. (1999). Music enhances sleep in preschool children. *Early Child Development and Care, 150*(1), 65–68.

Frost, J. L. (1992). *Play and playscapes.* Albany, NY: Delmar.

Frost, J. S., Wortham, S. C., & Reifel, S. (2012). *Play and child development* (4th ed.). Upper Saddle River, NJ: Pearson.

Gandini, L. (1984, Spring). Not just anywhere: Making child care centers into "particular" places. *Beginnings,* 17–20.

Garner, A., Skeen, P., & Cartwright, S. (1984). *Woodworking for young children.* Washington, DC: NAEYC.

Gonzalez-Mena, J., & Eyer, D. W. (2007). *Infants, toddlers, and caregivers* (7th ed.). New York: McGraw-Hill.

Greenman, J. (1998). *Places for childhoods: Making quality happen in the real world.* Redmond, WA: Exchange Press.

Greenman, J. (2005). Places for childhood in the 21st century: A conceptual framework. *Beyond the Journal: Young Children on the Web.* Retrieved from www.journal.naeyc.org/btj/200505/01Greenman.pdf

Greenman, J. (2007). *Caring spaces, learning places: Children's environments that work.* Redmond, WA: Exchange Press.

Haas-Foletta, K., & Ottolini-Geno, L. (2006, March–April). Setting the stage for children's success: The physical and emotional environment in school-age programs. *Child Care Information Exchange,* 40–44.

Harms, T., & Clifford, R. (2004). *Early childhood environment rating scale.* New York: Teachers College Press.

Hill, D. M. (1977). *Mud, sand, and water.* Washington, DC: NAEYC.

Hirsch, E. (1996). *The block book.* Washington, DC: NAEYC.

Johnson, J. E., Christie, J. F., & Wardle, F. (2005). *Play and early childhood development* (3rd ed.). Boston: Allyn & Bacon.

Jones, E., & Prescott, E. (1984). *Dimensions of teaching-learning environments: A handbook for teachers in elementary schools and day care centers* (2nd ed.). Pasadena, CA: Pacific Oaks College.

Keeler, R. (2008). *Natural playscapes: Creating outdoor play environments for the soul.* Redmond, WA: Exchange Press.

Koralek, D. G., Colker, L. J., & Dodge, D. T. (1993). *The what, why, and how of high-quality early childhood education: A guide for on-site supervision.* Washington, DC: NAEYC.

Moravcik, E., Nolte, S., & Feeney, S. (2013). *Meaningful curriculum for young children.* Upper Saddle River, NJ: Pearson.

National Association for the Education of Young Children (NAEYC). (1996). NAEYC position statement: Technology and young children—Ages three through eight. *Young Children, 51*(6), 11–16.

Nimmo, J., & Hallet, B. (2008). Childhood in the garden. *Young Children, 63*(1), 32–38.

Olds, A. R. (2001). *Child care design guide.* New York: McGraw-Hill.

Phillips, D. A. (1987). *Quality in childcare: What does research tell us?* Washington, DC: NAEYC.

Prescott, E. (2008, March–April). The physical environment. *Child Care Information Exchange,* 34–37.

Readdick, C. A. (1993). Solitary pursuits: Supporting children's privacy needs in group settings. *Young Children, 49*(1), 60–64.

Rosenow, N. (2008). Teaching and learning about the natural world. *Young Children, 63*(1), 10–13.

Seefeldt, C. (2002). *Creating rooms of wonder.* Beltsville, MD: Gryphon House.

Shade, D. (1996). Software evaluation. *Young Children, 51*(6), 17–21.

Sommer, R. (1969). *Personal space: The behavioral basis for design.* Upper Saddle River, NJ: Pearson.

Sutterby, J., & Thornton, C. D. (2005). Essential contributions from playgrounds. *Young Children, 60*(3), 26–33.

Wein, C. A., Coates, A., Keating, B., & Bigelow, B. C. (2005). Designing the environment to build a connection to place. *Young Children, 60*(3), 16–24.

White House Task Force on Childhood Obesity. (2010). *Solving the problem of childhood obesity within a generation.* Washington, DC: Office of the President.

Woodhouse, J. L., & Knapp, C. E. (2000). *Place-based curriculum and instruction: Outdoor and environmental education approaches.* Charleston, WV:

ERIC Clearinghouse on Rural Education and Small Schools.

Chapter 9

American Academy of Pediatrics (AAP), Committee on Public Education. (2001). Children, adolescents, and television. *Pediatrics, 107*(2), 423–426.

Bodrova, E., & Leong, D. J. (2003). Chopsticks and counting chips: Do play and foundational skills need to compete for the teacher's attention in an early childhood classroom? *Young Children, 58*(3), 10–17.

Bodrova, E., & Leong, D. J. (2007). *Tools of the mind: The Vygotskian approach to early childhood education* (2nd ed.). Upper Saddle River, NJ: Pearson.

Bronson, M. B. (2000). *Self-regulation in early childhood: Nature and nurture.* New York: Guilford Press.

Brown, S. & Vaughn, C. (2009). *Play: How it shapes the brain, opens the imagination, and invigorates the soul.* New York: Avery.

Carlson, F. (2009). Rough and tumble play 101. *Childcare Information Exchange, 188,* 70–72.

Centers for Disease Control (CDC). (2007). Childhood overweight. Retrieved from www.cdc.gov/nccdphp/dnpa/obesity/childhood

Csikszentmihalyi, M. (2008). *Flow: The psychology of optimal experience.* New York: Harper.

Dewey, J. (1910). *How we think.* London: D.C. Heath.

Ebbeck, M., & Waniganayake, M. (Eds). (2010). *Play in early childhood education: Learning in diverse contexts.* Victoria, AU: Oxford University Press.

Elkind, D. (1981). *The hurried child: Growing up too fast too soon.* Menlo Park, CA: Addison-Wesley.

Elkind, D. (2007). *The power of play: Learning what comes naturally.* Philadelphia: Da Capo Lifelong Books.

Frost, J. L. (2008, June). *Neuroscience, play and brain development.* Paper presented at IPA/USA Triennial National Conference, Longmont, CO. ERIC Document Reproduction Service No. ED427845.

Frost, J. S., Wortham, S. C., & Reifel, S. (2008). *Play and child development* (3rd ed.). Upper Saddle River, NJ: Pearson.

Ginsburg, K. R., Committee on Communications & Committee on Psychosocial Aspects of Child and Family Health.

(2007). The importance of play in promoting healthy child development and maintaining strong parent-child bonds. *Pediatrics, 119*(1), 183–196.

Groos, K. (1976/1901). *The play of man.* New York: Arno Press.

Hall, G. S. (1904). *Adolescence.* New York: D. Appleton.

Hassett, J. M., Siebert, E. R., & Wallen, K. (2008, March 25). Sex differences in rhesus monkey toy preferences parallel those of children. *Hormones and Behavior, 54*(3), 359–364.

Hughes, F. (2009). *Children, play, and development* (4th ed.). Boston: Allyn & Bacon.

Huizinga, J. (1971). *Homo Ludens: A study of the play-element in culture.* (3rd rev. ed.). London, UK: Maurice Temple Smith Ltd.

Isenberg, J. P., & Quisenberry, N. (2002). *Play: Essential for all children.* Position Paper of the Association for Childhood Education International. Retrieved from www.acei.org/wp-content/uploads/PlayEssential.pdf

Jarvis, P. (2006). "Rough and tumble" play: Lessons in life. *Evolutionary Psychology, 4,* 330–346. Retrieved from www.epjournal.net/filestore/ep043303462.pdf

Johnson, J. E., Christie, J. F., & Yawkey, T. D. (1999). *Play and early childhood development* (2nd ed.). Glenview, IL: Scott, Foresman.

Johnson, J. E., Christie, J. F., & Wardle, F. (2005). *Play and early childhood development* (3rd ed.). Boston: Allyn & Bacon.

Jones, E., & Reynolds, G. (1992). *The play's the thing: Teachers' roles in children's play.* New York: Teachers College Press.

Levin, D. E. (1998). *Remote control childhood: Combating the hazards of media culture.* Washington, DC: NAEYC.

Levin, D. E., & Carlsson-Paige, N. (2006). *The war play dilemma: What every parent and teacher needs to know* (2nd ed.). New York: Teachers College Press.

Orenstein, P. (2006, December 24). What's wrong with Cinderella? *New York Times Magazine,* Retrieved from www.nytimes.com/2006/12/24/magazine/24princess.t.html

Paley, V. G. (1993). *You can't say you can't play.* Boston: Harvard University Press.

Paley, V.G. (2004). *A child's work: The importance of fantasy play.* Chicago: University of Chicago Press.

Parten, M. B. (1932). Social participation among preschool children. *Journal of Abnormal Psychology, 27*(3), 243–269.

Patrick, G. T. W. (1916). *The psychology of relaxation.* Boston: Houghton-Mifflin.

Pellegrini, A. (1995). *School recess and playground behavior.* New York: State University of New York.

Pellis, S. M., & Pellis, V. C. (2007). Rough-and-tumble play and the development of the social brain. *Current Directions in Psychological Science, 16*(2), 95–98.

Piaget, J. (1962). *Play, dreams, and imitation in childhood.* New York: Norton.

Reifel, S., & Sutterby, J. A. (2009). Play theory and practice in contemporary classrooms. In S. Feeney, A. Galper, & C. Seefeldt (Eds.). *Continuing issues in early childhood education* (3rd. ed., pp. 238–257). Upper Saddle River, NJ: Pearson.

Reynolds, G., & Jones, E. (1997). *Master players: Learning from children at play.* New York: Teachers College Press.

Rogers, S. (Ed) (2011). *Rethinking play and pedagogy in early childhood education: Concepts, contexts, and cultures.* New York: Routledge.

Saracho, O., & Spodek, B. (Eds.). (1998). *Multiple perspectives on play in early childhood education.* Albany: State University of New York Press.

Schickedanz, J. A., Schickedanz, D. I., & Forsythe, P. D. (1993). *Understanding children.* Mountain View, CA: Mayfield.

Shonkoff, J. P., & Phillips, D. A. (Eds.). (2000). *From neurons to neighborhoods: The science of early childhood development.* Washington, DC: National Academy Press.

Smilansky, S. (1968). *The effects of sociodramatic play on disadvantaged pre-school children.* New York: Wiley.

Smilansky, S., & Shefatya, L. (1990). *Facilitating play: A medium for promoting cognitive, socio-emotional, and academic development in young children.* Gaithersburg, MD: Psychosocial and Educational Publications.

Spencer, H. (1963/1861). *Education: intellectual, moral, and physical.* Paterson, NJ: Littlefield Adams.

Trawick-Smith, J. (1994). *Interactions in the classroom: Facilitating play in the early years.* Upper Saddle River, NJ: Pearson.

United Nations General Assembly. (1989, November 20). *Convention on the Rights of the Child.* New York: United Nations.

Van Hoorn, J., Monighan Nourot, P., Scales, B., & Alward, K. R. (2007). *Play at the center of the curriculum* (4th ed.). Upper Saddle River, NJ: Pearson.

Williams, A. (2007, May 20). Putting the skinned knees back into playtime. *New York Times.* Retrieved from www.nytimes.com/2007/05/20/fashion/20retro.html.

Wolk, S. (2008). Joy in school. *The Positive Classroom, 66*(1), 8–15.

Chapter 10

Bowman, B. (Ed.). (2003). *Love to read: Essays in developing and enhancing early literacy skills of African American children.* Washington, DC: National Black Child Development Institute.

Campbell, D. (2000). *The Mozart effect in children: Awakening your child's mind, body, and creativity with music.* New York: Avon.

Chaillé, C., & Britain, L. (2003). *The young child as scientist: A constructivist approach to early childhood science education* (3rd ed.). Boston: Allyn & Bacon.

Children's Defense Fund. (2010). *The state of America's children 2010.* Washington, DC: Children's Defense Fund.

Colbert, J. (2003, August–September). Understanding curriculum: An umbrella view. *Early Childhood News,* 16–23.

Comenius, J. A. (1967). *Didactica magna.* (M. W. Keating, Ed., Trans.). New York: Russell & Russell. (Original translation published 1896.)

Consortium of National Arts Education Associations. (1994). *National standards for arts education: What every young American should know and be able to do in the arts.* Reston, VA: Music Educators National Conference.

Copple, C., & Bredekamp, S. (Eds.). (2009). *Developmentally appropriate practice in early childhood programs* (3rd ed.). Washington, DC: National Association for the Education of Young Children.

Council on Physical Education for Children (COPEC). (2000). *Appropriate practices in movement programs for young children ages 3–5: A position statement of the National Association for Sport and Physical Education*

(NASPE). Reston, VA: American Alliance for Health, Physical Education, Recreation & Dance.

Copley, J. V. (2009). *The young child and mathematics* (2nd ed.). Washington, DC: NAEYC.

Cuffaro, H. K. (1995). *Experimenting with the world.* New York: Teachers College Press.

Dixon, G. T., & Tarr, P. (1988). Extending art experiences in the preschool classroom. *International Journal of Early Childhood, 20*(1), 27–34.

Epstein, A. S. (2007). *The intentional teacher.* Washington, DC: NAEYC.

Feeney, S., & Moravcik, E. (1987). A thing of beauty: Aesthetic development in young children. *Young Children, 42*(6), 7–15.

Feeney, S., & Moravcik, E. (1995). *Discovering me and my world.* Circle Pines, MN: American Guidance Service.

Feeney, S., Galper, A., & Seefeldt, C. (Eds.). (2009). *Continuing issues in early childhood education* (3rd ed.). Upper Saddle River, NJ: Pearson.

Fields, M. V., Groth, L. A., & Spangler, K. L. (2004). *Let's begin reading right: A developmental approach to emergent literacy* (5th ed.). Upper Saddle River, NJ: Pearson.

Fröebel, F. (1885). *The education of man.* (J. Jarvis, Trans.). New York: Lovell.

Gabbard, C. P. (2004). *Lifelong motor development* (4th ed.). San Francisco: Benjamin Cummings/Pearson Education.

Gallahue, D. L., & Donnelly, F. C. (2007). *Developmental physical education for all children* (4th ed.). Champaign, IL: Human Kinetics.

Harlan, J. D., & Rivkin, M. S. (2004). *Science experiences for the early childhood years: An integrated affective approach* (8th ed.). Upper Saddle River, NJ: Pearson.

Holt, B. G. (1989). *Science with young children* (Rev. ed.). Washington, DC: NAEYC.

Hymes, J. L. (2001 [1947]). Planning ahead for young children. Speech to the National Association for Nursery Education. Reprinted in *Young Children, 56*(4), 62–94.

Hyson, M. (2008). *Enthusiastic and engaged learners: Approaches to learning in the early childhood classroom.* New York: Teachers College Press.

Katz, L. G. (2007). Standards of experience. *Young Children, 62*(3), 94–95.

Marlay, A. (1993). The importance and value of the development of aesthetic awareness in the education of young children. *Professional News, 1*(2), 19–27.

Mitchell, A., & David, J. (Eds.). (1992). *Explorations with young children.* Mt. Rainier, MD: Gryphon House.

Moravcik, E. (2000). Music all the livelong day. *Young Children, 55*(4), 27–29.

Moravcik, E., Nolte, S., & Feeney, S. (2013). *Meaningful curriculum for young children.* Upper Saddle River, NJ: Pearson.

Moskowitz, A. (1979). The acquisition of language. *Scientific American, 239*(5), 82–89.

Mulcahey, C. (2009). *The story in the picture: Inquiry and artmaking with young children.* New York: Teachers College Press.

Nager, N., & Shapiro, E. K. (Eds.). (2000). *Revisiting a progressive pedagogy: The developmental-interaction approach.* Albany, NY: State University of New York Press.

National Association for the Education of Young Children. (2009). *NAEYC Standards for Early Childhood Professional Preparation Programs.* Retrieved from www.naeyc.org/files/naeyc/file/positions/ProfPrepStandards09.pdf

National Association for Sport and Physical Education (NASPE). (2004). *Moving into the future: National standards for physical education* (2nd ed.). Reston, VA: American Alliance for Health, Physical Education, Recreation, and Dance.

National Council for the Social Studies (NCSS). (2010). *National curriculum standards for social studies: A framework for teaching, learning, and assessment.* Silver Spring, MD: NCSS.

The National Association of Music Educators (MENC). (1991). *MENC position statement on early childhood education.* Reston, VA: MENC. Retrieved from www.menc.org/about/view/early-childhood-education-position-statement

National Council of Teachers of Mathematics (NCTM) & National Association for the Education of Young Children (NAEYC). (2003). Learning paths and teaching strategies in early mathematics. *Young Children, 58*(1), 41–42.

National Research Council. (1996). *National science education standards.* Washington, DC: National Academy Press.

Neuman, S. B., Copple, C., & Bredekamp, S. (1999). *Learning to read and write.* Washington, DC: NAEYC.

Neuman, S. B., & Roskos, K. (2005). Whatever happened to developmentally appropriate practice in early literacy. *Beyond the Journal; Young Children on the Web,* 1–6.

Ogden, C., & Carroll, M. (2010). *Prevalence of obesity among children and adolescents: United States, trends 1963–1965 through 2007–2008.* Division of Health and Nutrition Examination Surveys, Atlanta, GA: CDC.

Ross, M. (1981). *The aesthetic imperative: Relevance and responsibility in art education.* Oxford: Pergamon.

Sanders, S. W. (2002). *Active for life: Developmentally appropriate movement programs for young children.* Washington, DC: NAEYC.

Schickedanz, J. (1999). *Much more than the ABC's.* Washington, DC: NAEYC.

Seefeldt, C. (Ed.). (2005). *The early childhood curriculum: Current findings in theories and practice* (3rd ed.). New York: Teachers College Press.

Seefeldt, C., Castle, S. D., & Falconer, R. (2009). *Social studies for the preschool/primary child* (8th ed.). Upper Saddle River, NJ: Pearson.

Skill Builders Pediatric Occupational Therapy. (2002). *Fine Motor Development 0 to 6 Years.* www.skillbuildersonline.com

West, J., Denton, K. L., & Germino-Hausken, E. (2000). *America's kindergartners.* Washington, DC: National Center for Education Statistics.

Chapter 11

Association for Supervision and Curriculum Development. (2002). *Overview of curriculum integration.* Alexandria, VA: Association for Supervision and Curriculum Development. Retrieved from www2.yk.psu.edu/~jlg18/506/ci_over.pdf

Baratta-Lorton, M. (1972). *Workjobs.* Menlo Park, CA: Addison-Wesley.

Berk, L. E., & Winsler, A. (1995). *Scaffolding children's learning.* Washington, DC: NAEYC.

Biber, B. (1969). *Challenges ahead for early childhood education.* Washington, DC: NAEYC.

Biber, B. (1984). A developmental-interaction approach: Bank Street College of Education. In M. C. Day & R. K. Parker (Eds.), *The preschool in action: Exploring early childhood programs* (2nd ed., 421–460). Boston: Allyn & Bacon.

Bloom, B. S., Mesia, B. B., & Krathwohl, D. (1964). *Taxonomy of educational* objectives (Vol. 1, The affective domain, Vol. 2, The cognitive domain). New York: David McKay.

Copple, C., & Bredekamp, S. (Eds.). (2009). Developmentally appropriate practice in early childhood programs (3rd ed.). Washington, DC: NAEYC.

Bredekamp, S., & Rosegrant, T. (Eds.). (1992). Reaching potentials: Appropriate curriculum and assessment for young children (Vol. 1). Washington, DC: NAEYC.

Bredekamp, S., & Rosegrant, T. (Eds.). (1995). Reaching potentials: Transforming early childhood curriculum and assessment for young children (Vol. 2). Washington, DC: NAEYC.

Carter, M., & Curtis, D. (1996a). Reflecting children's lives: A handbook for planning child centered curriculum. St. Paul, MN: Redleaf Press.

Carter, M., & Curtis, D. (1996b). Spreading the news: Sharing the stories of early childhood education. St. Paul, MN: Redleaf Press.

Cuffaro, H. K. (1995). Experimenting with the world. New York: Teachers College Press.

Edwards, C., Gandini, L., & Forman, G. (1998). The hundred languages of children (2nd ed.). Norwood, NJ: Ablex.

Epstein, A. S. (2007). The intentional teacher. Washington, DC: NAEYC.

Feeney, S. (2006, September). Which way should we go from here? Some thoughts about early childhood curriculum. Young Children: Beyond the Journal. Retrieved from http://journal.naeyc.org/btj/200609/FeeneyBT.pdf.

Goffin, S. G. (2001). Curriculum models and early childhood education: Appraising the relationship (2nd ed.). Upper Saddle River, NJ: Pearson.

Harlan, J. D., & Rivkin, M. S. (2007). Science experiences for the early childhood years: An integrated affective approach (9th ed.). Upper Saddle River, NJ: Pearson.

Helm, J., Beneke, S., & Steinheimer, K. (2007). Windows on learning: Documenting young children's work (2nd ed.). New York: Teachers College Press.

Helm, J. H., & Katz, L. (2001). Young investigators: The project approach in the early years. New York: Teachers College Press.

Hirsch, R. A. (2004). Early childhood curriculum: Incorporating multiple intelligences, developmentally appropriate practice, and play. Boston: Allyn & Bacon.

Hyson, M. (2008). Enthusiastic and engaged learners: Approaches to learning in the early childhood classroom. New York: Teachers College Press.

Jones, E., & Nimmo, J. (1994). Emergent curriculum. Washington, DC: NAEYC.

Katz, L. G. (1993). Dispositions as educational goals. Urbana, IL: ERIC Document Reproduction Service No. ED363454.

Katz, L. G., & Chard, S. C. (2000). Engaging children's minds: The project approach. Norwood, NJ: Ablex.

Katz, L. G. (2007). Standards of experience. Young Children, 62(3), 94–95.

Kostelnik, M. J., Soderman, A. K., & Whiren, A. P. (2010). Developmentally appropriate curriculum: Best practices in early childhood education (5th ed.). Upper Saddle River, NJ: Pearson.

Mitchell, A., & David, J. (Eds.). (1992). Explorations with young children. Mt. Rainier, MD: Gryphon House.

Moravcik, E., Nolte, S., & Feeney, S. (2013). Meaningful curriculum for young children. Upper Saddle River, NJ: Pearson.

Moravcik, E., & Feeney, S. (2009). Curriculum in early childhood education: Teaching the whole child. In S. Feeney, A. Galper & C. Seefeldt (Eds.). Continuing issues in early childhood education (3rd ed., pp. 218–237). Upper Saddle River, NJ: Pearson.

Nager, N., & Shapiro, E. K. (Eds.). (2000). Revisiting a progressive pedagogy: The developmental-interaction approach. Albany: State University of New York Press.

National Association for the Education of Young Children & National Association of Early Childhood Specialists in State Departments of Education. (2003). Executive summary early learning standards: Creating conditions for success. Young Children, 58(1), 69–70.

Phillips, D., Mekos, D., Scarr, S., McCartney, K. & Abbott–Shim, M. (2000, Winter). Within and beyond the classroom door: Assessing quality in child care centers. Early Childhood Research Quarterly, 15(4), 475–496.

Roopnarine, J. L., & Johnson, J. E. (Eds.). (2009). Approaches to early childhood education (5th ed.). Upper Saddle River, NJ: Pearson.

Schickedanz, J., Pergantis, M. L., Kanosky, J., Blaney, A., & Ottinger, J. (1997). Curriculum in early childhood: A resource guide for preschool and kindergarten teachers. Boston: Allyn & Bacon.

Seefeldt, C. (Ed.). (1999). The early childhood curriculum: Current findings in theories and practice (3rd ed.). New York: Teachers College Press.

Wheatley, K. F. (2003). Promoting the use of content standards: Recommendations for teacher educators. Young Children, 58(2), 96–101.

Wiltz, N. W., & Klein, E. L. (2001, Summer). "What do you do in child care?" Children's perceptions of high and low quality classrooms. Early Childhood Research Quarterly, 16(2), 209–236.

Chapter 12

Allen, K. E., & Schwartz, I. S. (1996). The exceptional child: Mainstreaming in early childhood education (3rd ed.). Albany, NY: Delmar.

Allington, R. L. (2009). What really matters in response to intervention. Upper Saddle River, NJ: Pearson.

Bowe, F. G. (2000). Birth to five: Early childhood special education. Albany, NY: Delmar.

Boyle, C. A., Boulet, S., Schieve, L. A., Cohen, R. A., Blumberg, S. J., Yeargin-Allsopp, M., . . . Kogan, M. D. (2011). Trends in the prevalence of developmental disabilities in U.S. children, 1997–2008. Pediatrics, 2011; peds.2010-2989; published ahead of print May 23, 2011. doi:10.1542/peds.2010-2989

Copple, C., & Bredekamp, S. (Eds.). (2009). Developmentally appropriate practice in early childhood programs (3rd ed.). Washington, DC: NAEYC.

Buysse, V., & Wesley, P. W. (Eds.). (2006). Evidence-based practice in the early childhood field. Washington, DC: Zero to Three Press.

Carta, J. J., Schwartz, I. S., Atwater, J. B., & McConnell, S. R. (1991). Developmentally appropriate practice: Appraising its usefulness for young children with disabilities. Topics in Early Childhood Special Education, 13(1), 1–20.

Division for Early Childhood (DEC). (2007). Promoting positive outcomes for children with disabilities: Recommendations for curriculum, assessment and program evaluation. Missoula, MT: Author.

Division for Early Childhood/National Association for the Education of Young Children (DEC/NAEYC). (2009). *Early childhood inclusion: A summary*. Chapel Hill: The University of North Carolina, FPG Child Development Institute.

Dunlap, L. L. (2009). *An introduction to early childhood special education: Birth to age five*. Upper Saddle River, NJ: Pearson.

Edmiaston, R., Dolezal, V., Doolittle, S., Erickson, C., & Merritt, S. (2000). Developing individualized education programs for children in inclusive settings: A developmentally appropriate framework. *Young Children, 55*(4), 36–41.

French, K. (2004). Supporting a child with special health care needs. *Young Children, 59*(2), 62–63.

Hall, L. J. (2009). *Autism spectrum disorders: From theory to practice*. Upper Saddle River, NJ: Pearson.

Hull, K., Goldhaber, J., & Capone, A. (2002). *Opening doors: An introduction to inclusive early childhood education*. Boston: Houghton Mifflin.

Kaplan-Sanoff, M., & Kletter, E. F. (1985). The developmental needs of abused children: Classroom strategies. *Beginnings, 2*(4), 15–19.

Kostelnik, M., Onaga, E., Rohde, B., & Whiren, A. (2002). *Children with special needs: Lessons for early childhood professionals*. New York: Teachers College Press.

McCormick, L., & Feeney, S. (1995). Modifying and expanding activities for children with disabilities. *Young Children, 50*(4), 10–17.

Mulligan, S. A. (2003). Assistance technology: Supporting the participation of children with disabilities. *Young Children, 58*(6), 50–53.

National Association for the Education of Young Children (NAEYC). (2005/2011). *Code of ethical conduct and statement of commitment* (Rev. ed.). Washington, DC: NAEYC.

Nemeth, K. N. (2009). *Many languages, one classroom: Teaching dual and English language learners*. Silver Spring, MD: Gryphon House.

Sandall, S. R., & Schwartz, I. S. (2002). *Building blocks for teaching preschoolers with special needs*. Baltimore: Brookes.

Snow, K. (2009). Disability is natural. (E-newsletter). Retrieved from disabilityisnatural.com/explore/pfl

Turnbull, A.R., Turnbull, R., Shank, M. & S. J. Smith. (2004). *Exceptional lives: Special education in today's schools* (4th ed.). Upper Saddle River, NJ: Pearson.

U.S. Department of Health and Human Services, Administration for Children and Families, Office of Head Start. (2008). Dual language learning: What does it take? Head Start dual language report. Retrieved from http://eclkc.ohs.acf.hhs.gov/hslc/tta-system/teaching/eecd

Wolery, M., & Wilbers, J. S. (Eds.). (1994). Including children with special needs in early childhood programs. *Research Monographs of the National Association for the Education of Young Children* (Vol. 6). Washington, DC: NAEYC.

Chapter 13

Barbour, C., Barbour, N. H., & Scully. P. A. (2011). *Families, schools, and communities: Building partnerships for educating children* (5th ed.). Upper Saddle River, NJ: Pearson.

Berger, E. H., & Riojas-Cortez, M. (2012). *Parents as partners in education: Families and schools working together* (7th ed.). Upper Saddle River, NJ: Pearson.

Brickmayer, J., Cohen, J., Jensen, I., & Variano, D. (2005). Supporting grandparents who raise grandchildren. *Young Children, 60*(3), 100–104.

Center for the Study of Social Policy (CCSP). (2004). *Protecting children by strengthening families: A guide book for early childhood programs*. Washington, DC. Retrieved from www.cssp.org

Christian, L. G. (2006). Understanding families: Applying family systems theory to early childhood practice. *Young Children, 61*(1), 12–20.

Copple, C. (Ed.). (2003). *A world of difference: Readings on teaching young children in a diverse society*. Washington, DC: NAEYC.

Diffily, D., & Morrison, K. (Eds.). (1996). *Family-friendly communication for early childhood programs*. Washington, DC: NAEYC.

Dombro, A. L., & Lerner, C. (2006). Sharing the care of infants and toddlers. *Young Children, 61*(1), 29–33.

Epstein, J. L. (2001). *School, family, and community partnerships: Preparing educators and improving schools*. Boulder, CO: Westview.

Galinsky, E. (1981). *Between generations: The six stages of parenting*. New York: Times Books.

Gennarelli, C. (2004). Communicating with families: Children lead the way. *Young Children, 59*(1), 98–99.

Gonzalez-Mena, J. (2001). *Multicultural issues in child care* (3rd ed.). Mountain View, CA: Mayfield.

Gonzalez-Mena, J. (2008). *Diversity in early education programs: Honoring differences* (5th ed.). Boston: McGraw-Hill.

Gonzalez-Mena, J. (2009a). *The child in the family and the community* (5th ed.). Upper Saddle River, NJ: Pearson.

Gonzalez-Mena, J. (2009b). What is the role of families in early care and education? In S. Feeney, A. Galper, & C. Seefeldt (Eds.), *Continuing issues in early childhood education* (3rd ed., 369–386). Upper Saddle River, NJ: Pearson.

Gonzalez-Mena, J., & Eyer, D. W. (2009). *Infants, toddlers, and caregivers*. Boston: McGraw-Hill.

Katz, L. (1980). Mothering and teaching—Some significant distinctions. In L. Katz (Ed.), *Current topics in early childhood education* (Vol. 3, 47–63). Norwood, NJ: Ablex.

Keyser, J. (2006). *From parents to partners: Building a family-centered early childhood program*. St Paul, MN: Redleaf Press.

Levine, J. A., Murphy, D. T., & Wilson, S. (1993). *Getting men involved: Strategies for early childhood programs*. New York: Scholastic.

National Association for the Education of Young Children (NAEYC). (1995). *Responding to cultural and linguistic diversity: A position statement*. Washington, DC: NAEYC.

National Association for the Education of Young Children (NAEYC). (2004). *Building circles, breaking cycles—Preventing child abuse and neglect: The early childhood educator's role*. naeyc.org/ece/pdf/duke.pdf

National Association for the Education of Young Children (NAEYC). (2005/2011). *Code of ethical conduct and statement of commitment* (Rev. ed.). Washington, DC: NAEYC.

National Association for the Education of Young Children (NAEYC). (2007). *Early childhood program standards and accreditation criteria: The mark of quality in early childhood education*. Washington, DC: NAEYC.

National Association for the Education of Young Children (NAEYC). (2009). *NAEYC standards for early childhood professional preparation programs.* Washington, DC: NAEYC.

Olson, M. (2007). Strengthening families: Community strategies that work. *Young Children, 62*(2), 26–29.

Powers, J. (2005). *Parent-friendly early learning: Tips and strategies for working well with families.* St. Paul, MN: Redleaf Press.

Riojas-Cortez, M., Flores, B. B., & Clark, E. R. (2003). Los niños aprenden en casa: Valuing and connecting home cultural knowledge with an early childhood program. *Young Children, 58*(6), 78–83.

Rogers, F. (1994). *You are special: Words of wisdom from America's most beloved neighbor.* New York: Penguin Books.

Sammons, W. A. H., & Lewis, J. M. (2000). What schools are doing to help the children of divorce. *Young Children, 55*(5), 64–65.

Turbiville, V. P., Umbarger, G. T., & Guthrie, A. C. (2000). Fathers' involvement in programs for young children. *Young Children, 55*(4), 74–79.

Turnbull, A. P., & Turnbull, H. R. III. (2001). *Families, professionals, and exceptionality: Collaborating for empowerment* (4th ed.). Upper Saddle River, NJ: Pearson.

U.S. Census Bureau, Housing and Household Economic Statistics Division, Fertility & Family Statistics Branch. (2008). America's families and living arrangements. Retrieved from www.census.gov/population/www/socdemo/hh-fam/cps2008.html

Chapter 14

Epstein, A. (2007). *The intentional teacher: Choosing the best strategies for young children's learning.* Washington, DC: NAEYC.

Feeney, S. (2012). *Professionalism in early childhood education: Doing our best for young children.* Upper Saddle River, NJ: Pearson.

Feeney, S., & Freeman, N. (2005, rev. ed.). *Ethics and the early childhood educator: Using the NAEYC Code.* Washington, DC: NAEYC.

Feeney, S., Galper, A., & Seefeldt, C. (Eds.). (2009). *Continuing issues in early childhood education* (3rd ed.). Upper Saddle River, NJ: Pearson.

Goffin, S. G., & Lombardi, J. (1988). *Speaking out: Early childhood advocacy.* Washington, DC: NAEYC.

Hymes, J. L., Jr. (1981). *Teaching the child under six* (3rd ed.). Upper Saddle River, NJ: Pearson.

Jones, E., & Reynolds, G. (1992). *The play's the thing: Teacher's roles in children's play.* New York: Teachers College Press.

Katz, L. G. (1995). *The developmental stages of teachers. Talks with teachers of young children.* Norwood, NJ: Ablex.

National Association for the Education of Young Children. (2005/2011). *Code of Ethical Conduct and Statement of Commitment* (rev. ed.). Washington, DC: NAEYC. Retrieved from www.naeyc.org/files/naeyc/file/positions/Ethics Position Statement2011.pdf

Rogers, F. (2003). *The world according to Mister Rogers: Important things to remember.* New York: Hyperion.

Stonehouse, A. (1994). *Not just nice ladies.* Castle Hills, NSW, AU: Pademelon Press.

name INDEX

Note: Page numbers followed by *f* or *t* refer to figures or tables.

subject INDEX

Note: Page numbers followed by *f* or *t* refer to figures or tables.